Israel and the Cyprus Question

Israel and the Cyprus Question

*Foreign Policy, Diplomacy and
International Relations 1946–1960*

Gabriel Haritos

BLOOMSBURY ACADEMIC
LONDON • NEW YORK • OXFORD • NEW DELHI • SYDNEY

BLOOMSBURY ACADEMIC
Bloomsbury Publishing Plc
50 Bedford Square, London, WC1B 3DP, UK
1385 Broadway, New York, NY 10018, USA
29 Earlsfort Terrace, Dublin 2, Ireland

BLOOMSBURY, BLOOMSBURY ACADEMIC and the Diana logo are trademarks
of Bloomsbury Publishing Plc

First published in 2018 in Greece as
Κύπρος, το Γειτονικό Νησί
Το Κυπριακό μέσα από τα Κρατικά Αρχεία του Ισραήλ, 1946–1960

First published in Great Britain 2023
Paperback edition published 2025

Series design by Adriana Brioso
Cover image: Courtesy of the I.D.F & Defense Establishment Archives,
Collection Ba'Makhane. Photographer Reuven, Yehudai, 1962.

A catalogue record for this book is available from the British Library.

A catalog record for this book is available from the Library of Congress.

ISBN: HB: 978-1-3503-5639-9
        PB: 978-1-3503-5643-6
        ePDF: 978-1-3503-5641-2
        eBook: 978-1-3503-5640-5

Typeset by RefineCatch Limited, Bungay, Suffolk

To find out more about our authors and books visit www.bloomsbury.com
and sign up for our newsletters.

Contents

Figures

Abbreviations

AAPSO	Afro-Asian Peoples' Solidarity Organization
AKEL	Progressive Party of Working People
AON	Youth Reconstruction Association
APOEL	Athletic Football Club of Greeks of Nicosia
CBS	Cyprus Broadcasting Service
CENTO	Central Treaty Organization
CIA	Central Intelligence Agency
CPSU	Communist Party of the Soviet Union
CTV	Cyprus Television
CYBARCO	Cyprus Building & Road Construction Company
CyBC	Cyprus Broadcasting Corporation (also RIK)
CYMEACO	Cyprus Middle East Construction Works Company
DEK	Democratic Union of Cyprus
EAK	Cypriot Union of Farmers
EDMA	United Democratic Reconstruction Front
EDON	United Democratic Youth Organisation
El-Al	Israel Airlines
EOKA	National Organisation of Cypriot Fighters
ERE	National Radical Union
FAO	Food and Agriculture Organization
FBIS	Foreign Broadcast Information Service
FRUS	Foreign Relations of the United States
GSEE	General Confederation of Greek Workers
ICFTU	International Confederation of Free Trade Unions
IDF	Israel Defense Forces
IDFA	Israel Defense Forces Archives
ILMA	Israel Labour Movement Archive
ISA	Israel State Archives
JCA	Jewish Colonization Association
JDC	Joint Distribution Committee
KATAK	Association of the Turkish Minority of Cyprus
KMA	Cypriot Maronite Arabic
KYP	Greek Central Intelligence Service
MAA	National Records and Research Service
MAKI	Israeli Communist Party
MAPAI	Workers' Party of the Land of Israel
MAPAM	United Workers' Party
MASHAV	Agency for International Cooperation
MECA	Middle East Communications Activity
MENA	Middle East News Agency
NAAFI	Navy, Army and Air Force Institutes

NATO	North Atlantic Treaty Organization
OAU	Organisation of African Unity
ORT	Organization for Rehabilitation and Training
PEO	Pancyprian Federation of Labour
POAS	Pancyprian Federation of Independent Trade Unions
PODG	Pancyprian Organisation of Democratic Women
PSE	Pancyprian Trade Union Committee
RAF	Royal Air Force
RIK	Cyprus Broadcasting Corporation (also CyBC)
SACME	Supreme Allied Command Middle East
SEK	Cyprus Workers' Confederation
SSNP	Syrian Social Nationalist Party
TMT	Turkish Resistance Organisation
UAR	United Arab Republic
UN	United Nations
UNESCO	United Nations Educational Scientific and Cultural Organization
UNPCC	United Nations Conciliation Commission for Palestine
WFTU	World Federation of Trade Unions
WIZO	Women's International Zionist Organization

Acknowledgements

I wish to offer my warmest thanks to His Most Godly Beatitude Theophilos III, Greek Orthodox Patriarch of the Holy City of Jerusalem and to the entire Greek Orthodox Patriarchate of Jerusalem for their hospitality at the Monastery of the Cross and the Monastery of Little Galilee (*Viri Galilaei*) on the Mount of Olives throughout my stay in Israel, and until the completion of my archival research. I would also like to extend my thanks to the Most Reverend Timotheos, Metropolitan of Vostra, Exarch of the Holy Sepulchre in Cyprus, and the Exarchate of the Holy Sepulchre in Cyprus, for their kindness in providing me with accommodation during my two months of research in Cyprus. The generous support I received from the entire Greek Orthodox Monastic Community in the Holy Land was a true gift and an experience to treasure for life.

I also wish to thank my academic supervisors, Theodosios Karvounarakis, Professor of International Relations at the Department of International and European Studies, University of Macedonia; Evanthis Hatzivassiliou, Professor of History at the Department of History and Archaeology, National and Kapodistrian University of Athens; and Amikam Nachmani, Professor of Political Science, Bar-Ilan University, for their valuable scientific assistance and encouragement.

I owe a great debt of thanks to the entire scientific and administrative staff of the Israel State Archives in Jerusalem for their unflagging support and courtesy, and in particular to former Ambassador Barouch Gilead, Editor in the Department of Documentation of the Israel State Archives, whose experience and knowledge proved invaluable. I also thank Galia Weissman, Research Consultant at the Israel State Archives, for her unceasing willingness to assist me in carrying out my research.

A special acknowledgement goes to the staff of the Press and Information Office of the Republic of Cyprus and the Cypriot Press Archives for providing every possible assistance during the two months I spent conducting supplementary research in Cyprus.

I cordially thank Betsy Rosenberg for editing the present English edition and for our excellent cooperation.

I would like to thank Bloomsbury Academic, my commissioning editor, Atifa Jiwa, and my assistant editor, Nayiri Kendir, for their trust and support.

Last but not least, I wish to thank my parents, Yiannis and Anna, for the support they provided throughout this undertaking, with all their love.

G. H.

Prologue

This study delineates Israel's position vis-à-vis the 'Cyprus Question' in the period between 1948 and 1960, and explores the international and regional correlations that determined the diplomatic actions of the young state towards the neighbouring isle. The book is based mainly on the classified reports of Israeli diplomats, declassified for the purposes of my research, and set forth here for the first time.

With Cyprus consistently in the background, the leading role in this narrative belongs to Israel's realpolitik and the factors that shaped it: the Arab–Israeli conflict and the fragile equilibrium of the Middle East and Eastern Mediterranean in the Cold War climate that prevailed throughout the world during that era. Meanwhile, the positions held by Cypriot political figures, the competition between Greek Cypriots and Turkish Cypriots, the manoeuvres of Athens and Ankara in a regional and global context, the potential spread of Nasserism in the area, and finally, the web of relations between Israel and Cyprus on the eve of the island's independence are likewise explored here and assessed in view of Israel's geopolitical interests.

When the book was originally published in Greek by Papazisis Publishers in 2018, it came as a surprise to the many readers both in Greece and Cyprus, for two reasons.

First, the heretofore unknown people and events that shaped developments are presented in the book for the first time.

Second – and in contrast to the way Greeks and Turks, Greek Cypriots and Turkish Cypriots relate the events of the period – for Israelis, the conflict over Cyprus presented yet another Middle Eastern problem; all other dimensions were of secondary importance.

Finally, when natural gas deposits were discovered in the Eastern Mediterranean, geography itself brought back the knowledge that, ultimately, the 'neighbouring isle' and the conflicts related to it had never ceased to be integral to Middle Eastern politics. Thus, many years later, we see that the Middle Eastern dimension of the Cyprus Question is resurfacing and questions very similar to those that occupied the decision-making centres during the distant 1950s have once again emerged. Current regional developments provide the impetus to consider this book with fresh eyes.

Gabriel Haritos
Jerusalem, November 2022

Introduction

Presented here is an account of Israel's foreign policy regarding events in Cyprus from 1946 until the declaration of Cypriot independence in August of 1960. Specifically examined are the international and regional factors that influenced Israel's vote at the United Nations on the Cyprus Question during the same period, and the subsequent establishment of diplomatic relations with the independent Republic of Cyprus, based on the departmental correspondence of Israel's Ministry of Foreign Affairs. Likewise examined are Israeli diplomatic reports and assessments highlighting the main characteristics of the realpolitik approach taking shape at the time and the criteria and decision-making processes of the newly formed Israeli diplomatic service.

The selection of the year 1946 as the starting point of the period under review was not a random one. Although the State of Israel was established two and a half years later, on 14 May 1948, the leadership of the *Yishuv*, the Jewish population in Mandatory Palestine, had turned its attention to neighbouring Cyprus and the release of thousands of Jewish Holocaust survivors detained in British camps around Famagusta since 1946. With Israel's independence, the British were less than eager to release the detainees in Cyprus. Israel interpreted London's reluctance as a deliberate attempt to prevent the reinforcement of the Israel Defense Forces (IDF), then facing the more powerful British-backed Jordanian Arab Legion in the Arab–Israeli War of 1948 (also called the Israeli War of Independence).

The issue of the continued internment of Jewish Holocaust survivors at the camps in Cyprus led to the first diplomatic crisis between Israel and Britain. It set the tone for the newly formed Israeli diplomatic service and highlighted the importance of Cyprus' geographical position for the regional security of Israel which was still vulnerable.

Another reason for beginning our investigation in 1946 is the correspondence of that date with the first fruitful interaction between Israel and the Greek residents of the island who were eager to be rid of British rule, and whose ultimate goal was *Enosis* (unification) with Greece.

Chapter summaries

Chapter 1 discusses the factors that shaped Israel's foreign policy and the concerns of its political leadership over what the state's position should be in the post-war, bipolar international system. Something we tend to forget nowadays is the fact that, in the early days of its independence, Israel's alignment with the West was not a foregone conclusion, given the ideological associations which had become entrenched in the Jewish population of Palestine during the British Mandate. The decisions ultimately adopted under the dominant influence of David Ben-Gurion and the key guidelines that the country's first foreign minister, Moshe Sharett, established for Israeli foreign policy, were critically important, in terms not only of Israel's position in the world, but also in the immediate region of the Middle East and the Eastern Mediterranean.

Chapter 2 analyses the intricate relations between Israelis and Greek Cypriots during the period 1946–9, when the detention camps were still in operation. The '*Enosis* Plebiscite' of 1950 and the appeal of the Cypriot Church to the Israeli foreign ministry for political support brought to light, for the first time, the official Israeli view of the Enosis movement. This coincided with an apparent shift in Britain's position from that of opposing the Zionist movement to eagerly assuming the role of Israel's protector in a completely hostile climate. Meanwhile, the first steps were being taken in the rapprochement between Israel and Turkey, a country oriented to the West and traditionally wary of the choices made by Arab leaders. It was within this regional web of relations that Israel established a diplomatic presence in Cyprus for the first time. As the consulate general of Israel opened its doors in Nicosia in late August 1950, a channel of communication was established with Britain, then in control of the neighbouring island.

Chapter 3 discusses the factors that determined Israel's attitude vis-à-vis Greece's repeated attempts to resolve the Cypriot question through the United Nations. Each of Israel's votes on the Cypriot question is examined and evaluated here in light of bilateral relations between Israel and the countries directly involved (Greece, Turkey, Britain). The chapter likewise investigates regional developments in the Middle East and the aspirations of the two superpowers, which led inevitably to the occasional convergence or divergence in the region throughout the turbulent period of 1954–8. Also examined are factors that were helpful in shaping Israeli relations on a local level with Greek Cypriots, Turkish Cypriots and the British authorities on the island during the struggle of the National Organisation of Cypriot Fighters (EOKA) to create new conditions.

Chapter 4 considers Israel's political leadership assessed the contents of the London-Zurich Agreements and analyses Israel's diplomatic overtures towards Athens and Ankara, to ensure that the two 'mother countries' would not prevent the independent Cypriot Republic from cultivating smooth diplomatic relations with the State of Israel.

Chapter 5 probes the interests of Israeli diplomacy in the orientation of Cyprus' regional foreign policy. Israeli diplomacy placed particular emphasis on the stance of the two communities on the island vis-à-vis Israel and the neighbouring Arab states.

Chapter 6 focuses on the tug-of-war Cyprus' political leadership, and particularly Archbishop Makarios, was subjected to by the Israeli and Arab sides during the Transition Period (February 1959–August 1960). Israel's diplomatic, entrepreneurial and political manoeuvring which aimed at establishing normal diplomatic relations between Israel and the Republic of Cyprus is examined here in depth. Israeli departmental reports shed light on the simultaneous efforts of the United Arab Republic (UAR), led by Gamal Abdel Nasser, as well as Lebanon, who shared the common goal of deterring Israeli infiltration of Cyprus and the legitimization of its political, diplomatic and institutional presence in the newly established Cypriot political system.

Chapter 7 presents a summary and discussion of the research findings.

Sources

The contents of the book are largely based on primary, unpublished archival sources. Specifically:

(a) The vast majority of source materials come from the Israel State Archives, the internal communications of the Israeli consulate general in Nicosia, the diplomatic representation of Israel in Athens, the diplomatic mission of Israel in Ankara, Israel's permanent representation to the United Nations, the Israeli embassies in London, Washington, DC, and elsewhere, as well as from the appropriately authorized divisions of the Israeli Ministry of Foreign Affairs. This book brings to light for the first time in English heretofore unexamined archival material related to Israel's foreign policy vis-à-vis the Cyprus question. The Israeli State Archives declassified the material at the author's request during the period 2012–14.

(b) The primary material used here derives from the Israeli Defence Forces Archives (IDFA) and relates exclusively to the detention of Jewish Holocaust survivors at the British camps in Cyprus, 1946–9. This material was declassified before the 1970s and became the object of systematic research, both in Israel and internationally. Supplementary archival material was also collected from the digital database of the Museum of Jewish Immigration from Cyprus, located in Atlit, Israel.

(c) An original addition to this study involves the use of primary archival material the author collected from the records of the so-called 'Milli Arşiv ve Araştırma Dairesi' (MAA, the National Records and Research Service), based in Kyrenia, Cyprus, and controlled by Turkish authorities.

(d) Subsidiary material included records from the Cypriot Press Archives at the Public Information Office of the Republic of Cyprus (PIO) based in Nicosia; from the archives of the Holy Archbishopric of Cyprus; the historical archives of the Pancyprian Federation of Labour (PEO); the archives of the Greek Orthodox Patriarchate of Jerusalem; the Israel Labour Movement Archive at the Pinhas Lavon Institute for Labor Movement Research in Tel Aviv; the online digitized archives of the US Department of State Foreign Relations of the United States (FRUS); and the Minutes of the Municipality of Rhodes Town Council meetings, filed in the Historical Archives of the Municipality of Rhodes, Greece. A sizeable number of Israeli reports from the period 1946–60 come from the digitized Israeli Press Historical Archive at the National Library of Israel in Jerusalem.

(e) Extensive use was also made of excerpted reports published in newspapers from Egypt, Lebanon, Jordan and Syria, as included in their Hebrew translation in the related reports, prepared by the Israeli Ministry of Foreign Affairs Research Division.

(f) Reports published in the local press of the Greek island of Rhodes press during the 1950s were retrieved from the digitized newspaper archive at the Central Public Library of Rhodes, Greece..

(g) Historical documents from the author's personal family archives.

(h) In addition to all of the above, broad use was made of Israeli and international historiography found chiefly at the National Library of Israel in Jerusalem, the Hebrew University of Jerusalem library, the Tel Aviv University central library and the Moshe Dayan Center for Middle Eastern and African Studies at Tel Aviv University. Extensively used as well were the specialized Cypriot bibliography of the Republic of Cyprus' Press and Information Office (PIO) and the library of the University of Cyprus in Nicosia.

This book is based on the author's PhD dissertation in International Relations entitled, 'Israel's Foreign Policy and Cyprus, 1946–1960', which was awarded by the Department of International and European Studies, University of Macedonia, Thessaloniki, Greece, on 20 October 2016.

The first edition of this book was published in May 2018 in Greek by the Athens-based Papazisis Publishers, under the title *Cyprus, the Neighboring Island – The Cyprus Question in Israel's State Archives (1946–1960)* [*Κύπρος, το Γειτονικό Νησί – Το Κυπριακό μέσα από τα Κρατικά Αρχεία του Ισραήλ, 1946–1960*].

This book is the English translation of the second edition of the latter, published in February 2020 by Papazisis Publishers.

The author's on-site archival research in Israel was conducted from June 2012 to August 2014, with supplementary archival research in Nicosia and Kyrenia conducted between March and May of 2016.

1

Israel and Cyprus

Between East and West

During the first three years of its independence, 1948–51, the fledgling State of Israel was ambivalent about its position within the international system influenced by the Cold War. After a brief period of diplomatic rapprochement with the Soviet Union, the proxy war in Korea between the USSR and the US opened the way for the Israeli administration headed by Prime Minister David Ben-Gurion to declare itself as pro-Western. This stance was further confirmed in 1955, when Israel was not even invited to attend the first Afro-Asian States Conference in Bandung, Indonesia – a conference considered essentially anti-Western.

At the time, only a few nautical miles west of the Israeli coastline, Cyprus' upgraded strategic role was expected to serve the regional interests of the West in the Eastern Mediterranean and Middle East. Moreover, the idea of Cyprus uniting with Greece had already matured in the minds of the Greek Cypriot majority of the island. The demand for Enosis had been around for some time, although it met with a violent rebuke from British colonialists in 1931. In the wake of the Second World War, however, the call of Enosis had acquired new momentum, as it became part of a general decolonization movement that was gradually reshuffling the maps of Africa and Asia. The 'Enosis Plebiscite' of January 1950 was a first indication that the countdown towards the end of British dominance in Cyprus had begun. It was only to be expected that the states of the Mediterranean Basin– including Israel, and each for its own reasons – would take an interest in a development such as this.

1.1 Israeli foreign policy: A question of orientation

The forerunner of what was later to become the Israeli diplomatic service was the Public Service College, founded by the Jewish Agency – an international organization established in 1908 for the purpose of helping to resettle Zionist Jews in Palestine. It was in Jerusalem that the Public Service College was instituted in the summer of 1946, headed by 36-year-old Walter Eytan, a young man of German Jewish origin and a graduate of the Humanities Division at Oxford University. Two years later, with Israel's declaration of independence in May 1948, Eytan was named director general of the newly formed Israeli Ministry of Foreign Affairs. Serving continuously until 1959, Eytan played a crucial role in shaping Israel's foreign policy as a confidante of its first foreign minister, Moshe Sharett, and his successor, Golda Meir, who took up the reins of the diplomatic service in 1956.

Upon assuming his duties in the summer of 1946, Eytan selected twenty-five young Jews, twenty men and five women studying at universities abroad as the nucleus of the first informal diplomatic service of the state-in-the-making. Only six weeks before the 29 November 1947 vote at the UN General Assembly to approve or reject the Partition Plan for Palestine, the Political Committee of the Jewish Agency officially entrusted Eytan with the task of introducing internal regulations to direct the international relations of the Yishuv. The international regulations Eytan drafted at the time later formed the basis for the Ministry of Foreign Affairs' organizational chart.[1]

Long before the proclamation of Israeli independence, there had been much deliberation among the political leadership of the Yishuv on the eventual form of the Jewish state. Such reflection was understandably intensified when Israel declared independence on 14 May 1948. In the Cold War climate that followed the Second World War, the fledgling state was expected to signify whether it would align itself with the East or with the West.

The Yishuv's most prominent political force had been the centre-left political party, Mapai (Mifleget Poalei Eretz Israel, Workers' Party of the Land of Israel). Founded on 5 January 1930, the party was the consolidation of leftist forces under Ben-Gurion, who led Mapai from its establishment until 1963 – with only a short, two-year interval (1953–5) at which time he was replaced by Moshe Sharett. From 1948 to 1967, Mapai dominated Israeli political life. The party drew the highest percentage of votes in all parliamentary elections held during the 1950s and remained the main pillar of practically every coalition government. Party leader Ben-Gurion served as prime minister from 1949 to 1953 and again from 1955 to 1963.

Before Israel's proclamation of independence, Mapai had viewed its international associations from a leftist ideological perspective. During the first three years of the state, various opinions were expressed in the party as to what 'position Israel should take in the world'. Aside from the dilemma of whether Israel should belong to the Western or Eastern bloc, the question of Israel's position had a direct impact on the shape of the new state and Israeli society in general.[2] Should it adopt communism, the ideals of which had inspired the Zionist kibbutz system and influenced a considerable proportion of Mapai members, or should it adopt a Western-style parliamentary democracy? Should it adopt capitalism and a free-market economy or opt for a fully fledged, state-regulated economy, and should that economy tend to socialism or perhaps to an intermediary system of controlled state interventionism? Should Jewish religious ideals be allowed to prevail over the principle of a secular society? Should

[1]   Walter Eytan, *The First Ten Years: A Diplomatic History of Israel* (London: Weidenfeld and Nicolson, 1958), 191–211.
[2]   Shabtai Roseene, *Basic Elements of Israel's Foreign Policy* (New Delhi: Indian Council of World Affairs, 1962), 11–13.

Israel aim at an institutionalization and further consolidation of religious tolerance, or pursue unequivocal separation of State and Religion as a whole? Should the legal and administrative systems instituted under the British Mandate continue to be applied or should Jewish law be implemented, or else should a solution be found to reconcile the diverse ideological currents reflected in the Israeli legal system that was taking shape? Should Israel pursue a civic solution of ratification and implementation of a constitution or should customary constitutional law, heavily influenced by pronounced Anglo-Saxon – i.e. British/colonial – traditions be allowed to prevail? And to what extent should the foreign policy of nascent Israel ultimately be influenced by recent armed struggles with the British?

The political leadership of the Yishuv now faced these dilemmas, intertwined ideologically as well as practically as related to foreign policy. Most enlightening as to the currents at play were the sessions of Mapai's Secretariat and Central Committee of 5 and 24 April 1948, respectively, held only a few weeks prior to Israel's proclamation of independence. The positions outlined at that time may be summarized as follows.

The first opinion, advocated mostly by Eliahu Elath, held that 'in the political field, the future of the state will be decided in practice by the Anglo-Saxons'. As such, it would be very detrimental to Israel if the impression received abroad was that Soviet economic and social models had been adopted domestically. On the other hand, Elath was not in favour of a complete ideological alignment with the West.

A second opinion, maintained by Mordechai Namir, was that Jewish communities in Eastern Bloc countries, would be in a position to determine Israel's fate as the state took its first steps.[3] Such a viewpoint obviously inclined more towards East European regimes, though it did not go so far as to adopt the social and economic model of the Soviet Union in full. This had been one of the fundamental differences between Mapai and the pro-Soviet Zionist opposition party Mapam (Mifleget ha-Poalim ha-Meuhedet, United Workers' Party) and persisted just as intensely even after Israel's declaration of independence.

A third position favoured 'extreme pragmatism'. Represented in the main by Pinhas Lavon, it held that Israel's foreign policy ought not to be ideologized. According to Lavon:

> Orientation means our readiness to have relations with anyone willing to have relations with us, with all those holding the keys of decision. If these be held by England – then it is England; if held by England and America – then England and America; if the keys of decision are held by the UN – then there are ten other, smaller countries and our orientation should thus lean towards these ten small countries; if to a certain extent they are held by Russia – then Russia, too. No room exists for partisan positions.[4]

---

[3] Uri Bialer, *'Our Place in the World': Mapai and Israel's Foreign Policy Orientation, 1947–1952* (Jerusalem: Magnes Press, Hebrew University of Jerusalem, 1981), 5.
[4] Ibid., 9–10, 13.

Ultimately, however, it was Ben-Gurion's position that prevailed. Combining all the aforementioned approaches, he emphasized that 'the Jewish Nation had no protector. The sole exception was the Jewish diaspora in the United States.' As for Britain's ambivalent attitude vis-à-vis Israel in the wake of its hasty withdrawal from Palestine, Ben-Gurion was of the opinion that Israel should seriously heed the shared interests of London and Washington in the Middle East, and that cultivating good bilateral relations with Britain would ensure equally good relations with the United States, where half the Jewish diaspora lived and was in a position to exercise political pressure on the White House. Nevertheless, Ben-Gurion insisted that the Soviet Union as an emerging superpower would be extremely useful to Israel, since it was there and in the various East European people's republics that the second-largest Jewish community lived.

Though at first glance, the latter position may appear to have embraced the extreme pragmatism of Pinhas Lavon, Ben-Gurion attached great importance to the influence which the Jewish diaspora was capable of exerting on the various decision-making centres. He found an ally in Moshe Sharett, his close associate at that time who was named foreign minister after the proclamation of Israeli independence.

But ambivalence within the party about whether it was more advisable to form an alliance with the East or the West continued even after independence. It was very clear to all party members that taking an extreme position would be anything but beneficial. Besides, in the aftermath of the 29 November 1947 vote at the UN General Assembly, it was no longer possible to ignore the fact that both the USSR and the US had backed the Partition Scheme, thus essentially pronouncing themselves in favour of establishing a Jewish state in Palestine. What is more, when in August 1948, the first two diplomatic missions of the US and the USSR[5] were both temporally housed on the premises of the Gat Rimon Hotel in Tel Aviv, the impressive sight of American and Soviet flags flying side by side sent out various positive messages to Israeli political leaders.[6] Nevertheless, during the first three years of the state, Israeli leaders chose a policy of 'Non-Alignment' vis-à-vis both superpowers.

In terms of post-war influence and regional affiliations, the directions Israeli policy took can be viewed on the one hand through its relations with the USSR and the US between 1948 and 1951, and on the other hand through its relations with the so-called Third World countries in 1955.

1.1.1 Israel and the Soviet Union

The Soviet Union and the People's Republics of Eastern Europe adopted a particularly favourable attitude vis-à-vis the newly founded State of Israel. The major milestones

---

[5] Cf. Isaac Alteras, *Eisenhower and Israel: US-Israeli Relations, 1953–1960* (Gainesville, FL: University Press of Florida, 1993), 1–9; and Yosef Govrin, 'Yakhasei Israel-Brit ha-Moatsot: Mi-Kinun Israel (1948) ad Peruk Brit ha-Moatsot (1991)' ['Relations between Israel and the USSR: From Israel's Independence (1948) until USSR's Dissolution (1991)'], in *Misrad ha-Khutz: 50 ha-Shanim ha-Rishonot* [*Ministry of Foreign Affairs: The First 50 Years*], ed. Moshe Yeger, Yosef Govrin and Arieh Oded (Jerusalem: Keter, 2002), 447.

[6] Walter Eytan, *Bein Israel la-Amim* [*Between Israel and the Other Nations*] (Tel Aviv: Masada, 1958), 126.

typifying the rapprochement between Israel and the Eastern Bloc can be summarized thus.[7]

On 17 May 1948, the Soviet Union became the first state to formally recognize Israel de jure, just three days after the formal proclamation of Israeli independence. Indeed, the first embassy officially established in Tel Aviv was that of the Soviet Union, on 10 August 1948; a few weeks later, on 6 September 1948, Israel's embassy in Moscow opened its doors, with Golda Meir heading the mission.[8]

The USSR was pushing for the dissolution of the UN Palestine Conciliation Commission (PCC) comprised of the US, France and Turkey, and encouraging the launching of direct talks between Israel and the Arabs without UN mediation. Moscow's position was fully embraced by the Israelis.

On 24 November 1948, the USSR submitted a draft resolution to the UN Special Political Committee, demanding that the Arab forces occupying Jewish territory be ordered to withdraw; the Soviet representative declared that: 'Israel was created as the result of an armed liberation struggle'. At the first UN General Assembly deliberation on the matter of Israel's membership in the organization, held on 19 December 1948, the USSR voted in favour of Israel's admission as did the USA, Ukraine, Argentina and Colombia, whereas Syria, Turkey and Iran voted against, and Britain, France, (nationalist) China, Belgium and Canada abstained. Consequently, Israel's admission to the UN was overruled, having fallen short of the statutory majority of seven votes in favour.[9]

Then, on 11 May 1949, the membership proposal introduced by the US representative[10] was unreservedly supported by the USSR and all the other Eastern Bloc countries,[11] and approved with nine votes in favour, Egypt against and Britain abstaining.

On 19 April 1950, Yakov Malik, head of the USSR's permanent mission to the UN declared his opposition to placing Jerusalem under international rule, asserting that such a solution 'pleases neither the Arabs nor the Jews'. As expected, Israel saluted this move on Moscow's part, given its reluctance to see a reinstatement of an international regime in Jerusalem.

The example of Israel's de jure recognition by the USSR was followed by the People's Republics of Poland, Czechoslovakia, Romania, Hungary and Bulgaria.[12] Czechoslovakia and Poland's contribution in terms of supplying weapons to the Israeli armed forces during the War of Independence (1948–9) was decisive for the outcome of the struggle,

---

[7] Govrin, 'Yakhasei Israel-Brit ha-Moatsot', 447.

[8] Golda Meir, *My Life* (New York: G. P. Putnam's Sons, 1975), 245–82. On Meir's appointment as Israel's ambassador to Moscow.

[9] Louis Shub, 'Israel and the United Nations', *American Jewish Year Book, 1950* (New York: American Jewish Committee, 1950), vol. 51, 385–6. Cf. Yossi Alper, *Medina Bodeda [A Country Alone]* (Tel Aviv: Matar, 2015), 39–41.

[10] Ibid.

[11] Govrin, 'Yakhashei Israel–Brit ha-Moatsot', 447.

[12] A. A. Ben-Asher, 'Israel ve-ha-Demokratiot ha-Amamiot be-Reshit Hakamat ha-Medina' ['Israel and the Peoples' Republics in the Early Years of Statehood'], in *Misrad ha-Khutz*, ed., Yeger, Govrin and Oded, 459–68.

particularly at a time when the US and the West had been reluctant to adopt an unequivocal position in favour of Israelis. Despite considerable difficulties involved in the resettlement of Eastern European Jews in Israel during the period 1949–50, the relevant authorities in Romania, Hungary and Poland eventually lifted all bureaucratic obstacles, though always with Moscow's blessing. The exception was Bulgaria which went so far as to facilitate the departure of its Jewish citizens, and was one of the first European countries to develop trade relations with the new state of Israel.[13] When Israel eventually decided to align itself openly with the West, Prime Minister Ben-Gurion did not neglect to commend the support of the Eastern Bloc countries during the early years of his country's independence. In his address at the Knesset (Israel's Parliament) plenary session on 5 November 1951, and despite his strong criticism of communism, Ben-Gurion declared that: 'nevertheless, we have not and will not forget the aid we had from Czechoslovakia. We appreciate the favourable attitude of the Polish government as to the Jewish *Aliyah* (Jewish immigration to Israel) and do indeed feel that both in Czechoslovakia and in Poland there is a genuine sympathy for us.'[14]

But it was not long before the differences between Israel's aspirations and the objectives pursued by Stalin's Soviet Union became glaringly apparent. The main points of friction were, on the one hand, the resettlement of the Soviet Jewish citizens in Israel and on the other, the supply of Soviet military aid to the Israel Defense Forces.

More specifically, Israel's absolute priority during the first years of its existence was to settle as many Jewish immigrants as possible in the country so as to gain a demographic advantage, to ensure domestic production through an influx of fresh workers and scientists, and to augment the armed forces. In the early 1950s, the Jewish community of the Soviet Union numbered about 2 million, which made it the second-largest Jewish community after that of the USA,[15] while the entire population of the State of Israel, including its Arab citizens, amounted to just over 1 million.[16] Under the circumstances, having USSR Jews settle in Israel was highest on the agenda of Golda Meir, who had just then assumed her diplomatic duties in Moscow. As she said on the eve of her departure, 'We wish to develop strong bonds of mutual friendship and understanding with the Soviet Union [. . .] and in this way, to forgestrong bonds directly with the Jewish element in the Soviet Union.'[17]

The Soviet Union, however, believed otherwise. Even in her first encounters with Valerian Zorin in Moscow, the deputy foreign minister left no room for doubt: 'There is and will be a Jewish Question only in those countries not on course towards the

[13] Ibid., 467–8.
[14] David Ben-Gurion, *Beayot ha-Medina: Mediniut Khutz shel Israel* [*The Problems of the State: The Foreign Policy of Israel*] (Jerusalem: Sherutei Modiin, 1951), 8.
[15] Leon Shapiro, 'World Jewish Population', *American Jewish Year Book, 1951* (New York: American Jewish Committee, 1951), vol. 52, 194–200.
[16] The composition of the Israeli population in an official report by the Israeli Central Bureau of Statistics, Ha-Lishka ha-Leumit li-Statistika, *Shishim Shana be-Re'ei ha-Statistika* [*Sixty Years from a Statistical Perspective*] (Jerusalem: Central Bureau of Statistics, 2008).
[17] *Al ha-Mishmar*, 'Fairwell Reception for Israeli Representatives to the Soviet Union', 27 August 1948, Statement by Golda Meir at a reception hosted by the Israel–USSR Friendship Alliance in Tel Aviv on 26 August 1948, shortly before assuming her ambassadorial duties in Moscow.

materialization of socialism. These will be the states of origin of Jewish émigrés and such will be the Jewish émigrés that Israel shall be called upon to integrate.' The same spirit and content appeared in *Pravda*, the official newspaper of the Communist Party of the Soviet Union (CPSU). In an article published 21 September 1948, the paper adopted the same line asserting that:

> The Jewish Question shall be tackled everywhere around the globe through social and intellectual progress. The solution to the Jewish Question is not solely conditioned by Israel's military feats – such a solution depends solely on the prevalence of Socialism over Capitalism. [. . .] Israel is not run by representatives of the working class. [. . .] The Jews of the Soviet Union are proud of their country, which they regard as their Homeland and Birthplace. They have no desire to settle in Israel, and East European Jews feel the same [. . .].[18]

Based on this reasoning, Moscow banned the Israeli embassy from publishing any printed material addressed to Soviet Jews urging them to settle in Israel. Meir's mandate in Moscow came to an end in July 1949, only a few months into her appointment. She was succeeded in the office by Mordechai Namir, the Mapai member who expressed the party's more pro-Soviet leanings. Meir had proven to be the wrong person to build bridges with the USSR, judging by the descriptions in her in memoirs about the way local authorities treated Jews there and the precautions the Jews of Moscow were forced to take in 1948 in order to attend their synagogue securely.[19]

Moscow's antagonism was due to the fact that as early as 1934, the USSR had established the 14,000 metres square Jewish autonomous province (Oblast) of Birobidzhan in Siberia, along the border with China. The understanding had been that all citizens of Jewish descent, hitherto scattered in various Soviet Republics would now be settled in the new province. For the USSR, Birobidzhan was the 'Soviet answer' to the Zionist movement in British-ruled Palestine.[20] If Moscow were to allow 2 million Russian Jews to settle in Israel, it would incur the wrath of the Arabs, something the Soviet government was loath to do.

An equally important concern for the Israeli side was the arms supply to its military forces. During the 1948 war, military aid had been sent primarily from Czechoslovakia and Poland.[21] It goes without saying that the USSR was cognizant of these arms supplies.[22] Israel expected its military cooperation with the Eastern Bloc to continue. As Ambassador Mordechai Namir, Meir's successor in Moscow, wrote in his memoirs,

---

[18] Mordechai Namir, *Shlikhut be Moskva* [*Mission to Moscow*] (Tel Aviv: Am Oved, 1971), 52; and Joseph Gordon, 'Soviet Union', *American Jewish Year Book, 1950*, vol. 51, 336–40.

[19] Meir, *My Life*, 247–54.

[20] Henry Srebrnik, 'Birobidzhan: A Remnant of History – The Jewish Autonomous Region in the Russian Far East', *Jewish Currents* (July–August, 2009): 16–18.

[21] A. A. Ben-Asher, 'Israel ve-ha-Demokratiot ha-Amamiot be-Reshit Hakamat ha-Medina' ['Israel and the Peoples' Republics in the Early Years of Statehood'], in *Misrad ha-Khutz*, ed. Yeger, Govrin and Oded, 449–67.

[22] Efraim Karsh, 'Israel', in *The Cold War and the Middle East*, ed. Yezid Sayigh and Avi Shlaim (Oxford: Clarendon Press, 1997), 156–60.

the Israeli military attaché met with officers of the Soviet Army in October 1948 to request weapons and training for the Israeli armed forces. He also proposed that weapon transit stations be established on land and sea to link the two countries. The Soviet Ministry of Foreign Affairs expressed serious reservations. If such a transaction were to become widely known it might lead to serious repercussions at a diplomatic level, 'since the UN prohibits the supply of weapons to all parties to the Arab-Israeli conflict'.[23] The Israelis deemed the Soviet refusal hypocritical and began to apprehend that nothing more could be expected from Moscow.

1.1.2 Israel and the United States

On 15 May 1948, just one day after Israel's proclamation of independence, Washington announced its de facto recognition of Tel Aviv's provisional government. For its part, the USSR went one better with de jure recognition of Israel on 17 May 1948 and consented to Czechoslovakia and Poland furnishing weapons to the IDF. The US State Department and the Pentagon appeared uncertain about what position to adopt vis-à-vis the Arab–Israeli conflict. The prevailing view in Washington was that, taking an unequivocally pro-Israeli position, was ill-advised for fear, that it would estrange the Arabs and most likely the entire Muslim world. It would also block American access to the wealth-producing resources of the Middle East.

Still, President Truman was amenable to the idea of rapprochement with Israel. The Jewish lobby and its powerful electorate and influence on the country's political life, combined with Israel's victory in the 1948 war so soon after the Holocaust had deeply affected public opinion. At President Truman's personal initiative, the US accorded de jure recognition to Israel on 31 January 1949[24] – six days after the first parliamentary elections in Israel – along with a generous financial grant (the equivalent then of #dl100 million) despite differences of opinion between Truman and powerful US diplomatic circles. The de jure recognition of Israel by the US encouraged Western European states (except for Greece, Spain and Portugal) to follow suit, along with Turkey, British Commonwealth member nations and the pro-Western countries of Central and Latin America.[25]

Washington was keen to find a middle course in its relations with Israel and the Arab world, as evidenced in a memorandum by the US National Security Council on 24 November 1947. The paper proposed the following main guidelines for US policy in the Middle East:

> The security of the Eastern Mediterranean and of the Middle East is vital to the security of the United States. It is in the national interest of the United States to have the respect, and insofar as possible, good will of all the peoples of the Near and Middle East, Jews and Arabs alike, and their orientation toward the West and away from the Soviet Union. The differences between the new Israeli state and

---

[23] Namir, *Shlikhut*, 73–6.
[24] Eytan, *The First Ten Years*, 9–14.
[25] Helmuth Lowenberg, 'Israel', *American Jewish Year Book, 1950*, vol. 51, 394–5.

neighbouring Arab states should be reconciled at least to the extent that Israel and the Arab States act in concert to oppose the Soviet aggression. We should provide advice and guidance in the solution of the economic, social and political problems of the area on an impartial basis, as between Israel and the Arab states, contingent upon the willingness of these countries to apply the maximum of self-help.[26]

It was on this basis that the United States undertook a series of diplomatic initiatives and negotiations to resolve the problems which had emerged after the 1948 war, in order to demonstrate its goodwill vis-à-vis all parties to the conflict. At Washington's instance, the UN formed the Palestine Conciliation Commission (PCC), which included the US, France and Turkey. The PCC's purpose was to resolve the issue of Palestinian refugees and the territorial disputes between Israel and the Arabs, and to promote the establishment of an international regime for the City of Jerusalem, in accordance with the Plan for the Partition of Palestine adopted by the UN 29 November 1947. The PCC's proposals satisfied neither the Israelis is nor the Arabs. More specifically, when American Secretary of State Dean Acheson met with his Israeli counterpart, Moshe Sharett, on 5 April 1949, he requested Israel's commitment to repatriate 200,000 Arab refugees and to accept the UN General Assembly resolution of 11 December 1948, placing the City of Jerusalem under international regime.[27] As expected, Israel did not accept this proposal, and Ben-Gurion declared before the PCC, 'Jerusalem is to Jews exactly what Rome is to the Italian and Paris to the French'.[28] Ben-Gurion's statement to the Knesset was along the same lines: 'The United States is a powerful country; Israel is a small and weak one. We may be crushed, but we will not commit suicide.'[29]

The PCC hit a similar impasse with respect to the implementation of an international regime in the City of Jerusalem, as called for by the Partition Plan of 1947, under which the city was to be divided into two zones, Jewish and Arab, with a High Commissioner appointed by the UN to oversee the city and ensure the status quo and the preservation of the Holy Places. The two zones would coincide with the areas already controlled by Israel and Jordan, respectively. The solution was rejected by both Israel and Jordan, along with the other Arab states.

Not surprisingly, the abortive diplomatic efforts gave the USSR a chance to propose the abolition of the PCC, to advocate direct talks between Israel and the Arabs, and to criticize the plan for the internationalization of Jerusalem which would be 'of no satisfaction either to the Jews or to the Arabs'. But with regard to *aliyah*, the Israelis had been aware since autumn of 1949 that the Soviets had no intention of helping out with

---

[26] Alteras, *Eisenhower*, 11.
[27] Estimates as to the exact number of Arab refugees as a consequence of Israel's victory in the war of 1948 varied. Whereas the Israelis spoke of some 539,000 persons, the PCC estimated their number at 700,000. In all likelihood, as many as 100,000 people fled to Lebanon, 80,000 sought refuge in Syria, 5,000–10,000 went to Iraq, 115,000–150,000 to the Gaza Strip and some 250,000–325,000 fled to Transjordan (East Bank). Cf. ibid., 13.
[28] Ibid., 16.
[29] Howard Sachar, *A History of Israel: From the Rise of Zionism to Our Time*, 3rd edn (New York: Knopf, 2007), 439–500.

their demographic reinforcement, nor were they willing to provide Soviet weapons to the Israeli Army.[30] It was precisely for such an opportunity that Prime Minister Ben-Gurion had waited to approach the United States.

The right moment came with the outbreak of the Korean War which proved to be a catalyst in shaping Israeli foreign policy. Israel grasped at the chance to side openly with the West, and to distance itself from aligning with the countries of the Eastern Bloc. The ensuing estrangement between Israel and the USSR led to the first break in their diplomatic relations and the closure of the Soviet embassy in Tel Aviv from February to July 1953. Israel perceived the brief diplomatic crisis with the USSR as a clear warning by Moscow to abstain from any regional security plans involving the US and the West in general.[31]

In July 1950, Israel condemned North Korean aggressiveness and in October of that year, Israeli Foreign Minister Moshe Sharett proclaimed his opposition to the Soviet demand for an immediate withdrawal of the Americans from the Korean peninsula. The friction between Israel and the USSR became all the more apparent when, on 9 January 1951, Moscow rejected the Israel-inspired peace plan to end the Korean War which amongst other things called for the withdrawal of all foreign military forces from the Korean peninsula.[32] At the same time, arrangements were being made for Prime Minister Ben-Gurion's first visit to the United States, due to take place on 3 May 1951. On the agenda for that visit were discussions about the prospects of Israel–US relations.

Ben-Gurion made it emphatically clear to President Truman that if the United States helped Israel develop a strong army with 250,000 personnel, such a force would in turn be in a position to help the United States, Britain and Turkey to counter Soviet encroachment in the Middle East. Moreover, Ben-Gurion hailed the US position on Korea, calling it 'a brave step against communist expansionism'.[33] Ben-Gurion's visit to the United States formally established Israel's pro-Western foreign policy, and the beginning of generous economic support provided by the US which has continued to the present day.

Although Harry S. Truman had declared Israel's destiny to be 'the cradle of democracy and progress' in the Middle East,[34] Washington did not lift the arms embargo which had been in place against Israel since 1947, either during Truman's term or later under Dwight Eisenhower. While the United States did not prevent France and Canada from supporting the IDF with know-how and military equipment, the American leadership did not back the military alliance of Britain, France and Israel against Egypt in the Suez Crisis of 1956;[35] as a result, Israel was compelled within a few months to withdraw from the Egyptian territory it had seized.[36] Subsequently, despite

---

[30] Cf. Section 1.1.1, above.
[31] Eytan, *Bein Israel*, 131.
[32] Govrin, 'Yakhashei Israel–Brit ha-Moatsot', 450. Young Sam Ma, 'Israel's Role in the UN during the Korean War', *Israel Journal of Foreign Affairs*, 4, no. 3 (2010): 81–9.
[33] Ibid.
[34] Alteras, *Eisenhower*, 18–19.
[35] Keith Kyle, *Suez* (London and New York: I.B. Tauris, 2003), 425–7.
[36] Ibid., 532–42.

the fact that Israel–US relations were influenced by the Eisenhower Doctrine (1957), according to which the US would distribute economic and military aid to any country in the region in order to stop the spread of communism in the Middle East, Washington did not intend to jeopardize its relations with Nasser's Egypt. Therefore, until 1963, the Americans remained determined not to reinforce Israel's military machine directly.[37]

1.1.3 Israel and the Third World

Despite Israel's brave steps forward in the three years 1948–51, the principle of 'Non-Alignment' with either of the two Cold War poles was promoted in local public opinion as the cornerstone of Israeli foreign policy. The term 'Neutrality' came up frequently in statements made by Foreign Minister Moshe Sharett. Such neutrality was at times perceived as an attempt to maintain an equal distance from East and West alike; at other times, neutrality was understood as the Zionist movement's non-alignment with either communism or capitalism, and Israel's hesitation to fully embrace the regional pursuits of either the US or the USSR. Nevertheless, members of the centre-left Mapai Party insisted that, irrespective of its leftist background, Israel should make it absolutely clear to everyone that it belonged to the 'Free World' in light of the strong presence of the Jewish diaspora in the West. On the other hand, however, the non-adoption of the communist social model did not necessarily mean that Israel would side with the Western forces against the Soviet Union and the countries within its sphere of influence.[38]

Yet another fact taken into account by the Israelis was that since 1950 – despite the winds of divisiveness blowing through the world at the time – Israel had managed to establish full diplomatic relations at an ambassadorial level with countries from both the capitalist West (USA, Britain, France, Italy, Belgium) and the communist East (USSR, Czechoslovakia, Romania, Poland). Meanwhile, by 1950, Israel had also been recognized, either de facto or de jure, by states of the so-called Third World, such as Bolivia, Brazil, Chile, Colombia, Costa Rica, Cuba, the Dominican Republic, Argentina, Ecuador, El Salvador, Haiti, Honduras, Nicaragua, Panama, Paraguay, Peru, the Philippines, Ceylon and Yugoslavia.[39] Indicative of the 'Non-Alignment' principle was the case of Israel's relations with China. More specifically, Nationalist China recognized Israel de jure in May 1948, though no diplomatic missions were delegated either to Tel Aviv or Taipei. In the winter of the following year, however, when Mao Zedong's communist regime prevailed, the Israeli Ministry of Foreign Affairs under Moshe Sharett proceeded to recognize the People's Republic of China – without previously consulting the United States. As such, Israel's diplomatic relations with West-leaning Formosa froze.[40]

---

[37] Mordechai Gazit, 'Timrurim Mukdamim be-Maslul Hizuk ha-Ksharim ha-Bitkhoniim Israel–Artsot ha-Brit' ['Initial Manoevres on the Path of Strengthening Security Relations with the United States'], in *Misrad ha-Khutz*, ed. Yeger, Govrin and Oded, 293–300.

[38] Bialer, *'Our Place'*, 9–13.

[39] Lowenberg, 'Israel', 394–5.

[40] Aharon Shay, *Sin ve-Israel* [*China and Israel*] (Tel Aviv: Yedioth Akharonot, and Chemed, 2016), 39, 43–7. Cf. Zev Sufott, 'Ha-Mediniut ha-Sinit shel Israel, 1950–1992' ['Israeli Policy toward China, 1950–1992'], in *Misrad ha-Khutz*, ed. Yeger, Govrin and Oded, 579–96.

Israel's non-alignment approach during the years 1948–50 was succeeded by a pronounced foreign policy shift to the West, triggered by the Korean War.[41] Yet the Western orientation of Israel's policy was not the true reason for its exclusion from the first Afro-Asian Conference, held in Bandung, Indonesia, from 18–24 April 1955. The criteria established by the organizing countries (namely India, Pakistan, Ceylon, Burma and Indonesia) for the selection of those entitled to take part in the Bandung Conference were primarily political and, in any case, not purely geographical.[42] Israel had not been invited in order to assure the attendance of numerous Arab countries in North Africa and the Middle East. Similarly uninvited had been South Africa, due to its racist regime, since inviting such a country would have meant the absence of all other African states. Nationalist China (Formosa) was not invited either so that the People's Republic of China would take part. Neither were North and South Korea invited since the conference organizers wished to avoid the impression that they identified with one or the pole of Cold War international reality.[43]

On the other hand, a considerable number of countries which actually attended the conference belonged to the Western world and were not negatively disposed towards Israel, specifically Turkey though it was already a member of NATO and the Baghdad Pact whilst also maintaining diplomatic relations with Israel.[44] Likewise in attendance was pro-Western Iran, which had recognized the Jewish state de facto in 1950, and this had not prevented Iranian citizens of Jewish descent from permanently settling in Israel. Iran also exported oil to Israel in defiance of the Arab embargo and the secret services of the two countries maintained close cooperation.[45] Other participants included Japan, the Philippines and Thailand, who were favourable to the West and had recognized Israel de jure.[46] Israel also maintained diplomatic missions in India and Burma, which were two of the five states hosting the Bandung Conference.[47] Interestingly, the local press in India and Burma was extensively critical of their

---

[41] Cf. 1.1.2.

[42] ISA/RG93/MFA/8693/2, Report under R.N. 1002/27.03.1955, by the Israeli Ministry of Foreign Affairs Research Division addressed to all Israeli diplomatic missions, included the entire text of the joint communiqué issued on 29.12.1954 by the prime ministers of India, Pakistan, Ceylon, Burma and Indonesia, in the matter of the decision to invite Afghanistan, Cambodia, the Central African Federation, People's Republic of China, Egypt, Ethiopia, Ghana, Iran, Iraq, Ivory Coast, Japan, Jordan, Laos, Lebanon, Liberia, Libya, Nepal, the Philippines, Saudi Arabia, Sudan, Syria, Thailand, Turkey, North Vietnam, South Vietnam and Yemen to the Afro-Asian Conference in Bandung. Also mentioned in that report was the fact that the Central African Federation had declined the invitation and that the Ivory Coast had not expressed an intention to attend the conference. In the end, neither the Central African Federation nor the Ivory Coast attended the Bandung Conference.

[43] John D. B. Miller, *The Politics of the Third World* (London: Oxford University Press, 1967), 18–24.

[44] ISA/RG93/MFA/8693/2, On 4 April 1955, only a few days before the start of the conference, the British House of Commons was debating the recent accession of Britain to the defence pact entered between Turkey and Iraq (the Baghdad Pact, Central Treaty Organization or CENTO, also acceded to later by Pakistan and Iran). Report under R.N. 1008/20.04.1955, from the Israeli Ministry of Foreign Affairs Research Division to all Israeli diplomatic missions quoted the entire minutes of session of 4.4.1955 at the House of Commons.

[45] Alper, *Medina Bodeda*, 39–41.

[46] State of Israel, *Government Year-Book 5715 (1954)* (Jerusalem: Government Printer, 1954), 133–48.

[47] Ibid., 134–6.

respective governments for not insisting on Israel's participation in the Bandung Conference. Such criticism focused mostly on the fact that the Jewish state was geographically part of the Middle East, as were most of the Arab countries taking part in the conference, and 'Israel had unjustly been "sentenced in absentia" without being given the opportunity to develop its positions during the Bandung Conference proceedings'.[48]

The Bandung Conference unreservedly endorsed Arab positions, and the final communiqué on 24 April 1955 stated:

> In view of the existing tension in the Middle East, due to the situation in Palestine and due to the risks that tension entails for world peace, the Afro-Asian Conference declares its support of the rights of the Arab people of Palestine and calls for the implementation of the United Nations Resolutions on Palestine and the achievement of a peaceful settlement of the Palestine question.

It had become clear by then that if such an effort were to succeed in rallying the Afro-Asian countries into a unified 'third pole' in the world order, the Third World could not accept Israel's positions in international fora, due mostly to the strong influence of Arab countries on the anti-colonial movement, but also to a lack of interest on the part of the other Asian and African countries in the outcome of the Arab–Israeli conflict.

The Israelis lent particular weight to the accurate assessment of Kumao Nishimura, Japan's ambassador in Paris, who shared his view about the outcome of the Bandung Conference with his Israeli counterpart, Yaakov Tsur, and the difficulties Israel would have to face with an 'unfriendly Third World'.[49] According to Nishimura, the importance of the conference was 'much higher than the West believes [. . .]' and Israel would find itself 'facing a cohesive group of countries with a potential comparable to that of the Latin American countries, which will fill the role of regulating the results of every UN resolution'. Japan's ambassador also foresaw the leading role Cairo would soon take on in the matter of the Arab–Israeli conflict, noting that 'the politician who emerged more prominent than any other at the Bandung Conference was Gamal Abdel Nasser' stressing that Egypt's dominant presence there had impressed everyone.

1.1.4 Fundamental pillars of Israel's foreign policy in the early 1950s

Although Ben-Gurion's visit to Washington in May 1951 heralded the shift of his country's external policy to the West, Israel did not join NATO or any other pro-West regional alliance. The fact was that NATO member states maintained special relationships with most of the Arab countries, and Israel's membership in the organization was liable to jeopardize the sizeable pool of Jews still in the USSR and the

---

[48] ISA/RG93/MFA/8693/2, Research Division, 1030/07.06.1955, Report by the Israeli Foreign Ministry's Research Division, Review of various publications in the Indian and Burmese press.
[49] ISA/RG93/MFA/8693/2, Research Division, 1034/13.6.1955, Tzur to UN Department.

People's Republics of Eastern Europe.[50] Meanwhile, immediately after Israel's proclamation of independence and until its open alignment with the West as a consequence of the Korean War, the government remained ambivalent about its position in the post-war bipolar international system.

The priorities of Israeli foreign policy were first made clear by Prime Minister David Ben-Gurion. Addressing the Knesset on 5 November 1951, he set forth the main pillars of Israel's international and regional policy, summarized as follows:[51]

1. By order of urgency, Israel's needs were ranked as follows: National security, Aliyah (Diaspora Jews coming to settle in Israel), development and productivity, unhindered contacts and connections with the Jewish diaspora, achieving peace with the Arab world and defending the principles of freedom and democracy on a regional and international level.
2. According to Ben-Gurion, foreign countries fell into three distinct categories, depending on their association with Israel: the first included countries unwilling to establish relations with Israel, either because they were hostile or because they had agendas of their own not directly linked to Israel, such as the Arab countries, Pakistan, Afghanistan and Ethiopia. The second category involved states with which Israel maintained relations on a governmental level but not on a popular level or with their Jewish communities, for example the Soviet Union and the People's Republics of Eastern Europe whom Ben-Gurion never ceased to refer to as 'self-proclaimed People's Republics'. In the third category were states with which Israel maintained relations on a governmental as well as a popular level, including their Jewish communities. A common feature of these countries was their compliance with Western-style parliamentary democracy. It is noteworthy that Ben-Gurion did not refer to specific countries that did not establish smooth diplomatic relations with Israel but were nevertheless deemed Western in terms of their parliamentary systems and their citizenry, Jewish and otherwise, whom they did not prohibit from settling in Israel. Greece was included in this *sui generis* category.
3. Since the Jews of the diaspora would be crucial in shaping Israel's relations to foreign governments, it was essential for Israel to maintain close contact with Jewish communities which were in a position to exert influence on decision making centres in those countries. In Ben-Gurion's opinion, this could only be achieved in countries which benefitted from a pluralistic, Western-style parliamentary democracy. Moreover, diaspora Jews living in the West constituted the main population source for Jewish repatriation (*aliyah*). As they lived in democratic systems, they were able to exercise their civil liberties and choose to

[50] Namir, *Shlikhut*, 116–18. At the farewell meeting on 14 April 1949 between Golda Meir, Ambassador of Israel to Moscow, and Soviet Foreign Minister Andreij Vishinsky, Meir stated amongst other things: 'We shall not violate our foreign policy principles, based on non-accession to organizations operating against the Soviet Union, the bonds of friendship with which are to us a fundamental concern [...]'.
[51] David Ben-Gurion, *Beayot ha-Medina: Mediniut Khutz shel Israel* [*The Problems of the State: The Foreign Policy of Israel*] (Jerusalem: Sherutei Modiin, 1951).

settle permanently in Israel without restrictions. Ben-Gurion concluded that only Western parliamentary democracies could guarantee the unimpeded exercise of civil liberties and thus would not prevent citizens of Jewish origin from 'making aliyah' to Israel.

4. Having sharply criticized the communist regimes, Ben-Gurion emphasized Israel's ideological, institutional and political identification with the parliamentary democracies of the West but also partially adopted the pragmatic stance of Mapai member Pinhas Lavon, adding that: 'The system of government in effect within each country is not our concern. [. . .] Our relations with specific countries cannot depend on their own domestic political system, whether we have already entered into cooperation with them or whether there is potential for developing such cooperation.' Albeit, in so saying, Ben-Gurion did not rule out the possibility of cooperation with non-Western countries.

5. Ben-Gurion concluded that Western countries were deluded in thinking that they could find a reliable ally in the Middle East other than Israel. Specifically referring to Nasser's Egypt, Israel's leading opponent at the time, Ben-Gurion cast doubt on attempts by the US, Britain and Turkey to include Egypt in the Middle East Command which was in the process of being formed, an ambitious venture that never materialized.

6. Ben-Gurion was convinced that it was only a matter of time before the West came to see Israel's importance in the region as well as its reliability as an ally. The Arab countries, despite the considerable size of their territories and populations, did not share the ideology and value system of the West. Thus, sooner or later, any attempt by the West to collaborate with the Arab world was doomed to failure. As he stressed in his speech before the Knesset on 5 November 1951:

> But how can it be that the United States and Britain believe Egypt will fight to defend democracy and freedom in the world, while at the same time, there is neither democracy nor freedom within Egypt itself? It was not Egypt's army that saved Egypt from Rommel. It was the armies of the British, the Australians, the New Zealanders, the Indians and the Jewish legions who fought on the side of the British army. If Egypt were ever supplied with American or British arms, it would not use them for any purpose other than fighting Israel. And that is exactly what we have already told the Americans and the British[52]

1.2 The importance of Cyprus to Britain and the Greek Cypriot factor

Having occupied Cyprus since 1878, Britain annexed the island in 1914, when the Ottoman Empire sided with Germany, Austro-Hungary and Italy in the First World

---

[52] Ibid., 16.

War. Under the 1923 Treaty of Lausanne, the Republic of Turkey recognized British sovereignty over the island, and in 1925, Cyprus became a British colony.

The importance of Cyprus for Britain was integral to the island's strategic location. According to Benjamin Disraeli, 'annexing Cyprus is not a Mediterranean move; it is an Indian move',[53] in the sense that by holding Cyprus, one would have control over the Suez Canal, itself a 'launching point and a bastion on the route to and from India'. At the time, the trade route was protected by the British presence in Malta and Gibraltar.[54] Then, too, Cyprus is located opposite the southern coast of Asia Minor, a very short distance away from Palestine, Syria and Lebanon, and, of course, the oil-producing countries of the Middle East.

In the aftermath of the Second World War and the beginning of the Cold War era, after Britain had withdrawn from India and Palestine, and its presence in the Suez Canal Zone was increasingly challenged, the position of Cyprus was greatly enhanced. The rationale behind Britain's continued presence on the island despite the anti-colonial tenor of the times, made it Britain's bastion in the Eastern Mediterranean enabling London to protect Ankara from the Soviet threat.[55] This argument was touted by Turkey[56] which wished to preserve total British control over Cyprus. Britain had no intention of withdrawing from Cyprus since this would have meant forfeiting its interests in the Middle East and the Greater Eastern Mediterranean region. As historian Robert Holland very aptly noted, 'It had always underlain British strategic thinking that the real value of Cyprus related to the scenario of a unilateral (that is, non-NATO) expedition to defend British national interests in the Levant.'[57]

On the other hand, the vast majority of the Cypriot population harboured a Hellenic national conscience and had expressed a strongly felt desire to unite with mainland Greece since the early decades of Greek statehood. The establishment of its first diplomatic presence in Cyprus dates back to 1833, when the position of a Greek vice consulate in Larnaca existed on paper, although owing to Ottoman diplomatic reservations, the arrival of Demetrios Margaritis, first vice consul of Greece, did not occur until 1846, twelve years after his appointment by the Greek Ministry of Foreign Affairs.[58]

[53] John Reddaway, *Burdened with Cyprus: The British Connection* (London: Weidenfeld & Nicolson, 1989), 9, quoted in Evanthis Hatzivassiliou, *To Kypriako Zitima, 1878–1960: I Syntagmatiki Ptychi* [*The Cyprus Question, 1878–1960: The Constitutional Aspect*] (Athens: Ellinika Grammata, 1998), 30–1.
[54] Konstantinos Katsonis, *I Kypros stous dromous tis Istorias* [*Cyprus on the Roads of History*] (Larnaca: 2002), 29.
[55] Charalampos Kafkaridis, 'O sovietikos kindynos kai i taftisi me ti Dysi os paragontes diamorfosis tis tourkikis politikis sto Kypriako (1945–1960)' ['The Soviet Threat and Identification with the West as Factors Shaping Turkish Policy on the Cyprus Question'], in *I Nea Tourkiki Igemonia* [*The New Turkish Hegemony*], ed. Nikos Moudouros and Michalis Michail (Athens: Papazisis, 2014), 47–8.
[56] Vyron Theodoropoulos, *Geopolitiki simasia: Mia metavallomeni ennoia* [*Geopolitical Importance: A Changing Concept*], in *Kypros: Geopolitikes exelixeis ston 21o aiona* [*Cyprus: Geopolitical Developments in the 21st Century*], ed. Vangelis Chorafas and Lefteris Rizas (Athens: Monthly Review Imprint, 2009), 86.
[57] Robert Holland, *Britain and the Revolt in Cyprus, 1954–1959* (Oxford: Clarendon Press, 1998), 146.
[58] Hellenic Republic, Ministry of Foreign Affairs, *Historic Record of the Presence of Greek Consular and Diplomatic Authorities in Cyprus*, March 2013.

In an effort to avert Greek Cypriot demands for unification with the Greek state, the British authorities established a legislative council in 1882. This legislative council, which was partially elected, included some Greek Cypriot representatives.[59] During the First World War, when the Austro-Hungarian and Bulgarian forces marched against Serbia, Britain, anxious to get Greece on its side, was prepared to concede Cyprus to Athens in exchange for joining the Entente and as part of a more broad-based regional cooperation agreement between Britain and Greece. The prospect was supported at the time by the prominent leader of Greek national liberation, Eleftherios Venizelos, then serving as prime minister.[60] However, in October 1915, The offer was extended again to the newly appointed anti-Venizelos Prime Minister, Alexandros Zaimis, on condition that Greece abandon neutrality – which favoured Germany – and join the Entente.[61] Greece turned down the British proposal, a fact attributed to its certainty that Germany would be the ultimate victor in the war.[62] When the rival Venizelos government was sworn in on 27 June 1917, Greece came out on the side of the Entente, but Britain did not put forward a new proposal to cede Cyprus to Greece.

The limited civil liberties granted to the inhabitants of Cyprus under colonial rule were not enough to avert the revolt of Greek Cypriots in October 1931 in what became known as the 'Oktovriana' (the 'October Events').[63] The unrest was triggered by Governor Sir Ronald Storrs' imposition of particularly onerous customs duties, despite the fact that such measures had previously been rejected by the Legislative Council. Greek Cypriot representatives on the Legislative Council resigned; amongst them was Metropolitan of Kition Nikodemos Mylonas, who later issued a written address to the Cypriots, inciting them to disobedience and proclaiming 'the Enosis of Cyprus with the Greek motherland'. Incidents erupted in practically all the towns of the island, culminating with the burning of the Governor's Palace in Nicosia on 21 October 1931. The uprising was violently suppressed by the British, and its leaders, including Metropolitan Mylonas of Kition, were exiled. However shocked public opinion and the Greek press may have been by the bloody uprising, Venizelos had no desire to disrupt relations between Greece and Britain and chose to wait for Britain's eventual concession of Cyprus to Greek rule.[64] But that never happened. Britain had no intention of ceding any of its sovereign rights, and Storrs' successor, Sir Richmond Palmer engaged in authoritarian practices throughout his mandate in Cyprus (1933–9). He abolished the Legislative Council and replaced it with an appointed consultative committee. He also imposed legislation aimed at ensuring strict control over primary and secondary education.[65] Palmer's overriding wish was to suppress the Enosis movement. The

[59] Hatzivassiliou, *To Kypriako Zitima*, 15–18.
[60] Yiannis P. Pikros, *O Venizelos kai to Kypriako* [*Venizelos and the Cyprus Questions*] (Athens: Filippotis Publishing House, 1980), 5–11.
[61] Ibid., 17.
[62] Ibid., 21.
[63] Doros Alastos, *History in Cyprus* (London: Zeno Publishers, 1976), 350–62. In the matter of the 'October Events' of 1931.
[64] Georgios Christopoulos and Ioannis Bastias (eds), *Istoria tou Ellinikou Ethnous* [*History of the Greek Nation*] (Athens: Ekdotiki Athinon, 1978), vol. 15, 351–2.
[65] Hatzivassiliou, *To Kypriak Zitima*, 55–9.

period during which he was governor of Cyprus came to be known as 'Palmerocracy' and is remembered as the harshest period of British colonial rule on the island.

On 31 March 1947, British military forces withdrew from the Dodecanese, ceding their place to the Greek military administration and marking the annexation of these islands to the Greek state. Over that same period, Britain was coming to grips with the fact that its continuing presence in Palestine would soon come to an end. Although the historical similarities with Cyprus were obvious, the British had already realized by 1946[66] that in light of developments in the region and the general trend towards decolonization, it was only a matter of time before the pro-Enosis movement once again took centre stage. In order to avoid any unpleasant surprises, the new governor of Cyprus, Lord Winster, upon taking up his duties in 1947, convened a meeting – referred to as a 'Consultory' Convention, urging the Church, the Left, the Turkish Cypriots and the Maronites to join in for the purpose of instituting a system of self-government under British rule.[67] The positions of Greek Cypriots were divided. The communist AKEL Party agreed to join in the convention, but the Greek Orthodox Church (the Ethnarchy) refused.

On 7 May 1948, only a week before the British definitively withdrew from neighbouring Palestine, Lord Winster announced the key points of the draft Constitution he intended to implement in Cyprus. Besides provisions related to elections, the representation of the island's communities at the Legislative Council and the purely consultative competences of community representatives on the Executive Council, the Constitution stipulated that the executive powers would be in the hands of the governor. The Legislative Council would commit to Cyprus remaining a member of the British Commonwealth. As such, Britain was declaring to all concerned that, contrary to the case of Palestine, it had no intention of leaving Cyprus. The Ethnarchy immediately rejected Winster's proposals whilst the Greek Cypriot delegates to the 'Consultory' demanded that ministerial duties also be assigned to Greek Cypriots. The British were not at all inclined to be flexible and the 'Consultory' was dissolved. Lord Winster resigned in October 1948 and was succeed by Sir Andrew Right, who retained the legislative reforms of the Palmerocracy[68] at a time when the Enosis movement was growing increasingly stronger.

---

[66] Ibid., 5–65.
[67] Cf. Clifton Daniel, 'Britain Proposes to Stay in Cyprus: Constitutional Plan Will Ban Legislative Discussion of Union with Greece', *New York Times* (1857 – Current file; 12 May 1948; ProQuest Historical Newspapers, The New York Times), 185: 18, in Murat Metin Hakki (ed.), *The Cyprus Issue: A Documentary History, 1878–2007* (London and New York: I.B. Tauris, 2007), 9–10.
[68] Hatzivassiliou, *To Kypriako Zitima*, 63–5.

2

Israel, the Greek Cypriots and Regional Realities

2.1 Cyprus as a place of detention for Jewish survivors of the Holocaust, 1946–9

Israeli historiography abounds in studies and testimonies about the detention camps that operated in Cyprus from mid-August 1946 to early February 1949. Those interned there were Jews who, after surviving the Holocaust, had been apprehended by British authorities in their effort to land clandestinely on the Mediterranean coast of Palestine which at the time was under British Mandate.

In 1939, Britain adopted a series of administrative measures proposed in the White Paper of that year, calling for, amongst other things, the establishment of an independent, bi-ethnic state in Palestine to be administered by its Arab and Jewish citizens, based on population ratios. Waiting for this to materialize, however, and in order to maintain the ratio between Jews and Arabs they deemed desirable, the British implemented a series of harsh restrictions on Jewish immigration as well as on the private acquisition of urban and rural property by Jewish parties or entities abroad. The White Paper of 1939 provided that within the next five years, only 75,000 Jews would be allowed to settle in Palestine. These measures triggered a reaction within the Jewish Zionist movement, which saw them as a breach of the League of Nations Mandate for Palestine and a contradiction of Lord Balfour's declaration in favour of creating a 'national home of the Jewish people' in Palestine.[1]

Shortly after the White Paper policy was issued in response to the Arab Revolt of 1936–9, the flow of Jewish immigration from Europe accelerated to such an extent that in 1940, the British set up a detention camp in the coastal town of Atlit, south of Haifa. Once there, clandestine Jewish immigrants were registered by the authorities, underwent medical examinations and awaited lawful entry visas to Palestine. Visas were awarded on a first-come, first-served basis and in accordance with established quotas, no more than 1,500 Jews per month. As a result, the camp in Atlit soon became congested with thousands of Jewish immigrants.

---

[1] For a better insight into the Zionist perception of political realities of the time, over the period of implementation of the White Paper and the administrative measures imposed in an effort to contain the Jewish element in Palestine, cf. P. Levinstein, *More-Derekh ba-Khok ha-Eretz Yisraeli* [*A Guide to Mandate Palestine Law*] (Jerusalem: Rubin Mass, 1947), 10–15.

Jewish organizations began a struggle against the British in Palestine, aimed primarily at liberating the immigrants detained in Atlit, thereby reinforcing their human resources and enhancing the effectiveness of their armed operations. In October 1945, an armed unit of the underground Palmach force invaded the Atlit camp and liberated all 208 of its detainees. By the end of 1945, the British were still at pains to contain the flow of Jewish immigration into Palestine,[2] so much so that the Arabs openly accused them of intentional foot-dragging.[3]

Faced with the reality of their inefficient measures, the British decided to intern the illegal immigrants in Cyprus, and on 13 August 1946, transferred the first group of 1,290 Jewish immigrants from modulated camps in Haifa to a coastal location on the neighbouring island known as 'Karaolos', near Famagusta. By the end of September, the overall number of detainees in Cyprus had reached 3,700, and in addition to five so-called 'summer camps' at Karaolos, eight 'winter camps' were set up at Dhekelia and Xylotymbou.[4] In the year that followed, the number of detainees in Cyprus rose dramatically, and by 14 May 1948, the day of Israel's proclamation of independence, the total number of Jewish immigrants held in Cyprus had reached many thousands.[5]

Jewish newspapers in Palestine published extensive accounts of the dire living conditions endured by the detainees in Cyprus, further fuelling already strong anti-British sentiment. The most powerful Jewish military organization, the Haganah, had been covertly sending special trainers to the Karaolos camps from the start to recruit and train detainees for active participation in the 'Shurot ha-Meginim' (literally, 'Defenders' Line') immediately upon reaching Palestine. Meanwhile, successive attempts were made to smuggle Jewish detainees aboard fishing boats from the Cypriot coast to Palestine – at best a highly risky venture.[6] Other Jewish military organizations and political factions sent their own representatives to Cyprus in order to increase the number of their supporters and fighters.

Meanwhile the British did their best to ensure 'normal life' in the camps, chiefly for public relations purposes and to maintain an air of calm. Already in September 1946, they had installed two British Army rabbis there so that the detainees would be able to celebrate the Jewish New Year as usual,[7] they also sent Hebrew teachers from Palestine to the camps. Moreover, in Cyprus itself, the local authorities did not attempt to bar the small Jewish community on the island from meeting with their Jewish brethren in the camps. On British authority, a modest number of local Jews, mostly British citizens and permanent residents of the island undertook the expansion of the existing Jewish

---

[2]　Arieh Kochavi, *Post-Holocaust Politics: Britain, the United States and the Jewish Refugees, 1945–1948* (Chapel Hill, NC: University of North Carolina, 2001), 63–4.

[3]　Ibid.

[4]　Morris Laub, *Last Barrier to Freedom: Internment of Jewish Holocaust Survivors on Cyprus, 1946–1949* (Berkeley, CA: Judah L. Magnes Museum, 1985), 18.

[5]　Menachem Weinstein, *Tzionut Datit be-Shulei Eretz-Israel: Tnuat 'Tora va-Avoda' be-Makhanot ha-Ma'atsar be-Kafrisin* [*Religious Zionism on the Outskirts of the Land of Israel: The 'Torah and Labour' Movement in the Detention Camps of Cyprus*] (Nir Galim: Beit ha-Edot le-Moreshet ha-Tzionut ha-Datit ve-ha-Shoah, 2001), 3–6.

[6]　Laub, *Last Barrier*, 26–30.

[7]　Weinstein, *Tzionut*, 168.

cemetery not far from the camps, at a site locally referred to as 'Marko' in the province of Nicosia. Indeed, it was the local authorities who paid for the expansion of the cemetery as well as for new headstones, carved and decorated in the traditional fashion by detainees at Karaolos.[8] Moreover, groups of detainees were regularly released from the camps and settled in Palestine, though always in accordance with the quotas of the White Paper of 1939. As the armed conflict in Palestine intensified, the British cut in half the number of discharges granted per month, from 1,500 to 750.[9]

On 31 March and again on 1 April 1948, the eve of the Arab–Israeli War, representatives of all Jewish political factions active in Cyprus since 1946 convened two extraordinary meetings in Tel Aviv. Their common objective was to help detainees escape from Cyprus and to induct them into the armed squadrons in Palestine.[10] Officers in the Drafting Division of the regular Israeli Army (being formed at the time) were to select and smuggle out the best trained detainees to serve in the Haganah Defenders' Line. The main criteria for the selection of conscripts, men and women, all 18 to 25 years old, single or married but childless, were their knowledge of Hebrew, their high level of performance in military training and professional experience that

---

[8] The Jewish cemetery at Marko (or Margo) has existed since the late nineteenth century, when the Jewish Colonization Association (JCA), with financing provided by Baron Maurice de Hirsch, vouched for the purchase of a rural plot of 4,500 metres square (0.45 hectares). That plot was to be administered by the Ahavat-Tzion ('Love of Zion') association, founded in 1892 and based in London. The purpose of the group was to establish a farm and livestock breeding settlement of Polish Jewish families who were British citizens in the area, the idea being that living conditions in Cyprus would be better than those in Palestine. However, a malaria epidemic put paid to those ambitions and by 1900, the farmland in Marko had been totally abandoned by the Jewish settlers of the association. After the death of Baron de Hirsch in 1896 and until the First World War, the JCA focused on the Jewish settlement, farming and stockbreeding activities in Palestine, acquiring bordering areas of land to establish Jewish communities. A similar investment model was also adopted in Cyprus, as a result of which the JCA had during the period 1900–10 purchased 13 kilometres square (1,300 hectares) of farmland in and around Marko, along the road between Nicosia and Famagusta. There were 16 Jewish families living in Marko in 1908, and by 1919 there were 169 Jewish inhabitants in the area, engaged solely in farming. Still, in the wake of the First World War, financial differences arose between the settlers and JCA's administrators. In 1923, the JCA decided to discontinue financing the settlement and to withdraw from Cyprus, selling off its farmland properties to a British entrepreneur, several local Cypriot farmers and the few remaining Jewish settlers established in the village of Kouklia, Famagusta Province. By 1950, all remaining Jewish residents in the area had already resettled in other Cypriot towns. Cf. (a) Yossi Ben-Artzi, 'Historical Perspectives of Jewish Rural Settlements in Cyprus', in *Historical Perspectives on Cypriot-Jewish Relations*, ed. Giorgos Kazamias and Giorgos Antoniou (Nicosia: University of Cyprus, 2015), 8–17; (b) Yair Seltenreich and Yossi Katz, 'Between the Galilee and Its Neighbouring Isle: Jules Rosenheck and JCA Settlements in Cyprus, 1897–1928', *Middle Eastern Studies*, 45, no. 1 (2009): 87–109; (c) Ata Atun, 'Initiative to Colonize Cyprus with Jews in the 20th Century', *International Journal of Academic Research*, 3, no. 3 (2011): 790–4. With regard to the expansion of the Jewish cemetery at Marko during the period 1946–9, see Yadin Rodan, 'The Forgotten Jews of Cyprus', *Eretz Magazine* (July–August, 2001): 26–36; and (d) Weinstein, *Tzionut*, 168.

[9] Yad Vashem, Shoah Resource Center, see *Cyprus Detention Camps*, available online: www.yadvashem. org (6 October 2022).

[10] IDFA 481/1949-41, The political factions participating in that meeting – Ha-Kibutz ha-Meukhad, Mapam, Ha-Kibutz ha-Artzi / Ha-Shomer ha-Tzair, ha-Poel ha-Mizrakhi, Yishuvei ha-Poel ha-Mizrakhi, ha-Oved ha-Tzioni, and ha-Tzionim ha-Klaliim – originated from all ideological currents. The meetings held on 31.3.1948 and 1.4.1948 were also attended by officers of the Drafting Division.

might prove useful in filling administrative service needs.[11] Ultimately, the mission was called off at the last minute due to the volatile circumstances prevailing in Palestine at the time.[12]

Shortly after the proclamation of Israel's independence on 14 May 1948 and the start of the first Arab–Israeli War, Britain attempted to undermine Israel's efforts in the battles against the Jordanian Arab Legion by announcing that no more visas would be granted to Jewish detainees in Cyprus from that point on.[13] By the second half of 1948, tensions in the camps had escalated dangerously. Reports filed by the General Staff of the Drafting Division detail accounts of violent protests[14] against inhumane conditions in the Dhekelia and Xylotymbou camps on 5 and 6 September of that year. In retaliation, the British imposed even harsher measures. On 28 September 1948, a detainee named Shlomo Hayimzon was shot and killed by British soldiers while attempting to escape. Those who did not manage to escape were arrested and subjected to humiliating treatment.[15] The situation was plainly out of control.

The refusal of the British to liberate the Jewish detainees and their violent treatment of them as well as their negative neutrality at the UN in matters vitally important to Israel (the status of Jerusalem, Israel's admission to the United Nations, the lifting of the embargo on weapons and so foth), acutely intensified the already strong anti-British sentiment in Israel. On 6 June 1948, a letter of protest, signed by Jewish detainees in Cyprus, was submitted to the UN General Assembly Secretariat detailing the inhumane conditions at Karaolos. The British Foreign Office began to realize that the Cyprus issue had to be resolved immediately.

After a series of backroom consultations, British Foreign Secretary Ernest Bevin decided in January of 1949 to close down the detention camps in Cyprus.[16] The first ship to embark from Cyprus carrying Jewish detainees with British consent arrived in Haifa on 25 January 1949.[17] The last Jewish detainee was released from the camp at Dhekelia on 10 February of that year.[18]

2.2 Cooperation between Israelis and Greek Cypriots 1946–9

No sooner had the detention camps in Karaolos become operational in mid-August 1946 than a relationship of cooperation was formed between the Greek Cypriots of

---

[11] IDFA 1003/1950-555, Israeli Army Drafting Division circular no. (גחל/791/3 – 12.4.1948).
[12] IDFA 1003/1950-555, Drafting Division (גחל/1541/2 – 27.4.1948).
[13] Natan Aridan, *Britain-Israel and Anglo-Jewry, 1949–1957* (London and New York: Routledge, 2004), 11, cf. Holland, *Britain and the Revolt in Cyprus*, 146.
[14] IDFA 1042/1949-137, Drafting General Staff, Report אס/1/7/8 – November 1948. Cf. Laub, *Last Barrier*, 47–50.
[15] IDFA 922/1975-397. A. Finkelshtein, *Shurot ha-Meginim be-Makhanot Kafrisin* [*The Defenders' Line in the Cyprus Camps*] (Tel Aviv: Agaf Mivtzayim – Agaf Mateh – Makhleket ha-Segel, Tzava ha-Hagana le-Israel, 1954), 132. Detailed report by the Operations Division of the Israeli Army General Staff on the 'Shurot ha-Meginim' of Jewish detainees in the British camps of Cyprus.
[16] Lowenberg, 'Israel', 399–400.
[17] *Davar*, 'Flotilla Ready for Its Mission "Exodus from Cyprus"', 25.1.1949.
[18] *Ha-Tzofeh*, 'Last Exiles Arrive from Cyprus', 13.2.1949.

Famagusta and the Jewish detainees – a relationship that was to continue until the definitive closure of the camps in early February 1949. The person who played a leading role in all this was Prodromos Papavassiliou.

Papavassiliou[19] was born in the village of Limnia, Famagusta Province, in May 1919. He attended the Commercial Secondary School of Famagusta from which he graduated in 1937 and went on to study economics at university. As a founding member of the Cypriot Corporative Movement, he served as the first secretary of the Commission of all the Corporations of Famagusta in 1937 and was elected to the five-member Secretariat of the Pan-Cypriot Corporative Commission (PSE). In 1941, he joined the AKEL Communist Party and was made a member of the Provincial Committee of Famagusta and the party's Central Committee. Papavassiliou was elected to the Municipal Board of Famagusta in the municipal elections of 1943 and 1946 on the ballot of Adam Adamantos, supported by AKEL. He joined the Cypriot Regiment of the British Army in June 1943, serving in Egypt, Libya, Transjordan and Greece. While serving in the Middle East, he met and befriended Jewish soldiers serving at the Royal Army Service Corps. This was his first contact with Zionist ideology and this is when he realized that the Jews of Palestine and the Greeks of Cyprus shared a common aspiration: to be free of British colonial rule. After his discharge from the army in May of 1946, Papavassiliou and two partners formed a company with the aim of undertaking customs clearance and cargo carriage and turning the company's attention to tourism later on.

In early August 1946, Charles Passman, general director of the Jewish Distribution Committee (JDC), a Jewish American humanitarian organization, informed Papavassiliou that the British intended to establish detention camps in Cyprus very soon for Jews who had attempted to enter Palestine illegally. The JDC requested Papavassiliou's assistance at every level, and he promptly agreed to provide it. As a member of the Famagusta Municipal Board, Papavassiliou entered into negotiations with the British authorities and managed to have the JDC registered as a charitable agency so it could benefit from favourable tax rates. This enabled the JDC to import essential items needed for the detainees without paying customs duties. Within only a short period, Papavassiliou, liaising with Morris Laub, head of the JDC's delegation in Cyprus, and in cooperation with members of the small Jewish community of the island, managed to set up a reception committee comprising medical doctors, nurses, teachers and administrative staff by 13 August 1946 – the day the first Jewish detainees arrived at the Karaolos camps. Papavassiliou then urged Mayor of Famagusta Adam Adamantos along with the local Greek Cypriot Corporative and farmers' organizations to adopt resolutions calling on the British to close down the detention camps and allow the Holocaust survivors to settle in Palestine. At the same time, Papavassiliou saw to the reception of Jewish officials, artists and others travelling from Palestine to Cyprus to

[19] Biographical notes on Prodromos Papavassiliou were obtained from the official website of the Municipality of Famagusta, available online: www.famagusta.org.cy (6 October 2022), the website of the Society for the Preservation of Historic Monuments of Israel, and a recorded interview with Prodromos Papavassiliou from June 2005 by Naomi Yizhar, former curator of the Museum of Jewish Immigration, housed in the refurbished premises of the detention camp at Atlit, North Israel.

visit the camps. These visitors included Golda Meir, subsequently minister of foreign affairs and prime minister of Israel, who had come to the island in November 1947 as a chargé d'affaires of the Jewish Agency to see first-hand the living conditions of the detainees in Karaolos, Dhekelia and Xylotymbou.[20]

The detainees formed close relations with Prodromos Papavassiliou, and affectionately called him 'Papa'. For his part, he made sure they did not lack for food and staples but this was not all. Papavassiliou saw to it that there would always be some means of transport waiting at the exit of tunnels dug by detainees through which letters and messages could be carried to and from the various Jewish military groups, along with illegal weaponry smuggled onto the island from Mandate Palestine.[21] These arms were to be used for the military training of detainees by Haganah cells at the Karaolos camps.[22] What is more, according to detainee testimonies, Papavassiliou helped a large number of them escape from the camps. He secured the cooperation of many anonymous Greek Cypriots living in Famagusta who, for a price, provided information on British movements and assisted Haganah cells by making their own cars, taxis and buses available to them. As documented in the extensive report by the Israeli Army General Staff's Operations Sector on the Shurot ha-Meginim activities in Cyprus, by the second half of 1946, the Haganah had recruited fifteen Greek Cypriots known to the detainees only by their code names. The amount of money administered by Haganah members during their missions in Cyprus included payments made to their Greek Cypriot collaborators,[23] whose true identity remains a mystery to this day.[24]

The accounts of detainees in Cyprus and the solidarity shown them by the island's Greek residents became more widely known through extensive coverage in the Israeli newspapers. Israeli appreciation towards the Greek Cypriots was particularly strong, not only because of the assistance given to the detainees between 1946 and 1949, but also because of their shared desire to be free of the British presence. In June 1949, after

---

[20] Laub, *Last Barrier*, 81–3.

[21] IDFA 922/1975-397; Finkelstein, *Shurot*, 42; and Museum of the Jewish Immigration in Cyprus: Testimony by Gad Hilb, Commander of the *Pan Crescent*, who recounts the actions of Prodromos Papavassiliou that contributed to the two ships, *Pan York* and *Pan Crescent*, setting out from Cyprus for Haifa in July 1948, Palyam Digital Archive, available online: www.palyam.org (accessed 6 October 2022).

[22] *Haaretz*, 'Cypriot Patriot and Zionist – Prodromos ("Papa") Papavassiliou, a Loyal Friend of Israel in Cyprus, 1919–2006', 1.1.2007, Testimony by Emmanuel Gutmann, Professor at the Department of Political Science, Hebrew University of Jerusalem, who while a student taught Hebrew at the detention camps in Cyprus from 1947 until the camps were closed in early February 1949.

[23] IDFA922/1975-39; Finkleshtein, *Shurot*, 18, 129, 134. The Israeli Army Operations Unit report on the activities of the 'Defenders' Line' [Shurot ha-Meginim] includes personal testimonies of Haganah envoys to the camps in Cyprus. One of them, Yosef Gadish, who was there from August 1948 to January 1949, reported that the Haganah 'made 1,000 Israeli pounds available monthly to cover the following expenses: [A, B, C,] D. Payment of Greeks who helped us transport individuals [E. . .]'.

[24] The database maintained by the website of the Society for the Preservation of Israel's Historic Monuments (Ha-Moatza le-Shimur Atarei Moreshet-Israel) is available online, www.maapilim.org.il (accessed 6 October 2022), providing ample information on the Museum of Cyprus Detention Camps outside the town of Atlit, in Northern Israel includes an alphabetical list of names of Greek Cypriots who helped Jewish detainees, either during their detention in the camps or in their attempts to flee. Aside from Prodromos Papavassiliou, all other Greek Cypriots are listed only by their first names, most of which are probably code names.

the camps were closed, Famagusta Mayor Adam Adamantos and Deputy Mayor
Christos Savvides paid a week-long visit to Israel, where local leaders gave them a
warm welcome. This was the first formal visit by Greek Cypriot officials to Israel, made
at the invitation of the Israeli government, and it received broad coverage in the local
press.

On 24 June 1949, Adamantos and Savvides travelled by air from Cyprus to Haifa
Airport, where they were met by Mayor Shabtai Levi.[25] On 28 June, they visited the
Israeli Parliament in Jerusalem and were received by Knesset Secretary Moshe Rosetti,
who expressed 'the warm appreciation of the State of Israel for the humane attitude of
the people of Cyprus and for the assistance that Cypriots offered to the Jewish refugees
during their internment there'.[26] That same day, they were given a guided tour by the
mayor of Jerusalem's Jewish sector, Daniel Auster.[27] On 1 July, they met with Tel Aviv
Mayor Israel Rokach,[28] and on 4 July, with high-ranking officials of the central
committee of the Histadrut Federation of Workers in Tel Aviv.[29]

Typical of the enthusiastic reception given to the Greek Cypriot dignitaries is the
extensive report published by the *Ha-Tzofeh* newspaper on 13 July 1949:

A modest ceremony of gratitude to the people of Cyprus and particularly the
citizens of Famagusta for their commendable attitude towards the detainees in the
Cypriot camps was held in the conference hall of the Jewish Agency in Tel Aviv,
during which Mr Savvides, Deputy Mayor of the city was presented with a cheque
for 2,000 Israeli liras as a first instalment of a donation towards the construction of
a children's playground in Famagusta. The donation was made jointly by the Israeli
government, the Jewish Agency and the Association of Municipalities and
Communities of Israel. Moshe Kohl, member of the board of directors of the
Jewish Agency, spoke most warmly of the people of Cyprus who so empathetically
felt for the dire circumstances the Jewish detainees in Cyprus had come under
and who did everything in their power to help them. He further stressed that,
besides the cash donation, an Israeli specialist would be dispatched to help
complete the construction of the children's playground in Famagusta. Deputy
Mayor Savvides thanked Mr Kohl with emotion.[30] The Municipality of Tel Aviv
also made a 300 Israeli Lira donation to the Municipality of Famagusta 'in
appreciation to the Famagustans for their gestures of friendship towards our
detained fellow Jews' [...].[31]

Israel did not forget the assistance of the Greek Cypriots to the Karaolos detainees.
Ten years later, in the award-winning American film *Exodus* (1960), based on the

[25] *Heruth*, 'Famagusta Mayor Visits Israel', 26.6.1949.
[26] Ibid., 'Famagusta Mayor Tours Jerusalem', 1.7.1949; and *Ha-Tzofeh* newspaper, 'Visitors to the Knesset', 29.6.1949.
[27] *Ha-Tzofeh*, column, 'Institutions and Personalities', 3.7.1949.
[28] *Heruth*, 'Famagusta Mayor Visits Tel Aviv City Hall', 4.7.1949.
[29] *Davar*, 'Guests from Cyprus at Histadrut Institutions', 7.7.1949.
[30] *Ha-Tzofeh*, 'Israel Makes Contribution for Cypriot Children', 13.7.1949.
[31] *Ha-Tzofeh*, 'Government Loan of 200,000 Israeli Pounds to City of Tel Aviv', 1.8.1949.

homonymous vessel used to carry Jewish Holocaust survivors from Germany to Haifa, the character of Plato Mandria was a clear reference to the personality of Prodromos Papavassiliou.[32] On 30 April 2018, the Municipality of Haifa inaugurated 'Papa' Square, named after Papavassiliou on Hubert Humphrey Road.[33]

Immediately after the closure of the detention camps and a few months before the Enosis Plebiscite of January 1950, Israeli public opinion held that Cyprus fully identified with its Greek roots. Most Israeli newspaper reports of that period, regardless of their ideologies, emphasized at every opportunity in their descriptions of life in the British camps the desire of Cypriot residents to shed the colonialist British yoke and realize their dream of unification with Greece. At the time, the average Israeli citizen assumed that the Greek Cypriot demand for Enosis was more than self-evident. And, of course, the desire of the Greeks in Cyprus to be rid of British rule was completely in line with the strong anti-British sentiment in Israel.

Still, despite the deeply felt solidarity Israeli society fostered towards Cypriot Hellenism, the Ben-Gurion government from very early on assumed a distinctly more reserved stance towards the Enosis movement. Israeli diplomacy had to take into serious consideration the international stakes of the time: the regional importance of Britain and Turkey, and the stand-offish attitude of Athens towards the fledgling Jewish state.

2.3 The inauguration of Israel's general consulate in Nicosia, 1950

With the closure of the detention camps in Cyprus in early February 1949 and the liberation of the last detainees in Karaolos, Dhekelia and Xylotymbou, the Ben-Gurion government was not inclined to aggravate relations with Britain. London maintained a negative neutrality towards Israel at the UN and abstained from voting on both motions to admit Israel. Ben-Gurion's government knew very well that in order for Israel to earn the trust of the United States and the West, it would have to improve its relations with Britain.[34]

Britain's de facto recognition of Israel came with the latter's proclamation of independence,[35] which did not, however, signal the start of normal bilateral relations. It was not until five months after the camps in Cyprus had closed that Israel appointed Mordechai Eliash, a jurist and academic, as its chargé d'affaires in London. Eliash presented his credentials to King George VI on 10 June 1949.[36] Yet it took another eleven months for Britain to recognize Israel de jure, on 28 April 1950.[37]

[32] George Th. Mavrogordatos, 'Greek Cypriots and Jews in *Exodus*: A Novel of Israel by Leon Uris', in *Historical Perspectives*, ed. Kazamias and Antoniou, 88–9.
[33] Embassy of Israel in Cyprus, 'Papa Square Inaugurated in Haifa', press release, 30.4.2018.
[34] Cf. 1.1.2 and 1.1.4.
[35] *Al ha-Mishmar*, 'First Secretary of British Diplomatic Mission Arrives', 11.5.1949.
[36] *Ha-Tzofeh*, 'King of England to Receive Israel's Chargé d'Affaires', 10.6.1949.
[37] Besides proceeding to de jure recognition of Israel, on 28.4.1949 Britain also acknowledged Jordan's annexation of East Jerusalem. The Foreign Office appointed an ambassador to Tel Aviv and two consuls to Jerusalem, one in the Israeli (Western Europe) sector of the city and one in the Jordanian (eastern) sector. Cf. *Davar*, 'Britain Recognises Israel and Annexed Territories', 28.4.1950.

As diplomatic relations between Israel and Britain became normalized, colonial Cyprus was the only nearby country not at war with the Jewish state. Cypriot harbours and airports were able to facilitate Israel's commercial transactions with other foreign countries, while also serving as the closest transit point for diaspora Jews on their way to settle in Israel. However, this was predicated on the existence of smooth relations between Israel and the British authorities in the neighbouring island.

As early as the summer of 1949, the Israeli Ministry of Foreign Affairs prepared to establish a diplomatic presence in Cyprus by placing an unpaid, honorary vice consul there. Initially, Gabriel Berdy, a British subject of Jewish descent and a permanent resident of Larnaca, was selected to fill the position. Berdy and his family had settled in the early twentieth century in Nicosia Province, as part of the Jewish farming settlement project financed by the Jewish Colonization Association (JCA) and Maurice de Hirsch, a German baron of Jewish descent.[38] In 1923, the JCA decided to discontinue financing the programme and in 1927, withdrew permanently from Cyprus, after selling off the large piece of farmland it had purchased in Marko.[39] The Jewish families living in Marko and the surrounding villages left, some of them for Israel, and others for Europe. The Berdy family were among the few Jewish families to remain in Cyprus and settle in the village of Kouklia, Famagusta Province.[40] When the British detention camps in Cyprus became operational in 1946–9, 30-year-old Gabriel Berdy offered his services to his detained co-religionists and, together with the few remaining members of the local Jewish community, saw to the maintenance of the Jewish cemetery in Marko.[41] In fact, Berdy himself worked closely with Papavassiliou, then a member of the Municipal Board of Famagusta, to assist the Jewish detainees in Karaolos as well as the underground Haganah cells on the island.[42]

By way of a memo addressed to the Ministry of Foreign Affairs on 19 September 1949, the Israeli Ministry of Immigration and Absorption (the Ministry of Aliyah) proposed that the duties of 'Aliyah officer' be assigned to Berdy along with the duties of honorary vice consul.[43] The aliyah officer was responsible for determining whether diaspora Jews applying for permission to settle in Israel met the conditions for obtaining travel documents, and then with issuing the special entry visas. The Aliyah Ministry's proposal was accepted by the Israeli Ministry of Foreign Affairs which sent a letter to Berdy on 21 September 1949, informing him in writing of his appointment as honorary vice consul of Israel in Cyprus and assigning him the additional duties of aliyah officer.[44] The Israeli Foreign Ministry's Division for Consular Affairs then sent

---

[38] Cf. Seltenreich and Katz, 'Between the Galilee'; and Ben Artzi 'Historical Perspectives', 13–17.
[39] Cf. 2.1 on the Jewish settlement in Marko, Province of Nicosia.
[40] Atun, 'Initiative to Colonize', 790–4. According to civil registry sources, in September 1946 there were four Jewish families living in the village of Kouklia, Famagusta Province. One of these was the family of Michael and Rosa Berdy. Their son, Gabriel Berdy, was 31 at the time. Since the Turkish invasion of Cyprus in 1974, Kouklia has been controlled by the Turkish Army and renamed Köprülü.
[41] Weinstein, *Tzionut*, 17.
[42] Cf. 2.2 above.
[43] ISA/RG130/MFA/2584/11, Ministry for Immigration and Absorption (Ministry of Aliyah) to the Ministry of Foreign Affairs (027/142/462/7573 – 19.9.1949).
[44] ISA/RG130/MFA/2584/11, Ministry of Foreign Affairs to Berdy (MH5990/21.9.1949).

Berdy's credentials on to Israel's diplomatic representation in London to complete the necessary process at the Foreign Office so they could then be forwarded to the British authorities in Cyprus.[45]

But although the credentials had already reached Berdy in Cyprus,[46] the Foreign Office's International Treaty Division sent a document to Israel's diplomatic mission in London on 14 December 1949 raising objections and invoking the opposition of the governor of Cyprus, who purportedly found that Berdy 'may perhaps not be entirely suitable for appointment as honorary Consul'. Moreover, Britain instructed Israel to appoint someone else to the position and recommended David Slonim, a British subject of Jewish descent permanently residing in Cyprus. Slonim was the owner of the Cyprus Palestine Plantation Company Ltd., a plant nursery in Pissouri, Limassol Province, who, it was believed, 'would be prepared to accept the appointment if it were offered to him'.[47] The Foreign Office letter unequivocally concluded: 'If your Government still desires to proceed with the appointment of Mr Berdy, we should not wish to withhold recognition from him.'[48] The Israeli chargé d'affaires in London transmitted the British ultimatum to Israel, proposing that Berdy's appointment be cancelled, 'as the Government of Cyprus would only make life difficult for him', while simultaneously suggesting that for reasons of prestige, Israel need not conform with Britain's demand to choose someone it considered more 'appropriate' to represent Israel's interests in the neighbouring island.[49]

Despite repeated attempts by Berdy to receive some kind of explanation from the local British authorities,[50] the reason for which he had unofficially been rendered *persona non grata* was never specified,[51] nor did the British authorities ever explain to him why David Slonim was 'more appropriate'.[52] The British position was not

[45] ISA/RG130/MFA/2584/11, Consular Affairs Division to Israel's Diplomatic Mission in London (7125/20/1171/7/ח – 28.11.1949).

[46] ISA/RG130/MFA/2584/11, Berdy to the Consular Affairs Division (1120/ר/1 – 6.12.1949).

[47] The Cyprus Palestine Plantation Company Ltd. had been registered with the relevant Cypriot corporate registry since January 1933. David Slonim, an agronomist of Russian Jewish origin, ran the farming unit in Pisouri. Cf. Mathopoulou, 'Pioneers', 39–41.

[48] ISA/RG130/MFA/2584/11, Foreign Office (SW1 Section) to the Israeli Embassy in London (T11876/31/385 – 14.12.1949).

[49] ISA/RG130/MFA/2584/11, Michael Comay, Head of the British Commonwealth Division, to Mordechai Kidron, First Secretary of the Israeli Embassy in London (ZL/PK/3568 – 19.12.1949).

[50] ISA/RG130/MFA/2584/11, Berdy to Zvi Avnon, Head of the Consular Affairs Division (not officially logged) and Comay to Kidron (FO/D/1120/17468 – 31.1.1950).

[51] ISA/RG130/MFA/2584/11, Comay to Walter Eytan, director general of the Ministry of Foreign Affairs (1561/20/1120/3/ח – 5.1.1950), and Kidron to Comay (ZL/RK/35055 – 16.1.1950).

[52] ISA/RG130/MFA/2584/11, Kidron to Comay (ZL/RK/35171 – 22.2.1950). Following the clarifications requested by Berdy in Cyprus, the British side reacted yet more vehemently to the prospect of Berdy's appointment. More specifically, in the cable cited above, Kidron writes from London to Comay:

> Dunbar (from the FCO Treaty Division) phoned me and in a most apologetic and hesitant manner said that the Cyprus Government had replied to his second enquiry in even stronger terms than the first. They now said that Mr Berdy would be definitely unacceptable to them, whereas the first time they had merely expressed the hope that his candidature would not be pressed. They again proposed Slonim.

groundless, however. In August 1948, Berdy had been arrested by the British on suspicion of helping Jewish detainees escape from Karaolos.[53] Nevertheless, Israel was reluctant to comply with London's orders, especially given the increased strain on diplomatic relations that preceded the definitive closure of the Cyprus camps in February 1949.[54] Thus, the Israeli Ministry of Foreign Affairs decided to tacitly reject the 'status quo' candidate indicated by the British.[55] In an effort to put the whole issue to rest, however, Israel was ultimately forced to revoke Berdy's appointment as well.[56]

But this was not the end of the saga. The Israelis wanted diplomatic representation on the island. At the same time, it became a matter of honour to teach a little lesson to the British Foreign Office, which insisted on having a say as to who would or would not be 'suitable' to defend Israeli interests in Cyprus. Thus, despite the financial cost, the Israeli Ministry of Foreign Affairs eventually decided to place a career diplomat in Cyprus, rather than an unpaid, honorary vice consul. By so doing, the British would not be able to raise objections as to the person selected to fill the post.[57]

The appointment of Ram Yaron (Yerachmiel Yaron, aka Robert Lustig) as Israeli consul in Cyprus on 1 June 1950 was by no means fortuitous. Yaron, who joined the diplomatic corps after a brief period of training, had served as head of police interrogations in Mandate Palestine while simultaneously acting as a Haganah informer, a fact possibly known to the British. After Israel declared independence, he was appointed Chief of Interrogations General Staff of the Israel Police Force.[58] The phrasing of a letter sent on 29 July 1950 by Zvi Avnon, director of the Israeli Foreign Ministry's Consular Affairs Division, to Avraham Kidron, Israel's ambassador in London, explains why Ram Yaron had been selected specifically to serve in Cyprus:[59] 'For reasons of good order, let it be remembered that since the aforementioned is an Israeli citizen, commissioned to Cyprus as an ordinary Foreign Affairs Ministry officer, there can be no issue of his arrival being predicated on previous approval by the competent British authorities.' When London learned of Yaron's placement, the Foreign Office remained absolutely silent for two weeks. Finally, on 14 August 1950, the *Agrément*[60] to Yaron's appointment was issued, though not before a number of reminders had been sent to the Foreign Office by the Israeli Embassy in London.[61]

[53] *Eleftheria*, 'Eleven Jewish Escapees Apprehended', 6.8.1948. Cf. Vasiliki Selioti, *Vretanika Stratopeda Evraion Prosfygon stin Kypro (1946–1949)* [*British Camps for Jewish Refugees in Cyprus (1946–1949)*] (Thessaloniki: Epikentro, 2016).

[54] ISA/RG130/MFA/2584/11, Comay to Kidron (FO/D/1120/20/13283 – 2.1.1950). Comay, when responding to Kidron, said, 'We feel no obligation to appoint Slonim based solely on the fact that the Cypriot authorities threw that particular name into the hat.'

[55] ISA/RG130/MFA/2584/11, Memorandum from Avnon to the British Commonwealth Division (28536/20/1120/ב/ח – 12.3.1950) and Comay to Kidron (FO/D/1120/20/23161 – 6.3.1950).

[56] ISA/RG130/MFA/2584/11, Avnon to Berdy (24001/20/1120/ז/ח – 9.3.1950).

[57] ISA/RG130/MFA/2584/11, Memo from Avnon to Comay (26894/20/1120/ב/ח – 6.3.1950).

[58] David Tidhar (ed.), *Entsiklopedia le-Khalutzey ha-Yishuv u-Vonav* (Tel Aviv: David Tidhar, 1952), vol. 5, 2288.

[59] ISA/RG130/MFA/2584/11, Avnon to Kidron (67981/20/1120/ז/ח – 29.7.1950).

[60] ISA/RG130/MFA/2584/11, Kidron to Comay (20/1171/ז – 14.8.1950).

[61] ISA/RG130/MFA/2584/11, Avnon to Kidron (MH10322 – 21.7.1950) and Comay to Kidron (MH10501 – 6.8.1950).

The Israeli consulate in Nicosia became operational on 28 August 1950, temporarily housed in a room of the Ledra Palace Hotel. The provisional recognition of Ram Yaron as consul general of Israel to Cyprus was published in the *Cyprus Gazette* two days later.[62]

News of the inauguration of an Israeli consulate in Nicosia was greeted with enthusiastic articles in the Israeli press, touting the fact that in Cyprus, a strong reminder of the years of hardship under British rule, the Jewish state now enjoyed an official diplomatic presence and could interact 'on equal terms with its former jailers'. Extensive coverage by the newspaper *Maariv* gave the impression that numerous Jewish families had filed aliyah applications with the newly appointed consul and that many residents of the neighbouring island were rushing to the consulate to obtain visas as soon as possible in order to seek care in Israeli hospitals. No other Israeli diplomatic mission abroad had created such a stir amongst Israeli journalists. In typical fashion, *Maariv* even listed the name of the sole consulate employee – a secretary to the consul, 'Mrs Shoshana Mizrahi of Jerusalem'.[63]

In 1950, there were six career diplomats who represented their countries, and the Israeli consul was one of them. The other five career diplomats were the consuls of Greece, Turkey, the US, Egypt and Lebanon. There were also fifteen honorary consuls, all of Greek-Cypriot origin, who represented each one of them.[64] Israel's consulate general acquired its permanent premises in October 1950,[65] at 2 Adonis Street in Nicosia.[66]

2.3.1 The first issues on the agenda of the newly founded Israeli consulate in Cyprus

2.3.1.1 *The Jewish community of Cyprus*

The Israeli consul's first concern was to rally the local Jewish element and establish the legal status of the Jewish community of Cyprus. According to the first monthly activity report filed by Ram Yaron for the month of September 1950,[67] the total number of Jews living in Cyprus – people of 'Jewish national conscience', as he described them – was just 200. Of these, 30 per cent were British citizens permanently established on the island, 5 per cent were Israeli citizens and the rest were citizens of third countries or stateless. Of Cyprus' Jewish inhabitants, 20 per cent spoke Hebrew, and most lived

62 ISA/RG93/MFA/2156/3, Yaron to the British Commonwealth Division, Monthly Activities Report of the Israeli Consulate in Nicosia.
63 *Maariv*, 'First day of Israeli Consulate in Cyprus – Family of Jewish immigrants requested visa to enter Israel – Patients want to be cured by our doctors – Duties of Yerachmiel Yaron focus of Middle East monitoring', 17.9.1950.
64 ISA/RG93/MFA/2156/3, Yaron to the British Commonwealth Division, Monthly Activities Report of the Israeli Consulate at Nicosia, September 1950.
65 ISA/RG93/MFA/2156/3, Yaron to the British Commonwealth Division, Monthly Activities Report of the Israeli Consulate in Nicosia, October 1950.
66 State of Israel, *Government Yearbook 5714 (1953–54)*, (Jerusalem: Government Printer, 1953), 160–1.
67 ISA/RG93/MFA/2156/3, Yaron to the British Commonwealth Division, Monthly Activities Report of the Israeli Consulate in Nicosia, September 1950.

in Larnaca. Yaron established contact with the local Jewish Welfare Committee which had been set up in order to provide humanitarian aid to internees of the Karaolos camps during the period 1946–9.

Elections for an acting board of directors of the Cyprus Jewish Community were held on 10 September 1950, though its members seemed less than eager to become more active, and only 32 came to vote. Furthermore, it was not long before intensely divisive trends manifested between the newly elected four-member board of directors and a sizeable number of Jews in the community who insisted that the Jewish Welfare Committee continue to represent them in practice. In September 1950, with Yaron's encouragement, the newly elected board of directors completed all legal formalities and obtained approval from the local authorities for the legal status of the Jewish community of Cyprus, based in Larnaca.[68] After numerous attempts, Yaron managed to rally the Jews of Cyprus around the Israeli consulate. In December of that year, the few Jews scattered throughout the island's larger towns were persuaded to attend the traditional religious ceremonies held at the Israeli consulate in Nicosia in observation of Hanukkah.[69]

As was the case in other countries where Israel maintained diplomatic missions, so, too, in Cyprus, the Israeli consul's first priority was to determine whether the local Jewish element was in a position to exert an influence over the decision-making centres. Yaron had realized early on that the local Jewish community had little to no influence over the local British authorities, or over the leadership of either of the two major communities on the island, the Greek Cypriot and Turkish Cypriot. In 1950, the Jews, living scattered in the towns, seemed reluctant to cultivate any sense of cohesion. Despite concerted efforts by the consuls who succeeded Yaron over the next few years, international Jewish organizations were not eager to provide financial support to the local Jewish community, mainly due to its limited membership.[70] More specifically, Consul Avraham Kidron, Yaron's successor, wrote to the Chief Rabbi of the British Armed Forces in November 1954, asking him to provide practical support for the Jewish presence on Cyprus. Kidron's main argument cited the significant number of Jews living on the island who, he said, ought not to be neglected. According to Kidron, in late 1954, a total of 59 Jewish families (126 people) lived in Cyprus: 25 Jewish families (52 persons) in Nicosia, 20 families (44 persons) in Larnaca, 6 families (12 persons) in Limassol, 4 families (7 persons) in Famagusta, 2 families (6 persons) in Kyrenia, 1 family (of 2 persons) in Morphou and 1 family (of 3 persons) in Marko.[71]

[68] Ibid.
[69] ISA/RG93/MFA/2156/3, Yaron to the British Commonwealth Division, Monthly Activities Report of the Israeli Consulate in Nicosia, December 1950.
[70] ISA/RG93/2155/4, The persistent pleas by Avraam Kidron for financial and institutional assistance to the Jewish Community of Cyprus over the second half of 1954 and through to early 1955, directed at Israel's Embassy in London and other Jewish bodies based in Britain and in Israel, fell on deaf ears: Kidron to Rekhavam Amir, Israeli Consul in London (1254/4/ק – 22.9.1954), Kidron to Amir, (1311/4/ק – 8.10.1954), Kidron to the Jewish Agency/Department of Education and Culture of the Jewish Diaspora (1619/4/ק – 17.12.1954) and Kidron to London's Anglo-Jewish Association (CSS/PR-23.12.1954).
[71] ISA/RG93/2155/4, Kidron to Y. Levi, Chief Rabbi of the British Armed Forces (letter dated 22.11.1954, not officially logged).

Although Kidron was known for his detailed departmental reports, this particular letter did not clarify whether the numbers he quoted were the same as those in the official records kept by the local authorities. He also failed to specify whether the Jewish families in Cyprus at the time were permanently established on the island or whether they were there temporarily for business purposes. Thus, Kidron gave the impression of wanting to exaggerate the actual size of the Jewish element in Cyprus, in an obvious effort to attract the interest of Jewish bodies, both in Israel and beyond, concerned about the needs of the Jewish diaspora. Ultimately, his endeavours came to naught.

2.3.1.2 *The British authorities' cold shoulder*

Over the first months of the Israeli consulate's operations in Nicosia, the Foreign Office's objections to the person to be appointed as Israel's vice consul in Cyprus still echoed in the air.[72] Britain may have recognized Israel de jure in April 1950, but the chill in their bilateral relations persisted.

Typical of the unpleasant situation was an incident that occurred when British customs authorities in Cyprus announced that diplomatic pouches addressed to the Israeli consul would be subject to special controls. The announcement triggered a most vehement reaction – both verbal and written – by Consul Yaron to the assistant secretary on consular affairs at the Foreign Office.[73] In the end, all diplomatic pouches were delivered to the Israeli consulate unopened, and the secretary of the colony apologized in writing. Nevertheless, no assurance was given that such incidents would not recur – a fact Yaron noted in his report.[74] Such 'special' treatment reserved by the British authorities for Consul Yaron was no doubt related to his resistance activities in Palestine under the Mandate.[75]

Meanwhile, the local press which espoused the positions of the British authorities was openly critical of Israel. An article published in the *Cyprus Mail* of 12 January 1951, reported that 150 diaspora Jews aboard the Turkish passenger vessel *Buntas*, heading for Haifa and intending to permanently settle in Israel, had been prevented from landing by the Israeli port authorities, and forced to return to Limassol because, according to the paper, 'the young State of Israel, unable to feed its rapidly growing population, has to refuse entry to unauthorised immigrants, just as did the British during the much-vilified Mandate'. The same article observed that 'one hears of Jews wishing to leave Israel owing to lack of opportunity there and being prevented from doing so. The "Wandering Jew" of the Biblical legend does not seem as yet to have escaped his misfortunes.'[76] The report drew strong reactions from Israel's Ministry of Foreign Affairs, which hastened to refute it as fabrication. According to the Israelis, the *Buntas* was transporting 202 Jewish immigrants, 4 Israeli citizens and 6 tourists who

---

[72] Cf. 2.3 on Gabriel Berdy's appointment.
[73] ISA/RG93/MFA/2156/3, Yaron to the British Commonwealth Division (2/כ/ד/ק – 8.11.1950).
[74] ISA/RG93/MFA/2156/3, Yaron to the British Commonwealth Division, Monthly Activities Report of the Israeli Consulate in Nicosia, November 1950.
[75] Cf. 2.3.
[76] ISA/RG93/MFA/2156/3, '150 Jews Turned Back from Israel', *Cyprus Mail*, 12 January 1951.

had all disembarked normally in Haifa on 27 December 1950.[77] Yaron responded with a strongly worded and lengthy letter to the *Cyprus Mail*, which was published on 17 January 1951.[78] During the second half of 1950 and early 1951, the climate between the Israeli consulate in Cyprus and the local British authorities was truly explosive, yet only a few months later, all had been forgotten.[79]

2.3.1.3 *The Cypriot left-wing trade unions: A critical attitude*

In addition to the cold shoulder of the British, the Israeli Consul was also faced with criticism from the local trade unionist movement. In October 1950, just a month after the inauguration of the Israeli consulate in Nicosia, Andreas Ziartides, secretary general of the leftist Pan-Cypriot Labour Federation (PEO), criticized the Israeli government's decision[80] to block the fifth annual convention of the left-wing Arab Trade Union Congress (Mwatamar al-'Umal al-Arab), scheduled to take place in Nazareth on 23 and 24 September 1950. The PEO's protest letter to the Israeli Consul dated 25 October 1950 stated its displeasure:

Please transmit our protest to the Israeli Government for this undemocratic, antilabour measure. We think that such measures are contrary to the declaration of the Israeli Government about Democracy and Freedom. We further believe that these measures are doing great harm to the interests of the Jewish People themselves, who are still in need of the international working-class solidarity and friendship. The banning of the Congress of a labour organization is a downright violation of the obligations of Israel undertaken by the signing of the UN Charter. You know Sir, that UN unanimously adopted a resolution on Trade Union Freedom. The violation of these obligations exposes the Jewish state and the Jewish People in the eyes of the democratic world.

One year earlier, in April 1949, the Arab Trade Union Congress had held its fourth annual convention in Nazareth. At the conclusion of the event, on 9 April 1949, a resolution was issued protesting measures that the Israeli Army had instituted against the Arab population in the aftermath of the 1948 Arab–Israeli War. By way of that resolution, the Arab Trade Union Congress stated its opposition to the special military administration regime imposed by Israeli security forces in Arab cities, towns and villages in the country's northern and southern regions. That convention had taken place under tense circumstances, having coincided with an extensive campaign by the Israeli police that resulted in the mass expulsion of Arab residents from their homes in

---

[77] ISA/RG93/MFA/2156/3, Comay to Yaron (3979/17.1.1951).
[78] ISA/RG93/MFA/2156/3, Consul General Yaron's letter to the *Cyprus Mail*, 17 January 1951.
[79] Cf. 2.4.2 and 2.4.2.1.
[80] PEO Historical Archive / International Relations Subsection / File: 'Israel, 1946–1962'. Ziartides' letter to Yaron (25.10.1950).

the centre of Haifa.[81] The following year, on 16 September 1950 and exactly one week prior to the scheduled opening day of the fifth annual convention of the Arab Trade Union Congress in Nazareth, the Israeli Army had arrested some Congress members as they were distributing leaflets in Haifa condemning the pro-government Jewish trade union, Histadrut, for its refusal to admit Arab trade unionists and workers.[82] It is clear that the decision of the Israeli authorities not to allow the Arab Trade Union Congress to hold its fifth annual convention in September 1950 was related both to the tensions manifested a year earlier and the volatile atmosphere created by the recent arrests of Congress members in Haifa.

Consul Ram Yaron immediately notified the PEO in writing that its letter of protest had been forwarded to the Ministry of Foreign Affairs.[83] He also filed a question with the competent division of the Ministry as to whether it would be advisable to offer an official response on behalf of the consulate.[84] Yaron was explicitly ordered to refrain from any confrontation with the Cypriot trade union.[85] But this was not the end of the matter. The PEO's protest was forwarded interdepartmentally by the Foreign Ministry to the office of Prime Minister Ben-Gurion,[86] so that Yaron would be prepared to respond to any additional protests from the PEO regarding that particular issue, the Arab Affairs Division of the Prime Minister's Office prepared a detailed report describing the special administrative regime Israel had imposed on Arab urban and semi-urban centres.[87] The official reason for not allowing the Arab Trade Union Congress to hold its convention was that the organizers had failed to file a timely application with Nazareth's Military Command, which was the competent authority to grant a 'permit to assemble'.[88]

---

[81] Adi Ofir, 'Sh'at ha-Efes' ['Time Zero'], in *Khamishim le-Arbaim u-Shmone: Momentim Bikortiim be-Toldot Medinat Israel* [*Fifty to Forty-Eight: Critical Moments in the History of the State of Israel*], ed. Adi Ofir (Jerusalem and Tel Aviv: Van Leer Institute and Ha-Kibbutz ha-Meukhad, 1999), 28.

[82] Baruch Kimmerling, 'Al-Naqba' ['The Naqbah'], in *Khamishim*, ed. Ofir, 38.

[83] ISA/RG93/MFA/2156/3, Yaron to PEO (C/C/K/10-29.10.1950).

[84] ISA/RG93/MFA/2156/3, Yaron to the British Commonwealth Division (13/ג/ק/פ – 31.10.1950).

[85] ISA/RG93/MFA/2156/3, British Commonwealth Division to Yaron (29710/2232/3/ה – 8.12.1950).

[86] ISA/RG93/MFA/2156/3, British Commonwealth Division to the Arab Affairs Department at the Office of the Prime Minister (5528/20/71/ו/ה – 8.11.1950).

[87] Mustafa Kabha, 'Khavrei ha-Knesset shel Reshimot ha-Lavian ha-Araviot bi-Tkufat ha-Memshal ha-Tsvai, 1948–1966' ['Knesset Members of Arab Satellite Parties and Their Activity during the Era of the Military Administration, 1948–1966'], in *Etgarim Bitkhoniim u-Medinim be-Mivkhan ha-Metsiut: Israel bein ha-Olam ha-Aravi ve-ha-Zira ha-Benleumit* [*Security and Policy Challenges in Practice: Israel between the Arab World and Global Reality*], ed. Michael Laskier and Ronen Yitzhak (Ramat Gan: Bar-Ilan University, 2012), 203–5. Four months before the end of the 1948 war and the signing of the armistice agreements in Rhodes, the Israeli government decided on 21.10.1948 to place areas of concentrated Arab populations under military command. After the war, there were 156,000 Arabs living in Israeli territory. Five local military commands were established for the cities of Nazareth, Ramla–Lod and Jaffa and the districts of Western Galilee in the north and the Negev Desert in the south. The regime imposed by the local military commands was defined by a number of 'Emergency Laws' the British had imposed in Palestine before the founding of the State of Israel. The military commands were abolished by law, passed by the Knesset on 1.12.1966, on the recommendation of the head of the Mossad intelligence service at the time, Isser Harel.

[88] ISA/RG93/MFA/2156/3, Arab Affairs Department / Office of the Prime Minister to the British Commonwealth Division (89/4/195 – 11.12.1950). Report by Barukh Yekutieli, special adviser to the Office of the Prime Minister on Arab matters.

The Israelis gave serious thought to the PEO letter of protest. It was the first time an official Cypriot organization had criticized Israeli policies vis-à-vis its Arab citizens; the first time, too, that the Israeli consulate had to address a sensitive issue – within only a few weeks of its opening. The criticism originated from the most powerful unionist organization of Cyprus which represented a large portion of the population, and at a time when the anti-colonialist reverberations of the Enosis Plebiscite were still strong. As such, the matter had to be handled by the Israeli consulate with great care if it wished to avoid setting an undesirable precedent for Israel's image among the Cypriots.

Apparently, the detailed report from the Israeli Prime Minister's Office was intended to brief Yaron thoroughly on the matter so that he would be in a position to counter any further actions taken either by the PEO or any other organization on the island. Correspondence records of the Israeli consulate in Nicosia indicate that the PEO did not respond and Yaron was not required to take further action.

The self-control demonstrated by the Israeli Ministry of Foreign Affairs in handling this incident served as an example for all consuls who succeeded Yaron in Cyprus throughout the 1950s. The Israeli consulate in Nicosia systematically avoided any confrontation with local public opinion – whether Greek or Turkish Cypriot – on any matter related to the living conditions of the Arab population in Israel and the Arab–Israeli conflict in general.

2.4 Israel and the Enosis movement, 1950–4

2.4.1 The reluctance of Ben-Gurion's government to provide political support for the Enosis movement

Only a few months before the consulate in Nicosia opened its doors, Israeli diplomacy found itself for the first time facing the Greek Cypriot demand for Enosis. On 6 March 1950, the Israeli Prime Minister's Office received a letter addressed to Ben-Gurion from Archbishop Makarios II dated 10 February 1950. The archbishop's letter was chronologically the first official Greek Cypriot document to be entered into the Israel State Archives.

First and foremost, Makarios II's letter included statistical data on the island's population distribution, based on a census carried out by British authorities in 1946.[89] It also laid out the events that preceded the plebiscite of January 1950, highlighting the determination of the overwhelming majority of inhabitants to unite the island with

---

[89] ISA/RG43/G/5570/10, Archbishop Makarios II's letter to Israeli Prime Minister David Ben-Gurion, 10.2.1950. Referring to the distribution of the population, he wrote: 'Cyprus, according to the latest official census (1946) has 450,114 inhabitants, of whom 361,199 are Greeks and 88,915 are Turks, Armenians, Maronites, etc., that is, over 80% of the population are Greeks ardently desiring and struggling for the termination of the British rule and their restoration into the Motherly arms.'

Greece.[90] Now known as the *Enotikon* (Pro-Union), the plebiscite was carried at all Orthodox churches on the island by collecting signatures on two consecutive Sundays (15 and 22 January 1950) at the end of the Sunday mass.[91] Makarios II's letter was more of a declaration. The same text was sent to other foreign leaders; it did not make any specific claim, and concluded as follows:

> Relying upon our just cause, we firmly believe that our national struggle will meet with a favourable response in the hearts of all the free peoples of the world and their Governments, for our struggle is in harmony with the oral principles of the allied struggle, for which Greece championing the cause of freedom gave herself up as a sacrifice, while Cyprus voluntarily offered everything she could in human life and material resources.
>
> In submitting the present communication, we deem it necessary to add that we are determined to carry on our national struggle without ceasing and by all internationally recognized legal means, until it is brought to a successful conclusion.[92]

It was not the prime minister but Walter Eytan, secretary general of the Israeli Ministry of Foreign Affairs who replied to the Cypriot archbishop with a brief and carefully worded letter, dated 8 March 1950. Without expressing an opinion as to the essence of the issue, the response referred neutrally to 'the people of Cyprus' and closed with an equally non-committal reassurance that Israel was 'taking an interest' in the developments unfolding on the neighbouring island. The letter read as follows:

> I am instructed by the Prime Minister, Mr David Ben-Gurion, to acknowledge receipt of your letter of 10th February 1950, in which you communicated to him the results of the plebiscite recently held in Cyprus.
>
> The people of this country, who take a deep interest in the welfare of the people of Cyprus, watched the progress and the result of the plebiscite with close attention.

---

[90] ISA/RG43/G/5570/10, ibid.:

> The Government having refused to carry out the plebiscite, we ourselves conducted it in a very peaceful and genuine manner. The result was that out of 224,747 eligible voters of over 18, including both sexes, 215,108 voted for union with Greece, that is 95,7% or over 80% of the whole population of the Island. The very small percentage of Greeks who abstained from voting is made up of Government officials and other persons dependent on the Government. By means of circulars and other measures the Government forbade them to participate in the plebiscite.

[91] Archbishop Makarios III Foundation, Ourania Kokkinou (ed.), *Apanta Archiepiskopou Kyprou Makariou III* [*The Collected Works of Archbishop Makarios III of Cyprus*] (Nicosia: Archbishop Makarios III Foundation, 1992), vol. 1, 415–17. Ethnarchic Circular dated 8.12.1949, signed by Archbishop Makarios II, Kleopas Metropolitan of Paphos, Makarios Metropolitan of Kition, Kyprianos Metropolitan of Kyrenia and Gennadios Metropolitan of Salamis, on conducting a pan-Cyprian referendum.

[92] ISA/RG43/G/5570/10, Archbishop Makarios II's letter to Israeli Prime Minister David Ben-Gurion, dated 10.2.1950.

The ties of neighbourhood which link our countries are a guarantee that nothing which touches the weal of the people of Cyprus passes unnoticed here.[93]

On 5 September, one week after the Israeli Consulate in Nicosia became operational, Metropolitan Kleopas of Paphos[94], interim prelate, locum tenens of the Archbishopric of Cyprus, sent a lengthy letter to Consul Ram Yaron, addressed to the Israeli Prime Minister's Office. Kleopas' letter differed significantly both in style and content from the one sent by Archbishop Makarios II who had died a few months earlier.

In no uncertain terms, Kleopas decried the stance maintained by British authorities towards Greek Cypriots in the wake of the January plebiscite. He stressed the fact that the British had banned the public rally in favour of Enosis, scheduled by the Ethnarchy to take place 3 September 1950.[95] The metropolitan made no effort to hide his displeasure:

Due to strong British diplomatic pressure, the delegation appointed by the Cyprus Ethnarchy failed to convince the Greek Government to take the matter into their hands. However, beyond the government premises, it met with the wholehearted support of the entire Greek nation. The Greek Parliament appealed to the British Parliament to intercede for the realization of the Cypriot and Panhellenic claim for the Union of Cyprus with Greece.

The letter concluded thus:

On behalf of our people, we denounce to the civilized world, the British Government's attitude and methods, which reflect on the reputation of the Western Democracies, and we call upon all friends of freedom to stand by the side of our wronged people struggling for its liberty. At the same time, we wish to stress that the attitude of the British Government may hurt our feelings but fails to dishearten or disappoint the Cypriot people. It rather strengthens their determination to carry on the struggle for the realization of their national aspirations, their Union with Motherland Greece, which is the only solution to the Cyprus problem. Trusting that in compliance with the principles of freedom and self-determination for all civilized people, You will not fail to give your sympathy and support to our cause.[96]

In reply to Kleopas of Paphos, the Israeli Ministry of Foreign Affairs chose to keep a distance. In his communication dated 18 October 1950, Michael Comay, head of the British Commonwealth Division at the Israeli Foreign Ministry, cited relevant instructions from Prime Minister Ben-Gurion in answering that 'the Israeli

---

[93] ISA/RG43/G/5570/10, Eytan to Archbishop Makarios II (FO/A/491/20/31564 – 8.3.1950).
[94] Archbishop Makarios II died on 28.6.1950, and until the election of Makarios III on 16.10.1950, Kleopas, Metropolitan of Paphos, was named locum tenens of the Archdiocesan throne. Cf. Archbishop Makarios III Foundation, Kokkinou (ed.), *Apanta Archiepiskopou*, vol. 1, 60.
[95] ISA/RG43/G/5570/1, Letter from the Metropolitan of Paphos, 5.9.1950, to the Office of the Israeli Prime Minister.
[96] Ibid.

Government, while not wishing to venture any opinion on the relations between Cyprus and the United Kingdom, will give its sympathetic consideration to the contents of your letter'.[97]

The statement that Israel 'was favourably disposed' towards the demand of the Greek Cypriots to be free of British colonial rule was not without context. It reflected the genuine sympathy in Israeli public opinion vis-à-vis the Greek Cypriots and found expression in both pro-government and opposition Israeli newspapers. Still, a review of newspaper coverage from that period reveals that Israel's political parties were divided over the possible withdrawal of the British from Cyprus. On the one hand, the ruling Mapai Party, as well as the revisionist right-wing opposition, were not in favour of British withdrawal from the neighbouring island, in contrast to the opposition, pro-Soviet Mapam Party. At the same time, all the Israeli newspapers of the period, regardless of party affiliation or ideological lines, lauded the Greek Cypriots' expressions of protest against the colonialist regime, as their goals were perfectly aligned with the ideological underpinnings of the Jewish armed struggle against the British Mandate.

Of particular interest is the manner in which the Israeli press covered the anti-British demonstrations of the Greek Cypriots during that period. On the one hand, the centre-left newspaper *Davar*, a mouthpiece for the pro-government Histadrut trade union, devoted extensive photo coverage of the Enosis Plebiscite with a caption that read: 'Cypriots Seek to Follow Their National Destiny'.[98] On the other hand, the incarceration of leftist Limassol Mayor Kostas Partassides and four members of the city's Municipal Board was praised by the Israeli Right. Partassides had been jailed for refusing to comply with a decision by British authorities to change the name of '28th of October Street' (a date celebrated in Greece as a national holiday) to 'Palmer Street'. In Israel, the right-wing opposition newspaper *Herut* grabbed the opportunity to launch a scathing criticism of the pro-British foreign policies of the centre-left Mapai Party and Ben-Gurion's government, noting that Israel had maintained place names from the Mandate era. *Herut*'s comment on Partassides' incarceration was: 'So this is what the residents of Cyprus do, though they are still under the British yoke, in contrast to us, two years after independence, with Tel Aviv's main thoroughfare continuing to go by the name of the anti-Semite Lord Allenby, and another major road in Tel Aviv retaining the name of the British King George.'[99]

Still, the main concern echoing in both the pro-government press and the right-wing opposition newspapers in Israel revolved around this issue: what would the East Mediterranean look like if the British were to leave Cyprus,[100] given the popularity of

[97] ISA/RG43/G/5570/10, Comay to Kleopas Metropolitan of Paphos (FO/D/42000/30/42310 – 18.10.1950).
[98] *Davar*, 'Cypriots Wish to Follow Their National Destiny', 27.1.1950 (10.11.2015), Commentary and photo coverage of the January 1950 Cypriot plebiscite.
[99] *Heruth*, 'Cyprus Sets an Example', 4.6.1950. Report on the incarceration of Partassides and the laudatory comments on the latter's defiant stance against the British authorities. The excerpt included here was published in the same newspaper as a political commentary column, 'On Right and Left', 5.6.1950. It is worth noting that the specific roads in central Tel Aviv retain these names to the present day.
[100] *Davar*, column 'Today', 'Demonstrations and Results', 2.7.1950.

the AKEL Communist Party on the neighbouring island? On that point, the newspaper *Herut*, in an article titled, 'Cyprus, Bastion of Communism', had this to say:

> Aided by the US and England, the Greek government managed to supress the rebellion within the country and evade the communist threat. Nevertheless, Greek communism, though suffering a serious blow in its own birthplace, was nonetheless able to dispatch acolytes further to the southeast and secure a strong bastion on the island of Cyprus. [...] As communists tend to do in all those countries under colonial rule, nationalist slogans prevail. They are doing exactly the same thing in Cyprus. They put forward the demand for 'Enosis' but intend an 'Enosis' flavoured with communism: Unification of Cyprus with the 'People's Republic' to be established in Greece in the future, given that, at the moment, their comrades there do not stand the slightest chance of controlling mainland Greece's current political regime. [...] Their leader in Cyprus, Ezekias Papaioannou, said recently: 'The British are setting up an air base and camps on the island. Rumours have it that they also want to construct a port. We are opposed to all of this.'[101]

At the other end of the spectrum, the newspaper *Al ha-Mishmar*, the official voice of the pro-Soviet positions of the Mapam Party, regularly ran long articles on the Cypriots' anti-colonial struggle, underscoring activities by AKEL and its members. Typical of the way in which the Israeli Left perceived the situation developing in Cyprus was a comment published in *Al ha-Mishmar* about the proposal made by Greek Prime Minister Nikolaos Plastiras on 2 May 1951 to the British government.[102] Plastiras had suggested therein that, in exchange for Enosis, Greece would commit to ceding two military bases to Britain – one in mainland Greece and one in Cyprus:

> This particular proposal by Plastiras is part of the effort waged by government leaders in Athens to reach a compromise with imperialism, a compromise that would present them as 'defenders of Enosis' albeit without tarnishing their 'friendship' with the imperialists. [...]. All Greeks on the island are unanimous in their determination to abolish British rule and unite the island with Greece. The plebiscite held in January of this year, upon the initiative of the Church, the AKEL political party and other Greek organizations, and in which 96% of all Greek men and women above the age of 18 took part, that determination was made unequivocally and unreservedly clear, without any 'good-will gesture' towards Britain. There can be no doubt that the efforts of the government in Athens to 'assuage' imperialism are not in consonance with either the spirit or the aspirations of the Greek population in Cyprus. The will of the people is to become fully liberated from the British and this is actually the reason why the Left on this island

---

[101] *Heruth*, 'Cyprus: Bastion of Communism – A "Fifth Phalanx" in the Heart of the Middle East', 16.5.1950. Cf. Yiannis Pikros, 'O Venizelos kai to Kypriako' ['Venizelos and the Cyprus Question'], in *Meletimata ghiro apo ton Venizelo kai tin Epochi tou* [*Studies on Venizelos and His Era*], ed. Thanos Veremis and Odysseas Dimitrakopoulos (Athens: Philippotis Editions, 1980), 260–2.

[102] Christopoulos and Bastias (eds), *Istoria*, vol. 16, 438.

declares itself ready to face even these harsh political conditions which prevail in monarchical Greece. [...] We, the Jews of Israel, feel especially connected to Cyprus – a place that once was a land of exile for hundreds of thousands of our people in detention. We recall the beautiful, humane treatment and the active Greek anti-imperialist solidarity, above all shown by the Left there. Our best wishes are with them, so they may emerge victorious from their struggle for the liberation of the island from this heavy yoke.[103]

Meanwhile, Israeli diplomacy chose not to engage in ideological dilemmas of this kind, nor did it seem to be affected by the anti-British sentiments of Israeli public opinion. The sole criterion the Israeli Ministry of Foreign Affairs felt it should take into account in shaping its position vis-à-vis the Cypriot demand for Enosis was the existing regional balance. The pro-West orientation recently adopted by the Ben-Gurion government called for normalization of relations between Israel and Britain. As explained in detail below, the realization of how necessary this was coming primarily through Ankara, which did not wish to see Britain leave the neighbouring island.[104]

On 20 October 1950, Makarios III was unanimously elected Archbishop of Nea Justiniana. Shortly before his first official visit to Athens on 13 March 1951, Makarios III dispatched a letter to foreign governments stressing the Greek origins of the great majority of the island's population and their will to exercise the right to self-determination. This was a precise implication that their ultimate objective was to unify Cyprus with the Greek state. In his letter, Makarios III deplored the repressive legislative measures imposed by British authorities against the Greek Cypriots and the Enosis movement, following the dissolution of the Consultative Committee and the rejection of Winster's proposals.[105] Dated 8 February 1951,[106] the letter was forwarded to the Israeli Consul in Nicosia and addressed to Moshe Sharett, Israel's Minister of Foreign Affairs.[107]

Michael Comey replied to the archbishop on Sharett's behalf:

I am instructed by the Minister of Foreign Affairs, Mr Sharett, to acknowledge your letter to him of the 8th February, 1951, and to assure you that the people of Israel take a deep interest in the welfare and constitutional progress of the inhabitants of the Island of Cyprus, and are anxious to promote the cordial neighbourly ties which exist between them.[108]

---

[103] *Al ha-Mishmar*, column by journalist M. Nakhumi, 'On Politics', 'How Will the Cypriot Question be Resolved', 5.6.1950.

[104] Cf. 2.4.2.

[105] Makarios' letter of 8.2.1951 to Israeli Foreign Minister Moshe Sharett was identical to that of 8.2.1951 sent to UN Secretary General Trygve Lie and the foreign ministers of most UN member states, in which he denounced the repressive measures Britain had recently enacted. Cf. Archbishop Makarios III Foundation, Kokkinou (ed.), *Apanta Archiepiskopou*, vol. 1, 85–7. The complete text of the letter.

[106] Archives of the Holy Archbishopric of Cyprus, Archbishop Makarios III Archives, ΛH 3/3. Letter of Archbishop Makarios III, 8.2.1951.

[107] ISA/RG93/MFA/2156/3, Yaron to Ministry of Foreign Affairs (13.2.1951, forwarded without reference number).

[108] ISA/RG93/MFA/2156/3, Comay to Makarios (FOD/420/159/51404 – 28.2.1951).

By way of that reply, the Israelis once again expressed implicit reservations towards the Greek Cypriot aspiration to self-determination and Enosis, keeping to the line established in the two previous letters sent in response to Archbishop Makarios II and Kleopas, Metropolitan of Paphos. While maintaining a clear distance from the feud between the Greek Cypriots and the British, here, too, Israel's laconic reply to the newly elected Makarios III suggested the possible advantage of accepting Winster's proposals or adopting another solution that would lead to 'constitutional progress'. Interestingly, whereas Makarios' letter refers to the 'people of Cyprus' as vectors of the right to self-determination, the term 'people' is nowhere to be found in the Israeli letter which refers instead to the 'inhabitants of the island of Cyprus', which includes those inhabitants of Cyprus not of Greek origin. Moreover, the intentional use of the phrase 'Island of Cyprus' instead of 'Cyprus' alone, implied that the Israeli government would not encourage the creation of a separate state entity in Cyprus, other than the one bestowed on it under the existing colonial regime.

2.4.2 Creating a new regional alliance amongst Israel, Turkey and Britain

Israel's reservations towards the Greek Cypriots' demand for Enosis were not without reason. It is not surprising that the rekindling of relations amongst Israel, Turkey and Britain, along with the stagnant diplomatic relations between Israel and Greece, would affect Israel's stance vis-à-vis the eventuality of a British withdrawal from the island across the sea. The auspicious prospects of cooperation with Ankara, combined with a strong British military presence in the East Mediterranean were for Israel an important guarantee of its security.

On the other hand, the Israelis had no wish to alienate the Greek Cypriots by adopting a negative stance on their demands. Enosis found many sympathizers in Israeli society, who associated it with their own desire to be rid of British rule. What is more, EOKA's organizational structure and operational tactics were reminiscent of the Zionist underground actions against the British.[109] Besides all this, memories of the support offered by Greek Cypriots to the Jewish detainees in Karaolos and the Haganah cells engaged there during the period 1946–9 were still quite vivid. Nevertheless, in the event of Cyprus uniting with Greece, Israel feared that Britain would abandon the Eastern Mediterranean completely. Under such circumstances, Israel had no reason to support or even encourage Cyprus' annexation by Greece, particularly in light of the pro-Arab stance taken by Athens.

More specifically, in the wake of Turkey's de facto recognition of Israel, sometime in mid-January 1950, an Israeli diplomatic mission had established itself in the Turkish capital. A couple of months later, in March 1950, Turkey, under Prime Minister Mehmet Semsettin Günaltay, became the first Muslim state to proceed to a de jure recognition of the State of Israel, as a result of which, the Israeli mission in Ankara came to be headed by an ambassador.[110]

---

[109] Holland, *Britain and the Revolt in Cyprus*, 53–4.
[110] Barouch Gilead, 'Shkhenoteinu: Turkia ve-Kafrisin' ['Our Neighbours: Turkey and Cyprus'], in *Misrad ha-Khutz*, ed. Yeger, Govrin and Oded, 371–2.

Since Turkey and Israel both aspired to deepen their attachment to the West, NATO and the latter's regional defence projections became the catalyst in the improvement of relations between the two countries. Meeting with his Israeli counterpart Abba Eban in February 1951, Turkish Ambassador to Washington Feridun Erkin presented the Turkish concerns vis-à-vis US misgivings about admitting Turkey to NATO. Turkey's membership in the North Atlantic Alliance would warrant the latter's security in view of the Soviet threat and in exchange, Turkey could safeguard Western interests in the Middle East.[111] In view of Turkey's participation in the Korean War and the voices of discontent heard in the country over the heavy losses to the Turkish Brigade, Ankara felt more than a little uneasy that NATO's doors remained closed to it. Israel shared similar concerns: capitalizing on the Korean War, the Jewish state had adopted an unequivocally pro-Western stance and in return expected defence and economic backing from the United States.

The most decisive factor in the tightening of relations between Israel and Turkey was Ankara's attitude vis-à-vis the Arab states. Having previously belied rumours according to which Turkey and Israel had entered into a secret military cooperation agreement in late January 1951, Mehmet Fuad Köprülü, Turkey's foreign minister at the time, met with Eliahu Sasson, Israel's ambassador to Ankara, and told him that Turkey had made the following recommendations to the member states of the Arab League: 'Quell your internal feuds, show realism and accept the fact that the State of Israel exists, and finally, adopt a pro-West attitude with no unnecessary reservations.' With these admonitory statements, Köprülü wished to make clear to the Arab states, and Egypt in particular, that in the event of an attempt to hinder international navigation in the Suez Canal, Turkey would side with the West.[112] At the same meeting, the Turkish foreign minister apparently told Sasson that he had warned the Arabs: 'Any country believing that it will remain neutral in the event of a Third World War is only nurturing illusions, as the term "neutrality" in the Russian vocabulary means siding with Soviet Russia.'[113] As far as Egypt's interference with international navigation was concerned, Turkey's stance was identical to that of Israel and coincided with the direction recently taken by the Israeli leadership, to do away, once and for all, with the 'Non-Engagement' policy,[114] despite the fact that Foreign Minister Moshe Sharett continued to espouse it, for domestic consumption.

Israel, had come to realize with some satisfaction, that Turkish rhetoric concerning the 'fraternal bonds between Turkey and the Muslim states' and 'cooperation between Turkey and the Arab states' was useful for public relations but did not affect Ankara's positive attitude vis-à-vis Israel. Furthermore, the concurring views of Turkey's two ruling parties with regard to the Soviet threat guaranteed Turkey's unequivocally

---

[111] ISA/RG93/MFA/8692/3, Research Division (253/3.4.1951). The Report includes an account by Abba Eban, Israel's ambassador to Washington, on the exchanges he had in mid-March 1951 with his Turkish counterpart, Feridun Cemal Erkin.

[112] ISA/RG93/MFA/8692/3, Research Division (226/26.2.1951). Included in this report is an account by Eliahu Sasson, Israel's ambassador to Ankara, on the working meeting he had in January 1951 with Turkish Minister of Foreign Affairs Mehmet Fuat Köprülü.

[113] Ibid.

[114] Cf. 1.1.3.

pro-West orientation. In January 1951, Ambassador Eliahu Sasson, head of the Israeli diplomatic mission in Ankara, detailed in his first annual report the way in which Turkey was addressing the possibility of a British withdrawal from the Suez Canal:

> Despite the recently observed tendency towards a Turkish–Arab rapprochement, Turkish public opinion demonstrated that with regard to issues of defence and security, it can distinguish between emotional slogans and the reality of the present situation. Almost all Turkish newspapers, even those strongly supporting relations of friendship and brotherhood between the Arabs and the Turks, were equally critical of Egypt's position on the matter of the Suez Canal. The Turks believe that Egypt cannot assume responsibility for the Canal, given its vital importance for the defence of the entire Middle East. The Turks believe that if the British withdraw from the Suez, the consequences will be catastrophic. The Turks do not hesitate to describe Egypt's extremist positions as 'irrational'. The prevailing attitude here leaves no room for misinterpretation: The Turks express their lack of confidence in the ability of Arab countries to defend themselves. There is no doubt that in the event of exacerbation of the Anglo-Egyptian crisis, Turkey will side with Britain.[115]

The Adnan Menderes government in Turkey, which came to power in the May 1950 elections, maintained good relations with Israel. During its term and over the first year of operations of Israel's diplomatic mission to Ankara, a bilateral transnational trade agreement was signed and the Israeli Press Office which was established in Istanbul quickly set about cultivating close relations with the local news media. The Turkish press maintained a favourable stance towards Israel's policies. Meanwhile, the Ministry of Aliyah provided training for Turkish public servants, particularly in social welfare agencies, on ways to implement a smoother settlement in Turkey of Turkish-speaking minorities fleeing communist Bulgaria in droves.[116] Moreover, ignoring the reactions of Arab states, Turkey raised no obstacles to its Jewish citizens relocating to Israel. Between 1948 and 1951, 40 per cent of Turkey's total Jewish population made aliyah to Israel. The vast majority of Jews from Turkey settled in the poorer areas of West Jerusalem, significantly boosting Jewish presence along the Green Line.[117]

Nevertheless, the concordant opinions of Israel and Turkey were not enough. Both countries needed a powerful ally in the region. Foreign Minister Köprülü could not have been more specific in saying to the Israeli Ambassador in Ankara: 'You need to understand that military cooperation between Israel and Turkey is predicated on a

---

[115] ISA/RG93/MFA/8692/3, Research Division (215/11.2.1951). Excerpt from Eliahu Sasson's report from Ankara, included in the Research Division report.
[116] ISA/RG93/MFA/8692/3, Research Division (212/8.2.1951). Sasson to the Middle East Division. Report of activities of diplomatic mission in Ankara, January 1951. Cf. Niyazi Kızılyürek, *Oi Tourkokyprioi, i Tourkia kai to Kypriako* [*The Turkish Cypriots, Turkey and the Cyprus Question*] (Athens: Papazisis, 2009), 184–5. In contrast to Turkish policy in Cyprus, Turkey dealt with the issue of Turkish minorities in Bulgaria in a completely different manner and encouraged them to leave their homes and relocate permanently to Turkey.
[117] Gabriel Haritos, 'The Jewish Community in a Multicultural Turkey', ELIAMEP *Middle East Mediterranean*, 3, no. 2 (May–August 2013): 17–20.

military cooperation between Israel and Britain.' Köprülü repeated this condition to the high-ranking officer of the Israeli Army, Moshe Dayan, when they met during the latter's official visit to Ankara in 1950. Similar advice was given by the Turkish ambassador in London to his Israeli counterpart, Eliahu Elath. The Israeli side was not indifferent to the Turkish suggestion: At UN Headquarters, Israel's permanent representation established contacts with the British mission, thanks to the intercession of Selim Sarper, head of the permanent Turkish mission.[118] Meanwhile, intense consultations had been launched amongst Britain, the US, Turkey and Israel on the possibility of establishing a joint Western defence mechanism in the Eastern Mediterranean, though Britain had already begun to consider eventually shifting the focal point of its military presence in the region away from the Suez Canal towards neighbouring Cyprus.[119]

For several reasons, the Israeli Foreign Ministry had adopted the position that, in the event of a new war in the region, Britain would be called upon to take on the bulk of defence in the Middle East. The protection of the Suez Canal was not of interest only to Britain, but to all member states of the Commonwealth. London was bound by defence treaties entered into with Iraq and Jordan. Key strongholds in Cyprus, Basra, Aden and Alexandria were all under British control.[120] For its part, the Foreign Office saw an alliance between Israel and Turkey as 'a reliable and effective support for British presence in the area in all possible aspects'.[121] It also described Israel as a 'bastion of democracy in the Middle East' as well as 'England's natural ally.' At the same time, British diplomats believed that, in the event of a Russian attack in the Middle East, one could not say with certainty that the Arab states would fall on the side of the West. Moreover, their military forces – with the single exception of the Jordanian Arab Legion – were not considered battle-worthy, compared to the Turkish and Israeli armies.

Israel continued to believe that notwithstanding these implications, the Foreign Office had no intention of adhering to a one-dimensional policy in the Middle East. In other words, the prevailing belief was that, in the event of a new war, Britain would not support either Turkey, Israel or the Arabs exclusively. The only thing certain to Israel was that the time had come to 'break the ice' with London and establish a foundation

[118] ISA/RG93/MFA/8692/3, Research Division (215/11.2.1951).
[119] ISA/RG93/MFA/8692/4, Research Division (380/16.10.1951). The Report features an account of the progress made in the consultation between the US, Britain and Turkey in the matter of the establishment of the Supreme Allied Command Middle East (SACME) against the background of the possibility of Egypt also being taken into account for that particular defence project. Egypt's ultimate refusal to take part therein seems to have seriously impacted developments in that enterprise which eventually failed.
[120] ISA/RG93/MFA/8692/3, Research Division (216/13.2.1951). Report by Eliahu Elath, Israel's ambassador to London, to the West Europe Division.
[121] Ibid. Particularly interesting was Elath's assessment, according to which the financial and military assistance provided by the US to Greece, Turkey and Iran was not associated with any formal commitment to provide military protection to those countries in the event of a Soviet invasion. Elath concluded that Britain's presence in the Middle East remained more important compared to that of the US.

for cooperation between Israel and Britain, while deepening sound bilateral relations already developed with the government in Ankara.

2.4.2.1 *The presence of Israeli entrepreneurs in Cyprus*

The British chilliness towards the Israeli consulate in Nicosia did not last long. Cyprus was proving itself to be quite welcoming to Israeli investors. Given the circumstances of the time, the presence of Israeli entrepreneurs on the island throughout the 1950s was of great importance, particularly in the public works sector. A relevant report by Eliezer Merom, the Israeli vice consul in Nicosia in charge of economic affairs, is indeed quite revealing as to Israeli entrepreneurship on the neighbouring island.[122]

By mid-1950, British military and political analysts had designated Cyprus as the most likely alternative if it proved necessary to relocate a sizeable volume of British military forces, in case of evacuation or partial withdrawal from the Suez Canal. In that same year, proceedings were launched towards the construction of an extended camp, featuring permanent military warehouses, in Dhekelia, a project with an estimated budget of £10 million. Works on the development of the first section of the Dhekelia camp construction project, worth £2 million, was launched in November 1952. Solel Boneh, Israel's most important developer of construction projects, was party to the venture, together with CYBARCO (Cyprus Building & Road Construction Company), a Cypriot construction company with Israeli interests. Interestingly, Solel Boneh had Israeli foremen and a logistical staff permanently established in Cyprus through the completion of the project. By mid-1953, the company had also made itself known in the maintenance work it carried out for the RAF warehouse facilities as well as other public infrastructure projects. Gradually, it began to expand its activities into the private sector.

In 1952, another Israeli company, Ha-Khevra ha-Merkazit le-Shikun u-Vinian (Housing and Building Central Company), founded a Cypriot subsidiary under the name Panta Selfter, and another company called the Cyprus Middle East Constructing Company (CYMEACO) in a joint venture with Greek Cypriot entrepreneurs. That same year, the Israeli Cyprus Drilling and Engineering Company Ltd was listed in the Cypriot Company Register and embarked on the construction of electricity infrastructure for the island's military camps. Given that British officials had reservations as to whether Cyprus was sufficiently equipped with appropriate infrastructures in the event that British forces would have to relocate from their actual base around the Suez Canal, it was understood that eventually it would be imperative to launch extensive public works for docking naval war crafts, loading and unloading military ammunition and facilitating the movement of troops throughout the island. Serious consideration was given to the construction of military warehouses and airports and extending the road network.[123] The Israeli construction companies saw

---

[122] ISA/RG93/MFA/2155/10, Eliezer Merom, vice consul in Nicosia to the British Commonwealth Division (031/101/ף – 7.5.1953). The report was prepared following a question from the Ministry of Finance regarding the taxable assets of Israeli entrepreneurs doing business in Cyprus.

[123] ISA/RG93/MFA/2156/3, Mordechai Gazit, first secretary of Israel's Embassy in London to the West Europe Division (65437/362/מ – 25.3.1953), Comments on presentation at an event hosted by the Royal Central Asian Society in London on 'Cyprus since the War and to This Day'.

these large-scale public works as a major business opportunity. Since they were unable to conduct business in the neighbouring Arab states, Cyprus was the only option open to them – with the exception of Turkey, where Solel Boneh had succeeded in developing a sizeable presence. In mid-1953, as the British authorities started construction on a major military base in Episkopi, Israeli construction companies were eager to take part in the venture. And other Israeli investors had likewise begun to take an interest in the Cypriot market, notably in the area of agriculture.

The Israeli business presence in Cyprus had become visible on 9 November 1950 when, in cooperation with the Louis Greek Cypriot travel agency, Israel's airline El-Al inaugurated regularly scheduled flights connecting Nicosia, Tel Aviv and Istanbul.[124] In the midst of this favourable climate, the Israeli Coastguard in March 1951 acquired a second-hand boat from the Cypriot Coastguard,[125] whilst Cypriot airports and seaports were developing into crucial transit hubs for Jews fleeing Iraq and Eastern Europe to settle permanently in Israel.

By 1954, Cyprus had become the most important British military and intelligence logistic centre in the region. All signs pointed to the likelihood that this development would attract even more Israeli investors to the island. The Israeli Ministry of Foreign Affairs, therefore, considered it essential for the consul who would succeed Ram Yaron to be someone who could efficiently handle trade-related issues. At the same time, the new consul would also have to act as an unofficial military attaché, since the regional cooperation between Israel and Britain was now in the fore.[126] The culmination of this rapprochement was the joint Israeli–British–French military operation against Egypt in October 1956.

2.4.2.2 *The resonance of the Enosis Plebiscite and Turkish Cypriot concerns*

As relations between Israel and Turkey evolved, Israeli diplomats began to turn their attention to regional matters that concerned their Turkish counterparts. One of these was the status of Turkish Cypriots on the neighbouring island. In 1951, the Israeli Foreign Ministry acquired a preliminary idea of how Turkish Cypriots perceived the results of the Enosis Plebiscite from Fuat Bayramoğlu, Turkey's consul to Jerusalem who had just completed his term in Nicosia. That was the main topic of a working meeting Bayramoğlu held on 25 April 1951 with an officer of the Middle East Division of the Israeli Ministry of Foreign Affairs.[127]

According to Bayramoğlu, the Turkish Cypriots had grave concerns about the Enosis movement. In fact, their representative appealed to Turkey to implement the

---

[124] ISA/RG93/MFA/2156/3, Yaron to the British Commonwealth Division, Activity Report for November 1950. Ceremony at the Nicosia Airport on 9.11.1950, date of El-Al's inaugural flight from Nicosia to Tel Aviv.

[125] ISA/RG93/MFA/2156/3, Yaron to British Commonwealth Division, Activity Report for March 1951 (225/100/ף – 16.4.1951).

[126] ISA/RG130/MFA/2584/11, Gideon Shomron of the British Commonwealth Division to Arthur Lourie, deputy director general of the Ministry of Foreign Affairs (6.3.1954, not officially logged).

[127] ISA/RG93/MFA/2156/3, Nissim Yaish, Middle East Division (Turkey Section) to Shmuel Divon, deputy director of the Middle East Division (39/51-30.4.1951).

same successful tactic which resulted in the annexation of the Hatay region (Alexandretta), formerly under Syrian sovereignty. They published this request through an open letter in the Turkish press.[128]

Kemalist Turkey had always taken an interest in the Turkish inhabitants of the island. Since the late 1920s, Ankara had made its presence in Cyprus known by financing newspapers, leaflets and associations in support of Kemalist ideals.[129] It was displeased, however, with British tactics that undermined the Kemalist regime's public relations efforts.[130] According to Bayramoğlu, the British governor did not seem averse to certain Turkish Cypriot officers wearing a fez when they appeared before him. The British administration continued to use the Ottoman alphabet and language in its official correspondence, exhibiting a typical reluctance to transcribe the official documents it issued into the new, Latin-character Turkish language. Such phenomena generated displeasure in Ankara and awkwardness among Turkish Cypriots.[131] Bayramoğlu claimed that the British never missed a chance to fan the flames amongst clashing figures in the Turkish Cypriot community, and sometimes even succeeded. But, despite the discomfort British tactics caused from time to time, the Turkish Cypriots as a whole did not want a change in the status quo. As Bayramoğlu emphasized, the Turkish Cypriots did not wish either for the British to withdraw from the island, nor for Cyprus to unite with Greece.

Bayramoğlu's assessment that in the event of a future referendum or plebiscite, 'the overwhelming majority of the island's dwellers would vote against unification with Greece' is interesting. In point of fact, he believed that, aside from the Turkish Cypriots, opponents to Enosis would include high- and middle-income classes of Greek Cypriot society, as they were well aware of the poor economic situation in Greece. He also believed that a considerable proportion of Greek Cypriot communists would also vote against Enosis, as he put it, 'because in doing so, they would be able to express their

---

[128] Cf. Umut Uzer, *Identity and Turkish Foreign Policy: The Kemalist Influence in Cyprus and the Caucasus* (London and New York: I.B. Tauris, 2011), 184–91; and Christos P. Ioannides, *In Turkey's Image: The Transformation of Occupied Cyprus into a Turkish Province* (New Rochelle, NY: Caratzas, 1991), 59–68.

[129] Alexis Rappas, *Cyprus in the 1930s: British Colonial Rule and the Roots of the Cyprus Conflict* (London and New York: I.B. Tauris, 2014), 94–5. The main proponents of Kemalist ideals in Cyprus were the newspapers *Ses* and *Söz* and the Nicosia-based Kardeş Ocağı association.

[130] James Allen McHenry, Jr, 'The Uneasy Partnership on Cyprus, 1919–1939: The Political and Diplomatic Interaction between Great Britain, Turkey and the Turkish Cypriot Community' (PhD diss., University of Kansas, Lawrence, KS, 1981), 224–8. During the interwar years and most particularly in the wake of the Oktovriana incidents in October 1931, the British embarked on a campaign aiming not only to combat the Enosis movement but Kemalist Turkish nationalism as well. In that spirit, they imposed restrictions on the activities of the Turkish consul general with regard to maintaining a balance in the Turkish Cypriot community. Ankara showed self-restraint, not wishing to disturb its relations with Britain, albeit without abandoning its efforts to instil Kemalist ideals within the local Turkish Cypriot community – efforts that gradually proved successful.

[131] Kızılyürek, *Tourkokyprioi-Tourkia* [*Turkish-Cypriots and Turkey*], 73–4, on the conflict within the Turkish Cypriot community over whether or not to adopt Kemalist ideals while under British rule. Cf. Yücel Bozdağlıoğlu, *Turkish Foreign Policy and Turkish Identity: A Constructivist Approach* (New York and London: Routledge, 2003), 45–50. On the Kemalist institutionalization of the Turkish Republic's Western orientation.

hatred of the monarchic fascist regime of Athens'. Israel's consul, Yaron, fully agreed with all of Bayramoğlu's assessments.[132]

The Israelis saw Turkey's concerns about the likelihood of Cyprus' accession to Greece as untimely and excessive, and the hopes of Greek Cypriots for Enosis as overly optimistic. In terms of what was being discussed in Greece at that time, the British Commonwealth Division of the Israeli Ministry of Foreign Affairs considered the assessment of nationalist currents in Greece which associated the country's entry into NATO with the call for Enosis as wishful thinking, par excellence.[133]

2.4.3 Greek and Israeli regional foreign policy: A story of incompatibility

As Israel and Turkey were gradually coming to terms with the fact that their regional interests were the same, Israeli diplomacy was realizing the lack of a similar convergence with Greece. In June 1951, the Research Division of the Israeli Ministry of Foreign Affairs described Greek–Israeli relations in the worst possible terms. Greece was one of a few countries in Europe which had not recognized Israel de jure. Athens did nothing to promote improved bilateral relations, adopting a consistently pro-Arab position at practically all international fora, including the UN, whilst maintaining particularly close bonds with Cairo. Each time the Israelis endeavoured to improve Greek–Israeli relations, Greek officials would respond that Athens could not afford to jeopardize its relations with Cairo unless Egypt first offered sufficient assurance that the future of the Greek diaspora there would not be jeopardized.[134]

Although the future of the Greek community in Egypt was a matter of negotiations between Athens and Cairo, according to Israeli reports, Egypt was no more favourably inclined towards its Greek citizens than toits other European inhabitants. Israel was convinced that ultimately, the forbearance shown by Athens to Cairo would not benefit its interests. Consequently, there was no reason why the anticipation of a signed agreement between Greece and Egypt – one which might never come to be – should delay the normalizing of relations between Greece and Israel. The prevailing view in the Israeli Ministry of Foreign Affairs was that Greece had been using its drawn-out negotiations with Egypt as a delaying tactic, because it did not actually wish to normalize or even improve relations with Israel for fear of upsetting Arab countries from which it hoped to gain support at international fora. The ostensible reason for Greece's pro-Arab stance at the UN was its demand for the immediate repatriation of orphaned Greek children living in neighbouring communist countries in the wake of the Greek Civil War.[135]

Another reason for the standstill between Israel and Greece was the substantial improvement which had taken place in relations between Israel and Turkey. Although

---

[132] ISA/RG93/MFA/2156/3, Yaron to the British Commonwealth Division (282/101/ק – 27.5.1951).

[133] ISA/RG93/MFA/2156/3, British Commonwealth Division to Yaron (123131/20/11011/ז/ח – 5.11.1951).

[134] ISA/RG93/MFA/8692/3, Research Division (287/5.6.1951). That report describes the web of relations between Greece and Egypt.

[135] ISA/RG93/MFA/8692/3, Asher Moissis, Honorary Israeli Consul in Athens, to West Europe Division (MH/sEO/0225-23.5.1951), and report by the Research Division (287/5.6.1951).

Greek–Turkish relations in the early 1950s were relatively normal, an extensive report filed in February 1951 by the Israeli Ministry of Foreign Affairs Research Division describes Greece's regional policy in the Eastern Mediterranean, citing 'diplomatic circles in Ankara' rather than the Greek Foreign Ministry in Athens which should have been the only valid source of information. According to this report, then, Greece had allegedly advocated the inclusion of Arab states in the Eastern Mediterranean defence formations of the West as a means of counteracting Turkey. More specifically, according to information obtained by the Israelis through their Turkish diplomatic sources, Greece was endeavouring to convince the West that Egypt (in view of its strategic position and plentiful military forces), Syria (because of its numerous airfields) and Lebanon (given its harbours and its geopolitical position) might serve as reliable partners in defending the Mediterranean. Naturally, these alleged Greek propositions or initiatives were deemed unacceptable by both Turkish and Israeli diplomats. The views of Turkey and Israel were in complete agreement. Because Turkey and Iran shared borders with the Soviet Union, they and not the Arab states required the protection of the West. The Arab states lacked sufficiently trained armed forces and their political leaders gave the impression that they were not ideologically aligned with the West.[136] On the other hand, the Israelis could not confirm that the allegations of these pro-Arab proposals indeed originated in Greece. Israel's diplomatic representation in Greece was quite limited, and the honorary consul in Athens, Asher Moissis, had little contact with the Greek Foreign Ministry and its decision-making centres. Nevertheless, in view of Greece's overall pro-Arab stance at international fora, Israel took the information it received from Ankara at face value.

Asher Moissis was equally pessimistic about the visit of Archbishop Makarios III to Athens in 1951. Although Greece was politically united with regard to Enosis, if the issue were brought before the UN, he feared, it would eventually lead Greece into an 'indirect war against Britain'. What is more, Athens believed it could count on the support of the Soviet Bloc which was vying against British influence, but this did not necessarily mean that the USSR would back Enosis. Then, too, the left-wing trade unions in Cyprus had already been in contact with high-ranking officials in Poland and Czechoslovakia in order to secure their support for the Cypriot issue at the next meeting of the UN General Assembly. Asher Moissis' conclusion – endorsed by the general staff of the Israeli Ministry of Foreign Affairs – was that 'Cyprus is, ethnologically speaking, the sole Greek territory where Communism is flourishing.' Clearly this did not make the best impression on the West, particularly at a time when Ankara never missed an opportunity to declare allegiance to the West.[137]

On the other hand, it is worth noting that neither the Greek nor the Israeli sides had made full use of certain significant opportunities for normalization or the improvement of bilateral relations, from 1948 until the eve of the first UN discussion on Cyprus in 1954.

---

[136] ISA/RG93/MFA/8692/3, Research Division (215/11.2.1951). The report includes an excerpt of a relevant report by the head of the Israeli diplomatic mission in Ankara, Eliahu Sasson, citing 'diplomatic circles in Ankara', without naming them.

[137] ISA/RG93/MFA/8692/3, Research Department (267/23.4.1951), Asher Moissis to the West Europe Division.

Despite the fact that negotiations and the subsequent signing of ceasefire agreements amongst the political leaderships of Israel, Egypt and Jordan had taken place in Greek territory, the island of Rhodes, the government in Athens chose not to capitalize on the situation by aligning itself with the United States, Turkey and the rest of the Western European states all of which had recognized the State of Israel de jure one after another since late January 1949.

The ceasefire agreements amongst Israel, Egypt and Jordan were a historic event of fundamental importance for the Arab–Israeli conflict. The Rhodes Armistice Agreements, signed under the aegis of the United Nations, finalized the de facto borders between Israel, Egypt and Jordan for the ensuing two decades. Talks between Israel and Egypt began on 12 January 1949 and concluded with the signing of the agreement on 24 February 1949, establishing the ceasefire and separating the (Egyptian) Sinai Peninsula from the (Israeli) Negev Desert. Immediately following, in early March 1949, negotiations began between Israel and Jordan and were concluded on 3 April 1949 with the signing of the ceasefire. The latter agreement set the Green Line separating the West Bank in Jordan from Israel, as well as the Israeli sector from the Arab sector in the city of Jerusalem.

The Greek government did not wish to take an active part in the progress of the negotiations in Rhodes. As the Swedish diplomat, Count Folke Bernadotte of Wisborg, was writing his memoirs on 13 May 1948, on the eve of the British departure from Palestine, the UN approached the Swedish Ministry of Foreign Affairs and requested contact with him in order to gauge whether he would accept a proposal to act as UN mediator if war erupted between the Jews and Arabs.[138] Their pessimism was justified, for the very next day, 15 May 1948, the first Arab–Israeli war broke out. On 17 May 1948, Bernadotte accepted the UN proposal and two days later he received a telegram from then UN Secretary General Trygve Lie appointing him chief negotiator in the Arab–Israeli conflict, the first effort of its kind at the UN.[139]

After the preliminary discussions in London and Paris, Bernadotte landed in Athens on 27 May 1948.[140] As he writes in his memoirs, he spent a pleasant evening in Athens with King Paul of Greece, Queen Frederica and the rest of the royal family. Bernadotte does not provide any details about the role which Greece might have taken on in the framework of this mission in the ensuing months. A social visit with the Greek royal family would not have been an appropriate occasion to discuss stenograms or protocols. This was the main reason we might never know what was discussed at that evening

[138] Count Folke Bernadotte was chosen by the UN on the basis of his endeavours at the start of the Second World War as lieutenant director general of the Swedish Red Cross when he was able, as a private citizen of a neutral country to maintain contact with high-ranking officials in Nazi Germany as well as Britain. After receiving detailed information about the horrendous conditions in the German concentration camps, he managed to obtain the release of 15,000 inmates on humanitarian grounds, citizens of Denmark, Norway and other Western European countries, and to have them transferred to Swedish hospitals in 'Bernadotte's White Buses'. Among the inmates were an unknown number of Jews. Cf. Folke Bernadotte, *The Curtain Falls* (New York: Alfred Knopf, 1945), 130–55, 21–40; and Sune Perrson, 'Folke Bernadotte and the White Buses', *Journal of Holocaust Education*, 9, no. 2 (2000): 237–68.
[139] Folke Bernadotte, *To Jerusalem* (London: Hodder & Stoughton, 1951), 1–5.
[140] Ibid., 17–18.

about Greece's role within the framework of Bernadotte's mission. Most possibly, he was himself unaware on the evening of 27 May 1948 until 10 o'clock of the following morning – the time of his departure from Athens to Cairo – whether or not a decision had been reached about how Greece might assist in the UN diplomatic initiative to bring about a settlement of the conflict between the new State of Israel and the Arab countries which had declared war against it. In any case, at that time, it was too early to anticipate that the UN initiative negotiated by Bernadotte would have ended in direct negotiations between the adversaries.

According to Bernadotte's memoirs, the possibility of direct negotiations on the Greek island of Rhodes had first come up during a face-to-face meeting with Egyptian Foreign Minister Mahmood El-Nokrashy Pasha.[141] Bernadotte's initial visit to Rhodes took place four days later, on 14 June 1948, at which time he was received by the mayor of Rhodes, Gabriel Haritos. Bernadotte spent a day on the island verifying that conditions there were adequate for likely protracted formal talks in terms of housing, transportation and media networks.[142] On 18 June 1958, Bernadotte, accompanied by the rest of the UN delegation, among them the Greek diplomat Constantine Stavropoulos,[143] returned to Rhodes where they stayed till the end of the month.[144]

The Greek Ministry of Foreign Affairs wished to stay as far as possible from anything to do with the talks between Israel and the Arabs. This is evident from the description given by Greek diplomat, Themistoklis Chrysanthopoulos, who was serving at the time as a representative of the Greek Ministry of Foreign Affairs on Rhodes, the capital of the Dodecanese, a region which only a few months earlier became an integral part of Greece. Chrysanthopoulos recalls:

> One day, without any warning Folke Bernadotte landed at Rhodes airport with his delegation. Bernadotte was appointed by the UN as the first negotiator for a settlement of the Israel-Palestine issue, [...] All members of the UN delegation stayed at the *Grand Hotel des Roses*. Soon after the Arab delegations arrived, each of which included public figures, princes, minsters, generals [...].[145]

The selection of Greek territory as the location for these negotiations might have marked the beginning of an improved diplomatic standing for Greece at a regional

[141] Ibid., 81–2.
[142] Ibid., 92–5.
[143] Constantine Stavropoulos was the UN secretary general's special envoy to the talks on the Korean conflict (1951–2) and UN legal advisor from 1952 until 1974, when he was elected to the Greek Parliament as a member of the right-wing Nea Dimokratia political party after the fall of the military regime. Between 12.3.1975 and 28.11.1977, he served as deputy foreign minister in the Karamanlis government. Cf. Antonis Makridimitris, *Oi Ypourgoi ton Eksoterikon tis Elladas 1829–2000 [Foreign Ministers of Greece 1829–2000]* (Athens: Kastaniotis, 2000), 121.
[144] Bernadotte, *To Jerusalem*, 108–33.
[145] A portion of a lecture by former Ambassador Themistoklis Chrysanthopoulos at an evening organized by the Cultural Foundation of the Dodecanese 'Kleovoulos o Lindios', which published transcripts of all the lectures presented at the event in the pamphlet: Politistikon Idryma Dodekanisou, 'Kleovoulos o Lindios' [Cultural Foundation of the Dodecanese 'Cleobulus the Lindian'], *I Apeleyftherosi tis Dodekanisou (31 Martiou 1947) [The Liberation of the Dodecanese (31st of March 1947)]* (Athens: Politistikon Idryma Dodekanisou 'Kleovoulos o Lindios', 1997), 60.

level. The credit was given to the mayor of Rhodes, Haritos, for the excellent services rendered by the local Greek authorities to facilitate the months-long negotiations by the chief UN negotiator, Ralph Bunche[146] and the director general of the Israeli Ministry of Foreign Affairs, Walter Eytan, who had headed the Israeli negotiation team and who heaped praise on the constructive role of the Municipality of Rhodes[147] well beyond the demands of protocol. Such praise could have been appropriately capitalized upon in a variety of ways by Greek future governments not only at a diplomatic and institutional level but also to promote its image. Promoting peace in the Middle East would earn multiple benefits, improving relations between Greece and Israel, as well as with the Arab world. Had Greece acquired such a role in the events unfolding in the region, perhaps the fate of the Greek diaspora in Egypt would have been different and the Greek communities in the Middle East might not have been uprooted. Nevertheless, for reasons unknown, the opportunity was lost.

Neither the Israeli nor the Greek government – each for its own particular reasons – took advantage as much as they might have of the normalization which had begun to form in Jerusalem between the Israeli government and the Greek Orthodox Patriarchate of Jerusalem. After the signing of the Armistice Agreement in Rhodes between Israel and Jordan and the division of Jerusalem into Israeli and Jordanian sectors, there was regular bilateral contact between Israel and the representatives of various Christian organizations in the city. In January 1950, the Greek Orthodox Patriarchate dispatched Epiphanios, Archbishop of Philadelphia, as its envoy to Israel. Upon taking office, Epiphanios reviewed the situation of the 15,000 members the Greek Orthodox community then living in Israel. In September of that year, the archbishop was named head of a Patriarchal Committee to negotiate the property rights on Patriarchate-owned assets in Israel with the Israeli government and the Jewish National Fund (Keren Kayemet LeIsrael). Those negotiations concluded with long-term leases on certain church properties.[148] According to the report by the Research Division of the Israeli Ministry of Foreign Affairs,[149] in April 1951, Timotheos I, Greek Orthodox Patriarch of Jerusalem, reassured the Israeli Ministry of Religious Affairs that a solution would also soon be found to the issue of long-term leases on patriarchal property situated within the Israeli enclave of Mount Scopus (Har ha-Tzofim). Later, these properties were used to rebuild the new wings of Hadassah Hospital and extend the buildings on the Hebrew University of Jerusalem campus. At that meeting, the Israeli

---

[146] Letters of thanks dated 6.10.1948 and 6.4.1949 from Ralph Bunche, UN negotiator in the Arab-Israeli talks for the armistice agreement between Israel, Egypt and Jordan, to then Mayor of Rhodes Gabriel Haritos (from the author's family archives). The next year, Ralph Bunche was awarded the Nobel Peace Prize for his role in the Rhodes negotiations.

[147] Letter of thanks dated 28.2.1949 (FA/198/49) from Walter Eytan to Mayor of Rhodes Gabriel Haritos (from the author's family archives).

[148] Monastic Register ('Monachologion') of the Greek Orthodox Patriarchate of Jerusalem, 129–130 / Historical Archives of the Greek Orthodox Patriarchate of Jerusalem.

[149] ISA/RG93/MFA/8692/3, Research Division (268/29.4.1951). The report describes the meeting held in mid-April 1951 at the King David Hotel in Jerusalem, between Timotheos I, Greek Orthodox Patriarch of Jerusalem, Yaakov Herzog, head of the Christian Communities Division of the Israeli Ministry of Religious Affairs and adviser to Ministry of Foreign Affairs on Jerusalem-related matters, and Avraham Granot, director general of the Jewish National Fund (*Keren Kayemet le-Israel*).

side gave reassurances that the Patriarchate would be facilitated in importing and exporting foreign exchange, that its property rights within Israeli territory would be protected and that the status quo with respect to Holy Places[150] would be preserved, as preserved under the British Mandate. As a sign of the harmonious coexistence between the Greek Orthodox Patriarchate of Jerusalem and the State of Israel, an official letter was drafted on 24 November 1951, signed by Archbishop Epiphanios of Philadelphia (Amman) to the Israeli Ministry of Foreign Affairs so the latter could invoke its contents at the 6th Session of the UN General Assembly. The letter read as follows:

> The Greek Orthodox Patriarchate of Jerusalem is pleased to mark once again the friendly relations of good understanding subsisting between it and the Government of Israel. During the past year, the matter of our properties throughout Israel and Jerusalem has been satisfactorily settled, by being released from the Custodian of Abandoned Property. The rights and privileges of the Patriarchate in accordance with the Status Quo have been respected and satisfactorily kept. Facilities for unrestricted access from and through Israel territory to the Christian Holy Places in Jerusalem have been accorded securely and in dignity. We know well that the Israeli Government has acted thus in accordance with its basic and permanent policy and we are sure that same policy will continue in the future, Israel thus fulfilling faithfully its obligation to the Christian World.[151]

Letters identical in content and written for the same purposes had been drafted on behalf of other Christian organizations based in Jerusalem, namely, Yeghishe Derderian, locum tenens of the Patriarchal Throne of the Armenian Apostolic Patriarchate in Jerusalem; Alberto Gori, Latin Patriarch of Jerusalem; George Hakim, Greek Catholic Archbishop of the Galilee; and Jacob, Archbishop of the Coptic Church of the Near East.[152]

To this end, Ioannis Moschopoulos, then Greek consul in Jerusalem, had written a letter dated 20 November 1951 to the Israeli Ministry of Foreign Affairs, offering his

---

[150] On the status quo of Holy Places in Palestine under the British Mandate, cf. Kobi Cohen-Hattab, *La-Tur et Irushalayim: Ha-tayarut be-Eretz Israel bi-Tkufat ha-Mandat ha-Briti, 1917–1948* [*Touring in Jerusalem: Tourism in Eretz-Yisrael during the British Mandate, 1917–1948*] (Jerusalem: Yad Yitzhak Ben Zvi, 2006), 93–6. On the administrative competences of the first British military governor of Jerusalem, Sir Ronald Storrs, in relation to maintaining the status quo of the Holy Places, cf. Yaakov Reuveni, *Mimshal ha-Mandat be-Eretz Israel: Nituakh Histori-Medini* [*Administration of the British Mandate in Palestine: A Historical and Political Analysis*] (Ramat Gan: Bar-Ilan University, 1993), 59–63. Later, Storrs was named governor of Cyprus, and it was during his term that the 'Oktovriana' ('October Events') uprising took place in 1931. Cf. 1.2 above.

[151] ISA/RG130/MFA/4364/9, Research Division (408/28.11.1951). Titled 'On the issue of Jerusalem, in view of the upcoming UN General Assembly', that report by the Research Division includes a report by Herzog citing a series of letters sent by prelates of various Christian organizations based in Jerusalem. It included the letter dated 24.11.1951 by Archbishop Epiphanios, Archbishop of Philadelphia, head of the Patriarchal Delegation of the Greek Orthodox Patriarchate of Jerusalem in Israel, a letter from the consul general of Greece in Jerusalem, Ioannis Moschopoulos, and the Spanish consul in Jerusalem, Antonio de la Cierva y Lewita, who was of Jewish descent.

[152] Ibid.

own positive assessment of the contacts between the Greek Orthodox Patriarchate and Israel.[153] In his letter, Moschopoulos wrote, among other things:

> It is with particular pleasure that I avail myself of this opportunity to pay tribute to the manner in which relations between the authorities of the new State and the Patriarchate have and are being conducted. All questions relating to the property of the Patriarchate in the New City of Jerusalem and elsewhere in the State have been satisfactorily cleared up. We are confident that such matters as are still outstanding between the Patriarchate and the Government of Israel will be satisfactorily settled in the regular process of relations between them. The status and rights of the Patriarchate and the Greek Orthodox Community in Israel have been confirmed and guaranteed – regular meetings are held between a Patriarchal mission and Israeli Government representatives on mutual relations and these are held in a spirit of cordiality and good will. The Greek Orthodox religious personnel enjoy full freedom of passage from one part of Jerusalem to the other. Moreover, special arrangements have been made for free access to the Old City of considerable numbers of Greek Orthodox worshippers in Israel on the occasion of the Holy Days of our Church. In consultation with the leaders of the Greek Church in Greece, plans are being drawn up for large-scale pilgrimages through Israel to the Old City of Jerusalem and to Bethlehem. In making these plans we are confident of the cooperation of the Israel Government, its central and Jerusalem local authorities.[154]

An identical letter was submitted by the consul general of Spain in Jerusalem – Spain having been amongst those Western European states that, like Greece, had yet to recognize the Jewish state de jure.[155] Nevertheless, though these circumstances partly contributed to Greece's de facto recognition of Israel in 1952,[156] they were not sufficient to fully normalize relations between the two countries.

Last but not least, neither the Greek nor the Israeli side fully capitalized on a highly symbolic event which might have, under the circumstances of the time, developed their bilateral relations in more ways than one. More specifically, for the first time since the end of the Italian occupation of the Dodecanese Islands and during the British provisional military administration there, free municipal elections were held in Rhodes on 6 August 1946, the eve of the formal accession of the Dodecanese to Greece the following year. A little less than two months later, on 1 October 1946, at the third meeting of the newly elected Municipal Board, and with the encouragement of the mayor, Haritos, it was decided to change the name of the central square of the medieval

---

[153] Ibid.
[154] Ibid.
[155] Netanel Lorch, 'Yisrael–Sfarad: Kinun Yakhasim Diplomatiim' ['Israel–Spain: Establishment of Diplomatic Relations']; and Shmuel Hadas, 'Yisrael u-Sfarad: Nativ Metupal' ['Israel and Spain: A Careful Path'], in *Misrad ha-Khutz*, ed. Yeger, Govrin and Oded, 398–403 and 404–13. Spain recognized Israel de jure in January 1986.
[156] Cf. 2.4.3.1 below.

Jewish Quarter (the *Judería*) from Piazza del Principe (Prince's Square) to Plateia Evraion Martyron (Jewish Martyrs Square). According to the minutes of that meeting, the renaming of the square was approved 'in memory of the Jews of Rhodes, our fellow citizens, who met with a deplorable death in German concentration camps during the last war'.[157]

This fine gesture was essentially the first public acknowledgment of the Jewish Holocaust in Greece since the end of the Second World War, and this, by a democratically elected local Hellenic administrative authority.[158] In fact, it was possibly the first commemoration of Jewish Holocaust victims at a European level. Nevertheless, despite the positive impact the publicity of such a move would have had on public opinion in both Greece, Israel and the world, the instance was not leveraged for communication purposes and was completely ignored by the political leaderships of both states.

The details of this event were reported by the Mayor of Rhodes Gabriel Haritos to the members of the Israeli delegation who arrived on the Greek island in order to take part in the UN-led Armistice talks with their Egyptian and Jordanian counterparts in 1949. An article published in the Israeli newspaper *Al ha-Mishmar* on 25 January 1949, describes an informal visit of the members of the Israeli delegation to the home of Haritos, during which the latter spoke about his initiative to honour the memory of the Rhodian Jews killed during the Holocaust. On the subject of establishing full diplomatic relations between Greece and Israel, the Israeli paper wrote: 'the Mayor added informally that although the Greek government did not recognize the State of Israel, the Greek people recognize Israel in their hearts [. . .]'.[159]

2.4.3.1 Greece's de facto recognition of Israel in 1952

Greece's reluctance to improve relations with Israel began to subside sometime in February 1952. It was then that the Greek government notified the honorary Israeli consul in Athens, Asher Moissis, that it intended to recognize Israel de facto and that the full normalization of relations between Greece and Israel would take place as soon as negotiations between Greece and Egypt were successfully completed with regard to the protection of all Greek community rights. The Greek government also proposed that an agreement with Israel be signed immediately establishing direct air connections between the two countries and calling for intense negotiations on a transnational trade agreement. The Israelis promptly agreed to both proposals.

Greece's positive about-face towards Israel, according to a report by the Israeli Ministry of Foreign Affairs,[160] was due, first and foremost, to pressure from the US State

---

[157] Municipality of Rhodes, Minutes of the 3rd Municipal Board meeting, 1.10.1946 (3/1.10.1946), Archives of the Municipal Board.

[158] Historical Account of the Jewish Community of Rhodes, official website of the Jewish Community of Rhodes, available online: www.jewishrhodes.org (accessed 6 October 2022). Cf. Willard Manus, *This Way to Paradise: Dancing on the Tables* (Athens: Lycabettus Press, 1998), 60.

[159] *Al ha-Mishmar*, 'Recognition in Their Hearts', 25.1.1949.

[160] ISA/RG130/MFA/4364/10, Research Division (458/21.2.1952). Includes a report dated February 1952 by Gershon Avner, head of the West Europe Division.

Department on the Greek Foreign Ministry after behind-the-scenes communications between the Israeli embassy in Washington and American officials had been conducted. The Israelis believed that Athens had begun to realize that, ultimately, despite the anti-Israel positions it had adopted, Egypt was not so eager to introduce measures protecting the rights of its Greek inhabitants. Furthermore, Israel's Ministry of Foreign Affairs believed Greece had come to realize that it did not need Arab support at international fora with regard to its difference with neighbouring communist countries, as the support provided by countries of the West was clearly more effective. It was also believed that the general spirit of understanding between the Israeli government and the Patriarchate of Jerusalem in the matter of Church properties had provided a positive thrust in the relationship between Israel and Greece. Finally, the same report cited the conviction that certain unnamed individuals who had recently been appointed to key positions in the Greek Foreign Ministry, would have a positive impact on the course of Israeli–Greek relations.

The decision of Athens to settle the issue of the Greek diaspora in Egypt before attempting normalization with Israel was seen by the Israelis as having a double meaning: either that Athens had been using negotiations with Cairo as a pretext for not improving relations with Israel, or that Cairo was dragging its heels in talks with Greece because it wanted to delay normalization between Israel and Greece for as long as possible. In that regard, Israel considered Greece to be a 'hostage of Egypt'. The prevalent feeling was that because of the 'hostage situation', Sofoklis Venizelos, Greek foreign minister and vice president of the Greek government, on an official visit to Syria and Lebanon in May 1952, was quoted as declaring to the Syrian and Jordanian media that, 'Because of its good relations with the Arab states, Greece does not recognize Israel nor does it intend to.' When Arye Levavi, deputy director of the West Europe Division of the Israeli Ministry of Foreign Affairs, asked Greece's consul general to Jerusalem, Ioannis Moschopoulos, to clarify this statement, the latter denied the report, and implied that there was still a long way to go before de jure recognition and full normalization of bilateral relations.[161] The Israeli Foreign Ministry did not put much store in the words of the Greek consul. On the contrary, it chose to maintain its optimism after Greece's de facto recognition. Indicative of this was the unusually long report by the Israeli ambassador to Ankara, Eliahu Sasson, containing a particularly detailed account of an otherwise ceremonial and very laconic exchange he had had with the Greek monarch, Paul I and his wife, Queen Frederica, at a reception hosted in honour of the royal couple in Istanbul during their official visit to Turkey in early June 1952.[162]

The immediate effect of Greece's de facto recognition of Israel was a change in the official title of Greece's consul general to Jerusalem to 'Greece's Diplomatic

---

[161] ISA/RG93/MFA/8692/5, Research Division (507/9.6.1952). Included in that report: (a) The report dated 25.5.1952 by Arye Levavi, head of the Eastern Europe Division, to Ioannis Moschopoulos, Greece's consul general to Jerusalem, regarding statements attributed to Foreign Minister Sofoklis Venizelos, transmitted over Syrian State Radio in Damascus on 21.5.1952; and (b) The letter of reply sent by the latter to the former, dated 31.5.1952.

[162] ISA/RG93/MFA/8692/5, Research Division (531/6.8.1952).

Representative to the Israeli Government'. Similarly, Asher Moissis' title which up to that time had been Israeli 'Honorary Consul to Athens' was changed to 'Diplomatic Representative of Israel in Greece',[163] giving an impression, however slight, that bilateral diplomatic relations had improved. The same year, on 15 July 1952, an intergovernmental agreement was signed establishing direct airline connections between Israel and Greece, reflected in Israeli departmental reports as a widespread feeling that full normalization of bilateral relations was approaching.

But the feeling proved erroneous. Greek–Israeli relations remained frigid, despite the adoption of more grandiose terminology. The airline connection agreement, though it was eventually enacted, was never endorsed by the Greek Parliament. Last, despite the fact that the recently appointed Greek consul general to Jerusalem Angelos Vlachos regularly held talks with the Israeli Ministry of Foreign Affairs, which had moved from Tel Aviv to Jerusalem by then, Greece did not acknowledge the legitimacy of the Israeli government's decision to move the Ministry to Jerusalem. As Angelos Vlachos himself wrote in his memoirs, Greece fully supported the UN Security Council's opinion, shared by other countries[164] such as the United States, Britain, France, Italy, Australia and Turkey, that the relocation of the Israeli Foreign Ministry from Tel Aviv to Jerusalem was 'an arbitrary act transgressing Jerusalem's special international status'.[165] Thus, as far as Greece and the overwhelming majority of the international community were concerned, the requirement for ambassadors and consuls to travel to Jerusalem in order to meet with Israeli government officials was just a matter of practical necessity and nothing more.

Regardless, Israeli diplomats, whether by design or because they truly believed it to be so, assumed that the meetings held in Jerusalem with their foreign counterparts showed their tacit approval of the controversial decision on the apart of the Israeli government. The argument they put forward was that even the consul from Greece, a country that had only recently recognized Israel de facto, travelled to Jerusalem for meetings with officials at the Ministry of Foreign Affairs.[166]

[163] State of Israel, *Government Yearbook 5714 (1953–54)*, 162. In the list of Israeli diplomatic missions abroad, the title of Asher Moissis in Athens was changed from 'Diplomatic Representative (Honorary)' to 'Diplomatic Representation–Athens'. For the adoption of complex terminology related to diplomatic representation between Israel and Greece during the 1950s, cf. Amikam Nahmani, *Israel, Turkey and Greece: Uneasy Relations in the East Mediterranean* (London: Frank Cass, 1987), 112–18.

[164] ISA/RG93/MFA/8692/5, Research Division (518/11.7.1952). This Research Division report includes the responses of foreign governments to Israel's decision of 4.5.1952, to move its Foreign Ministry headquarters from Tel Aviv to Jerusalem. The Israeli decision was implemented on 13.7.1953. For an account of the Ministry's transfer, cf. Rekhavam Amir, 'Haavarat Misrad ha-Khutz li-Yerushalayim – 1953' ['Moving the Ministry of Foreign Affairs to Jerusalem – 1953'], in *Misrad ha-Khutz*, ed. Yeger, Govrin and Oded, 34–40.

[165] Angelos Vlachos, *Mia fora ki enan kairo enas diplomatis* [*Once Upon a Time a Diplomat*] (Athens: Estia, 1999), vol. 4, 60–3.

[166] ISA/RG93/MFA/8692/8, Research Division (740/24.3.1954). This report includes an account of Ministry of Foreign Affairs activities over the first eight months after moving its headquarters to the new premises, with specific references to the meetings between ministry officials at the time and various foreign diplomats, including Angelos Vlachos, accredited to the Israeli government. Cf. Vlachos, *Enas diplomatis*, 60–3.

2.4.3.2 *The Cephalonia Earthquake and the perspectives in Greek–Israeli relations, 1953–4*

An earthquake registering 6.2 on the Richter scale that shook the Ionian Islands in August 1953 greatly dampened the optimism that had filled Israeli diplomacy after Greece's decision to recognize Israel de facto in the previous year. That earthquake caused serious loss of human lives and extensive material damage on the islands of Zakynthos, Ithaca and Cephalonia. On 12 August 1953, as soon as news of the event became known, an Israeli Navy flotilla engaged in manoeuvres in international waters in the Aegean Sea rushed to Cephalonia to offer assistance to those hit. US and British warships which also happened to be in the area responded likewise. According to a detailed report by Moshe Sasson, first secretary of Israel's diplomatic representation in Athens, the Greek government was shown to be ill-prepared to cope with the situation in Cephalonia.[167] According to Sasson, despite the fact that the Greek government and the press praised the multitude of foreign states which provided humanitarian aid and financial assistance, the fact that the crews of Israeli warships were freeing civilians from the rubble was initially kept quiet by the Greek news media, even though the Israeli diplomatic representation in Athens kept Greek journalists apprised of their activities. It was only when the rescue operation by Israeli sailors in Cephalonia became more widely known that the Greek press started to publish extensive articles praising Israel's assistance, 'with the exception of two newspapers, loyal to the [Greek]Ministry of Foreign Affairs', as Sasson writes in his report.

In the same report, Sasson relates that even while Israeli warships were in Cephalonia and their crews were rescuing civilians from the rubble, Stefanos Stefanopoulos, minister of foreign affairs in the Papagos government, rejected Israel's formal offer of humanitarian aid. In fact, the Greek government, in a document to the Israeli diplomatic representation in Athens, stated that: 'under the circumstances, an acceptance of your proposal is not deemed necessary'.[168] Sasson also noted that although the Greek government had requested assistance from US and British warships in the emergency, they justified their refusal to officially accept Israeli assistance with the excuse that 'they were unable to see exactly how warships could be in a position to help those trapped'. While all this was going on in Athens, Israeli sailors in Cephalonia were still pulling people out of the rubble.

Upon completion of the rescue missions in Cephalonia, the Israeli flotilla called in at the port of Piraeus, once again to a cold reception by the Greek political leadership. Sasson reports that:

> No representative of the Greek Ministry of Foreign Affairs came to meet the flotilla. No official appeared at the port of Piraeus either to welcome it or see it off.

---

[167] ISA/RG93/MFA/8692/7, Research Division (725/15.9.1953). Included in that report is an account dated August 1953, by Moshe Sasson, first secretary of Israel's Diplomatic Representation to Athens, to the West Europe Division.

[168] ISA/RG93/MFA/8692/7, Research Division (726/15.9.1953). The letter dated 17.8.1953 sent by Stefanos Stefanopoulos, Greek Minister of Foreign Affairs, to Moshe Sasson.

Contacts with the local port authorities were kept to the absolute minimum. The customary visit paid by the head of the Israeli crew to the Greek Prime Minister's office took place on the initiative of Israel's Diplomatic Representation in Athens, and though it had originally been announced that the Head of the Church of Greece would visit the Israeli vessels already anchored in Piraeus, the visit was cancelled at the last moment without any specific reason being given.[169]

According to Sasson, the Chief of the Hellenic Navy General Staff tried to explain that the reason no special attention was paid to the Israeli flotilla for its assistance was that a national day of mourning had been decreed by the Greek government. The explanation was not at all convincing. As Sasson points out in the same report, when the US warships called in at Piraeus on their way back from the quake-stricken areas, the decreed national mourning did not prevent the Greek government from giving them the warmest of welcomes. And although letters of thanks followed – one from former Greek consul general in Jerusalem, Dimitrios Pappas, to Israeli Foreign Minister Moshe Sharett,[170] and one from the Central Council of Jewish Communities to Prime Minister David Ben-Gurion,[171] the Israeli diplomats could not hide their disappointment at the coldness of the Greek government.

Israel believed that the political behaviour of Athens was due primarily to its customary avoidance at all costs of upsetting the Arabs, particularly the Egyptians, and to its fear of public criticism because:

there was no way [the Greek government] could justify the total absence of the Greek fleet and its failure to provide assistance to its citizens. In contrast, a navy as fledgling as Israel's was able to demonstrate disproportionately extensive activity. According to the Greek government, the country's public opinion could more easily avoid making such comparisons with the US or British fleets and could thus more easily justify the weaknesses demonstrated by the Greek government machinery. Praising Israeli assistance carried the risk of highlighting the inability of the Greek government to mobilise the Greek fleet into a state of operational readiness.

Thus, yet another chance for rapprochement between Greece and Israel went by the board, and, as Moshe Sasson concludes in his extensive report, 'despite the sentiment of affection and gratitude expressed by Greek public opinion and, from a certain point on, by the Greek press, ultimately Israel's humanitarian aid, which essentially was provided against the will of the Greek government, will ironically not bear political benefits in the near future'. The Israeli Ministry of Foreign Affairs Research Division agreed with

---

[169] Ibid.
[170] Ibid. The letter dated 24.8.1953 from former Consul General of Greece to Jerusalem Dimitrios Pappas to Moshe Sharett.
[171] Ibid. The letter dated 23.8.1953 from the Central Council of Jewish Communities in Greece to Israeli Prime Minister David Ben-Gurion, signed by Secretary General Isaac Emmanuel and Vice President David Sam Amarilio.

this conclusion, and forwarded Sasson's report to other Israeli diplomatic missions.[172] Last but not least, it is worth noting that, contrary to what occurred in Greece, the humanitarian aid sent to areas of two other powerful earthquakes which happened to occur the same year, in Turkey[173] and in Cyprus,[174] went a long way towards improving relations between Israel, Turkey and Britain.

In the aftermath, Greece took pains to change initial impressions. A year later, in June 1954, when an Israeli Navy flotilla called in once again at the port of Piraeus as part of a training exercise in the Mediterranean, Athens adopted a totally different attitude, apparently in an effort to dissipate the negative impressions it had made. One week prior to the flotilla's arrival, the Israeli diplomatic representation circumvented the Greek Foreign Ministry and directly contacted the Royal Palace and was reassured by the Master of Ceremonies that if the Greek monarch was in Athens, he would decorate two of the officers of the Israeli Navy who had participated in the rescue of the quake victims the summer before.

News of the Israeli Navy's visit was unreservedly publicized through the Athenian press, along with particularly flattering remarks about Israel's assistance the previous summer. On 26 June 1954, the two Israeli naval officers were decorated by the master of ceremonies of the Greek Royal Palace. That day, the decorated Israeli officers laid a wreath on the Tomb of the Unknown Soldier at Syntagma Square, marking the first time such an event had ever occurred.[175]

Thus, whereas in 1952 the Israelis had been particularly optimistic about progress in bilateral relations after the Greek de facto recognition and Israel's improved diplomatic representation – albeit in name only – by 1954, it was clear that the full normalization of Greek–Israeli relations would remain uncertain. In fact, Israel believed that so long as Egypt held Greece hostage with regard to the fate of the Greek diaspora there, Greek reticence towards Israel would remain unchanged. When in December of the same year, Greece appealed to the UN for the first time in the matter of Cyprus, Greek–Israeli relations remained cool. In contrast, regional cooperation between Israel, Turkey and Britain was expanding more and more.

---

[172] Ibid.
[173] ISA/RG93/MFA/8692/6, Research Division (648/7.4.1953). Report on Israeli rescue operation in the towns of Yenice and Gönen in the Dardanelles, hit by a 7.5 MS earthquake in March 1953, leaving many dead.
[174] ISA/RG93/G/5570/10. Israel provided humanitarian aid (sending tents and other necessities) to the residents of the Province of Paphos after the earthquake of 10.9.1953.
[175] ISA/RG93/MFA/8693/1. Research Division (930/19.7.1954). Report by Moshe Sasson with details of a two-day visit by the flotilla of the Israeli Navy to Piraeus on 25 and 26 June 1954.

3

Israel's Stance on the Cyprus Question
before the United Nations

3.1 Israel's assessment of the intentions of the Cypriot ethnarchy and Greece to bring the Enosis issue before the UN, 1951–3

In mid-February 1951, the Israeli press reported the words of Greek Prime Minister Sofoklis Venizelos before the Hellenic Parliament to the effect that 'Greece will never yield in the matter of Cyprus', indicating that Greece was adopting the Greek Cypriot demand for Enosis.[1] Despite the official Greek position, according to which a *sine qua non* condition for a solution to the problem would be an amiable settlement between Athens and London, another view expressed was that Britain would never give in to Greek demands without substantial diplomatic pressure. The Greek Church sided with this view and Archbishop Spyridon, the head of the Church, in a coordinated effort with Archbishop Makarios III, had been endeavouring to bring the Cyprus question before the United Nations. Asher Moissis, Israel's honorary consul to Athens, believed that such a move would be endorsed by 'the democratic states, including those of the Soviet Bloc, whose aim was to undermine Britain's global influence'. In fact, he did not rule out the possibility of a Greek appeal to the UN as early as September 1951, a fact the Israelis felt was liable to trigger an undeclared war between Greece and Britain.[2]

In Cyprus, Venizelos' statements before Parliament were enthusiastically received by the right-wing and the Church. Still, Ram Yaron, Israel's consul general in Nicosia, noted, leftist circles expressed reservations as to the intentions of 'Venizelos' reactionary government', and believed that, in exchange for Cyprus' accession to Greece, Athens would be willing to allow the US and Britain to establish military bases on the island.[3] Nevertheless, the volume of rumours about Greece's prospective recourse to the UN also mobilized Cypriot left-wing trade unions to contact governmental and trade union organizations in Poland and Czechoslovakia in an effort to secure East European

---

[1] For example, *Al ha-Mishmar*, 'Greece Seeking Cyprus Accession', 16.2.1951.
[2] ISA/RG93/MFA/8692/3, Research Division (267/23. 4.1951). Asher Moissis to the West Europe Division, March 1951.
[3] ISA/RG93/MFA/2156/3, Yaron to the British Commonwealth Division, Activity Report for February 1951 (79/100/פ – 7.3.1951).

support for Greece's appeal to the UN, for the obvious purpose of removing the prospect of an intra-NATO arrangement.[4]

According to Israel's initial appraisal, the Greek intention to bring the issue of Cyprus' accession before the UN would indeed have been encouraged by the USSR and the rest of the communist states. On the other hand, such support was liable to become something of a headache for Athens, tactically speaking,[5] as it was bound to trigger reactions on the part of Greece's 'natural' allies in the West, most particularly Britain and the British Commonwealth states supporting it. In addition, the West would take very seriously the fact that 'the communist element within Greek Cypriot society was flourishing'.[6] As far as Turkey was concerned, the Israelis had foreseen since March 1951 that sooner or later, it would be impossible for Turkey to remain indifferent to movements by Greece and the Greek Cypriots. Indeed, in April 1951, Ankara announced that it intended to send a multi-party delegation to Cyprus to meet with leaders of the Turkish minority on the island and make an on-site assessment of the situation.[7]

Nevertheless, the Greek government made it clear to Makarios III that Greece had no intention of directly confronting Britain and that the solution of bringing the issue before the UN was not advisable. As Israeli consul general to Nicosia Yaron learned, Archbishop Spyridon of Greece had purportedly sent a letter to UN Secretary General Trygve Lie requesting that the issue be debated in the upcoming session.[8] Yet, at the same time, the Greek prime minister denied rumours that Greece would file a formal request with the UN regarding the Cyprus issue, stating that 'the current conjuncture does not allow for the issue of Cyprus to be rekindled, though it remains a valid issue' – a statement construed by Israeli diplomacy as a tactical move to avoid upsetting Greek relations with the British, since the Foreign Office was in a position to prevent Greece's accession to NATO.[9]

Many aspects of the divergence of opinions in the relations of the Greek government with Makarios III were reminiscent of the negative feelings induced in the Metropolitan of Paphos and then locum tenens prelate of the Archiepiscopal See, Kleopas of Paphos, during his visit to Athens after the 1950 Enosis Plebiscite.[10] Such divergence of opinions, however, was of no surprise to the Israelis, given that Athens had no wish to oppose London on the eve of the Greek accession to NATO. On the other hand, the likelihood of recourse to the UN was exploited by Left and Right alike in Cyprus, as well as by prominent members of the clergy. It was thus that in May 1951, Kyprianos, Metropolitan

---

[4]   ISA/RG93/MFA/8692/3, Research Division (267/23 – 4.1951). Asher Moissis to the West Europe Division, March 1951.
[5]   ISA/RG93/MFA/2156/3, British Commonwealth Division to Yaron (114050/20/11011–29.4.1951).
[6]   ISA/RG93/MFA/8692/3, Research Division (267/23.4.1951), Asher Moissis to the West Europe Division, March 1951.
[7]   ISA/RG93/MFA/2156/3, Yaron to the British Commonwealth Division, Activity Report for April 1951 (307/100/פ – 8.5.1951).
[8]   Ibid.
[9]   ISA/RG93/MFA/2156/3, Yaron to the British Commonwealth Division, Activity Report for May 1951 (458/100/פ – 22.6.1951).
[10] Cf. 2.4.1 on the contents of the letter sent on 5 .9.1950 by Kleopas, Metropolitan of Paphos, to the Office of Israeli Prime Minister David Ben-Gurion.

of Kyrenia, raised anew the issue of sending a Cypriot delegation abroad to rally support for bringing the Enosis issue before the UN. In the Israeli opinion, this particular initiative by Kyprianos of Kyrenia was meant to underscore the failure of the newly elected Archbishop Makarios III to secure the support of the Greek government and to highlight his ineffectual handling of the entire issue.[11]

Greece's intention of having recourse to the UN in an effort to terminate British rule on this island off the coast of Israel triggered interest amongst Israeli diplomats, who began to follow the moves of Greeks and Greek Cypriots more closely. Fully aware that at the time, the main purpose of Greece, Turkey and Israel was to be included in NATO's plans for regional security, the Israeli Foreign Ministry determined that Greece would not jeopardize its alliance with Britain or undermine normal relations with Turkey by exacerbating existing disputes. Thus, the statements made by Greek politicians about appealing to the UN, or even the call of Archbishop Makarios III for 'Enosis and nothing but Enosis,'[12] were perceived by Israeli diplomats as moves meant to impress public opinion both in Greece and Cyprus. Ram Yaron, having reviewed Greek activities for the period of 1950–1, reported that 'given the situation in the Middle East, it is deduced that bringing the issue of Cyprus before the UN would not yield any substantial results. Even those statements made by Greek officials were obviously not meant to request the island's incorporation into Greece, but apparently to make an impression, and nothing more than that.[13]

3.2 Israel's attitude vis-à-vis the question of Cyprus at the 9th Session of the UN General Assembly, 1954

After considerable vacillation, the Papagos government finalized its decision in June 1954 to bring the question of Cyprus before the General Assembly of the United Nations. Constantine Stavropoulos, head of the UN Secretariat General Office of Legal Affairs, reportedly explained to Mordechai Kidron, deputy head of Israel's permanent representation to the UN, that 'what the Greek Government was really after was not an immediate annexation of Cyprus so much as to reach an agreement to conduct a referendum under international observation so the will of the island's citizens could be directly expressed'.

---

[11] ISA/RG93/MFA/2156/3, Yaron to the British Commonwealth Division, Activity Report for May 1951 (458/100/ק – 22.6.1951) and British Commonwealth Division to Yaron (20/11011/ז/ח – 3.7.1951).

[12] ISA/RG93/MFA/392/10, Moshe Sasson, first assistant at the Middle East Division to the Israeli Embassy in Washington (62181/11/אר – 7.5.1952). Included speculations about the possibility of Greece's recourse to the UN, as well as excerpts from Makarios' statements on the occasion of festivities in commemoration of the 25 March Greek national holiday. Cf. Archbishop Makarios III Foundation, Kokkinou (ed.), *Apanta Archiepiskopou*, vol. 1, 142–3. Circular dated 17.3.1952 by Archbishop Makarios on Greek National Day, 25 March.

[13] ISA/RG93/MFA/2156/3. Yaron to the British Commonwealth Division Activity Report for November 1951 (943/100/ק – 10.12.1951). Cf. Evangelos Averoff, *Istoria Hamenon Efkairion (Kypriako 1950–1963)* [*A Story of Missed Opportunities (Cyprus Issue 1950–1963)*], 2nd edn (Athens: Estia, 1982), vol. 1, 21–33.

Despite the optimistic official declarations, Greece did not believe the struggle to be waged at the General Assembly would be an easy one. According to Stavropoulos, the Greek government was fully aware that Cyprus had never been under Greek rule, that the Turkish minority was opposed to Enosis, and therefore, complications were to be expected in the relations between Athens, London and Ankara.[14] Stavropoulos' personal belief as to potential difficulties between Greece and Turkey were not consistent with the way Athens presented those matters. Athens appeared not to implicate Turkey at all – at least not officially.[15] What Alexis Kyrou, general director of the Hellenic Ministry of Foreign Affairs, in charge of diplomatic manoeuvring on the Greek side was seeking by way of recourse to the UN was a controlled diplomatic confrontation with Britain, with the ultimate goal of achieving a bilateral agreement between Greece and Britain resulting in Enosis.[16]

In an effort to explain the reasons behind the Papagos government's recourse to the UN at this particular conjuncture, Avraham Darom, head of the Israeli diplomatic representation to Athens, filed a relevant report citing the view of officials in the Greek government and Ministry of Foreign Affairs.[17] The Greek government, he felt, had been left with no choice but to 'give in' to the Enosis movement,[18] since, as he observed, the prevalent position was that Greece could not accept 'even one Greek remaining under the rule of the British crown, at a moment when Britain was ready to grant independence to such states as Sudan or other African countries, far less developed and less civilized than Cyprus, the sole area in Europe still under a colonial regime'. Whereas the desire of the Greek government had been to see the issue settled by way of an agreement with Britain, London showed no willingness to negotiate the future of Cyprus.

According to Darom, the recourse to the United Nations was the only solution. This conclusion was bolstered by the fact that the Greek Cypriot demand for Enosis was extremely popular in Greek public opinion. At the same time, the Church was expressing an intense interest in the Cyprus question, not only because of Archbishop Makarios' actions, but also because of the strong support the latter was being provided by Archbishop Spyridon. Since 1951, Makarios had been vociferously criticizing the governments of Sofoklis Venizelos and Nikolaos Plastiras for hesitating to have recourse to the UN in order to promote Cypriot claims for self-determination, accusing

---

[14] ISA/RG93/MFA/2156/7, Mordechai Kidron, deputy head of Israel's Permanent Representation to the UN, to the UN Division of the Israeli Ministry of Foreign Affairs (9.6.1954, not officially logged). Kidron's meeting with Constantine Stavropoulos, director general of the Legal Department of the UN Secretariat General, on 4.6.1954. Cf. Averoff, *Istoria Hamenon Efkairion*, 29–41, in the matter of the influence of Archbishop Makarios III's moves and the religious hierarchy in Greece and in Cyprus, on the eve of Greece's first recourse to the UN in 1954.

[15] Menelaos Alexandrakis, Vyron Theodoropoulos and Efstathios Lagakos, *To Kypriako 1950–1974: Mia endoskopisi* [*The Cyprus Question: An Introspection*] (Athens: Elliniki Evroekdotiki, 1987), 95–9. Assessments of Greek diplomacy as to Turkey's positions on the issue of Cyprus during the period 1950–4.

[16] Evanthis Hatzivassiliou, *Stratigikes tou Kypriakou: I dekaetia tou 1950* [*Strategies in the Cyprus Question: The 1950s*], 2nd edn (Athens: Patakis, 2005), 113–14.

[17] ISA/RG93/MFA/2155/10, Avraham Darom, Israel's diplomatic representative in Athens to the Western Europe and UN Divisions (2041/חמ – 30.4.1954).

[18] Cf. Alexandrakis, Theodoropoulos and Lagakos, *To Kypriako*, 22.

their governments of undercutting national interests.[19] The Greek government sensed that public opinion would begin to believe that its political leadership was lagging behind the Church[20] as far as national issues were concerned, since the Church had increasingly emerged as the main exponent of the 'genuine patriotic voice'. Makarios' appeal to Greek public opinion and particularly the country's youth was made abundantly clear during his layover in Rhodes from 18 to 20 March 1954, on his way to Nicosia from Athens. The former head of the Israeli diplomatic representation in Athens, Asher Moissis, happened to be in Rhodes at the time and filed a detailed report with the Israeli Foreign Ministry describing the popular welcome the island residents gave Makarios, as well as the serious incidents that followed. On 19 March 1954, during a student demonstration, the British cosulate in Rhodes was severely damaged, 25 students and ten police officers were injured.[21]

Last, Prime Minister Alexandros Papagos' personality played an important part in Greece's decision to have recourse to the UN regarding the Cyprus question, since he aspired to Cyprus' becoming a Greek territory under his mandate. Also important was the influence of Alexis Kyrou on the Greek government's decisions on the issue of Cyprus. Of Cypriot descent, Kyrou had backed the Greek Cypriot uprising of October 1931 (the 'Oktovriana') in 1931, while serving as Greek consul general on the island and in defiance of the express government position of maintaining neutrality. As a result of his actions, Kyrou was recalled from Cyprus.[22] In 1954, as general director of the Greek Ministry of Foreign Affairs, Kyrou personally determined the content of Greece's recourse and had the last say over every diplomatic move.[23]

3.2.1 The British factor

With the forthcoming UN debate on the Cyprus issue in view, Israeli diplomacy was called upon for the first time to adopt a formal position. The grid of relations between Israel and Britain was directly linked to the maintenance of the latter's military presence on the neighbouring island – a presence linked in turn to Israel's security. On the other

---

[19] Cf. Archbishop Makarios III Foundation, Kokkinou (ed.), *Apanta Archiepiskopou*, vol. 1, 158–60. A typical sample of the criticism aimed by Makarios at the Greek governments of the period 1950–2 was his speech transmitted by Athens Radio Station on 25.7.1952.

[20] Hatzivassiliou, *Stratigikes*, 105. Cf. ISA/RG93/MFA/2155/10, Moshe Sasson, second secretary of the Israeli Diplomatic Representation in Athens to the West Europe Division (מס/1856 – 14.2.1954). Description of the enthusiastic expressions of support for Makarios upon his arrival in Athens on 12.2.1954.

[21] ISA/RG93/MFA/2155/10, Asher Moissis, former honorary consul of Israel to Athens to the West Europe Division (MH/1980-6.4.1954). Cf. *Proodos Dodekanisou*, 'Cyprus Ethnarch Makarios arrives in Rhodes today at 8:45 am', 18.3.1954. Ibid., 'Rhodes gives warm welcome to leader of the Cypriot Liberation Struggle', 19.3.1954. Ibid., 'Rhodes youth clash with police outside British Consulate – The militant protest of the Dodecanese – The injured citizens and police', 20.3.1954. Ibid., 'Archbishop Makarios tells *Proodos*: Rhodians demonstrated their love of freedom and their frustration with the rigid stance of the British against the Cypriots', 21.3.1954.

[22] In the matter of the dispute between Eleftherios Venizelos and Alexis Kyrou over the handling of the Cyprus issue, during the period 1930–1, cf. Pikros, 'O Venizelos', 263–81.

[23] Hatzivassiliou, *Stratigikes*, 105–18. Cf. Alexis Kyrou, *Elliniki Exoteriki Politiki* [*Greek Foreign Policy*] (Athens, 1955), 389–400.

hand, according to a relevant proposal by Gershon Avner, the secretary of the Israeli embassy in London, if Israel were to openly support British pursuits at the UN vote, it should first try to obtain as many benefits as possible from London. Consequently, Avner suggested, it should be made clear to the British that the government of Israel had yet to decide on its position, and that Israel's reticence on the matter was in fact a reaction to Britain's reservations blatantly demonstrated in international fora, when it came to matters of vital importance to Israel.[24]

At the opposite pole, of Israel's intent to try to 'discipline' London while reaping certain practical benefits, Cyprus' strategic position was a reminder of how important the continued presence of the British on the island was for Israel. The Israeli consulate in Nicosia had no doubts that the 'British will be here for many years to come,'[25] a belief based on indisputable facts: large-scale, costly public works of a military nature, underway in Cyprus since the early 1950s and involving Israeli construction companies[26] were now proceeding at a fast pace with long-term timelines. Owing to Britain's withdrawal from the Suez Canal following its agreement with Egypt on 27 July 1954, London was giving more prominence to Cyprus' geopolitical role. At the local Cypriot level, and in order to deflect Greek demands for Enosis, Britain was expected to counter with an offer granting a constitution and instituting either a limited or broader autonomy. In no event, however, would the British relinquish their full control.

Besides all of the above, Israel was at the time seeking clear reassurances from Britain that even after withdrawing from the Suez Canal, it would continue to contribute to the preservation of stability in the region.[27] In spite of relevant correspondence exchanged between the Israeli ambassador to London, Eliahu Elath, and British foreign minister Anthony Eden in October 1954,[28] Ben-Gurion wanted express reassurance from London that Israel would not be left defenceless in the event of a war with Egypt. A few weeks before the debate on Greece's recourse before the UN, Britain reiterated its promise with a written assurance from Sir John Nicholls, the British ambassador in Tel Aviv, to Ben-Gurion.[29] Based on these facts – and regardless of what each side wanted in exchange – the Israelis had no reason to displease Britain, which was committed to protecting the Jewish state from its military bases in Cyprus in the event of an Arab attack.

[24] ISA/RG93/MFA/2156/7, Avner Gershon, Adviser to Israel's Embassy in London, to Israel's Permanent Representation at the UN (40401/41/בא – 5.8.1954).
[25] ISA/RG93/MFA/2156/7, Eliezer Marom, Israel's vice consul in Nicosia, to the British Commonwealth Division (1113/102/ק – 15.8.1954).
[26] ISA/RG59/GL/12561/17, Israeli consulate in Nicosia to the Economic Affairs Division (1988/02/ק – 14.12.1953). Details on the activities of Israeli construction companies in Cyprus since 1952, with data on the size of their respective investments and their cooperation in the area of public works of military interest. Cf. above 2.4.2.1.
[27] ISA/RG93/MFA/8693/2, Research Division (957/28.11.1954). British Foreign Minister Anthony Eden's address to the House of Commons on 2.11.1954, during which he raised the issue of the protection of Israel by Britain in the event of an attack by Egypt.
[28] ISA/RG93/MFA/8693/1, Research Division (945/26.10.1954). Eden's letter of 19.10.1954 to Elath, Israel's ambassador to London, in response to a letter from the latter dated 22.9.1954 to the former (Research Division 937/4.10.1954).
[29] ISA/RG93/MFA/8693/2, Research Division (954/22.11.1954). The letter of 14.11.1954 from Britain's ambassador to Tel Aviv, Sir John Nicholls, to Prime Minister Ben-Gurion.

3.2.2 The Turkish factor

Israel's assessment of the attitude it would be called upon to adopt vis-à-vis Turkey was along the same lines. Turkey's diplomatic representation in Tel Aviv had informed Walter Eytan, director general of the Israeli Ministry of Foreign Affairs, that Turkey would oppose putting the Cyprus issue on the agenda of the UN General Assembly, and asked Israel to endorse the same position.[30] Nevertheless, Turkey appeared to be particularly troubled and undecided as to the tactics it should adopt towards striking a balance amongst a number of factors: on the one hand, Turkey wanted to align itself with the British perspective so that the Greek recourse would be held off the UN General Assembly agenda; on the other, it wanted to ensure that measures would be taken to protect the Turkish Cypriot population; and at the same time, it wished to avoid upsetting relations with its NATO partners, Greece and Britain.[31] Thus, the best solution as far as Turkey was concerned, and the way to avoid dealing with such difficult tactical questions, was for the Cyprus issue not to be debated at all.

In view of the impending vote, Israeli diplomacy had to choose which position to take vis-à-vis the concerns expressed by Turkey. Initially consulted was Yohanan Meroz, who had served as secretary of the Israeli diplomatic mission to Ankara during the period 1951–4. It was his opinion that Israel had a number of critical reasons to fully back Turkey, whichever stance it took.[32] One of his main points was the excellent bilateral relationship between Turkey and Israel, in contrast to the Greek 'retrenchment policy' – as he called it – vis-à-vis Israel. He also believed that Greece's recourse would receive support from Arab states that followed an anti-British policy and wished to undermine Turkey's regional interests. Regardless of the particular motives that any individual Arab government might harbour, the Arab countries as a whole would use their votes to retain influence over the Greek decision-making centres. And finally, Meroz speculated that Turkey would sooner or later be left with no choice other than to align itself with Britain.

Meroz's arguments were not without merit. The fact that Israel deemed its relations with Turkey at the time as 'excellent' is confirmed by the yearly activity report for 1953, prepared by Yohanan Meroz himself in January 1954, shortly before his term in Ankara ended and he was transferred to Washington.[33] Turkey was the only Muslim country to maintain normal diplomatic relations with Israel. Typical of the excellent bilateral relations were various articles in the Israeli press favourable to Turkey, on a variety of

[30] ISA/RG93/MFA/2156/7, West Europe Division to the Israeli Embassy in London (3934/ד –26.8.1954). Included Eytan's memo of 24.8.1954 on his meeting with the second secretary of the Turkish Diplomatic Mission in Tel Aviv on 23.8.1954.
[31] ISA/RG93/MFA/2156/7, Michael Pragai, adviser to Israel's Permanent Representation to the UN, to the UN Division (224/818/גמ – 10.9.1954). Working meeting held with his Turkish counterpart, Arkant.
[32] ISA/RG93/MFA/2156/7, Yohanan Meroz, first secretary at the Israeli Embassy in Washington to the UN Division (54/09/5/בי – 10.9.1954). Cf. Alexandrakis, Theodoropoulos and Lagakos, *To Kypriako*, 95–9. On Turkey's stance towards Greece over the Cyprus issue during the period 1950–4.
[33] ISA/RG93/MFA/8692/8, Research Division (823/15.2.1954). Meroz, first secretary of Israel's Diplomatic Mission to Ankara, to West Europe Division. Report on relations between Israel and Turkey in 1953.

occasions: from the Israeli offer of humanitarian aid to the victims of an earthquake in the Dardanelles, to the festivities at the Hebrew University of Jerusalem marking the 500th anniversary of the fall of Constantinople,[34] to the anniversary of the proclamation of the Republic of Turkey, to which the English-language *Jerusalem Post* dedicated its main editorial. Similarly, the Turkish press ran pro-Israeli commentaries on various issues relevant to Israeli foreign policy – from the suspension of diplomatic relations between the USSR and Israel to the controversial transfer of headquarters of the Israeli Ministry of Foreign Affairs from Tel Aviv to West Jerusalem; meanwhile, any criticism of Israeli policy was carefully couched in the mildest of terms. Throughout 1953, Turkish scientists and civil servants had made various study visits to Israel, while Israeli technocrats offered their services to the Turkish public sector in the areas of education, agriculture and industry. Despite deep displeasure on the part of the Arab states, Israel and Turkey in 1953 made significant inroads in developing their trade relations, improving diplomatic relations to embassy level,[35] posting an Israeli military attaché to Ankara, and signing an intergovernmental cooperation agreement for cultural exchanges, while Israeli construction companies undertook technical projects on infrastructure directly related to Turkey's role in NATO. Subsequently, Yohanan Meroz's report on progress in bilateral relations made during 1953 concluded with this characteristic phrase, 'Israel came to Turkey to stay.' In view of the prevailing facts, such a conclusion could not be truer.

Yohanan Meroz was the ultimate supporter of the pro-Turkish position, which at that time was fully endorsed by the Israeli Foreign Ministry. He believed that a 'vague' stance by Israel on the Cyprus question would not only harm his country's relations with Turkey, but that Ankara would perceive it as inexplicably inconsistent. On the contrary, he predicted that if Israel were to vote against the Greek position, 'it would make the Greeks take stock of just how small Israel's "numerical" value actually is in the UN', particularly on an issue where every vote counts.[36]

3.2.3 The Greek and Greek Cypriot factors

As for Israel's stance toward Greece, Gershon Avner, secretary of the Israeli Embassy in London, made this suggestion: deliver a clear message to the effect that Israel will not support the Greek recourse, and express disappointment over the friction in Israel's relations with Greece as a result of the long-drawn negotiations with Egypt over the Greek diaspora there. A stance of this kind, Avner believed, would have no major repercussions since having committed to proceed to a de jure recognition of Israel after the vote at the UN, 'it would be highly likely that Athens would once again fail to keep its promise'. Then, too, he concluded:

---

[34] *Davar*, '500 Years of Turkish Istanbul', 10.6.1953. Commemorative festivities hosted on 8.6.1953 in the auditorium of the Hebrew University of Jerusalem Law School to mark the 500th anniversary of the Fall of Constantinople to the Turks. *Davar*, 'Celebrating the Walls of Istanbul', 12.6.1953. Extensive press coverage of festivities in Turkey marking the 500th anniversary of the Fall of Constantinople to the Ottomans.

[35] *Davar*, 'Turkey to Upgrade Diplomatic Mission to Embassy', 26.1.1953.

[36] ISA/RG93/MFA/2156/7, Meroz to the UN Division (54/09/5/מ – 10.9.1954).

even if we support the Greeks, there will be no change in our relations, a fact we have accepted by now. They will simply tell us that they will review the matter after the General Assembly and then they will fool us again, as they have done three or four times in recent years. Only if they are willing to commit themselves in writing that they will proceed to de jure recognition immediately following the General Assembly, only then would it be worth our while to re-examine the issue.[37]

As for Israel's stance vis-à-vis the Greek Cypriots, Vice Consul to Nicosia Eliezer Marom estimated that even if the Greek position were not supported at the UN, there would be no negative impact on relations with the Greek Cypriots since their main focus was on trade. And what is more, 'many Greek Cypriot entrepreneurs are not in favour of the island's annexation to Greece and in general, they preferred not to mix their trade interests with their political convictions'.[38] Israel's diplomatic restraint immediately following the plebiscite of 1950 left no room for a different approach.[39] Nor did the Israelis offer any indication of support for Enosis rhetoric on the eve of the General Assembly. Whatever exploratory remarks the Greek consulate in Nicosia had made, Eliezer Marom took them to be a courtesy rather than an explicit request for Israeli support. Besides, the Israelis believed such a request should be accompanied by an express commitment from Athens that it would immediately proceed to a de jure recognition of the State of Israel.[40] Nevertheless, an open letter from Nicosia Mayor Themistocles Dervis to all consulates in the city – including that of Israel – protesting British legislative measures against Greek Cypriots triggered no expression of sympathy on the part of Israel. This was in fact indicative of the Israeli consul's decision not even to acknowledge receipt of the letter.[41]

Still, Marom made no secret of his sense that it was wrong to ignore the moral and ideological basis of the Greek Cypriots' hopes for self-determination and their desire to be rid of British colonial rule which struck a definite chord in Israeli public opinion. Memories of the armed struggle with the British in Palestine were still fresh, as were those of the assistance provided by the Greek Cypriots to the Jewish detainees in Cyprus between 1946 and 1949.[42]

3.2.4 The Arab factor

Another contributing factor to the Israeli stance at the first UN debate on the Cyprus question was the persistent rumour that the Arab states intended to support Greece. That feeling was indeed corroborated not only by Yohanan Meroz in Washington[43] and

---

[37] ISA/RG93/MFA/2156/7, Avner to Israel's Permanent Representation to the UN (40401/41/גא – 5.8.1954).
[38] ISA/RG93/MFA/2156/7, Marom to the British Commonwealth Division (1113/102/ק – 15.8.1954).
[39] Cf. 2.4.1.
[40] ISA/RG93/MFA/2156/7, Marom to the British Commonwealth Division (1113/102/ק – 15.8.1954).
[41] ISA/RG93/MFA/2156/7, Avraham Kidron, Israel's Consul in Nicosia, to the British Commonwealth Division (1229/102/ק – 13.9.1954).
[42] Cf. 2.2.
[43] ISA/RG93/MFA/2156/7, Meroz to the UN Division (54/09/5/מי – 10.9.1954).

Eliezer Marom in Nicosia[44] but by the Greeks themselves, who made no attempt to gain Israel's support. Still, on 10 September 1954, only a few days before the 9th UN General Assembly Session, Egyptian state radio aired a statement by the Political Affairs Commission of the Arab League, urging Arab representatives to:

> make contact with the parties involved to prevent the Cyprus issue from being placed on the UN General Assembly agenda in an effort to have the matter settled amicably. If these efforts fail, only then should the Arab states not decline to have the issue placed on the agenda. In such case, the Arab states should work towards the adoption of a joint resolution text calling upon both parties to settle the issue by demonstrating mutual understanding.[45]

Only by assessing the tone of this statement, did the Israelis realize that the Arab states had not agreed to present a united front in favour of the Greek recourse.

Yet another manifestation of a lack of uniformity in the Arab attitude vis-à-vis the Cyprus issue occurred in early September 1954, when the opposition Syrian Social Nationalist Party (SSNP)[46] (Partie Social Nationaliste Syrien / Al-Hizb as-Suri al-Qawmi al-'Ijtima'i) issued a statement claiming that Cyprus belonged not to Britain, nor to Greece or Turkey, but rather to 'Greater Syria'. The statement was published in the English-language *Egyptian Gazette* in mid-September 1954.[47] According to the SSNP, the indigenous Cypriots had been of Syrian origin and spoke the Assyrian language, and despite the fact that nowadays the islanders were Greek- and Turkish-speaking, Cyprus had never ceased, culturally and geographically, to form part of Syria, and as such, should be placed under Syrian rule. Obviously, this position did not reflect the official stance of the Syrian government. The country was still in turmoil following the military coup which had occurred in February of 1954.

Nevertheless, the Israelis made the heretical position of the SSNP known to the Greeks. On instructions from Moshe Sasson, head of Israel's diplomatic representation in Athens, the consul to Nicosia, Avraham Kidron, posted anonymous envelopes to newspaper editors in Greece containing the SSNP statement just as it had appeared in the *Egyptian Gazette* only in Greek translation.[48] By resorting to these machinations, like something out of a novel in terms of invention, the Israelis had sought to gauge public opinion and the climate at the decision-making centres in Greece.

---

[44] ISA/RG93/MFA/2156/7, Marom to the British Commonwealth Division (1113/102/ק – 15.8.1954).

[45] ISA/RG93/MFA/392/10, Israeli embassy in Washington to the British Commonwealth Division (YS/54/09/36-15.9.1954).

[46] The Syrian Social Nationalist Party (SSNP, *Parti Social Nationaliste Syrien / Al-Hizb as-Suri al-Qawmi al-'Ijtima'i*), founded in 1932, advocates the creation of 'Greater Syria' that includes Lebanon, historic Palestine, Jordan, Iraq, Cyprus, the Mediterranean coast of Turkey (Alexandretta and Cilicia) and the Sinai Peninsula. In past decades, it was the main oppositional voice against the policies of the Ba'ath governing party.

[47] ISA/RG93/MFA/2156/7, *Egyptian Gazette*, 'Cyprus Should Belong to Syria, Say Nationalists', 14.9.1954. On the matter of 'Greater Syria' and the SSNP's ideological background, cf. Yosef Olmert, *Suria ha-Modernit* [*Modern Syria*] (Tel Aviv: Misrad ha-Bitakhon, 1997), 62–4. Cf. 3.2.5 below.

[48] ISA/RG93/MFA/2156/7, Sasson to the Research Division (366-7/2/אח – 21.10.1954). Detailed description of the tactics to distribute the SSNP statement to the Greek press.

A few days later, the SSNP statement was published by certain Greek newspapers. However, it caused no reaction either in Greek public opinion or at the Greek Ministry of Foreign Affairs. The release of the SSNP statement in Greece did not compromise Greek–Arab relations. Quite the contrary, in fact. The Press Office of the Syrian Embassy in Athens was immediately mobilized, with the result that a few days later, the Athenian newspapers published lengthy articles highlighting the Arab states' support for the Greek claim before the UN. Israel's peculiar attempt to create a distraction thus ended with nary a whimper.

3.2.5 Israel's vote on the issue of Cyprus at the 9th Session of the UN General Assembly

The 9th Session of the UN General Assembly was set to open on 21 September 1954. A few days earlier, intensive consultations had been underway between the Israeli Ministry of Foreign Affairs and its diplomatic missions in London, Ankara, Athens, Nicosia, Washington, DC, and New York in order to finalize the Israeli stance vis-à-vis the Greek demand for the right of Cypriot citizens to self-determination. A related report drafted by the UN Division at the Israeli Ministry of Foreign Affairs summarized the fundamental positions that were adopted.[49]

First, Israel decided to vote in favour of placing the Cyprus issue on the General Assembly agenda. It was indeed a matter of principle for Israeli diplomacy that any issues relevant to the right of a people's self-determination should be brought before the UN. The adoption of such a position was based on the outcome of the vote held on 29 November 1947 before the UN in the matter of the Partition Plan for Palestine, which for the Israelis had been the first step towards acquiring territorial sovereignty and international political recognition. Since that time, Israel had always been favourable to debates before the UN on requests for self-determination by populations under colonial regimes.

The Israelis were conscious that the ultimate goal of Greece and the Greek Cypriots was Enosis – which meant the end of British rule on the island. The fact that Britain had no intention of withdrawing from Cyprus was featured in all the Israeli reports, and all of them concurred that Britain's presence on Cyprus reinforced Israel's defences against Egypt and Syria. London, clearly intending to retain British control of Cyprus indefinitely, proposed that the dispute should be resolved at a constitutional level. As far as Greece was concerned, Israel made no effort to hide its frustration with the coldness Athens demonstrated towards the Jewish state and its reluctance to proceed to a de jure recognition of Israel, on the one hand, and the consistently pro-Arab stance Greece maintained both regionally and internationally on the other. The Israelis were aware that such a position was mainly due to Greece's concern about the future of the Greek diaspora in Egypt and its need to secure numerous Arab votes in its favour at the UN. Meanwhile, the fact that Greece was amongst the few Western states which did not

---

[49] ISA/RG93/MFA/2156/7, UN Division to the British Commonwealth Division, the Israeli embassy in London and Israel's consulate in Nicosia (30519/מ – 14.9.1954).

maintain an equal distance in the Arab-Israeli conflict was also a matter of grave concern for Israeli diplomacy. By contrast, Turkey, though Muslim, showed a disregard for Arab criticism and continued to maintain relations with Israel which were described as very good to excellent.

Israeli interdepartmental correspondence reveals that the Cyprus issue was viewed primarily in terms of the bilateral relations with Britain, relations which were expected to remain unaffected by Greek Cypriot demands for self-determination which might otherwise lead to the accession of the neighbouring island to pro-Arab Greece. It was also becoming clear that Turkey was not pressing Israel to adopt a strictly pro-Turkish stance – possibly in the knowledge that, one way or another, the Israelis desperately needed the British protective shield in Cyprus.

Thus, Israel decided not to back the Greek claim, which, if granted, would open the way for Cyprus' accession to Greece. At the same time, Israel sought maximum assurance from Britain that it would remain in Cyprus, specifically, in exchange for a UN vote favourable to its interests vis-à-vis the Cyprus issue. Israel hoped to see the lifting of legislative restrictions in Cyprus imposed by Britain on the import and distribution of Israeli agricultural produce in the local market, a simplified procedure for issuing residence and work permits to Israeli citizens, the awarding of contracts to Israeli companies and the option to use raw materials from Israel for work undertaken by Israeli construction companies on the island as well as an increase in the number of flights operated by the Israeli national airlines to and from Nicosia Airport.[50]

Aside from the foregoing, Israel decided to oppose a referendum to be held in Cyprus under the aegis and monitoring of the UN, as that would likely pave the way for Enosis. Nevertheless, for tactical reasons, it was decided that Israel's intention should not be disclosed to the British, at least not until Israel's mostly economic demands were met.

On 16 August 1954, Greece had formally lodged a claim before the Secretariat of the UN General Assembly, titled 'Implementation, under the Aegis of the United Nations, of the Principle of Equal Rights and Self-Determination in the Case of the Population of the Island of Cyprus'.[51] To buttress the arguments of the Greek claim, Archbishop Makarios had submitted a memorandum to Dag Hammarskjöld, secretary general of the UN, dated 22 August 1954, requesting the placement of Greece's claim on the agenda of the 9th Session of the General Assembly with an acknowledgment of the islanders' right to self-determination.[52]

The 9th Session of the UN General Assembly commenced on 21 September 1954. Three days later, a vote was held to determine whether the Greek claim would be put on the session agenda. Over the objections of the British,[53] the request was approved by

[50]   ISA/RG93/MFA/2156/7, Moshe Yuval, head of the Research Division, to the UN Division and British Commonwealth Division (classified report, not recorded as incoming document, September 1954).

[51]   Kyrou, *Elliniki Exoteriki Politiki*, 443–50; and Archbishop Makarios III Foundation, Kokkinou (ed.), *Apanta Archiepiskopou*, vol. 1, 434–9. The complete text of the Greek appeal.

[52]   Archbishop Makarios III Foundation, Kokkinou (ed.), *Apanta Archiepiskopou*, vol. 1, 258–60.

[53]   Stephen G. Xydis, 'The UN General Assembly as an Instrument of Greek Policy: Cyprus, 1954–1958', *Journal of Conflict Resolution*, 12, no. 2 (1968): 142.

30 to 19 with 11 abstentions.[54] Whereas 39 states had been expected to vote for and 9 to oppose adding the issue to the agenda, the anti-colonial bloc from Latin American states appeared divided on the Greek proposal.[55]

Israel voted in favour of placing the proposal on the General Assembly agenda. As Alexis Kyrou wrote in his autobiographic monograph about Greece's diplomatic moves, the Israeli vote was 'the only pleasant surprise',[56] expressing indirectly his disappointment with the negative votes or abstentions on the part of some other states whose support he had been counting on. The Greek side was stunned by Israel's favourable vote on 24 September 1954. In fact, Archbishop Makarios, wishing to take advantage of this turn of events, sent a letter of appreciation to Israeli Prime Minister Ben-Gurion in an effort to elicit information about Israel's expected position regarding Greece at the UN debate of December 1954.

Makarios' letter to Ben-Gurion, dated 28 September 1954, reads:

Honourable Sir,

On behalf of the Greek people of Cyprus and as their elected political and spiritual leader, I wish to thank you, as well as the other members of your Government, warmly, for the support you have given through your delegation at the United Nations to the demand of the Cypriot people for self-determination, by voting in favour of including the Greek appeal on Cyprus in the Agenda of the General Assembly.

This noble gesture of yours, emanating from the principles and spirit of the United Nations, is an expression of the liberal ideals which so nobly characterise your people; it has raised in the conscience of the peoples of the World the prestige of the UNO, and their confidence in it as an Organisation striving for the establishment of Freedom and Justice.

We have no doubt that your Government will continue the same attitude of supporting the Cyprus Question until a favourable decision regarding the self-determination of the people of Cyprus is finally taken by the United Nations.

---

[54] Votes in favour were cast by the following states: Egypt, Haiti, Afghanistan, Burma, Yugoslavia, Guatemala, Greece, Indonesia, Ecuador, Iceland, Israel, China, Costa Rica, Cuba, Belarus, Lebanon, Mexico, Nicaragua, Ukraine, Uruguay, Poland, El Salvador, Saudi Arabia, Russia, Syria, Thailand, Czechoslovakia, Yemen, Philippines and Honduras. Votes against were cast by: Britain, Australia, Belgium, France, Denmark, Dominican Republic, Canada, Colombia, Liberia, Luxemburg, New Zealand, Norway, South Africa, Netherlands, Paraguay, Peru, Sweden, Turkey and Chile. Abstentions by: Ethiopia, Argentina, Venezuela, Bolivia, Brazil, USA, India, Iran, Iraq, Pakistan and Panama. Cf. Kyrou, *Elliniki Exoteriki Politiki*, 287.

[55] ISA/RG93/MFA/263/6, International Organisations Division to Director General Gideon Rafael and the UN Division (dated 27.12.1954, no incoming document record available). Impressions of the Israeli permanent representation to the UN of the voting held on 25.9.1954 and 15.12.1954, in the matter of Cyprus. Cf. Stephen G. Xydis, *Cyprus: Conflict and Conciliation, 1954–1958* (Columbus, OH: Ohio State University Press, 1967), 12.

[56] Kyrou, *Elliniki Exoteriki Politiki*, 287.

We thank you warmly and convey to your honour the feelings of deep gratitude and respect of the people of Cyprus.[57]

Archbishop Makarios' letter received no response from Israel which exercised the 'policy of silence' its consulate in Nicosia had followed a few weeks earlier in neglecting even to acknowledge Mayor Dervis' open letter.[58] A report submitted by Abba Eban, head of Israel's permanent representation to the United Nations, explains why Israel did not respond to Makarios' 'fit of friendliness' immediately after the vote on 24 September. Having established the concept of 'a people's right to self-determination' as a separate issue, Eban drew a parallel between the Greek use of this principle with regard to Cypriot citizens and the invocation of the principle by (pro-Arab) Indonesia at the same session against the (pro-Israel) Netherlands over its control of the island of Irian (today known as Papua Barat, Province of Indonesia.) In substance, Eban believed, the aim of both countries was not so much to secure self-determination for the inhabitants of the islands as the desire to annex them. 'Neither Greece nor Indonesia suggest that the inhabitants on the respective islands gain independence; what each of said countries is actually pursuing is to annex such islands to their respective national territories,' he noted. Regardless of what Abba Eban believed about the true motives of Greece and Indonesia, the Israeli side – for its own obvious reasons – did not wish to see territorial sovereignty regulated or modified by such votes. Eban clearly expressed this position in his report: 'It is of paramount importance for Israel to reinforce those tendencies already developing within the UN, against any territorial changes being brought about by virtue of an international decree.' In other words, he implied, the concession of a constitution to Cyprus and Irian would resolve both disputes in such a way that their demands for self-government or 'self-determination' would be satisfied, without requiring Britain and the Netherlands to withdraw – 'because the majority of the UN member states wished it so'. Eban's report was crystal clear: 'It is my conclusion that we should not have any reticence as to unreservedly backing the United Kingdom and the Netherlands in the matters of Cyprus and Irian, respectively, all the more since there are solutions to be found that do not necessarily favour colonialism.'[59]

The Greek claim was debated at the session of the Political Committee on 14–15 December 1954. According to the report of Israeli representatives who had followed the procedure, Alexis Kyrou's speech made a very good impression.[60]

[57] ISA/RG93/MFA/2156/7, British Commonwealth Division to the Israeli embassy in London and the Israeli consulate in Nicosia (9234/7 – 25.10.1954). Attached was the 28.9.1954 letter from Archbishop Makarios to Prime Minister David Ben-Gurion.

[58] Cf. 3.2.3.

[59] Israel State Archives, Naomi Barzilai (ed.), *Documents on the Foreign Policy of Israel* (Jerusalem: Government Printer, 2004), vol. 9, 650–1, no. 384. Eban to Rafael (93.01/2210/18- 26.9.1954).

[60] ISA/RG93/MFA/263/6, International Organisations Division to Director General Gideon Rafael and the UN Division (27.12.1954, not officially logged). The impressions of Israel's Permanent Representation to the UN during the voting of 25.9.1954 and 15.12.1954 on Cyprus.

As for Turkey, the arguments put forward by Selim Sarper, head of Turkey's permanent representation to the UN, were based mainly on the geographical proximity of Cyprus to the Turkish coast as well as on the ethnicities of the local population. The contents of his speech made an unfavourable impression on numerous diplomatic missions – including that of Israel. Specifically, as described in the relevant Israeli report,[61] an awkward silence fell over the hall when the Turkish diplomat drew a parallel between the Greek claim for recognition of the right of Cypriot citizens to self-determination and the Nazi Anschluss of Austria. In fact, the Israeli diplomats seemed upset by the 'anti-Greek, anthropological and racial remarks' delivered by Selim Sarper from the UN podium regarding the genetic origins of the Greek Cypriots.[62]

At this point, it is worth noting that the arguments made by Sarper as head of the Turkish permanent representation at the 9th Session of the UN General Assembly were the precursor to the official line adopted by Turkey over the ensuing years. In 1956, with the start of the EOKA struggle, the Press Office of the Turkish embassy in London issued a pamphlet in English which once again compared the policy of Greece on the Cyprus issue with the ideological foundations of Nazi Germany's foreign policy. The Turkish embassy's pamphlet stated the following:

> Article 1 of the Programme of the German National Socialist Party underlined the need for all Germans to unite solidly around the principle of self-determination in order to establish a Greater Germany. The Nazi party programme will continue to be cited as an historical example of how a noble principle can be corrupted and misused to serve aggressive aspirations.[63]

This pamphlet developed arguments similar to those Sarper had offered two years earlier regarding the racial origins of Greek Cypriots:

> The total population of the island is about 500,000. Of this, about 120,000 are of indubitable Turkish origin and culture, as a perfectly natural consequence of three centuries of the existence of Cyprus as an integral part of Turkey; 11,000 are of various races and faiths. The remaining 370,000 are claimed by the Greek Government to be Greeks. In fact, from the ethnic point of view, almost the whole of this community belongs to the category of peoples dispersed in the Eastern Mediterranean who are referred to as 'Levantines'. This Cypriot branch of the 'Levantines' has nothing in common with the Greeks other than the Greek

---

[61] Ibid.
[62] Cf. Kyrou, *Elliniki Exoteriki Politiki*, 399–405. Alexis Kyrou's comments on Selim Sarper's arguments.
[63] Republic of Turkey, *Turkey and Cyprus: A Survey of the Cyprus Question with Official Statements of the Turkish Viewpoint* (London: Turkish Embassy, Press Attaché's Office, 1956), 41.

Orthodox faith under the influence of which it has adopted a certain dialect of the Greek language.[64]

The Arab states viewed the Cyprus issue from a completely different perspective, in light of Britain's role – and that of the West in general – in the Eastern Mediterranean and the Middle East. Many Arab delegations, led by Saudi Arabia, wanted to hear a clearer explanation of what the phrase, 'Cyprus' defensive importance in the region,' actually meant. The Arab delegates who were aligned with Greek positions repeated this rhetoric but posed reasonable questions: 'Just who does the West mean to protect with its presence in Cyprus? The Arabs? If so, protect them from whom? From themselves?'

Yemen opted for an unequivocally favourable stance vis-à-vis the issue of self-determination for the inhabitants of Cyprus, and furthermore, made a commitment to back the island's request for accession to Greece while at the same time juxtaposing its own claim for recognition of the right to self-determination for those populations in the southern part of the Arabian Peninsula under Saudi Arabian rule. In contrast, Lebanon and Iraq sided with Turkey and Britain, thereby confirming information published in the Cypriot press, according to which certain Arab states had already, since October 1954, decided to endorse the British, irrespective of their differences with London and Paris as to the self-determination of Morocco, Tunisia or various areas in Asia.[65] An extensive report in the 15 October 1954 edition of the Cypriot paper *Ethnos*, which cited Greek diplomatic sources in New York, outlined all the reasons for the inability of certain Arab countries to support the Greek position. The reasons allegedly contributing to this development were numerous: first, Britain's acquiescence to leave the Suez Canal and to vacate its air bases in Iraq played a significant role. At the same time, it seemed the Arab world had been disappointed by Greece's de facto recognition of Israel in 1952. On the other hand, the British were said to be committed to stamping out the smuggling of Israeli products into Arab countries, which is why they had increased customs controls in Cyprus. However, notwithstanding these assessments which became public after the fact, no pro-British Arab regime wanted to see Britain depart from Cyprus.

---

[64] Ibid., 22–33. Over the years, and particularly after the Turkish invasion of Cyprus in 1974, the Turkish academic community began to adopt theories that were not limited to questioning the national origins of the Greek Cypriots, but of all modern Greeks. One such example was an article by Yaman Örs, a professor at the University of Ankara Faculty of Medicine, titled ,'Certain Basic Misconceptions in the Field of History: Ancient Greeks, the West and the Modern World', published in 1976 by the Institute of International Relations of the Faculty of Political Science of the same university. Örs maintained that Greek Cypriots and all modern Greeks in general have no genetic or racial connection whatsoever to the ancient Greeks and concluded that the only influence of ancient Greeks over modern-day Greeks is limited to 'tricks in politics and diplomacy', inherited from the ancients. Cf. Yaman Örs, 'Certain Basic Misconceptions in the Field of History: Ancient Greeks, the West and the Modern World', *The Turkish Yearbook of International Relations* (Ankara: University of Ankara, Institute of International Relations, Faculty of Political Science, 1974), vol. 14, 106 and 112–13.

[65] ISA/RG93/MFA/2156/7, Israeli Consulate in Nicosia to Rafael, Research Division, UN and West Europe divisions and Israel's Diplomatic Representation in Athens (1354/102/פ – 18.10.1954). The document comments extensively on a report published in the Cypriot newspaper *Ethnos* in the 15.10.1954 edition.

Finally, it is worth noting that during the two-day UN session on the Cyprus question, Syria's opposition nationalist party, the SSNP, reiterated its standard request to place Cyprus under Syrian rule, and thereby, a call for a public statement by the Syrian government that Cyprus belonged to Syria and Syria alone.[66] Not surprisingly, the SSNP resolution, though it drew the attention of international news agencies and newspapers in Syria and Egypt, was otherwise ignored.[67]

Also, not surprisingly, Greece's positions met with rigid resistance from Britain and its steadfast allies. New Zealand's representative, Sir Leslie Munro, took it upon himself to suggest postponing the debate for 'a more appropriate time', since the subsequent vote was liable to jeopardize relations between Greece, Britain and Turkey.[68] Greece and the countries of Latin America reacted most vehemently to this, arguing that New Zealand had essentially raised the resolution adopted at that same session (namely, the resolution of 24 September 1954 to place the Greek claim on the agenda), which required a two-thirds majority of all UN member states.[69] The Norwegian representation then took up the baton and moved to vote on New Zealand's request to postpone the debate on the Greek claim. Norway's motion passed with 45 votes in favour, 15 against and 12 abstentions. New Zealand's proposal to postpone the debate on the Greek claim was then put to the vote. This time, 28 states (including Britain, Turkey, Iraq, Lebanon and other traditionally pro-colonial Western states) voted in favour, 15 states (Greece, the Latin American countries and India) voted against, and 16 countries abstained (Israel, Saudi Arabia, Yemen and Egypt).

Still, New Zealand's proposal failed to get the two-thirds majority vote required under Article 124 of the Rules of Procedure. Following this procedural tumult, the Greek claim was debated as to substance.[70]

The Israeli delegation attempted to make good use of the tumult. According to a relevant report by Israel's UN Division at the Ministry of Foreign Affairs,[71] the Israeli delegation took the opportunity to engage in a series of back-room manoeuvring with Latin American countries, urging them to oppose New Zealand's delaying tactics more vehemently. As a result, Israel hoped, Britain would be persuaded that it needed more allies and seek Israel's support directly. If Israel voted in favour, the requisite two-thirds majority would most likely be satisfied and London might commit in turn to accommodate Israel's financial claims in the matter of Cyprus.[72] Yet Britain did not do so, as it had become clear meanwhile that, one way or another, it would be impossible to secure a two-thirds majority and avert the debate on the substance of the Greek

---

[66] Cf. 3.2.4.
[67] ISA/RG93/MFA/2156/7, Research Division (1668/‎ – 21.12.1954), and Research Division to the Israeli Consulate in Nicosia (158/534/‎ – 3.1.1955). The SSNP's resolution was transmitted by the Associated Press correspondent in Damascus by the English-language Syrian newspapers *Daily Star*, and the Egyptian newspaper *Al-Ahram* on 17.12.1954.
[68] Kyrou, *Elliniki Exoteriki Politiki*, 302–6, regarding the Greek reaction to New Zealand's proposals.
[69] Ibid., 305.
[70] Ibid., 305–8.
[71] ISA/RG93/MFA/263/6, International Organisations Division to Rafael (27.12.1954, not marked for entry).
[72] ISA/RG93/MFA/2156/7, UN Division to British Commonwealth Division the Israeli Embassy in London and the Israeli Consulate in Nicosia, (30519/‎ – 14.9.1954).

claim. In fact, according to the Israeli report, once it transpired that New Zealand's efforts would come to nought, the British representation tried to create the impression that it, too, had been taken by surprise by the muscled intervention of New Zealand – causing the delegates present, including the Israelis, to raise an eyebrow or two.[73]

At the 15 December 1954 session, New Zealand submitted a draft resolution, with a series of amendment proposals by Colombia and El Salvador and a preamble which began: 'Considering that, for the time being, it does not appear appropriate to adopt a resolution on the question of Cyprus [...].'[74] The Greek side believed this phrasing left room to raise the Cyprus issue before the UN in the near future. Thus, the draft resolution submitted by New Zealand, incorporating the amendment proposals by El Salvador and Colombia, was sustained by the Plenum. Resolution 814(IX) was upheld both by states which sided with Greece and those aligned with Britain and Turkey[75] whereas the USSR and all the Eastern Bloc countries abstained, scorning the formulation of the draft as much too moderate and criticizing the tactics employed by the colonial countries of the West to manipulate the process.[76]

Thus, Israel's vote was 'lost' within the ultimate unanimity of what were initially conflicting currents. In this way, Israel could side step the Enosis issue, and at the same time, avoid upsetting relations with both Britain and Turkey. What is more, it could use the opportunity to promote the practical facilitations it had been pursuing in Cyprus vis-à-vis the British authorities but refrain from irking the Greeks and Greek Cypriots, and eventually vote in favour of placing the Greek claim on the agenda for the first vote on 24 September 1954 – at no diplomatic cost whatsoever. Finally, the gracious thank you letter from Makarios to Prime Minister Ben-Gurion undoubtedly opened a new channel of communications between Israel and the Greek Cypriots, which Israeli diplomats could exploit if and when they wished to in future.

In assessing the Greek move to bring the Cyprus issue before the UN, the Israeli Ministry of Foreign Affairs concluded that, given the unfavourable balance of powers in the world vis-à-vis its interests, Greece had done its best to focus international

---

[73] ISA/RG93/MFA/263/6, International Organisations Division to Rafael (27.12.1954, not marked for entry). Indicative was the description of the incident in the UN Division's report to Rafael: 'On the fringes of the session, the British attempted to leak the information that New Zealand's delegate was acting exclusively on his own initiative, so much that they themselves had been taken by surprise (if that was believed is anyone's guess) [...]'. Cf. Kyrou, *Elliniki Exoteriki Politiki*, 307–8.

[74] Xydis, 'The UN General Assembly', 143. The original text of the Preamble: 'Considering that for the time being, it does not appear appropriate to adopt a resolution on the question of Cyprus [...].'

[75] ISA/RG93/MFA/263/6, Minutes A/2881 of the 16.12.1954 meeting of the 1st Political Committee of the UN General Assembly which include the results of the voting held on 15.12.1954. Votes in favour: Afghanistan, Argentina, Bolivia, Brazil, Canada, China, Colombia, Costa Rica, Cuba, Denmark, Dominican Republic, Ecuador, Egypt, El Salvador, Ethiopia, Greece, Guatemala, Haiti, Honduras, Iceland, India, Indonesia, Iran, Iraq, Israel, Lebanon, Liberia, Mexico, Netherlands, New Zealand, Nicaragua, Norway, Pakistan, Panama, Paraguay, Peru, Philippines, Saudi Arabia, Sweden, Syria, United Kingdom, United States, Venezuela, Yemen. Abstained: Australia, Belgium, Burma, Soviet Socialist Republic of Belarus, Chile, Czechoslovakia, France, Luxembourg, Poland, Thailand, Turkey, Soviet Socialist Republic of Ukraine, Union of South Africa, USSR, Uruguay and Yugoslavia. No country voted against.

[76] ISA/RG93/MFA/263/6, International Organisations Division to Rafael (27.12.1954, not recorded as incoming document).

attention on what was happening in Cyprus. It therefore came as no surprise that the General Assembly decision did not disappoint Britain.[77] Still, London was not completely satisfied since ultimately the issue of Cyprus had been put to a debate.[78] In that sense, Israel viewed the contents of Resolution 814 of the 9th Session of the UN General Assembly as something of a Pyrrhic victory for the British.

3.3 Israel's stance on the Cyprus issue at the 10th Session of the UN General Assembly, 1955

3.3.1 Greece's pro-Arab position

Although the UN did not recognize the right to self-determination by the Cypriot population, the outcome of the 9th Session both in Greece and in Cyprus was favourable. The issue of Cyprus had achieved prominence on the international political scene and the wording of Resolution 814 left Athens with plenty of room for further diplomatic manoeuvring.

The determination of the Greek side to bring the Cyprus issue before the UN in future was officially voiced by Greek Prime Minister Alexandros Papagos himself in his address to Parliament on 7 February 1955.[79] Israel's consul in Nicosia, Avraham Kidron, was informed by the Ethnarchy that this was to take place at the very next UN session.[80] The intention was further confirmed by Archbishop Makarios in an interview with the British *Daily Mail*, published on 25 March 1955, in which he noted that 'this claim will not be put forward only by Greece, but also by Arab countries and Latin American countries'.

Makarios' assertions that the Arab countries would take a more active role this time with regard to the Cyprus question naturally piqued the interest of the Israelis. It was rumoured at that time that the Egyptian government had suggested to Greece that it might appeal to the UN – either on its own or in conjunction with the Greek government – for recognition of the right of the people of Cyprus to self-determination. In fact, according to Israeli interdepartmental reports, Cairo claimed it would be willing to take diplomatic action at the UN and support Greece on the Cyprus issue if Athens

---

[77] Xydis, *Cyprus: Conflict and Conciliation*, 13–14. As Xydis himself observed, there had been no discussion on the drafts of a resolution, according to which the General Assembly would either give its 'blessing' to the recognition of the principle of self-determination for the inhabitants of Cyprus or at least encourage Britain and Greece to engage in direct negotiations to settle the issue.

[78] ISA/RG93/MFA/8693/2, Research Division (998/21.3.1955). The assessment of Resolution 814(IX) by the Israeli Ministry of Foreign Affairs coincides with that of Alexis Kyrou, who attached particular weight to the phrase 'for the time being'. Cf. Xydis, *Cyprus: Conflict and Conciliation* , 14.

[79] Hellenic Parliament, Parliamentary Archives, 3rd Term, 3rd Session, vol. 1, 690–727. Cf. ISA/RG93/ MFA/263/3, Daily News Bulletin/2638/8.2.1955, Foreign Press Office, Office of the Prime Minister, Kingdom of Greece; and Xydis, *Cyprus: Conflict and Conciliation*, 16–17. Cf. Archbishop Makarios III Foundation, Kokkinou (ed.), *Apanta Archiepiskopou*, vol. 2, 447–514.

[80] ISA/RG93/MFA/2156/7, Kidron to the British Commonwealth Division (184/100/ק – 9.2.1955).

condemned the military cooperation agreement which had been concluded that year between Turkey and Iraq.[81]

EOKA's armed struggle began on April 1st. The same month, Archbishop Makarios made his presence felt at the Afro-Asian Conference which took place in Bandung, Indonesia, on 18–24 April 1955. Invited as an observer in his capacity as head of the Church of Cyprus and representative of the island's inhabitants, Makarios grasped the opportunity to distribute a detailed report on the situation in Cyprus[82] to all the delegations in attendance and to make contact with diplomatic circles and representatives of foreign countries known to be anti-colonialist. Greece was also present at the Bandung Conference as an observer, and naturally helped Makarios to make contacts.

The Bandung Conference drew Israel's interest, first because it had not been invited to participate, and second because the Arab–Israeli conflict was the focal point of the meetings and of the text of the final declaration.[83] Meanwhile, Israel was closely following the activities of all non-Arab states at the conference – including Greece.[84]

The Greek presence in Bandung aimed at securing the broadest possible Arab support for the new recourse in the matter of Cyprus at the UN. In the aftermath of the UN General Assembly vote in December of the previous year, the Athens News Agency featured Arab reports casting a favourable light on the fact that 'Greece had not recognised Israel,' and as such, the Arab states backed Greece's position on the Cyprus question.[85] In addition, the 22 April meeting held on the fringes of the Bandung Conference between Archbishop Makarios and Gamal Abdel Nasser[86] was highly publicized, and capped off the warm welcome Egyptian authorities had reserved for the Cypriot leader 10 days earlier when he travelled to Egypt to meet with government officials and prominent members of the Greek Cypriot diaspora in Egypt.[87]

The final Bandung Declaration adopted the Arab views on the Palestinian issue in full while condemning colonialism in all its manifestations. A few weeks later, Greece's permanent representation to the UN submitted a written protest and a precursor to its new claim on the Cyprus issue to the Secretariat General. Greece's document, which the Secretariat General forwarded to all Permanent Representations on 10 May 1955, conveyed a strongly anti-colonialist sentiment. Armed conflicts in Cyprus were already underway and the Greek government described the British presence on the island as a

---

[81] ISA/RG93/MFA/263/3, Israel's Diplomatic Representation in Athens to the West Europe Division (436-6/אהב – 29.3.1955). Cf. 3.3.2.1 below.

[82] Archbishop Makarios III Foundation, Kokkinou (ed.), *Apanta Archiepiskopou*, vol. 2, 33–5.

[83] Cf. 1.1.3.

[84] ISA/RG93/MFA/263/3, Darom to the West Europe Division (635-6/אהב – 10.5.1955). Special note was made of the fact that the Greek government had dispatched its own observer to the Bandung Conference.

[85] ISA/RG93/MFA/263/3, West Europe Division to Israel's Diplomatic Representation in Athens (9234/ח – 4.1.1955). In attachment: the Press Review Report by the Athens News Agency, with opinion pieces published on 16.10.1954 in the Egyptian daily *Al-Qahira* and the Jordanian *Falastin* under the characteristic headlines 'Greece's Wisdom' and 'The Arab States on Greece's Side', respectively.

[86] Archbishop Makarios III Foundation, Kokkinou (ed.), *Apanta Archiepiskopou*, vol. 2, 35.

[87] Ibid., 30–2.

'regime of colonial domination which abuses its powers and turns against the will of the people, violating its rights, which are recognized and guaranteed by the UN Charter'.[88] The language used by the Greek Foreign Ministry was in complete accord with the anti-West, anti-colonialist spirit of the Bandung Declaration.

Taking all this into account, the Israelis anticipated that the second Greek appeal in relation to Cyprus would be of a more markedly 'anti-West' nature than the first one.[89] At the same time, as Israel's diplomatic representative to Athens, Avraham Kidron, observed, the Greek Ministry of Foreign Affairs appeared to expect a great deal of Arab diplomatic support, particularly from Egypt.[90] In fact, he speculated that Archbishop Makarios' visit to Cairo in April 1955 aimed at rallying more Arab countries, such as Saudi Arabia, Yemen and even pro-West Lebanon, around Egypt's pro-Greek line. Aside from the important role which the Greek Cypriot communities were being called upon to assume in Egypt, it was also believed that the Greek diaspora in Latin America was in a position to influence governmental decision-making centres there. A clear indication of the power wielded by the Greek diaspora in those countries were the resolutions adopted by the parliaments of Uruguay and Chile in favour of recognizing the right to self-determination for the inhabitants of Cyprus.[91]

Naturally, the stance of the United States was also of great interest to the Israeli diplomatic representation in Athens. In his report on the aftermath of the 9th Session of the UN General Assembly, Avraham Darom noted that, during the first half of 1954, the State Department had tried to convince the Greek side that it was not a good time to bring the issue of Cyprus before the UN. At least this is how the American decision to abstain was interpreted, a decision which Israel believed it would inevitably repeat at the 10th Session. In June 1955, the Greek press was teeming with rumours that the US was once again endeavouring to prevent a new recourse by Greece, and that the US was mediating from the sidelines to open the way for direct bilateral negotiations between London and Athens.[92] Anxious to avert a new debate on the issue before the United Nations, Britain advocated a Tripartite Conference between Britain, Greece and Turkey for late August 1955, but when this did not succeed, the Greek government decided to bring the issue of Cyprus before the UN again.

This time, in contrast to the events leading up to the 9th Session, the Greek side approached Israel as well. On 8 June 1955, Greece's new ambassador to Washington, George Melas met with Israel's permanent representative to the UN Abba Eban and relayed Athens' hope that Israel would support the Greek position,[93] a hope reiterated a month later when Eban visited the Greek embassy in Washington, DC, on 6 July 1955.[94]

---

[88] ISA/RG93/MFA/2156/7, British Commonwealth Division to the Israeli Consulate in Nicosia (9234/ד – 30.5.1955). Darom to the UN and West Europe divisions (635-6/אחב – 10.5.1955) and Greece's permanent representation to the UN Secretary General.
[89] ISA/RG93/MFA/2156/7, Darom to the UN and West Europe divisions (635-6/אהב – 10.5.1955).
[90] ISA/RG93/MFA/263/6, Darom to the West Europe Division (753–6/אהב – 31.5.1955).
[91] Ibid.
[92] ISA/RG93/MFA/263/6, Moshe Sasson to the West Europe Division (845-6/אהב – 10.6.1955).
[93] ISA/RG93/MFA/263/6, West Europe Division to Israel's diplomatic representation in Athens (4255/ח – 15.7.1955).
[94] ISA/RG93/MFA/263/6, West Europe Division to Israel's diplomatic representation in Athens (4255/ח – 27.7.1955).

At both meetings, Eban's response to Melas was more than reserved. During the initial meeting, he emphasized that the Israeli Ministry of Foreign Affairs would consider the Greek request, while keeping in mind Israel's good relations with Britain and Turkey. At the later meeting, he once again raised the issue of Greece's de jure recognition of Israel. In response to Eban, Melas promised that upon his return to Athens for consultation, he would bring the matter up with the Greek Ministry of Foreign Affairs. The Israelis were not optimistic that Melas would take any meaningful action or that anything positive would come of it,[95] and their trepidations proved well founded. They were never actually informed whether Israel's request – as Eban had expressed it to Melas – was ever transmitted to Athens or if it had been turned down. Meanwhile, Greece filed the request to put the Cyprus issue on the agenda of the 10th Session of the UN General Assembly as the tripartite talks between Britain, Greece and Turkey got underway. Scheduled for 29 August 1955,[96] George Melas was to take part in it, hence direct communication with him was difficult.[97] In view of the upcoming UN session, Israel perceived the desperation of the Greeks for Arab support which made it unlikely in the extreme that they would recognize Israel de jure.[98]

3.3.2 Israel's concerns about the priorities of Turkey's regional policy

The Arabs' unequivocal support for Greek positions and the increasing likelihood that Greece would delay its de jure recognition of Israel convinced Israel that there was absolutely no reason to support them at the upcoming session. At the same time, Israel was ambivalent about supporting Turkey's positions on the Cyprus issue. Although both Ankara and Jerusalem were adamant in their objection to British withdrawal from the neighbouring island, Israel was concerned about Turkey's military advances towards the Arab world.

There were two fundamental issues behind Israel's reticence to openly support Turkey's stance: the signing of a military cooperation agreement between Turkey and Iraq on 24 February 1955 (the 'Baghdad Pact') and Turkey's participation in the Afro-Asian Conference in Bandung in April of that year.

3.3.2.1 *The military cooperation agreement between Turkey and Iraq (Baghdad Pact)*

In a joint statement released on 12 January 1955, Turkey and Iraq established an agenda on the issues that constituted a basis for negotiations ultimately aimed at signing a military and political cooperation agreement. Israel perceived this development as yet another step towards its gradual but complete marginalization from Western security planning in the Middle East. Bilateral military agreements had already been concluded

---

[95] ISA/RG93/MFA/263/6, Darom to the West Europe Division (1112–6/אהב – 2.8.1955).
[96] Ibid.
[97] ISA/RG93/MFA/263/6, Darom to the West Europe Division (1220-6/אהב – 23.8.1955).
[98] ISA/RG93/MFA/263/6, Eliahu Sasson, Israel's ambassador to Rome, to the Research Division (61/צר – 12.9.1955).

by the United States, Britain and Turkey with states such as Egypt, Jordan and Pakistan, which were hostile to Israel. The potential for a Turco-Iraqi rapprochement was of grave concern to the Israelis. Israel's permanent representative to the UN, Abba Eban, laid out these preoccupations in detail to US Secretary of State John Foster Dulles,[99] whilst Maurice Fischer, Israel's ambassador to Ankara, sought similar clarification from Turkish Prime Minister Adnan Menderes.[100]

At the meeting between Fischer and Menderes on 27 January 1955, in the presence of Turkish Foreign Minister Fuat Köprülü and Ministry Director General Nuri Birgi, the Israelis sought clarification about the spirit of the joint Turco-Iraqi communiqué of 12 January 1955 which referred to a Turkish guarantee of Iraq's safety, both in the event of threats from outside the Middle East region and 'risks originating from within the Middle East', a formulation which could only have meant Israel. Moreover, Israel requested information on how exactly the Turkish government intended to implement UN resolutions on the issue of Palestine – an issue that was purportedly being discussed at the time by Turkish officials in Baghdad, Damascus and Beirut. In other words, Israel wished to clarify whether Ankara had ultimately decided to align itself diplomatically with the Arab states, interpreting the phrase, 'implementation of UN Resolutions on the issue of Palestine', as follows: (a) Retreat of the Israeli military forces back to the line established in the Partition Plan of 1947 – in other words, the annulment of everything which had been agreed to during negotiations in Rhodes in which Iraq had not taken part and was therefore not bound to comply with the cease fire; (b) The return of Palestinian refugees to the land occupied by Israel in 1948 – whereby the demographic balance in Israel's territory would drastically change; and (c) The institution of an international special status for the city of Jerusalem, under the auspices of the United Nations – a prospect the Israelis found completely unacceptable.

Menderes attempted to appease the Israelis with the claim that the agreement between Turkey and Iraq was aimed solely at responding to a Soviet threat in the Middle East. Trying to dissipate initial impressions even further, Menderes put forward the argument that if his government intended to disrupt relations with Israel, it would have entered into a deal with the Arab League, not just with pro-Western Iraq. This was not a very convincing argument, as the Arab League at the time mainly echoed Egypt's anti-Turkish positions. Menderes promoted his country's intention to become a balancing factor, capable of palliating differences between Israel and pro-Arab regimes. Finally, Menderes left open the option of not placing special emphasis on the Palestinian issue in the text of the memorandum of understanding in the matter of cooperation between Turkey and Iraq, inasmuch as 'an appropriate formulation would be found' and Turkey would 'notify Israel in advance should any part of the memorandum of understanding touching upon the issue of Palestine'. Meetings along these lines were also held in Jerusalem between Prime Minister and Foreign Minister Moshe Sharett

---

[99] ISA/RG93/MFA/8693/2, Research Division (990/14.2.1955), Letter by Abba Eban to John Foster Dulles, US secretary of state (31.1.1955).

[100] ISA/RG93/MFA/8693/2, Research Division (987/8.2.1955). A confidential report dated 27.1.1955 by Maurice Fischer, Israeli chargé d'affaires in Ankara, on the working meeting held with Turkish Prime Minister Adnan Menderes on that date.

and Turkish Consul Şefkati İstinyeli, as well as in Rome between Israel's ambassador to Italy, Eliahu Sasson, and Turkey's foreign minister, Fuat Köprülü.[101]

Despite repeated reassurances by Turkey, Israel's fears proved justified. The agreement for military cooperation between Turkey and Iraq, signed on 24 February 1955, did nothing to set Israel's mind at ease.[102] Article 5, in particular, left room for 'any other member state of the Arab League or any other state actively concerned with the security and peace in this region' to enter into the Turco-Iraqi alliance. Moreover, despite the fact that none of the covenant's articles made reference to the Palestinian issue or to any of the relevant UN resolutions, the accompanying letters exchanged between Adnan Menderes and his Iraqi counterpart, Nuri Al-Said, specified that both Turkey and Iraq would 'work in close cooperation for effecting the carrying out of the United Nations resolutions concerning Palestine'. As was to be expected, Israel's disappointment was extensively aired in a multi-page letter from Maurice Fischer to the Turkish minister of foreign affairs.[103] But it was too late. The agreement between Turkey and Iraq had already been signed.

3.3.2.2 *Turkey's participation in the Bandung Conference*

In a joint communiqué issued by the prime ministers of India, Pakistan, Ceylon, Burma and Indonesia on 27 December 1954, twenty-five countries were invited to attend the Afro-Asian Conference, scheduled to take place in the city of Bandung, Indonesia, between 18–24 April 1955.[104] Despite a recommendation by India and Burma, Israel was not invited to take part.[105] The reason for Israel's exclusion from the conference was the organizing governments' wish to solicit the participation of the Arab states in the Middle East and North Africa. The assertive leadership of Nasser predominated throughout the conference and, as was to be expected, the final declaration was fully aligned with the Arab stance vis-à-vis the issue of Palestine.[106]

Aside from the clearly anti-Western and anti-colonial nations of Africa and Asia, some of those more positively inclined towards the West took part in the Bandung Conference as well, including Turkey. Turkey's participation might have been of less concern to Israel, but for the agreement Turkey had concluded with Iraq in February of

---

[101] ISA/RG93/MFA/8693/2, Research Division (997/21.3.1955), Fischer to Fuat Köprülü, Turkish minister of foreign affairs (17.3.1955).

[102] ISA/RG93/MFA/8693/2, Research Division (996/9.3.1955). Full text of the Memorandum of Understanding for Mutual Cooperation between Turkey and Iraq (24.02.1955) and the accompanying statement by Turkish Prime Minister Adnan Menderes to his Iraqi counterpart, Nuri Al-Said.

[103] ISA/RG93/MFA/8693/2, Research Division (997/21.3.1955), Fischer to Köprülü (17.3.1955).

[104] ISA/RG93/MFA/8693/2, Research Division (1002/27.3.1955). The joint declaration by the prime ministers of India, Pakistan, Ceylon, Burma and Indonesia, reflecting the decision to invite to the Bandung Conference the following 26 states: Afghanistan, Cambodia, Central African Federation, People's Republic of China, Egypt, Ethiopia, Ghana, Iran, Iraq, Ivory Coast, Japan, Jordan, Laos, Lebanon, Liberia, Libya, Nepal, Philippines, Saudi Arabia, Sudan, Syria, Thailand, Turkey, North Vietnam, South Vietnam and Yemen. The Central African Federation declined the invitation, and the Ivory Coast did not respond to the invitation at all.

[105] Cf. 1.1.3, above.

[106] Ibid.

that year. The Israeli government followed Turkey's ambiguous stance with some concern as questions arose with regard to the scope and quality of relations Ankara was pursuing with Arab states.[107] Nevertheless, after Britain's reassuring accession to the Baghdad Pact on 4 April 1955,[108] Israeli diplomacy chose not to further exacerbate relations with Ankara. Thus, over the following months, Israel chose not to probe why the Turkish representatives expressed no reservations as to the final text of the Bandung Declaration.

In the summer of 1955, as the date approached for the vote on whether Greece's request would be placed on the agenda of the 10th Session of the UN General Assembly, Turkey sought Israel's favourable vote on its own positions. As part of that effort, Nurettin N. Akıncı, Turkey's ambassador to Israel, asked to meet with the deputy director general of the Israeli Ministry of Foreign Affairs, Arthur Lourie, in Jerusalem. The meeting was held on 18 August 1955, at which time Akıncı submitted a memorandum detailing Turkey's positions on the Cyprus issue. After promising Akıncı that Turkey's positions 'would be taken under serious advisement', without however reassuring him that Israel would support them, Lourie found an opportunity to ask why Turkey had participated in the Bandung Conference and why Akıncı's country had not reacted to what was said there on behalf of the Arabs. The Turkish diplomat seemed surprised and attempted to explain his country's position, citing speculation by various journalists, rather than the opinion of his ministry. Lourie did not conceal his scepticism over these vague explanations, particularly since the Israeli Ministry of Foreign Affairs was at that time under pressure to decide whether or not it would support Turkey at the UN regarding the Cyprus issue.[109]

3.3.3. Britain's guarantee of Israel's safety

When Britain announced that it would accede to the memorandum of understanding between Turkey and Iraq for military cooperation, Israeli concerns were largely dissipated. On 30 March 1955, Sir John Nicholls, the British ambassador to Israel, relayed a message from the foreign secretary, Anthony Eden, to the Israeli prime minister and foreign minister, Moshe Sharett, to the effect that the Foreign Office did not intend to endorse the statements of Menderes and Al-Said in the matter of UN resolutions on the Palestinian issue.[110] In so doing, Britain eliminated the anti-Israel

---

[107] Cf. 3.3.2.1.

[108] Cf. 3.3.3.

[109] ISA/RG93/MFA/263/6, West Europe Division to Israel's Diplomatic Representation in Athens (9234/ח – 22.8.1955). Attached is the report dated 18.8.1955 filed by Arthur Lourie, deputy director general of the Israeli Ministry of Foreign Affairs, on the meeting he had with the Turkish ambassador to Tel Aviv, Nurettin K. Akıncı.

[110] ISA/RG93/MFA/8693/2, Research Division (1005/10.4.1955), Letter by Sir Jack Nicholls, Britain's ambassador to Tel Aviv, to Prime Minister Moshe Sharett (30.3.1955). On the Turco-Iraqi pact: 'Sir Anthony Eden adds in his message that he will make it clear in his statement to Parliament that, in acceding to the Turco-Iraqi pact, Her Majesty's Government are not associating themselves with the letters which are exchanged at the time of its signature between the Turkish and Iraqi Governments.' Indeed, on that same date (30.3.1955), Eden, in addressing the House of Commons, made this elucidative statement which was of great importance to Israel.

nature of the letters that might otherwise have threatened the implementation of the Turco-Iraqi pact. Such a move on the part of the British was met with satisfaction by the Israelis, and Sharett's declaration that regional balance had thus been reinforced. He did, however, highlight the risks arising from an irrational bolstering of the Iraqi arsenal.[111]

In light of such developments, Israel had no reason not to back Britain at the UN – not just on the Cyprus issue, but on all of London's pursuits in the Middle East. At the time, the Israeli Foreign Ministry had contemplated proposing to London that other issues of interest to Israel, such as the right to free transit through the Suez Canal to and from Israel, should be included on the agenda of the upcoming 'Tripartite Conference on the Eastern Mediterranean'.[112] The idea was soon abandoned as it was generally believed that the countries directly involved (Britain, Greece and Turkey) would not wish – each for their own reasons – to bring to the table issues that might complicate their tripartite encounters even further.[113]

Against this background, on the eve of the 10th Session of the UN General Assembly, Israel's main concern was to avoid disrupting relations with Britain and the British authorities in Cyprus, which were dealing with the EOKA. In fact, it is worth noting that already in the early weeks of the bombing attacks on the British, there had been rumours that the EOKA fighters had been trained by Israelis.[114] Historical references associating Greek Cypriot EOKA with the Jewish armed struggle against the British in Palestine, and the cooperation behind the scenes between the Greek Cypriots and the Jews in the Karaolos detention camps,[115] raised suspicions amongst local British authorities and led them to make mountains out of molehills. For instance, the request by the Greek Cypriot football team, APOEL, to travel to Israel for training with Tel Aviv's Hapoel team was considered suspect.[116] Then, too, the British embassy in Tel Aviv complained to the Ministry of Foreign Affairs that Israel's newly appointed consul to Nicosia, Avraham Kidron, had held a ceremonial meeting in September 1955 with Archbishop Makarios and other officials of the Ethnarchy.[117] Rumours that Israel was backing EOKA became so persistent[118] that Avraham Kidron made every attempt to allay British suspicions. As part of his efforts, he decided to pay regular visits to the colonial secretary, for fear that restrictions might be imposed on Israeli subjects entering and staying in Cyprus[119] or on Israeli construction firms which had undertaken major public works projects for military purposes at Dhekelia and Episkopi.[120] Kidron

---

[111] ISA/RG93/MFA/8693/2, Ibid. Sharett's letter in response to Nicholls (6.4.1955).

[112] ISA/RG93/MFA/263/6, Darom to the West Europe Division (1096-201/אחא – 26.7.1955). Proposal to submit the relevant démarches to London, Athens and Ankara.

[113] ISA/RG93/MFA/263/6, West Europe Division to Darom (9531/ח – 7.8.1955).

[114] ISA/RG93/MFA/2156/7, Kidron to the British Commonwealth Division (869/102/ק – 24.8.1955).

[115] Cf. 2.2.

[116] ISA/RG93/MFA/2156/7, Kidron to British Commonwealth Division (260/102/ק – 22.2.1955).

[117] ISA/RG93/MFA/2156/7, Kidron to Gideon Shomron, Head of British Commonwealth Division (260/102/ק – 22.2.1955).

[118] Holland, *Britain and the Revolt in Cyprus*, 57.

[119] ISA/RG93/MFA/2155/10, Kidron to the British Commonwealth Division (1492/101/ק –27.12.1955).

[120] *Davar*, 'Will the British Leave Cyprus?: "Heated" Climate on the Island', 23.5.1955. On the intensified activities of the British security forces in Cyprus. Cf. 2.4.2.1 on Israeli entrepreneurial activity in Cyprus.

reached the point of reporting to the British authorities that malicious rumours were being spread about purported Israeli involvement in the island's troubles. The colonial secretary responded in writing to reassure the consul that the authorities would take his statement into account and that until the matter could be resolved, there would be no change in the bureaucratic process for Israeli visitors arriving in Cyprus.[121]

Nevertheless, the possibility remains that the climate of suspicion over an alleged connection between Israel and EOKA was intentionally fomented by the authorities in Cyprus in an effort to prevent such a situation in future. A review of Israeli archival material reveals no Israeli assistance of any kind to the EOKA cause. In fact, particularly during the early months of the troubles, Israel took every opportunity to declare its support for the local British authorities. Indicative of this was Israel's willingness to respond promptly to a British request for a supply of specially trained dogs to bolster law enforcement operations.[122]

The outbreak of the EOKA struggle occurred during a time when high-ranking officials from Israel's Ministry of Foreign Affairs were in frequent contact with their British counterparts in Cyprus over issues of regional security. One of these Israeli officials was Gideon Rafael, a special Middle East adviser to Foreign Minister Moshe Sharett. Reporting on developments in Cyprus, where he happened to be for consultations in mid-June of 1955, Rafael described the situation as volatile. According to him, there was a wide divergence of opinions among members of the island's political and military leaderships. The military purportedly kept pressing the governor for harsher repressive measures, while British government officials feared that harsher measures would provide Greece and Greek Cypriots with an opportunity to internationalize the Cyprus issue, and they wished to avoid active involvement with the UN at all costs.[123]

In the same report, Rafael conjectured that the British would probably not preclude relinquishing their political control over Cyprus to Athens at some future time – on condition that 'a sovereign British military base' remained on the island. Also of interest is the impression he formed from the talk among certain unnamed British officers that EOKA had been encouraged by the Americans for the ultimate purpose of securing a permanent presence on the island with the establishment of a NATO military base. An excerpt from Rafael's report states that 'the British suspected the US of encouraging Greek extremists, so it [the US] could come up at the appropriate time with a compromise proposal whereby the political governance would be relinquished to the Greeks and a military base would be given to NATO to secure a US presence on the island'.[124] However, British suspicions over the American encouragement of EOKA and their full-fledged involvement in the armed struggle of Greek Cypriots against the British is corroborated neither by secondary historical sources nor by subsequent

---

[121] ISA/RG93/MFA/2155/10, Kidron to the British Commonwealth Division (1492/101/ק – 27.12.1955).

[122] ISA/RG93/MFA/2155/10, Kidron to the British Commonwealth Division (463/101/ק – 2.5.1955).

[123] ISA/RG93/MFA/2155/10, Gideon Rafael, Special Adviser to the Ministry of Foreign Affairs on Middle East issues to Israeli Prime Minister and Minister of Foreign Affairs Moshe Sharett (24.6.1955, not recorded as incoming document). Rafael's report on the meetings he had in Cyprus with British military officials on the issue of defence cooperation between Israel and Britain.

[124] Ibid.

Israeli reports. Apparently what Rafael intended to convey in his report was that British officials may well have assumed that the Israelis knew more about US intentions.

3.3.4 Israel's vote on the Cyprus issue at the 10th Session of the UN General Assembly

In light of the circumstances discussed above, Israel was again faced with the diplomatic issue of the peoples' right to self-determination for the inhabitants of Cyprus – and of course the possibility of the island's unification with Greece – from the perspective of Israeli dependence on Britain's military presence in the area. In this sense, Israeli diplomats encountered fewer dilemmas at the 10th Session of the UN General Assembly than they had the year before.

The Israelis believed that Greece could count on the support of the Arab League – dominated by Egyptian influence – as well as the bloc of traditionally anti-colonialist Latin American states. Israel also believed that Archbishop Makarios, having participated in the Bandung Conference, would secure the support of a considerable number of African and Asian countries which had adopted an unequivocally pro-Arab stance during the Bandung Conference that year. Under the circumstances, Greece would not be eager to jeopardize crucial Arab and other anti-colonialist votes at the upcoming UN session by improving diplomatic relations with Israel. Furthermore, negotiations between Greece and Egypt over the future of the Greek diaspora were still unresolved, as were efforts to safeguard the interests of the Greek Orthodox Patriarchate of Jerusalem within Jordanian territory. Indicative, too, were the assessments of the Greek consul general in Nicosia, Rodis Roufos-Kanakaris, who expressed the pessimistic belief that Greek-Israeli relations were not likely to be normalized in the immediate future. The experienced Greek diplomat's assessment may also have testified to the awkward position Greece might find itself in if it became the target of a sudden 'attack of friendship' by the Israelis. Such a reversal would be hard to explain to Arab supporters, particularly in the context of the Cyprus issue.[125]

Under these circumstances, Israel had little to gain at a regional or bilateral level by supporting Greek positions. On the contrary, there was every chance that the rumours artfully cultivated by the British to the effect that 'Israel was behind EOKA' would be confirmed. On the other hand, 1955 had been a problematic year for relations between Israel and Turkey as well. The signing of the Turco-Iraqi pact had been met with suspicion by the Israelis, as had Turkey's participation in the pro-Arab Bandung Conference.[126]

In anticipation of the debate on the Cyprus issue at the 10th Session of the UN General Assembly, and based on the significant regional developments of 1955, it seemed that backing Britain's positions would be the most advisable way for Israel to

---

[125] ISA/RG93/MFA/2155/10, Avraham Giladi, administrative officer at Israel's consulate in Nicosia, to the British Commonwealth Division (579/101/ף – 30.5.1955). Assessment by Rodis Roufos-Kanakaris, Greek consul general in Nicosia.
[126] Cf. 3.3.2.1 and 3.3.2.2.

go. It is worth noting that Consul Avraham Kidron's reports on these developments, beginning with the EOKA armed struggle and the incidents that followed to the end of 1955, were cautious and neutral.[127]

That being said, an unequivocally pro-British vote by Israel would have displeased both Athens and Ankara. It would have lessened the chance for normal diplomatic relations between Greece and Israel but it might also have incited Ankara to take further pro-Arab actions, a prospect Israel wanted to prevent.

The line proposed by Israel's ambassador in Rome, Eliahu Sasson, who had considerable experience in Ankara, coincided with that of Sharett, Israel's prime minister and minister of foreign affairs at the time: Neither Greece nor Turkey would be backed in the voting on Cyprus – whether in regard to the placement of the issue on the UN Session agenda or at the debate on the merits of the question, if the topic were ultimately included on the agenda. In order to justify this particular stance, the argument should be, 'Israel has no wish to back one friendly state against another, equally friendly state.'[128]

The Greek proposal to include the Cyprus issue on the agenda of the 10th Session was voted down.[129] Israel, despite its usual inclination to back requests for agenda placement on any issue related to decolonization,[130] chose this time to abstain on the matter of Cyprus. In their comments on the outcome of the vote, the Israelis focused on the positions adopted by the Arab states. More specifically, the votes in favour cast by Egypt, Saudi Arabia, Yemen and Syria came as no surprise, but Lebanon's vote in favour was unexpected, since it had backed pro-West Iraq the year before. Moreover, the Israelis noted with interest that certain important participants in the Bandung Conference ultimately refrained from backing the Greek proposal, among them Iran, India, Burma, Indonesia, the Philippines and Ethiopia.[131]

3.3.5 The position of the Israeli prime minister and Foreign Minister Moshe Sharett on the Cyprus issue, 1955

A review of Israeli foreign policy on the issue of Cyprus at this historic juncture would be incomplete without an account of the consequential personal views of Moshe

---

[127] ISA/RG93/MFA/2156/7, Indicatively: (a) Kidron to the British Commonwealth Division (408/101/ק – 10.4.1955), Description of the early days of the EOKA struggle. Consul Avraham Kidron recounts the sequence of the events of those days without comment but expressing the belief that EOKA's actions could continue and that the British side should be expected to react decisively. Subsequent reports throughout 1955 were along the same neutral lines. (b) Kidron to the British Commonwealth Division (1313/102/ק – 21.11.1955). The comparison of the *modus operandi* of the Jewish armed groups in Palestine at the time of the British Mandate, to the way EOKA was operating in Cyprus in 1955 is of particular interest in this report. Contrary to his previous reports, Kidron criticizes EOKA's recruitment of underage students.

[128] ISA/RG93/MFA/263/6, Eliahu Sasson to the Research Division (61/רצ – 12.9.1955).

[129] Xydis, 'The UN General Assembly', 144.

[130] ISA/RG93/MFA/2156/7, UN Division to the British Commonwealth Division, Israel's embassy in London and Israel's consulate in Nicosia (30519/מ – 14.9.1954). Cf. 3.2.5.

[131] ISA/RG93/MFA/8693/3, Research Division (1096/28.12.1955). Review by the International Organisations Division of the proceedings of the 10th Session of the UN General Assembly.

Sharett, the man who practically and substantively determined Israel's international orientation from the founding of the Jewish state to the mid-1950s. A close associate of Israel's first prime minister, Ben-Gurion (and later his political opponent), Sharett had also served as foreign minister during the early years of Israeli independence, having the first and last word on the structure, staffing and workings of the administration.[132] During his two short-lived terms as head of coalition governments (26 November 1954–29 June 1955 and 29 June 1955–3 November 1955), Sharett also retained the office of foreign minister. When Ben-Gurion returned to the political scene to form a coalition government on 3 November 1955, Sharett was once again sworn in as foreign minister, serving until 18 June 1956 when he resigned and left politics for good. He was succeeded by a new foreign minister, Golda Meir.

Sharett outlined his recommendation vis-à-vis Israel's position on the Cyprus issue in response to a letter from Peretz Bernstein of the Centre-Right 'Pan-Zionist Party' (Mifleget ha-Tzionim ha-Klaliim). Bernstein had held the office of minister of trade and industry in the first coalition government under Sharett (26 January 1954–29 June 1955), and their relationship on both a political and personal level was very good.

Bernstein had been asked by a Greek journalist what Israel's position would be on Cyprus should Greece's claim come up for debate at the approaching UN Session. Since Bernstein was not personally familiar with the issue, he had written to Sharett for information on the matter so that he would be able to a give the journalist a well-reasoned answer.[133]

Sharett's highly enlightening reply, dated 6 July 1955, set forth his concerns and views on the criteria determining Israel's stance:

Dear Mr Bernstein,

I appreciate the fact of your having contacted me and will be happy to answer your query.

With reference to the issue of Cyprus as well as to the claim for said island to become part of Greek national territory, we are indeed – as in many other international issues – caught between a rock and a hard place. Practically speaking, we have no reason to turn Greece against us, nor do we desire to take any hostile action against Britain or Turkey, although in the light of specific estimations, it would be in our interest to see Cyprus remaining under British rule rather than becoming a Greek colony.

Also considered as a question of principle, this is not a simple issue:

On one hand, we have a moral obligation to remain the advocates of the principle of self-determination of those peoples still struggling for their independence.

---

[132] Walter Eytan, 'Sherut ha-Khutz' ['Diplomatic Service'], in *Misrad ha-Khutz*, ed. Yeger, Govrin and Oded, 21–9.
[133] ISA/RG93/MFA/263/6, Letter dated 3.7.1955 from Peretz Bernstein, former Minister of Trade and Industry and member of the Centre-Right *Ha-Tzionim Ha-Klaliim* [General Zionists] political party, to Moshe Sharett, Prime Minister and Minister of Foreign Affairs.

In that sense, however, it would not be easy for us to adopt a position such as to result in leaving the Turkish minority unprotected, all the more since under the current circumstances, said minority has, vis-à-vis the Greek majority, the same position we had in relation to the Arab majority under the British Mandate.

So far, we have been able to elude adopting a clear-cut position in favour of one or the other side. As of the last UN General Assembly, we voted in favour of the issue of Cyprus being put on the agenda for debate, endorsing Greece's request. That vote was consonant with our principle of acknowledging the right of any country to ask that any issue it considers important be placed on the agenda for debate. By voting then, we did not adopt any position as to the merits of the problem. Fortunately for us, the dispute was resolved by way of a compromise proposal which was agreed to by the delegations of both Britain and Greece, and which we had no problem voting for. That resolution made no reference to the merits of the issue, but only deferred the debate for some time in the future. Meanwhile, it became known that upon Britain's initiative, a Tripartite Convention[134] would soon take place between Britain, Greece and Turkey – all three of which are NATO member states – in an effort to arrive at a commonly acceptable solution. Needless to say, we have been enthusiastically supporting this effort and most sincerely hope that it bears fruit.

So much for the background of the issue.

You may tell the Greek journalist that we fervently desire a peaceful solution to the issue, namely one that would best serve the legitimate interests of all three states involved, since we mean to maintain friendly relations with all three of them.

You may also incidentally note to the journalist that it is Greece that has not been helping to develop balanced relations with us, which is not the case between ourselves and either of the other two countries:

Whereas England and Turkey have fully recognised Israel within a short time of the founding of our State and established diplomatic relations with us, Greece is still hesitant to normalise its relations with us, thereby essentially relieving us of any obligation towards it.[135]

Private though it was in essence, this letter from Israeli Foreign Minister Sharett, who at the time was also Israel's prime minister, was transmitted interdepartmentally to the Israeli diplomatic missions in Nicosia, Athens and Ankara. In it, Sharett outlined the general framework of Israel's foreign policy vis-à-vis the Cyprus question. The main pillars that shaped Israel's foreign policy with regard to the fate of Cyprus were as follows: (a) Israel's dependence on Britain and Turkey at the regional security level;

---

[134] In the matter of the Tripartite Conference on the Eastern Mediterranean, which took place in London, 29.8.1955–7.9.1955, with the participation of Britain, Greece and Turkey, and the matter of the background and the outcome of the conference: Hatzivassiliou, *To Kypriako Zitima*, 73–6; Evanthis Hatzivassiliou, *Britain and the International Status of Cyprus, 1955–59* (Minneapolis, MN: University of Minnesota, 1997), 35–8; and Holland, *Britain and the Revolt in Cyprus*, 69–75.
[135] ISA/RG93/MFA/263/6, Sharett to Bernstein (503/55-6.7.1955).

(b) Israel's endeavour to maintain normal relations with Turkey; (c) Greece's refusal to normalize diplomatic relations with Israel and its pro-Arab stance at international fora; (d) Israel's need for the British presence in Cyprus to reinforce its security in the region; and (e) Israel's need to maintain as low a profile as possible at the UN in any matter involving the Cyprus issue.

Apart from such conclusions, however, Sharett expressed his personal view on the Cyprus issue in his journal. On 6 July 1955, the day he wrote to Bernstein, Sharett noted in his diaries:

> I dropped by the Ministry of Foreign Affairs and looked into current issues. Quite unexpectedly, I received a very courteous letter from Peretz Bernstein asking about our position on the issue of Cyprus. I replied with a detailed letter and explained to him what, according to our opinion, the background of the issue is, since on one hand we have Britain and Turkey and, on the other hand, there is Greece. What matters is that under no circumstances do we want to see Enosis materialise.[136]

Sharett's negative attitude towards the prospect of unification with Greece is not surprising. What is surprising, is the parallel Sharett drew between the position of the Jewish minority vis-à-vis the Arab majority in Palestine under the British Mandate and the position of the Turkish Cypriot community vis-à-vis the Greek Cypriots in 1955. For the average Israeli of the time, such a parallel meant that Greek Cypriots were committing atrocities against innocent civilians, women and children, similar to the organized attacks on Jewish settlements committed by armed Arab factions in British-held Palestine in 1920, 1921, 1929 and 1936–9, which were indelibly marked in the collective memory of the Yishuv, particularly the bloody incidents of 23 and 24 August 1929. During that time, rumours had spread about an imminent change in the status quo of the Muslim Holy Sites in the Old City of Jerusalem, allowing Jews to pray in the courtyard of the Al-Aqsa Mosque. Arab public opinion was outraged, and armed factions attacked the Jewish quarters of Jerusalem, Safed (Tsfat), Tiberias, Hebron, Jaffa and Haifa. In two days, the tiny Jewish settlements of Motsa, Beer Tuvia and Hulda were razed, and residents who did not manage to flee were slaughtered. The bloodiest attack took place in the Jewish quarter of Hebron on 24 August 1929, leaving 64 dead civilians, many of them women and children. The event went down in Israeli history as the 'Hebron Massacre'. Throughout the 1950s, those massacres were often cited in Israeli political discourse, rekindling intense anti-Arab public sentiment.[137]

In his letter to Bernstein that July, Sharett undoubtedly distorts the prevailing conditions in Cyprus and does not do justice to EOKA in comparing the Greek Cypriot

---

[136] Moshe Sharett, *Yoman Ishi 1955* [*Personal Diary 1955*] (Tel Aviv: Sifriat Maariv, 1978), 1084.

[137] *Davar*, 'Our Fallen: Our tortured, massacred and dead who fell in the struggle to defend our sacred homeland', 2.9.1929. A list of names of the victims of that two-day attack on 23–24.8.1929, by town, district and age, was published on the front page. Cf. Benny Morris, *Medina Akhat, Shtei Medinot: Yisrael-Falastin* [*One State, Two States: Israel-Palestine*] (Tel Aviv: Am Oved, 2012), 26–7; and Baruch Kimmerling and Yoel Migdal, *Falastinim: 'Am be-Hivatzruto* [*Palestinians: A People on the Making*] (Jerusalem: Keter, 1999), 85.

majority to the Arab perpetrators of the Hebron Massacre of 1929. Throughout 1955, EOKA fought exclusively against British targets, not against the Turkish Cypriot population. Moreover, Israeli Consul to Nicosia Avraham Kidron, in an ad hoc report he prepared on 24 April 1956, confirms that until that time, relations between Greek Cypriots and Turkish Cypriots were 'more or less good'.[138] It is also noteworthy that throughout Sharett's term in government, this historical reference was not expressed or implied in any departmental report or internal memo at the Israeli Ministry of Foreign Affairs.

Sharett's views on the Cyprus issue, as expressed in his letter, are also interesting because of their political expediency. Specifically, relations between Greek and Turkish Cypriots had until that time never been at the epicentre of the broader regional nexus between Turkey and Israel. During Sharett's term in office, Turkey did not request Israel's assistance or active involvement in the protection of Turkish Cypriots from EOKA or Greece. Israeli diplomatic manoeuvring aimed at maintaining British domination on the neighbouring island, which was precisely the reason Enosis was undesirable. However, there was never a suggestion of any 'moral obligation', let alone an intention on Israel's part to act as a 'quasi-motherland' for Turkish Cypriots.[139]

What Moshe Sharett wished to convey to the Greek journalist at his meeting with Bernstein was Israel's displeasure at Greece's stubborn refusal to recognize the Jewish state de jure. Although the entire letter was officially transmitted to the Israeli diplomatic missions in Athens, Ankara and Nicosia, it was ultimately fortunate that the historical parallels contained in it did not enter Greek and Greek Cypriot public opinion, otherwise Greece would have had yet another good reason to stall on normalizing relations with Israel.

In light of the above, two questions arose: how would Sharett handle the situation in Cyprus if conflicts between the Greek and Turkish Cypriots erupted on the island? How eager would Israel be to protect the Turkish minority from the Greek majority?

These questions remain unanswered for the following reason: on 3 November 1955, Ben-Gurion made a dynamic comeback in the country's political scene and assumed the prime ministership once again. Nevertheless, his coexistence with Sharett proved difficult and clashes within the Mapai ruling party worsened to the point that Sharett resigned from his post as foreign minister on 18 June 1956, effectively ending his political career.

3.4 The Israeli position on the Cyprus issue at the 11th UN General Assembly Session, 1956

3.4.1 The eventful realignments of 1956

Without question, 1956 was a year of major political upheavals in Israel as well as in Cyprus and Greece. In Greece, parliamentary elections were held on 19 February 1956, from which the ERE (Ethniki Rizospastiki Enosis, National Radical Union) political

---

[138] ISA/RG93/MFA/263/3, Kidron to British Commonwealth Division (1971/102-26.4.1956). Cf. 3.4.2.2.
[139] Israeli interest in protecting the rights of the Turkish Cypriot minority was first expressed at a purely intra-ministerial level in November 1958. Cf. 3.6.5.1 on the content of Loker's memo to Meir.

party, led by Konstantinos Karamanlis, emerged victorious. Initially, Spyridon Theotokis was appointed foreign minister of the newly elected government, but Evangelos Averoff (aka Evangelos-Tositsas) assumed the post in the reshuffle of 28 May 1956.[140] Meanwhile in Israel, Ben-Gurion had returned to active political life after winning the parliamentary elections in July 1955. In June 1956, Golda Meir took the helm of the Ministry of Foreign Affairs after the eventful resignation of Moshe Sharett, who for years had set priorities for Israel's foreign policy. In Cyprus, the outbreak of the EOKA armed struggle on 1 April 1955,[141] the failure of the Tripartite Conference for the Eastern Mediterranean in August–September 1955,[142] the unsuccessful negotiations between Makarios and Governor Harding,[143] ending with the exile of Archbishop Makarios, Bishop Kyprianos of Kyrenia, Reverend Stavros (Papastavrou) Papagathangelou of the Holy Church of Faneromeni in Nicosia and Polykarpos Ioannides, former editor of the newspaper *Efimeris* on 9 March 1956,[144] all turned international attention to the island.[145] Once again, the Greek government decided to appeal to the UN, at a moment when international sentiment was extremely critical of the repressive measures applied by the British. This time, British policy in Cyprus was not only criticized by the Eastern Bloc countries, but by many Western and British Commonwealth countries as well.[146] These included Israel, where the local press emphasized more and more the commonalities between the Cypriot struggle and the Jewish armed struggle under the British Mandate.

Nonetheless, the 26 July decision by Nasserist Egypt to nationalize the Suez Canal and renounce the Anglo-Egyptian Treaty which stipulated that the Suez Canal Company, with Britain and France as majority shareholders, would control this important sea route, played a pivotal role in shaping Israeli foreign policy.[147] Nasser's move adversely affected the interests of Britain and France as well as the international community, as it essentially invalidated the 1888 Convention of Constantinople on the protection of international navigation. Meanwhile, strengthened economic ties between Egypt and the Soviet Union, and a significant acquisition of arms from Czechoslovakia in late 1955, added a Cold War aspect to the Suez Crisis, making the situation in the Middle East extremely tense.

The nationalization of the Canal would also have serious repercussions for Israel, both in military and economic terms. It was in imminent danger of being commercially isolated, and the Egyptian military machine, strengthened by the Soviet Union, represented a major threat to Israel's territorial integrity. Having appealed to France to

---

[140] Xydis, *Cyprus: Conflict and Conciliation*, 45. Theotokis was heavily criticized by the opposition forces in Greece and the Ethnarchy in Cyprus for his actions after the exile of Makarios to the Seychelles.
[141] Holland, *Britain and the Revolt in Cyprus*, 108–32.
[142] François Crouzet, *Le Conflit de Chypre 1946-1959* [*The Cyprus Conflict 1946–1959*] (Brussels: Émile Bruylant, 1973), vol. 2, 685–707; Hatzivassiliou, *To Kypriako Zitima*, 73–6; Hatzivassiliou, *Britain and International Status*, 35–8; and Holland, *Britain and the Revolt in Cyprus*, 132–41.
[143] Crouzet, *Conflit*, 708–68; and Hatzivassiliou, *Britain and International Status*, 54–65.
[144] Crouzet, *Conflit*, 774; and Holland, *Britain and the Revolt in Cyprus*, 210–14.
[145] Crouzet, *Conflit*, 783.
[146] Ibid.
[147] Kyle, *Suez*, 135–8.

equip its armed forces[148] and after concerted diplomatic communication with Britain, Israel invaded the Gaza Strip and the Sinai Peninsula on 28 October 1956. This marked the start of the Sinai Campaign (Operation Kadesh) in which Britain, France and Israel joined forces against Nasserist Egypt.

Intense pressure exerted by US President Dwight Eisenhower, who calculated political costs to the imminent US presidential elections against the risk of the Canal coming under Soviet control, brought a ceasefire into effect at midnight of 6 November 1956.[149] The United Nations adopted Canada's motion for a resolution to station a UN Peacekeeping Force in the Sinai Peninsula and Gaza in order to guarantee free navigation in the Suez Canal and the Straits of Tiran in the Red Sea, and ensure the withdrawal of Israeli troops from all occupied Egyptian territories.[150] The outcome of the campaign was perceived as an Egyptian victory over Britain and France. Israel expressed dissatisfaction over the stance adopted by the US, which had the effect of reinforcing its relations with and its dependency primarily on Britain and to a lesser extent, on France.[151]

The Suez Crisis once again demonstrated the geopolitical importance of Cyprus to the British and their allies, providing as it did a bridgehead for British paratroopers and ground forces participating in the landing at Port Said.[152] At the same time, Britain was beginning to realize that the explosive situation in Cyprus could not continue, with EOKA tangibly intensifying its armed activity in November 1956. The Foreign Office advocated a constitutional way out of the Cyprus problem that would ensure Britain's continued military presence on the island and more or less satisfy the Greek Cypriot desire to engage in the decision-making process. For its part, Athens maintained a moderate stance, with Prime Minister Karamanlis' statement before the UN General Assembly on 22 November 1956, that Greece demanded recognition of the Cypriots' right to self-determination, that it did not seek 'territorial expansion' and that it was eager to find ways to safeguard the rights of the island's Turkish minority.[153] Athens continued to negotiate with the British with a view to terminating Makarios' exile and establishing a regime of self-determination for Cyprus 'as soon as possible, without setting a pressing timeframe'. The conciliatory messages conveyed by Athens seemed well received by the British media, but EOKA meanwhile began to intensify its armed operations in the belief that 'no pseudo-constitution would resolve the problem'[154], and in November 1956, Britain imposed yet more repressive measures which further exacerbated the situation.

---

[148] Zach Levey, 'Israel's Foreign Policy Orientation, 1952–1959' (PhD diss., Hebrew University of Jerusalem, Jerusalem, 1993), 249–51.

[149] Kyle, *Suez*, 469–76.

[150] Ibid., 532–48. Cf. Alexandros Koutsis, *Mesi Anatoli: Diethneis Scheseis kai Politiki Anaptyxi [Middle East: International Relationships and Political Development]* (Athens: Papazisis, 1992), vol. A, 175–9.

[151] Chaim Herzog, *The Arab–Israeli Wars: War and Peace in the Middle East from the War of Independence through Lebanon* (New York: Vintage Books, 1984), 138–40.

[152] Crouzet, *Conflit*, 840.

[153] Ibid., 842.

[154] Ibid., 843–4.

3.4.2 The Israeli assessment of developments in Cyprus

The start of EOKA's armed struggle in April 1955 and the lengthy negotiations between the new governor, Sir John Harding and Archbishop Makarios, which began in early October of that year,[155] were two events that aroused the interest of the Israeli Ministry of Foreign Affairs. The issue that concerned Israel most was the manner in which British presence would be maintained on the neighbouring island – a matter of fundamental importance for Israel's security.

Israel's consul in Nicosia, Avraham Kidron, was not optimistic that negotiations between Makarios and Harding would lead to any kind of agreement. As to the 'formula' proposed by London, he described it as 'political acrobatics',[156] noting the ambiguities it contained: 'As Britain is a party to the United Nations Charter and the Potomac Declaration, it is not the intention of Her Majesty's government that the principle of self-determination should never be applied to Cyprus.' Britain was aware of the significance acquired by the principle of self-determination in the international system, yet it sought to maintain sovereignty in Cyprus for an unspecified time. The justification was that the situation in the Middle East and the Eastern Mediterranean, and Britain's commitments to protect its own interests and those of its allies in the region had to be taken into consideration. These commitments arose from 'already existing alliances and treaties', such as the 1923 Treaty of Lausanne, the Baghdad Pact, the Anglo-Turkish Convention of 1878[157] and the Tripartite Declaration of the US, Britain and France on maintaining the balance of power between Israel and the Arab states.[158] According to this line of reasoning, therefore, the application of the self-determination principle to Cyprus was not of timely concern. Kidron, referring to the positions of Governor Harding, Archbishop Makarios and EOKA leader Georgios Grivas, while negotiations were leading nowhere,[159] essentially agreed with the astute observation of Konstantinos Karamanlis that on certain points of the 'formula' advanced by the British, the right to self-determination was 'practically unrecognisable'.[160]

The only optimistic aspect of the Makarios–Harding talks was simply that they continued. According to the assessment of the Greek Consul in Nicosia, this was mainly due to the diplomatic pressure exerted by Washington and the Greek government's encouragement of Makarios not to abandon the effort. In Kidron's view, however, the most important reason for the ongoing negotiations was that they boosted Karamanlis' chances of winning the upcoming parliamentary elections in February

---

[155] Holland, *Britain and the Revolt in Cyprus*, 159; and Nikos Kranidiotis, *Oi Diapragmatefseis Makariou–Harding, 1955–1956* [*The Negotiations between Makarios and Harding, 1955–1956*] (Athens: Olkos, 1987), 91–5.

[156] ISA/RG93/MFA/2156/7, Kidron to West Europe Division (1666/102-6.2.1956).

[157] Hatzivassiliou, *To Kypriako Zitima*, 76–83, on the British views put forward during the negotiations between Harding and Makarios.

[158] ISA/RG93/MFA/2156/7, Gazit to the Research Division (392/מ – 25.1.1956), Statements of Sir John Harding on the BBC's *Panorama* broadcast (23.1.1956). Harding expressly includes the 'alliances and treaties binding on Britain in the region' and the Tripartite Declaration of 25.5.1950 relating to the Arab–Israeli conflict.

[159] ISA/RG93/MFA/2156/7, Kidron to the British Commonwealth Division (1531/102/ק – 4.1.1956).

[160] Hatzivassiliou, *To Kypriako Zitima*, 78.

1956. Otherwise, if Makarios and Harding suspended talks, Greece was liable to be 'neutralized' within the NATO framework – and Greek Prime Minister Konstantinos Karamanlis' right-wing ERE political party would lose the elections.[161]

On the other hand, as the Israeli diplomatic delegation in Ankara noted, the Menderes government did not want to seem condescending towards the issues being negotiated between Makarios and Harding, fearing that the opposition would accuse him of 'betraying the Turkish brothers living on the island'.[162] The prevailing climate was reflected in the stern tone of Foreign Minister Fuat Köprülü's statement that Turkey would never agree to 'the true ultimate objective of Makarios and Greece, which was for Cyprus to come under Greek state sovereignty'.[163]

In early February 1956, after months of negotiations, Makarios indirectly accepted the provisions of the 'formula'. At the same time, he brought to the negotiating table decision-taking arrangements on internal governance matters, which would originate from the Cypriot people through a parliamentary system, with the governor holding a constitutional position as head of state.[164] The 'national consultation' convened by Makarios over the weekend of 30 January–1 February 1956,[165] as well as the meeting between Makarios and Grivas at Kykkos Monastery on the evening of 28 January 1956,[166] had already taken place. Makarios and Grivas discussed whether the 'revised formula' on self-determination proposed by Harding should be accepted or not, stressing, albeit, the need to provide guarantees for self-determination during the Transitional Period as well, such as Greek majority representation on the Legislative Council. Although Grivas warned Makarios that Harding's propositions were nothing more than a trap,[167] he reluctantly accepted the 'revised formula' as the basis for negotiations and ordered a two-week ceasefire, on condition that amnesty should be granted to all those who had participated in EOKA's operations as of 1 April 1955. The 'national consultation' that ensued over the next two days was eventful, as proponents of Bishop Kyprianos of Kyrenia criticized Makarios' actions as treasonous.[168] However, the main issue of disagreement which led to the eventual breakdown of negotiations between Makarios and Harding was the British refusal to accept Makarios' requests to grant amnesty to EOKA fighters and to appoint a Greek Cypriot minister as head of internal security matters.[169]

---

[161] ISA/RG93/MFA/2156/7, Kidron to the British Commonwealth Division (1561/102/ק – 11.1.1956). Cf. Holland, *Britain and the Revolt in Cyprus*, 200. US Secretary of State John Foster Dulles had made it clear to the British Foreign and Commonwealth Office that: 'it was an issue of major importance to avoid any incidents in Cyprus', before 19.2.1956, the day when the parliamentary elections would be held in Greece. Cf. Hatzivassiliou, *Britain and the International Status*, 56.

[162] ISA/RG93/MFA/2156/7, Barouch Gilead, Second Secretary of Israel's Consulate in Nicosia, to West Europe Division (4409/3612/אנ – 11.1.1956).

[163] Ibid. Statements of Turkish Foreign Minister Fuat Köprülü, to the Anadolu News Agency and the Turkish press (25.1.1956).

[164] Hatzivassiliou, *To Kypriako Zitima*, 79.

[165] Holland, *Britain and the Revolt in Cyprus*, 197–8.

[166] Kranidiotis, *Diapragmatefseis*, 68–74.

[167] Hatzivassiliou, *Britain and International Status*, 56.

[168] Holland, *Britain and the Revolt in Cyprus*, 197–8.

[169] Hatzivassiliou, *To Kypriako Zitima*, 80.

The lengthy negotiations between Makarios and Harding were a matter of concern for Israeli diplomacy, but not with respect to the extent of self-determination obtained on the island or the internal political system that would be formed there. Israeli interest focused rather on the continuing presence of Britain's military forces and the terms of the agreement that would ensure its continuing presence in Cyprus.

Although the Makarios–Harding negotiations featured prominently in the reports filed by the Israeli Consul in Nicosia, they were not of major concern to Israel's Ministry of Foreign Affairs. The application of the principle of self-determination in Cyprus and the way in which political decisions would be taken on the neighbouring island were secondary issues for the Israelis. What most interested them at that time was ensuring British military support in the event that Israel's territorial integrity was threatened by Arab countries, specifically Nasser's Egypt. An indication of the importance of this matter to Israel was the special attention paid by Mordechai Gazit, first secretary of the Israeli embassy in London, to an excerpt from the BBC's televised interview with Governor Harding on 23 January 1956. When asked by a journalist whether Cyprus would no longer serve as a military base for Britain in the event of the island's unification with Greece, he replied:

> For us, the British, Cyprus is directly concerned with all our military effort in the Middle East. It is the nerve centre of our whole Middle East military organization; it could be used for military and air operation; it could be used for assembling reinforcements and for sending them through there. It is possible that we might want to use Cyprus as a base for operations in which the Greeks would not be directly associated. Our treaties in the Middle East might well involve us in military commitments-treaties to which the Greeks were not a party, such as the Baghdad Pact, the Anglo-Jordanian Treaty, the Tripartite Declaration over Israel or the protection of British lives and property [...].[170]

3.4.2.1 *Israeli assessment of Britain's decision to exile Makarios*

Britain's decision to exile Archbishop Makarios, Bishop Kyprianos of Kyrenia, the priest of the Church of Faneromeni in Nicosia and the secretary of Nicosia's bishopry on 9 March 1956 was troubling,[171] but not surprising to Israeli diplomacy. The main concern of the British was to overcome EOKA. They continued negotiating with Makarios for the sake of appearances, but wanted to be the ones to set the terms.

The Israelis believed that, under the circumstances, resorting to exile would not produce positive results for the British in the long term. Besides, exiling the leaders of the October 1931 revolt had only postponed the problem without resolving it.[172] As such, Makarios' exile was described by the Israelis as an 'unintelligent British move'. In

---

[170] ISA/RG93/MFA/2156/7, Gazit to Research Division (392/מג – 25.1.1956).
[171] Holland, *Britain and the Revolt in Cyprus*, 211–14; Crouzet, *Conflit*, 775–85; Petros Papapolyviou, 'O ektopismos tou Makariou stis Seychelles' ['The Exile of Makarios to the Seychelles'] (Cypriot) *Kathimerini*, 15.6.2014.
[172] Cf. 1.2.

fact, the British Commonwealth division of Israel's Ministry of Foreign Affairs believed it certain that by taking such action, the British themselves would be forced to 'canonise Makarios, which would provide further impetus to the Cypriots' struggle for freedom and bring themselves to an impasse from which they would be able to escape only by bringing Archbishop Makarios back with pomp and ceremony – and, in the end, they would be obliged to satisfy all his demands'.[173]

The exile of Makarios made a negative impression on Israeli public opinion. This sudden decision of British authorities in Cyprus reminded the Israelis of the 1,580 Jews banished to the island of Mauritius in the Indian Ocean in 1940, when they were captured trying to enter Mandate Palestine,[174] and of the three-year detainment of Jewish Holocaust survivors in the camps at Karaolos.[175] Makarios' exile and the execution of Cypriot fighters combined with the extensively stringent measures on the island starkly highlighted the historic parallels linking EOKA's struggle with the armed struggle of Jews against the British in Palestine just a decade earlier.

While EOKA's armed struggle continued, Israelis observed British attempts to pave the way for a constitutional self-governance regime. Clear indications of this were proposals submitted to the British government by Constitutional Commissioner Lord Radcliffe in November 1956.[176] This intent was tainted albeit by the statement of British Secretary of State for the Colonies Alan Lennox-Boyd to the House of Commons on 19 December 1956, which brought partition to the forefront by acknowledging the right of separate self-determination for both Greek and Turkish Cypriots.[177] This development raised considerable concern for the Greek side. Despite the deep importance of Lennox-Boyd's statement to subsequent developments in the Cyprus issue, it should come as no surprise that Israel did not pay particular attention to it. During the period of November and December 1956, immediately after the Suez Crisis, Israel's political leadership faced a variety of serious diplomatic challenges. More than ever, Israel was focused on maintaining Britain's presence in the region, not on how it would handle the inter-community balance on the island. Therefore, to the extent that it affected the Israelis, Radcliffe's propositions were satisfactory for the following reasons: Cyprus would remain under British sovereignty for as long as the regime of self-determination was in force, the British governor or the London government would maintain full control of international relations and defence of the neighbouring island and, as a result, Britain would be able to comply with its commitments regarding Israel's security.[178]

[173] ISA/RG93/MFA/2156/7, British Commonwealth Division to Kidron (9234/ד – 16.3.1956).
[174] Yad Vashem, 'Mauritzius', from the digital database for the study of the Jewish Holocaust, available online at: www.yadvashem.org.il (6 October 2022). Report published by the Yad Vashem World Holocaust Remembrance Centre on the exile of illegal Jewish immigrants to the island of Mauritius in the Indian Ocean. The exiles, all of them Holocaust survivors, had been captured by the British as they were attempting to reach the shores of Palestine, then under British Mandate. They were held captive for five years (1940–5).
[175] Cf. 2.1.
[176] Hatzivassiliou, *To Kypriako Zitima*, 86–90.
[177] Ibid., 90–1.
[178] ISA/RG93/MFA/2156/7, Cyprus Public Relations Division, *Lord Radcliffe's Terms of Reference: Cyprus Embargoed*, No. 5, 14.9.1956, Pamphlet (Nicosia: [Government of Cyprus]).

On the other hand, however, neither Israel nor any other country in the region could afford to turn a blind eye to the reality. The situation in Cyprus had placed Britain in a tenuous diplomatic position, both locally and internationally. Though Israeli diplomats carefully refrained from openly expressing their concerns to the Foreign Office, they saw plainly that British hopes to bring the situation under full control through further repressive measures were utterly unbased. All indications were that EOKA's struggle would not subside anytime soon.[179] As the Israelis observed the intensity of the bloody events on the island, they realized that the self-governance regime Britain intended to implement would not be accepted by the Greek Cypriots nor would forcibly imposing it be an easy feat.[180]

3.4.2.2 *The developments in Cyprus and their effect on bilateral contacts between Greece and Israel*

The arrest of Archbishop Makarios on 9 March 1956 and his exile to the Seychelles came as a shock to the Greeks. These developments seemed to go against Konstantinos Karamanlis' pre-election optimism with respect to the prospects of the Makarios–Harding negotiations, and provided the left-wing opposition with an opportunity to criticize the right-wing government party. Initially the Greek government did not prohibit spontaneous protests in the country's major cities but, subsequently, it imposed strict police measures which it justified by saying that they were instigated by communists with a view to destabilizing the country. The newly appointed Israeli diplomatic representative in Athens, Avraham Darom, did not agree. In a relevant report on events in Greece, he wrote:

> The government's view was not substantiated by any clear testimony and, despite the fact that the anti-communist measures are still in force, no communist has been brought to trial. On the other hand, although one might well conclude that the largely anti-British demonstrations will lead to further destabilisation, the demonstrations themselves are not necessarily driven or organized by the communists alone.[181]

Moreover, Avraham Darom noted the uneasiness that prevailed in Athens following Makarios' sudden banishment. The Greek ambassador to London was recalled while the Greek government provided assurances behind the scenes that diplomatic relations with Britain would not be severed, as also confirmed by the British ambassador in Athens, Sir Charles Peake. Nevertheless, no one was surprised by the Greek decision to ask the UN secretary general to put the Cyprus issue up for debate at the next General

---

[179] ISA/RG93/MFA/2156/7, Kidron to British Commonwealth Division (2164/14-102-6.7.1956).
[180] ISA/RG93/MFA/2156/7, Kidron to British Commonwealth Division (2405/102-10.10.1956). Cf. ISA/RG93/MFA/3122/38, Her Majesty's Stationary Office (HMSO), *Constitutional Proposals for Cyprus: A Report Submitted to the Secretary of State for the Colonies by the Right Hon. Lord Radcliffe, GBE* (London: HMSO, 1956); and Crouzet, *Conflit*, 849–927.
[181] ISA/RG93/MFA/263/6, Darom to West Europe Division (2126/20.3.1956).

Assembly. In Athens, meanwhile, the idea of submitting a request for an extraordinary resolution by the UN Security Council was also discussed. Such a move was certain to lead to a British veto, but it would also give the Greek side a chance to draw greater international attention to the Cyprus question. This caused uneasiness, as the minister of public administration under Karamanlis, Konstantinos Tsatsos, informed Darom cryptically that, 'The government is taking all measures necessary and we shall see how things develop before we decide on what further action to take.'[182]

While the Greek government appeared ill at ease, the British ambassador in Athens seemed quite untroubled both by the situation in Cyprus and relations between Britain and Greece. As Darom wrote in his report of 20 March 1956, Britain's priority, according to Peake, was 'to defeat EOKA's terrorism and, once this was accomplished, then a way would be found to continue discussions with the ultimate objective of implementing a regime of constitutional self-government'. According to Darom, Peake seemed certain that 'there are many players in Cyprus who are prepared to work with the British to reach an agreement on the future self-governance regime. However, they don't dare publicly express their opinion in fear of EOKA's response.'[183]

Israel did not share this view, believing that either the British could not see or did not want to face reality. Darom's assessment, shared by the Israeli Ministry of Foreign Affairs,[184] was that the British 'error in thinking that the Enosis issue was contrived and that it does not reflect the national sentiments of the Greek Cypriots. [...] Armed activity is not going to stop in Cyprus unless the British are prepared for bloodshed on the island. Even if they should reach this point and such a decision, international public opinion will not remain indifferent.' As regards the continuation of negotiations, Israeli diplomacy insisted that banishing Makarios was yet another tactical mistake for which London would sooner or later pay a heavy price. The 'reinstatement' of Makarios was merely a matter of time, and when it came about, the British would be compelled to sit down with him again at the negotiating table. The Israelis never openly expressed these views to the British.[185]

The situation became increasingly complex when on 23 April 1956, armed conflict spread between the island's Greek and Turkish inhabitants. As Israeli Consul Avraham Kidron reported from Nicosia,

clashes between the communities began after the events of 23.4.1956, when two members of EOKA entered the Turkish sector of Nicosia and attempted to kill a Greek-Cypriot policeman. However, they killed a Turkish Cypriot colleague of his by mistake. A manhunt ensued, during which one more Turkish Cypriot was killed. That is the reason fighting immediately broke out as the Turkish Cypriots sought retaliation. The British authorities imposed a curfew on the city's Turkish sector on 24.4.1956 in an attempt to defuse the situation, but to no avail.

---

[182] Ibid.
[183] Ibid.
[184] ISA/RG93/MFA/2156/7, British Commonwealth Division to Kidron (9234/ד – 16.3.1956) Kidron's reply to the British Commonwealth Division (1805/102-12.3.1956).
[185] Cf. 3.4.2.1.

Kidron concludes with the assessment that the bloodshed would continue and that 'it will be difficult for normal relations to resume between the two communities, which have so far been more or less good'.[186]

In 1956, international public attention over the repressive measures put in place by the British authorities intensified. The same was true for political and intellectual circles, public opinion and the press in Israel. Only three days after the news of Makarios' exile, the rector of the Hebrew University of Jerusalem, Benjamin Mazar, sent a message of support for the Cypriot cause to Konstantinos Kavassiadis, rector of the Aristotle University of Thessaloniki.[187]

Beginning in early May 1956, on the eve of the execution of Karaolis and Dimitriou,[188] and throughout that month, the pro-government newspaper *Ha-Boker* published regular reports from its Cyprus correspondent, Shlomo Shetkol, who gave a favourable account of the struggle of the Greek Cypriots and condemned the practices of the British. In his nine reports, Shetkol likened the situation on the island to that of the Jewish struggle against the British in Palestine, before the declaration of Israeli independence. *Ha-Boker* was the first Israeli newspaper to publish an interview with Georgios Grivas, the leader of EOKA who was wanted by the authorities. Shetkol revealed that he had managed to meet Grivas at his hideout with the help of some Greek Cypriot secondary school students. When he left Cyprus, Shetkol thanked the Israeli consulate in Nicosia for the help it had provided him.[189]

Other Israeli newspapers released articles in the same vein, much to Britain's displeasure. The Press Office of the British Armed Forces in Cyprus sent Avraham Kidron 500 British propagandist pamphlets, asking him to forward them to the Israeli media. The leaflets were accompanied by a letter from the head of the Press Office which read:

Dear Mr Kidron,

I am informed by recent British visitors to Israel that there is widespread ignorance among the Israeli public about the British case for remaining in Cyprus.

I feel that it is of the utmost importance in the interests of friendly relations between our two peoples that this misconception should be eliminated, if only because the presence of Britain in Cyprus provides a very strong source of support to Israel in the event of a major Arab aggression on her frontiers. If sovereignty were to pass to Greece and the British merely had a leased base on this island, it would be very doubtful whether it could be used against Arab wishes.

---

[186] ISA/RG93/MFA/263/3, Kidron to the British Commonwealth Division (1971/102-26.4.1956).
[187] ISA/RG93/MFA/263/6, The cable of 11.3.1956 from the rector of the Hebrew University of Jerusalem, Benjamin Mazar, to the rector of Aristotle University of Thessaloniki, Konstantinos Kavassiadis, reads as follows: 'Your cable received yesterday by Hebrew University with full sympathy and understanding. Watching closely fight of our Cyprus neighbours for emancipation. We pray for speedy peaceful settlement, conforming to ideals of freedom and self-determination.'
[188] Holland, *Britain and the Revolt in Cyprus*, 129–32.
[189] ISA/RG93/MFA/2156/7, Letter of thanks dated 27.5.1956 from Shlomo Shetkol to the Israeli consulate general in Nicosia.

In order to do something to make the true facts quite clear to influential Israeli citizens, both official and private, I am sending you herewith 500 copies of a pamphlet we have produced for British servicemen entitled 'Why We Are in Cyprus'.[190]

In conclusion the letter to Kidron noted that 'the Israeli public should also be made aware of Greek policy in the event of Cyprus passing under its sovereignty'. Attached to the letter was a transcribed excerpt from *Foni tis Patridas* (*Voice of the Motherland*), a programme broadcast by Athens Radio for Cyprus which referred in the warmest of terms to the historical ties between Greece and the Arab world. It spoke of a common struggle against colonization and the prospects of cooperation between Greece and Egypt, Jordan, Syria, Lebanon, Iraq and Saudi Arabia, once the British were out of Cyprus and Enosis became a fact.[191]

British efforts to sway Israeli public opinion proved fruitless nor was any attempt in this regard made on the Israeli side. The dramatic events in Cyprus left no room for alternative interpretations. On the eve of the execution of two young Cypriot fighters, Michail Karaolis and Andreas Dimitriou, the young Queen Elizabeth was besieged by international pleas for their pardon. The Speaker of the Greek Parliament, Konstantinos Rodopoulos, urged his foreign counterparts to put pressure on London to avert the execution. The Speaker of the Israeli Parliament, Yosef Shprinzak, responded to Rodopoulos' appeal and sent a cable to his British counterpart, calling for the reprieve of Michail Karaolis. The wording of Shprinzak's cable clearly stressed the moral ground of the Cypriot armed struggle for freedom and self-determination:

> In response to a moving appeal from the Speaker of the Greek Parliament, I would beg you on humanitarian grounds to consider using your good offices to seek to prevent the execution of the Cypriot Michael Karaolis. Whatever may have been the nature of the deed, Karaolis acted in the belief that he was fighting for the liberty and self-determination of his people. I trust that you will find it possible to intervene for the reprieve of Karaolis as a human act of clemency.[192]

When Evangelos Averoff, the new Minister of Foreign Affairs, assumed office, Greece submitted a package of proposed resolutions on the Cyprus issue to the US and British governments. These resolutions determined that constitutional elections would take place for a parliament comprising a Greek Cypriot majority, while the British governor would retain his powers in matters of defence and foreign policy and responsibility for issues of public order over a one-year period. In the course of the next five to eight years, Cypriot citizens would exercise the right of self-determination,

---

[190] ISA/RG93/MFA/263/6, The letter dated 21.7.1956 with ref. no. PR/1 from Colonel J. M. White, an official with the Press Office of the British Armed Forces in Cyprus, to Kidron.

[191] Ibid. Attached to White's letter to Kidron was the English translation of the transcribed excerpt from the programme, 'I Foni tis Patridos' ['Voice of the Motherland'], broadcast by the Athens Radio Station on 23.5.1956 to Cyprus, via retransmission from Rhodes.

[192] ISA/RG93/MFA/263/6, West Europe Division to Darom (236/٦ – 13.5.1956).

whereupon a referendum would be held to determine whether or not they wished to unite the island with Greece. In the event that Cyprus proceeded to unification with Greece, the Greek proposal provided for specific issues regarding the citizenship of Turkish Cypriots, the establishment of two British military bases – one in Cyprus and one in Greece – as well as the establishment of two or three free ports in Cyprus to serve Turkish trade without requiring payment of customs duties to the Greek state.[193] The potential for creating 'free ports' in Cyprus piqued Israel's interest in the hope that Greece would be willing to facilitate not only Turkish commerce, but Israeli trade as well.

The customary initial meeting took place on 9 July 1956 between the Israeli diplomatic representative in Athens, Avraham Darom, and Evangelos Averoff. The two focused exclusively on developments in the Cyprus issue and particularly on the recent Greek proposals. Averoff wished to pass on a number of messages to the Israelis. In response to Turkish claims that in the event of Enosis, Greek military forces would land on nearby Turkish shores, Averoff was adamant that such a possibility was unthinkable. Both Greece and Turkey, which was friendlier to Israel, were members of the North Atlantic Alliance. Though not explicitly stated by the Greek foreign minister, one might deduce from this that as relations between NATO member Turkey and Israel were good, relations between Israel and NATO member Greece must also be good.

Averoff took things a step further. At the aforementioned meeting, he stressed the economic importance of Cyprus not only for Greece and Turkey but for Eastern Mediterranean countries in general – and in particular for Israel. Among other ideas he put forward, in the event of Enosis, two or three free ports would be established to serve Turkish trade without paying Greek customs duties.[194] This, according to Averoff, would not only boost the Turkish economy but would also be of great benefit to other neighbouring countries, including Israel. The Greek Minister of Foreign Affairs referred extensively to Israel, stating that 'given its industrial development, Israel is the country that will benefit most from such an arrangement',[195] without, however, specifying which Greek measures would benefit the Israeli side.

According to the reviewed Israeli archival material, these Greek proposals were the first to link Israeli regional interests to the policy Greece hoped to implement in Cyprus. Nevertheless, Averoff made it clear to Darom that Greece's de jure recognition of Israel was not a timely matter for discussion. The need to rally Arab votes in favour of Greek positions at the impending UN General Assembly took precedence.[196]

Averoff's approach undoubtedly proved a pleasant surprise for his Israeli counterpart. On the other hand, Darom was convinced that the proposals from Athens would not be accepted by the British.[197] Indeed, he believed that, as far as the Cyprus issue was concerned, Greece had very little room to manoeuvre. At a general session of

---

[193] Hatzivassiliou, *To Kypriako Zitima*, 84–5.
[194] Ibid.
[195] ISA/RG93/MFA/263/6, Darom to the West Europe Division (2680/9.7.1956), Customary meeting with the Greek minister of foreign affairs, Evangelos Averoff.
[196] Ibid.
[197] Hatzivassiliou, *To Kypriako Zitima*, 85–6.

Parliament to discuss Greece's next moves with regard to Cyprus, Avraham Darom expressed his concerns about the position Greece then held on the international diplomatic chessboard, saying among other things:

The feeling that Greece is more internationally isolated than ever, with regard to the Cyprus issue, grows day by day. In any event, however, even if to some it seems that this is untimely, Greece seems determined to raise this issue again at the next UN General Assembly.

In fact, the Greek government has no other choice, since the issue of Cyprus has become a national issue. And no government, other than a military dictatorship, would have the power to announce that the issue of Cyprus should be put off indefinitely until there is a better chance for a more desirable outcome.

And what would happen next? It is difficult to predict developments after the General Assembly, when Greece will most certainly fail once again. Is this something the government will leave to EOKA? Will it try to coerce its allies, turning to the Russians or the Non-Aligned? Will it try to reach a compromise with the Turks? Will it be able to continue along the same lines, failing again and again at the UN?

I will not even attempt to answer such difficult questions and prefer to let time provide the answers.[198]

On 27 October 1956, when the British, French and Israeli military forces were making their final preparations before invading Egypt, London rejected Averoff's proposals on Cyprus.[199] No one was surprised, and apparently, neither was Greece.

3.4.2.3 Upset in Turco-Israeli relations and the possibility of a pro-Greek Israeli reversal, 1956

When it became known in mid-January 1955 that the signing of a military cooperation agreement between Turkey and Iraq was imminent, Israeli political leaders were concerned. Britain's intervention and reassurances from the Foreign Office that Israel would not be threatened by the Baghdad Pact set the Israeli Foreign Ministry's mind at ease for the time being.[200] Nevertheless, the events that followed cast a shadow over bilateral relations between Ankara and Jerusalem, as the pessimistic Israeli predictions seemed to be coming true.

A sober indication of Turkey's revised foreign policy for the Middle East emanated from the remarks of the director general of the Turkish Ministry of Foreign Affairs, Nuri Birgi, to Israel's ambassador to Ankara, Maurice Fischer, on 11 November 1955. A report by Israel's diplomatic delegation to the Turkish capital contains Birgi's

---

[198] ISA/RG93/MFA/263/6, Darom to the West Europe Division (2756/23.7.1956).
[199] Hatzivassiliou, *Britain and International Status*, 80.
[200] Cf. 3.3.2.1.

comments word for word, as he explicitly outlined Turkey's diplomatic priorities at that time:

> The Soviet threat to Turkey is very real and the Arab–Israeli conflict is an obstacle to forming an overall security mechanism for the Middle East. Thus, we have before us two possibilities: We either wait until the Arab–Israeli conflict is resolved, or have a security mechanism for the Middle East formulated immediately. As a result of the Soviet threat, Turkey has decided to take immediate action and must now choose between siding with Israel or with the Arabs. Because of their majority population and the breadth of territory under their control, Turkey prefers the Arabs. [...] Turkey will have to take care not to create needless obstacles in its approach to the Arabs. For this reason, and as regards issues of security, Israel should gradually withdraw to the side-lines – at least until the Arab-Israeli conflict is resolved. In addition, Turkish officials will refrain from public declarations of friendship with Israel, as they could be interpreted by the Arabs as being hostile to them.[201]

As evident in the ensuing months, Ankara followed this tactic to the letter. On the other hand, both the Turkish Foreign Ministry, with its communiqué to the Israeli government in May 1955, and Turkey's foreign minister himself in a meeting with Maurice Fischer in Ankara in late December 1955,[202] provided assurances that 'Turco-Israeli relations would not be negatively affected,' and therefore Israel had nothing whatsoever to worry about.

Nevertheless, the Israelis remained uneasy. Throughout 1955, Turkey kept its distance from Israel and expressed support for Arab positions in various ways. Aside from its participation in the Bandung Conference,[203] Turkey made systematic efforts to draw Lebanon and Jordan into the Baghdad Pact. For example, in May 1955, Turkey took part in the Pan-Arab Economic Summit in Beirut. A month later, during an official visit by Iraqi monarch Faisal II to Ankara, Turkish President Celâl Bayar took the opportunity to stress the need 'for a resolution to the issue of Palestine in conjunction with the Arab countries'.

During the same period, Turkey criticized Israel for isolated armed incidents between Israel, Syria and Egypt along the border of the Golan Heights and the Gaza Strip.

Statements by Bayar while on an official visit to Jordan in November 1955 also caused a reaction in Israel. Addressing senior officials of the Arab Legion at a military outpost along the ceasefire line and on the Jabal al-Radar promontory, where the entire

---

[201] ISA/RG93/MFA/8693/3, Research Division (1122/20.3.1956). The report by the Research Division includes the report by the second secretary of Israel's Diplomatic Mission in Ankara, Barouch Gilead, with an overview of relations between Israel and Turkey from the signing of the cooperation agreement between Turkey and Iraq (Baghdad Pact) on 12.1.1955 to March 1956.

[202] ISA/RG93/MFA/8693/3, Research Division (1103/25.1.1956). The document includes a report by Israel's Chargé d'Affaires in Ankara Maurice Fischer on his meeting with Turkish Foreign Minister Fuat Köprülü, who had recently assumed office.

[203] Cf. 3.3.2.1 and 3.3.2.2.

Mediterranean coastline of Israeli territory was visible to the naked eye, Bayar told the officers of the Jordanian armed forces: 'Don't be surprised if one day you see the Turkish Army fighting alongside the Arab Legion against the invader, if Jordan should ever come under attack.'[204] The Turkish president's statements did not only raise eyebrows in Israel, but in Turkey as well. The following month, opposition party legislators sent a parliamentary inquiry to the Turkish Grand National Assembly about whether Turkey had, in fact, committed to engaging in an armed struggle against Israel in defence of Jordan's territorial integrity. Foreign Minister Fuat Köprülü, who was called upon to respond, attempted to allay fears with a vague mention of adherence to the principles and decisions of the UN in regard to the Palestinian issue, and Turkey's contribution to maintaining world peace, citing as an example the deployment of Turkish troops to the Korean War.[205] In this way, the Turkish government gave Israel the impression that nothing was out of the question, but it stopped short of confirming anything that had been said or implied.

Nuri Birgi, director general of the Turkish Foreign Ministry, had informed the Israelis in so many words of the public relations interests Turkey had to serve. Regardless of the grandiose public statements coming from official lips, however, Turkey's prominently pro-Arab stance was due to deeper issues. The Iraqi government was not in a position to convince other powerful Arab countries, such as Egypt and Syria, to enter into the pro-West Baghdad Pact. According to Israeli assessments, Turkey would have to make an effort to expand its influence over the remaining pro-West Arab countries in the region – Jordan and Lebanon – in order to include them, either officially or unofficially, in this new framework of regional cooperation which served British interests.

With such assumptions in mind, Israel demonstrated tolerance and patience with what it sometimes heard from Ankara, in the full knowledge that the axis with Turkey was invaluable and irreplaceable. Nevertheless, after the Suez Crisis broke out in late October 1956, Turkey recalled its ambassador from Tel Aviv on 26 November in a show of solidarity with the Arab world. This act left the Israelis with the impression that Ankara had decided to 'switch camps' after all and to re-evaluate its relationship with the Jewish state.

The Turkish ambassador was recalled shortly before the Cyprus question was to come up for debate before the UN General Assembly. Israel's Ministry of Foreign Affairs had been engaged at the time in final consultations on its position vis-à-vis Greece and the Greek Cypriots and it had not forgotten that Turkey carefully avoided linking differences with Greece to its relations with Israel. Specifically, in the pogroms of 6 and 7 September 1955, Turkish mobs attacked Greek residents of Istanbul and their properties, but incidentally vandalized Jewish properties in the city as well. The Israeli Ministry of Foreign Affairs was taken aback when the Turkish diplomatic mission in Tel Aviv hastened to apologize officially for those violent incidents, because precisely then, Turkish officials were touting in every way possible the importance of

---

[204] ISA/RG93/MFA/8693/3, Research Division (1101/18.1.1956). Report from the second secretary of Israel's Diplomatic Mission in Ankara, Barouch Gilead.
[205] Ibid.

ties between their country and the Arab world.[206] This gave the Israelis pause, and they began to perceive the web of Greek–Turkish differences in a new light, as the UN debate on the Cyprus issue neared.

Thus, on 28 November 1956, just two days after the recall of the Turkish ambassador, Foreign Ministry Director General Walter Eytan sent a written recommendation to Foreign Minister Meir, to the Office of Prime Minister Ben-Gurion and to Israel's permanent representation at the UN, proposing to support the Greek positions on the Cyprus question at the upcoming General Assembly, and noting:

> I am under the impression that this action by the Turks [that is, recalling their ambassador from Tel Aviv] should remove any reservations we may have as to the issue of our stance on the Cyprus issue. In my opinion, there is no longer any obstacle preventing us from supporting the Greek claims. Besides, this would also make us more sympathetic to the bloc of Afro-Asian countries.[207]

3.4.3 The Israeli vote on the Cyprus issue at the 11th Session of the UN General Assembly

On 15 November 1956, the Cyprus question was entered on the agenda for the 11th Session of the UN General Assembly,[208] and Israeli diplomacy was once again faced with a decision on the stance it would adopt.

Following Makarios' exile to the Seychelles, the Greek government was left with no choice but to appeal once again to the UN, though it knew this would not end the deadlock. Entering this appeal was not just a means of exerting pressure on the British but a way of raising Greek Cypriot morale following the arrest and exile of Makarios, as Prime Minister Karamanlis posited before the Greek Parliament.[209] The Greek draft resolution sought the recognition of the Cypriot people's right to self-determination.[210]

This time, however, Britain submitted its own appeal to the United Nations, with a request to 'consider the external attempt to change the status of Cyprus by force and subversion, and the methods used by those in Greece who supported terrorism in Cyprus'.[211]

---

[206] ISA/RG93/MFA/8693/3, Research Division (1122/20.3.1956). The Research Division report includes a report by the second secretary of Israel's Diplomatic Mission to Ankara, Barouch Gilead, providing an overview of Turkish–Israeli relations from 12.1.1955 to early March 1956.

[207] ISA/RG93/MFA/3122/38, Eytan to Meir and the Israeli Permanent Representation to the UN, copied to the Office of the Prime Minister, the British Commonwealth, Western Europe and the UN Divisions, the Israeli embassy in London and Israeli's diplomatic representation in Athens (4241/א – 28.11.1956).

[208] Crouzet, *Conflit*, 860.

[209] Xydis, 'The UN General Assembly', 144–5.

[210] Ibid., *Cyprus: Conflict and Conciliation*, 573–8. The application of 13.3.1956 submitted by Greece's permanent representative to the UN to the secretary general of the UN regarding, 'Application, under the auspices of the United Nations, of the principle of equal rights and self-determination of peoples in the case of the population of the Island of Cyprus', and the memorandum of 12.6.1956.

[211] Ibid., 579–80. The application of 12.10.1956 submitted by United Kingdom's permanent representative to the UN to the secretary general of the UN for the purpose of including the appeal in the agenda of the 11th Session of the UN General Assembly: 'Support from Greece for terrorism in Cyprus', and the Explanatory Memorandum of 12.11.1956.

Greece responded to the British request with a second draft resolution which provided for the establishment of an international commission of inquiry composed of the representatives of seven UN member states who would investigate British charges against the Greek state for supporting Cypriot terrorists and, concurrently, look into Greek complaints about violations of human rights by British authorities in Cyprus.[212]

To determine its stance, Israel had to consider a number of criteria. The tension in Cyprus naturally evoked memories of the Jewish armed struggle against the British. Turkey, however, had recalled its ambassador from Tel Aviv as a token of support for the Arab world, protesting the Israeli advance into the Sinai Peninsula. This move, as Israel understood it, showed Ankara's intention to secure as many Arab votes as possible at the UN in favour of its positions on the Cyprus issue, but also revealed its intent to boost its regional role in the spirit and objective of the pro-British Baghdad Pact. Meanwhile, however, the after-effects of the Suez Crisis pressured Israel to give careful thought to its close ties with Britain.

According to the assessment of Israel's diplomatic representative in Athens, Avraham Kidron, the Greek efforts at the UN had no hope of success.[213] Nevertheless, Kidron noted with great interest the heightened activity and concerted efforts of the Greek Ministry of Foreign Affairs to secure as many favourable votes as possible in the forthcoming balloting. Evangelos Averoff was named to head up the Greek delegation that would take part in the General Assembly. Meanwhile, during September–October of 1956, senior Greek officials were sent off to persuade various governments that they should adopt a pro-Greek stance. Speaker of the Greek Parliament Rodopoulos visited Austria, France, Spain and Portugal. Minister without Portfolio Grigorios Kassimatis visited India, Burma, Ceylon, Indonesia and the Philippines; and a senior official from the Ministry of Foreign Affairs was dispatched to the remaining Asian countries. Minister of Transport and Public Works, Georgios Rallis, visited the Scandinavian countries, Belgium, the Netherlands and Luxembourg. MP Petros Garoufalias joined diplomatic delegations to the People's Republics of Eastern Europe and the Director of the 4th Department of the Ministry of Foreign Affairs toured Latin America.

In assessing the contacts made by Greek officials abroad, and according to information he had garnered, Darom noted that the Greek line of argument varied from case to case.[214] Specifically, in the so-called 'anti-colonialist' countries, Greece appeared to be highly critical of Britain's colonial policy whilst offering assurances that Greece did not intend to place Cyprus under Greek sovereign rule while allowing the 'British colonial' bases to remain on the island. Its only objective was a genuine realization of the right to self-determination for the residents of Cyprus. In this way, it countered any reservations voiced by some Third World countries, predominantly India, which were not eager to support Greek positions, either because they were thought to mask expansionist tendencies,[215] or because they were seen as essentially

---

[212] Xydis, 'The UN General Assembly', 145.
[213] ISA/RG93/MFA/263/6, Darom to the West Europe Division (2756/23.7.1956). Cf. 3.4.22.
[214] ISA/RG93/MFA/263/6, Darom to the West Europe Division (3165/23.10.1956).
[215] Xydis, *Cyprus: Conflict and Conciliation*, 41–2. India's positions on the Cyprus issue. Statements by the head of India's Permanent Representation to the UN Krishna Menon before the Political Committee.

pro-British.[216] In contrast, the Greek line of argument to NATO member states stressed the risk of a potential rise of the Left should the efforts of the Karamanlis government fail, while at the same time, maintaining its determination to seek a solution acceptable to the NATO states involved in the Cyprus conflict, namely Britain and Turkey.

Avraham Darom found the multifaceted nature of the Greek line of argument East and West to be not entirely appropriate. Greece was not stating its positions clearly but 'ultimately painting a blurred picture which would hardly produce positive results'.[217] Via his contacts with Greek and British officials in Athens, Darom concluded that the Cyprus issue would be among the last items discussed when the General Assembly vote took place in February of 1957. According to the Israelis, this was not a matter of chance. They believed that both Britain and Greece intended to delay debate over the Cyprus question as long as possible, in the hopes that a compromise would be reached in the meantime.[218]

Purely in Greek-Israeli terms, Darom noted that since his meeting with Evangelos Averoff on 9 July 1956 and until the Suez Crisis in late October of that year, no Greek official had made any rapprochement to secure a favourable Israeli vote during the upcoming UN balloting.[219] This was interpreted as resulting from the increased tension between Israel and Egypt.[220] At the same time, statements from the Arab world in favour of Makarios and the placement of Cyprus under Greek control were arriving fast and furious. An example of many reports in this vein is an extensive one from Alexandria, published in the Cypriot newspaper *Ethnos* on 30 May 1956, which noted that:

> A reliable Egyptian source stated that the Arab countries will intervene and act within the framework of the United Nations for Makarios' immediate release, and will also strongly support the idea of placing Cyprus under Greek rule. The same source notes that the Arab countries do not intend to press Greece to concede military bases to them in Cyprus.[221]

---

[216] ISA/RG93/MFA/263/6, Darom to Asia Division (2566/11.6.1956). Darom sets out the Greek concerns arising from the statements made by India's ambassador in Athens, John Thivy, during a press conference on 8.6.1956. Thivy expressed the view that India had not yet adopted a position on the Cyprus issue due to Eden's tactical shift in declaring that Britain supposedly 'no longer intends to maintain its bases in Cyprus', while during the same period, the Greek side offered assurance that in the event of the island's Enosis, 'British interests in the region would not be prejudiced', implying that the British military forces would ultimately remain on the island. Thivy's statements allegedly alarmed Athens at the time, primarily due to India's significant influence over the Afro-Asian countries. Darom to the West Europe Division (2636/27.6.1956). Cf. *Kathimerini* and *Estia* (7.6.1956 and 8.6.1956 respectively), on the controversial statements by Prime Minister Konstantinos Karamanlis on the intention of the Greek government to agree to keep the British bases in Cyprus after the island's unification with Greece.

[217] ISA/RG93/MFA/263/6, Darom to West Europe Division (3165/23.10.1956).

[218] Ibid.

[219] Ibid.

[220] Herzog, *Arab–Israeli Wars*, 111–14, 141.

[221] ISA/RG93/MFA/263/6, *Ethnos*, 30.5.1956.

Apparently, Greece did not want to risk losing favourable Arab votes, and thus did not pursue further contact with the Israeli side.

Nevertheless, as strange as it may sound, the views in Israel's Ministry of Foreign Affairs turned in favour of the Greek position, as reflected in a report from the meeting held on 21 October 1956, under the newly appointed Minister of Foreign Affairs, Golda Meir.[222]

At the meeting a question was raised about whether or not the EOKA struggle should be defined as terrorism. In an effort to secure Israel's support for the upcoming UN vote, Britain had argued that EOKA's operations were no different from the raids carried out by paramilitary Arab Fedayeen who entered Israel clandestinely from Jordan, Syria and Egypt to attack targets in urban centres. This line of reasoning was not adopted by the Israeli Ministry of Foreign Affairs, which concluded that, unlike the attacks of the Fedayeen 'which were truly acts of terrorism driven from abroad', the EOKA struggle was not. 'There is a nation in Cyprus fighting to realise its will, and it is supported from the outside.' In other words, Israel did not agree with Britain's theory and concluded that EOKA's activities were a struggle to liberate a nation, not acts of terrorism. The report documenting the content of the meeting of 21 October 1956 concluded: 'As regards Greece's political claim, we believe that if the people who live in Cyprus want a specific situation, then who are we to oppose it at a time when we ourselves called for a National Home?' Nonetheless, it was understood that if Israel were to openly adopt such a stance, it would have to deal with the displeasure of Turkey, 'which, compared to Greece, is clearly more important to Israeli interests', the report noted.

Thus it was decided that Israel would support the motion to include both the Greek and British requests regarding the Cyprus issue in the agenda of the General Assembly. On the substance of the matter, an attempt would be made to support Greece against Turkey. Israel would also support any initiative on peace negotiations. In an attempt to maintain a carefully balanced stance, it was decided that the Israeli permanent representative to the UN would explain his vote, emphasizing the historical ties between Israel and the Greek Cypriots,[223] along with the fact that Israel fully understood Ankara's concerns over protecting the Turkish minority on the island. Of interest was the Israeli assessment that Turkey would ultimately find an appropriate way to avoid siding with Britain until the very end and that it would prefer a compromise with Greece, 'even to the detriment of its own minority'.[224]

The overall sense seemed to be that open support for Greece on the Cyprus issue would not impair British–Israeli relations. The meeting had taken place just a week

---

[222] ISA/RG93/MFA/263/6, Meir Meir, UN Division of Political Affairs to the Israeli Diplomatic Mission in Ankara, with a copy to the Israeli permanent delegation to the UN, the Israeli embassy in London, the Israeli diplomatic mission in Athens, Western Europe and British Commonwealth Divisions (23.10.1956, not recorded as incoming document, top secret). Decisions of the meeting of 21.10.1956 on the Israeli stance in the forthcoming vote on the Cypriot issue during the 11th Session of the UN General Assembly.

[223] Cf. 2.2.

[224] ISA/RG93/MFA/263/6, Meir Meir (23.10.1956).

before the Suez Crisis broke out when Israeli, British and French mobilizations were well underway. It is not out of the question, then, that Israel's impending and cautious pro-Greek turn on the Cyprus issue was a response to the potential international outcry that was sure to follow a planned invasion of Egypt. An 'anti-colonialist' Israeli vote on Cyprus would make a strong counter-argument to censure the Arabs and the Non-Aligned. Nevertheless, it is impossible to guess what the Israeli Ministry of Foreign Affairs might have decided had the 21 October 1956 meeting taken place *after* the launch of British–French–Israeli operations against Nasserist Egypt.

On 25 October 1956, three days before the Suez Crisis, the Ministry of Foreign Affairs had sent a memo to Israel's permanent representative to the UN with instructions on how to handle the Cyprus issue at the 11th Session:[225]

> The Israeli delegation will support Britain's wish to include its request in the agenda referring to Greek involvement in Cyprus, since Greece also wishes to discuss this request. The Israeli delegation will support Greece's requests with regard to the right of self-determination for the Cypriot people and the adoption of measures to protect human rights. [...] The Israeli delegation will support a resolution calling for the commencement of peace negotiations. Depending on the motions for resolutions to be submitted, the Israeli delegation, after first consulting with the Ministry of Foreign Affairs, will take any actions necessary to make it possible to support Greece over Britain, without causing any detriment to Turkey.[226]

This puzzling formulation demonstrates Israel's intention to draw closer to Greek positions without disrupting its relations with Turkey or Britain – no simple matter. The discrepancies in it followed from the change of leadership in the Israeli Ministry of Foreign Affairs. For a number of reasons, the newly appointed foreign minister, Meir, wished to advance her country's diplomatic relations with the Third World, primarily with the African countries just then breaking free of colonialist repression, and in order to achieve that goal, Israel had to prove that it did not stand with the supporters of colonialism. Given the circumstances, it is quite possible that Meir anticipated the international response, and first and foremost the reaction of the Eastern Bloc and Third World countries, to Israel's involvement in the Franco-British operation. An anti-colonialist vote on the Cyprus question would show that Israel was ideologically opposed to colonialism and give the international community to understand that Israel's participation in the Suez War was a defensive act against Nasserist expansionism.

Notwithstanding her motives, Meir gave the impression that she was not in alignment with the views of her predecessor, Moshe Sharett, with regard to the Cyprus issue and the situation on the island in general.[227] Perhaps this was because she had herself visited the Karaolos detention camps as an envoy of the Jewish Agency, and had

[225] Israel State Archives, Barouch Gilead, ed., *Israeli Foreign Policy Documents* (Jerusalem: Government Printer, 2008), vol. 11, 822–5 no. 502, UN Division to the Israeli Permanent Delegation to the UN (25.10.1956).
[226] Ibid., 824.
[227] Cf. 3.3 5.

seen first-hand the assistance offered by Greek Cypriots to the detainees and the Haganah cells.[228] Perhaps she also hoped that Greek-Israeli relations would improve during her term in office.

The Suez War broke out just one week after the Ministry of Foreign Affairs meeting on 21 October 1956, and Israel launched its 'Operation Kadesh' in the Sinai Peninsula on 29 October.[229] Turkey decided to recall its ambassador from Tel Aviv as a token of support for the Arab world.[230] This played havoc with Israel's decision to support the Greek positions on the Cyprus issue before the UN.[231]

The strong anti-West after-effects of the military invasion of Suez[232] put Israel in a difficult position. Its embassies around the world actively engaged in trying to convince the international community that Israel's participation in the Franco-British campaign against Egypt was a defensive act, but their arguments fell on deaf ears. Meanwhile in Greece, the press was focused more on developments in Cyprus than on the Suez Crisis. Still, it was practically impossible in pro-Arab Greece to elicit statements or reports favourable to Israel.[233]

As Yehuda Horam,[234] secretary of the Israeli diplomatic representation in Athens, noted in his report, he had tried to find an opportunity to approach the Greek Ministry of Foreign Affairs with the information that Israel intended to support the Greek positions at the impending UN General Assembly. However, because he had been unable to make contact, he proposed that Israel should about-face in favour of Greece during the UN vote without informing Athens in advance. Horam believed that Israel's favourable attitude would come as a pleasant surprise to the Greeks, and might in fact improve bilateral relations in future.

Ultimately, despite the decisions taken, the Israeli turn in favour of Greece was never expressed at the 11th Session of the UN General Assembly, and moreover, as evidenced in Israeli archival materials, Meir's intentions were never made known to Athens either. The turbulence caused by the Suez War, the distance Washington kept from the military operations against Egypt and the withdrawal of the British, French and Israelis from Egyptian territories[235] forced Israel not to diverge from the British line in any way. As the vote on the Cyprus issue drew close, the Foreign Office sent Israel a written plea to support the British positions.[236] Harold Macmillan who had just

[228] Laub, *Last Barrier*, 81–3. Cf. 2.2.
[229] Kyle, *Suez*, 347–52.
[230] Cf. 3.4.2.3.
[231] ISA/RG93/MFA/263/6, Eytan to Golda Meir and the Israeli permanent delegation to the UN, with copies to the Prime Minister's Office, British Commonwealth, Western Europe and UN Divisions, the Israeli embassy in London and the Israeli diplomatic mission in Athens (4241/א – 28.11.1956). Cf. 3.4.2.3.
[232] Kyle, *Suez*, 392–6.
[233] ISA/RG130/MFA/3122/38, Horam to Eytan (0/16-3.1.1957).
[234] Ibid.
[235] Kyle, *Suez*, 478. US President Dwight Eisenhower, in a message to Israeli Prime Minister Ben-Gurion, harshly criticized the latter's statements made in a speech before the Knesset that Israel did not intend to withdraw from the Sinai.
[236] ISA/RG130/MFA/3122/38, Sir John Nicholls, the British Ambassador in Tel Aviv, to Eytan (2212/57-7.2.1957). Nicholls sought Israeli support at the UN about the issue of Cyprus, attaching a draft motion for a resolution that turned against Greece for the aid provided to EOKA's armed struggle.

become prime minister was determined to bridge the differences between London and Washington on managing the balance in the Middle East,[237] and Israel knew perfectly well that a restored British–US axis could advance Israeli interests in the region. Nevertheless, Israel avoided committing to London's request, thinking it prudent to maintain a wait-and-see position, in the hope that by the time the Cyprus vote came around, either the US would take a diplomatic initiative of some sort to defuse tensions,[238] or else Turkey would indicate its interest in restoring relations with Israel.

In the long run, this 'wait and see' approach proved beneficial for Israel: On 1 February 1957, Gideon Rafael from the UN Division and Abba Eban, Israel's permanent representative to the UN, met with the latter's Turkish counterpart, Selim Sarper. Sarper admitted off the record that the recall of the Turkish ambassador from Tel Aviv 'had been a mistake'. In fact, he revealed that the ambassador's recall had been decided at the urging of Britain and the US in order to 'save' the Baghdad Pact and the pro-British Iraqi government. Sarper noted that Ankara wished to smooth out bilateral relations with Israel as soon as possible. Specifically, in relation to the Cyprus issue, he asked the Israelis to mediate and persuade anti-colonialist Latin American countries[239] to refrain from supporting any proposal for direct negotiations between Britain and the Greek Cypriots – something Turkey wished to avoid at any price.[240]

Although this development was important for the prospect it offered of improving disrupted Israeli–Turkish relations, the Israeli side made no move to engage in mediation and did not reveal its planned position on Cyprus to London.[241] And based on Israeli archival materials, there is no evidence of contact between the Israeli permanent delegation to the UN and Greek officials at that time.

In the end, the issue of Cyprus was discussed before the First Political Committee and the General Assembly with neither Greece nor Britain submitting a request for a vote.[242] Both the committee and the General Assembly adopted the proposal from the Indian delegation, which was drafted in an very neutral tone. Decision No. 1013 (XI) reflected the belief that the matter should be resolved 'in an atmosphere of peace and freedom of expression', and that a 'peaceful, democratic and just solution' would be found 'in accord with the purposes and principles of the Charter of the United Nations', in the hope that 'negotiations will be resumed and continued to this end'. The text was inspired by India's permanent representative Krishna Menon.

Neutral though it was, the motion before the Political Committee was certainly not colourless. In Krishna Menon's opinion, the Cyprus question would best be approached

---

[237] ISA/RG130/MFA/3122/38, Eytan to Elath (30.1.1957, not recorded as incoming document).

[238] Claude Nicolet, *United States Policy towards Cyprus, 1954–1974: Removing the Greek-Turkish Bone of Contention* (Mannheim and Mohnesee: Bibliopolis, 2001), 95–6. The US was in favour of 'a decision on which all involved parties would agree' in a situation where relations between the US and Britain were being tested due to the after-effects of the Suez Crisis. Cf. ISA/RG130/MFA/3122/38, British Commonwealth Division to the Israeli embassy in London (20.2.1957, not marked as official entry).

[239] Turkey reintroduced the same request in August 1958. Cf. 3.6.4 and 3.6.5.

[240] ISA/RG93/MFA263/6, Rafael to the UN Division (2.2.1957, not recorded as incoming document).

[241] ISA/RG130/MFA/3122/38, British Commonwealth Division to Israeli Embassy in London (20.2.1957, not recorded as incoming document).

[242] Xydis, 'The UN General Assembly', 145.

on the basis of a discrete Cypriot nationality to which all island residents belonged, regardless of their origin, religion or language. In his argument, he postulated that, 'though many Cypriots speak Greek, it does not mean that they are Greek, no more than the citizens of the United States who speak English are British'. In fact, he expressed the hope that Greek Cypriots would realize that Cyprus' independence was the only solution to the problem and affirmed that India saw Cyprus as the birthplace of its inhabitants, with a right to be recognized as a discrete nationality, and to have their birthplace established as an independent state. Finally, it should be noted that the Indian diplomat essentially formulated the same views he had put forth at the 9th and 10th Session of the UN General Assembly in 1954 and 1955.[243]

Decision No 1013 (XI) was adopted by a large majority, with Greece, Britain and Turkey voting in favour. Israel opted to abstain, and its representative Amiel Najjar, in his report on the process, described the Indian proposal as 'nondescript and colourless', although it 'managed to salvage the situation at the very last moment', and fortunately, he added with some relief, it had not been necessary for him to open his mouth.[244]

Under its new political leadership, the Israeli Ministry of Foreign Affairs had initially decided to support the Greek positions, largely for reasons related to the general Middle East realignment in 1956. However, in the end, Israel's pro-Greek about-face was never manifested, in part because of the unfavourable fallout of the Suez Crisis, and in part because of the behind-the-scenes admission of the Turks that recalling their ambassador from Tel Aviv had been a mistake.

Under the circumstances, Israel once again avoided taking a clear position on the Cyprus issue, which, even if it had wanted to, would have been difficult to carry off. At the 11th Session, Israel found itself isolated from friends and foes alike because of the Suez Crisis and all that followed. Years later, Golda Meir described in her memoirs the tense climate created around Israel at those meetings:

> We have no family here. No one who shares our religion, our language or our past. The rest of the world seems to be grouped into blocs that have sprung up because geography and history have combined to give common interests to their peoples. But our neighbours – and natural allies – don't want to have anything to do with us, and we really belong nowhere and to no one, except on ourselves.[245]

In the midst of such an international outcry, Britain had become Israel's only supporter on the global chess board. Thus, if Israel decided to stand with Greece 'as a matter of principle', the only certainty was that it would alienate its last supporter. In addition to the foregoing, however, Washington's ever-increasing influence in the Middle East was an additional factor that Israel had to keep in mind – and Israel was

---

[243] Ibid., *Cyprus: Conflict and Conciliation*, 41–2.
[244] ISA/RG93/MFA/263/6, Amiel Najjar to the Israeli permanent representation to the UN (854/26.2.1957), Najjar's cable read verbatim as follows: 'The issue of Cyprus unfolded as expected. A toned-down Indian proposal somehow salvaged the situation at the last moment and received 44 votes. I didn't even open my mouth.'
[245] Meir, *My Life*, 317–18.

thus forced to reassess and review its adopted decision to support the Greek positions on the Cyprus issue at the 11th Session.[246]

Nevertheless, though circumstances forced the Israelis to remain firmly hitched to Britain's wagon, they were reluctant to consent to Greece's condemnation because it had supported EOKA – which London described as 'terrorist'.

The minutes of the 21 October 1956 meeting at the Israeli Ministry of Foreign Affairs reveal that Israeli diplomacy was unwilling to turn a blind eye to the national liberation aspect of EOKA. Thus, the fact that Israel chose to abstain at the 11th Session implies that something had begun to change in the way events on the neighbouring island were being assessed.

3.5 The Israeli stance on the Cyprus issue at the 12th Session of the UN General Assembly, 1957

Throughout 1957, Israeli diplomacy focused on the after-effects of the Suez Crisis and specifically on Israel's relations with the United States,[247] which had been critical of the British, French and Israeli joint military operations against Egypt. Turkey's pro-Arab stance and its recall of the ambassador from Tel Aviv the previous November, continued to be a matter of great concern for Israel. As Greek–Israeli relations remained cold, the Israelis opted to maintain a neutral attitude towards all matters related to the Cyprus issue. In any event, all indications were that the time was approaching for a change in the status quo, and the Israelis waited to see how things would turn out. In 1957, the Israeli consul in Nicosia began focusing for the first time on the political landscape emerging within Cyprus, in both the Greek and Turkish Cypriot communities.

3.5.1 Israeli concerns and speculations on British intentions and American pursuits in Cyprus

The decision of the British government to release Makarios from his exile in the Seychelles was officially announced in Cyprus at 6 pm local time on 29 March 1957 over BBC Radio, albeit, rumours of his release had been circulating since Greek Independence Day on 25 March.[248] The Israeli consul general in Nicosia, Peretz Leshem, gave a detailed account of the spontaneous celebrations and the uneasiness of the British authorities as to whether they should continue to implement the strict security measures which were still in force. The general feeling was that something very important was about to change. There was an atmosphere of optimism and anticipation reminiscent of the Jewish celebrations in Palestine on 29 November 1947, when the

---

[246] ISA/RG130/3122/38, British Commonwealth Division to the Israeli embassy in London (20.2.1957, not recorded as incoming document).

[247] Kyle, *Suez*, 477–9. On the disapproving reaction of US President Dwight Eisenhower to the statements made by Israeli Prime Minister David Ben-Gurion that Israel would not withdraw from the Sinai.

[248] Vlachos, *Enas Diplomatis*, 329–31.

UN General Assembly adopted the Partition Plan for the establishment of the State of Israel.

Leshem's report of 29 March 1957 gives a vivid account of the intense joy in the streets and the fragile balance in those days:

> Already since the previous evening, on March 28, 1957, prayers of gratitude were offered in Greek churches. The Greek population turned out full of enthusiasm and marched down the streets, waving Greek flags; young people participated in large numbers, dancing and singing in football stadiums and along the major roads of the city. Taxis and trucks drove through the streets carrying young people, even primary school children, throughout Nicosia shouting 'EOKA' and 'Enosis'. Church bells rang joyously all night long. At around 11 at night, I saw groups a happy crowd consisting of 80–100 persons standing outside the residence of the Greek Consul-General with Mr. Vlachos and his spouse and their assistants greeting them at the door. Police forces stood motionless and watched, despite the fact that there were many among the cheering crowd for whom curfew should be imposed due to their age. Such rallies have continued since then and up to now, March 29, 1957. Greek flags were raised at many houses, as they had a couple of days before on Greek Independence Day. But watching what is happening in the streets, there seems to be more to it than just flag-waving. The whole atmosphere was reminiscent of what it was like on the streets of Israel, on the eve of November 29, 1947. Stores and offices were closed and the people felt that an era was coming to an end and another was beginning, and that all their wishes would come true.[249]

Makarios' release marked the beginning of many changes. Leshem was a party not only to the hopes of the Greek Cypriots to be rid of colonial rule, but also to the concerns of the entrepreneurs on the island – regardless of their ethnic origins – about the possible economic impact that a political shift might bring. Naturally, the uncertainty felt by British officers at every level was also palpable.[250]

What most concerned Israel at that time was whether the next political regime – about which everyone was in the dark – would bring Greece face to face with Turkey, perhaps allowing the Arab regional element to make its presence felt not only in Cyprus itself, but in the region as a whole. Another issue preoccupying the Israelis was the discontinuation of military construction works and the cancellation of contracts for projects which had already been assigned to Israeli companies.[251] When it was decided in August 1957 to suspend emergency security measures, there was a sense that Britain

---

[249] ISA/RG93/MFA/2156/7, Peretz Leshem, Israeli consul in Nicosia to the British Commonwealth Division (369/102-29.3.1957). On 29 November 1947, the UN adopted the Partition Plan for Palestine which called for the establishment of two states, Jewish and Arab. The news was met with frenzied celebrations in the Jewish communities of British-held Palestine.

[250] ISA/RG93/MFA/2156/7, Leshem to the British Commonwealth Division (3519/102-26.6.1957). Assessments by local British officials, public figures from the Greek Cypriot community and foreigners living on the island for decades.

[251] Ibid.

would significantly curtail its military presence on the island.[252] The Israelis hoped that Britain would not leave Cyprus in a disorderly manner – as in the case of Palestine – and that before turning over its authority, it would first make arrangements for all unresolved issues pertaining to the fragile balance in the Eastern Mediterranean.

At the same time, the United States stepped up its diplomatic presence in the region. A start had already been made in November 1956, when the US demanded that the British, French and Israelis withdraw from the Egyptian territory they had occupied during the Suez Crisis.[253] The Bermuda Talks in late March 1957 between US President Eisenhower and British Prime Minister Macmillan aimed at restoring the 'special relationship' that linked the two countries and at aligning their regional policies on issues of common interest. One of these was the balance of power in the Middle East and the Eastern Mediterranean. Britain welcomed the Eisenhower Doctrine, whereby the US would provide economic aid to pro-West regimes in the region. With regard to Cyprus in particular, the island would be more useful to Western regional plans as a military base than as a British colony.[254] In fact, according to historian Claude Nicolet, the Bermuda Talks allegedly played a key role in Britain's decision to release Makarios from exile, thus placing its negotiating strategy on new footing.[255] The same assessment was borne out by interdepartmental communications within the Israeli Ministry of Foreign Affairs. The Israelis believed that the decisions of the British to release Makarios and to appoint the more moderate Sir Hugh Foot as governor of Cyprus on 3 December 1957 were dictated by Washington.[256]

The Israeli Consul noted that his American counterpart, Taylor Belcher, made his presence increasingly felt in the summer of 1957 with public appearances and press conferences. 'He makes frequent appearances, but without having anything to say,' as Leshem pointedly noted, adding that, 'this energetic man who visits the leaders of both the Greek and Turkish communities and loves to be in the spotlight' wants to demonstrate that Britain is not the same as it once was and that 'if the US were in Cyprus, all the problems would have been resolved more easily'.[257] It follows from the review of Israeli diplomatic correspondence and the manner in which Leshem described American activity in Cyprus that the Israelis were not sufficiently aware of the tentative contacts being made by American diplomat Julius Holmes in London and Athens. In reality, Belcher's movements in Cyprus were all but superficial. From August to October of 1957, the US promoted a package of proposals known as the 'Holmes

[252] ISA/RG93/MFA/2156/7, Leshem to the British Commonwealth Division (102/2029-13.8.1957).
[253] Nicolet, *United States Policy towards Cyprus*, 77–98 and 99–102.
[254] United States Department of State, John P. Glennon (ed.), *Foreign Relations of the United States, 1955-1957: Soviet Union, Eastern Mediterranean* (Washington, DC: United States Government Printing Office, 1989), vol. 24, 464–7 no. 231–4. Cf. Giannis Sakkas, *I Ellada, to Kypriako kai o Aravikos Kosmos 1947-1974* [*Greece, the Cyprus Question and the Arab World 1947-1974*] (Athens: Patakis, 2012), 128–9.
[255] Nicolet, *United States Policy towards Cyprus*, 96–7; and Kyle, *Suez*, 542–3.
[256] ISA/RG93/MFA/2156/7, Leshem to the British Commonwealth Division (102/2119-24.10.1957), On Britain's decision to replace the intransigent Sir John Harding and appoint Sir Hugh Foot in his stead in December 1957.
[257] ISA/RG93/MFA/2156/7, Leshem to the British Commonwealth Division (102/2116-18.9.1957).

Mission' to resolve the Cyprus problem.[258] Specifically, in his letter of 6 June 1957, American diplomat – and US consul general in Tangier at the time – Julius Holmes, suggested to Secretary of State John Foster Dulles that a ten-year period of autonomy should be instituted in Cyprus, with the British governor retaining veto powers on a wide range of governance issues. This period would end with a referendum under NATO supervision. If the island's inhabitants voted in favour of Enosis in the referendum, the British would have to accept the outcome, and the minority rights of the Turkish Cypriots would be protected under special constitutional provisions. Meanwhile, starting from the period of the ten-year autonomy, Cyprus would be included in NATO's operational zone and the British would keep their bases on the island, regardless of the outcome of the referendum. The proposal met with a favourable response at the State Department and Holmes made concerted contacts in London, Athens and Ankara from August to October 1957 in order to sound out the governments concerned. London rejected the 'Holmes Mission' in October 1957, marking the end of the first US attempt at mediation in the Cyprus issue, aside from unofficial communications carried out by Dulles' personal friend, the Greek American businessman Spyros Skouras.

Beyond the erroneous impressions Israel had received from Leshem in Nicosia, information concerning American intentions for Cyprus was scant, as indicated by other diplomatic reports from that period. In a communication prepared on 14 July 1957, the head of the Israeli diplomatic delegation in Ankara, Moshe Alon, wrote that NATO Secretary General Paul-Henri Spaak had already recommended to the governments of Greece and Turkey that Cyprus should be made an independent state, guaranteed by UN member states which would be duly endorsed by both Athens and Ankara.[259] According to Alon, this piece of information was confirmed by the Belgian consul general in Ankara a month later.[260] But the information proved false.[261] Since Israel was not a member of NATO it was not in a position to receive prompt and reliable information on the manoeuvres or intentions of the US with regard to the Cyprus issue at the time.

3.5.2 The Turkish tactic of 'Islamization' of the Cyprus issue, according to Israeli diplomatic reports

On 17 April 1957, Athens was celebrating Makarios' arrival, but an entirely different climate prevailed in Ankara. The Turkish press condemned the release of 'the murderer, the despicable peasant priest', and expressed strong concerns about the British stance

---

[258] Nicolet, *United States Policy towards Cyprus*, 86–90.

[259] ISA/RG93/MFA/263/6, Moshe Alon, Israeli chargé d'affaires in Ankara, to the Western Europe and Research Divisions (520/3612/אנ – 14.7.1957).

[260] ISA/RG130/MFA/3122/38, Alon to the West Europe Division (594/3612/אנ – 16.8.1957) Reassurance of Belgium's ambassador in Ankara that the US were in full agreement with Spaak's proposal, confirming the content of Alon's report to the West Europe Division (Cf. 520/3612/אנ – 14.7.1957).

[261] Nicolet, *United Stated Policy towards Cyprus*, 111–12. On the contacts of NATO Secretary General Paul-Henri Spaak with Greece, Turkey and Britain and the US stance towards his proposals on Cyprus.

towards the Cypriot issue and the future status quo.[262] Turkish journalists did not hesitate to speak of Britain's possible exclusion from the Baghdad Pact.[263] Reactions in Turkey were even more indignant when, according to a Turkish paper, New York Governor Averell Harriman allegedly invited Makarios on an official visit to the United States. Turkish organizations acted immediately and telegraphed protests to Harriman while the Anadolu News Agency wondered 'how a well-known US public figure could have invited a man like Makarios, a murderer, the leader of terrorism, whose hands are soaked in blood'.[264] The outcry about this in Turkey led the Israeli embassy in Washington to investigate the facts regarding Harriman's invitation. It was ultimately ascertained that the governor of New York had sent Makarios a wire congratulating him on his release and expressing the hope that both men would meet 'at the earliest opportunity', sometime in the future. Those close to Governor Harriman noted that Makarios could never be invited to New York without prior consent from the State Department, an unlikely circumstance, given that 'such a move would obviously displease the British'.[265] Regardless of the report's denial, the release of Makarios had outraged Turkish public opinion and the local newspapers were claiming with near certainty that Turkey's diplomatic relations with Greece would undergo a review, and the Turkish ambassador might even be recalled from Athens.[266]

Despite growing tensions in Turkey, the Israelis believed it unlikely that Ankara would openly confront Greece let alone Britain, the US or NATO. Their assessment was quickly confirmed. When Makarios arrived in Athens, Menderes spoke about Britain's policy with caution and moderation.[267] American officials, too, described the atmosphere of the Cyprus talks between Turkey, Greece and Britain at the NATO conference in Bonn that May as 'much more low-key than expected'. In fact, US Secretary of State John Foster Dulles was quoted as saying, 'there is hope that the situation will improve' on the island.[268]

Despite the foregoing, Israel scrutinized Turkey's new tendency to stress the religious aspect of the Cyprus issue. Israel interpreted this as a Turkish tactic to rally Arab support, both regionally and at the UN. It is worth noting that in the midst of the Turco-Syrian crisis in the summer of 1957, as Turkey gathered its military forces along the border and was seemingly ready to invade Syria, the pro-Soviet government in

[262] ISA/RG93/MFA/263/6, Alon to the West Europe Division (3.4.1957, not recorded as incoming document).
[263] Ibid. Published in *Hakimiyet*, 2 April 1957.
[264] ISA/RG93/MFA/263/6, Alon to the West Europe Division (21.4.1957, not recorded as incoming document).
[265] ISA/RG93/MFA/263/6, Shimshon Arad, first secretary of the Israeli embassy in Washington to the US, Western Europe and British Commonwealth Divisions (2.5.1957, not recorded as incoming document).
[266] ISA/RG93/MFA/263/6, Alon to the West Europe Division (342/3612/אנ – 21.4.1957), Articles appearing in the newspapers *Cumhuriyet* (21.4.57) and *Ulus* (19.4.57).
[267] ISA/RG93/MFA/263/6, Alon to West Europe Division (338/3612/אנ – 21.4.1957).
[268] ISA/RG93/MFA/263/6, West Europe Division to the Israeli diplomatic representation in Athens (14.5.1957, not recorded as incoming document). An excerpt of the letter of 9.5.1957 from the Israeli embassy in Washington is included, on the perceptions of the senior US diplomat Fraser Wilkins. When the independence of the Republic of Cyprus was later declared, Wilkins was named US ambassador in Nicosia from 1960 to 1964.

Damascus declared that it was willing to grant Makarios asylum in the event that Britain would block him from returning to Cyprus after his release. The pro-government Turkish newspaper *Hakimiyet* described the Syrian initiative as 'prostitution in the eyes of the Muslim world, for which Syria will soon be asked to pay a high price'.[269]

The pro-Makarios statements coming from Damascus gave Ankara the opportunity to play its 'Islamic' card in the diplomatic world, not only to highlight the religious aspect of the Cyprus conflict, but to draw closer to the Arab world. Perhaps the first signs of the 'Islamization' of Turkey's regional policy in the Middle East appeared in 1957, although the Kemalist regime in the country's interior took a completely different approach to the political dimension of Islam. But that did nothing to stop the Turkish government from encouraging demonstrations against Makarios' release in the rural towns of the interior – demonstrations which gradually took on an intensely religious character, as noted by the Israeli ambassador in Ankara, Moshe Alon.[270]

The Israelis watched with interest and restrained concern as Turkey sought to approach the Arab world by emphasizing their common Muslim identity. In fact, it endeavoured to artificially overcome any religious or dogmatic differences by attempting to recruit pro-West Arab states against their common enemy: the Christian Greek Cypriots. The West realized that Ankara was obliged to follow this tactic at the time in order to preserve the Baghdad Pact. In this way, Turkey would ensure the support of Jordan and Afghanistan which had strong ties to the West. Statements made by King Saud bin Abdulaziz Al-Saud of Saudi Arabia, calling on all Muslim countries to defend the interests and rights of their co-religionists 'in Kashmir, Algeria and Cyprus' caused a sensation. The statements were put to good use by the pro-government Turkish press through strongly pro-Arab reports, as Alon noted.[271]

When bilateral relations with the Turks remained strained, Israeli diplomats were seriously worried as they waited to see how far their Turkish colleagues would go with the 'Islamization' of the Cyprus issue, and what else they would be forced to offer the Arabs in exchange for their support of Turkish positions *en masse* at the UN.[272] Besides, the religious element of the Arab–Israeli conflict was decidedly more explosive than what was primarily a nationalistic conflict in Cyprus.

3.5.3 Assessments of the Israeli consulate in Nicosia concerning political trends among Greek and Turkish Cypriots

In November 1957, Israeli Consul General Peretz Leshem drafted a detailed report to diplomat Reuven Shiloakh, a close associate and adviser to Foreign Minsiter Meir, on

---

[269] ISA/RG93/MFA/263/6, The Israeli diplomatic mission in Ankara to the West Europe Division (281/3701/אן – 2.4.1957).

[270] ISA/RG130/MFA/3122/38, Alon to the West Europe Division (313/3612/אן – 11.4.1957.)

[271] ISA/RG130/MFA/3122/38, Alon to the West Europe Division (451/3612/אן – 7.6.1957). Article in the pro-government newspaper *Hakimiyet* (7.6.1957) on the plea of King Saud of Saudi Arabia under the headline: 'King Saud wants Cyprus turned over to Turkey'.

[272] ISA/RG130/MFA/3122/38, Alon to the West Europe Division (313/3612/אן – 11.4.1957).

the internal situation in Cyprus.[273] What made this report extraordinary was that, for the first time, attention was being paid to factors affecting internal political differences both within Greek Cypriot and Turkish Cypriot societies. Leshem did not propose which stance Israel should adopt vis-à-vis the two communities. He had not been asked to do so. Israeli diplomacy merely wished to have insight into the political balance in Cyprus, while gathering information about what would determine the ensuing status quo.

This first local 'political mapping' of Cyprus heralded an end to viewing developments in Cyprus exclusively in light of Israel's relations with Britain, Turkey and Greece. Leshem foresaw that the era of 'Israeli neutrality' on Cyprus would have to end. The countdown to the final settlement had begun. Leshem concluded that 'not adopting a specific stance on the Cyprus issue may come to haunt us in the future. It is much better to adopt a specific stance – even if it is unpopular with some of the parties concerned.'

3.5.3.1 *The Greek Cypriot political scene*

According to Leshem, the attitude of the Greek Cypriot community towards the British regime on the island comprised four elements: the Church, the two trade unions – the Pancyprian Federation of Labour (PEO) and the Cyprus Workers' Confederation (SEK) – and EOKA, the armed movement.[274]

According to Leshem's report, the most important influence over the Greek Cypriot community was the Church. Its influence was based on 'pressure levers' which determined key events and activities, like marriages, christenings, divorces, etc. These levers were reinforced even more by the Greek schools in Cyprus which loyally followed the ideology of the Church.

The local trade unions were another major influence in the Greek Cypriot community. The institution of trade unionism had been established decades earlier, and the most important labour union on the island in terms of organization was the PEO, with more than 30,000 members. Politically, it was the voice of the Left and was affiliated with the World Federation of Trade Unions (WFTU).

According to Leshem, both the Church and the PEO wished for a rapid collapse of the British regime and a recognition of the absolute right of Cypriots to unfettered self-determination. Nevertheless, Leshem was convinced that once Britain ceased to rule the island, key ideological differences between the Church and the Greek Cypriot Left would come to light.

At the opposite end of the ideological spectrum from PEO was the Cyprus Workers' Confederation (SEK), established in 1944. Politically, it was aligned with the Right and a member of the International Confederation of Free Trade Unions (ICFTU). Compared to PEO, it exerted less influence, with no more than 8,000 members in 1957.

---

[273] ISA/RG93/MFA/2156/7, Leshem to Reuven Shiloakh, special adviser to the Ministry of Foreign Affairs (102/2295-18.11.1957).
[274] Ibid.

As for recognition of the Right to self-determination, the Church, PEO and SEK all shared the same view. However, it was assumed that after the British withdrawal, SEK and the Church would join forces politically and ideologically.

Finally, the way in which the Israeli Consul portrayed EOKA and its influence over the Greek Cypriot community is particularly interesting. Leshem believed the number of active EOKA members was actually small and that its main achievement had been deterring the vast majority of Greek Cypriots from cooperating with British authorities. Thus, in addition to the armed struggle it had successfully waged against the British, EOKA, Leshem believed, was also a mechanism for the suppression of the Greek Cypriots. As evidence of this, he reported that EOKA fighters often executed Greek Cypriots 'who believed that guerrilla warfare was going nowhere'. In his report, he described the organization as fighting for national liberation, though he noted that at the intra-community level, it often acted 'as a conspiratorial mechanism for silencing any voice rising in opposition, with the result that many people did not dare to publicly criticise its actions'.[275]

Leshem also referred to the social aspect of EOKA's activity. He had formed the opinion that the Greek Cypriot bourgeoisie were allegedly afraid to take a stand against EOKA 'for fear of attracting the interest of its armed fighters'. They worried that an eventual annexation by Greece would weaken their economic power and this was the principal reason that they transferred their money abroad, mainly to Britain. On the other hand, Greek Cypriot farmers, who were thought to be more ideologically influenced by the Church, appeared to believe that unification with Greece would enhance their economic status and level of education. As Leshem wrote in his report, it was for this reason that the rural areas were more strongly aligned with the revolutionary current of the guerrilla war.

Leshem's first report on the Greek Cypriot community and the reports that followed reflect his de-mythification of EOKA, so adamantly that he came close to deconstructing its ideology. It is possible that the official information provided by the British regime may have coloured his departmental views. The Israeli Ministry of Foreign Affairs, both within the ministry and in the outside world, did not go the trouble of drawing such conclusions regarding EOKA's role. Nevertheless, the Israeli consul's criticism of the methods used by EOKA against Greek Cypriot dissidents was hardly flattering.

3.5.3.2 *The Turkish Cypriot political scene*

In the same report, Leshem describes the political scene in the Turkish Cypriot community.[276] The political associations there were much simpler. The indisputable leader of the Turkish Cypriots was Dr Fazıl Küçük and his political group, KATAK (Kıbrıs Adası Türk Azınlık Kurumu, Association of the Turkish Minority of the Island of Cyprus, which later developed into Kıbrıs Türk Milli Birlik Partisi, Turkish Cypriot

---

[275] Ibid.
[276] Ibid.

National Union Party). For as long as the British remained on the island, Küçük's goal was to maintain absolute political equality between Turkish and Greek Cypriots. However, once the British withdrew from the island, their aim changed to partition (*Taksim*). Nevertheless, Leshem continued, the idea of partition was also perceived as a difficult compromise. The Turkish Cypriot leadership believed that all of Cyprus should revert to Turkey because before British rule was established, the island had belonged to the Ottoman Empire, not Greece.

According to the Israeli consul, there were two key characteristics of the Turkish Cypriot minority: its universal support of Küçük, and its dedication to Kemalism and the imperatives of Ankara's government.[277] In the early 1950s, the Turkish Cypriot community had marginalized those who remained attached to the old social structures, the diehards who served the political expediency of the British.[278]

The first time Leshem focused attention on Turkish Cypriot politics was Turkish Independence Day, celebrated on 29 October 1957, when the Turkish consul in Nicosia held a formal reception, attended by the two most powerful figures in Turkish Cypriot politics, Fazıl Küçük and Rauf Denktaş. Leshem's first impression of Rauf Denktaş was quite positive, and he described him flatteringly as a:

talented jurist who will no doubted play an important public role one day. Various circles view him as the likely alternative to Küçük. He recently resigned from public office to practice law and focus on the educational and cultural activities of the Turkish community. This will certainly help him gain experience so that, when the right time comes, he will be able to fulfil his future political duties.[279]

3.5.3.3 Israel's image in Cypriot society

Diplomatic reports from 1957 reflect Israel's interest in learning how it was perceived by Cypriot public opinion. According to Consul Leshem, the armed struggle of the Jews in Palestine and their ultimate victory over the British forces added to Israel's popularity in the Greek Cypriot community. However, these positive perceptions were reversed when Israel joined forces with Britain in the Suez Crisis and turned against Nasserist Egypt, which had unequivocally supported the Greek positions on the Cyprus issue.[280] As far as Cypriot public opinion was concerned, Israel may not have been amongst the powers opposing Greek pursuits but it was certainly not one of those that wanted to see the British withdraw from the island.

[277] Niyazi Kızılyürek, *Kemalismos* [*Kemalism*] (Athens: Mesogeios Publisher, 2006), 55–90 and 109–10. The key ideological pillars of Kemalism. Kemalist 'Pan-Turkism' and the position of the Turkish Cypriot community on the island from the mid-1940s onwards.
[278] Cf. 2.4.2.2.
[279] ISA/RG93/MFA/2156/7, Leshem to the British Commonwealth Division (102/2138-31.10.1957).
[280] ISA/RG93/MFA/2156/7, Leshem to Shiloah (102/2295-18.11.1957).

On the other hand, Israel should not have expected much from Greek Cypriot public opinion. Perhaps with the exception of commerce,[281] after it opened its consulate in Nicosia in late August 1950 and onwards, Israel did not make any particular effort to cultivate stable relations with local businesspeople – aside from the British authorities. It maintained a similar stance towards local political players. As to the Church of Cyprus, which was a leading factor in politics, Israeli diplomacy kept its distance. This was a conscious decision, dating back to the days following the Enosis Plebiscite in 1950. Despite repeated efforts by Cypriot hierarchs or Nicosia Mayor, Themistocles Dervis, to establish a channel of communication with the Israeli government, the latter responded either with cold-shoulder telegrams or total silence.[282]

A few months after the release of Makarios, Leshem suggested that Israel should start taking the political power of the Church very seriously and stop ignoring it. He believed that the time had come to bridge communications with the majority of the island's residents; otherwise, when the British withdrew, the diplomatic cost would be great. Despite his repeated criticism of EOKA's methods, Leshem believed it was unwise to ignore the common ideological background linking the struggle of the Greek Cypriots against the British with the fight to liberate the Jews of Palestine. It was therefore not possible to ignore the leading role played by the local Church in this national effort.[283] The Israeli Consulate insisted on not missing any more opportunity at rapprochement with the Cypriot Church, believing that any gesture of goodwill would be positively received. The congratulatory telegram sent by the Bishop of Salamis, Gennadios, to the Israeli Consulate in 1957 on the ninth anniversary of Israel's independence could serve as a good excuse to forge a new beginning in relations between Israel and the Church of Cyprus.[284]

Throughout 1957, Leshem's repeated pleas were unheeded by his superiors. The following year, however, Israel made its presence known in the Greek Cypriot community. Once again, it was a conscious decision.[285]

---

[281] Ibid. On the basis of data reported with respect to the commercial transactions between Cyprus and Israel in 1956 and the first nine months of 1957, it appears that Israeli exports to Cyprus were five times the value of the respective Cypriot exports to Israel. Specifically: imports of Israeli products into Cyprus in 1956 amounted to £551,000 Cyp while Cypriot exports to Israel amounted to £113,300 Cyp. During the first nine months of 1957 (1/1–30/9), exports of Israeli products to Cyprus amounted to £411,000 Cyp while Cypriot exports to Israel amounted to only £129,600 Cyp. The report does not indicate the source of the above economic data. Also, ISA/RG59/GL/12561/7, David Hess, Director of the Ministries Audit Sector of the Public Independent Audit Authority to Dr Dienstein, director of the Foreign Exchange Division of the Ministry of Finance (3152/17-17.1.1957). Financials of investments by the Israeli construction firm Solel Boneh in Cyprus, in cooperation with the local company Cybarco. Cf. 2.4.2.1.

[282] Cf. 2.4, 3.1 and 3.2.5.

[283] ISA/RG93/MFA/2156/7, Leshem to the British Commonwealth Division (102/3402-3.6.1957).

[284] Ibid.

[285] Cf. 3.6.1.1.1.

3.5.4. The Israeli vote on the Cyprus issue at the 12th Session of the UN General Assembly

On the eve of the 12th Session of the UN General Assembly, the Israeli Ministry of Foreign Affairs once again refrained from showing its hand on the Cyprus issue. In fact, it was the first time the Ministry advised its Consul in Nicosia to refrain from all actions or social appearances that could be interpreted either positively or negatively by either opposing side.[286] It was indicative that in July 1957, after much debate, Leshem and his American counterpart decided not to attend the funeral service of their common friend, Demosthenes Stavrinides, co-founder and publisher of the newspaper *Eleftheria*, to avoid giving rise to talk that might affect the positions of their respective countries on current developments on the island.[287]

Despite a variety of assessments about the future status quo in Cyprus, Israel continued to take it for granted that the island was still under British rule. Nevertheless, although proceedings at the 12th Session had already begun, Israel's Ministry of Foreign Affairs had not yet determined what stance it would take. This time, too, there was no particular reason for Israel to support either the Greek or Turkish position, given that both Athens and Ankara sought the exclusive support of the Arab countries. Thus, for the Israelis, it seemed that aligning themselves with Britain was probably the only way to go.

On the other hand, having already suffered negative fallout from the Suez Crisis, and because Foreign Minister Golda Meir was intent, for various political and economic reasons, on strengthening ties between her country and the Third World, it was essential for Israel to shed the stigma of the 'loyal ally of colonialists'. For this reason in particular, and specifically with regard to the Cyprus problem, Israel was wary of again appearing to be hitched to Britain's wagon. Besides, even London now seemed eager to defuse tensions and negotiate, having released Makarios and replaced the uncompromising Harding with the more moderate Hugh Foot as the island's governor. Though the Israelis claimed to be awaiting instructions from the British Ambassador in Tel Aviv on what stance to adopt at the upcoming UN vote on the Cyprus question,[288] in reality they had already decided to follow the tried-and-true approach of abstaining.

On 20 September 1957, the issue of Cyprus was put on the agenda of the 12th Session with the revised Greek petition, from which it expunged the phrase, 'British atrocities against Cypriots', which naturally provoked reactions from Britain, Turkey and the Committee Secretariat.[289] On 9 December 1957, Greece submitted a draft resolution before the Political Committee. The Greek arguments demonstrated that British policy in Cyprus did not follow the spirit and letter of Resolution 1013 adopted by the 11th Session.[290] Once the revised draft resolution, jointly submitted by Canada, Denmark, Chile and Norway as well as Greece, was accepted, the Greek proposal was approved by the Political Committee with 33 votes in favour, 20 against

---

[286] ISA/RG93/MFA/2156/7, British Commonwealth Division to Leshem 3607/102-4.8.1957.
[287] ISA/RG93/MFA/2156/7, Leshem to the British Commonwealth Division (102/3607-15.7.1957).
[288] ISA/RG93/MFA/2156/7, British Commonwealth Division to Leshem (736/22.9.1957).
[289] Xydis, 'The UN General Assembly', 149.
[290] Ibid., 150. Cf. 3.4.2.

and 25 abstentions. The revised text included the phrasing suggested by Evangelos Averoff, whereby the General Assembly expressed the hope that further negotiations and discussions would take place with a view to applying the right of self-determination in the case of the people of Cyprus.[291] The adoption of this phrasing, which contained the peoples' right to self-determination, was seen by the Greek side as a moral vindication and was portrayed to the Greek public as a diplomatic success. However, during the General Assembly balloting on 14 December 1957, the resolution was not adopted after all, having failed to receive the required two-thirds majority.

Israel opted for abstention in both votes. In its document to the consulate general in Nicosia, the Israeli Ministry of Foreign Affairs explained the Israeli stance as follows:

> While we would unreservedly vote in favour of a draft resolution seeking to initiate negotiations between the concerned parties without any reference to the right of self-determination, our Representation to the UN was instructed to abstain in the event a draft resolution including the right of self-determination was proposed, so as to avoid having to take a stand on the Cyprus conflict.[292]

Israel followed the line of the United States[293] and the other Western countries which, either by voting against or by abstaining, failed to support Greek positions.

3.6 The Israeli stance on the Cyprus issue at the 13th Session of the UN General Assembly, 1958

The year 1958 proved to be a landmark in Israel's regional foreign policy. The military coup in Iraq on 14 July 1958, which resulted in the deposition of the pro-West Hashemite royal family and the establishment of a military regime led by Abd-al-Karim Qasim, was the catalyst. This development gradually distanced Iraq from the West and from the Baghdad Pact, which included Britain and the most significant pro-West Muslim countries in the region: Turkey, Iran and Pakistan. The same year, Nasserist Egypt joined Syria to form the United Arab Republic (UAR), thus fuelling the belief that the Soviet Union was striving to increase its influence in the Middle East.

These realignments highlighted the need to restore the pro-West axis between Israel and Turkey. In the summer of 1958, Ankara and Jerusalem put an end to their diplomatic chill dating back to January 1955, when the Turco-Iraqi military agreement was concluded, and the Turkish ambassador to Tel Aviv was recalled in November of

---

[291] Ibid. The exact phrasing: 'that further negotiations and discussions will be undertaken promptly and in a spirit of cooperation with a view to applying the right of self-determination in the case of the people of Cyprus'.

[292] ISA/RG93/MFA/2156/7, British Commonwealth Division to Leshem (917/23.12.1957).

[293] Nicolet, *United States Policy towards Cyprus*, 110–11. On the US stance on the Cyprus issue at the 12th Session of the UN General Assembly.

the following year, immediately after the Suez Crisis.[294] The rapprochement between Turkey and Israel drastically affected Israel's stance on the Cyprus issue.

Meanwhile, the new British prime minister, Harold Macmillan, had already begun working on a complex – and extremely difficult to implement – plan for a tridominium of Britain, Greece and Turkey. The Macmillan plan was never proposed. It was, however, indicative of Britain's intent to avoid displeasing Turkey, which wanted to prevent Cyprus from coming under Greek control at all costs. The regional realignments increasingly underscored Turkey's strategic importance for Western interests.[295] Notably, London was willing for the first time to discuss a potential concession of the island's sovereignty, on condition that it would be able to maintain sovereign military bases there.[296]

3.6.1 The Foot Plan and Israeli assessments

Sir Hugh Foot had joined the service of the Colonial Office in 1929, and was first assigned to Palestine where he became known for his tolerant way of speaking with both Jews and Arabs. He was assigned to Cyprus in 1943 when London decided to relax the strict measures it had imposed after the October events of 1931 (Oktovriana). These circumstances made Foot popular among the Greek Cypriots. During Harding's term of office in Cyprus, Foot, then governor of Jamaica, applied for an assignment in Cyprus in the belief that he would be able to help reduce tensions there. His outline of the policy guidelines he wished to follow was seized on by the Foreign Office as an opportunity to buy time and find some way to break the deadlock.[297]

The Foot Plan provided for a seven-year period of self-governance, during which Greek and Turkish Cypriots would remain free of external interventions, with a view to coming up with a mutually acceptable political solution. At the end of the seven years, the solution would be implemented. Notwithstanding, London made clear to the new governor that the declaration of 19 December 1956 (regarding the 'double' right to self-determination) was still valid – although Foot disagreed with its contents.[298] During the seven-year transitional period, measures would be taken to build trust between the British authorities and Greek Cypriots, helping to restore normalcy. One of the measures Foot had in mind was the release of all political prisoners.[299]

The Foot Plan met with a strong reaction from Ankara, which saw the possibility of partition it desired slipping further and further away.[300] The uprising of the Turkish Cypriots in January 1958 and the cold reception Foot received in Ankara from Menderes on his visit to secure Turkish support for his plan were two significant events

---

[294] Cf. 3.3.2.1.
[295] Hatzivassiliou, *To Kypriako Zitima*, 96–101, on Harold Macmillan's idea for a tridominium in the summer of 1957.
[296] Ibid., 99–100.
[297] Holland, *Britain and the Revolt in Cyprus*, 213–15 and 224–5.
[298] Ibid., 225.
[299] Nikos Christodoulides, *Ta schedia lysis tou Kypriakou (1948–1978)* [*Plans for Solution of the Cyprus Problem (1948–1978)*] (Athens: Kastaniotis, 2009), 110–19.
[300] Hatzivassiliou, *To Kypriako Zitima*, 101–3.

which proved to the British that when Turkey wanted to impose its views, it knew just how to do it.[301]

The Israelis followed the unfolding of events in Cyprus with interest. According to a relevant report by Consul Leshem,[302] the Foot Plan aimed at placating the Greek Cypriot majority, and this would anger the Turkish Cypriots and heighten tensions between the two communities. The resulting climate served the purposes of the British and their intention to maintain military bases on the island, since friction between the Greek and Turkish Cypriots would justify the need to restore and preserve order at any moment. Leshem linked Foot's proposals to the fact that in March 1958, the British allowed the Greek Cypriots to celebrate Greek Independence Day, describing it thus:

> In the past two years, parades by the Greek Cypriot population were banned. This year, a permit was granted to hold a parade on Greek Independence Day under specific conditions. After church services had concluded, large parades were held, where mostly schoolchildren participated, holding Greek flags. I watched one of the parades in the city where youth and people affiliated with the nationalist right-wing party participated. On the one hand, there were pupils in uniform and marching bands and, on the other hand, there were trade unions marching in another direction in the city. There were many citizens watching along the parade route, but the number of spectators was not very large and there was no overcrowding. From time to time, whenever a class of school children would pass by singing, there was applause. This right-wing parade passed in front of the Greek Consul-General's residence as he stood on the balcony with members of his diplomatic mission and a close associate of Makarios, and Orthodox Church officials. [...] The day passed without incident and those who are familiar with the situation confirm that this parade was more massive and better organised than any others. The Governor is to be commended for being so understanding; he is the one who made it possible to grant parade permits. Although this was a very special day, security forces did not make an appearance, except for traffic police so that the streets could be given over to the parades. Undoubtedly, the Greek Cypriots saw all of this as a great victory in their fight, as the celebrations, the sports events held that afternoon, and the city all decorated with Greek flags – all of these things together were far from reminiscent of the fact that all those parading were British citizens and parading on British soil.[303]

As Leshem observed, Foot's tolerance of the Greek Cypriots did not always meet with positive results. The freedom of expression enjoyed by Greek Cypriots exacerbated relations with the Turkish Cypriots, while in other cases, it gave rise to increased

[301] Holland, *Britain and the Revolt in Cyprus*, 227–33, on Turkey's objections to the Foot Plan and events in Cyprus involving the Turkish Cypriots in January 1958. Cf. ISA/RG93/MFA/2156/7, Leshem to the British Commonwealth Division (102/2531מם – 28.1.1958), on Ankara's encouragement to the Turkish Cypriots to proceed with mobilizations and protests.
[302] ISA/RG93/MFA/2156/7, Leshem to the British Commonwealth Division (102/2440מם – 5.1.1958).
[303] Ibid. (102/2765מם – 27.3.1958).

tensions between the Greek Cypriot Right and Left. It was no coincidence that during the 25 March celebrations, there were essentially two types of parades – 'rightist' and 'leftist'. As early as mid-January 1958, there were serious outbreaks of violence between the Right (who enjoyed the support of the Church and EOKA) and the Left (aligned with the Communist AKEL and members of the PEO trade union). The murders of Michail Petrou and Ilias Ttofaris by two masked perpetrators on 21 January 1958, were attributed to EOKA. Leshem assigned most of the blame for this to Grivas, 'who is apparently attempting to do what he did in Greece following World War II and transfer the Greek Civil War to Cyprus'.[304]

Although violent incidents of this type had not yet become widespread – due to the conciliatory interventions of Makarios with the officials of PEO, as Leshem noted[305] – the negative impression made on the Israeli diplomat by Grivas' role in Cyprus coloured the contents of his other reports, which as noted, were not at all flattering to EOKA. For example, the effectiveness of certain measures announced by the organization, like the boycott of imports and distribution of British consumer goods, or the elimination of English-language signs on Greek Cypriot shops, were more likely due to the fears of ordinary people, than to their patriotism. A description of the climate prevalent in the Greek Cypriot community in Leshem's report of March 1958 is indicative:

> EOKA continues to put pressure on the population and, from time to time, murders people. [...] The Governor made repeated appeals via radio addresses to avoid violent incidents and explained the need for calm and restraint. However, all of this does not preclude new armed action that could strain relations between the majority of the population and British authorities. The boycott EOKA declared of British products only serves to increase such tension. The organisation aims to intimidate commercial agents and importers into not ordering or marketing British goods, and to intimidate consumers into not buying or using them. Recently, EOKA appeared in masked groups, ordering people not to go to gambling cafes, lottery stands, or billiard halls. In fact, they succeeded in putting an end to festivities held in the homes of ordinary citizens whenever a relative was released from prison. Their argument was that not all political prisoners had been released yet and so it was not yet time for frivolous enjoyment. [...] The population fears EOKA.[306]

Whether the foregoing descriptions reflect the truth or not, it is certain that these particular reports by Leshem from Nicosia encouraged a pro-Turkish stance at the Israeli Ministry of Foreign Affairs. This is confirmed by the historian and Israel State Archives researcher Professor Amikam Nachmani, according to whom 'reports from Israeli diplomats in Nicosia, Athens and Ankara utterly dismissed the authenticity of Enosis, thereby facilitating the decision to support the Turkish side'.[307]

---

[304] Ibid. (102/2508מס – 23.1.1958).
[305] Ibid. (102/2531מס – 28.1.1958).
[306] Ibid. (102/2712מס – 17.3.1958).
[307] Amikam Nachmani, *Israel, Turkey and Greece: Uneasy Relations in the East Mediterranean* (London: Frank Cass, 1987), 100.

3.6.1.1 *The Israeli consulate's concerns over Israel's image in Cypriot public opinion*

Despite the biased reports of the consul in Nicosia, Israeli diplomacy monitored developments in Cyprus during the first months of 1958 without taking an official position in favour of either side. In mid-February, Leshem travelled to Israel to take part in a broad-based consultation at the ministry which arrived at the following conclusions: 'Although in principle we are ideologically in favour of the application of the right of people to self-determination, this position is not acceptable either to the Greeks or the Turks.'[308] Essentially, this was a restatement of the views expressed by Israel's permanent representative to the UN, Abba Eban, in regard to what he considered the actual content of Greece's first appeal on the Cyprus question at the 1954 General Assembly.[309] Thus, according to the Israeli view, both the Enosis sought by the Greek Cypriots and the partition pursued by the Turkish Cypriots were perceived as demands that were incompatible with the principle of the peoples' self-determination and, essentially, Cyprus was a battleground for the expansionist aspirations of Britain, Turkey and Greece.[310]

Regardless of how the situation in Cyprus was assessed, for the first time the Israelis became seriously concerned about 'the sympathetic feelings shown by the majority of the island's population for Nasser, resulting in less sympathy for Israel'.[311] This pro-Arab stance among Greek Cypriots was due not only to the fact that Israel did not support Greek initiatives at the UN, but also to the quality and quantity of commercial transactions between Israel and the merchants of the island who were mostly Greek Cypriots. Israel had not been importing as much Cypriot agricultural produce as it might have done and it was likewise clear from financial figures that the bilateral trade relations were heavily weighted in favour of Israeli businesses. Moreover, the number of Israeli tourists had dropped dramatically as a result of the unrest. Ultimately, the Ministry of Foreign Affairs came to realize that as a result of its reluctance to take a clear stand on the Cyprus issue, the islanders had no way of knowing Israel's diplomatic intentions and this left the way open for pro-Nasserists to air their views with growing frequency in the local Greek Cypriot press.

The lack of substantive communication with the Greek Cypriots became abundantly clear in early January 1958, when it was learned that a Greek Cypriot delegation was to take part in the anti-colonial Afro-Asian Conference being held in Cairo at that time. As had previously occurred in Bandung, pro-Palestinian views were impressively propounded by representatives of all countries.[312] Taking part in the Cairo conference

---

[308] ISA/RG93/MFA/2156/7, Leshem to the British Commonwealth Division (102/2609מס – 20.2.1958), conclusions from the meeting of 13.5.1958 of the British Commonwealth Division, which was attended by Leshem.

[309] Israel State Archives, Barzilai (ed.), *Documents*, vol. 9, 650–1, no. 384, Eban to Rafael (93.01/2210/18-26.9.1954). Cf. 3.2.5.

[310] ISA/RG93/MFA/2156/7, Leshem to the British Commonwealth Division (102/2609מס – 20.2.1958).

[311] Ibid.

[312] ISA/RG93/MFA/1008/5, Research Division (377/מ – 14.1.1958), overview of the sessions at the 'Afro-Asian People's Solidarity Conference', during which Egypt and the USSR played a dominant role. The conference was also attended by Western countries, including Greece as an observer.

were members of the Greek Cypriot community in Egypt while the Cypriot Ethnarchy was represented by Savvas Loizides.[313] A few months later, in April 1958, and contrary to what had transpired in previous years, no representative of the Church of Cyprus sent a message of good wishes to the Israeli consul on Israel's Independence Day. Leshem interpreted this silence as 'a clear message from Makarios' people that they have grown desperate over Israel's stance on the Cypriot Issue at the UN'.[314]

These small – though significant – indications did not pass unnoticed. The Ministry of Foreign Affairs began to consider inviting Cypriot journalists to Israel in order to encourage the publication of articles friendly to Israel, primarily in the Greek Cypriot press. However, an invitation addressed to Greek Cypriot journalists alone might have given rise to negative comments not only from Turkish Cypriot colleagues, but also from British authorities.[315] Thus, although the need to pursue some kind of overture towards the neighbouring island was indisputable, the ministry soon abandoned the idea.

Nevertheless, a suitable opportunity was not difficult to find. Israel's 10th Independence Day was coming up on 14 May 1958, and the consulate marked the occasion with a piano recital at the Royal Theatre in Nicosia featuring the famous Israeli pianist Pnina Salzman. Salzman was already well known in Cyprus, as she had appeared there in 1954,[316] but this time, her recital was to be covered more extensively by the Greek Cypriot and English-language press.[317] Her performances were recorded by the Cyprus Broadcasting Service and the newly established public television station, CTV. Although British, Turkish and Turkish Cypriot officials were invited, the Israeli consulate placed more weight on attracting the Greek Cypriot public – and it was successful.[318]

That year, Leshem was pleased to note the tolerance shown by Greek Cypriot journalists when they learned that Israel had allowed British war planes to fly through Israeli airspace while transporting military personnel to Jordan after Nasser supporters attempted to overthrow the Jordanian king.[319] Nevertheless, the Israeli consul's assessment that Israel was 'scoring points' with Cypriot public opinion was overly optimistic. Two widely advertised piano recitals and relatively mild reporting by the Greek Cypriot newspapers on Israeli anti-Arab policy were not enough to offset Nasser's enthusiastic declaration of support for the Greek Cypriot cause, made while

[313] ISA/RG93/MFA/2156/7, *Athens News*, January 1958.
[314] ISA/RG93/MFA/2156/7, Leshem to the British Commonwealth Division (102/2880מס – 22.4.1958). Cf. 3.5.3.3.
[315] ISA/RG93/MFA/2156/7, Leshem to the British Commonwealth Division (2609מס /20.2.1958), British Commonwealth Division to Leshem (162/ 24.3.1958), Leshem to the British Commonwealth Division and Press Office of the Ministry of Foreign Affairs (102/27660מס – 30.3.1958), British Commonwealth Division to Leshem (285/19.5.1958).
[316] *Cyprus Mail*, 'Pnina Salzman's Recital – A Style Reminiscent of Liszt', 18.3.1954.
[317] *Times of Cyprus*, 'A Social Scrapbook of the Week – Recording Artist', 11.5.1958; *Times of Cyprus*, 'World Famous Pianist Here', 14.5.1958; Giorgos Arvanitakis, 'Salzman's Recital', *Eleftheria*, 17.5.1958; and *Haravgi*, 'Pnina Salzman in Limassol', 18.5.1958.
[318] ISA/RG93/MFA/2156/7, Leshem to the British Commonwealth Division (41/29680מס – 15.5.1958).
[319] Ibid. (102/31580מס – 6.8.1958).

Archbishop Makarios was visiting Cairo early in the summer of 1958.[320] It was then, too, that the Israelis became aware of the public relations advantage to be gained by strengthening ties with the local trade union movement.

3.6.1.1.1 Zeev Levin's contacts with Cypriot trade unionism and his political interventions in favour of the Greek Cypriots

During the turbulent months of 1958, Israel managed to make a favourable impression on Greek Cypriot public opinion, thanks to repeated visits by Zeev Levin, a member of the Political Affairs Department of the Histadrut Executive Committee, the largest trade union in the country. The Histadrut was closely linked institutionally to Ben-Gurion's Mapai governing party and considered by Israelis to be a kind of 'state within a state'.

Both Mapai and the Histadrut were ideologically aligned with the centre-left. At an international level, though, the Israeli trade organization belonged to the ICFTU. The ICFTU adopted more Western-capitalist ideological models and was at the opposite pole of the distinctly leftist World Federation of Trade Unions (WFTU). In Cyprus, the leftist PEO belonged to the WFTU,[321] while the newer SEK was a member of the ICFTU, like the Israeli Histadrut.

In May 1958, the ICFTU appointed Zeev Levin as its delegate to Cyprus. He was called upon to advise structural changes within SEK, which would allow the latter to absorb ICFTU funds. In an article he published on 19 June 1958 in the Israeli daily newspaper *Davar*,[322] Levin outlined the official positions of the Histadrut and gave an account of the contacts he had made during his recent first visit to Cyprus. In the article, he made no secret of the fact that the main purpose of his activity on the island was to strengthen SEK against the PEO, which was an older trade union with more members and affiliated with the Left. Support for SEK was deemed essential to making the trade union movement more pluralistic. To support this undertaking, Levin made extensive reference in his article to the violent reprisals during that time in Morphou between the 'right-wing SEK' unionists and the 'leftist PEO'.

Levin's first visit to Cyprus in 1958 had attracted the attention of the Greek Cypriot press.[323] In his statements to them, he explained that the main purpose of his visit was to help with the organizational restructuring of SEK and to enable it to protect workers' rights more effectively. However, the visit soon took on a political character when he

---

[320] Cf. 3.6.2.
[321] Cf. 2.3.1.3 on criticism by the PEO regarding policies followed by the Israeli government against Arab trade unionists in Nazareth.
[322] Zeev Levin, 'The Free Trade Union Movement in Cyprus increases its organizational power: Successfully resisting pressure from the communist trade unions', *Davar*, 19.6.1958.
[323] *Fileleftheros*, 'Zeev Levin, the representative of the International Confederation of Free Trade Unions (ICFTU), arrived in Cyprus yesterday – He will help the Cypriot Free Trade Union Movement with its organizational development – The ICFTU's positions on the Cyprus problem', 20.5.1958; *Eleftheria*, 'A delegate of the International Confederation of Free Trade Unions (ICFTU) arrived in Cyprus yesterday – He will help in the organisational plan of Cypriot Free Trade Unions', 20.5.1958; and *Times of Cyprus*, 'Unionist Visits Cyprus', 20.5.1958.

was called upon to speak publicly about ICFTU's positions on the Cyprus problem, a speech which was extensively cited in the 20 May 1958 edition of the *Fileleftheros* newspaper:

> During its latest congress, which this year was held in Tunis, the ICFTU reaffirmed its support of the just demand of the Cypriot people for self-determination and called for negotiations for a democratic and fair solution to the Cyprus problem so as to apply the principle of self-determination. It urged the British government to lift emergency measures, release all political prisoners against whom no charges have ever been brought, and allow the return of Makarios and his fellow exiles, and of the Secretary-General of SEK (the Free Trade Unions of Cyprus) Mr Michalakis Pissas [...].[324]

In response to a reporter's question about whether the Israeli trade union movement endorsed ICFTU's political positions on the Cyprus question, Levin stated that: 'The Histadrut fully supports the resolution of the ICFTU Congress favouring the application of self-determination for the Cypriot people.'[325] As could be expected, Zeev Levin's public statements in favour of the Greek Cypriots annoyed the British, but nevertheless, Consul Leshem noted, the Greek Cypriot press implied that Levin had voiced not only the positions of ICFTU but those of the Israeli government as well.[326]

In early July 1958, the ICFTU held a meeting at its Brussels headquarters attended by SEK General Secretary Michalakis Pissas. In his address, Pissas condemned the British for the ongoing detention of Greek Cypriot political prisoners and the biased attitude of the local authorities in favour of Turkish Cypriots at the expense of Greek Cypriots. In an official statement, the ICFTU adopted the SEK's positions and condemned the armed actions of the Turkish Cypriot Turkish Resistance Organisation (Türk Mukavemet Teşkilatı, TMT), describing 'Turkish brutalities against the Greek population on the Island.'[327] As to the political detainees, the ICFTU's statement read:

> The ICFTU Steering Committee asked the British Government once again to inform it on the legal and judicial measures being taken in the case of detainees and their chances for release. In examining the Judicial Body's report, we took particular note of the British government's statement that of the 127 detained

---

[324] *Fileleftheros*, 'Mr Zeev Levin, the representative of the International Confederation of Free Trade Unions (ICFTU), arrived in Cyprus yesterday', 20.5.1958.

[325] Ibid.

[326] ISA/RG93/MFA/2156/7, Leshem to British Commonwealth Division (102/306סב – 27.5.1958). Cf. *Fileleftheros*, 'Remarkable activities and achievements of the free workers' movement in Cyprus – A large number of Cypriot workers wish to join the Free Trade Unions – Statements of the ICFTU Representative, Mr Levin, to *Fileleftheros*', 25.5.1958. *Eleftheria*, 'Free trade unions grow bigger and bigger – The first Cypriot Convention of Miners last Sunday was a great success – All together, united, under the honourable flag of the Ethnarch – The General Secretary of SEK, Mr Mich. Passas, should be freed and returned – Labour issues', 4.6.1958; and *Eleftheria*, 'The movement of Free Trade Unions', 6.6.1958.

[327] Holland, *Britain and the Revolt in Cyprus*, 263–5; and *Eleftheria*, 'Serious actions of the International Confederation of Free Trade Unions (ICFTU) for the Cypriot Issue', 19.7.1958.

trade unionists, 82 of those named in our report have already been released. To verify the accuracy of this claim, we asked our member in Cyprus [from the SEK] to provide us with a list of trade unionists currently being held. Cyprus reported that 78 trade unionists are currently detained, despite the fact that they have been released from time to time. A large number of them have already been detained for two or three years. When we lodged a protest with the Governor of Cyprus, Sir Hugh Foot, we sent him a list of detainees we received from our member in Cyprus, and stressed to him that the information given to the International Labour Organisation was not consistent with the list in our hands, which was prepared by the Cyprus Workers' Confederation (SEK). Therefore, we requested that the Governor of Cyprus review his list and correct the one sent to the International Labour Organisation.[328]

On 8 August 1958 – a few weeks after the ICFTU statements – Zeev Levin visited Cyprus for a second time, and once again his presence there took a strongly political turn.[329] Levin's activities were reported on by the Greek Cypriot press in highly favourable terms. He initiated a joint conference on 13 August, with participants from the main trade unions of the island, regardless of ideology or ethnic origin. The conference which took place at the Majestic Hotel in Nicosia, was attended by representatives of the SEK (Loukis Efstathiades and Giorgos Georkas), PEO (Andreas Ziartides and Michalakis Michailides), POAS (Andreas Christou and Kyriakos Nathanail) and the Turkish Labour Federation (Niaz Tagli, Mustafa Emin and Osman Arif).[330] In fact, it was decided to establish joint bicommunal cooperation committees 'which shall deal with cases involving the interests of workers of the two communities'.[331]

The conciliatory tone of the joint statement by Greek and Turkish Cypriot trade unionists, apart from being a victory for all Cypriot labour activists, was an important personal achievement for Levin himself – particularly in the midst of intercommunal turbulence. On 18 August, he visited the Karaolos camp at which 200 Greek Cypriot political prisoners were interned, including four trade unionist members of the Famagusta Free Labour Centre to ascertain the conditions there.[332] The next day, he visited the Agyrta camp in the Kyrenia Province where 90 Greek Cypriot political prisoners were being held, two of them prominent SEK members, and also to Kyrenia Castle where 32 Greek Cypriot political prisoners were detained, eleven of them trade

---

[328] *Eleftheria*, 'Serious Actions'.
[329] *Fileleftheros*, 'An Israeli Trade Union leader will arrive in Cyprus tomorrow', 7.8.1958.
[330] Pantelis Varnava, *Koinoi Ergatiki Agones Ellinokyprion kai Tourkokyprion: Gegonota mesa apo tin Istoria* [*Common Labour Struggles of Greek Cypriots and Turkish Cypriots: Events in History*] (Nicosia, 1997). Cf. Press release published on 15.8.1958 in the newsletter *I Foni tis PEO*; and *Fileleftheros*, 'Joint appeal by Greek and Turkish trade unions in favour of peacekeeping', 14.8.1958.
[331] *Eleftheria*, 'Cypriot workers are encouraged to avoid provocations or any other actions that might renew intercommunal tension on the island – An appeal was issued yesterday, following a joint conference, and signed by representatives of all Greek and Turkish Labour Unions – Statements by the International Representative, Mr Zeev Levin', 14.8.1958.
[332] *Eleftheria*, 'Mr Zeev Levin visited the prisoners in Karaolos yesterday'; *Fileleftheros*, 'Mr Levin in Karaolos', 19.8.958.

unionists.[333] During his ten-day stay on the island, Levin expanded his circle of contacts and gained popularity. Consul Leshem noted that thanks to Levin, Greek Cypriot public opinion about Israel had improved dramatically.[334] Levin was highly praised in the Israeli press for his achievements in Cypress,[335] although the fact that his actions clearly favoured the Greek Cypriots was more or less ignored.

Then came 'Black October', with bloody clashes between British security forces and Greek Cypriots,[336] which culminated on 8 November 1958, with the bombing of the Navy, Army and Air Force Institute (NAAFI) canteen at Nicosia Airport, which killed two British soldiers and wounded seven others. In reprisal, the British decided to dismiss all 4,000 Greek Cypriots employed by the NAAFI and the RAF, replacing them with British personnel.[337] A week later, another 25 Greek Cypriot fixed-term workers employed by the Nicosia Airport Civil Aviation Authority were also dismissed,[338] and all Greek Cypriots were banned from entering Nicosia Airport. In the days that followed, another 35 Greek Cypriot workers employed at the Episkopi garrison were let go.[339] All Cypriot trade unions condemned the actions of the authorities, and the SEK requested assistance from the ICFTU. In the midst of this, Zeev Levin was asked to return to Cyprus in his capacity as representative of the ICFTU to try and convince the British to revoke the mass dismissals.[340]

On 14 November, Levin arrived in Cyprus, and on the same day, accompanied by SEK officials, visited Greek Cypriot trade unionist political prisoners at the Kokkinotrimithia detention camp.[341] He also met with representatives of PEO and other independent Greek Cypriot trade union organizations.[342]

Levin's communications with British officials of the local government and Governor Foot himself[343] proved fruitless.[344] However, his efforts in support of Greek Cypriot trade unionists were extensively covered with flattering reports in both the Greek Cypriot and Israeli press.[345] Before returning to Israel, Levin held a press conference in

[333] *Fileleftheros*, 'Mr Levin visited trade unionist political prisoners', 20.8.1958.
[334] ISA/RG93/MFA/2156/7, Leshem to the British Commonwealth Division (102/31810מס – 19.8.1958).
[335] *Davar*, 'Zeev Levin returns from Cyprus', 27.8.1958.
[336] Holland, *Britain and the Revolt in Cyprus*, 290–1; and Andreas Karyos, 'O Mavros Oktovris tis Kyprou' ['Cyprus' Black October'] (Cypriot) *Kathimerini*, 1.3.2015.
[337] Holland, *Britain and the Revolt in Cyprus*, 291. Cf. *Cyprus Mail*, '4,000 are told: Go Home – Security ban on Greek Cypriots at airfields', 11.8.1958; and *Kypros*, 'Greek NAAFI employees hospitalized in the General Hospital', 10.11.1958. Greek Cypriot airport workers were among those injured in the bomb blast at the Nicosia Airport snack bar.
[338] *Fileleftheros*, 'Mr Levin, the representative of the International Confederation of Free Trade Unions (ICFTU), arrived yesterday in Cyprus for the case of workers fired from the RAF-NAAFI', 15.11.1958.
[339] *Haravgi*, 'Under a new circular of the military authorities – No Greek is allowed to enter the Nicosia airport – Civil Aviation employees dismissed yesterday', 15.11.1958.
[340] ISA/RG93/MFA/2156/7, Leshem to the British Commonwealth Division (102/33900מס – 17.11.1958).
[341] *Fileleftheros*, 'Mr Levin, the representative of the International Confederation of Free Trade Unions (ICFTU), arrived yesterday in Cyprus in relation to workers fired from the RAF-NAAFI', 15.11.1958.
[342] *Fileleftheros*, 'The mobilization to re-employ those dismissed', 16.11.1958.
[343] *Eleftheria*, 'A delegation of dismissed workers will meet with the Governor today', 16.11.1958. Levin met with Foot, Chandley, and Fallows on 15.11.1958. On the following day, Levin also attended the meeting between the delegation of Greek Cypriot trade unions and Foot.
[344] *Eleftheria*, 'The governor excluded the reemployment of 4,000 redundant workers', 18.11.1958.
[345] ISA/RG93/MFA/2156/7, *La-Merkhav*, 'Israeli representative mediates revocation of mass dismissals in Cyprus', 23.11.1958.

Nicosia, criticizing the governor and describing the collective dismissals as 'a form of political blackmail by the British against Greek Cypriots'. The Greek Cypriot press cited Levin's statements on the prevailing political situation according to which 'the ICFTU is opposed to violence from either side. However, the British must deal with the situation in which Cyprus claims the right to self-determination. Had the Cypriot people been able to exercise that right, the two pilots would not have died.'[346]

The British interpreted Levin's public statements as an attempt to 'legitimise terrorism' and complained vehemently to Israeli Consul Leshem.[347] Leshem argued that Levin had travelled to Cyprus as a representative of the ICFTU and was not expressing the views of the Israeli government. Nevertheless, there was no doubt that Zeev Levin's activities on the island significantly improved Israel's image with the Greek Cypriots. Coincidentally, on the very day the issue of mass dismissals at Nicosia Airport came up, an intercommunal delegation of trade unionists was just returning to Cyprus following a 14-day training visit to Israel at the invitation of the Israeli Ministry of Labour.[348] The complimentary comments by Greek Cypriot and Turkish Cypriot unionists about their stay in Israel, in combination with Levin's statements which were just then prominently played up in the local newspapers, further stimulated pro-Israeli feelings in local public opinion.

Ten days after Levin left Cyprus, Greek Cypriot trade unionists – SEK members detained in the Pyla detention camp – wrote an open letter published in *Eleftheria* publicly thanking Levin for his efforts on their behalf:

> The trade union officials and active members detained in the Pyla detention camp, Ioannis Kyriakides, Stelios Vlachos, Vasos Papadopoulos, Christodoulos Pavlides, Evgenios Nikola, Stelios Rossides, Georgios Kollios and Nikos Lambrou, feel it is their duty to also express through the press their sincere gratitude, on behalf of the 220 trade unionists who are being held hostage at the Pyla detention facilities, to ICFTU representative Mr Zeev Levin for his tireless and ongoing efforts to upgrade the living conditions of the island's working classes, and particularly for his efforts to settle the justified demand of the RAF and NAAFI workers who were unfairly, and for no reason whatsoever, dismissed.[349]

---

[346] *Ethnos*, 'Statements by the ICFTU representative: The dismissals of RAF workers are political blackmail against Greeks – free trade unions have declared they are in favour of the peoples' self-determination – The British would never have been killed', 21.11.1958. *Fileleftheros*, 'The rally of dismissed RAF-NAAFI workers in Varosha – Yesterday's statements by Mr Zeev Levin', 21.11.1958. *Eleftheria*, 'Mr Levin stated yesterday that the authorities practice political blackmail through the collective dismissals of workers – What the Governor told him during their third meeting yesterday – Disarming response by Mr Levin to a British journalist on the matter of "violence"', 21.11.1958; Excerpts from the press conference held by Zeev Levin at Majestic Hotel in Nicosia on 20.11.1958.

[347] ISA/RG93/MFA/2156/7, Leshem to the British Commonwealth Division (102/3439סמ – 5.12.1958). The Governor's trade union adviser, T. E. Fallows, expressed his discontent to Leshem over Zeev Levin's statements in favour of the Greek Cypriots.

[348] ISA/RG93/MFA/2156/7, Published reports in the newspapers *Davar*, 13.11.1958, and *Al Ha-Mishmar*, 13.11.1958. Also, *Davar*, 'One-third of Cypriot population sides with trade union movement', 20.11.1958. Detailed report.

[349] *Eleftheria*, 'The trade unionists, members of SEK, detained in Pyla thank Mr Levin', 27.11.1958.

In just three short visits to Cyprus, Zeev Levin managed to build a wide network of contacts with the island's labour movement in both communities and significantly improve his country's image in the Greek Cypriot community. This, combined with excellent recommendations by American diplomats in Washington, who characterized him as 'the most obvious choice for Israel's representation to the island'.[350] These recommendations came after Levin's appointment as an ICFTU to Greece, which Levin visited for the first time in January 1959, where he met with the leadership of the General Confederation of Greek Workers (GSEE) and Greek government officials, in order to help both sides with GSEE's organizational restructuring. During his stay in Greece, Levin established close contacts with the US embassy in Athens and managed to earn their trust.[351] Levin's excellent analytical and mediating skills,[352] combined with the 'green light' from the US State Department, led the Israeli Ministry of Foreign Affairs to immediately recruit Levin to its diplomatic service, and thus, in July of 1959, he was named Israel's consul general in Nicosia at a moment that was critical not only for the Cyprus issue, but for the outcome of Cypriot–Israeli relations.[353] Very soon, Levin proved to be the best choice possible.

3.6.1.1.2 Turkish Cypriot public opinion and Israel: 'Filistin' or 'İsrail'?

In 1958, the Turkish Cypriots saw Gamal Abdel Nasser in a negative light, given his unequivocal support of the Greek Cypriots. However, the fact that the Ankara government was taking a positive stance towards the pro-West Arab regimes left little room for the Turkish Cypriot leadership to display sympathy towards Israel.

Fazıl Küçük was the owner and editor-in-chief of the daily newspaper *Halkın Sesi*. At the time, the newspaper espoused the official political line followed by the Turkish Cypriot community. In addition to its daily edition in Turkish, it also published an English edition every Monday. According to archival material, the first written exchange between the Israeli consulate and Fazıl Küçük concerned the English edition, specifically, the *Halkın Sesi* masthead which featured next to its logo a square box showing a map of the Eastern Mediterranean depicting the close proximity of Cyprus

---

[350] ISA/RG93/MFA/263/6, Yapou to Israel's Diplomatic Mission in Ankara and Israel's Diplomatic Representation in Athens (796/10.6.1959). The report of 26.5.1959 by Moshe Erell, adviser to the Israeli embassy in Washington. Cf. 5.2.1.

[351] United States Department of State, Glenn W. LaFantasie (ed.), *Foreign Relations of the United States, 1958–1960, Eastern Europe; Finland; Greece; Turkey* (Washington, DC: United States Government Printing Office, 1993), vol. 10, part 2, 656, no. 256, Telegram from the US embassy in Athens to the US embassy in Brussels describing the contacts between ICFTU delegate Zeev Levin with both the leadership of GSEE and US embassy officials in Athens.

[352] ILMA IV-219A-1-41. During his stay in Athens from late January to mid-February 1959, Levin sent three detailed reports to Reuven Barkat, director of the Histadrut Political Department, dated 28.1.1959, 10.2.1959 and 17.2.1959 (not recorded as incoming documents). Despite his short stay in Athens and although he could not communicate with local trade union and government officials without the help of a translator, Levin managed to quickly understand the complexities of the post-civil war political realities in Greece and correctly assess and evaluate personal antagonisms between the GSEE leadership, personalities of the local trade union opposition within GSEE, Prime Minister Karamanlis' views, while Minister of Labour Aristidis Dimitratos was promoting his own political ambitions at that specific period of time.

[353] Cf. 5.2.1.

to the Turkish coastline (40 nautical miles) contrasted with the far greater distance between Cyprus and Greece (575 nautical miles). In addition, the names of all the countries in the area, namely Turkey, Greece, Syria and Libya, were written in Turkish. The Mediterranean coast of Egypt was unnamed. This particular map piqued the Israeli consul's interest, as Jordanian and Israeli territories were drawn as a single territory under the name 'Filistin', i.e. Palestine (Figure 3.1).

On 5 January 1958, Peretz Leshem sent a brief letter to Fazıl Küçük, addressing him only in his capacity as editor-in-chief of *Halkın Sesi*, and omitting – apparently with intention – his political position. The letter read:

Dear Dr, Küçük,

My attention has been drawn to the map of the Eastern Mediterranean area which you print at the head of the English Weekly Edition of 'Halkın Sesi'.

There the area of Israel and part of the Hashemite Kingdom of Jordan is marked 'Filistin'.

I am sure you agree that the drawing and the block are outdated.

I believe that your paper too should take into account historical events which occurred almost ten years ago and which are recognised by Turkey, which maintains diplomatic relations with Israel, but not with an imaginary 'Filistin'.

With best regards,
Yours sincerely,
P. Leshem
Consul of Israel.[354]

For six months after the letter was sent, *Halkın Sesi* disregarded the suggestions by the Israeli consul. Finally, the English edition of 26 May 1958 featured an altered map in the masthead. Specifically, the word 'Filistin' was deleted (Figure 3.2). The boundary between Israel and Jordan was demarcated by a dotted line, while the borders of the other countries on the map were marked with a solid line. In this manner, Israeli territory was shown on the map in Fazıl Küçük's newspaper. Nevertheless, the word 'İsrail' was not added.[355]

---

[354] ISA/RG93/MFA/1428/11, Leshem to Küçük (2430/13-5.1.1958).
[355] (a) MAA-GZ/HSE1958051901, The Turkish word 'Filistin' (Palestine) was displayed for the last time on the map of the weekly English edition of *Halkın Sesi*, published 19.5.1958; and (b) MAA-GZ/HSE1958052601, The map in the masthead of *Halkın Sesi*'s weekly English edition changed on 26.5.1958.

Figure 3.1 On 19 May 1958, the word 'Filistin' (Palestine) appeared for the last time on the masthead of *Halkın Sesi*'s weekly English edition. *Source*: Photograph from the Milli Arşiv ve Araştırma Dairesi: MAA-GZ/HSE1958051901. *Note*: The Milli Arşiv ve Araştırma Dairesi (National Archives and Research Department) is based in Kyrenia, within the remit of the Turkish regime controlling Cyprus' northern territory since August 1974.

Figure 3.2 On 26 May 1958, *Halkın Sesi*'s weekly English edition, the word 'Filistin' is deleted and Israeli territory is delineated by the ceasefire line agreed upon in 1949 between Israel and the neighbouring Arab countries. However, the designated area was not named 'İsrail' (Israel). *Source*: Photograph from the Milli Arşiv ve Araştırma Dairesi: MAA-GZ/HSE1958052601.

3.6.2 Makarios' visit to Cairo in June of 1958, viewed through Israeli diplomatic reports

In February 1958, Nasserist Egypt and Syria formed the United Arab Republic (UAR) and one of the first foreign political leaders to officially visit the UAR was Archbishop Makarios. As soon as his decision to embark on this visit became known, he made clear that he had not received approval for it from the Greek government. Seeking to downplay the significance of this initiative as much as possible, Athens stressed that the visit to Egypt was 'independent of it'. Makarios himself reaffirmed the same with frequent statements to the Cypriot press.[356]

The Israeli diplomatic delegate in Athens, Jeonathan Prato, understood Greece's reservations perfectly well. In his report on the matter commenting on Makarios' decision to declare solidarity with Gamal Abdel Nasser, he wondered 'what practical benefits might result from this visit, a few days before the new British plan for resolution is announced. The arrival of Makarios shall annoy all those involved; not just the British and Turks, but the Americans as well.'[357] The development was viewed in the same way by the Israeli chargé d'affaires in Ankara, Moshe Alon, and the secretary of the Greek embassy in Ankara, Alexis Stefanou, who confirmed that 'the Greek government was not happy'. According to Alon, Stefanou said that Athens had tried to persuade Makarios either to cancel his visit to the UAR, or at least postpone it. Makarios, however, was waiting to hear the official word on whether solutions for the Cyprus issue proposed by the West would be more satisfactory. The Greek government was not in a position to offer him convincing answers, as the Macmillan Plan had not yet been released and Makarios was unwilling to listen to further exhortations.

As Moshe Alon noted, the visit of Makarios to Cairo had placed Athens in a difficult position vis-à-vis Britain and the US. The Americans had already pointed out to Averoff that the Cyprus question should be resolved at the NATO level and not through collective UN procedures where communist countries would seize the opportunity to become actively involved in the issue with the sole intent of weakening the cohesion of the North Atlantic Alliance. In reality, Greece did not disagree with the American assessment, but it naturally expected its allies to guarantee that its interests in Cyprus would not be compromised. Alon concluded that, under these circumstances, instead of feeling protected by its 'natural allies', Athens had been backed into a corner not only by them, but by its own earlier decisions.[358]

The Cairo visit also raised concerns for Turkey, but for different reasons. Citing sources within the Turkish Ministry of Foreign Affairs, Moshe Alon concluded that Ankara did not want Nasser to become involved in the Cyprus issue either. In fact, it was unsure as to how to deter such a possibility without affecting its delicate relationships with the Baghdad Pact member states and other Arab or African–Asian neutralist countries. Therefore, in anticipation of the announcement of the Macmillan

---

[356] Archbishop Makarios III Foundation, Kokkinou (ed.), *Apanta Archiepiskopou*, vol. 3, 372–5.
[357] ISA/RG93/MFA/263/6, Jeonathan Prato, Israeli chargé d'affaires in Ankara, to the Middle East Division (679/3.6.1958).
[358] ISA/RG130/MFA/3122/8, Alon to the West Europe Division (546/3612/אנ – 16.6.1958) Greece's position was presented to Alon by Alexis Stefanou, second secretary of the Greek embassy in Ankara.

Plan, Turkey chose to wait and see before deciding how to handle Makarios' visit to Cairo. As Alon had learned, the Turkish government instructed newspaper editors in Turkey to tone down their language criticizing the Nasser regime and not to touch upon the issue of the United Arab Republic interest or potential involvement in the Cyprus question at all.[359]

The Israelis carefully monitored the various conflicting interests as they emerged in response to Makarios' visit, and anxiously assessed its impact. For Israel, the matter of most import was, first, what Makarios sought to gain from the UAR, and second, whether Nasser truly intended to take a more active role in the neighbouring island.

On 1 June 1958, – just two weeks before the Macmillan Plan was to be announced,[360] Makarios flew to Cairo from Athens, where he was living permanently after his return from exile. His visit to Cairo lasted ten days.

As one might expect, all the Greek Cypriot newspapers gave extensive coverage to the enthusiastic welcome staged for the archbishop by the Egyptian authorities and members of the Greek Cypriot community in Egypt at Cairo Airport on the morning of 1 June 1958. Both Makarios and President Nasser were wildly cheered, with the crowd holding numerous placards with slogans like, 'Long live the anti-imperialist struggle of the Cypriot people,' 'Long live all peoples struggling against colonialism' and 'Long live Nasser and Makarios.'[361] Immediately after his arrival, Makarios praised the Nasserist regime's 'reform work' which 'draws general admiration', and expressed his gratitude to Egypt for its support of 'the demand of the Cypriot people for freedom and self-determination'.[362]

That evening, Anwar Sadat, General Secretary of the National Union – the only political party in the UAR – and a close associate of Nasser's, hosted a formal dinner in Makarios' honour. In his remarks at the dinner, Sadat linked the coordinated military attack by Britain, France and Israel against his country in 1956 to developments in the Cyprus issue, noting that there are 'blood ties between the people of Cyprus and the people of the UAR' – and continuing that 'there cannot be peace and security for us, unless Cyprus gains independence. Although Cyprus is only 40 miles from Syria, we believe that it must gain independence. The 30 million people of the United Arab Republic continue to support what Cypriots' desire.'[363] All the Greek Cypriot newspapers, regardless of their ideological leanings, responded enthusiastically to Sadat's statements.

In his response to Sadat's speech, as reported by the correspondent in Cairo and published in the *Fileleftheros* on 3 June 1958, Archbishop Makarios stated that:

---

[359] ISA/RG130/MFA/3122/8, Alon to the West Europe Division (539/3612/אנ – 9.6.1958). Alon was informed by the French ambassador in Ankara, who had received pertinent information from reliable sources he did not name.

[360] Cf. 3.6.3.

[361] *Haravgi*, 'We want to decide our future on our own – Speech by the Ethnarch before a number of officials in Cairo – Unlimited solidarity from the United Arab Republic', 3.6.1958.

[362] Ibid.

[363] *Fileleftheros*, 'Egypt and Cyprus shall fight the holy war together in favour of freedom of the people – Egypt finds Turkish claims on Cyprus unacceptable – "We share this anticolonial spirit", the Ethnarch declared', 3.6.1958.

Cyprus belongs to the Afro-Asian group because we share the same anti-colonial spirit sweeping through these continents. Great Britain involved the Turks in the Cyprus matter on the grounds that our island is near Turkey. However, isn't Cyprus near Syria? Yet, as you stated, you support our struggle for independence. We wish to decide our future for ourselves. We cannot accept the continuation of colonialism. Only a free Cyprus can pursue the case of freedom in the Middle East.[364]

That day, the leftist newspaper *Haravgi* published additional statements which were also attributed to Makarios in his response:

In his response, the Archbishop said he was deeply moved by the warm welcome extended to him by officials and the people of Egypt. Being here – he noted – for a moment felt like being in Cyprus. Makarios dismissed the British claims that Cyprus is allegedly necessary to them for defending the 'free world' and stressed that life itself has proven that they want Cyprus, not to safeguard freedom, but as a base for attacking Arab peoples. [...] As long as Cyprus is deprived of its freedom – Makarios concluded – both the security and freedom of Middle Eastern countries shall be at risk.[365]

In reading these two excerpts from the Cairo reports, it is easy to see that the exact contents of Makarios' response could not be surmised. Conflicting texts, words and expressions could leave significant gaps in the minds of a third-party reader – including the Israeli Ministry of Foreign Affairs.

Nevertheless, the Greek Cypriot press expressed a unanimous hope that Nasser's Egypt would play an active role in what was then a crucial phase in the Cyprus issue. Emphasis was placed on 'the direct involvement of the Arab factor in the Cyprus dispute', something which 'would be occurring for the first time',[366] and it was noted that the UAR 'does not want bases on the island, like Britain, or division, like Turkey, but supports the Cypriot people's demand for self-determination'. In fact, Greece was urged to rely on the power of the UAR which 'represents the vast majority of the Arab world'.[367] Finally, as the day for Makarios' departure from Cairo approached, Cypriot reports indicated that most likely 'an appeal would be lodged in connection with the Cyprus question under the auspices of a broad-based group of Arab-Asian and other anti-colonial states' at the upcoming UN General Assembly.[368] The subtle impression

---

[364] Ibid.
[365] Haravgi, 3.6.1958. Cf. Archbishop Makarios III Foundation, Kokkinou (ed.), *Apanta Archiepiskopou*, vol. 3, 143–4.
[366] *Haravgi*, 'New and bright prospects', 6.6.1958.
[367] *Fileleftheros*, 'The Ethnarch's visit to Cairo attracted international interest – It opens up a range of new prospects for the further successful management of the national issue of Cyprus at international level – The Arab world stands in solidarity on the issue of Cyprus', 5.6.1958. *Haravgi*, 'New and bright prospects', 6.6.1958. *Alitheia*, 'The initiative of Makarios in Egypt paved new promising ways – The Turkish factor tends to be ostracised', 9.6.1958.
[368] *Eleftheria*, 'Concrete achievements favouring Cyprus as a result of the Ethnarch's visit to Cairo – Reliable information that the appeal to the UN shall be under the auspices of a wide group of Arab-Asian and other anticolonial states – Turkish allegations have collapsed – The issue of Cyprus is now promoted as an urgent matter of justice, freedom, and peace', 10.6.1958.

created here is that the Greek Cypriot press was downplaying Greece's role in impending developments, compared to Nasser's more powerful United Arab Republic.

In Israel, the excellent relations between Makarios and Nasser had been known since the Bandung Conference in 1955.[369] However, the manner in which Anwar Sadat's remarks to Makarios were reported by the Cypriot and Greek newspapers raised concerns among Israeli diplomats.

The currently known text of Anwar Sadat's address to Makarios on the evening of 1 June 1958 reads:

> On behalf of the 30 million people of the United Arab Republic, I welcome the brother and beloved fighter and leader of the heroic Cypriot people. Our peoples have much in common. In addition to other noble causes, we are linked by a common period in 1956, when a sick man in London thought that the Cypriot people would be put down by fire and sword, and exiled their leader, Archbishop Makarios. Then, the same sick man attacked Egypt. The United Arab Republic shall fight for the independence of Cyprus. There cannot be peace and security for us unless Cyprus gains its freedom. Although Cyprus is only 40 miles from Syria, we believe in its independence. The 30 million people in the Arab Republic shall forever defend what Cypriots want.[370]

At that time, transmission was very slow, and information was often distorted when reported by the press. However, with regard to the unresolved Cyprus question and the ongoing Arab–Israeli conflict, every word was charged with meaning. The Israeli diplomatic representative in Athens, Jeonathan Prato, relying on the day's newspaper reports about Sadat's statements on Cyprus, concluded that: 'the UAR shall fight for the independence of Cyprus because the independence of Cyprus is a prerequisite for the peace and security of the United Arab Republic'.[371] He noted, however, that Sadat made no mention of 'Enosis' or 'Self-Determination', and spoke rather of an independent Cyprus 'within Nasser's sphere of influence' in defence of which the UAR would be 'ready to do battle'.[372] Based on this reasoning, the question that remained was who the UAR would be willing to fight in order to defend the independence of the neighbouring island.

Israeli concerns grew a few days later when the Greek Community in Cairo held an official luncheon in honour of UAR President Gamal Abdel Nasser and Archbishop Makarios at the Semiramis Hotel in the Egyptian capital. At the event, which took place on 4 June, Nasser stated:

> We support the freedom of Cyprus because unless Cyprus is free, our own freedom or independence cannot be guaranteed. The UAR supported the demand for self-determination, not only in principle, but also because the British used Cyprus to

---

[369] Cf. 1.1.3 and 3.3.2.2.
[370] Archbishop Makarios III Foundation, Kokkinou (ed.), *Apanta Archiepiskopou*, vol. 3, 143–4.
[371] ISA/RG93/MFA/263/6, Prato to the Middle East Division (679/3.6.1958).
[372] Ibid.

attack us. An enslaved Cyprus shall always be a risk to us [. . .] When certain people heard I am consulting with Archbishop Makarios, they took advantage of the opportunity to accuse me of conspiring and planning to send weapons from Egypt to Cyprus. Nothing will stop us from supporting Cyprus.[373]

As expected, due to Makarios' visit, the extensive reporting and Egypt's combative declarations of support for Cyprus, Nasser's popularity among Greek Cypriots soared. At a time when the slightest remark could convey a variety of meanings, Leshem included a statement in his report which was attributed to Makarios among others: 'Once Cyprus has a regime of its own, it shall decide whether it shall accede to Greece or the British Commonwealth or the United Arab Republic.' Leshem failed to mention the name of the newspaper which had published this statement that essentially portrayed the UAR as akin to a motherland, protecting the Greek Cypriots. However, primary archival sources and reports in the Greek Cypriot press show that Makarios never said anything of the sort. Nevertheless, the false information Leshem included in his report provided yet another serious cause for Israeli concern.[374]

In June 1958, the flood of reported statements (both true and false) gave Israel the impression that the newly formed UAR might well include Cyprus in its expansionist plans. A start in this direction had already been made the previous February, when Syria came under Nasser's absolute control. In fact, according to Israel's pessimistic assessments, it would not be long before Iraq, Lebanon and Jordan were led along a similar path.[375]

Based on this line of thinking, if the Egyptian sphere of influence were to extend to Cyprus, Israel might suddenly find itself surrounded by pro-Nasserist regimes. From this perspective, public statements by Nasser and Sadat to Makarios linking 'Cyprus' independence' to the safeguarding of UAR security concerned the Israelis far more than the actual contents of the soon to be released Macmillan Plan.

3.6.3 The Macmillan Plan and Israeli concerns about UAR influence in Cyprus

Just before the release of the Macmillan Plan, Turkey declared that the only acceptable solution to the Cyprus issue was partition. The Turkish Grand National Assembly unanimously adopted a resolution to that effect on June 16, 1958,[376] and the government encouraged mass protests in major cities nationwide.[377] According to the Israeli chargé d'affaires in Ankara, Moshe Alon, such protests 'aimed at sending a message abroad that the government had the people's mandate to take action and to decide the fate of

[373] Archbishop Makarios III Foundation, Kokkinou (ed.), *Apanta Archiepiskopou*, vol. 3, 145–7.
[374] ISA/RG93/MFA/2156/7, Leshem to the British Commonwealth Division (102/3028מס – 5.6.1958).
[375] Cf. 3.6.4.
[376] ISA/RG130/MFA/3122/38, Reuven Roubach, first secretary of the Israeli diplomatic mission in Ankara to the West Europe Division (559/3612/אנ – 23.6.1958). Cf. Archbishop Makarios III Foundation, Kokkinou (ed.), *Apanta Archiepiskopou*, vol. 3, 377.
[377] ISA/RG130/MFA/3122/38, Roubach to the West Europe Division (559/3612/אנ – 23.6.1958). Cf. Holland, *Britain and the Revolt in Cyprus*, 249–50.

Turkish Cypriots on the island, even by force'.[378] It was not long before the Turkish Cypriots revolted. In early June 1958, Cyprus was still reeling from the impact. It was clear that tensions would increase over the following weeks, and the British would seek reinforcements to control the situation. For the first time, the Israeli consulate prepared to evacuate Israeli citizens living on the island.[379]

On 19 June 1958, British Prime Minister Harold Macmillan presented Parliament with a new set of proposals known as the 'Macmillan Plan' to resolve the Cyprus question. Under this plan, Britain would maintain sovereignty on the island for seven years, and Greece and Turkey would each appoint a 'government representative' to assist the British governor. A new constitution would be established to ensure the institutional separation between the Greek and Turkish Cypriot communities by assembling two separate houses of representatives, with powers to set laws for 'purely communal affairs'. The government would consist of four Greek Cypriot and two Turkish Cypriot ministers. The two Greek and Turkish 'government representatives' would also be members of the cabinet. After the seven-year period, British military bases would remain in Cyprus, and a shared sovereignty under Britain, Greece and Turkey would be considered. Nevertheless, the British government's statement of 19 December 1956 which paved the way for final partition would remain in effect.[380]

Naturally, the Greeks and Makarios rejected the plan, describing it as pro-partition. Moreover, if the Macmillan Plan were to go into effect, Turkey would – for the first time since 1878 – acquire institutional powers in the Cypriot political system. On the other hand, while Turkey initially demanded the establishment of a Turkish military base on the island during the seven-year interim period with a view to leaving the door open for partition at the first opportunity,[381] as the weeks of negotiation went by, it adopted an increasingly temperate stance.

Ultimately, on 25 August 1958, Ankara formally announced that it would accept the Macmillan Plan as a basis for negotiation.[382] No one was surprised by this development.[383] It had been indicated by the statements of Turkish Cypriot leader Fazıl Küçük in Ankara on 11 June 1958, immediately following his meeting with Turkish Foreign Affairs Minister Fatin Zorlu. At that time, Küçük recognized the points establishing Turkey's political presence on the island and leaving open the prospect of partition as

[378] ISA/RG130/MFA/3122/38, Alon to the West Europe Division (571/3612/אב – 23.6.1958). Cf. Holland, *Britain and the Revolt in Cyprus*, 250–5; and Christodoulides, *Schedia Lysis*, 126–7.
[379] ISA/RG93/MFA/2156/7, Leshem to the British Commonwealth Division (102/3690מ – 17.6.1958). Cf. Holland, *Britain and the Revolt in Cyprus*, 253–4.
[380] Hatzivassiliou, *To Kypriako Zitima*, 103–8. Holland, *Britain and the Revolt in Cyprus*, 259–62; and Christodoulides, *Schedia Lysis*, 122–9. Critical overview of the Macmillan Plan.
[381] ISA/RG130/MFA/3122/38, Roubach to the West Europe Division (580/3612/אב – 27.6.1958), Roubach was informed by the press officer of the Turkish Ministry of Foreign Affairs that the 'Turkish government shall agree to an interim period on the island under British rule, but only if it is immediately allowed to set up a Turkish military base in Cyprus, and provided that the island's eventual partition, upon expiry of the interim period, is not ruled out.'
[382] ISA/RG130/MFA/3122/38, Roubach to the West Europe Division (746/3612/אב – 30.8.1958). The 25.8.1958 bulletin issued by the *Anadolu* news agency, including the relevant statements by Turkish Minister of Foreign Affairs Fatin Zorlu, is attached.
[383] Christodoulides, *Schedia Lysis*, 120–37.

positive aspects of the Plan. The Israeli delegation to Ankara concluded that Turkey had essentially accepted the Plan as early as June 1958.[384]

On 1 October 1958, Turkey appointed its then consul general in Nicosia, Burhan Işın, as the 'government representative' called for in the Macmillan Plan.[385] Moshe Alon described this move as 'a wise decision by the Turkish government' in the sense that, although Turkey could have appointed another dignitary to serve as 'government representative', it did not do so because publicity surrounding his arrival on the island would further exacerbate the already tense situation. Similarly, Alon saw Athens' stubborn refusal to accept the Macmillan Plan as 'non-productive'.[386] In reality, the appointment of the Turkish consul to the position of 'government representative' on the part of Ankara was clearly meant to make a positive impression, coming after intense behind-the-scenes pressure on the Foreign Office by the United States.[387] It was most certainly not evidence of Turkey's prudence, as it no longer mattered whether Ankara conducted itself with civility. What mattered was the fact that over the objections of Athens and Makarios, the Macmillan Plan was beginning to be put into effect. Before their eyes, Greece and the Greek Cypriots now witnessed the unfolding of baleful *fait accompli*.

The Israeli consulate in Nicosia closely monitored developments and avoided any show of sympathy with either side. During that time, Leshem was reluctant to facilitate contact between a Turkish Cypriot employee of the local Ministry of Agriculture and Israeli government officials regarding the importation of fertilizers from Israel for use on farmland owned by Turkish Cypriots. In addition, Leshem was asked to intervene in finding entrepreneurs who would undertake the distribution of Turkish Cypriot agricultural products in the Israeli market. The consul was fully aware of the political aspect of this – seemingly innocent – request. An effort by the Turkish Cypriots was already underway to prepare a response either to a trade embargo by the Greek Cypriots or even the possibility of partition. They wished to develop an economy for their community that would be as self-reliant as possible and unaffected by Greek Cypriot actions. Leshem avoided involving Israeli state officials when approached with such requests, either directly or indirectly. However, he provided the contact information of private Israeli citizens and entrepreneurs who might be interested in expanding the Turkish Cypriot market.[388]

At the same time, though, the Israelis did not fail to notice the Greek Cypriots' increasing tendency to seek support from the UAR, Nasser and the Arab world in general. And this tendency was not without reason. In September 1958, the Arab League approved a resolution whereby its member states would support the Greek Cypriot claim for self-determination in the event that it came before the UN. As the 10 September telegram from Makarios thanking the secretary general of the Arab League stated:

[384] ISA/RG130/MFA/3122/38, Roubach to the West Europe Division (790/3612/אב – 19.9.1958). The 11.9.1958 bulletin issued by the *Anadolu* news agency, including Küçük's statements, is attached.
[385] Holland, *Britain and the Revolt in Cyprus*, 284. Cf. ISA/RG130/MFA/3122/38, Alon to the West Europe Division (0/68-1.10.1958).
[386] ISA/RG130/MFA/3122/38, Alon to the West Europe Division (827/3612/אב – 2.10.1958).
[387] Nicolet, *United States Policy towards Cyprus*, 128.
[388] ISA/RG93/MFA/2156/7, Leshem to the Economic Affairs Division, Israeli Ministry of Foreign Affairs (102/31050סמ – 1.7.1958).

On behalf of the Cypriot people, we wish to express our grateful thanks for the Arab League's decision in favour of the self-determination of Cyprus, which is deeply appreciated. Please convey our gratitude to League Member-States for this decision, which confirms the commitment of Arab peoples to the cause of freedom and justice. We also wish to affirm the Cypriot people's solidarity with the noble cause of Arab nationalism and cooperation, which we believe is a factor in peace and freedom in the Middle East.[389]

Makarios' reference to 'the Cypriot people's solidarity with the cause of Arab nationalism', which was presented as a 'factor in peace and freedom in the Middle East', reflects the starkly different views of the state of things in the region by the Greek Cypriot leadership on the one hand, and Israel on the other. While for Makarios, Arab nationalism was a factor in peace and stability, for Israel, Arab nationalism represented the main destabilizing factor and most ominous threat.

It was not long before the Israelis began to wonder whether the UAR had finally found a way to infiltrate Cyprus more assertively, reinforcing EOKA's arsenal and improving its operational effectiveness. They had not forgotten that during the Suez Crisis of 1956, and while the British military troops were focused on taking control of the Canal, Egyptian secret services had allegedly contacted EOKA members, who provided them with information about British activities on the island. While fighting in Egypt was underway, EOKA was escalating its activity, resulting in 76 dead and 160 wounded British.[390] In recalling the recent past, the Israelis could not preclude the possibility of EOKA's alignment with Nasser. The British response to Israeli concerns was reassuring. It argued that EOKA received sufficient support from Greece and had no need of reinforcements from the UAR or any other country. Additionally, the British estimated that 'an alliance between Nasser and Grivas would infuriate the Cypriot Left', and that Nasser's regime was ideologically closer to the communist AKEL than to the Right-nationalist EOKA.[391] The British claims were not convincing, however. Israel believed that Nasser's engagement with Cyprus was not based on ideological grounds, given that he maintained excellent relations with all Greek Cypriot political parties.

Meanwhile, there was a deluge of diplomatic developments. Both Athens and the Ethnarchy were focusing on how to avoid further *faits accomplis* in Cyprus due to the implementation of the Macmillan Plan and on how to initiate negotiations between Greece and Turkey on the future status of the island, now with a view to establishing an independent Cypriot state.[392] Britain's determination to proceed with the implementation of the Macmillan Plan (to the point where London would not rule out the possibility of a Greek exit from NATO – if Athens insisted on rejecting the Macmillan Plan – and remaining in a 'neutral Balkan zone' together with

---

[389] Archbishop Makarios III Foundation, Kokkinou (ed.), *Apanta Archiepiskopou*, vol. 3, 417.

[390] Sakkas, *Kypriako kai o Aravikos Kosmos*, 62–3.

[391] ISA/RG130/MFA/3122/38, Roubach to the West Europe Division (897/3612/אב – 27.10.1958), An assessment by the first secretary of the British embassy in Ankara on the likelihood of links between the UAR and EOKA in Cyprus.

[392] Hatzivassiliou, *To Kypriako Zitima*, 111–14.

Yugoslavia).[393] All this in conjunction with the ongoing brutalities in Cyprus aimed at strengthening the Turkish arguments in favour of partition may have influenced Makarios' proposal for a solution to independence in September 1958. In his telegram of 27 September 1958 to Sir Roger Allen, the British ambassador in Athens, the archbishop wrote:

> On 22 September, in an interview with Miss Barbara Castle, an MP and the Vice-Chair of the Labour Party, I said that the Cypriot people would accept as a solution to the issue of Cyprus a constitution for self-government for an agreed-upon period, at the end of which the Island shall be granted independence. The status of independence shall be guaranteed by the United Nations, and it shall not be subject to changes without the consent of the United Nations. I now wish to formally submit these proposals to Her Majesty's Government.[394]

Questions were raised as to what behind-the-scenes discussions had been taking place between Greece, Great Britain, Turkey and the US,[395] and whether or not Makarios' statements to Castle had actually taken the Greek government by surprise.[396] But all of this was of little interest to the Israelis. What concerned them most at that time was something much simpler: how regional balances in the Eastern Mediterranean and Israeli regional interests in particular would be affected by this political volte-face in Cyprus.

The summer of 1958 in particular was a time of concern about security and territorial integrity as a result of Nasser's growing influence in the region. The establishment of the United Arab Republic, the subversion of Iraq's pro-West regime and the frightening prospect of Nasserization in Jordan and Lebanon increased the threat of a coordinated Arab military attack on Israel. The possibility of being surrounded by pro-Nasserist regimes held catastrophic implications for the Jewish state. Under these circumstances, the Israeli Ministry of Foreign Affairs underscored the immediate need to normalize relations with Turkey, the only Western Muslim

---

[393] Ibid., 108–9.
[394] Archbishop Makarios III Foundation, Kokkinou (ed.), *Apanta Archiepiskopou*, vol. 3, 178–9. Cf. Stavros Panteli, *A New History of Cyprus* (London and The Hague: East-West Publications, 1984), 207, in David French, *Fighting EOKA: The British Counter-Insurgency Campaign on Cyprus, 1955–1959* (Oxford: Oxford University Press, 2015), 272. According to Panteli, on 7.9.1958, Makarios had informed the Greek government in confidence that given the British determination to implement the Macmillan Plan, he would consider accepting an interim period of self-government, at the end of which the island would gain independence, guaranteed by the United Nations.
[395] Nicolet, *United States Policy towards Cyprus*, 116–22. On behind-the-scenes diplomatic activity to revise the conditions of the Macmillan Plan.
[396] Dimitri S. Bitsios, *Cyprus: The Vulnerable Republic* (Thessaloniki: Institute for Balkan Studies, 1975), 78–80. Bitsios vividly describes his own embarrassment and that of Konstantinos Karamanlis when they learned from Barbara Castle of Makarios' statements regarding independence. Evangelos Averoff describes a similar sense of surprise experienced by the Greek government: 'Thus, on 20 September (announced on the 22nd), quite suddenly and apparently feeling anxious, he did something which, though correct in substance, was quite wrong in its execution. He told the English Labour Party's prominent member, Barbara Castle, who has always helped us, that he would accept conditional independence as a solution to the Cyprus question [. . .].' Cf. Averoff, *Istoria*, vol. 2, 74–6; and Xydis, *Cyprus: Conflict and Conciliation*, 514.

country in the region with which it shared common security issues.[397] Thus, behind-the-scenes talks between Israeli and Turkish diplomats, which had already begun in September 1957, were intensified. The overturning of the pro-West regime in Iraq in July 1958 hastened the discussions, and by August 1958, the secret rapprochement between Israel and Turkey had become a reality.

At precisely the same time, Turkish diplomacy had focused attention on Cyprus, adding its own dimension to the Israeli–Turkish rapprochement. Besides, Makarios' June visit to Cairo and Nasser's proclamations of support for the Greek Cypriots had already attracted Israeli interest and concern that the UAR would include the neighbouring island in its expansionist plans.[398]

3.6.4 The Turkish–Israeli rapprochement, 1958

As noted, in 1 February 1958, when Syria and Egypt united to form the United Arab Republic, Egyptian President Gamal Abdel Nasser envisioned the creation of a unified Arab state under his leadership, organized according to the ideological model of the regime he led in Egypt. Nasserism was particularly popular in the Arab community of the time, and this was cause for concern amongst the pro-West regimes of the region. The Iraqi and Jordanian monarchies decided to form a competing entity at the opposite end of the ideological spectrum of the UAR, and on 14 February 1958 established the short-lived Arab Federation.[399]

Then, on 14 July 1958, the Iraqi monarchy was overthrown by a military coup led by Abd al-Karim Qasim, who changed the country's political system to a 'republic', with a prominent pro-Nasserist identity. On 2 August, Iraq, under its new constitutional polity, withdrew from the Arab Federation, while political turmoil threatened Lebanon and Jordan, where Nasserist groups were attempting to seize power. The Lebanese government asked Washington to deploy military forces and safeguard the country's pro-West orientation. A similar appeal was made to Britain by the Jordanian monarchy. Both Washington and London responded immediately to these requests. Britain in particular dispatched troops from its military bases in Cyprus,[400] and Israel allowed British military planes to use its national airspace on the flight to Jordan. This enraged the USSR, which then accused the Israeli government of complicity in Western aggression,[401] while simultaneously mobilizing its own troops along the borders with

[397] Cf. 3.6.5.
[398] Cf. 3.6.2 Israeli concerns over statements by Gamal Abdel Nasser and Anwar Sadat about Cyprus in June 1958.
[399] Cf. John Jessup, *An Encyclopaedic Dictionary of Conflict Resolution, 1945–1996* (Westport, CT: Greenwood Press, 1998).
[400] Nicolet, *United States Policy towards Cyprus*, 124–5. Cf. Koutsis, *Mesi Anatoli*, 182–4, 252–5, 309–12, 377–80, developments in Egypt, Syria, Lebanon, and Iraq in the summer of 1958.
[401] Israel State Archives, Barouch Gilead (ed.), *Documents on the Foreign Policy of Israel* (Jerusalem: Government Printer, 2001), vol. 13, 65–6 no. 38 – [ISA/RG130/MFA/2327/4]. Israeli embassy in Moscow to the Eastern Europe Division (863/1.8.1958), Soviet criticism of Israel's decision to make its airspace available in order to facilitate the RAF in its operations in Jordan. Ibid., 96 no. 55. By resolution of the UN Security Council, following a marathon session which took place from 8.8.1958 to 12.8.1958, it was decided that US and British troops would withdraw from Lebanon and Jordan, respectively. Troop withdrawal was completed in October 1958.

Turkey. The chain of developments that summer led Turkey and Israel to settle their diplomatic differences with alacrity so they would be able to confront their common regional opponents.[402]

The rapprochement between Israel and Turkey did not come about out of the blue. Starting in September 1957, Israeli Foreign Minister Golda Meir had made a priority of smoothing relations with Turkey. Over a number of months, the Israeli ambassador in Rome, Eliahu Sasson, held behind-the-scenes meetings with senior Turkish diplomats and Turkish Foreign Minister Fatin Zorlu himself.[403] The formation of the UAR increased concerns. Between June and July of 1958, Turkish and Israeli experts held intensive meetings in Rome to consider ways of halting the spread of Nasserism into neighbouring Arab countries.[404] Upon successfully completing these sessions, it was decided that the Turkish and Israeli foreign ministers would meet in due course to seal the agreements reached. No specific date was set for such a meeting, however.[405]

As a consequence of the Nasserist military coup in Iraq on 14 July1958, the meeting between Zorlu and Meir was moved up. On 2 August, the day the dissolution of the Arab Federation was announced, Meir and Zorlu held a top secret meeting in Zurich to finalize their countries' coordinated moves in view of the apparent political destabilization of Jordan and Lebanon, incited by Nasser.

Nevertheless, regional cooperation between Turkey and Israel could not be achieved without a price. Turkey sought the mediation of the Jewish lobby in the USA to secure generous financial aid for itself. Israel wanted Turkey to restore bilateral diplomatic relations and return its ambassador, who had been recalled from Tel Aviv in November 1956 during the Suez Crisis.[406] Zorlu avoided promising an imminent restoration of diplomatic relations with the justification that Turjey would need the support of Arab countries at the upcoming 13th Session of the UN General Assembly, where the Cyprus issue would be discussed again. At the same time, he demanded that Israel overtly support Turkish positions on Cyprus. During his meeting with Meir, Zorlu did not specify exactly what Israel's assistance would entail.[407] However, in order to override any hesitation his Israeli counterpart might have, he argued that, 'Israel has no obligation towards Greece. Greece is amongst the countries opposing Israel in every Western or international forum, as well as at every NATO summit.' Meir completely agreed with Zorlu's finding.[408] Thus, when the Turkish foreign minister flew to New York in mid-August to attend the emergency session of the UN Security Council on the situation in Jordan and Lebanon, he met with Abba Eban, with whom he agreed that the two countries would cooperate within the UN framework 'on any matter pertaining to their interests'.[409]

---

[402] Nachmani, *Israel, Turkey and Greece*, 74–8.

[403] Israel State Archives, Gilead (ed.), *Documents*, vol. 13, 793 no. 418.

[404] Ibid., no. 425, Shiloakh to Ben-Gurion and Golda Meir (11.8.1958), Report on the meeting held between Israeli and Turkish experts in Rome from 26.6.58 to 2.7.1958 (ISA/RG130/MFA/3752/15).

[405] Ibid., 793, no. 418.

[406] Cf. 3.4.2.3.

[407] Turkey made its claims more specific a few months later, in November 1958. Cf. 3.6.5.

[408] Ibid., 805, no. 425 (ISA/RG130/MFA/3752/15).

[409] Ibid., 814–15, no. 426, Abba Eban, head of Israel's permanent representation to the UN, to Shiloakh (18.8.1958) (ISA/RG130/MFA/3752/15).

On 29 August 1958, the rapprochement between Turkey and Israel was sealed at a secret meeting in Ankara between prime ministers David Ben-Gurion and Adnan Menderes. According to Israeli archival sources, long classified, there is no written record of exactly what was said at that meeting,[410] but in 2001, the Israel State Archives released a top secret report which stated simply that the two prime ministers focused on 'military, economic, and political issues, and on the fields of science and culture'.[411]

3.6.5 Israeli pro-Turkish manoeuvres on the Cyprus issue at the UN

The looming threat of the Macmillan Plan disappointed the Greek Cypriots, who once again pinned their hopes on Greece, Yugoslavia and other non-NATO states in the upcoming UN session.[412] Küçük and the Turkish Cypriots, on the other hand, viewed the plan in a positive light and were eager to see how Ankara would move to implement it.[413] As the opening of the 13th Session of the UN General Assembly approached, the convergence of Britain and Turkey on the issue was becoming ever more clear. During talks at the British embassy in Ankara, a British official told his Israeli counterpart that he believed 'the Turks were convinced of the sincerity of British intentions, and were cooperating to implement the plan'.[414] Indeed, on 25 August 1958, Turkey formally accepted the Macmillan Plan and on 1 October, named its 'government representative' to Cyprus.[415] One month later, on 22 September, the Cyprus question was placed on the agenda of the 13th Session,[416] marking the start of a particularly tense period in diplomatic activity.

When Zorlu asked Meir in July of that year for Israel's active support on the Cyprus question, he did not specify precisely what he was seeking.[417] The time for that came a few months later: in November 1958, Turkey asked Israel to act as mediator in Latin America and garner support for Turkish rather than Greek positions at the upcoming UN vote.[418] The reason behind Turkey's request was this: Turkey had not developed a significant diplomatic presence in Latin America. As the Israelis phrased it in their reports, the Turkish presence in that part of the world was 'zero to none'. The Latin American countries had considerable voting power at the UN because of their unified stance against colonialism. As for the Cyprus issue in particular, the majority of Latin American votes had previously been cast in favour of

---

[410] Ibid., 818, no. 428.

[411] Ibid., 819–20 no. 429 [ISA/RG130/2450/9].

[412] Nicolet, *United States Policy towards Cyprus*, 128–31. Cf. ISA/RG93/MFA/2156/7, Leshem to the British Commonwealth Division (102/3119במ – 7.7.1958)

[413] Cf. 3.6.3; and ISA/RG93/MFA/2156/7, Roubach to the West Europe Division (790/3612/אנ – 19.9.1958), Küçük's statements on the Macmillan Plan following consultations with the Turkish government in Ankara were characterized as 'extremely moderate as regards the British plan'.

[414] ISA/RG93/MFA/2156/7, Roubach to the West Europe Division (822/3612/אנ – 1.10.1958).

[415] Cf. 3.6.3.

[416] Xydis, 'The UN General Assembly', 152.

[417] Cf. 3.6.4.

[418] ISA/RG130/MFA/3122/38, Maurice Fischer, assistant to the director general of the Ministry of Foreign Affairs, to Arieh Aroch, Israeli ambassador to Rio de Janeiro (700/4.11.1958). On the Turkish request for Israeli mediation with South American countries and on Moshe Tov's actions in New York.

Greek positions. This was not just a matter of ideology but the result of successful Greek diplomacy in Latin America, the extensive Greek diaspora and powerful Greek shipowners active there. At the 12th Session of the UN General Assembly, the permanent representatives of Guatemala, Bolivia and Panama had lent substantial support to Greek positions.[419]

Israel, on the other hand, had made its presence felt in Latin America since its very first months of its independence through the technical aid offered in collaboration with local Jewish entrepreneurs. Israeli embassies in Montevideo and Buenos Aires were opened as early as 1949, and by 1955, a broad network of Israeli diplomatic missions – embassies and consulates – had been deployed in the region. When Israel transferred the Ministry of Foreign Affairs from Tel Aviv to Jerusalem, Bolivia, Chile, Colombia, Costa Rica, the Dominican Republic, Ecuador, El Salvador, Haiti, Panama, Uruguay and Venezuela also moved their embassies from Tel Aviv to West Jerusalem, thus formally recognizing the city as the capital of the Jewish state (whereas Israel's traditional allies, such as Britain, France and the US, made no such move, nor did any other Western country – except the Netherlands).[420] In light of the above, it was only natural that Turkish diplomacy turned to Israel, in the hope of leveraging its influence in Latin America and weakening the strong pro-Greek front which had formed there in the 1950s.

In exchange for Israeli mediation, Turkey promised that, after the UN vote, the Turkish ambassador would be reappointed to Tel Aviv, and bilateral diplomatic relations with Israel would be fully restored. However, this could not happen before the UN vote, since Turkey would thereby lose Arab votes – an argument Israel fully appreciated.

Thus, Israel agreed to the Turkish request and to this end, recruited Moshe Tov, an Israeli diplomat of Argentinian descent and a member of Israel's permanent representation to the UN. Tov had served for a number of years in the Division of Latin America in the Ministry of Foreign Affairs and was considered the most appropriate person to conduct exploratory contacts with Latin American representatives. It was through his handling of matters and personal contacts that Israel had managed to cultivate strong ties with the Latin American Bloc since its earliest presence as a member state of the UN. The diligence displayed by Tov in promoting Turkish positions on the Cypriot issue was impressive. The main reason for this was very succinctly summed up by Turkish Foreign Minister Fatin Zorlu: 'Israel has no obligation to Greece.'[421]

Zorlu's conclusion was not without basis: according to Israeli archival material, Greece had omitted to ask Israel for a favourable vote, or any comparable diplomatic assistance, or, at the very least, for a 'constructive' abstention. As pointed out in October 1958 by Jeonathan Prato, head of Israel's diplomatic representation to Athens, the

[419] Xydis, *Cyprus: Conflict and Conciliation*, 480.
[420] Yoel Bar-Romi, 'Israel, ha-Umot ha-Meukhadot u-Medinot Amerika Latinit: Hirhurim al Shanim Rekhokot' ['Israel, the United Nations and the Latin American States: Reflections from Distant Years'], in *Misrad ha'Khutz*, ed. Yeger, Govrin and Oded, 754–69.
[421] Cf. 3.6.4.

Greek Ministry of Foreign Affairs had never explored whether and to what extent Israel would support Greek positions at the UN on the Cyprus question. Prato was likely disappointed with his personal meeting with Evangelos Averoff in early September of that year. The Greek foreign minister had merely thanked Israel for abstaining during the 12th Session 'despite the anomaly in diplomatic relations between our two countries', without so much as expressing the hope that in time bilateral relations would be improved or normalized.[422] In November 1958, one month before the UN vote, Prato reiterated that in any event, Greece did not expect support from Israel, based on reports from Angelos Vlachos (who in the meantime had returned from Cyprus and taken over the department of the Greek Ministry of Foreign Affairs, which dealt with the Cyprus issue) and other officials in Athens. According to Prato, not only did Athens choose to discount a favourable Israeli vote, it never even asked for one.[423] Based on official reports of the period, Israeli diplomacy did not face a dilemma when it came to support for the Turkish side. Indeed, Israel's permanent representation to the UN was placed at the disposal of Turkey, which sought the implementation of the Macmillan Plan in order to pave the way towards self-determination for Turkish Cypriots – with the ultimate goal of partitioning the neighbouring island.[424]

Moshe Tov's first Latin American contact was Brazil's permanent representation to the UN. As Tov stated in his report, the Brazilians emphasized their commitment to anti-colonialism. As for the issue of Cyprus, however, Tov perceived that they seemed willing to revisit their position, taking into serious consideration the political and military balance in the Mediterranean, and the importance of military bases on the island, both for NATO and the West in general.[425] This initial Israeli foray set the tone for the key arguments Tov presented to the remaining Latin American diplomats. Specifically, while up to that time the Turkish side stressed the need to safeguard the rights of Turkish Cypriots, Tov shifted the interest of his interlocutors to the need for ensuring that Cyprus remain within the Western sphere of influence. His key argument was that this would be possible only through the agency of Turkey and Britain, and not Greece. Meanwhile, Tov sought to undermine the anti-colonial slant of the Greek requests by depicting Enosis as a clear manifestation of Greek nationalist expansionism, which he linked to Soviet attempts at expanding their influence in the Middle East. Tov's letter to his personal friend, the foreign minister of El Salvador, Alfredo Ortiz Mancia, dated 12 November 1958, is revealing in this respect:

> My dear Minister and Friend;
>
> I recall that during your stay in New York, I spoke to you of the Cyprus problem as one of the factors most harmful to the policy of the West in its struggle against communist influence. The Cyprus problem as such is a bloody fiction invented by a group of extremists, which has confused the political leaders of Greece but which is basically Soviet inspired. But taking advantage of the anti-colonialist trend, so

---

[422] ISA/RG93/MFA/263/6, Prato to Eytan (182/ı – 8.10.1958).
[423] ISA/RG130/MFA/3122/38, Prato to Eytan (0/23-12.11.1958).
[424] Xydis, *Cyprus: Conflict and Conciliation*, 516.
[425] ISA/RG130/MFA/3122/38, Fischer to Aroch (700/ 4.11.1958).

laudable and just in principle but which at the same time has served as a cover-up for much rotten merchandise, this topic has arisen and since been most skilfully managed by the Soviets in the General Assembly for reasons which are obvious.

Attached you will find an editorial which has appeared in a Spanish New York daily, and which, I believe, reflects the historical background of the matter as well as the special characteristics which surround it.[426] It is obvious that Cyprus is a bulwark for the defence of the Mediterranean. And the Russians want to destroy it. Actually the Greek position does not defend the designs of annexation of a territory to which its claims are none too convincing.

At the time of your stay in New York, I mentioned to you how concerned I was about this matter. As the constant target of Soviet aversion and hatred, we could not view favourably a solution that would strategically weaken the status quo in the Mediterranean in favour of the forces of aggression. In our estimation, the Turkish point of view contains a fair solution as it meets with the interests of the two ethnic groups which inhabit the island and yet maintains constant the defensive factor in which we have so great an interest.

El Salvador, up to now, has supported the Greek stand, spurred no doubt by the romantic lure of anti-colonialism, which in this case can however not be applied. We know that this year, the reasons set down by Turkey are creating an impression in other countries of Latin America. It would be of prime importance that the Delegation of El Salvador be in a position to favour a more constructive tendency than in the past.

The topic of Cyprus will no doubt come up in the First Committee next week and a change in the stand of El Salvador would be highly beneficial and perhaps decisive. Of the twenty Latin American countries, only eight supported Greece during the last Assembly; we know for certain that some of them are seriously considering a change in position.

I trust, my dear Minister, you will forgive this intrusion, but I consider it an obligation on my part to relate to you my concern, in the certainty that you will realise the high motives which prompt me to write you on this matter.[427]

Mancia's response was not long in coming:

My dear Moshe,

I am pleased to acknowledge receipt of your confidential communication of the 12th [November 1958] in which you expound your most interesting view vis-à-vis the current state of the Cyprus question, the reasons and background of this problem and the interests and motives which, in your judgement, promote and heighten them.

---

[426] Moshe Tov does not specify any further details about the cited publication (name of the Spanish newspaper, date of publication, author, etc.). No copy of the report was included in the reviewed archival material.

[427] ISA/RG130/MFA/3122/38, Moshe Tov's letter of 12.11.1958 to Alfredo Ortiz Mancia, the foreign minister of El Salvador at the time.

In reply, I take pleasure in assuring you that I have not only read your valuable exposition with all due attention but that I deem the motives and point of view therein expressed most important.

I should like to add further that I have written to the Permanent Delegation of El Salvador to the UN about this matter [. . .].[428]

El Salvador's stance did indeed change, supporting the solution of 'direct negotiations amongst the parties involved', meaning Greece, Britain and Turkey, in order to resolve the question within the context of NATO.[429]

Meanwhile, the Israeli embassy in Rio de Janeiro began to mobilize, urged on by Tov's assessment that – with regard to the Cyprus issue – Brazil might deviate from its consistently anti-colonialist line. This led Turkey's ambassador in Brazil, Şefkati İstinyeli, to contact prominent journalists in the country, in order to promote Turkish positions on the Cyprus question in the local media. Israeli diplomats also mediated a meeting between İstinyeli and Colombian embassy officials there. The Turkish ambassador faithfully reiterated Tov's Cold War arguments, just as they had been laid out in writing to El Salvador's foreign minister a few days prior.[430]

Behind-the-scenes manoeuvring by Israel in support of Turkish positions was greatly appreciated, not just by Turkish diplomats who were closely monitoring the effort, but also personally by Foreign Minister Fatin Zorlu himself, who carefully heeded the instructions he received from Tov on 17 November 1958, at the offices of the Israeli mission to the UN. Nevertheless, despite the flurry of activity, the Israeli side admitted that, in effect, influencing the vote of the Latin Americans was far from simple. Both the Brazilian Ministry of Foreign Affairs and a significant number of local journalists declared loudly that they had no intention of supporting Turkish positions.[431] In a final attempt to persuade the Latin Americans, Tov himself arranged a face-to-face meeting between Zorlu and the heads of all South American representations to the UN. At that meeting, Zorlu realized how difficult the undertaking had turned out. In describing the meeting, Tov admitted that it had been a 'fiasco' for which he cast sole blame on the Turkish foreign minister. According to Tov, Zorlu gave the impression that he was not at all inclined to handle even a cursory dialogue with the diplomats before him. He repeated the argument again and again that '60% of Greek Cypriots are communists, and as such, the Greek Cypriots represent a direct threat to Western interests', adding that Turkey was the only reliable defender of Western interests in the Middle East and the Eastern Mediterranean. The Latin Americans, however, had expected to hear well-supported arguments – particularly from such a cool-headed individual.[432]

[428] ISA/RG130/MFA/3122/38, El Salvador Foreign Minister Alfredo Ortiz Mancia's letter to Moshe Tov (20.11.1958).
[429] ISA/RG130/MFA/3122/38, Mancia to Moshe Tov (4.12.1958).
[430] ISA/RG130/MFA/3122/38, Israeli embassy in Rio de Janeiro to Israel's permanent representation to the UN (233-3/ב – 17.11.1958).
[431] ISA/RG130/MFA/3122/38, Aroch to the Latin America Division (629-104015/19.11.1958).
[432] ISA/RG130/MFA/3122/38, West Europe Division to Israel's diplomatic mission to Ankara and Israel's diplomatic representation to Athens (2.12.1958), Moshe Tov's telegram (26.11.1958) to the UN Division.

Despite the unfavourable signs, Tov advised Zorlu against abandoning the effort, noting that Turkey must not under any circumstances fail to respond to Makarios' possible attendance at the General Assembly. In Moshe Tov's opinion, it was essential for Fazıl Küçük to attend all the sessions and votes before the UN in person.[433] In addition, he suggested that Turkey should also seek US help in exerting pressure on the Latin Americans.[434] A few days later, on 20 November 1958, at a meeting in Washington, American Secretary of State John Foster Dulles reassured Zorlu that the US would contact 'a few Latin American countries'.[435] As the Israelis later learned, the Americans made similar contact with the pro-West Arab states before the vote on the Cyprus issue.[436]

3.6.5.1 Israeli critique of the Greek positions

On 22 September 1958, the issue of Cyprus was placed on the agenda of the 13th Session of the UN General Assembly. Greece sought to suspend the implementation of the Macmillan Plan,[437] and a few days later, Averoff proposed its suspension to his British counterpart, Selwyn Lloyd, in exchange for withdrawing the Greek request for a discussion of the Cyprus question before the UN. Lloyd rejected the proposal, however.[438]

According to a report drafted on 23 September 1958, by Michael Comay, assistant director general of the Israeli Ministry of Foreign Affairs,[439] Evangelos Averoff met with the permanent representatives of South and Central American countries at the UN at which time the Greek foreign minister allegedly stated that Greece was now ready to accept the idea of 'limited independence' for Cyprus. According to information brought to Comay's attention by the Latin American diplomats who had attended this meeting, the term 'limited independence' used by Averoff meant that both the British and 'other NATO member states' would be able to maintain military bases on the island 'sine die', on condition that the Cypriot people be granted self-governance. According to Comay's report, Averoff allegedly told Latin American diplomats that 'should the Cypriot people wish full independence or accession to Greece in the future, they should submit a relevant request to the UN General Assembly requiring a two-thirds majority for approval'. Averoff argued that the main reason for rejecting the idea of the partition of Cyprus was the absence of any natural and clear-cut geographical division between the Greek and Turkish populations on the island.

When a Mexican diplomat asked Averoff whether an independent Cyprus might become a member of the British Commonwealth, Averoff allegedly answered in the

[433] ISA/RG130/MFA/3122/38, Moshe Tov to Comay (582X-17.11.1958), On the meeting between Moshe Tov and Zorlu in New York.
[434] Ibid.
[435] ISA/RG130/MFA/3122/38, Comay to the Israeli Embassy in London (21.11.1958).
[436] Cf. ISA/RG130/MFA/3122/38, Israel's diplomatic mission to Ankara to the West Europe Division (969/3612/אנ – 25.11.1958). Cf. 3.6.5.2.
[437] Xydis, 'The UN General Assembly', 152.
[438] Ibid.
[439] ISA/RG130/MFA/3122/38, Comay to the Israeli diplomatic mission in Ankara and the Israeli diplomatic representation in Athens (23.11.1958).

affirmative, adding that 'for political reasons, we will not be able to state this publicly as yet'. The position Averoff expressed with regard to the inclusion of a future independent state in the Commonwealth coincided with information in the hands of the Israeli Diplomatic Envoy to Athens, Jeonathan Prato. The latter cited statements by Angelos Vlachos, who reasserted that such a possibility would be acceptable to the Greek side, on condition that 'the Cypriot people shall decide the matter. However, for the time being, this issue is not up for discussion'.[440]

According to Comay's report, Evangelos Averoff's words drew mixed reactions from the Latin Americans. The countries that wished to remain true to their anti-colonialist beliefs thought that Greece was essentially adopting a pro-NATO stance, as NATO forces would be allowed to remain on the island and an independent Cyprus could be incorporated into the British Commonwealth. On the other hand, Latin American countries which were seemingly more inclined to deviate from their traditionally anti-colonialist stance interpreted Averoff's statements as a clear indication that Greece, in contrast to its past positions, was now subscribing to milder views on colonialism. In light of this, Israel concluded that the Latin Americans were surprised to hear – and unpleasantly so – the revised positions of the Greek foreign minister. Though until then, the Latin American Bloc had adopted purely anti-colonial (and thus pro-Greek) positions on the Cyprus question, they now had to decode what Athens was after.[441]

On 25 November 1958, Greece submitted a draft resolution calling upon Britain to assist the Cypriots in establishing a regime of independence after a period of 'genuine and democratic self-governance', during which safeguards would be provided to protect the rights of the Turkish minority and allow its participation in public administration. Moreover, the draft resolution recommended the establishment of an international committee to facilitate its practical implementation.[442] According to the account related by the Israeli diplomatic mission to Ankara, the Turkish side described the stipulations of the Greek draft resolution as 'an expected tactical move' aimed at satisfying the British, the US and NATO, while in reality Athens' key objective for Enosis still applied. This was the main argument advanced by Ankara in asking Israel not to stop its efforts to gather as many Latin American votes in favour of Turkey as possible before the upcoming vote.[443]

The Greek proposals were regarded with suspicion by the Israeli Ministry of Foreign Affairs as well. With the disclosure of Comay's report of 23 November 1958, which was based on information passed on by Latin American diplomats after their meeting with Averoff,[444] the deputy director of the British Commonwealth Division, Zvi Loker,

[440] ISA/RG93/MFA/263/6, Prato to the West Europe Division (237/ג – 26.11.1958). Reply to Comay (23.11.1958).
[441] ISA/RG93/MFA/263/6, Comay to the Israeli diplomatic mission in Ankara and the Israeli diplomatic representation in Athens (23.11.1958).
[442] Xydis, 'The UN General Assembly', 152.
[443] ISA/RG130/MFA/3122/38, Roubach to the West Europe Division (969/3612/אב – 25.11.1958), The position of the Turkish Ministry of Foreign Affairs on the Greek draft resolution.
[444] ISA/RG93/MFA/263/6, Comay to the Israeli diplomatic mission in Ankara and the Israeli diplomatic representation in Athens (23.11.1958).

submitted a relevant memo to Foreign Affairs Minister Golda Meir, criticizing the Greek proposals on the following points:[445]

(a) The Greek side has given no assurances about the termination of 'terrorism [by EOKA] on the island, nor that the Turkish minority's rights would be safeguarded'.
(b) There is no international precedent for United Nations protection of a national minority living in a sovereign state – obviously implying that such an arrangement might be implemented against the interests of Israeli state sovereignty in the future in relation to the Arab (Palestinian) minority within Israeli territory.
(c) According to references in Comay's report on the positions Averoff set out for the Latin Americans, the Greek proposals allowed for the possibility that, in the future, the UN General Assembly would decide on the accession (or not) of a sovereign state [Cyprus] to another [Greece], meaning that the UN would be vested with the authority to intervene in the territorial sovereignty of a UN member state. Thus, Cyprus would become an 'independent state on condition'.

Israeli concerns, as outlined in Loker's memo – in addition to the previously agreed-upon commitment to Turkey at the upcoming vote on the issue of Cyprus – in essence expressed Israel's apprehension that a precedent that might be set, at the UN level, which would in future challenge Israeli sovereign rights internally or regionally – by reason or because of the existence of the Arab minority living in Israel. Finally, Loker's memo posed the rhetorical question of whether 'Cyprus itself was actually ready to gain independence' – and, by extension, whether Greece itself was ready to accept the existence of a truly independent Cyprus.[446]

Aside from drawing parallels between the manner in which the Cyprus problem was being handled and its potential impact on Israel in the future, Zvi Loker's concerns include an additional point of interest: For the first time, an official document of the Israeli Ministry of Foreign Affairs takes note of the importance of Turkish Cypriot minority rights, bringing to mind the personal views expressed in 1955 by Meir's predecessor, Moshe Sharett who was both Israeli foreign minister and prime minister.[447]

3.6.5.2 The vote on the Cyprus issue at the 13th Session of the UN General Assembly

In anticipation of the vote on the Cyprus issue, draft resolutions had been submitted to the First Committee by Greece, Britain, Turkey, Colombia, Iran and Belgium, and one draft resolution had been jointly submitted by Ceylon, Ethiopia, Haiti, Iceland, India,

---

[445] ISA/RG130/MFA/3122/38, Zvi Loker, deputy director of the British Commonwealth Division to Golda Meir, Eytan, Comay and the UN and West Europe divisions (Internal Memo, 24.11.1958).
[446] Ibid.
[447] Cf. 3.3.5.

Ireland, Nepal, Panama, Sudan and the United Arab Republic. Britain's draft resolution[448] sought to terminate EOKA's armed activity which Greece was accused of shielding, while at the same time seeking a political solution through direct negotiations. Turkey's draft resolution[449] likewise called for the termination of EOKA's armed activity but also for the institution of measures to stop the riots. As regards the Turkish Cypriots, Turkey argued that any new political regime would have to be approved by both communities, otherwise, the community that withheld its approval would not have to comply with it. Essentially, Turkey was calling for the institution of a separate right to self-determination for each of the two communities, whatever that might entail.[450] For its part and through its own draft resolution,[451] Greece called upon Britain to cooperate with a view to Cypriot independence, following an interim period of self-governance, with guaranteed rights for the Turkish Cypriot minority. The Greek draft resolution provided for the establishment of a 'Good Offices Commission', consisting of representatives from five UN Member States, though these were not named in the draft. Colombia's draft resolution[452] called for assigning a more active role on the island to the UN through the deployment of observers who would prepare periodic reports on the situation there. Columbia also proposed that a collective UN body should be given the authority to mediate. Iran's draft resolution[453] called for the launching of negotiations between Britain, Greece and Turkey, involving representatives from both Cypriot communities. Belgium's draft resolution was identical to Iran's, and called upon 'all parties involved' to work to end terrorism and foster a 'climate of cooperation' to resolve the dispute in accordance with the principles of the UN Charter.[454] Finally, the draft resolution submitted by 10 'neutral' countries[455] and led by India's Permanent Representative Krishna Menon, called for the termination of hostilities, a resumption of negotiations with a view to self-government and the prevention of the island's partition ('the preservation of its integrity').

Moshe Tov worked behind the scenes to merge the proposals of Colombia and Iran. However, seeing that Colombia would not yield, he urged the Iranian representative to revise his submitted proposal so as not to split the Latin American votes.[456] According to Israeli reports from that period, Iran revised its initial proposal at Israel's prompting because it was convinced that Israel's influence would rally the Latin American votes.

[448] ISA/RG130/MFA/3122/38, Memo from Britain's Permanent Representation to the UN.
[449] ISA/RG130/MFA/3122/38, UN General Assembly document ref. no. A/C.1/L/223, dated 22.11.1958, includes the full text of the Turkish draft resolution, as submitted to the 1st Committee.
[450] Xydis, *Cyprus: Conflict and Conciliation*, 516.
[451] ISA/RG130/MFA/3122/38, UN General Assembly document ref. no. A/C.1/L.222, dated 22.11.1958, includes the full text of the Greek draft resolution, as submitted to the 1st Committee.
[452] ISA/RG130/MFA/3122/38, The telegram of 28.11.1958 from Israel's permanent representation to the UN to Michael Comay, director general of the Israeli Ministry of Foreign Affairs, includes the full text of the Colombian draft resolution.
[453] ISA/RG130/MFA/3122/38, Memo from Britain's permanent representation. Cf. Xydis, *Cyprus: Conflict and Conciliation*, 517.
[454] Ibid., 518.
[455] Ibid., 517.
[456] ISA/RG130/MFA/3122/38 Moshe Tov to Comay (670X-4.12.1958), Behind-the-scenes contacts in view of the revised Iranian draft resolution.

Iran's revised draft resolution[457] provided for the establishment of a committee involving Britain, Greece and Turkey, as well as representatives from the island's two communities for the purpose of deliberating on the interim regime and ultimate resolution. A key feature of the draft was that there should be no provision for UN involvement in the peace process, so that a political solution could be reached within NATO. The Iranian proposal was in line with American pursuits, and Britain and Turkey were prepared to accept it, albeit according to information available to the Israelis, Greece seemed to favour the proposal submitted by the 'Neutralists' instead.[458]

The revised Iranian draft resolution was approved by the First Committee with 31 votes in favour, 22 votes against and 28 abstentions. The proposal of Iran, a Muslim member state of the 'Baghdad Pact', garnered the pro-West votes – both Arab and non-Arab – with the US as focal point.[459] Naturally, Israel also voted in favour of the revised Iranian draft resolution. Greece, Guatemala, Iceland, India, Ireland, Nepal, Panama, Yugoslavia, Bolivia, Ceylon, Ethiopia and the USSR, along with the other eight people's republics, voted against it. Among the Arab countries, only the UAR and Yemen took the side of Greece. Pro-West Jordan, which had abstained during the previous session, now voted in favour of the Iranian draft resolution. Lebanon, Iraq, Saudi Arabia, Sudan, Morocco and Tunisia abstained.[460] The majority of Arab countries did not support the Greek positions, and according to the Israelis, this was due to behind-the-scenes interventions by the Americans.[461] In fact, according to a report by the Israeli diplomatic mission to Ankara, it was alleged that the State Department had begun in mid-November 1958 to reassure the Turkish government that it would make the appropriate contacts with Arab capitals. Apparently, the US was already aware of the coordinated Israeli and Turkish diplomatic manoeuvres to rally the Latin American Bloc, and of the difficulties faced by Fatin Zorlu.[462]

Ultimately, the revised Iranian draft resolution was not put to a vote before the Plenary. After behind-the-scenes consultations involving Greece, Turkey, Britain, the US, Mexico and Iran, the Mexican representation submitted a short and generally worded draft resolution on 5 December 1958. The Mexican proposal, which called on the parties to agree on a 'peaceful, democratic and just solution, in accordance with the Charter of the United Nations' was adopted with Resolution No. 1287 (XIII) of the UN General Assembly, both Greece and Turkey voting in favour.[463]

---

[457] Xydis, *Cyprus: Conflict and Conciliation*, 517–19. Cf. ISA/RG130/MFA/3122/38, A document from Turkey's Permanent Representation to the UN includes the revised Iranian proposal.

[458] Nicolet, *United States Policy towards Cyprus*, 130–1. Cf. ISA/RG130/MFA/3122/38, Moshe Tov to Comay (670X-4.12.1958). Behind-the-scenes contacts between Moshe Tov and the representatives of Iran, Colombia, Turkey and Britain, in order to convince Colombia to accept the revised Iranian proposal; however, that was not made possible.

[459] Xydis, 'The UN General Assembly', 153. Cf. Nicolet, *Unites States Policy towards Cyprus*, 128–31; and Xydis, *Cyprus: Conflict and Conciliation*, 520.

[460] Israel State Archives, Gilead (ed.), *Documents*, vol. 13, 833 no. 438.

[461] Cf. Nicolet, *United States Policy towards Cyprus*, 128–31.

[462] ISA/RG130/MFA/3122/38, Israeli diplomatic mission to Ankara to the West Europe Division (969/3612/אנ – 25.11.1958), US moves to influence the vote of pro-West Arab countries.

[463] United Nations, *Yearbook of the United Nations, 1958* (New York: Department of Public Information, 1958), part 1, chapter 6, 76, Vote of the 1st Committee (4.12.1958). Cf. Xydis, 'The UN General Assembly', 153; and ibid., *Cyprus: Conflict and Conciliation*, 523–4.

In assessing what had taken place at the 13th Session of the UN General Assembly with respect to the Cyprus question, Israeli diplomacy focused on the way in which Greece had handled the situation. According to Israeli diplomatic reports, Greece's promising pro-Arab foreign policy did not bring the expected gains. Of all the Arab states, only the UAR and pro-Nasser Yemen stuck by Athens to the end. It was also noted that ties between Greece and the UAR would be further strengthened in the immediate future. The Israelis predicted that Cairo, in exchange for its support, would seek similar backing from Greece on its own regional concerns which would further alienate Greece not only from Israel, but from its 'natural' allies in the West.

As Jeonathan Prato noted, the reaction in Greece to what had occurred at the UN was very critical of the Western countries – particularly the United States. Criticism of the West was expressed in the strongest of terms both by right-wing and left-wing newspapers in Greece.[464] Based on the climate he observed at a political level, Prato predicted that following the UN vote, the position of Greece would be weakened in the event of immediate negotiations with Britain and Turkey on the future status of Cyprus.[465]

3.6.6 Assessing Israel's stance on the Cyprus issue at the 13th Session of the UN General Assembly

The secret agreement on the rapprochement between Turkey and Israel in August 1958 clearly delineated Israel's foreign policy views on the Cyprus issue. Turkey had asked Israel to put it in contact with the Latin American Bloc in order to undermine support for Greek positions on the Cyprus problem. Israel responded favourably and eagerly assumed the role of mediator to seal its rapprochement with Ankara. Furthermore, the Israelis knew that the rapprochement was in line with Washington's priority in the region, namely, a settlement on Cyprus within the context of NATO. From an Israeli standpoint, such a settlement would severely impede Nasser's expansionism – and by extension, Soviet penetration into the Middle East.

As indicated by Israeli diplomatic reports of that time, the Israelis were not certain whether Greece had been apprised of their behind-the-scenes activity during the 13th Session.[466] It was not long before they realized that the Greeks and Greek Cypriots had been informed about the Israeli manoeuvring. That is apparent from the telegram of 17 February 1959 from Prato to Walter Eytan, director general of the Israeli Ministry of Foreign Affair. Jeonathan Prato referred in this telegram to the contacts Zeev Levin had made in Athens with the GSEE in his capacity as the delegate to the International Confederation of Free Trade Unions ICFTU. During his stay in Athens, Levin was also in frequent contact with Michalakis Pissas, the General Secretary of the Cyprus Workers Confederation (SEK), whom he had already met in Cyprus during his numerous visits to the island in 1958.[467] Among other things, Prato wrote the following:

---

[464] ISA/RG130/MFA/3122/38, West Europe Division to the Israeli diplomatic mission to Ankara (1574/10.12.1958). Cf. Nicolet, *Unites States Policy towards Cyprus*, 128–31.

[465] ISA/RG130/MFA/3122/38, West Europe Division to the Israeli diplomatic mission to Ankara (1574/10.12.1958). Long extract from Prato's report to the West Europe Division.

[466] Averoff, *Istoria*, 104–45; and Bitsios, *Cyprus*, 92–6. In describing the events of the 13th Session of the UN General Assembly, neither Evangelos Averoff nor Dimitris Bitsios referred to Israel's stance.

[467] Cf. 3.6.1.1.1.

'During a friendly chat, Pissas told Levin that the Cypriot leadership is disappointed and deeply saddened by Moshe Tov's activity aimed at drawing the support of Latin Americans for the Turks at the session.'[468] Perplexed, Jeonathan Prato asked Walter Eytan what exactly Pissas meant to say 'by those strange words'.

It is debatable whether it was Israeli influence that ultimately determined how the Latin Americans voted. It is, however, a fact that during the 13th UN Session, their voting positions vis-à-vis Greece and the Greek Cypriots changed significantly compared to their previous votes at the UN. For example, at the 12th Session in 1957, the majority of Latin American states had voted in favour of the Greek proposal, both before the First Committee and the Plenary[469] whereas during the 13th Session, only 3 Latin American countries voted against the revised Iranian proposal, 6 voted in favour of it, and the remaining 11 chose to abstain. It was the large number of abstentions which most disappointed Athens.[470]

Israel's behind-the-scenes initiatives earned Turkey's warmest gratitude, while the fact that these actions were disclosed to Greece and the Greek Cypriots cast a dark shadow over Greek–Israeli relations, one that could not easily be overlooked. Israel was able to keep a safe distance from the Cypriot dispute, as it had more or less during previous sessions. Besides, Turkey had already sought alternative ways to safeguard its interests and requested assistance from Britain and the US – two countries which were in a position to influence the outcome of the vote much more effectively than Israel could.

In order to properly assess, and perhaps even to judge Israel's decision to become involved unofficially in the Cyprus question at the critical 13th Session, the following factors must be taken into account: first, Israel had to prove itself credible with regard to its commitments to Turkey and Britain, the latter of which had also requested Israel's support on the issue of Cyprus.[471] Moreover, the bitter aftertaste of the Suez Crisis still lingered when Golda Meir realized during the 11th Session of the UN General Assembly that her country was a state 'without a family' but with many critics.[472] Providing support to the 'major stakeholders', meaning the US, Britain and Turkey, gave Israel an additional sense of security at the diplomatic level – in the hopes that it might cash in on its good deeds in the future.

However, even if Turkey had not requested assistance, there was no good reason for Israel to support Greece at the time. The United Arab Republic had clearly sided with them and by adopting this stance, Nasser's regime aimed to expand its influence over the Eastern Mediterranean, consistently targeting the unwanted Israeli presence in the region. Israel's decision not to support the Greek positions was thus directly linked to its overall effort to impede Nasser's regional plans as effectively as possible.[473] Besides, as Turkish Foreign Minister Fatin Zorlu had astutely noted to his Israeli counterpart: 'Israel has no obligation to Greece.'

---

[468] ISA/RG93/MFA/263/6, Prato to Eytan (41/ᴎ – 17.2.1959) Levin's contacts in Athens.
[469] UN, *Yearbook of the United Nations*, 1957 (New York: UN, Department of Public Information, 1957), part 1, chapter 6, 76.
[470] UN, *Yearbook of the United Nations, 1958*, part 1, chapter 6, 76.
[471] ISA/RG130/MFA/3122/38, British Commonwealth Division to the Israeli consulate in Nicosia and the Israeli embassy in London (578/17.11.1958). The British embassy in Tel Aviv asked Israel to support the British draft resolution.
[472] Cf. 3.4.3.
[473] Nachmani, *Israel, Turkey and Greece*, 98–101.

4

Israel and the London–Zurich Agreements
on Cyprus

The non-specific phrasing of Resolution No. 1287 (XIII) of the UN General Assembly, approved by all three countries involved in the Cyprus issue, merely reiterated the Plenary's confidence that 'continued efforts will be made by the parties to reach a peaceful, democratic and just solution, in accordance with the Charter of the United Nations'.[1] Nonetheless, it was already clear from the results of the commission meeting that Greece had been diplomatically weakened.[2] On the other hand, Archbishop Makarios' statement to British Labour MP Barbara Castle in September 1958 indicated that he, too, would be willing to accept the solution of an independent Cyprus given the determination of London and Ankara to implement the otherwise unwelcome Macmillan Plan.[3] Immediately after the Plenary vote, Averoff responded favourably to Fatin Zorlu's initiative to embark at once on Greek–Turkish negotiations towards Cypriot independence.[4]

4.1 Israel's information about negotiations between Greece, Turkey and Great Britain in view of the London–Zurich Agreements

During the period of negotiations between Greece, Turkey and Britain leading to the London–Zurich Agreements, Israel's only source of information was the Turkish Ministry of Foreign Affairs.[5] As a result, the reports from the Israeli chargé d'affaires in Ankara, Moshe Alon, reflected reality as depicted by the Turks, and their one-sidedness must be taken into account in assessing the content of the Israeli diplomatic reports at a time when information from Israel's diplomatic representatives in Athens and London was scant to nil.

---

[1] See 3.6.5.
[2] See 3.6.4.
[3] Nicolet, *United States Policy towards Cyprus*, 134; and Christodoulides, *Schedia Lysis*, 132–3.
[4] Christodoulides, *Schedia Lysis*, 132–4, on the initiative taken by Fatin Zorlu.
[5] About the meetings and negotiations between the Greek government and Archbishop Makarios, see Angelos Vlachos, *Deka Chronia Kypriakou* [*Ten Years of the Cypriot Question*] (Athens: Estia, 2003), 235–71.

According to Alon's reports, Turkey was giving up on the idea of partition while Greece acknowledged that the 'Cypriot people' consisted of two communities. A 'federal union' would be established in Cyprus to join the two communities under the auspices of the West and NATO, and British military bases would remain on the island. The details of this bicommunal arrangement would be determined between Greece and Turkey, but Great Britain was expected to take part in the negotiations at a later stage. The thorn in the side of the Greek–Turkish negotiations was Ankara's concern about a possible annexation of Cyprus by Greece at some future time, which is why Ankara insisted on its right to prevent such an occurrence with a military intervention, thus calling into question the guarantees offered by the UN and even NATO.[6] Greece opposed this demand at all costs, as it wished to forestall a de facto partition of the island at a later date.[7] Britain reassured Turkey and urged both sides to continue their preliminary negotiations despite the air of pessimism promoted by Greek and Turkish media in mid-January 1959. While the British Embassy in Ankara observed the change in the way Turkey perceived the Cyprus issue following the vote at the 13th Session,[8] the Greek side could not hide its scepticism about Ankara's intentions, or its misgivings about Britain's pro-Turkish attitude. That was the impression Jeonathan Prato had from Greek diplomatic circles[9] in Athens. Michael Comey who headed the West Europe Division of Israel's Ministry of Foreign Affairs, received the same impression from the Greek diplomatic representative in Jerusalem, Pavlos Pantermalis.[10] The Israelis wrongly believed that the US was involved in the negotiations to a significant extent, and that the visits of its former Turkish Ambassador George McGhee to Athens in early February 1959 were related to Cyprus.[11] Clearly, based on the assumptions in these departmental reports, Israel had no tangible information about the precise agenda of the negotiations. Despite the persistent efforts of Israeli diplomats, Ankara, London and Athens did not leak any details of substance. In fact, the Foreign Office refused to provide information to the Israeli embassy in London, making it clear that 'any leaks of information would be of no benefit and only absolute secrecy can help ensure progress of these contacts'.[12] From late January 1959, leaks of information and assessments ceased entirely from the Turkish side as well.[13]

The Zurich Conference (5–11 February 1959) with the participation of the prime ministers and foreign ministers of Greece and Turkey culminated in the signing of an agreement on 11 February 1959, which provided for the main pillars of the structure and operation of an independent bicommunal Cypriot state.[14] In London,

[6] ISA/RG93/MFA/3122/38, Alon to West Europe Division (82/3612/אנ – 27.1.1959).
[7] ISA/RG93/MFA/263/6, Alon to West Europe Division (27/3612/אנ – 12.1.1959).
[8] Ibid., Roubach to West Europe Division (49/3612/אנ – 19.1.1959).
[9] Ibid., Prato to Comay (4/77-28.1.1959).
[10] Ibid., Comay to Prato (8/30-31.1.1959).
[11] Ibid., Yehoshua Almog, 1st secretary of the Israel's dDiplomatic representation to Athens to West Europe Division (160/5.2.1959). He cites a conversation with his counterpart at the US embassy in Athens, Sam Berger. Cf. Nicolet, *United States Policy towards Cyprus*, 140–7, on the US priorities and operations during the Greek–Turkish negotiations on the Cyprus issue.
[12] ISA/RG130/MFA/3122/38, Moshe Ofer, 1st secretary of Israel's embassy in London to the British Commonwealth Division (406/30.1.1959).
[13] ISA/RG130/MFA/3122/38, Roubach to West Europe Division (137/3612/אנ – 30.1.1959).
[14] The Archbishop Makarios III Foundation, Kokkinou (ed.), *Apanta Archiepiskopou*, vol. 3, 642–51.

on 19 February 1959, the prime ministers of Greece, Turkey and Britain, and the representatives of the two communities, Makarios and Küçük, signed the Zurich Agreement and the agreements linked to it: the Treaty of Guarantee and the Treaty of Alliance between the Republic of Cyprus, Greece and Turkey.[15]

4.2 The repercussions of the London and Zurich Agreements on Greece and Turkey, according to Israel's diplomatic reports

4.2.1 Repercussions on Greece

Commenting on Greek press reports, Jeonathan Prato concluded that the signing of the Zurich Agreement had brought a 'sense of relief' to Athens.[16] Though some disappointment was expressed that the vision of Enosis would not be realized, the prevailing view was that 'the Cypriot issue was finally settled' and that it was high time to improve relations with Turkey. Concerns about the difficulties of implementing the agreement were countered by the argument that, given the circumstances, the Karamanlis government had handled matters in the best possible way. At the opposite pole of this positive assessment was the view espoused by the left-wing *Avgi* newspaper, which the Israelis noted with interest. *Avgi* was the only paper to criticize the outcome, arguing that the aim of the agreement had been to protect the imperialist interests of the Western powers in the region, and that this intra-NATO arrangement essentially targeted the neighbouring Arab states. The newspaper went so far as to urge the Arabs to react, recalling the military operations of Britain, France and Israel in Egypt in 1956 and the US intervention in Lebanon the summer of 1958.

The debate held in the Greek Parliament to ratify the London and Zurich Agreements lasted five days (23–28 February 1959), and was marked by the opposition's harsh criticism of the Karamanlis government. The result of the no confidence vote put forward by the opposition on 28 February 1959 was only to be expected. Out of 288 members of the Greek senate, 170 voted in support of the government and approved its conduct in Zurich and London, contra 118 votes from the opposition.[17]

In his extensive report to the West Europe Division of Israel's Ministry of Foreign Affairs, Jeonathan Prato emphasized the points raised by the opposition in the debate at the Greek Parliament.[18] Those critical of the agreements called them treasonous because the idea of Enosis had been abandoned, the Turkish minority was granted equal rights to those established for the Greek majority, the agreement framework was essentially based on 'trilateral cooperation' between Greece, Turkey and Britain, precisely as laid down by the Macmillan Plan and, finally, the implementation of the agreements was precarious, relying as it did almost exclusively on Turkish benevolence.

---

[15] Ibid., 628–36.
[16] ISA/RG93/MFA/263/6, Prato to West Europe Division (208/15.2.1959).
[17] Archbishop Makarios III Foundation, Kokkinou (ed.), *Apanta Archiepiskopou*, vol. 3, 652–812. Extracts from the Minutes of the Greek Parliamentary sessions on the London–Zurich Agreements (23–28.2.1959).
[18] ISA/RG93/MFA/263/6, Prato to West Europe Division (318/9.3.1959).

Furthermore, Liberal Party leader Sofoklis Venizelos argued that as soon as his party rose to power, it would rescind the agreements and continue to strive for Enosis – a position Prato described as 'extremely demagogic'.

The main argument of the Karamanlis government was that the London–Zurich Agreements abolished British rule on the island and restored friendly relations between Greece, Turkey and Britain. As for the issue of Cypriot independence, the government held that 'it did nothing more than support the independence solution that Archbishop Makarios himself, the only representative of the Greeks of Cyprus, had put forward on the eve of the recent UN General Assembly'. Jeonathan Prato called this 'outright hypocrisy on the part of the Greek government' since the independence agreed upon is very different from what Makarios envisioned', adding moreover that 'it is common knowledge that Makarios was faced with a fait accompli which he tried to reverse up to the very last moment'.[19]

Though in public Greek officials expressed optimism regarding the smooth implementation of the London–Zurich Agreements, in private meetings with Prato, it was clear that they were well aware of the difficulties involved. In the first place, both Athens and Turkey were legitimately concerned about whether the Greek Cypriots and Turkish Cypriots sincerely intended to coexist within this particular bicommunal constitutional framework.[20] The Greek side worried mostly about the role a strong communist element might play within the Greek Cypriot community, the popular nationalist sentiments and slogans, and the stance Makarios would take should any difficulty arise amid the smooth operation of civil structures in the new state. In particular, as the adviser to the Greek embassy in Ankara, Vyron Theodoropoulos, observed at a meeting with Israeli diplomat Eytan Ronn, who was also serving in the Turkish capital at the time,[21] the London–Zurich Agreements set in motion a complex system of checks and balances which would be inept at preventing major nationalist disputes between the two communities. Theodoropoulos believed that possible difficulties in the smooth implementation of the agreements might also arise from the 'concentrated communist element within the Greek community which is vulnerable to external anti-West influences and thus uses right-wing nationalist slogans in the service of the left'.[22] He also predicted that, should the difficulties in implementing the agreements increase, Makarios would not be willing to ask Athens for assistance and would then revive the request for Enosis because 'he is a highly ambitious man who would prefer, above all, to maintain his popularity and political power'. Therefore, Theodoropoulos continued, under such circumstances, the Greek government would

[19] Ibid.
[20] ISA/RG93/MFA/263/6, Prato to Fischer (266/27.2.1959), Angelos Vlachos' concerns about the goodwill of the parties involved to implement the agreements.
[21] ISA/RG93/MFA/263/6, Eytan Ronn, 1st secretary to the Israeli diplomatic mission to Ankara to West Europe Division (230/3612/אנ – 2.3.1959).
[22] Theodoropoulos' argument on the use of 'right-wing' nationalist slogans by the political forces of the Left coincides with the views of the Israeli revisionist Right. The use of nationalist slogans by the Cypriot Left had been noted already in 1950 by the right-wing Israeli opposition newspaper *Heruth*, in an article titled 'Cyprus: Bastion of Communism – A "Fifth Phalanx in the heart of the Middle East"', 16.5.1950. Cf. 2.4.1.

be powerless to persuade Makarios to implement the London–Zurich Agreements unless the power of the island's communist element were contained in time.

The strictly confidential report by the head of Israel's Diplomatic Mission in Ankara, Moshe Alon, was along the same lines. Citing a conversation with the ambassador of Switzerland in Ankara, Eric Ernst Kessler, Alon wrote that:

> based on reliable information that the Swiss Ambassador obtained from one of his colleagues in Ankara [author's note: without naming him], a secret agreement was reached between Karamanlis and Menderes to fight the communists in Cyprus together. The aim of the plan of action was to expel or weaken the 'activists' on the island if there is good cause to believe that the Cypriot communists are collaborating with the Soviets or other extreme leftist circles [author's note: outside of Cyprus].[23]

Kessler's information proved correct. In Zurich on 11 February 1959, a secret 'Gentlemen's Agreement' was signed between Karamanlis and Menderes. Article 2 of the agreement stipulated: '2. The two Prime Ministers agreed to assist the President and Vice-President of the Republic of Cyprus respectively to outlaw the Communist Party and communist activity [...]'.[24]

4.2.2 Repercussions on Turkey

Throughout 1958, Turkish public opinion, the newspapers and state radio, covered the events in Cyprus by presenting partition as the only way to ensure protection of the Turkish Cypriots. Militant demonstrations with slogans such as 'Partition or Death' and inflammatory statements about Makarios, Grivas and Greece were the order of the day in the political news. Following the UN vote in December 1958, and in particular, after the opening of Greek–Turkish negotiations in early 1959, the tone in the Turkish news media changed dramatically. As stressed by the Israeli consulate in Istanbul, the news coverage regarding progress in the negotiations was intensive, continuous and coloured by respectful words for both Averoff and Zorlu. Within a two-month period, the presentation of the Cyprus issue in Turkish media was nothing like it had been in the recent past. As a result, the London–Zurich Agreements concluded in February 1959, found Turkish public opinion properly prepared.[25] Thus, when Greek military officials working at NATO headquarters in Izmir returned in early March 1959 or when the screening of an anti-Greek film was banned in Istanbul, there was no reaction from the press or from political groups which a few months earlier became enraged about

---

[23] ISA/RG93/MFA/263/6, Alon to West Europe Division (223/3612/אנ – 2.3.1959); and Benedikt Wirthlin, Swiss Embassy, 'Swiss Ambassador – February–March, 1959', attached with email to Gabriel Haritos, 2015. Eric Ernst Kessler was Ambassador of Switzerland in Ankara from 1957 to 1962.

[24] Archbishop Makarios III Foundation, Kokkinou (ed.), *Apanta Archiepiskopou*, vol. 3, 637–9. The same agreement established that Greece and Turkey would give their vote to the Republic of Cyprus to become a full member of NATO. Cf. Stephen G. Xydis, *Cyprus: Reluctant Republic* (The Hague and Paris: Mouton, 1973), 413 and 519.

[25] ISA/RG93/MFA/256/8, Israeli consulate in Istanbul to West Europe Division (1545/213-25.2.1959).

anything Greek.[26] Nevertheless, as the Israelis noted, it was difficult to assess exactly what the average Turkish citizen believed about the Cyprus arrangement, since the press and the radio at the time were under the complete control of the government.[27]

Be that as it may, Prime Minister Menderes was lucky for another reason. After narrowly escaping death in a plane crash on his way to London, he won public sympathy and the mass demonstrations opposition circles were preparing upon his return to Turkey under the slogan 'Partition or Death' did not take place. On the contrary, capitalizing on public sympathy because of the accident, the state machinery acted effectively and organized a grandiose popular welcome, which, according to Alon, was certainly not as spontaneous as the newspapers suggested.[28] As a result, given the circumstances, the tension which had been expected to result from the opposition to the government's abandonment of partition was dissipated. Nevertheless, Makarios and Grivas did not suddenly become more popular in Turkey and the opposition newspapers expressed their reservations about whether the Turkish Cypriots were sufficiently safeguarded from future discrimination.

On a diplomatic level, Turkish officials shared virtually the same concerns as those expressed in Athens. Based on Alon's contacts with representatives of both the government and the opposition,[29] the communist element on the island, the extreme Right and the strong nationalist sentiments in both communities might, it seemed, have seriously hampered the practical implementation of the agreements. Seeing that Athens did not have absolute control over the political powers on the island, Turkish officials did not dismiss the possibility that a number of Greek Cypriots who were opposed to the London–Zurich Agreements could claim that neither Makarios nor Küçük were democratically empowered to co-sign agreements – and therefore, the agreements were not binding on the island's citizens. The Turkish opposition was also critical of the agreement, and apprehensive about finding enough educated Turkish Cypriots to fill their 30 per cent quota in the administration of the new state. Nevertheless, despite concerns and insecurities over the resolution of the problem, Ankara felt confident that it was in full control of the Turkish Cypriot community and its leadership, and optimistic about its ability to effectively influence the political balance in the future Cypriot state.

4.3 Prospects for improved diplomatic relations between Israel and Greece and Israel and Turkey following the London–Zurich Agreements

The London–Zurich Agreements pleased Israel for a number of reasons. The resolution of the ongoing conflict in Cyprus provided a measure of stability in Israel's immediate

---

[26] Ibid. (1572/4.3.1959).
[27] ISA/RG92/MFA/263/6, Alon to West Europe Division (223/3612/אנ – 2.3.1959).
[28] Ibid.
[29] Ibid.

environment. Moreover, the country's main pillar of security, the British military presence in the Eastern Mediterranean, was also safeguarded now. The stance adopted by Israeli diplomacy during the critical 13th Session of the UN General Assembly and its behind-the-scenes interventions in the matter of Cyprus further strengthened Israel's ties to Britain and the US, while at the same time marking the beginning of a new and better era in Turco-Israeli relations which had been so upset by the Suez Crisis and its aftermath.

The Israeli perspective towards the Cypriot diplomatic arrangement emphasized the fact that two historical opponents, Greece and Turkey had dared to sit down at the negotiating table and ultimately managed to resolve their differences. This approach reinforced the standing argument of Israeli governments of the era who claimed that a solution to the Palestinian problem could not be achieved through conferences and votes at the UN. Only direct negotiations between Israel and the Arabs could result in a realistic, long-term and mutually acceptable solution. This was the argument Israel's diplomatic representative in Athens, Jeonathan Prato, believed should be highlighted, particularly by the pro-government Israeli newspapers.[30]

Now that the gaping wound of the Cyprus question had closed, Israel hoped the way would be open to improving relations with Greece – a Western country that maintained close relations with Nasser's Egypt – and to fully restoring diplomatic relations with Turkey.

At the same time, Israel was interested in establishing full diplomatic relations with Nicosia, provided the latter was not discouraged either by Arab-friendly Athens, or by Muslim Turkey, which wanted to be seen on its best behaviour with the Arab world. For the Israelis, it was clear that the quality and extent of bilateral relations with independent Cyprus would be decisively influenced by the way in which both mother countries – Greece and Turkey – viewed the Arab–Israeli conflict.

4.3.1 Prospects for the normalization of Israeli–Greek diplomatic relations

Ever since Israel's declaration of independence in 1948, its prospects for normalizing diplomatic relations with Greece had been up in the air. Athens had not recognized the newly established Jewish state de facto until 1952, after which the Greek consulate in Jerusalem was renamed the Greek Diplomatic Representation to the Israeli Government[31] and concurrently, two honorary Greek consulates, one in Tel Aviv and one in Haifa, became operational. From the time of Israel's independence and throughout the 1950s, Athens had consistently refused to recognize the Jewish state de jure, its main justification being the need to garner Arab votes at the UN in support of its positions on Cyprus.[32] After the favourable settlement of the Cyprus issue, Israel believed that the time had come to put an end to what was described in the corridors of the Ministry of Foreign Affairs as the inexplicably frigid relationship with Greece.

---

[30] ISA/RG93/MFA/263/6, Prato to West Europe Division (37/2 – 13.2.1959).
[31] Cf. 2.4.3 and 2.4.3.1 on Greece's de facto recognition of Israel in 1952.
[32] ISA/RG93/MFA/263/6, Prato to West Europe Division (208/15.2.1959).

Once the London–Zurich Agreements had been signed and the Cyprus issue was on its way to being resolved, the Israelis began to prepare for a diplomatic rapprochement with Greece, now that Athens was no longer dependent on Arab votes at the UN. This was one of the reasons that immediately following the signing of the Zurich Agreement Walter Eytan, director general of the Israeli Ministry of Foreign Affairs, met informally with the editors-in-chief of the Israeli press, as he routinely did. During the 1950s, most Israeli newspapers of the period followed specific party lines. But where matters of foreign policy and defence were concerned, the editors of all the newspapers – whether party, trade union or privately owned, and either supporters or opponents of the government – set aside their journalistic ethics and eagerly followed a specific line as requested by the government in power.[33] Thus, on 12 February 1959, at his meeting with the editors, Eytan encouraged the publication of opinion pieces on the need to normalize Israel's relations with Greece, Turkey and independent Cyprus. These opinion pieces would be directly aimed at the average Israeli reader and would outline the position of the Ben-Gurion government, namely, that the Arab–Israeli conflict can be resolved only through direct negotiations, not through the UN. However, the ulterior motive of these pieces was to reach the foreign ministries of Greece (and less urgently, Turkey) in order to lay the ground for smoother relations with both Athens and Ankara.[34]

On 13 February 1959, all the Israeli newspapers dealt with the Zurich Agreement, essentially outlining the Israeli diplomatic approach. The pro-government *Ha-Boker* wrote:

The historic decision taken in Switzerland will set a future example, not only for Cyprus, but also for relations between other peoples in the region. If the independence of the neighbouring island is agreed upon at the London talks – and it is believed that England will be satisfied with keeping its bases on the island – and the implementation of the Zurich Agreement is not hindered, then this will not simply constitute an act of humanitarianism, bringing many years of bloodshed to an end. It will also prove that with good will, it is possible for people to overcome the hatred of generations for the sake of a happier future. [...] If there is one nation in the region that welcomes such an agreement without expecting anything in return, then that nation is Israel. After all, by congratulating the Cypriot people, we are also congratulating Greece and Turkey for their success in bringing this cold war in our region to an end, and doing away with prejudice. [...] The Greek–Turkish war that ended with Ataturk's victory was the start to a peaceful settlement between these two countries. Despite the harsh accounting of that war, the two countries realised that the repatriation of the large Greek population from Turkey

[33] Yitzhak Galnoor and Dana Blander, *Ha-Maarekhet ha-Politit bi-Israel* [*The Political System in Israel*] (Tel Aviv and Jerusalem: Am Oved and Israel Democracy Institute, 2013), 688–9; and Yehiel Limor and Rafi Mann, *Itonaut: Isuf Meida, Ktiva va-Arikha* [*Journalism: Collecting Information, Writing and Editing*] (Tel Aviv: Open University of Israel, 1997), 43–7.

[34] ISA/RG93/MFA/263/6, Eytan to Prato (15.2.1959 no official reference), Statements by Eytan to the editors of Israeli newspapers.

to their birthplace – although most would never have expected something like that to happen – finally brought about a normalization in their relations. For its part, Greece opened its arms to receive the uprooted Greeks. Human pain was overcome, and these two peoples jointly adopted a modus vivendi, which ultimately saw them fighting as allies in World War II. We mention this historic example, which has been described in hundreds of books, in order to point out yet another example that could evolve in a similar manner. It is certain that the results of this agreement [author's note: Zurich] will not only be met with praise. It raises concerns in our own region; questions of transformation that could even touch the hearts of those who hate Israel and dream of its destruction. [...] Our relations with Turkey and Greece are not particularly sound, due to the Arab influence. Ankara has withdrawn its ambassador – though without severing our diplomatic relations, while Greece has not yet recognised us, even on a de jure basis. But now is not the time to discuss this. And we should also not forget that these two countries, Greece and Turkey, will be called upon to play an important role in the rapprochement between the peoples of this region, including Israel. Even if such a thing seems utopian right now, let us not despair. [...] Let us hope that Israel will find a neighbour in Cyprus that will not only have good services to offer to the world's community of nations but will also help to bring peace to our neighbourhood for all the people in our region.[35]

On the same day, an analysis published in the independent (non-partisan) newspaper *Ha-Aretz* concluded:

Three factors made the solution to this complex problem possible: Firstly, the decision to abandon the 'holy' claims that prevented any chance of reaching an agreement. Secondly, the initiative undertaken by one of the parties to put forward a new moderate position – and I mean Makarios' proposal regarding the island's independence instead of Enosis. Thirdly, the two-party agreement to carry out direct negotiations. Without even one of these three factors, it would have been impossible to arrive at such a settlement and the conflict in Cyprus would have escalated further and been the cause of further bloodshed. [...] Israel hopes to develop amicable relations with the new neighbouring state in a way that will improve the relations of Israel with both Greece and Turkey – its two other neighbours in the Eastern Mediterranean.

The English-language newspaper *Jerusalem Post* took the same lines as *Davar* (the official mouthpiece of the pro-government trade union, Histadrut). It called upon the Israeli government to 'find the right paths that would lead to the hearts of the future leaders of the new state of Cyprus', and voiced the opinion that 'while land borders are often the source of conflict, maritime borders in their majority constitute a cradle of

---

[35] ISA/RG93/MFA/263/6, Eliezer Yapou, deputy director of the West Europe Division, to Prato (212/15.2.1959), and the West Europe Division to the Israeli diplomatic mission in Ankara and Israeli consulate in Istanbul (220/16.2.1959). Excerpts from Israeli published articles.

friendship'. The left-wing opposition newspaper *Al ha-Mishmar* highlighted the ties of friendship between Israel and the Greek Cypriots, 'who expressed their humanity towards the multitude of Jews held at British camps on the island'. In this article, *Al ha-Mishmar* made a special reference to Zeev Levin, an executive member of the Histadrut, who 'recently took on an important mission to foster cooperation between the trade unions of both communities on the island and approached the British authorities to defend the Greek employees who had been fired from their jobs as a result of the suppressive measures the British used against the local populace'.[36]

Jeonathan Prato forwarded the above publications to the office of the Greek prime minister, the Greek Ministry of Foreign Affairs and the editors of the Athenian newspapers. The response was not what he had hoped for. Aside from one brief, general reference by the Athens News Agency, no Greek official was willing to advance the reports further and none of the newspapers reprinted them, neither after the signing of the Zurich Agreement,[37] nor after the meeting in London which ended on 19 February 1959.[38]

The Israeli side was concerned about this cold indifference to their overture, and worried too that Greece and the Greek Cypriots had been briefed about Moshe Tov's pro-Turkish manoeuvers at the 13th Session of the UN in December. These apprehensions were confirmed in mid-February, when SEK General Secretary Michalakis Pissas and Zeev Levin happened to be in Athens at the same time and Pissas relayed to Levin the great disappointment Makarios had expressed over Israel's pro-Turkish stance at the UN. Levin, who had been unaware of this, was quite surprised. When Prato learned of the secret goings-on, he informed Foreign Walter Eytan and suggested that full diplomatic relations be established as soon as possible with the independent Cypriot state – where Greek Cypriots would have first say – before Athens had a chance to predispose them negatively.[39]

In order to explore Greek intentions, but also to prevent anything worse from happening, Jeonathan Prato immediately requested a meeting with the Vice President of the Greek Government, Panagiotis Kanellopoulos. The meeting took place on 20 February 1959 – the day after the signing of the London Agreements which would shape subsequent political reality in Cyprus. The exchange between Kanellopoulos and Prato was particularly enlightening, according to the description included in a report Prato sent to the West Europe Division of the Israeli Ministry of Foreign Affairs on 23 February 1959.[40]

According to Prato's report, in assessing the agreements on Cyprus, Kanellopoulos believed that:

> Greece could no longer uphold a policy that would perpetually fuel a dispute with its western allies and put the preservation of the cultural ideals of the enlightened

[36] Cf. 3.6.1.1.1 on Zeev Levin's activity in Cyprus in 1958.
[37] ISA/RG93/MFA/263/6, Prato to Yapou (232/19.2.1959).
[38] Ibid. (246/24.2.1959).
[39] ISA/RG93/MFA/263/6, Prato to Eytan (41/ɔ – 17.2.1959) Cf. 3.6.5 and 3.6.6 on Israel's behind-the-scenes support for Turkey at the 13th Session of the UN General Assembly.
[40] Ibid., Prato to West Europe Division (241/23.2.1959).

world at risk. The settlement does indeed require that the idea of annexing the island be abandoned, but this occurred due to circumstances that should not be viewed as final and irreversible, or that they are able to undo an inevitable historical process. Besides, the union of all regions of Greece was not achieved at once and the most important result [author's note: of the agreements on Cyprus] is that the primary obstacle to realising the wishes of the Cypriot people was overcome, and this was none other than bringing the British sovereignty of the island to an end. The government was forced to rid itself of the burden that prevented it from fulfilling its primary duty, which was to dedicate itself to addressing the daunting economic and social problems facing the Greek people. As long as the matter of Cyprus remained unresolved, the hands of the Greek government were tied [...].

For his part, Prato tried to assess the London and Zurich agreements as well as Greek intentions regarding a potential improvement in relations with Israel, since the Cyprus issue had now been resolved. As he told Kanellopoulos,

the relations between our two countries will also be affected positively. The solution to the problem was accepted in Israel with satisfaction, since it distances a risk to peace close to our borders and because this solution was achieved through direct negotiations. [...] The creation of the state of Cyprus, which is in essence a 'little Greece', brings Greece that much closer to the state of Israel. With this in mind, it is my opinion that the relations between our two countries need to be re-evaluated. As long as the conflict in Cyprus was escalating, we avoided raising the issue of our bilateral relations, since we understood the delicate position of Greece. I hope that now that the Greek government is no longer burdened by the matter of Cyprus, as you said, it will have the time to address the issue of Greece's de jure recognition of Israel in an objective and realistic manner [...].

In conclusion Prato gave Kanellopoulos to understand that Israel believed this to be an excellent opportunity to normalize Greek–Israeli diplomatic relations in full, with 'a momentum that should not be ignored'.

In reply, Kanellopoulos pointed out that 'still pending is the problem of the Greek community in Egypt, whose situation is becoming more dire as time goes by', thus conveying the message to his interlocutor that the Greek de jure recognition of Israel was not yet on the table. However, Prato countered that Athens should no longer associate the open question of the Greek community in Egypt with the normalization of Greek–Israeli relations. In his report, Prato wrote:

I pointed out to Kanellopoulos that Egypt's treatment of foreign nationals living there does not depend on whether their countries of origin have good or bad relations with Israel. Egypt's attitude toward foreign nationals stems from the extreme nationalism of Nasser's regime, which shall not be stopped or deterred simply because Greece maintains a 'diplomatic mission' in Jerusalem and not an official embassy – a difference that no one grasps. I mentioned the cases of Italy, France and Britain, which recently signed agreements with Egypt, despite their friendship with Israel. I also mentioned the case of West Germany, which, despite threats from Egypt, signed a reparations agreement with Israel.[41] I also added that if he would permit me to express my opinion of the policy Greece was following, I would say that I believe the stance being displayed by Greece regarding its special relation to Israel could quite possibly be viewed by Egypt as a weakness, and nothing more. If that is in fact the reality, then it is primarily Greek interests that are not being promoted [...]

As Jeonathan Prato wrote in his report, Kanellopoulos chose not to expand on the issue. 'He provided me with a vague assurance that he would discuss the matter with the Prime Minister and the Minister of Foreign Affairs,' and with that, the meeting came to an end.[42]

A few days later, on 25 February 1959, Prato met with Angelos Vlachos,[43] a member of the Greek delegation at the Zurich and London negotiations and an old acquaintance of the diplomatic service of Israel, since the time he had served as a representative of Greece in Jerusalem. Vlachos reiterated most of what Kanellopoulos had said regarding Cyprus. The de jure recognition of Israel, he clarified, was not a matter for the present time. In fact, he described Greek–Israeli relations as 'excellent' and the pending recognition as 'a mere formality, of which Athens is ever aware'.

The Israelis did not seem surprised by Greece's postponement of de jure recognition. On the other hand, signals from Athens regarding the possible establishment of diplomatic relations between Israel and Cyprus were not disheartening. At the meeting between Prato and Vlachos, the Greek diplomat hinted that Athens did not intend to hinder such a development – but would not encourage it either. According to Vlachos' words, as included in Prato's report to Maurice Fischer, the assistant director general of the Israeli Ministry of Foreign Affairs, 'it is natural for the new state to want to maintain good relations with its neighbours and Israel has much to offer Cyprus from its own experience in the field of development and improvements in the standard of living of its citizens. Cyprus is in need of such assistance [...].'[44]

4.3.2 Prospects for improvement in Israeli–Turkish relations

In the summer of 1958, the change of regime in Iraq, the political instability in Jordan and Lebanon, and the increasing influence of Nasser on the Arab world all acted as a catalyst for Israel and Turkey to renew their collaboration behind the scenes. The objective for both the Israelis and the Turks was to contain the risk of Nasserization in pro-West Arab states of the region. Nevertheless, during the same period, Turkish diplomacy was equally concerned about the continuing unrest in Cyprus, and was

[41] On 10 September 1952, West Germany signed a bilateral agreement with Israel based on which Bonn would pay reparations to Israel for Nazi war crimes committed against the Jewish people during the Second World War, for a total amount of DM3 billion (deutschmarks) paid in instalments.
[42] ISA/RG93/MFA/263/6, Prato to West Europe Division (241/23.2.1959).
[43] ISA/RG93/MFA/263/6, Prato to Fischer (266/27.2.1959).
[44] Ibid.

seeking ways to ensure that the outcome of the pending vote at the 13th Session of the UN General Assembly in the matter of Cyprus would not compromise its interests. For this reason, the Turkish side asked for Israel's active support, given the significant influence of Israeli diplomats in Latin America which traditionally supported Greek positions on the Cyprus question.[45] The Israelis decided that since there was nothing on the cards in terms of relations with the Greek government, they might as well seize the opportunity and mobilize behind the scenes in support of Turkish positions. Diplomatic contacts between Israel and the countries of Latin America, and the guidance personally offered to Fatin Zorlu by Israel's permanent representation to the UN helped the Turkish cause in various ways.[46] Thus, the formerly solid 'pro-Greek' Latin American front was split in the vote of 4 December 1958, so that Greece essentially secured only the votes of the pro-Soviet Eastern Bloc, Yugoslavia and other neutral Afro-Asian countries, while in the Arab world, only the United Arab Republic and pro-Nasser Yemen supported the Greek positions.[47]

Israel expected something tangible in return for its diplomatic contributions at the UN but Turkey acknowledged them with words alone. According to the commitments Fatin Zorlu had made to Golda Meir in July 1958, and subsequent to what had allegedly been agreed between Ben-Gurion and Menderes during their secret meeting in Ankara on 29 August 1958,[48] in exchange for Israel's good services at the UN, Turkey would proceed to fully normalized diplomatic relations with Israel and reinstate its ambassador in Tel Aviv.

On 25 December 1958, Reuven Shiloah, Meir's closest confidante and special adviser to the Israeli Ministry of Foreign Affairs on political matters, travelled to Ankara. The purpose of the visit was to formulate a joint strategy against Nasser, who had recently made strong anti-communist statements. Nasser's motive in this had been to boost pro-Nasser voices at the State Department and various governments in the West. The apparent change in Egypt's tactics worried both Turkey and Israel. On the other hand, the new Iraqi regime was not entirely clear about the direction it would choose to follow at a political and diplomatic level. Iraq's relations with the West seemed fragile. Still, Turco-Iraqi relations did not appear to have deteriorated yet. Turkey had to maintain a fine balance indeed, just when its relations to Israel were on a positive track.

Shiloah and Zorlu were in absolute agreement over the common approach they should follow in Washington with regard to Qasim's regime in Iraq. Tensions flared, however, when the topic of restoring Turco-Israeli diplomatic relations came up. Zorlu admitted that both he and Prime Minister Adnan Menderes had promised Meir and Ben-Gurion that immediately after the vote on Cyprus, Turkey would normalize diplomatic relations with Israel in full and the Turkish ambassador would be returned to Tel Aviv. However, the situation had changed significantly. According to Shiloah, Zorlu argued that 'prior to the vote at the UN, he believed all Arabs would vote against

[45] Cf. 3.6.3.
[46] Cf. 3.6.5.
[47] Cf. 3.6.4 and 3.6.5.2.
[48] Israel State Archives, Gilead (ed.), *Documents*, vol. 13, 818 no. 428. Cf. 3.6.4.

Turkey', and therefore intended to proceed with the triumphant move of immediately reopening the Turkish embassy in Tel Aviv. 'But what can be done now, when only the UAR and Yemen voted against Turkey? What can we do now that the remaining Arab countries either openly supported Turkey or abstained, thus essentially serving Turkish interests?'[49] So, according to the Turkish way of thinking, 'it would not be wise on behalf of Ankara – at this point in time – to harm its own relations with the Arabs by restoring its diplomatic relations with Israel, and particularly in such a spectacular manner'. Reuven Shiloah's furious reaction was met with a cool-headedness from the Turkish foreign minister that bordered on polite indifference.[50]

After this unexpected development, the Israelis realized that what had actually prevented Turkey from normalizing diplomatic relations with Israel was not the Cyprus issue. After all, up until the eve of the 13th Session of the UN General Assembly, Cyprus had never been a key issue in the regional cooperation between Israel and Turkey. For Turkey, the vote on Cyprus was nothing more than a very important pretext to kick-start the meaningful collaboration of the two countries on a regional level. For Israel, the clandestine intervention in favour of the Turkish positions was an excellent opportunity for Israel to end its isolation at international fora and at the same time prove to both friends and enemies that it was in a position to influence the outcome of votes at the UN.

The true reason for the Turkish–Israeli rapprochement at that time did not lie in the developments in Cyprus. It was the new state of affairs taking shape in the Middle East and the increasing influence of Nasser in the Arab world, a fact that was of equal concern for both Israel and Turkey. At the same time, Turkey's relations with the Arabs stood in the way of an official normalization of ties with Israel. If Turkey honoured its commitment regarding the establishment of embassies in Ankara and Tel Aviv immediately after the vote on Cyprus, it would only have increased Nasser's popularity in Iraq, while undermining the stability of the pro-West Arab regimes in the region. The potential of pro-Nasser currents gaining ground in Jordan, Lebanon and elsewhere would clearly not benefit Turkey, nor, of course, Israel.

In May 1959, Moshe Sasson, deputy director of the Israeli Ministry of Foreign Affairs Middle East Division, expressed the following concerns:

> In the end, to what extent is it useful for us to continue pretending during our talks with the Turks that there is supposedly no other issue hindering the reopening of our embassies, apart from the matter of Cyprus? Is it perhaps preferable to put the question to them clearly, or is it in our best interest to leave them with the impression that they are successfully managing to hide the real cause [author's note: relations between Turkey and the Arab countries] from us? There are gains to be had in both cases. It is, however, essential to clarify the situation and take our decisions.[51]

---

[49] Israel State Archives, Gilead (ed.), *Documents*, vol. 13, 837 no. 440, Shiloah to the Israeli Ambassador in Rome, Eliahu Sasson (5.1.1959). On the Shiloah–Zorlu meetings (25.12.58–31.12.1958).
[50] Ibid.
[51] Ibid., 845–9, no. 443, Moshe Sasson, deputy director of Middle East Division, to Eliahu Sasson (25.5.1959); and ibid., 849 (endnote 2 of no. 443). Eliahu Sasson to Moshe Sasson (28.5.1959) (ISA/RG130/MFA/3750/1).

In response, Israeli ambassador to Rome Eliahu Sasson – who had coordinated behind-the-scenes contacts between Turkish and Israeli officials at the Italian capital in the summer of 1958 – agreed that relations between Turkey and the Arabs were the real reason behind Ankara's reluctance to reopen its embassy in Tel Aviv, and not the outcome of the Cyprus issue. He nonetheless seemed to understand Turkey's cautious stance towards the Arab countries, particularly as it borders on remote and generally unpredictable Syria, on the one hand, and unstable Iraq, on the other. Eliahu Sasson's remarks concluded by saying that ultimately it might be preferable for the Israelis to let matters lie and exert no further pressure on Ankara regarding the embassies. 'Besides,' he added, 'any relationship with Turkey – whether above board or not – is beneficial for Israel one way or another'.[52]

Consequently, Israeli diplomacy had no other option but to tolerate this peculiar 'secret romance' with Turkey, in the hopes that Ankara would maintain its influence in Iraq and prevent the spread of Nasserism in the Middle East.[53]

[52] Ibid.
[53] Cf. Ofra Bengio, *The Turkish–Israeli Relationship: Changing Ties of Middle Eastern Outsiders* (London: Palgrave Macmillan, 2004), 45–8.

5

Israel and Cyprus in the Transition Period

5.1 Israel's assessments and concerns about the orientation of regional foreign policy in the soon-to-be independent State of Cyprus

Being under British rule throughout the 1950s, Cyprus was the only neighbouring state entity with which Israel had developed normal diplomatic, political and commercial relations. An Israeli consulate had opened in Nicosia as early as August 1950.[1] The Cypriot ports and airports were Israel's closest gate to the West. The British military presence on the island largely guaranteed the security of the State of Israel, highly cognizant as it was at the time of its diplomatic, political and economic isolation in the Middle East. As a result, Israel had good reason to be interested in developing full diplomatic relations with the independent Republic of Cyprus, and a presence in the only non-Arab state of the region with shared maritime boundaries.

According to the popularized and fairly optimistic view expressed by the Israeli press at the time, the Republic of Cyprus, a non-Arab country with a European and mostly non-Muslim population, would have no reason not to be friendly towards Israel. The Arab–Israeli conflict was of no concern either to the Greek Cypriot or Turkish Cypriot residents of the island. Throughout the 1950s, Greek Cypriot merchants and businessmen had dealings both with neighbouring Arab countries and with Israel. Both Israel and independent Cyprus adopted similar state structures and their societies had much in common. The principle of separation of powers, the representative parliamentary democracy, the multi-party system, freedom of the press, the existence and function of a variety of religious institutions and organizations, the free-market economy, the active trade unions, women's place in society, and the broad middle class were only some of the common points in the two countries' sociopolitical structure. These common characteristics were in a position to provide a solid footing for political cooperation based on common values. Finally, Israeli public opinion had not forgotten the support shown by the Greek Cypriots to the Jewish Holocaust survivors detained at the British camps in Karaolos between 1946 and 1949.[2]

---

[1]   Cf. 2.3.1.
[2]   Cf. 2.1, 2.2 and 4.3.1.

Nevertheless, the reality was much more complex. The London–Zurich Agreements had changed the state of things in the Eastern Mediterranean. The new Cypriot state would share maritime boundaries with Israel, Lebanon and the United Arab Republic (Egypt and Syria), while the British military bases would remain on the island. On the other hand, the communities of Greeks and Turks living on the island, which until recently had been at odds with each other, were expected to maintain a particularly fine political balance while at any given moment they might negatively affect the already fragile Greek–Turkish relations. Athens and Ankara had to work closely together in order to implement the agreements, and thus, along with Britain, become the guarantors not just of the stability in the Republic of Cyprus, but also of smooth cooperation within the NATO framework. Right after the signing of the London–Zurich Agreements, Israel tried to gauge its chances of improving bilateral relations with Greece and Turkey. The results were discouraging, as both motherlands, each for its own reasons, did not wish to jeopardize relations with the Arab states.

Meanwhile, Israeli diplomats received indications that Greece would not raise obstacles to the potential establishment of full diplomatic relations between Israel and the future independent Cyprus.[3] At the same time, Turkey, which had already developed good behind-the-scenes relations with Israel,[4] was sure not to object to such a prospect either.

In the period between the day after the signing of the London–Zurich Agreements and the official proclamation of independence of the Republic of Cyprus, the consulate general of Israel in Nicosia had to coordinate actions and make contacts with multiple aims: First, factors that could potentially affect the decision-making centres of the newly established Cypriot state had to be assessed. Then, the ground had to be prepared for establishing full diplomatic relations. At the same time, however, it was necessary to counteract any sign of Arab pressure on Cypriot leadership which might compromise Israel's presence in the region.

5.2 The impact of Greek and Turkish Cypriots on relations between independent Cyprus and Israel

Israel's main concern was the position which the independent State of Cyprus would assume vis-à-vis the Arabs – and in consequence with Israel. As to this issue, the assessments of Peretz Leshem, Israel's consul general to Nicosia, were pessimistic, as indicated by three extensive reports he prepared in February and March of 1959.[5]

The Greek Cypriots were divided over the handling of major political and economic issues in the early days of independence. The question of whether or not independent

---

[3] Cf. 4.3.1.
[4] Cf. 4.3.2.
[5] ISA/RG93/MFA/263/6, Research Division (59/10.3.1959), Three reports by Leshem to the British Commonwealth Division on the internal political situation in Cyprus are included. The first two reports were drafted in February 1959 and the third one on 4.3.1959.

Cyprus would join the British Commonwealth and remain in the pound sterling monetary zone, and the role of the Ethnarchy and the Left in the country's political life were only a few of the burning issues that would play a decisive role in the political balance, and also in the physical features of the new state. Nevertheless, Leshem noted one of the few points of consensus among Greek Cypriot political powers, Left and Right: the necessity to consolidate relations between Cyprus and the Arab world. In the report Leshem prepared in the days before the Zurich negotiations, he notes a general sense that the 'the difficult days are over'.[6] EOKA had announced an indefinite suspension of operations. Shops, cinemas and entertainment venues were reopened. Military patrols were decreased. British senior staff, who had until recently handled public healthcare and education for the two communities were replaced by Greek and Turkish Cypriots, and on New Year's Day 1959, the governor held his customary meetings with Makarios and Küçük. The climate was changing day by day. When the London Agreement was finally signed and Greek Cypriot political prisoners were released, Cyprus began to change. The only reminders of the fact that, only a few months earlier, the island had been plagued by bloody skirmishes were the expressions of gratitude in the local press to the Arab world for supporting Cyprus in its struggle against the British. Right-wing Greek Cypriot papers were full of praise for Nasser and his stance at the UN, while the left-wing papers hailed the consistently anti-West positions of the United Arab Republic.

Another area of concern for the Israeli consul was the commercial relationship between Cyprus and neighbouring Arab countries. Trade was controlled mostly by active Greek Cypriot entrepreneurs, and up until October 1956, their commercial transactions with Egypt had thrived.[7] The Suez Crisis, however, had severed British diplomatic relations with Egypt and as a result, Cyprus had stopped exporting to the extremely profitable Egyptian market. This had a significant impact on the island's economy. Israel feared that an independent Cyprus would give Greek Cypriot entrepreneurs and merchants the green light to restart business dealings with Egypt and thereby strengthen political relations between Cyprus and the UAR. In his March 1959 report, Leshem assessed the island's relationship with Israel in correlation to its commercial ties with Arab markets:

> We must remember that the Greek Cypriots do not like us, even though there was a time they appreciated us thanks to our victory in our liberation struggle. Nevertheless, they 'love' any buyer or, more to the point, any cheap supplier who will secure high and easy profits. They believe British dominance over local trade will continue, unless we learn to buy products from both Greek Cypriots and Turkish Cypriots, for as long as the latter are trying to build their own independent market. We must bear in mind that the Turks' lack of commercial acumen,

---

[6] ISA/RG93/MFA/2156/7, Leshem to British Commonwealth Division (102/8-59/8.1.1959), and Leshem to British Commonwealth Division (102/185/59-25.2.1959).

[7] ISA/RG93/MFA/2156/7, Leshem to British Commonwealth Division (192/162/59-18.2.1959), Comparative statistical data on the value of exports and imports between Cyprus and the countries of Egypt, Lebanon, Syria, Jordan, Libya, Iraq, Sudan and Israel in the period 1953–8. Cf. 5.3 and 6.2.1.

compared to that of the Greeks, may put an end or weaken any efforts that have been made so far to create their own independent market when this new political arrangement comes into force on the island.

We must expect a major recession in the growth rate of the [author's note: Cypriot] state, as well as the emergence of problems in the functioning of the public sector. This recession, which will not only be the result of new hiring in the public sector, or the difficult negotiations with the British [author's note: about the military bases], or the function of institutions and the exercise of duties by public officials, but also in the commercial sector. In spite of the long-term education provided by the British regime, the majority of the people retained a Levantine mentality and many predict that the Greek practices and the example of Athens will eventually dominate public life here.[8]

The Israelis were aware that the Greek Cypriots dominated the commercial sector, while the Turkish Cypriots did not have a particularly strong presence on a local or regional level. It was also obvious that economic relations between Greek Cypriots and the Arab markets were more beneficial than their transactions with Israel.

As a result of these pessimistic assessments, Israel pinned its hopes on the enhanced political role that the Turkish Cypriot community was expected to play in the new state. The vice president's veto power on foreign policy issues and the established quota favouring the involvement of the Turkish Cypriot community in executive government and public administration were reassuring for Israel. It was believed that in this way, the pro-Arab feelings of the Greek Cypriots would be mitigated, thus allowing the newly independent neighbouring state to maintain a balanced distance vis-à-vis the Arab–Israeli conflict. After the signing of the London–Zurich Agreements, Leshem concluded that:

> Israel will have to promote its interests on the island through the Turks. The Greek majority is not allied to us, either in politics or in the commercial sector. It is our natural rival in the 'old' markets of the region and will seek to dominate on a regional level. When Cyprus becomes a fully-fledged UN member, it will most likely side with our opponents over the majority of issues related to our region.[9]

Leshem had expressed the same view as early as January 1959, before the Greek–Turkish agreement was signed in Zurich.[10] Not coincidentally, Israel's concerns grew as Egypt and Syria were allegedly preparing to appoint consuls to Cyprus.[11] Egypt, stronger than ever, was getting ready to return to Nicosia and reopen its consulate which had been closed in November 1956 when diplomatic relations with Britain were suspended in light of the Suez Crisis.

---

[8] ISA/RG93/MFA/263/6, Research Division (59/10.3.1959), Leshem to the British Commonwealth Division.
[9] Ibid.
[10] ISA/RG93/MFA/2156/7, Leshem to British Commonwealth Division (102/143/59-12.1.1959).
[11] ISA/RG93/MFA/2156/7, Leshem to British Commonwealth Division (102/56/59-19.1.1959).

On the other hand, there were also positive signs. Nikos Kranidiotis, a close associate of Archbishop Makarios who lived permanently in Athens and was already rumoured to be up for appointment as ambassador of the Cypriot Republic in Athens, allegedly wanted to advance relations between independent Cyprus and Israel in the areas of agriculture and trade, and to invite special Israeli advisers to the island. Speaking to an Israeli businessman who was already active on the island, Kranidiotis responded to the question of whether this would be detrimental to Cyprus' relations with Arab countries that 'circumstances dictate good relations with the Arab countries of the region', but 'if Ghana has managed to be on good terms with both Israel and the Arabs, why shouldn't Cyprus be able to do the same?'[12] The position that Ghana maintained on the Arab–Israeli conflict could well have served as a good example for Cypriot foreign policy. Ghana was the first country in West Africa which, immediately after its decolonization and independence in 1957, established full diplomatic relations with Israel. In exchange, Israel implemented a broad spectrum of development programmes in the areas of agriculture, irrigation and public health. This did not stop the African country from establishing diplomatic relations with all Arab countries without becoming embroiled in dilemmas relating to the Arab–Israeli conflict.[13]

Israeli diplomatic reports of that period contained conflicting opinions and unconfirmed information as to whether Cyprus would be friendly towards Israel or not. Having no other, more reliable sources, Israeli diplomats waited to learn from the press about the intentions of Makarios and Küçük. An extensive article in the English-language daily *Cyprus Mail*, which included statements by both leaders of the new state, was not particularly enlightening.[14] Makarios' first public speech on 1 March 1959, the day of his official return to the island, did not present a clear view of his views on Cyprus' position in the world. An excerpt from his remarks related to international relations left much room for interpretation:

> Around our seas spread today troubles between three continents and the disputes of two worlds. In this environment, we Cypriots are called upon to play the role of a conciliator and coordinator. We are called upon to turn our country into a golden bridge which will unite and not disrupt oppositions. We are called upon to turn our island into a big artery which will unite spiritually and physically, North and South, East and West. The work is not easy. Big efforts and colossal work are

---

[12] ISA/RG130/MFA/3570/12, Zeev Shek, adviser of the Israeli embassy in London to British Commonwealth Division (1108/25.2.1959). It includes everything that Nikos Kranidiotis allegedly said to Israeli businessman Rudolf Goldstein, who ran an agricultural holding in Cyprus at the time.

[13] Ghana maintained balanced diplomatic relations with Israel and the Arab countries from 1957 to 1973. After the Yom Kippur War in October 1973, Ghana was forced to take a position on the Arab–Israeli conflict, when the Organisation of African Unity (OAU) decided that all of its member states must suspend diplomatic relations with Israel. The same stance was adopted by all member states of the OAU except Malawi, Swaziland and Lesotho. Ghana and Israel fully restored diplomatic relations in 2011, with the opening of their embassies in Tel Aviv and Accra, respectively. Cf. Arieh Oded, 'Israel ve-Afrika: Hebetim Historiim ve-Politiim' ['Israel and Africa: Historical and Political Perspectives'], in *Misrad ha-Khutz*, ed. Yeger, Govrin and Oded, 615–29.

[14] ISA/RG93/MFA/2156/7, *Cyprus Mail*, 'White Paper: The full text: Women will have the vote; Army may be conscripted', 24.2.1959.

needed. We are a small people who can become strong only through the power of Spirit and the grandeur of Morality. Only Spirit cannot be tied by geographical boundaries. A small people like us can play a big role. The mission of the Cyprus Republic is very high and sacred [...].[15]

As he witnessed the aftermath of the London–Zurich Agreements in Cyprus, Leshem took note of developing trends in his reports. He believed that the Greek Cypriots were not reconciled to the idea that the Turkish Cypriot vice president had the institutional power to influence political decisions, equivalent in practice to the power of the Greek Cypriot president. Public statements by Makarios and Küçük, and press reports in both communities, laid emphasis on the concept of 'Good Will'. Yet, according to Leshem, this mutual 'good will' was the main issue. The secret hope of the Greek Cypriots was that once the British departed, the rights of Turkish Cypriots would ultimately be curtailed and figure less than the rights they had believed they were entitled to. On the other hand, the Turkish Cypriots would ostensibly insist on applying the London–Zurich Agreements to the letter, while endeavouring as well to establish a condition of 'community autonomy' and avoid being rendered vulnerable to the stronger Greek majority.

'If Cyprus was a car, Makarios would be the driver, but Küçük would handle the accelerator and the brake,' was the oft-heard quip in the diplomatic circles of Nicosia.[16] Israeli diplomacy had long since realized that this uniquely 'unified' and 'independent' Cyprus consisted of two separate political systems. According to the Israeli interpretation of reality, the Greek Cypriot political system was headed by Archbishop Makarios, though he faced strong criticism from the nationalist Right and to a certain extent from the Left/Communist opposition as well, while Fazıl Küçük's leadership of the Turkish Cypriots was unquestionable. Albeit the more nationalist views of Rauf Denktaş drew considerable attention.

At the time of the London–Zurich Agreements, the consulates of Greece, Turkey, the US, West Germany, Lebanon and Israel were operating in Nicosia. According to Israeli assessments, it was only a matter of time before the consulates of Egypt and Syria, which constituted the United Arab Republic, were reopened. This inevitability was a cause of grave concern for the Israelis, given the pro-Arab leanings they observed in the Greek Cypriot community.[17] Owing to the pro-Turkish stance they had adopted at the 13th Session of the UN General Assembly,[18] the Israelis resolved to edge closer politically to the Greek Cypriot community before Nasser's Egypt could install a diplomatic mission and gain a stronger foothold on the island. This, notwithstanding the fact that Israel deemed relations with the Turkish Cypriots absolutely crucial.

[15] ISA/RG93/MFA/2156/7, *Cyprus Mail*, 'A glorious era lies ahead for Cyprus', 2.3.1959.
[16] ISA/RG93/MFA/2156/7, Leshem to British Commonwealth Division (102/199/59-4.3.1959).
[17] Cf. 5.2.
[18] Cf. 3.6.5.

5.2.1 The Greek Cypriot factor

On 20 February 1959, one day after the successful completion of the London Conference, Walter Eytan made a statement to the Israeli press. Israel, he said, was prepared to recognize the Republic of Cyprus and establish full diplomatic relations immediately after its formal proclamation of independence.[19] The following day, Israeli Prime Minister Ben-Gurion congratulated the Greek and Turkish governments on reaching an agreement, and noted that Israel looked forward to establishing friendly relations with the Republic of Cyprus, 'another non-Arab state which has been added to the region'.[20] During the press conference for foreign journalists in Tel Aviv on 21 February 1959, Ben-Gurion praised the way in which the Cyprus issue had been resolved, described the process of direct negotiations between Greece and Turkey as a successful model for settling international differences, and expressed the hope that it could be applied to the Arab–Israeli conflict:

> I believe that the independence of Cyprus is proof of the benefits to be gained when former enemies meet, talk about their common issues and come to an agreement. They [author's note: the Greeks and Turks] once fought against each other. They were enemies. But rationality prevailed and they came to an agreement, even though it seemed there was no hope. If the UN could do exactly the same with us and our Arab neighbours, I am convinced this would be to our benefit, and bring us together to solve our differences on our own.[21]

Leshem conveyed these statements to Makarios upon the latter's return to Cyprus on 10 March 1959. Their meeting took place at a reception in his honour held by Aristotelis Frydas, the Greek consul to Nicosia.[22] Leshem spoke to Makarios about the renewed stream of tourists from Israel now that the state of emergency had been lifted, but also about deploying special advisers from Israel in areas of primary development along the lines of technical assistance which his government was offering to recently decolonized countries. Just two years earlier, the Israeli Ministry of Foreign Affairs had set up the International Aid Sector, which was responsible for providing technical assistance and Israeli advisers to Asian and African countries which had recently gained independence. These development programmes focused on public healthcare, agriculture, livestock breeding and industrial and housing development. Naturally, Israeli companies undertook the construction of any necessary public works. Through its involvement from 1957 and during the 1960s, Israel had strengthened its diplomatic relations with those countries as they absorbed logistical support from Israel in

---

[19] *Davar*, 'Israel congratulates Turkey and Greece', 22.2.1959.
[20] *Maariv*, 'Ben-Gurion attempting to reassure Arab countries – Ready for peace in an hour, but disappointed with Nasser – Hopes for good relations with Cyprus', 22.2.1959.
[21] Ibid.
[22] ISA/RG93/MFA/263/6, Leshem to Loker (1011/238/59-15.3.1959).

exchange for favourable votes at the UN and other international fora on Israel-related issues.[23]

Makarios' reactions were particularly guarded. He expressed his wish to establish full diplomatic relations with Israel, emphasizing that Cyprus should cultivate friendly relations with all the countries in the region. On the other hand, he did not hide his concern about the strained relations between Israel and the Arabs. His reserved stance worried the Israelis, who expected to hear a clearer commitment to establishing full diplomatic relations with the Cypriot state.

5.2.1.1 *The Greek Cypriot ministers of the Transitional government*

The same awkward climate prevailed even after the Governor's official announcement on 5 April 1959, that he had accepted the line-up of the 'Transitional Committee', which would serve as a provisional government. The ministers would formally take office on 1 May 1959 although essentially, the Council of Ministers was convened and began exercising public powers as early as mid-April.[24] The members of the Transitional government were as follows: Paschalis Paschalides (Commerce and Industry), Glafcos Clerides (Justice), Polycarpos Georkadjis (Labour), Antonis Georgiades (Transport and Public Works), Tassos Papadopoulos (Interior), Riginos Theocharis (Economy), Niyazi Manyera (Health), Osman Örek (Defence) and Fazıl Plümer (Agriculture). The Greek Cypriot and Turkish Cypriot Ministers were selected by Archbishop Makarios and Fazıl Küçük, respectively.[25]

Although the main aim of the Transitional Committee was to fill the power gap until the withdrawal of the British regime and until the independent Republic of Cyprus was officially declared, its composition was an indicator of Makarios' personal preferences and the ideology that would shape the ensuing political situation. The people Makarios chose to make up the Council of Ministers were not from the Left. He did not choose 'old politicians' who had been involved in local administration or in trade unions under British rule. As ministers he selected lesser-known figures, nearly all of them in their 30s, who had demonstrated their loyalty to him and had been involved, each in his own way, in the EOKA struggle.[26]

The common element in Leshem's reports after his face-to-face meetings with the new Greek Cypriot ministers was that they all carefully avoided talking about foreign policy issues, which – as they claimed – would be handled by Makarios himself. That aside, the Israeli Consul did not know them personally and was therefore unable to

---

[23] The International Aid Sector (ha-Mador le-Siua Benleumi) was renamed in 1960 the Agency for International Development Cooperation (ha-Makhlaka le-Shituf Peula Benleumi), better known in Israeli documents by its acronym 'Mashav'. From 1960 to 1967, Mashav oversaw development programmes in West and Sub-Saharan Africa (Guinea, Ghana, Liberia, Ivory Coast and others), in Indochina (Burma, Thailand, Laos) and Latin America. During the same period, Mashav took part in programmes under the auspices of international organizations (FAO, UNESCO, etc.).

[24] ISA/RG93/MFA/2156/5, Leshem to British Commonwealth Division (102א/345/59-14.4.1959).

[25] Ibid. (102א/316/59-6.4.1959).

[26] ISA/RG93/MFA/263/6, Loker to Golda Meir (3.4.1959).

surmise their views on future relations between the Republic of Cyprus and Israel.[27] The deputy director of the Israeli Ministry of Foreign Affairs British Commonwealth Division, Zvi Loker, detected Leshem's objective difficulty in time and recommended to Foreign Minister Meir that she seek the opinion of Zeev Levin as well. As a member of the Executive Committee of the Histadrut, the country's largest trade union, Levin had personally met most of the newly appointed Greek Cypriot ministers during his three trips Cyprus in 1958 as an envoy of the ICFTU.[28] His presence on the island had drawn positive comments from Greek Cypriot public opinion, and in Israel he was considered to have the deepest knowledge of conditions in the neighbouring island.

Meir agreed with Loker's proposal and brought Levin back to the forefront on matters related to Israeli foreign policy in Cyprus. By April 1959, the Cypriot press had already learned that in the following months, Levin would be named consul general in Nicosia.[29]

This choice was welcomed by the US. At the end of May 1959, US diplomat Murat Williams had just completed his mandate at the State Department's Office of Greek–Turkish and Iranian Affairs. A few weeks before his placement at the US Embassy in Tel Aviv, he was asked by the adviser to the Israeli embassy in Washington, Moshe Erell, what he thought of Levin's posting as consul in Nicosia. In 1958, Levin, in his capacity as ICFTU representative, had come into contact with the leadership of GSEE and was also in constant contact with the American embassy in Athens, earning its trust. Over the next few months, the Americans watched Levin's activities in Cyprus with interest. Williams was complimentary about Levin's personality and capabilities, believing him to be the 'most natural choice to represent Israel in Cyprus', given the considerable number of contacts he had cultivated on the island.[30]

Zeev Levin was to assume his new duties in Nicosia in early July 1959. But until then, Consul Leshem had to navigate the first critical months of the Transitional Period, during which he was called on to coordinate efforts to strengthen Israel's presence in Cyprus while readying the ground for his replacement. It was clear to the Israelis that the newly appointed Cypriot officials and Greek Cypriot businessmen were not fully aware of the broad potential for Cypriot–Israeli cooperation. For this reason, the Israeli Ministry of Foreign Affairs decided to launch public relations

---

[27] ISA/RG93/MFA/2156/5, Leshem presented his personal impressions to the British Commonwealth Division with separate reports on the following members of the Transitional government: Andreas Azinas, Deputy Minister of Agriculture (102א/337/59-13.4.1959); Antonis Georgiades, Minister of Transport and Public Works (102א/504/59-18.5.1959); Riginos Theocharis, Minister of Economy (102א/530/59-25.5.1959); Paschalis Paschalides, Minister of Commerce and Industry (102א/529/59-25.5.1959); Polycarpos Georkadjis, Minister of Labour (102א/536/59-27.5.1959); Tassos Papadopoulos, Minister of Interior (102א/547/59-28.5.1959).

[28] Cf. 3.6.1.1.1.

[29] *Times of Cyprus*, 'Zev Levin Ambassador – Israel's new envoy talks to the *Times of Cyprus*: Plans for an all-out friendship drive', 14.4.1959.

[30] ISA/RG93/MFA/263/6, Yapou to Israeli diplomatic mission in Ankara and Israeli diplomatic representation in Athens (796/10.6.1959), The report dated 26.5.1959 by Moshe Erell, adviser to the Israeli Embassy in Washington, in which he describes a discussion he had with US Diplomat Murat Williams. Cf. 3.6.1.1.1 and 3.6.6.

initiatives that would promote mutual benefits in such areas as entrepreneurship, trade and tourism.

In mid-March 1959, the head of the Ministry of Foreign Affairs Press Office, Yehuda (Harry) Levin, proposed a set of initiatives to spearhead Israel's appeal to Cypriot public opinion.[31] Specifically, he recommended distributing printed informational material in Greek and in Turkish, inviting Cypriot journalists to visit Israel with a view to publishing relevant articles in the local press, broadcasting radio and television shows promoting Israel in a positive light, urging commercial, professional and charitable Cypriot associations to establish contacts with their respective Israeli counterparts, and staging cultural events to promote Israel in Cyprus.

Within two weeks, the recommendations of the Press Office were already being implemented. In April 1959, the Israeli airline El-Al and the Israeli Tourist Organisation, in cooperation with the Israeli Consulate and a Greek Cypriot tour operator, organized a visit for ten Cypriot journalists to Israel. In the same month, Cypriot television CTV for the first time broadcast extensive reports about Tel Aviv, Jerusalem and the Israeli kibbutz movement, shortly before the main evening news.[32] At the initiative of the consulate in Nicosia,[33] an exhibition of works by Greek Cypriot painter George-Paul Georgiou was held in early April 1959 at the Bezalel Academy of Arts in Jerusalem. The event received wide press coverage in Cyprus, since it was the first time that a Greek Cypriot artist had attracted such attention in Israel.[34] One month later, on the eve of the eleventh anniversary of Israel's declaration of independence, the Israeli consulate in Nicosia bought a painting by the artist, portraying Jewish detainees attempting to escape from the Karaolos detention camps.[35]

However, Israel's evident communication overture to Cyprus was met with immediate opposition from Lebanon, the only Arab country with diplomatic representation on the island at that time. The invitation of El-Al and the Israeli Tourist Organisation in April 1959 was extended not only to journalists but also to twelve tour operators from both communities. The consul of Lebanon to Nicosia, Michel Farah, made it clear to the Greek Cypriot tour operators that if they accepted Israel's invitation, their professional cooperation with Lebanon and the other Arab countries would be suspended immediately.[36] The Greek Cypriot tour operators who worked with Lebanese, Egyptian and Syrian airline companies and travel agencies chose to heed the Lebanese consul's warnings. As a result, only Turkish Cypriot tour operators visited Israel.

---

[31] ISA/RG130/MFA/3570/12, Yehuda (Harry) Levin, director of the Media Department at Israeli Ministry of Foreign Affairs, to Yitzhak Ben-Yaakov, deputy director of the same division (19.3.1959).
[32] ISA/RG93/MFA/2156/7, Leshem to British Commonwealth Division (102/362/59-17.4.1959).
[33] Ibid. (102/366/59-19.4.1959).
[34] *Ethnos*, 'Mr G. Georgiou's exhibition in Jerusalem', 8.4.1959. *Cyprus Mail*, 'Israel hails Cypriot painter', 12.4.1959. *Times of Cyprus*, 'The Island's "Ambassador of Art" shows his work to Israel', 12.4.1959. *Ethnos*, 'Gauguin of Cyprus – The work of Mr Georgiou a huge success – Favourable criticism in Israel', 16.4.1959.
[35] *Times of Cyprus*, 'Israel buys Georgiou picture', 11.5.1959.
[36] ISA/RG93/MFA/2156/7, Leshem to British Commonwealth Division (102/333/59-10.4.1959).

This incident heralded similar Arab interventions, putting Greek Cypriot businessmen, merchants and government officials in a difficult position. Paschalis Paschalides, the Transitional government's Minister of Commerce and Industry was the first Greek Cypriot politician who was faced with this unprecedented reality in Cyprus.[37] Both he and the other Greek Cypriot tour operators, along with the British officials who were still performing their administrative duties,[38] watched helplessly as this unexpected aspect of the Arab–Israeli conflict unfolded in Cyprus. Although they were all sympathetic to Leshem's objections and critical of the attitude of his Lebanese counterpart, they were unable to intervene. Both Israelis and Greek Cypriots had come to realize that any type of cooperation between them would be a difficult undertaking. Arab pressure would mount in the following months with the ultimate aim of preventing the independent Cypriot state from maintaining any contact at all with Israel, whether at a transnational or a business level.

Nevertheless, certain Greek Cypriot ministers of the Transitional government and other official organizations on the island took the initiative to contact the Israelis and create appropriate conditions for further cooperation in their areas of competence. Of these first contacts, the most interesting was Minister of the Interior Tassos Papadopoulos, who on his own initiative, brought together Greek Cypriot farmers, members of the Executive Committee of the Eniaion Dimokratikon Metopon Anadimiourgias (United Democratic Reconstruction Front, EDMA)[39] Israeli development organizations engaged in the areas of water supply and irrigation, citrus farming, and the distribution and standardization of agricultural products.[40] Papadopoulos suggested training Cypriot farmers in Israel with a view to applying Israel's crop-growing methods on their return. Following contacts between Consul Leshem with Papadopoulos and members of EDMA, it was suggested that the Israeli Ministry of Agriculture and the pro-government trade union organization Histadrut take the next steps.

In April 1959, Teddy Kollek, director general of the Israeli Prime Minister's Office, visited Cyprus and met with Paschalis Paschalides, the Minister of Commerce and Industry in the Transitional government. Paschalides expressed interest in conducting a joint advertising campaign aimed at attracting tourists to Cyprus and Israel.[41] The two corresponded over the following months so that their ideas could be implemented immediately after the independence of the Republic of Cyprus had been declared.

Meanwhile, Tassos Papadopoulos expressed interest in the housing programme the Israeli government was implementing, and told Teddy Kollek that they might undertake

---

[37] Ibid. (102/352/59-14.4.1959), On the stand adopted by Greek Cypriot entrepreneurs and Paschalis Paschalides.

[38] Ibid., (102/465/59-11.5.1959).

[39] On 1 April 1959, EOKA fighters established the political movement 'United Democratic Reconstruction Front' (EDMA). EDMA's establishment was welcomed by Archbishop Makarios and George Grivas. A few months later, on 17 November 1959, Ioannis Clerides and Themistoklis Dervis founded the 'Democratic Union of Cyprus' (DEK), bringing together the anti-Makarios factions mainly from the Greek Cypriot Right.

[40] ISA/RG93/G/5570/10, Leshem to British Commonwealth Division (8554/59-10.8.1959).

[41] Ibid., Leshem to Kollek (102א/479/59-14.5.1959).

similar public works in Cyprus.[42] Kollek responded to Papadopoulos' request and in November 1959, the director of the Ministry of Labour's Department of Housing and Urban Planning, David Tanneh, went on a fact-finding visit to Cyprus, accompanied by a qualified staff member.[43] After his visit to Nicosia, Larnaca, Limassol and Famagusta, Tanne drafted a technical report containing a set of proposals for the urban reconstruction of the Cypriot urban centres, with the prospect of the competent agencies from both countries cooperating in the near future.[44]

Dr Konstantinos Spyridakis, president of the Greek Education Council in charge of Greek education on the island during the Transitional Period,[45] appealed to Consul Leshem for information on the Israeli national education system and asked whether it might be possible for Greek Cypriot teachers and educators to receive additional training through seminars or special training schools for teaching staff in Israel. Leshem forwarded Spyridakis' request to the Israeli Ministry of Foreign Affairs, suggesting that it send him information from the Ministry of Education and the Organization for Rehabilitation and Training (ORT) educational organization which oversaw the technical and vocational training schools in Israel.[46]

The Supreme Court of Cyprus sent a questionnaire to the secretariat of the Tel Aviv District Court, asking how the Israeli justice system had dealt with legislation and case law from the end of the British Mandate period in Palestine to the formation and operation of the Israeli court system.[47] Judge Yehoshua Eisenberg, answered the questionnaire while Judge Chayim Cohen drafted a detailed report on the question and sent it to the Supreme Court of Cyprus. Cohen had been Secretary of the ad hoc Israeli committee entrusted with ensuring a smooth transition from the British law of the Mandate to the national law that would become effective in view of Israel's proclamation of independence in the years 1947–8. On the Cypriot side, Judge Kostas Zannetides, adviser to Minister of Justice Glafcos Clerides, sought the assistance of Israeli Consul General Leshem to obtain information about the Judicial Authority Israel had recently instituted.[48] The Israeli Ministry of Justice sent Zannetides an English translation of the 'Law on Courts'.[49]

Finally, in December 1959, the possibility of establishing a Cypriot-Israeli Chamber of Commerce was proposed, and the necessary contacts were made between Greek Cypriot businessmen and members of the Tel Aviv and Jerusalem chambers of

[42] Ibid., Zeev Levin, consul general of Israel to Nicosia, to Teddy Kollek, director general of the Prime Minister's Office (10/972/59-31.8.1959).
[43] Ibid., Levin to Division of International Development Cooperation in the Ministry of Foreign Affairs (1399/59-12.11.1959).
[44] Ibid., David Tanneh to Kollek (804/45-5.1.1960).
[45] No member of the Transitional government had been entrusted with competences of the Minister of Education.
[46] ISA/RG93/MFA/2156/5, Leshem to British Commonwealth Division, with a copy to Comay, director general of the Ministry of Foreign Affairs, and to the Press Office (102א/361/59-17.4.1959).
[47] ISA/RG93/MFA/2156/7, Sufott to Leshem (1094/24.5.1959), and the Secretariat of the Supreme Court of Cyprus to the Secretariat of the District Court of Tel Aviv (S.C.554/11.4.1959).
[48] ISA/RG93/MFA/2156/5, Leshem to the Israeli Ministry of Justice through the British Commonwealth Division (102א/577/59-7.6.1959).
[49] Ibid., Leshem to Judge Kostas Zannetides (102a/666/59-30.6.1959).

commerce.[50] The Israelis hoped that in this way they would be able to deter the Arab countries from preventing the Greek Cypriots from doing business in Israel.[51]

5.2.1.2 The anti-Makarios Right

There were political figures from the anti-Makarios Right who condemned the London–Zurich Agreements. Their criticism focused on the exclusion of Enosis from the agreement and on the way Makarios had handled the negotiations. One of the leading voices of the anti-Makarios faction was the long-standing Mayor of Nicosia, Themistocles Dervis.[52] As a member of the large Greek Cypriot committee of leaders, Dervis had travelled to London on 15 February 1959 at Makarios' invitation, just before the signing of the agreements on 19 February.[53] After the signing, Dervis and fellow members of the largely right-wing delegation, accused Makarios of failing to consult with them on the specifics of what had been agreed to, and accused him of inviting them to London simply as a pretext and a means of keeping up appearances.

As Mayor of Nicosia, Dervis was named head of the 'Mayors' Front' which criticized the role of the pro-Makarios 'Consultive Convention' formed at that time and accused Makarios of appointing lackeys. The very unpleasant climate between Makarios and a section of the Right is aptly rendered in a statement Dervis issued on 30 October:

> We, the Mayors, were not present at yesterday's meeting of the Consultative Convention, because it no longer functions as a Consultative Body. Most members represent none other than the Archbishop himself. The situation is so grave, that it is time for the Archbishop to stop taking all decisions himself as a dictator. We believe that any decisions should be taken by the Convention and implemented by the Archbishop. The members of the Consultative Convention are always presented with a fait accompli. We, the Mayors, will take a stand against this method to the best of our abilities. The dictatorship period is over.

Makarios' response was equally scathing:

> If Cyprus was indeed a fascist country, then Mr Dervis would not have been able to unleash his tongue in this manner and unrestrainedly insult EOKA's fighters, even if his relations to the Organisation were not good during the struggle. As regards the 'Mayors' Front', consisting of the Mayors of six Cypriot towns, I am very much afraid that this 'front', established with such delay, can be misconstrued and gives rise to many questions. This front should have existed during the armed struggle against our foreign dominators. But there were internments camps and many dangers then [...].[54]

[50] ISA/RG130/MFA/3570/12, Levin to the Economic Affairs Division (03-21/1581/59-10.12.1959).
[51] Ibid. (03-17/1587/59-10.12.1959), Presence of the Israeli company Sapan in Cyprus.
[52] Themistocles Dervis had served as mayor of Nicosia during the periods 1929–31, 1943–6, 1949–53 and 1953–9.
[53] ISA/RG93/MFA/2156/7, Leshem to British Commonwealth Division (102/143/59-12.2.1959).
[54] Archbishop Makarios III Foundation, Kokkinou (ed.), *Apanta Archiepiskopou*, vol. 4, 331–2.

Following a political gathering held at a cinema in Nicosia, the political group Democratic Union of Cyprus (DEK) was established on 17 November 1959, under the leadership of Themistocles Dervis and Ioannis Clerides. The DEK was the official voice against Makarios in the days before the first presidential elections scheduled for 13 December 1959. Running against Makarios was Ioannis Clerides, father of the Transitional government's minister of justice, Glafcos Clerides. Ioannis Clerides' candidacy represented a significant number of Greek Cypriots who were against the London–Zurich Agreements; he was supported, as to be expected, by the right-wing DEK and by a portion of voters from the left-wing AKEL. Archbishop Makarios emerged as the winner of those presidential elections with 66.85 per cent of the vote, while Ioannis Clerides received 33.15 per cent.[55]

Before the Democratic Union of Cyprus had even been formed, and while the political conflict intensified between the supporters and opponents of Makarios, the Israelis tried to determine whether the Greek Cypriot right-wing opposition was leaning favourably towards Israel and what positions it intended to adopt on issues of regional foreign policy. Sources available to the Israelis were scarce and the information gathered was unclear. Contrary to what was happening in other countries with a strong Jewish presence, where local Jewish communities informed their Israeli consulates on the politics of their area, the Jewish community in Cyprus was small and its access to Greek and Turkish Cypriot decision-making centres was minimal.[56] This had already been reaffirmed in September 1950, as soon as the Israeli consulate opened its doors in Nicosia.[57] Subsequently, the Israeli consul's sources of information were limited to private meetings with other foreign diplomats on the island, with British officials and a limited number of figures in the local community who expressed their personal views, depending on their ideological beliefs. Gaps in information had to be filled via publications in the local press, which had to be very carefully evaluated in order to reach reliable conclusions.

But Themistocles Dervis, with whom Israeli Consul Leshem was in personal contact, was an exceptional source, not only because he was the mayor of Nicosia, but because his wife, Katia, was of Hungarian-Jewish descent.[58] An invitation extended to Dervis from the mayor of Tel Aviv, Chaim Levanon, to visit Israel with his family and attend the 50-year anniversary celebration of the city's founding was an excellent opportunity for the Israeli Ministry of Foreign Affairs to hear first-hand the views of the main representative of the anti-Makarios opposition.[59] Dervis accepted and spent four days in Israel, from 4 to 8 June 1959.[60]

---

[55] Ioannis Clerides' loss in the elections marked the ultimate dissolution of the Democratic Union of Cyprus.

[56] Cf. 2.1.

[57] Cf. 2.3.1.1.

[58] ISA/RG93/MFA/2156/7, Leshem to British Commonwealth Division (102/574/59-5.6.1959), and Leshem to British Commonwealth Division (41/29680 מ – 15.5.1958).

[59] ISA/RG93/MFA/2156/7, Leshem to British Commonwealth Division (102/574/59-5.6.1959).

[60] *Eleftheria*, 'Dr Dervis leaves tomorrow for Tel Aviv', 3.6.1959; *Haravgi*, 'Themistocles Dervis leaves for Israel', 5.6.1959; and *Ethnos*, 'Mayor Themistocles Dervis returns from Israel', 9.6.1959.

Dervis, on a one-day tour of the Israeli sector of Jerusalem, was approached discreetly by Zev Sufott, an official from the British Commonwealth Division of the Ministry of Foreign Affairs. Sufott's effort to form an opinion of Dervis' character and political views[61] left him unimpressed. Dervis, he noted, was 'against one and all'. According to Sufott's report, Dervis persistently criticized the British and their policy in Cyprus, both prior to and following the signing of the London–Zurich Agreements. He also strongly criticized the way in which Makarios had handled the negotiations. He spoke contemptuously of the ministers in the Transitional government, calling them 'Makarios' kindergarten'. Furthermore, his anti-communist views and negative comments concerning AKEL policy were perceived by the Israelis as confirmation of the publications in the Turkish Cypriot press, particularly *Bozkurt*, which denounced Dervis for his 'extreme nationalist views'.[62]

Sufott concluded that Makarios' right-wing opponents, who were against Cypriot independence were totally incompatible with the positive light in which Israel viewed the results of the London–Zurich Agreements. Thus, the Israelis could find no point of consensus with the positions of Themistocles Dervis. Indicatively, during the rest of his visit to Israel, further contact between him and other Israeli officials was evaded, nor was he given any further publicity, apparently so as not to give Makarios the impression that Israel was siding with the opposition.[63]

Sufott's negative impression of the positions of Dervis was supplemented by Leshem who described Dervis as a person

> with extreme nationalist views, who is however inflamed by totalitarian attitudes, whether they come from the Right or the Left. He is a person who has always voiced his opinion strongly, without considering the consequences, and his position in public life is weak within the framework of the current political regime, which will undoubtedly remain in power over the next few years [...].[64]

Finally, Dervis claimed that 'Cyprus has no need of an army' and that the agreement for a military alliance between Cyprus, Greece and Turkey signed on 28 October 1959 was just another one of Makarios' mistakes.[65] Both claims reaffirmed the belief that the positions of the right-wing Makarios opposition, as represented by Dervis, did not conform to the way in which the Israelis perceived regional reality.[66]

During the political confrontation leading up to the presidential elections of 13 December 1959, it became clear that the issue was whether popular opinion would approve or reject what had been agreed to in Zurich and London – regardless of the fact that the agreements had already been signed. Ioannis Clerides' defeat, in contrast to the clear electoral victory of Archbishop Makarios, and the subsequent dissolution

---

[61] ISA/RG93/MFA/2156/7, Sufott to Leshem (1134/7.6.1959).
[62] Ibid. (11414/9.6.1959).
[63] Ibid.
[64] Ibid., Leshem to British Commonwealth Division (102/623/59-18.6.1959).
[65] Cf. 6.1.
[66] ISA/RG130/MFA/3751/26, Levin to British Commonwealth Division (1317/59-3.11.1959).

of the Democratic Union of Cyprus confirmed Israeli assessments regarding Dervis' presence in the Greek Cypriot political scene.

As for the character and political role of Georgios Grivas, it is worth noting that Israeli diplomatic reports were very terse – both those prepared prior to the signing of the London–Zurich Agreements and those signed later on. They recognized his fighting spirit and ability to dramatically influence developments on the island. As had been thoroughly outlined, Grivas' aim to achieve Enosis was incompatible with the regional interests of Israel in the Eastern Mediterranean, due to the ties established between Israel, Britain and Turkey throughout the 1950s. Following the signing of the London–Zurich Agreements and Makarios' prevalence on the internal political scene of Cyprus, the Grivas–Makarios confrontation in 1959 was described in neutral terms. Grivas' departure from Cyprus strengthened the Israeli conviction that the era of his great political influence had come to an end.[67]

5.2.1.3 The position of the leftist AKEL Party

Relations between Israel and the Greek Cypriot Left were idiosyncratic. Since the early days of its establishment in the mid-1950s, the Israeli Consulate in Nicosia had been the recipient of complaints from the leftist PEO concerning the living conditions of the Arab population in Israeli territory.[68] In addition, starting in early 1949, Ben-Gurion's centre-left government adopted West European parliamentary models, and gradually began to align itself with the West on a diplomatic and political level,[69] while consolidating the country's relations with the Turco-British axis.[70] By the late 1950s, and a mere ten years into statehood, Israel had become one of the most pro-West countries in the Middle East. This fact made it difficult to establish channels of communication between Israel and the Greek Cypriot Left, whose leading representative was the AKEL Communist Party.

An additional factor in the distancing of the Cypriot Left from Israel was the rivalry between the leftist PEO and the newer SEK, representing trade unions of the Right. The latter was a member of the international confederation ICFTU, which was often represented in Cyprus by Zeev Levin, a member of the Executive Committee of the Israeli Federation of Labour, the Histadrut – a member of the same international confederation. Levin's activities in Cyprus in 1958 had focused on providing financial support for the institutional restructuring of SEK, so that it could continue to act as an effective counterweight against the broad influence exerted by the leftist PEO in trade union activity. His contacts in Cyprus reinforced the efforts made by the SEK leadership to rehire the Greek Cypriot workers who had been fired *en masse* by the local British authorities for purely political reasons. Levin's intervention received broad press coverage on the island, giving the impression that SEK's status vis-à-vis the PEO had

---

[67] ISA/RG93/MFA/263/6, Leshem to British Commonwealth Division (102/249/59-17.3.1959). Cf. 5.2.1.3.
[68] Cf. 2.3.1.3.
[69] Cf. 1.2.
[70] Cf. 2.4.2.

been enhanced with the support of the ICFTU's Israeli envoy.[71] Although the PEO never criticized Zeev Levin's actions aimed at having the Greek Cypriot workers rehired, it was nonetheless clear that the presence of the Israeli ICFTU representative was associated with right-wing SEK.

Still, and despite the lack of communication between the official political leadership of the Greek Cypriot Left with Israel, there were AKEL members who had cultivated important ties with the Jewish state. Specifically, Prodromos Papavassiliou, who was a member of AKEL and a city council member of the Famagusta Municipality, had played an important role while British detention camps were in operation during the 1946–9 period, actively helping Jewish detainees to escape and reach Israel, in order to join the ranks of the newly formed regular Israeli Army as soon as possible.[72] The collaboration between Papavassiliou and the Israelis later extended to politics. Thanks to his personal contacts, Famagusta Mayor Adam Adamantos, who was supported by AKEL, visited Israel in June 1949 at the invitation of the government. It was the first time a Greek Cypriot mayor had ever visited Israel. During Adamantos' visit, the municipalities of Haifa and Tel Aviv offered financial assistance for technical works in Famagusta as an expression of gratitude for the help its citizens had offered the Jews held on the island.[73] Another example was the case of Kostas Partassides, a senior member of AKEL and for many years the mayor of Limassol. His imprisonment in 1950 and 1955 had earned him words of praise in the Israeli press for his courageous stand against the British colonial regime.[74] In 1954, under Partassides' mayorship, the Municipality of Limassol contacted the Municipality of Haifa requesting technical assistance in carrying out extensive public works to improve the city's sewer system. The Municipality of Haifa responded positively and sent staff from its technical department and special advisers to Limassol, from 1954 to early 1957.[75]

Meanwhile, newspapers espousing the views of the pro-Soviet Mapam opposition party continued to praise and promote AKEL and its actions throughout the 1950s. The various reports filed by Israeli diplomats about the disputes between EOKA and the Greek Cypriot communists maintained what was clearly a more favourable stance towards the latter, confirmed by the socialist ideology of Ben-Gurion and his governing party, Mapai, and particularly after it was learned that Grivas' followers were guilty of murdering members of the Left.[76] Whereas none of this seemed to interest AKEL leadership, the Israeli publications and departmental reports in favour of the AKEL faction on the neighbouring island did not in any way change the unwavering pro-West stance of the Ben-Gurion and Sharett coalition vis-à-vis regional security.

Consequently, the Israeli side did not attempt to establish meaningful contact with the leadership of the illegal AKEL, though it could have done so had it wished to. In his

---

[71] Cf. 3.6.1.1.1.
[72] Cf. 2.2 On the activities of Prodromos Papavassiliou.
[73] Cf. 2.2.
[74] Cf. 3.4.1.
[75] ISA/RG130/MFA/2028/12, Avraham Ehrlich, civil engineer, Division of Public Health, Municipality of Haifa, to the Ministry of Foreign Affairs (10.9.1959).
[76] Cf. Sofia Argyriou, *To ethniko kinima ton Ellinokyprion* [*The National Movement of the Greek Cypriots*] (Athens: Asini, 2017), 403–7.

July 1959 assessment of Israel's relationship with the various political powers on the island, Zeev Levin noted that 'so far, we have developed absolutely no relationship with the powerful communist faction', without however suggesting that this state of affairs should be changed.[77]

Throughout the 1950s, Israel and the Greek Cypriot Left had been unable to coordinate a channel of communications for the relationships that were developing between the Israelis and certain prominent figures who happened to be AKEL members or supporters and held important positions in local government and business. In any case, these did not propound an anti-West party line which was by definition unfriendly to Israel.

On the eve of the first presidential elections in December 1959, Israel indicated that it did not wish to improve its relations either with the left-wing trade unions, or AKEL. Nevertheless, in their reports, the Israeli diplomats did not typically disparage the Left or its members and took care to maintain good relations with some of them. The explanation for this peculiar affection from afar is this.

Israeli diplomats assumed that the Greek Cypriot communists did not wish to be controlled by the right-wing, post-civil war monarchy in Athens, which was clearly anti-communist and had outlawed the Greek Communist Party. For this reason, even though AKEL was not against the candidacy of the anti-Zurich Ioannis Clerides – since behind-the-scenes meetings for their potential support of Makarios had already failed[78] – the Israelis believed that the communists would ultimately not stand against Cypriot independence as instituted by the London–Zurich Agreements. At the same time, the Israeli government was pleased by the fact that Cyprus would not become part of Greek territory, since Athens maintained strong ties with the Arab countries, displayed a pro-Arab stance at international fora and seemed unwilling to recognize Israel de jure.[79] Thus, based on Israeli speculation, the independence of Cyprus was acceptable both to Israel and AKEL, though for completely different reasons. Consequently, Israel had nothing to gain by improving relations with AKEL.

[77] ISA/RG93/MFA/2156/7, Points made by Zeev Levin during a broad-based meeting held on 2.7.1959 at the Israeli Ministry of Foreign Affairs on the bilateral relations of Cyprus and Israel, in view of Levin's assignment to Nicosia. Cf. 6.1.1 on the meeting of 2.7.1959.

[78] ISA/RG93/MFA/263/7, Levin to British Commonwealth Division, with copies to Middle East Division and the Diplomatic Representation of Israel to Athens (1517/59-30.11.1959). Meetings between the communists and Makarios, during which they discussed their support of his candidacy in the upcoming presidential elections of 13.12.1959. According to Levin's report, members of EDMA had reacted against such a prospect, while similar objections were allegedly voiced by the American consulate. Levin's belief led to the conclusion that the communists:

> would also take into account the votes that would go to the 'Democratic Union of Cyprus' of Dervis and Ioannis Clerides, in order to present them as their own negotiating tool with Makarios, in view of the coming elections for the House of Representatives. It is possible that the communists may wish to continue their negotiations with Makarios, although it seems that the pressure exerted on Makarios from many sides, including the American Consulate here, will prevent him from reaching any kind of agreement with them.

[79] Cf. 4.3.1.

Israel was aware that both the AKEL communists and the supporters of the nationalist Right had a positive stance towards the Arab countries – and particularly towards Gamal Abdel Nasser. On the other hand, neither AKEL nor the Right held enough electoral power to significantly influence Cypriot–Israeli relations at a transnational level. Given the new political balances of the London–Zurich Agreements, the final word on whether or not full diplomatic relations would be established between Israel and Cyprus rested with Archbishop Makarios, who personally handled matters of foreign policy, and Fazıl Küçük, who was constitutionally empowered to exercise his veto on matters of international relations involving the future Cypriot state. No matter how Israel approached AKEL, there would be absolutely nothing to gain. On the contrary, it could cause additional difficulties. In any event, according to Israeli assessments, Makarios' decision not to include AKEL members or sympathizers in the Transitional government was far from arbitrary.

Finally, the Israelis were obliged to take seriously the fact that from December 1955 to the eve of the presidential elections of 1959, AKEL had been banned. More specifically, a few weeks after a state of emergency was declared in Cyprus,[80] Governor Sir John Harding outlawed AKEL on 13 December 1955, based on criminal provisions regarding 'illegal associations', along with organizations controlled by AKEL (Anorthotiki Organosi Neolaias, Youth Reconstruction Association, AON; the Cypriot Union of Farmers, EAK; and the Pancyprian Organisation of Democratic Women, PODG). He also banned the leftist publications *Neos Dimokratis*, *Theoritikos Dimokratis*, *Anexartitos* and *Empros* and the Turkish language *İnkilâpçı*. At the same time, the British authorities began making arrests, not only of party members but also members of the leftist trade union organization, PEO, though the latter was not banned.[81]

On 8 November 1959, about a month before the first presidential elections in Cyprus, Israeli Consul Leshem met with Governor Foot to discuss the issue of legalizing AKEL and the place of the Left in the island's political life.[82] The governor was not opposed to legalizing AKEL and acknowledged that the communist factor in Cyprus could not be ignored, though he also expressed his personal opinion that AKEL was not connected to Moscow. Nevertheless, he was unwilling to bear the responsibility for such a decision, apparently because he wished to avoid opening up another electoral front that would make things difficult for Makarios. As he told Leshem, he wanted 'the Cypriots to deal with the matter themselves', specifically Makarios himself, given that 'Küçük had stated that this matter does not concern his community'. Foot was initially reluctant to bear the brunt of legalizing AKEL, since he believed that it was up to Makarios to decide the matter. Ultimately, however, the governor did legalize AKEL, with a special decree, published a day later in the special issue, no. 4280/2.12.1959, of

---

[80] Archbishop Makarios III Foundation, Kokkinou (ed.), *Apanta Archiepiskopou*, vol. 2, 622–8. The official announcement of 26.11.1955 by the Public Information Office declaring Cyprus to be in a state of emergency.

[81] Ibid., 128–9.

[82] ISA/RG93/MFA/392/10, Leshem to British Commonwealth Division (1385/59-11.11.1959).

the official *Cyprus Gazette*.[83] Thus, although in April 1959 the Foreign Office had said it was pleased to see that Makarios had not included members of the Left in the Transitional government,[84] in December of that year, it appeared not to take into account the 'Gentlemen's Agreement' between Karamanlis and Menderes, signed under confidential reference in Zurich on 11 February 1959, according to which 'the two Prime Ministers agreed to assist the President and Vice-President of the Republic of Cyprus respectively in order to outlaw the Communist Party and communist activity'.[85] On 13 December 1959, the day of the first presidential elections and just ten days after AKEL was legalized, the British administration published a circular expressing its conclusion that the Cypriot communist movement was linked to the Greek Communist Party – which in turn identified ideologically with the Soviet Union.[86]

Israeli diplomacy was not interested in decrypting what Britain intended to do with regard to the communists in Cyprus. Instead, it chose to keep its distance from AKEL's party organizations, not just during the Transitional Period, but throughout the 1950s. Had Israel adopted a more communist-friendly stance in Cyprus, it would have been merely one more thorn in its relations with post-civil war Greece and would likely have upset both its even-keeled relations with blatantly anti-communist Ankara or London, and the US, where the prospect of legalizing a communist party on the island caused grave concern.[87] Thus, even after the British governor legalized AKEL, Israel avoided opening channels of communication with the party. After all, things were still unclear, both regarding the future relations of Makarios and the communists, and the burning question of full diplomatic relations being established between the Republic of Cyprus and Israel. Finally, it is worth noting that while Ben-Gurion was in office, and despite his left-wing background and that of the governing Centre-Right party Mapai, the main opposition in Israeli politics came from the more extreme leftist party Mapam, which espoused explicitly pro-Soviet views.[88]

---

[83] *The Cyprus Gazette* (Extraordinary), No. 4280, 2.12.1959. Cf. Colony of Cyprus, *Legislation of the Year 1959 – Subsidiary Legislation* (Nicosia: Government Printer, 1960), vol. 2, 511–12 (Supplement No. 3). With the special decree of 1.12.1959 by Governor Foot, published in a special issue of the *Cyprus Gazette* on 2.12.1959, the legal restrictions on the operation of AKEL and of other political organizations under its auspices, as well as on the publication and circulation of leaflets supporting their views were lifted. Cf. *Haravgi*, 'Restrictions against AKEL and other people's organisations are lifted', 3.12.1959.

[84] ISA/RG93/MFA/2156/5, Ofer to British Commonwealth Division (4052/17.4.1959). The Foreign Office expresses its satisfaction regarding the fact that Makarios did not include any AKEL members in the Transitional government.

[85] Archbishop Makarios III Foundation, Kokkinou (ed.), *Apanta Archiepiskopou*, vol. 3, 637–9; and Xydis, *Cyprus: Reluctant Republic*, 413 and 519.

[86] Cf. Archbishop Makarios III Foundation, Kokkinou (ed.), *Apanta Archiepiskopou Kyprou Makariou III*, vol. 2, 716–19. The complete text of the explanatory circular issued by the British authorities on 13.12.1955.

[87] Nicolet, *United States Policy towards Cyprus*, 143–5.

[88] Cf. Gabriel Haritos, 'I Araviki Psifos sto Israil: Apo ta 'Kommata-Doryforous' tis Dekaetias tou '50 ston Eniaio Araviko Sindiasmo tou 2015' ['The Arab Vote in Israel: From the "Satellite-Political Parties" of the '50s to the Joint Arab List in 2015'], Policy Paper 5/2015 (Nicosia: Cyprus Center for European and International Affairs, University of Nicosia, 2015), 14–17. On the pro-Soviet leanings of the Mapam Party in the political reality of Israel in the 1950s. Cf. 1.1 and 1.1.4.

5.2.1.4　Statements made by Makarios to the Washington Star on relations between Cyprus, Israel and the Arabs

The interview Canadian journalist Marie Grebenc conducted with Makarios, published on 5 July 1959 in the American *Washington Star*[89] and later reprinted in the British *Daily Express* had a large impact both in Cyprus and abroad. In that interview, the archbishop seemed to express clear positions on the decisions he was poised to make about the management of the country's internal political landscape, particularly concerning his relations with Grivas, the West and Britain, and on the regional foreign policy of the new state.

In the same interview, Makarios made clear that he would no longer tolerate any involvement by Grivas in local politics. In the article, Makarios commented on Grivas' criticism of the way negotiations between Turkey and Britain had been conducted. 'Grivas will simply have to be made to understand that it is I, Makarios, and not Grivas, who is responsible and in authority here in Cyprus,'[90] he said,

> Grivas very often speaks without knowing the facts. He is an emotional man, easily swayed by what people tell him. He should not listen to everything those around him say. In the next few days, I shall have to write to him that he must be more careful in what he says about what we are doing here. Of course, I cannot tell him directly to be quiet [...] I believe it would be a serious mistake for him to enter politics.[91]

Makarios seemed equally clear about relations between the Republic of Cyprus and Britain. Contrary to the anti-British positions expressed in the local political scene, the archbishop took a stand in favour of the inclusion of Cyprus in the British Commonwealth and keeping the Cypriot pound within the monetary zone of the pound sterling, as he believed these options would benefit the local economy. After praising the attitude of Greek Prime Minister Konstantinos Karamanlis during the negotiations, he criticized the US stand on Cyprus at the UN, saying he felt 'not just disappointment. The word should be 'resentment'. It will be quite a long time before that is forgotten.'[92] Nevertheless, he asserted, his own negative sentiments about this would not hinder him from seeking US financial assistance in order to support the Cypriot economy.

The authenticity of the interview with Marie Grebenc[93] was strongly questioned by Archbishop Makarios, who hastened to claim it was fabricated. Makarios denied making critical remarks about Georgios Grivas and declared that he had not met with

---

[89]　ISA/RG130/MFA/3570/12, Marie Grebenc, 'Makarios views Cyprus future: Sees Grivas' role more restricted', *Washington Star*, 5.7.1959.

[90]　Ibid.

[91]　Ibid.

[92]　Ibid.

[93]　In the Cypriot press and related statements made by Archbishop Makarios on the publication of the interview in question, the surname of the journalist is wrongly rendered as Kreenberg instead of the correct surname which is Grebenc.

the journalist nor referred to his relations with Grivas in any interview.[94] The statements Makarios was alleged to have made about Grivas riled public opinion in Cyprus. Notably, a month later, on 8 August 1959, Makarios was still refuting the content of that interview, claiming in a statement to the Athens News Agency that Grebenc 'had totally distorted the truth'.[95] These persistent refutations persuaded neither Grivas nor his supporters.[96]

The article in the *Washington Star* was discussed in Cyprus for a long time, since it highlighted the points of tension between Makarios and Grivas. Yet the same article was also the focus of much attention within Israel's Ministry of Foreign Affairs – for a totally different reason: Israeli interest focused on an excerpt from the interview about prospects for relations between Cyprus and its Middle Eastern neighbours. In the article, the archbishop was quoted as saying:

> I, myself, lean in my sympathies to the Arab countries. I have been in the United Arab Republic three times and regard Nasser as a personal friend. We will, of course, establish relations with the UAR first – but then, they do not want us to have relations with Israel. We need to be friendly with both groups. I will have to persuade our Arab friends to let us be friendly with Israel, too.[97]

Those words spurred the Israeli press to publish a multitude of ominous predictions about the future of relations with the neighbouring island, which was soon to become independent.[98]

Makarios' interview with the *Washington Star* coincided with the end of Peretz Leshem's term in Nicosia, and their final meeting lacked what would otherwise have

[94] Archbishop Makarios III Foundation, Kokkinou (ed.), *Apanta Archiepiskopou*, vol. 4, 283. Makarios' statement on the content of the publications in the *Washington Star* and the *Daily Express* is as follows:

> The report from Nicosia published in the Daily Express newspaper, which includes certain statements supposedly made by me, which refer to General Georgios Grivas-Digenis, are totally false. I have never given any interview since I arrived in Cyprus to a *Daily Express* correspondent, nor have I spoken to any other journalist about the leader of EOKA in a way that has given the impression there is disagreement between us. My relations with the General are excellent, we regularly exchange letters as friends and we have never disagreed on any matter to date.

[95] Ibid., 294–5. The excerpt of Makarios' interview to the *Athens News Agency* which concerns his interview with Marie Grebenc is as follows:

> I am sorry to have to declare categorically once more that Ms Kreenberg, for reasons unknown to me, has totally distorted the truth. I have never claimed, nor could have claimed, that I organised and managed the armed struggle in Cyprus. From the outset, the organisation and management of the struggle was handled exclusively by Digenis. It was more than obvious after all that the struggle was managed by a military figure with extensive experience and skills.

[96] Archbishop Makarios III Foundation, Kokkinou (ed.), *Apanta Archiepiskopou*, vol. 4, 611–12. The letter of 7.7.1959 from Renos Kyriakides to Fotis Papafotis, with a handwritten note by Georgios Grivas attached. Grivas expressed the conviction that Makarios' interview was authentic and that he had indeed stated all that Grebenc reported.

[97] ISA/RG130/MFA/3570/12, Marie Grebenc, 'Makarios views Cyprus future: Sees Grivas' role more restricted', *Washington Star*, 5.7.1959.

[98] ISA/RG130/MFA/3570/12, For example, *Ha-Aretz*, 'Makarios: We shall ask the UAR for permission to establish relations with Israel', 6.7.1959.

been a ceremonious atmosphere. Their main topic of discussion was the archbishop's interview, which had met with such a range of reactions. Makarios claimed that his words had been misquoted, both with regard to the statements he made about his relationship with Grivas, and about future relations with Israel. He had been put in a very awkward position, he insisted, following the completely false and fabricated article.[99]

Of greater concern for Israel was whether or not Makarios' statements were true regarding the supposed 'permission' he hoped to receive from the UAR in order to proceed with the establishment of normal diplomatic relations with Israel. This was also the main issue discussed during the first meeting between newly appointed Israeli Consul Zeev Levin and the archbishop.[100] While Makarios insisted that the content of the news report was false, the Israelis received information to the contrary which they found to be more convincing. More specifically, Grebenc was said to have shown Governor Foot the complete transcription of the interview prior to its publication. As soon as he read it, he contacted Makarios and advised him to smooth over his statements concerning Grivas, but Makarios allegedly refused to go back on any of them and insisted on having the interview published as is.[101] The Israelis were likewise persuaded by American Consul Taylor Belcher, who told Levin that Grebenc had shown him the text of the interview immediately after it took place and shortly before she filed it for publication in the *Washington Star*. According to Belcher, when he asked Grebenc how she had managed to get such emotionally charged statements on Grivas from Makarios, who was usually reserved, Grebenc answered that she had simply charmed him.[102] Belcher was convinced that Makarios' statements to the *Washington Star* had been faithfully conveyed in full – particularly those concerning Grivas and that in making these statements, Makarios hoped to end Grivas' political interference and to oust him from the political stage before it was too late, so as to avoid any unpleasant surprises at the upcoming presidential elections in December 1959.[103]

The very day after the interview was published in the *Washington Star*, a group of Israeli journalists travelled to Cyprus to meet with Makarios and Fazıl Küçük. The two leaders set the minds of the journalists at ease, promising that Cyprus would establish diplomatic relations with Israel following independence; the Israeli press noted as well that the archbishop had expressed a desire to visit Israel 'in due course'.[104] The pro-government organ *Ha-Boker* provided unusually wide coverage of a formal visit paid to the archbishop by a few members of the Jewish Women's International Zionist Organization (WIZO), who happened to be in Cyprus at the time.[105] Meanwhile, the

[99] Ibid.
[100] ISA/RG93/MFA/392/10, Levin to British Commonwealth Division (736/59-16.7.1959).
[101] ISA/RG93/MFA/263/7, Levin to British Commonwealth Division (761/59-22.7.1959), Confidential report. Levin does not name his sources.
[102] ISA/RG93/392/10, Levin to British Commonwealth Division (736/59-16.7.1959).
[103] United States Department of State, LaFantasie (ed.), *Foreign Relations of the United States, 1958–1960*, vol. 10, part 1, 789–90 no. 327. Belcher to State Department (25.7.1959, telegram). It is noted that the last two paragraphs of the telegram in question have remained confidential up until the publication of this book.
[104] ISA/RG130/MFA/8317/7, *Ha-Aretz*, 7.7.1959.
[105] Ibid., *Ha-Boker*, 8.7.1959.

left-wing newspaper *Al ha-Mishmar* praised Makarios and Küçük for their words of wisdom, which confirmed that Cyprus and Israel would establish diplomatic relations despite Arab objections.[106]

Nevertheless, Levin's impressions upon embarking on his consular duties in Cyprus were identical to the assessments of his predecessor with regard to the Greek Cypriot disposition. It was clear that Makarios was eager to align with the Arab countries, particularly Nasser's Egypt,[107] and hesitant about expanding contact with Israel. A visit by an official delegation from Cyprus to Cairo in July 1959 was taken as a clear indication of Greek Cypriot intentions. Among the delegates were Nikos Kranidiotis, a close associate of Makarios, Antonis Georgiades, minister of transport and public works who was considered a Grivas proponent, Paschalis Paschalides, minister of commerce and industry, and Andreas Azinas, deputy minister of agriculture. Zeev Levin believed that with this move, Makarios wished to demonstrate respect for Nasser, to increase his popularity in Cyprus and to explore areas of potential cooperation between Cyprus and the UAR, but also perhaps to convince Nasser 'to give the Cypriots his permission to establish diplomatic relations with Israel as well'.[108]

However, to the contrary, during the same period, Makarios prevented Labour Minister Polycarpos Georkadjis and Agriculture Minister Fazıl Plümer from visiting Israel, with the official excuse that no Cypriot official was allowed to travel abroad before the mixed committee meeting in London[109] ironed out the details of the constitutional provisions. On the other hand, just before the Cypriot delegation was to leave for Cairo, Makarios suggested to Levin on his own initiative that the minister or deputy minister of agriculture in the Transitional government should go to Israel and explore prospects for cooperation with Israeli counterparts.[110] The mixed messages Makarios was sending about the outlook for Cypriot–Israeli relations had become deeply troubling to the Israelis.

5.2.2 The Turkish Cypriot positions vis-à-vis relations between Israel and Cyprus

Israel's relations with the Turkish Cypriots were much more clear-cut due to the fact that the entire community was rallied around Küçük. Some isolated and more radical nationalists who supported the popular Rauf Denktaş were the exception, though even they did not question matters of leadership.[111] Küçük faithfully followed Ankara's orders and seemed determined to ensure that the London–Zurich Agreements would

---

[106] Ibid., *Al ha-Mishmar*, 9.7.1959.
[107] Cf. 5.2.
[108] ISA/RG93/MFA/263/7, Levin to British Commonwealth Division (102/756/59-22.7.1959), and Levin to British Commonwealth Division (801/59-30.7.959).
[109] ISA/RG93/MFA/392/10, Levin to British Commonwealth Division (736/59-16.7.1959).
[110] ISA/RG93/MFA/263/7, Levin to British Commonwealth Division (102/718/59-12.7.1959), Content of Levin–Makarios meeting on 11.7.1959.
[111] ISA/RG93/MFA/263/7, Leshem to British Commonwealth Division (6.7.1959, not officially logged).

be applied to the letter in safeguarding the rights and privileges instituted for Turkish Cypriots.

Israeli Consul Peretz Leshem's first meeting with Fazıl Küçük on 24 March 1959 immediately after the signing of the London–Zurich Agreements was far less ambiguous than his 10 March meeting with Makarios had been.[112] Küçük was explicit about his intention to establish normal diplomatic relations with Israel, to join the British Commonwealth and the pound sterling monetary zone, and to become fully aligned with the West, both politically and diplomatically, in regard to regional issues of security. What reassured the Israeli consul was Küçük's confirmation that the Turkish Cypriots could theoretically cooperate equally well in political terms with the moderate Greek Cypriot Right or Left. Nevertheless, Küçük explained that he did not intend to back the potentially consolidated Left not only because of its strong influence among Greek Cypriots but also because Turkey would clearly oppose such an eventuality.

After the signing of the London–Zurich Agreements Küçük viewed his enhanced institutional role as an excellent opportunity to improve the living conditions of the Turkish Cypriots in the new state. The refusal of the Greek Cypriot suppliers to do business with the Turkish communities in 1958 had resulted in their economic stagnation and Küçük believed that strengthening ties between Israel and the Republic of Cyprus was directly linked to the reconstruction and development of the Turkish Cypriot economy. Küçük's long-term goal was for his community to become self-sufficient in the primary and secondary sectors and to cease their dependence on the Greek Cypriot majority. Though he did not say so openly, it was clear that he wanted his community to be prepared for the possibility of partition, if and when that came to pass, and wished to encourage logistical support from Israeli suppliers and technical advisers in the areas of agriculture, small-scale manufacturing and trade. To the Israeli consul, it was crystal clear that the Turkish Cypriots had not forgotten the possibility of partition any more than the Greek Cypriots had forgotten Enosis.

The Turkish Cypriots sought to enhance the Israeli presence on the island, and given Ankara's encouragement to do so, Küçük had no qualms about backing Israel's aspirations in Cyprus at a diplomatic level. Moreover, the Greek Cypriots' strong affinity for the Arab countries and for Nasser in particular gave Küçük ample leeway to tell the Israelis exactly what they wanted to hear.

A few days after the publication of Makarios' controversial statements in the *Washington Star*,[113] the Turkish Cypriot leader seized the opportunity once again to stress that his community fully understood Israel's concerns. At his farewell meeting with the outgoing Consul Peretz Leshem, on 8 July 1959, Küçük expressed the view that 'we regret the fact that Nasser wanted to prevail one way or another in all the countries of the region'. He confirmed that the Turkish Cypriot community 'is aware of the necessity to cultivate a bold relationship of cooperation between Israel and Cyprus', and that he would personally commit to working consistently to achieve that goal.[114]

---

[112] ISA/RG93/MFA/2156/5, Leshem to British Commonwealth Division (102א/276/59-25.3.1959). Cf. 5.2.1; and ISA/RG93/MFA/263/6, Leshem to Loker (1011/238/59-15.3.1959).
[113] Cf. 5.2.1.2.
[114] ISA/RG93/MFA/263/7, Levin to British Commonwealth Division (102/698/59-9.7.1959).

It was not long before Fazıl Küçük proved true to his word. According to a confidential report by Zeev Levin, based on statements by Deputy Minister of Agriculture Andreas Azinas, Makarios had asked Küçük to either join the Cypriot representation travelling to Cairo in July 1959[115] himself or to send one of the Turkish Cypriot ministers of the Transitional government. Küçük refused and wrote to Makarios that the group traveling to Cairo represented only the Greek Cypriots, not the Turkish Cypriots.[116]

Aside from Küçük, there were other Turkish Cypriot officials who expressed views that were reassuring to Israeli ears. Turkish Cypriot attorney Ümit Süleyman, who filled in for Minister of Defence Osman Örek while the latter was in London participating in the work of the mixed constitutional committee,[117] expressed his concern to Levin about the Greek Cypriot desire to affiliate with the UAR and the Arab world in general. According to Süleyman, the Greek Cypriots' pro-Nasser intentions stood in sharp contrast to the reason for creating a bicommunal Cypriot Army. The fears expressed behind the scenes by the Turkish Cypriots were in full accordance with the Israeli assessment of the reality prevailing in the region. In fact, in talking to Levin, Süleyman expressed his complete agreement that if Cyprus became a satellite of the UAR, the independent Cypriot state would inevitably distance itself not only from the West 'but also from Turkey and Israel, which were the main pillars of western democracy in the region'.[118]

In the area of trade, Turkish Cypriot entrepreneurs clearly had limited financial capacity and were not able to compete with Greek Cypriot private initiative. The Turkish Cypriot Chamber of Commerce took it upon itself to submit a long list of investment proposals to Israel focusing on the establishment and operation of small craft undertakings for wine-making, perfumery, juice and soft drink production, canning, olive production, packing, tanning, plastic goods, ceramics, carob processing, shoemaking and textiles.[119] This initiative had been set in motion by Rauf Denktaş in full compliance with Küçük's express political will to make the Turkish Cypriots economically independent of the Greek Cypriots. In fact, in November 1959, in an interview with the newspaper *Davar*, a mouthpiece for the pro-government trade union organization Histadrut, Küçük spoke of the Israeli communal agricultural units, the kibbutzim, as the model for his vision of Turkish Cypriot economic development.[120]

---

[115] Cf. 5.2.1.4.
[116] ISA/RG93/MFA/263/7, Levin to British Commonwealth Division (102/756/59-22.7.1959); and ISA/RG93/MFA/3570/12, Levin to British Commonwealth Division (949/59-27.8.1959).
[117] ISA/RG93/MFA/2156/5, Levin to British Commonwealth Division (102א/310/59-3.4.1959).
[118] ISA/RG93/MFA/263/7, Levin to British Commonwealth Division (102א/767/59-23.7.1959); and ISA/RG93/MFA/3570/12, Middle East Division to Yaacov Caroz, head of the 'Tevel' section of the Israeli secret services (796/פק – 27.7.1959). Meeting of Levin-Ümit Süleyman. On Caroz's competences during the period 1958–61, cf. his autobiography published after his death (1993) by Israel's Ministry of National Defence, Yaacov Caroz, *Ha-Ish Baal Shnei ha-Kovaim* [*The Man with two Hats*] (Tel Aviv: Misrad ha-Bitakhon, 2002), 123–54.
[119] ISA/RG130/MFA/3570/12, Letter dated 25.7.1959 from Kemal Rüstem, president of the newly formed Turkish Cypriot Chamber of Commerce, to Levin (not officially logged), and Levin to Economic Affairs Division (3/828/59-6.8.1959).
[120] *Davar*, 'Küçük: Israel's achievements should serve as an example to Cyprus', 11.1.1960.

It was no coincidence that during the same period, the trend among the Turkish Cypriots was to ask foreign companies interested in doing business on the island to have two commercial representatives in Cyprus – one for each community.[121]

Rauf Denktaş had something similar in mind. As a representative of the Federation of Turkish Cypriot Associations, he thought he would approach the Israeli consul to suggest that a Turkish Cypriot delegation visit Israel to learn more about the Israeli education system, the adult education system and the organization of kibbutz farm production. Denktaş also suggested that the Israelis should send logistical equipment and special advisers to the Turkish Cypriot community.[122] The Denktaş proposals were warmly received by the Agency for International Development Cooperation of the Israeli Ministry of Foreign Affairs, and in August 1959, Denktaş held a round of meetings with Levin with a view to specifying the scope of the three-member Turkish Cypriot representation, 'the first Turkish Cypriot mission to visit Israel', as Levin emphasized in his reports. Ultimately, it was decided to send three young Turkish Cypriots who, during their ten-day stay in Israel, would be trained in youth camps on kibbutzim. Upon their return to Cyprus, the three trainees would in turn train their peers in a number of agricultural spheres (developing irrigation systems, managing cooperative unions, instituting youth groups living in small rural communities, etc.).[123] After repeated postponements, the teenagers' guardians did not allow their children to travel to Israel.[124] At first, the plan was postponed till the spring of 1960, but it did not materialize at that time, either.

The fundamental difficulty facing the Turkish Cypriot proposals to attract investors was the non-response of Israel's private sector. Zeev Levin's efforts to stimulate interest in the Turkish Cypriot market amongst the entrepreneurs of his country were fruitless even though he told them that the Turkish Cypriot Chamber of Commerce had already begun to attract western European investors.[125] Nonetheless, what was most important in a purely political context was that the Turkish Cypriot political leadership was more than willing to attract Israeli entrepreneurs and strengthen its ties with Israel at every level. But for all that, the Greek Cypriot side was clearly restrained.

5.3 Assessment of Israel's contacts with the Greek and Turkish Cypriot communities in 1959

Throughout 1959, the Israelis kept a close watch on the two communities of the new independent Republic of Cyprus and their potential relations with Israel. This was no easy task, given that the Greek and Turkish Cypriots applied different criteria in their assessment of the situation in the Middle East. In essence, the Israelis had to form an

[121] ISA/RG130/MFA/3570/12, Levin to Economic Affairs Division (3/828/59-6.8.1959).
[122] ISA/RG130/MFA/3570/12, Rauf Denktaş to Levin (29.7.1959, not officially logged).
[123] ISA/RG130/MFA/3570/12, Levin to Division for International Development Cooperation (102/913/59-20.8.1959).
[124] ISA/RG130/MFA/3570/12, Denktaş to Levin (387/5/59-28.11.1959).
[125] ISA/RG130/MFA/2156/7, Levin to British Commonwealth Division (102/804/59-30.7.1959).

opinion of two distinct political realities – Greek Cypriot and Turkish Cypriot – which were politically compelled to coexist, and to shape and implement a single 'Cypriot' foreign policy.

Immediately after the signing of the Zurich and London Agreements, the major question posed by the Israelis was whether and to what extent Archbishop Makarios intended to maintain a balanced position between Israel and the Arabs, given his close ties to Gamal Abdel Nasser's Egypt. The Israeli side was aware of the objective reasons pushing Makarios to back the UAR – and thus to show reticence towards Israel.

A few days after Makarios' victory in the presidential elections of 13 December 1959, deputy secretary general of the Israeli Ministry of Foreign Affairs, Yaakov Tzur, noted that the factors adversely affecting future relations between Cyprus and Israel were based on the following assumptions.[126]

First, diplomatic relations between Greece and Israel remained cold and it was believed that, despite reassurances, ultimately Athens would not encourage Makarios to adopt a more positive stance towards the Jewish state.

Another factor that would significantly influence Makarios' decisions regarding the UAR was the need to safeguard the economically robust community of 15,000 Greek Cypriot nationals in Egypt. Since Athens too adhered to a pro-Arab policy over its concerns for the future of the Greek diaspora in Egypt, Israelis feared that Makarios would follow suit. The assessment that Greek Consul to Nicosia, Aristotelis Frydas, expressed to his Israeli counterpart, Zeev Levin, was unsettling, since in his view, the existence of the Greek minority in Egypt reduced the likelihood of Cyprus establishing diplomatic relations with Israel. Asked to comment on this vantage point, Israel's diplomatic representative to Athens, Jeonathan Prato, posited that in the event that Cyprus and Israel ultimately did establish diplomatic relations, it would have an adverse effect on relations between Greece and the UAR. Levin and Prato concluded that 'as far as the issue of bilateral relations between Cyprus–Israel is concerned it is essential to terminate Cyprus' dependence on Greece'. Both men wondered how this could be achieved during the Transitional Period, given that it was natural for the Greek Cypriots to look to Athens for guidance on issues of foreign policy and security.[127]

Finally, Makarios was on friendly terms with Nasser himself due to the consistent support Egypt had provided to the Cypriot anti-colonialist struggle. Indicative of this was the UAR's pro-Greek stance during the 13th Session of the UN, which quite justifiably the Greek Cypriots had not forgotten.

Aside from existing political adversities, prospects for economic relations between Israel and the Greek Cypriots could have been better. Statistics on imports and exports for both countries for the period 1953–9 revealed that Israeli exports to Cyprus were many times higher than Cypriot exports to Israel. Conversely, the balance of trade between Cyprus and the Arab countries was more favourable for Cypriot entrepreneurs

[126] ISA/RG93/MFA/392/10, Yaakov Tzur, deputy secretary general of the Israeli Ministry of Foreign Affairs, to Avraham Harman, Israel's ambassador in Washington (21.12.1959, not recorded as incoming document, top secret).

[127] ISA/RG93/MFA/263/7, Levin to British Commonwealth Division (156/59-26.11.1959), and Prato to British Commonwealth Division (1373/1.12.1959).

and producers.[128] In this regard, Cypriot Minister of Commerce and Industry Paschalis Paschalides was right to point out to Zeev Levin that such negative economic data did nothing to encourage the Greek Cypriot political leadership to make an overture towards Israel, when the Arab markets were proving to be more willing to support the Cypriot economy.[129] Levin himself admitted that throughout the 1950s, Israel had failed to develop a stable economic presence on the island, or to cultivate long-term partnerships with local businesses. Under British rule, Israeli investors had mainly pursued public works of a military nature,[130] but the era of colonialism was now past.

Therefore, as far as Zeev Levin could surmise, Archbishop Makarios' statements in the *Washington Star* in July 1959[131] should hardly have come as a surprise or have frustrated anyone at the Israeli Ministry of Foreign Affairs. Indeed, Cyprus had many reasons to wait for Arab permission – particularly from Nasser's Egypt – before deciding to develop diplomatic and economic relations with Israel. However, since Egypt would not consent, Israel was forced to take the necessary steps to prevent the Republic of Cyprus – the only neighbouring non-Arab state in the region – from becoming a satellite of the hostile Arab countries.

On the other hand, there were some positive aspects to Israel's aspirations. Specifically, at the local Cypriot level, immediately after the signing of the London–Zurich Agreements and throughout 1959, the Turkish Cypriot leadership unreservedly supported Israeli positions. Fazıl Küçük, urged on by Ankara, seized any opportunity to state that he fully shared Israel's concerns, openly expressed his objection to any effort by Makarios to turn towards the UAR and proclaimed loudly and clearly that he would work within the framework of his institutional role to help Cyprus establish full diplomatic relations not only with the neighbouring Arab countries, but also with Israel. Meanwhile, the Turkish Cypriots sought to attract Israeli investments to the island to strengthen their economy. Rauf Denktaş, who was then assumed to succeed Fazıl Küçük someday, supported this approach.

At the same time, Britain, through Governor Foot, repeatedly reassured the Israeli Consul that he was in favour of full diplomatic relations between Cyprus and Israel. In fact, he continued to denigrate the importance of Makarios' choices at a regional level, pointing out to the Israelis that, in any event, the British bases would continue to serve as a security factor for Israel even after the proclamation of Cypriot independence.[132]

The uninterrupted functioning of Israel's Consulate General in Nicosia since August 1950 was another encouraging point. This fact constituted a sort of 'diplomatic *fait accompli*' for a subsequent course of bilateral relations with independent Cyprus. Should the Israeli consulate cease to operate, independent Cyprus would inevitably adopt a pro-Arab position in the Arab–Israeli conflict. Nevertheless, Makarios had made it clear that he was not willing to take on this additional burden, particularly as

---

[128] Cf. 6.2.1.
[129] ISA/RG93/MFA/392/10, Levin to British Commonwealth Division (1093/59-17.9.1959).
[130] Cf. 2.4.2.1.
[131] ISA/RG93/MFA/392/10, Levin to British Commonwealth Division (1093/59-17.9.1959). Cf. 5.2.1.4.
[132] ISA/RG93/MFA/392/10, Levin to British Commonwealth Division (1385/59-11.11.1959), Content of the Levin – Foot meeting on 8.11.1959.

he insisted that Cyprus, 'situated between three continents and two worlds', aspired to play the role of mediator in the disputes between the neighbouring countries.[133]

In spite of everything, the factor that would best serve Israel's aspirations in Cyprus was precisely the bicommunal character of the Cypriot system. The veto powers of the Turkish Cypriot vice president on foreign policy issues were a critical safeguard guaranteeing that Israel's ten-year official diplomatic presence in Cyprus would continue. At the same time, Makarios could use the Turkish Cypriot veto, based on which Cypriot–Israeli relations could be advanced, as an alibi amid Arab pressure. Thus, throughout 1959, the Israelis gradually began to realize that the Cypriot bicommunal state structure afforded them plenty of room to manoeuvre – with the Turkish Cypriots emerging as valuable assistants.

Meanwhile, however, Israel noted with interest the assessments of American diplomacy, as expressed on 26 May 1959, to the adviser to the Israeli embassy in Washington, Moshe Erell, by US diplomat Murat Williams, who had served in the State Department's Office of Greek, Turkish and Iranian Affairs between 1956 and 1959.[134] According to Williams, as long as the Turks and the Greeks continue to approach the Cyprus issue in good faith, one could predict that over the years, the importance of the national factor in Cypriot politics would diminish and the political system, instead of relying on the Turkish camp on one side, confronted by the Greek camp on the other, a clear division of political forces will emerge on its own and the political chasm between the two communities will be mitigated. In other words, there will be mixed, bicommunal parties. This development would initially be easier to advance amongst the Greek Cypriots and later the Turkish Cypriots. For the moment, the Turkish people at grassroots level behaved like a consolidated entity, which accepted without question Ankara's aspirations and guidance. In contrast, the Greeks of Cyprus were already showing some early signs of political emancipation from Athens.

Despite Murat Williams' interesting observations, the United States did not seem to care about the internal political process that could take place in the future independent Cypriot state – with the exception of its unequivocal objections to the legalization of the AKEL Communist Party.[135] The Americans had other issues to focus on which were of immediate practical significance, such as maintaining the communication mechanism MECA (Middle East Communications Activity) linking the State Department with US diplomatic missions and CIA substations in the Middle East and North Africa; maintaining the FBIS (Foreign Broadcast Information Service) that was broadcast by the neighbouring Middle East countries, and the transponder of the Voice of America radio station.

The possibility of establishing 'mixed parties' in Cyprus at some time in the future was never the intention of the US – not then and not later. Nevertheless, the views expressed by Murat Williams, the adviser to the American embassy in Tel Aviv, were of

---

[133] ISA/RG93/MFA/2156/7, *Cyprus Mail*, 'A Glorious Era Lies Ahead for Cyprus', 2.3.1959. Cf. 4.2.

[134] ISA/RG93/MFA/263/6, Yapou to Israel's diplomatic mission in Ankara and to Israel's diplomatic representation in Athens (796/10.6.1959), Includes an excerpt from the Erell report to the British Commonwealth Division (26.5.1959).

[135] Nicolet, *United States Policy towards Cyprus*, 140–5.

concern to the Israelis, not only with regard to events on the neighbouring island, but on account of what was happening in Israel just then.

Williams' views as conveyed by the Israelis through their departmental reports betrayed surprise and bewilderment.[136] At the time, relations between the Jewish majority and the Arab minority in Israel were being tested. After the 1948 War, the Israeli government had placed towns and villages with sizeable Arab populations under military command.[137] On the political level, a new practice had begun, in which Arab satellite-parties supported Ben-Gurion's ruling party, Mapai and other Zionist parties that participated in various coalition governments.[138] In the 1950s, the Israeli government decided to safeguard ethnic homogeneity in the decision-making centres, but to allow Arab citizens a parliamentary voice – albeit through controlled party mechanisms.[139] When the Israelis heard Williams' views, they were not certain whether his theories about 'mixed parties' in Cyprus had been adopted by top officials at the State Department. It would have been problematic for the Israeli Ministry of Foreign Affairs if the US intended to test the 'mixed party' model in Cyprus, on the premise that the same thing could be implemented in Israel.

It is possible that Williams' views led the Israelis to further accelerate their efforts to ensure a diplomatic presence in the future Republic of Cyprus as soon as possible, before the bicommunal character of the Cypriot political system was weakened. Otherwise, if the bicommunal balance struck by the London–Zurich Agreements were upset, the succeeding situation – as Williams described it – would favour the Greek Cypriot community, which was stronger in terms of population and economy, and which had significant reasons to maintain a pro-Arab policy. If the 'mixed party' model were to be adopted, the Turkish Cypriots would gradually be assimilated into the bicommunal party mechanism and sooner or later, their political influence would diminish to nothing. If that were to happen, the Israelis feared, pro-Israeli Turkish Cypriot voices would no longer be in a position to influence decision-makers, and as a result, Cyprus would become a satellite of the neighbouring Arab countries – with the blessings of Greece.

Under these circumstances, before the bicommunal state structures were in place, as established by the London–Zurich Agreements and for as long as a bicommunal separation remained to the benefit of the Turkish Cypriot minority, Israel determined that it would have to develop contacts within and outside Cyprus in order to maintain

---

[136] ISA/RG93/MFA/263/6, Yapou to Israel's diplomatic mission in Ankara and to Israel's diplomatic representation in Athens (796/10.6.1959). Includes an excerpt from the Erell report to the British Commonwealth Division (26.5.1959).

[137] Military command in the Arab urban and semi-urban centres in Israel lasted until 1966. Cf. Kabha, 'Khavrei ha'Kneset', in *Etgarim Bitkhoniim u-Mediniim*, ed. Laskier and Yitzhak (Ramat Gan: Bar-Ilan University, 2012), 203–18.

[138] Haritos, 'Araviki Psifos', 8–15.

[139] Ibid.; and ISA/RG93/MFA/8694/1, Alexander Dotan, Israeli Foreign Ministry Press Office to Research Division (1432/11.6.1958). An exception to the rule was the Mapam pro-Soviet opposition party, and later the Maki Communist Party (Ha-Miflaga ha-Komunistit ha-Yisraelit), which had included citizens of Arabic origin in their ranks. This fact attracted the attention of Israeli internal security services.

a diplomatic presence on the island and establish full, normal diplomatic relations with the independent Cypriot state, which could not then become a satellite of the UAR. This was the ultimate goal of a long series of diplomatic manoeuvres set in motion the day after the signature of the London–Zurich Agreements, and lasting until diplomatic relations were established with the young Republic of Cyprus on 17 August 1960.

6

Independent Cyprus and the Arab–Israeli
Tug of War

6.1 Israel's diplomatic manoeuvring in view of Cyprus' declaration of independence

As previously noted, Israel's first major initiative in an effort to approach the business and media world in Cyprus in April 1959 did not go unnoticed. The state El-Al airlines and the Israeli Tourism Organisation invited a select group of Cypriot journalists and travel agents to visit Israel, causing an unprecedented reaction from Michel Farah, the Lebanese consul in Nicosia.[1] The Lebanese warnings to immediately sever any relations between the major tourist agencies of Cyprus and the rest of the Arab countries prevented the Greek Cypriot travel agents *en bloc* from accepting Israel's invitation. Lebanon's successful intervention was the start of a series of similar anti-Israeli actions during the Transitional Period. Spearheading the campaign was the consulate of Lebanon, the only Arab country with a diplomatic representative on the island, aided by the wide popularity which Nasserist Egypt and Gamal Abdel Nasser enjoyed in the Greek Cypriot community. It was only a matter of time before the two countries comprising the UAR, Egypt and Syria reopened their consulates in Cyprus. UAR relations with Britain were normalized and it was viewed in a positive light by the Greek Cypriots due to Nasser's continued political support of Greek positions on the Cyprus issue throughout the 1950s, and because of the personal friendship which had developed between the Egyptian leader and Archbishop Makarios. All of this troubled the Israelis.

During the Transitional Period (February 1959–August 1960) that preceded the declaration of independence of the Republic of Cyprus, and before the UAR had diplomatic representation in Nicosia, Israel sought to take advantage of 'Nasser's absence' while it lasted and establish its own political, economic and diplomatic influence on the island. In this way it hoped to show Cypriot political leaders that full bilateral diplomatic relations with Israel would be to their mutual advantage.

---

[1] Cf. 5.2.1.1.

6.1.1 Israel's views on forming bilateral relations with Cyprus: The meeting at the Israeli Ministry of Foreign Affairs on 2 July 1959

When Consul Peretz Leshem's term in Nicosia came to an end in the summer of 1959, and he was replaced by Zeev Levin, a broad-based meeting took place on 2 July at the Ministry of Foreign Affairs in Jerusalem to discuss the next steps Israel would take during the Transitional Period until Cyprus declared independence. According to the London–Zurich Agreements, the declaration was to take place on 19 February 1960.[2] During the first half of 1959, Israeli diplomacy had realized the extent to which Cypriot–Israeli relations were affected by the bicommunal balance on the island[3] as well as by Israel's bilateral relations with both motherlands, Greece and Turkey.[4] Likewise, the activity of the Lebanese consulate in Nicosia[5] foreshadowed the growing influence of the Arab factor in the region, a cause of great concern.

At the Israeli Ministry of Foreign Affairs meeting on 2 July 1959, the important role of the Turkish Cypriots was highlighted though the fact that it was not in Israel's best interests to publicize its mutual understanding with the Turkish Cypriot side was clearly recognized. Also recognized was the fact that the Greek community was the majority on the island and, for this reason, it would be ill-advised to give the impression that it supported or was supported solely by the Turks who were the minority.[6] On the other hand, Turkey and the Turkish Cypriots were deemed to be 'the most important means of defence against the Arab provocations' that were expected to intensify in Cyprus over the following months. It was clear that Turkey 'owed Israel a favour', after the significant diplomatic support it had provided during the critical 13th Session of the UN.[7] Nevertheless, Israel realized that it would not be wise to link its own policies or economic goals to the similar pursuits of Turkey or Britain on the eve of Cypriot independence. It was therefore decided that Israel would have to discreetly intensify its development of bilateral trade relations and render the Israeli market more attractive to Greek Cypriot entrepreneurs – who had total control of the local economy – by encouraging the import of Cypriot products to Israel and providing the new neighbouring state with logistic assistance in as many sectors as possible.

With respect to Arab diplomatic and economic activity in Cyprus, the meeting concluded that Israel should avoid any action that would 'open yet another Arab–Israeli front'. It would have to be made clear, mainly to the Greek Cypriot side, that Israel did not aim to involve the island in the Arab–Israeli dispute, and to both sides, that it was in the interest of the Republic of Cyprus to maintain normal political, diplomatic and economic

---

[2] ISA/RG93/MFA/2156/7, Minutes of the meeting of 2.7.1959 held at the headquarters of Israel's Ministry of Foreign Affairs in Jerusalem, under the chairmanship of deputy director general of the Ministry Michael Comay. Those present at the meeting were: director of the British Commonwealth Division Zvi Loker, the next consul general of Israel to Nicosia, Zeev Levin, director of the Middle East Division Moshe Sasson, Deputy Director of the West Europe Division Dr Eliezer Yapou, Assistant to the West Europe Division Helen Barkay, Assistant to the Economic Affairs Division Zeev Shatil, and Zev Sufott from the British Commonwealth Division.
[3] Cf. 5.3.
[4] Cf. 4.3.1 and 4.3.2.
[5] Cf. 6.2.3.
[6] ISA/RG93/MFA/2156/7, Minutes of the meeting of 2.7.1959. Michael Comay's proposal.
[7] Cf. 3.6.6.

relations of equal measure and friendship, with both the Arabs and Israel. Consequently, if some Arab countries, like Lebanon or the UAR, demanded that Cyprus cease all contact with Israel, Cypriot leadership would have to realize that this position on the part of the Arab world constituted a gross intervention in the internal affairs of an independent state and as such, Israel would be justified in expecting Cyprus to reject it.[8]

At the same time, the signing of the agreement for a military alliance between Greece, Turkey and Cyprus in Athens on 28 October 1959 highlighted the regional aspect of the overall settlement reached in the London–Zurich Agreements. As stated in Article 2 of the agreements, all three countries were obliged to prevent and jointly address any threat to the territorial integrity and sovereignty of the Republic of Cyprus. Article 4 stipulated that Greece and Turkey would maintain 950 and 650 troops on the island respectively, and that these numbers could be increased if jointly requested by the president and vice president of the Republic of Cyprus. Article 5 set out the joint responsibility of Greek and Turkish military officers to train the bicommunal Cypriot Army.[9]

The wording of Article 2 provoked a reaction from Nasser's Egypt. From the Egyptian point of view, the military agreement of 28 October 1959 essentially framed the operational capabilities of the British military bases in Cyprus.[10] After all, the choice of 28 October 1959 as the date for signing the trilateral agreement held historical connotations: Egypt could not forget that on the same date three years earlier, the joint Anglo-French military intervention had begun at Suez, together with Israel's 'Operation Kadesh' in the Sinai.[11] Likewise, in July of 1958, a few months before the Agreements were signed, the RAF had flown soldiers from Cyprus to Jordan to quash pro-Nasser protests there against the pro-West monarchical regime, with Israel's permission to use its airspace, and the US had sent its own military forces to Lebanon to prevent a similar change in regime.[12]

As the new regional landscape became more clearly delineated with the signing of the trilateral military agreement of 28 October 1959, so did the political scene in Cyprus itself. In the presidential elections 13 December 1959, Makarios and Küçük became the official leaders of Cyprus.[13] Soon, on 19 February 1960, the British would

---

[8] ISA/RG93/MFA/2156/7, Minutes of the meeting of 2.7.1959. Michael Comay's proposal.
[9] Archbishop Makarios III Foundation, Kokkinou (ed.), *Apanta Archiepiskopou*, vol. 3, 636.
[10] ISA/RG130/MFA/3751/26, Levin to British Commonwealth Division (1317/59-3.11.1959). Includes comment from the Cairo radio station on the Cyprus–Greece–Turkey defence agreement, concluding that this action aims to compromise the security and territorial integrity of the UAR. According to Levin's report, the content of the radio programme was reprinted by the Greek Cypriot press without further comment.
[11] Cf. 3.4.
[12] Cf. 3.6.4.
[13] ISA/RG105/PRES/50/17, On 15.12.1959, the president of Israel, Yitzhak Ben-Zvi, sent a congratulatory telegram to Makarios on his election:

His Excellency Archbishop Makarios, President Elect of Cyprus, Nicosia

On the occasion of the election of Your Excellency as first President of the new Republic of Cyprus, it is my great pleasure to offer you my warmest greetings and congratulations on my own behalf and on behalf of the people of Israel. I wish you every success in the historic mission of consolidating Cyprus independence and I look forward to the continued growth of neighbourly relations between our two countries. I am glad to take this opportunity in conveying to the people of Cyprus my best wishes for their lasting prosperity and wellbeing.

Izhak Ben-Zvi
President of Israel

complete their withdrawal from the island and the Republic of Cyprus would declare independence. By then it was hoped that an agreement over the territorial, legal and administrative status of the British military bases on the island would be signed, and the mixed constitutional committee would provide the final text of the Cypriot Constitution. Based on these facts, there was precious little time left for the Israelis to decide exactly what their next moves would be to ensure the establishment of full diplomatic relations with the neighbouring island.

6.1.2 Israel's diplomatic manoeuvres in view of the declaration of Cypriot independence and the 20 December meeting at the Israeli Ministry of Foreign Affairs

On the day of the first presidential elections in Cyprus, the Middle East Division of the Israeli Ministry of Foreign Affairs issued a warning, based on classified information[14] and articles in the Egyptian press,[15] that the UAR was planning to establish a diplomatic mission in Nicosia in the coming weeks. In this manner, the UAR sought to reinforce its influence on Makarios and his political milieu so as to forestall the establishment of diplomatic ties between Cyprus and Israel.[16] The Israelis did not hide their concerns over the attitude Greek Cypriots might adopt, in view of their many reasons for aligning with Cairo. Nevertheless, it was repeatedly confirmed that the Turkish Cypriot vice president faithfully followed orders from Ankara which prohibited Cyprus from becoming a satellite of the UAR. Given the above, Golda Meir, Israel's minister of foreign affairs called an urgent meeting with her Turkish counterpart, Fatin Zorlu.

In a confidential telegram, the Middle East Division ordered Eliahu Sasson, Israel's ambassador in Rome to contact his Turkish counterpart, Mehmet Cevat Açıkalın, or the adviser to the Israeli embassy in Paris, Mordekhai Sneerson, to arrange a personal meeting between Sasson and Zorlu.[17] After contacts were made, it was agreed that the Sasson–Zorlu meeting would take place in Paris.[18]

When Sasson arrived in Paris, the Middle East Division sent a confidential telegram to Mordekhai Sneerson describing in detail the course Israel's diplomats had chosen for dealing effectively with the prospect of Makarios yielding to the demands of the UAR.[19] As described below, this would become Israel's adopted course until 16 August 1960, when Cyprus finally declared independence after several postponements.

The Israeli reasoning for this course was as follows: The London–Zurich Agreements stipulated that the Turkish Cypriot vice president had the right to veto any decisions regarding the security, defence and international relations of the Republic of Cyprus.[20]

---

[14] Cf. 6.2.2.
[15] ISA/RG130/MFA/3570/12, Research Division (1407/ℷ – 15.11.1959), Article in Egyptian daily *Al-Ahram* (7.11.1959), according to which the UAR was opening its consulate in Nicosia on 1.2.1960.
[16] ISA/RG130/MFA/3736/3, Middle East Division to Eliahu Sasson (1147/13.12.1959).
[17] Ibid.
[18] ISA/RG130/MFA/3736/3, Middle East Division to Alon (517א – 14.12.1959).
[19] ISA/RG130/MFA/3736/3, Middle East Division to Mordekhai Sneerson, Adviser to the Israeli Embassy in Paris (912ל – 18.12.1959).
[20] Archbishop Makarios III Foundation, Kokkinou (ed.), *Apanta Archiepiskopou*, vol. 3, 629.

This meant that Fazıl Küçük would be able to prevent the operation of a Cypriot consulate or embassy in any Arab country unless a Cypriot consulate or embassy was also opened in Israel. Küçük could also exercise his veto power if Makarios agreed to establish an Arab embassy in Nicosia without agreeing to an equivalent Israeli diplomatic mission in Cyprus. But, of course, it was not a good idea to embark on bilateral diplomatic relations with an unpleasant diplomatic incident.

In view of the above, Israel decided to recognize the Republic of Cyprus on the day it declared its independence. The same day, Israel would also officially announce the upgrading of the Consulate General of Nicosia to an embassy. Such a development would present the Greek Cypriots with a *fait accompli*. Makarios would not be able to refuse an upgraded diplomatic presence for Israel, and if he raised objections, Küçük could be mobilized.

As reflected in the related departmental telegrams, this development was a 'well-guarded secret'. The Israelis feared Makarios would ask Israel a priori not to upgrade its consulate to an embassy. If something like that were to happen, Israel would have to comply. On the other hand, the Arab countries would hasten to establish their own embassies in Cyprus, resulting in a *fait accompli* in their favour. Nevertheless, Israel wanted to avoid a situation like that which prevailed in Greece where Israel maintained a low-ranking diplomatic delegation, whereas the Arab countries operated full embassies. With the passing years, the Greek government either did not wish to or was no longer able to change its cold demeanour vis-à-vis the Jewish state and was unwilling to proceed with the de jure recognition. Although the Middle East Division pointed out that this 'well-guarded secret' should not be revealed even to Turkish Minister of Foreign Affairs Fatin Zorlu, since 'even he was not worthy of trust',[21] Israel's plans had become known in Athens, Nicosia – and apparently, Cairo as well. Specifically, on 21 April 1959, the Greek English-language *Athens News* reprinted a full account of Israel's 'seventh-seal secret' which had appeared in the Athenian paper *To Vima*. Fearing that the Arab countries, and particularly the UAR would initiate their own 'seventh-seal secret' Jeonathan Prato at the Diplomatic Mission in Athens contacted the editor-in-chief of the *Athens News* and tried to convince him that the report in *To Vima* had been based on erroneous information.[22]

At the 19 December meeting between Eliahu Sasson and Fatin Zorlu which took place in Paris, complete agreement was reached on the need to prevent the UAR from taking initiatives in Cyprus. Sasson pointed out that the UAR aimed at bringing together the anti-West political forces of the Greek Cypriot Right and Left, with the ultimate objective of removing the British bases from the island and creating a breach

[21] ISA/RG130/MFA/3736/3, Middle East Division to Sneerson (912ל – 18.12.1959), The instructions given to Sneerson to help him prepare Eliahu Sasson for the meeting with Fatin Zorlu in Paris included the following: 'The plan is a well-guarded secret to be kept from the Greeks, as they might call on our Consul in Cyprus and ask him not to make an announcement about Israel's intention to operate an Embassy. Since we cannot even trust Zorlu, we suggest that you do not tell him of our plan.'
[22] ISA/RG130/MFA/3570/12, Prato to West Europe Division (115/נ – 21.4.1959), and Eytan to Prato (859/נ – 22.4.1959).

between the Republic of Cyprus and the West. Something like this would have had a grave impact on the security of the Turkish Cypriots, of Turkey and of Israel.

Zorlu dismissed Israel's concerns as unfounded and claimed that Makarios would not allow an anti-West climate to prevail in Cypriot foreign policy.[23] Nevertheless, he ordered the Turkish consul in Nicosia to continue the close cooperation with his Israeli counterpart so that they could jointly address the situation that would take shape once the UAR established a diplomatic mission.[24]

Sasson neglected to convey to Zorlu Israel's request that if Makarios subscribed to a pro-Arab line, Turkey should order Küçük to exercise his veto power. This greatly frustrated Foreign Minister Meir.[25] In the ensuing period the Israelis tried in vain to meet with specific Turkish officials and highlight precisely this issue.[26] The Ministry of Foreign Affairs in Israel became even more alarmed when it learned from Turkish diplomats that all the Arab countries in the Levant, the Persian Gulf and North Africa were preparing to open embassies in Nicosia as soon as Cyprus declared its independence.[27]

With the declaration scheduled for 19 February 1960, the Israeli Ministry of Foreign Affairs called a meeting on December 20, 1959 to discuss the matter.[28] Taking part in the meeting were Yaakov Tzur, director general of the Ministry of Foreign Affairs, Maurice Fischer and Shmuel Bentzur, assistant directors general, Zeev Levin, Israeli consul general to Nicosia, Avraham Kidron, director of the Research Division, Moshe Sasson, deputy director of the Middle East Division, Eliezer Yapou, deputy director of the West Europe Division, Pinhas Eliav, deputy director of the USA Division, Zvi Loker, deputy director of the British Commonwealth Division, Zev Sufott, assistant to the British Commonwealth Division, and Abba Gefen, head of the Director-General's Office.

The meeting focused on two main issues: Firstly, the diplomatic actions Israel's Ministry of Foreign Affairs would take on the day of Cyprus' declaration of independence; second, behind-the-scenes initiatives to rebuff the efforts of the UAR, Lebanon and the rest of the Arab states to prevent the establishment of diplomatic relations between Cyprus and Israel.

With respect to the first issue, it was decided that on 19 February 1960, the expected date of Cyprus' declaration of independence, Israel would recognize the new state on the spot and announce its intent to elevate its consulate in Nicosia to an embassy and to appoint Zeev Levin as provisional director of the embassy office. A few days later, the

---

[23] ISA/RG130/MFA/3736/3, Eliahu Sasson to Middle East Division (34/פד – 18.12.1959), Content of Eliahu Sasson – Zorlu meeting in Paris.
[24] Ibid., Alon to Eliahu Sasson (863/א – 23.12.1959).
[25] Ibid., Golda Meir to Eliahu Sasson (142ר – 20.12.1959), Golda Meir's telegram read as follows: 'I am surprised by the fact that you did not tell Zorlu to ask Küçük to exercise his veto if Makarios decides to act against our interest.'
[26] Ibid., Middle East Division to Levin (509/28.12.1959).
[27] Ibid., Middle East Division to Eliahu Sasson (51/מפר – 25.12.1959).
[28] ISA/RG130/MFA/3570/12, Minutes of the meeting of 20.12.1959.

Israeli Ministry of Foreign Affairs would ask the Cypriot leaders to accept Zeev Levin's credentials as ambassador of Israel to Cyprus.

As to the second issue, it was decided that action would be taken on many levels and addressed to numerous recipients. More specifically, the meeting of 20 December 1959 concluded with the following seven points:

To continue the close collaboration with the Turkish government, so that, if Makarios refused to accept the Israeli Consulate's upgrade to an embassy, Ankara could order Küçük to exercise his veto power and force Makarios to establish equivalent diplomatic relations with both Israel and the Arab countries.

To send a senior diplomat with the rank of ambassador to meet unofficially with the Greek Minister of Foreign Affairs, Evangelos Averoff in Athens. The Israeli envoy would ask Greece to refrain from any action that would encourage Makarios to prohibit the immediate operation of the Israeli embassy in Nicosia.

To seek the assistance of the Israeli embassy in London in finding other means of pressuring Makarios. The Israeli embassy in Washington would proceed along the same lines and contact the competent office at the State Department.

To seek the assistance of certain leading figures who might effectively influence Makarios. More specifically, it was decided to ask Spyros Skouras, a Greek American multimillionaire businessman and CEO of Twentieth Century Fox to meet with the archbishop, whom he knew personally. The Israelis hoped that Skouras would travel to Nicosia in early February, two weeks before independence was declared and prevent Makarios from succumbing to pressure from the UAR. Spyros Skouras knew many people at the White House; he was in direct communication with the elected presidents of the United States[29] and with the Karamanlis government. In 1957, when Makarios was exiled to the Seychelles, Skouras had asked his personal friend President Eisenhower to intervene so that the British would release Makarios and persuade him to accept a political solution for Cyprus.[30] But Skouras' relations with the Jewish lobby in the US were likewise excellent, as were his communications with Israeli leaders established during visits to Israel in 1945 and 1949.[31] Israel's Ministry of Foreign Affairs considered Skouras' mediation efforts supremely important. Indicative of this was the heading 'Operation Spyros Skouras' on all official documents issued by the Ministry of Foreign Affairs concerning attempts to approach Makarios through the Greek American tycoon.

---

[29] Nicolet, *United States Policy towards Cyprus*, 85. On the communication between Eisenhower and Skouras.

[30] Louis Galambos and Daun Van Ee (eds), *The Papers of Dwight David Eisenhower: The Presidency: Keeping the Peace* (Baltimore, MD, and London: Johns Hopkins University Press, 2001), vol. 18, 269–70 no. 209, 302 no. 236. Cf. Nicolet, *United States Policy towards Cyprus*, 96–7. On the release of Archbishop Makarios.

[31] Ilias Chrissochoidis (ed.), *Spyros P. Skouras, Memoirs (1893–1953)* (Stanford, CA: Brave World, 2013), 126–31.

In a similar spirit, Anselmos Mourtzoukos,[32] the second vice president of the Central Board of Jewish Communities in Greece, was asked to meet with his personal friend, Themistoklis Tsatsos, who headed the Greek delegation at the mixed constitutional committee. The Israelis speculated that Themistoklis Tsatsos was positively predisposed towards Israel and that he might have a major influence over Makarios' decisions.[33]

To increase the number of Israeli tourists in Cyprus throughout January 1960 in order to highlight the benefits of private initiatives from Israel on the Cypriot economy.

Foreign Minister Meir invited all editors of the Israeli press to a private meeting where she would ask them to prohibit their reporters from interviewing Makarios prior to Cyprus' declaration of independence. The prohibition was intended to avoid drawing attention to Israeli activities and thus prevent the UAR and Lebanon from stepping up their own communications on policy with Cyprus.

A few days after that meeting, it was also decided that Israel would not insist on Cyprus adhering to the principle of reciprocity. In other words, when the Israeli Embassy went into operation in Nicosia, Israel would not require Cyprus to open its own embassy in Jerusalem or Tel Aviv. However, if Cyprus did not agree to upgrade the Israeli consulate to an embassy, that would be perceived as a hostile act.[34]

Having decided on which initiatives to set in motion, the Israelis began to reach out to foreign diplomats to hear their views. Of particular interest were the assessments of the Turkish ambassador in Rome, Mehmet Cevat Açıkalın, which arrived at the following conclusion: precisely because the anti-Makarios opposition was susceptible to Nasser's anti-West influence, Makarios would have many reasons to seek pro-West support. As a result, Israel's objective to establish full diplomatic relations with Cyprus would fall on very welcome ears in Nicosia.[35] The relevant report by the Israeli ambassador in Rome, Eliahu Sasson, who had met with Açıkalın, stated among other things:

The Turkish Ambassador believes that the Arabs will do everything within their power to increase their influence on the island and force the fledgling Cypriot Republic to implement the same regional and international policy as theirs, namely an anti-Israeli policy in line with the [author's note: Afro-Asian] neutral countries.

[32] Raphael Frezis, *I Israilitiki Koinotita Volou* [*The Israelite Community of Volos*], 2nd edn (Volos: Epikoinonia, 2002), 200–1; Anselmos Mourtzoukos was a businessman from Volos of Jewish origin. After the war, he settled in Athens, where he was a member of various Jewish organizations. From June 1958 to May 1961, he was second vice president of the Central Board of Jewish Communities in Greece.
[33] ISA/RG93/MFA/263/7, Levin to Prato, with copy to the British Commonwealth and West Europe divisions (991/59-1.9.1959). Confidential telegram, according to which Themistoklis Tsatsos was in constant contact with Levin and sometimes informed him about proceedings in the mixed constitutional committee.
[34] ISA/RG130/MFA/3570/12, Tzur to Levin (867/23.12.1959).
[35] ISA/RG130/MFA/3736/3, Eliahu Sasson to Fischer and Middle East Division (51/מפר – 25.12.1959), Assessments by the Turkish Ambassador in Rome, Mehmet Cevat Açıkalın.

He also believes that at an appropriate time, the Arabs will not hesitate to cooperate with members of the former EOKA and with Grivas against Makarios, should the latter not fall into step with them. Furthermore, they [author's note: the Arabs] would not hesitate to cooperate with the Cypriot communists. The fact that in the presidential elections, Makarios' rival candidate won a significant share of votes proved to the Arabs that the ground was ready on the island for action against Makarios and that there were elements in Cyprus who were ready to move against him if requested. Consequently, Açikalin concluded that all the non-Arab actors in the region, including Israel, needed to strengthen Makarios' influence and position, as he de facto became increasingly dependent on the West and would want, due to his own personal interests, to curb Arab influence on the island as far as possible.[36]

In the end, Açikalin advised the Israelis 'to get closer to Makarios', no less so than to Küçük. Makarios, he said, had many reasons to approve the establishment of full diplomatic relations with Israel.

US consul general in Nicosia Taylor Belcher shared this view and noted that there were growing indications that Makarios would sooner or later seek Western support. Although Makarios was interested in establishing diplomatic relations with the UAR, Belcher surmised that he was not entirely sure about what position to adopt vis-à-vis Israel, which was 'exactly why he prefers to do nothing for the time being'.[37]

In the early days of January 1960, Israel began to approach diplomatic players and officials who were in a position to influence Makarios. The Foreign Office had instructed Governor Sir Hugh Foot to find an appropriate way to make it clear both to Makarios and to members of his opposition that Great Britain was in favour of full diplomatic relations between Israel and Cyprus.[38] Concurrently, Ankara instructed Vice President Küçük to exercise his veto if it became necessary.[39]

The US State Department fully backed the establishment of diplomatic relations between Israel and Cyprus in the belief that strengthening trade and tourism between them would help deter the anti-West forces in the region, namely Nasser's Egypt. The main US concern however was the threat of a USSR foothold in Cyprus through a consolidation of the communists on the island. Eventually, the Americans believed, AKEL communists would aim at neutrality for Cyprus in the international sphere, much like the UAR. Nevertheless, if it came to that, they would not interfere in order to promote Israel's diplomatic aspirations. In an attempt to justify this stance, Owen Jones, the director of the Office of Greek, Turkish and Iranian Affairs at the State Department, claimed that the US was still on the sidelines and had not yet formed a particularly close relationship with Cypriot leadership, so any intercession on their part would be unproductive.[40] However, the reality was that during the Transitional Period, the

---

[36] Ibid.
[37] ISA/RG93/MFA/1008/1, British Commonwealth Division to Levin (524/103.1קפר – 14.1.1960).
[38] ISA/RG93/MFA/1431/19, Ofer to British Commonwealth Division (4235/103.3קפ – 8.1.1960).
[39] ISA/RG93/MFA/1008/1, Middle East Division to Levin (526/103.1קפר – 15.1.1960).
[40] Ibid., Erell to British Commonwealth Division (387/15.1.1960), Content of the meeting Erell-Owen Jones, director of the Office of Greek, Turkish and Iranian Affairs of the State Department. Cf. 6.1.4.

US was primarily concerned with ensuring its own presence on the island at a purely practical level.[41] For the Americans, Israel's presence in Cyprus was not a priority. Washington made it subtly clear to the Israelis that they would have to look after their own interests, and that they should expect nothing more from the US.

As 19 February 1960 approached, the day Cyprus was due to proclaim its independence, Israel did not know with any certainty how Athens and Makarios would react to the announcement of the Israeli consulate's upgrade to embassy status. Maurice Fischer, assistant director general of the Ministry of Foreign Affairs met with Evangelos Averoff in Athens in January 1960 but did not obtain any assurances.[42] Perhaps, Fischer considered, a meeting with Archbishop Iakovos of the Greek Orthodox Archdiocese of North and South America would bring results,[43] but such a meeting did not take place. Another idea was to contact Zenon Rossides through the Foreign Office but that did not happen either, because Rossides, they believed, was more influenced by the Americans than the British, and Makarios seemed less influenced by Rossides than by Nikos Kranidiotis.[44] As for Themistoklis Tsatsos, though there was no doubt about his good intentions, he was evidently more concerned at the time with the text of the Cypriot Constitution than with Israel's relations with Cyprus.[45] That point aside, Tsatsos' frequent trips abroad made it impossible for him to meet with Jeonathan Prato, the head of Israel's diplomatic representation in Athens.[46] When Anselmos Mourtzoukos finally managed to meet with him for a few minutes, Tsatsos limited himself to some general remarks and compliments and avoided any substantive disclosures.[47]

It is true that Israeli diplomacy had received reassuring messages about its pursuits, not just from Ankara and London, but indirectly from Makarios himself. Nevertheless, it could not ignore the growing Arab infiltration of the Greek Cypriot community,[48] nor could it ignore Küçük's conviction that Makarios was essentially 'the Arabs' man' and even if he declared that he had no objections to diplomatic relations with Israel, he only did so under repeated pressure from Küçük. In fact, on 10 January 1960, shortly before the end of his meeting with Levin, Küçük summarized Makarios' tactics with the pointed statement that, 'Everyone knows that Makarios changes his mind from one day to the next . . .,'[49] which only heightened Levin's suspicions.

The day of Levin's meeting with Fazıl Küçük, the entire island was shocked to learn that anti-Jewish slogans and swastikas had been scrawled over the walls of private

[41] Cf. 5.3; and Nicolet, *United States Policy towards Cyprus*, 140–5. On US aspirations with regard to Cyprus during the Transitional Period.
[42] Israel State Archives, Barouch Gilead (ed.), *Documents on the Foreign Policy of Israel* (Jerusalem: Israel State Archives, Government Printer, 1997), vol. 14, 622 no. 400, Fischer to Golda Meir.
[43] ISA/RG93/MFA/1008/1, Sufott to Levin (1652/103.1קפר – 3.1.1960). Cf. ISA/RG93/MFA/1007/5, Tzur to Levin (511/103.2קפר – 4.1.1960), and Levin to Tzur (4.1.1960, not recorded as incoming document).
[44] Ibid., Levin to British Commonwealth Division (159/103.1קפר – 5.1.1960).
[45] Ibid., Levin to Israel's Diplomatic Representation in Athens (45/103.1קפר – 10.1.1960).
[46] Ibid., Prato to Levin (134/21.1.1960).
[47] Ibid., Prato to Levin (214/9.2.1960), Meeting between Mourtzoukos and Tsatsos in Athens on 8.2.1960.
[48] Cf. 6.2.
[49] Ibid., Sufott to Loker (24.1.1960), Overview of Levin's contacts in Cyprus during the period 1.1.1960–24.1.1960.

businesses, hotels and nightclubs in the centre of Famagusta. The Greek Cypriot newspapers were filled with commentary and photographs.[50] The local Jewish community protested vehemently; Andreas Pougiouros, the mayor of Famagusta who was supported by AKEL, Ezekias Papaioannou, AKEL general secretary, the Famagusta Veterans Union, the local EDMA organizations and Makarios himself all condemned the incident with official statements and announcements broadcast particularly over local radio.[51] The following evening, swastikas and anti-Semitic slogans like 'Jews out of Cyprus' and 'Death to the Jews' appeared at a centrally located church in Limassol and on the walls of the house where an Israeli employee of the CYBARCO construction company lived.[52]

Following the uproar over this, Consul Levin broke the ice and asked Makarios to meet with him the very next day, 11 January. The matter of the swastikas and slogans on the Famagusta buildings took but a few minutes of their time. The main issue at hand was the prospect for bilateral relations between Cyprus and Israel. Makarios reiterated that he wanted Cyprus to establish diplomatic relations with all the countries in the region 'despite the pressure he was under to support one or the other side'. In reference to the number of embassies Cyprus would establish, Makarios said there would be only four of them, in Athens, Ankara, London and Washington. Concerning the neighbouring countries of the Eastern Mediterranean, Makarios stated that Cypriot consulates would operate in Cairo, Beirut and Israel. As for the consulate to open in Israel, he did not specify whether it would be based in Tel Aviv or the western sector of Jerusalem.[53]

A week later, on 18 January 1960, it was officially announced that negotiations in London between Britain, Greece, Turkey and the two Cypriot communities had broken down. As a result, the date for announcing Cypriot independence was postponed till 19 March 1960.[54] The breakdown in negotiations was due to a dispute over the territory to be occupied by the British bases. The British wanted to tie up a significant amount of agricultural land for operational purposes. Britain, Greece and Turkey were allegedly surprised to see Makarios and Küçük presenting a united front and refusing to agree to the British terms. But the failed negotiations did not merely delay the declaration of Cypriot independence; Britain also held up financial aid of a sizeable amount to the local economy.

---

50 ISA/RG93/MFA/1431/25, *Alitheia*, 'Swastikas were placed on shops of Varosha', 11.1.1960. *Kypros*, 'The Ethnarch condemns the Swastikas', 11.1.1960. On 12.1.1960, similar articles were published in the newspapers *Fileleftheros*, *Eleftheria*, *Haravgi*, *Ethniki* and *Ethnos*. Swastikas were drawn in the centre of Famagusta, on the walls of a store owned by M. I. Louizides, the Amathous company, Savoy Hotel, Chadzichambi Theatre, Triton Navigation Company, Nikos Vassileiou Tailors and George Kolokassides shop.
51 ISA/RG93/MFA/1431/25, Levin to Tzur (161/113.14-11.1.1960), Makarios' announcement is included: 'I unreservedly condemn these acts, which were undoubtedly the work of irresponsible individuals. The perpetrators must be found immediately and punished.'
52 Ibid., Levin to British Commonwealth Division (107/113.14קפר – 20.1.1960). For example, *Haravgi*, 'Youths drew swastikas in Limassol last night', 12.1.1960.
53 Ibid., Levin to Tzur, copies to the British Commonwealth and the Middle East divisions (162/113/14-11.1.1960).
54 ISA/RG93/MFA/1008/1, *Maariv*, 'Independence postponed for a month – London conference on Cyprus at an impasse', 19.1.1960.

In taking stock of this development, the Israelis concluded that Makarios' objections to the territorial and administrative arrangements proposed by the British regarding the territory for the bases was essentially the result of pressure from Grivas, the right-wing opposition and the communists. According to Zvi Loker, the deputy director of the British Commonwealth Division of the Israeli Ministry of Foreign Affairs, the complication was nothing more than a 'simple geographic – statistical problem' which would soon be resolved. Meanwhile, the postponement of the proclamation of Cypriot independence had a twofold impact: On the one hand, the UAR would have more time to intensify its efforts and convince Cypriot leadership to suspend any contact with the Jewish state; on the other, Israel could use the additional time to implement the decisions taken during the 20 December 1959 meeting in a more effective way.[55] The standstill in negotiations would have to be exploited as much as possible.

6.1.3 'Operation Spyros Skouras'

The key question that continued to worry the Israelis had not been answered. Makarios may have reassured Zeev Levin on 11 January that Cyprus would establish diplomatic relations with Israel and open a Cypriot consulate either in Tel Aviv or Jerusalem, but no one could dismiss the possibility that the archbishop's words were a pretext. All indications were that the time had come to set 'Operation Spyros Skouras' in motion, as had been decided at the meeting of 20 December 1959.[56]

In early January 1960, a week before the acts of vandalism in Famagusta, Israeli ambassador to Washington Avraham Harman met with Spyros Skouras and asked him to meet with Makarios in Nicosia. Skouras accepted Harman's request to persuade Makarios that it would be in Cyprus' best interest to cultivate full diplomatic relations with Israel, in spite of Arab pressure, but he set two key conditions. The first was that his meeting with Makarios should take place in utter secrecy. The second was to be fully informed in writing about the benefits that would follow from the establishment of normal diplomatic relations with Israel.[57]

Harman assured Skouras that his meeting with the archbishop would not be divulged to anyone. The second of Skouras' conditions was covered in an extensive report by Yaakov Tzur, the deputy director general of the Israeli Ministry of Foreign Affairs, outlining the economic benefits Cyprus would gain through its diplomatic relations with Israel. In his report, Tzur wrote that Israeli technical advisers specializing in public works, citrus farming and healthcare services were even then working in Cyprus. He outlined the long-standing presence of the Solel Boneh construction company on the island and noted that a total of 4,000 Israeli tourists had visited Cyprus in 1959, far exceeding the number of visitors from other countries in the region.[58]

However, Yaakov Tzur was not completely honest. He included in the report a long list of companies interested in making a variety of investments in Cyprus (for the

[55] Ibid., Loker to Levin (57/103.1קפר – 19.1.1960).
[56] Cf. 6.1.2.
[57] ISA/RG93/MFA/1431/19, Harman to Tzur (850/5.1.1960).
[58] ISA/RG93/MFA/1431/19, Tzur to Harman (958יי /7.1.1960).

manufacture of batteries, plastic goods and cosmetics, mineral mining and others). These companies had indeed filed applications with the committee of the Israeli Ministry of Foreign Affairs Economic Division, which was competent to approve state funding for these investment programmes abroad. What was not mentioned in the report was that most of those applications had either been withdrawn, deemed unsustainable or rejected by the committee.[59] Obviously Skouras could never learn those details.

Having received the reassurances he asked for, Spyros Skouras left for Nicosia on 3 February 1960. He met first with Consul Zeev Levin for further clarifications and to again request a guarantee that his contact with Makarios would remain secret and later in the day he met with the archbishop.

In his discussion with Skouras, Makarios reiterated exactly what he had told Levin on 11 January 1960 regarding the number of Cypriot embassies and consulates to be established and in which countries. He also made it clear that, particularly with regard to the Arab–Israeli conflict, that he expected independent Cyprus to 'maintain neutrality, following the example of Switzerland'. In so saying, Makarios sought to emphasize that his understanding of the word 'neutrality' was not the same as that of Gamal Abdel Nasser and the rest of the Afro-Asian countries.[60] This put Israel's mind further at ease regarding Makarios' true intentions. As for Skouras, after briefing Zeev Levin on the meeting, he left Nicosia but continued with his scheduled business meetings in Beirut, Cairo and Athens[61] before returning to America. 'Operation Spyros Skouras' had been a success.

6.1.4 The standstill in negotiations in Cyprus, February–July 1960, through Israeli diplomatic reports

On 18 January 1960, it was announced that the declaration of Cypriot independence would be postponed, from 19 February of that year, the date originally stipulated in the London–Zurich Agreements, to 19 March of the same year. This first postponement of independence marked the beginning of a long period of stagnation in the negotiations. The questions that remained unresolved were the land to be occupied by the two British bases in Dhekelia and Akrotiri, the individual administrative and legal arrangements related to their special status, and issues pertaining to the sovereignty of the Republic of Cyprus should Great Britain decide to withdraw its military presence from the island in future. The mixed constitutional committee also dealt with serious issues, as there was a divergence of opinions on the division of Greek and Turkish

[59] ISA/RG93/MFA/1430/8, Fischer to Economic Affairs Division (123/511.3קפר – 12.1.1960), Attached to Minutes No. 12/27.12.1959 of the meeting of the Foreign Projects Committee at the Israeli Ministry of Foreign Affairs on the applications submitted for funding in relation to investments by Israeli businesses in Cyprus.
[60] ISA/RG93/MFA/1008/1, Tzur to Levin (522/103.1קפר – 14.1.1960).
[61] ISA/RG93/MFA/1007/15, Levin to Tzur and British Commonwealth Division (198/3.2.1960), and Levin to Tzur and British Commonwealth Division (4.2.1960, not recorded as incoming document).

municipalities, the ratio of Greek Cypriots to Turkish Cypriots in public administration and the special status of religious groups (Armenians, Maronites and Latins).[62]

The impasse between Makarios and the British seemed insurmountable. The 19 of March came and went without resolution, and negotiations seemed at risk of being terminated. In his speech on 1 April 1960, the fifth anniversary of the EOKA struggle, Makarios spoke of the 'continuation of the liberation struggle' and of declaring independence even without Britain's consent. On the other hand, as Zeev Levin noted in his reports, with the delay of financial aid from Britain to Cyprus, opposition to Fazıl Küçük began to be voiced,[63] led by Rauf Denktaş, who by late May 1960 had reached the point of declaring that only partition and double unification would resolve the Cyprus issue.[64] The irony was that while the mixed constitutional committee completed its work and signed the final text of the Cypriot constitution on 6 April 1960,[65] it seemed as though the London–Zurich Agreements would not be put into practice after all, so long as the status of the British bases was pending.[66]

And then an unexpected development took place. The Adnan Menderes government in Turkey was overturned on 27 May 1960 by a military coup and General Cemal Gürsel took power.[67] Despite initial fears that the change in the Turkish regime would further complicate the situation in Cyprus, the new regime quickly demonstrated that it wished to give the negotiations fresh impetus. In early June, Fazıl Küçük arrived in Turkey to find out what line the new government intended to follow. Upon returning to Cyprus, he reassured Consul Zeev Levin that Ankara planned to push for an end of the impasse on the status of the British bases and to implement the London–Zurich Agreements as soon as possible.[68] Thus, by the end of June, significant progress had

[62] Diane Markides, 'I Metavatiki Periodos, Fevrouarios 1959–Avgoustos 1960' ['The Transitional Period, February 1959–August 1960'], in *Istoria tis Kypriakis Dimokratias* [*History of the Republic of Cyprus*], ed. Petros Papapolyviou (Nicosia: Fileleftheros Publishing, 2010), vol. 1, 21–4 and 26–31. Cf. ISA/RG93/MFA/1431/19, Levin to British Commonwealth Division (34/103.3קפר – 7.1.1960).

[63] Ibid., Levin to British Commonwealth Division (567.103.3קפר – 6.4.1960).

[64] Ibid. (793/103.3קפר – 25.5.1960).

[65] Archbishop Makarios III Foundation, Kokkinou (ed.), *Apanta Archiepiskopou*, vol. 3, 652–6. The texts of speeches by Tsatsos, Clerides, Bridel, Bilge and Denktaş. Cf. ISA/RG93/MFA/1007/17, The final text of the Cypriot Constitution was signed in Nicosia on 6.4.1960 by the chairman of the mixed constitutional committee, the Swiss constitutionalist Marcel Bridel and the head of the Greek representation Themistoklis Tsatsos, the Turkish representation Suat Bilge (sitting in for Nihat Erim who was not on the island that day), the Greek Cypriot representation Glafcos Clerides and the Turkish Cypriot representation Rauf Denktaş. The announcement by Committee Chairman Marcel Bridel caused a stir, as he expressed regret that the final text did not provide for the possibility of Greek Cypriots entering into marriage with Turkish Cypriots due to the refusal of the latter. The excerpt from Bridel's announcement on 6.4.1960 stated the following:

> There is only one point which I must confess I greatly regret not having seen fully implemented. This is the question of free marriage between members of the two communities. In view of the fact that three delegations had agreed to include this principle in the Constitution, I expected the Turkish Cypriot Delegation to also accept it. This grieved me very much.

Cf. *Times of Cyprus*, 'Five signatures and the draft Constitution is completed', 7.4.1960.

[66] ISA/RG93/MFA/1431/19, Levin to British Commonwealth Division (611/103.3קפר – 20.4.1960).

[67] Ibid., Reuven Nall, sub-director of the British Commonwealth Division, to Levin (408/101.1-29.5.1960).

[68] Ibid. (883/103.3קפר – 15.6.1960).

taken place in negotiations and finally, on 6 July 1960, all parties agreed on the scope and legal status governing the bases, as well as the amount of British financial aid to Cyprus.[69]

As Zeev Levin had learned behind the scenes, shortly before the final signatures were penned, Fazıl Küçük had at the very last moment raised the issue of changing the terms of the London–Zurich Agreements stipulating the ratio of participation by members of his community in the public sector. In particular, he wanted an immediate agreement that the representation of Greek Cypriots and Turkish Cypriots in the civil services would be at a ratio of 70:30. After a lengthy private conversation, Makarios and Küçük agreed that this issue would be settled legislatively over the next five years. Having received these assurances, Küçük was persuaded to sign,[70] thus opening the way for the proclamation of Cypriot independence in August 1960. For their part, the Israelis began to prepare their next move.[71]

The successful outcome of the negotiations was no surprise to anyone. From February to July 1960, it never once occurred to the Israelis that the London–Zurich Agreements would not be implemented. They assessed the hard line Makarios kept to during negotiations, along with his public statements, as shows of strength aimed at impressing public opinion and his Greek Cypriot political detractors rather than the British themselves.[72] What was surprising, however, was the fact that Makarios and Küçük presented a united negotiating front against the British, if only for a short period of time. As historian Diana Markides has noted, this was the only time in the recent history of Cyprus that Greek and Turkish Cypriots adopted a common line in their negotiations without pressure or guidance from the two motherlands.[73] This had surprised not only the Turks and the Greeks, but the Israelis as well. In its reporting of events, the Israeli daily *Maariv* commented in its 19 January 1960 edition:

> In the last 24 hours, it became obvious that the conference was heading towards an impasse. Great Britain wanted large areas of land around the military bases to serve as a 'buffer zone'. Makarios refused, as 20–30% of the island's agricultural production and the main exportable product comes from these areas. One of the most remarkable features of this conference was the united front presented by the Greek and Turkish leaders – Makarios and Küçük – who, one year ago represented their communities as adversaries. Makarios and Küçük will stay in London for two more days in order to hold informal talks. [...] Makarios could not accept the blocking of 120 square miles for the British bases. British political observers believe that the settlement of the issue shall depend on the following two factors:

---

[69] Ibid. (950/103.3קפר – 29.6.1960).
[70] Ibid. (993/103.3קפר – 6.7.1960).
[71] Ibid., Nall to Levin (490/101.1קפר – 6.7.1960).
[72] ISA/RG93/MFA/1008/1, Levin to British Commonwealth Division (197/103.1קפר – 2.2.1960): 'The problems relating to the territory occupied by the military bases and their legal status have not yet been resolved and it seems that Makarios either does not want to or cannot handle them at an internal political level. Cypriot public opinion accepts the new postponement of independence provided that there is no further concession.'
[73] Markides, 'I Metavatiki Periodos', 26–30.

Firstly, on whether guarantees will be given to Makarios that Britain is only interested in the purely military role of the bases and that the Cypriot government shall exercise its enlarged administrative sovereignty over the land occupied by the bases; secondly, on the amount of the financial aid to be given by Britain to the island after its independence. However, as other political observers note, Grivas' shadow and statements from Athens helped shape Makarios' position on the question of the bases.[74]

Nevertheless, a few months later, it became clear that the Makarios–Küçük alignment was opportunistic and that there would be no end to bicommunal competition, which Israeli diplomacy had by now learned to manage.[75]

But what worried the Israelis most during this period, apart from the intensive infiltration of Cyprus by the Arabs,[76] was the reluctance of the US to support Israel's diplomatic aspirations. The assertion of Owen Jones, director of the State Department's Office of Greek, Turkish and Iranian Affairs, that the US had not had time to develop close relations with the Cypriot political leadership and was therefore not in a position to influence Makarios regarding the establishment of diplomatic relations with Israel,[77] convinced no one, neither the staff of the Israeli Ministry of Foreign Affairs in Jerusalem,[78] nor Consul Zeev Levin in Nicosia.[79] In fact, according to Levin, his American counterpart Taylor Belcher held frequent meetings not only with Makarios but with all the other actors on the Greek Cypriot political scene – except of course AKEL. While the arrival of British financial aid was being delayed due to the impasse in the negotiations about the military bases, American economic influence on the island steadily increased. Jones' view completely contradicted the explicit commitment made by the adviser to the American embassy in Tel Aviv, Murat Williams, that the US would do everything in its power to help establish full diplomatic relations between Cyprus and Israel, not only for political but also for very important economic reasons.[80] The Israelis believed that, if Cyprus' economy remained in recession, the communist party would sooner or later exploit the poverty of rural Cyprus to attack Makarios. As a result, US economic aid would not only bolster political support for Makarios,[81] but also strengthen US presence and counteract Soviet influence. Likewise, the US did not wish to see the development of a 'neutral' and pro-Soviet foreign policy in Cyprus along the lines of Nasserist Egypt.

---

[74] ISA/RG93/MFA/1008/1, *Maariv*, 'Independence postponed for one month – London conference on Cyprus at an impasse', 19.1.1960.
[75] Cf. 6.1.1, 6.1.2 and 6.1.3.
[76] Cf. 6.2.
[77] ISA/RG93/MFA/1008/1, Erell to British Commonwealth Division (387/15.1.1960). Cf. 6.1.2.
[78] Ibid., Jaacov Barmore, 1st Assistant to the US Division to Erell (6/103.1ר פק – 1.2.1960).
[79] Ibid., Levin to British Commonwealth Division (170/103.1ר פק – 4.2.1960).
[80] ISA/RG93/MFA/1008/1, Sufott to Levin (27/103.1ר פק – 12.1.1960), Content of meeting between the Israeli diplomatic official, who is not named, with Murat Williams, Adviser to the US Embassy in Tel Aviv.
[81] ISA/RG93/MFA/1431/19, Sufott to Sneerson (1613/6.1.1960).

With the approach of August 16, 1960, the date Cypriot independence was to be declared, State Department secrecy was a cause of concern for Israel. The Israelis mistakenly assumed that the US was unwilling to support their pursuits because it did not wish to clash head-on with Nasser.[82] Israel's only consolation was that at least they had realized early enough that they could not count on Washington's help,[83] and that they would have to advance their interests by whatever diplomatic means they had at their disposal.

6.1.5 Bilateral meetings between Greek Cypriot and Israeli officials from February to July 1960

The period extending from February to early July 1960 was filled with conflicting indications on whether and to what extent the terms of the London–Zurich Agreements would be implemented. As for behind-the-scenes communication between the Israelis and Greek Cypriots, the standstill in negotiations was by no means a time of idleness. Intensive efforts by the UAR and Lebanon were underway to subvert any collaboration between Cyprus and Israel.[84]

This was the first time in Israeli – Cypriot relations that a potential collaboration was discussed between Israel's intelligence agencies and corresponding bodies in Cyprus entrusted with setting up similar services from scratch in the future Republic of Cyprus. More specifically, the Transitional government's Minister of the Interior, Tassos Papadopoulos, approached Consul Zeev Levin with a request to contact the founder and head of the Military Intelligence Service at the time, Major-General Chaim Herzog.[85]

According to Levin's report to the British Commonwealth Division,[86] the meeting between Papadopoulos and Herzog took place on the island that January in absolute secrecy. Papadopoulos outlined the problems he was facing in the reorganization of the Cypriot police force, and his main concern, the appropriate way of staffing it. As he saw it, the present police force in Cyprus was largely staffed by persons with close ties to the outgoing British regime and as such, he did not trust them. In addition, Papadopoulos explained the practical difficulties he faced in his efforts to establish a Cypriot counter-intelligence agency: Britain refused access to confidential files, and he did not yet have properly trained staff at his disposal. In fact, officials from KYP, the Greek Central Intelligence Service (KYP) and Scotland Yard had already visited Cyprus, in order to assist in the training and staffing of the Cyprus secret service, but 'their proposals had not been to his satisfaction', Levin reported, but included no further details.

[82] ISA/RG93/MFA/1008/1, Erell to British Commonwealth Division (416/103.1קפר – 2.2.1960).
[83] Nicolet, *United States Policy towards Cyprus*, 140–5. On the priorities of US policy in Cyprus during the Transitional Period. Cf. 5.3.
[84] Cf. 6.2.
[85] During his military service, Chaim Herzog (1918–97) established the Military Information Service in 1948 and served as its director during 1948–50 and 1959–62. After retiring, he joined the diplomatic service of Israel's Ministry of Foreign Affairs and later the Labour Party. He was the sixth president of Israel, with two consecutive terms (1983–8 and 1988–93).
[86] ISA/RG93/MFA/1008/1, Levin to British Commonwealth Division (150/103.1קפר – 1.2.1960).

Tassos Papadopoulos had asked Chaim Herzog and the departments he headed for help in the proper training of an effective Cypriot counter-intelligence service and a trustworthy police force and the activities of foreign countries within Cypriot territory able 'to prevent the spread of internal factors'. Although he did not name these 'internal factors' Herzog and Levin speculated that the Cypriot Minister may have been alluding to the communists or anti-Makarios right-wing factions, who were ideologically aligned with Metropolitan Kyprianos of Kyrenia. One way or another, it is interesting to note that Levin and Herzog did not suppose that Papadopoulos may have had the Turkish Cypriots in mind as well.

In his response to Papadopoulos, Herzog said that the problems Cyprus was facing in 1960 were identical to those Israel had dealt with immediately after the British withdrawal from Palestine. Herzog suggested that Papadopoulos should visit Israel himself for further briefing or else invite members of Israel's Military Intelligence Service to Cyprus for extended consultations. The meeting ended inconclusively and archival material from the period ending with the declaration of Cypriot independence in August 1960 contains no reference to a further meeting between Papadopoulos and Herzog, or any other related communications between Cypriot and Israeli officials. However, the possibility that such meetings did in fact take place cannot be discounted. The Israeli Ministry of Foreign Affairs security services, in a confidential memo dated 26 February 1960, instructed Consul Levin not to include references in his report to 'the responsibilities of the Mossad, or which related to the activities of military personnel or other national security agencies'.[87]

In April 1960, the general staff of Israel's armed forces asked for Zeev Levin's views on the possibility of cooperation between Cyprus and Israel, in view of the staffing and organization of the bicommunal Cypriot Army.[88] The Israeli Army was exploring the possibility that conditions would permit the implementation in Cyprus of a bilateral military cooperation model similar to Israel's agreements with Burma and Ghana – countries to which Israel had provided extensive logistic support coordinated by Israel's Agency for International Development Cooperation at the Ministry of Foreign Affairs.[89] This agency implemented programmes to train, staff and organize the armed forces of Third World countries which had recently become decolonized. In both Burma and Ghana, training schools for conscripts and officers of the navy, infantry and air force were in operation, under Israeli guidance and funding, while special seminars were also held in administrative oversight. As Cyprus was amongst those countries achieving their independence after a long period of colonization, Israeli armed forces began to consider the possibility of expanding their activity to the neighbouring island, together with the Ministry's competent Agency for International Development Cooperation (Mashav).

[87] Ibid., Y. Lanir (or Y. Lenir), Security Officer, Israeli Ministry of Foreign Affairs, to Levin (511/7/103.1קפרר – 26.2.1960).
[88] ISA/RG93/MFA/1008/1, Mordechai (Mocha) Limon, deputy director general, Department of Emergency Economic Planning, Ministry of Defence, to Levin (235/190/מט – 25.4.1960).
[89] Cf. 5.2.1 on the International Support Section (*ha-Mador le-Siua Benleumi*) of Israel's Ministry of Foreign Affairs, established in 1957, which three years later, in 1960, evolved and was renamed the Division of International Development Cooperation, known as 'Mashav'.

Levin's answer was categorically negative.[90] His main argument was that, based on the London–Zurich Agreements, the Cypriot government would have to ask for the assistance of the three guarantor powers. Furthermore, Levin believed that both communities were at that time gathering weapons 'just to be prepared' – in secret from one another – and that relations between Greek and Turkish Cypriots were governed by mutual suspicion. Israel's presence in the sensitive area of defence would further complicate the fragile balance, and therefore Israel had to keep a distance from the underlying competition between the two communities.

Nevertheless, Levin was not as resistant to establishing a military training programme in Cyprus to prepare teenagers before they enlisted in the regular army, modelled on the scouting-type 'Youth Brigades' (the Gdudey Noar or Gadna) that were popular in Israel at the time. Levin actually suggested training in Israel and later setting up a similar preparatory military training programme for Turkish Cypriot youth before their induction into the Cypriot Army. Levin's alternative proposal was offered during an exchange of views with Rauf Denktaş in August 1959. At that time, Denktaş had expressed particular interest in having Turkish Cypriot youth train in Israel primarily in the areas of agricultural production, agricultural economics and so forth.[91] The review of relevant archives up to the declaration of independence of the Republic of Cyprus in August 1960 does not indicate any further actions on the feelers put out by Israel's armed forces or on Levin's alternative proposal. In any event, the Israeli consul was categorically against visits by Israeli Army officials to Cyprus 'even unofficially' during the Transitional Period.

In mid-May 1960, Levin met with Spyros Kyprianou for the first time, upon the latter's initiative.[92] It was rumoured that 31-year-old Kyprianou, a close adviser to Makarios, was destined for a key position in the Ministry of Foreign Affairs – either as Cypriot ambassador to London, or even minister of foreign affairs. Kyprianou wanted to learn what Israel considered to be Cyprus's role in the Eastern Mediterranean. He also wanted to reassure Levin that Makarios would honour his commitment and maintain an equal distance on the Arab–Israeli dispute. Nevertheless, he did not fail to mention that, given the difficulties Makarios was then facing in his negotiations with the British over the land occupied by their military bases, he considered it crucial to politically support the UAR as a counterweight to British pressure. On the other hand, Kyprianou reaffirmed that Makarios would not adopt an anti-Israeli stand. Citing a recent conversation he had with UAR's minister of foreign affairs, Mahmood Fawzi, Kyprianou told Levin that, in his opinion, Egypt did not intend to impose sanctions on Cyprus if the latter decided to maintain friendly relations with Israel.

Although Kyprianou's assurances were apparently not enough to convince Meir,[93] Levin determined that his Cypriot interlocutor did not intend to mislead him, as his comments in the relevant report indicate: 'Kyprianou does not raise any suspicions, and we get the impression that he does not lie and that he is ethical. We convey his

[90] ISA/RG93/MFA/1008/1, Levin to Limon (694/103.1קפרו – 6.5.1960).
[91] Cf. 5.2.2.
[92] ISA/RG93/MFA/1007/15, Levin to British Commonwealth Division (739/103.2קפרו – 18.5.1960).
[93] Ibid., Nall to Levin (394/16.2קפרו – 22.5.1960).

words just as they were spoken. However, it is possible that to some extent, Kyprianou's words may also express his personal views.'[94]

6.1.6 Israel's diplomatic manoeuvres leading up to the day of Cyprus' Declaration of Independence, 16 August 1960

On 12 July 1960, four weeks prior to the official declaration of Cypriot independence, Israeli Foreign Minister Golda Meir approved[95] the report of Israeli Consul Zeev Levin[96] in which he recommended specific steps to ensure the establishment of diplomatic relations with the Republic of Cyprus. Levin's suggestions were based, first, on the decisions which had been taken at Israel's Ministry of Foreign Affairs on 20 December 1959,[97] and second, on developments between January and July of 1960, namely, that Athens did not adopt the role of adviser to Makarios regarding bilateral relations between Cyprus and Israel, a fact that set Israel's mind at ease. After the tough negotiations over the legal status of their bases in Cyprus, the British believed it would be a bridge too far to dictate Makarios' position on the Arab–Israeli conflict. Britain was the focus of UAR criticism at a time when relations between Makarios and Nasser were excellent and, as such, a pro-Israeli intervention by London might have had exactly the opposite effect. The US for its part expected Cyprus to maintain an equal distance from the Arabs and Israel, something Makarios was already aware of. Nevertheless, the Israelis seemed displeased by the State Department's reluctance to take further action in support of their pursuits.[98] The only practical support remaining to Israel was the veto power of the Turkish Cypriot vice president. That aside, Küçük's veto could well prove useful as a convincing alibi for Makarios vis-à-vis both the Arab governments and critics at home, in the event that he was obliged to refrain from raising objections to Israel's intentions. Nevertheless, it would certainly have been a 'bad start' if Cypriot–Israeli bilateral relations were to lead to the first constitutional rift between Makarios and Küçük.

Israeli diplomacy had decided to repeat the round of meetings held at the beginning of that year, when Cypriot independence was expected to be declared on 19 February 1960.

Meir approved the following steps:[99]

Asking Ankara to mobilize the Turkish Consulate in Nicosia to give Küçük the necessary instructions. In essence, the Israelis wanted Turkish reassurance that the Turkish Cypriot vice president would not hesitate to exercise a veto in the event

[94] Ibid. (799/103.2קפר – 27.5.1960).
[95] ISA/RG93/MFA/1431/19, Haim Yahil, director general, Israel's Ministry of Foreign Affairs, to Levin (17.7.1960, not recorded as incoming document).
[96] Ibid., Levin to Yahil (1010/103.3קפר – 12.7.1960).
[97] Cf. 6.1.2.
[98] Nicolet, *United States Policy towards Cyprus*, 140–7. Cf. 5.3 Commentary on Williams' views.
[99] ISA/RG93/MFA/1431/19, Levin to Yahil (1010/103.3קפר – 12.7.1960), and Yahil to Levin (17.7.1960, not recorded as incoming document).

that Makarios did not agree to equal diplomatic representation for both Israel and the Arab countries.

Following up on contacts with Athens in order to prevent undesirable Greek intervention in the matter of normal bilateral relations between Cyprus and Israel.

Re-establishing contact with Britain which was deemed able to effectively influence Makarios, given that Cyprus' removal from Cairo's sphere of influence would serve the interests of both Britain and Israel.

Encouraging massive Israeli tourism to Cyprus during the month of August 1960, in order to show Cypriot leadership and the public of both communities that good relations with Israel would benefit the local economy.

Implementing to the letter all diplomatic steps decided on at the meeting on 29 December 1959 regarding the announcement of the upgrade from consulate to embassy, on the day Cypriot independence was declared, so that the Israeli Ambassador could present his credentials to Makarios a few days later.

In keeping with the above, Maurice Fischer, assistant secretary general of the Ministry of Foreign Affairs visited Ankara and Athens once again to ascertain their views. In Athens, the position adopted by Averoff was particularly encouraging. Averoff pointed out that he had told both the Greek consul in Nicosia, Georgios Christopoulos, and the Greek Cypriot ministers that Cyprus must establish equivalent diplomatic relations with Israel and the Arab countries. He also mentioned that Makarios considered asking the Israelis to show tolerance and wait a while before upgrading their consulate in Nicosia to an embassy. Averoff had allegedly prevented Makarios from doing so, warning him that sooner or later Cyprus might find itself facing precisely the same difficulties Greece had faced for years due to its stance on the Arab–Israeli conflict.

Fischer was pleasantly surprised by Averoff's position, which was clearly in favour of establishing normal relations between Cyprus and Israel. In fact, as included in his report, Evangelos Averoff allegedly urged Makarios to enter into diplomatic relations with Israel, telling him that 'it would be preferable to deal with a one-time wave of wrath from the Arabs than a chronic disease later on'.[100] A few days later, on 22 July 1960, at his farewell meeting with Jeonathan Prato, the outgoing Israeli diplomatic representative to Athens, Averoff reassured the Israelis yet again that suitable instructions had been given to the Greek consul in Nicosia so that Makarios could do what was necessary to ensure equal diplomatic representation for Israel and the UAR.[101]

When Maurice Fisher travelled to Turkey, however, he found that the new military regime was not planning to change its positive stand towards Israel's intentions in

[100] ISA/RG93/MFA/1008/4, British Commonwealth Division to Levin (635/18.7.1960). Cf. ISA/RG130/MFA/2293/8, Fischer to Yahil (394/ב – 18.7.1960), and Israel State Archives, Gilead (ed.), *Documents*, vol. 14, 640 no. 412.
[101] ISA/RG93/MFA/1008/1, British Commonwealth Division to Levin (640/103.1קפר – 24.7.1960), and ISA/130/MFA/2293/8, Prato to Yahil (402/ב – 22.7.1960). Cf. Israel State Archives, Gilead (ed.), *Documents*, vol. 14, 639–40 no. 412.

Cyprus. The country's new minister of foreign affairs, Selim Sarper,[102] who was familiar to Israeli diplomats as head of Turkey's permanent representation to the UN,[103] reassured him of this. Sarper seemed hesitant though with regard to the need for Küçük to exercise veto powers. Nevertheless, he reassured Fischer, Makarios had already committed himself to deciding jointly with the vice president on anything related to the installation of foreign embassies in Cyprus.

On 10 August 1960, a meeting was held at Israel's Ministry of Foreign Affairs, chaired by Ministry Director General Haim Yahil. The topic was the final stage of diplomatic actions to be taken in view of the Cypriot declaration of independence on 16 August 1960.[104] Zeev Levin, who had travelled to Jerusalem specifically for that purpose, was present at the meeting. Levin confirmed that Makarios and Küçük had agreed to operate four Cypriot embassies (in Athens, Ankara, London and Washington) and ten consulates in ten countries, including the UAR, Lebanon and Israel. In fact, Turkey's consul to Nicosia, Vecdi Turel, promised to do whatever possible on behalf of his country so that the Republic of Cyprus would be represented at the same diplomatic level both in Israel and the Arab countries.

It was decided at the meeting that on 15 August 1960, the eve of the declaration of Cypriot independence, Israeli President Yitzhak Ben-Zvi and Prime Minister David Ben-Gurion would send a congratulatory telegram to Makarios. On 16 August 1960, upon receipt of the telegram from Makarios addressed to all member states of the UN and asking for their recognition of the Republic of Cyprus, Israeli Foreign Minister Meir would immediately send a telegram recognizing the new state. Concurrently Meir would send a second telegram to Makarios announcing the upgrade of Israel's consulate in Nicosia to an embassy, and appointing Zeev Levin as temporary chargé d'affaires. On 16 August 1960, Levin, in his new capacity, would hand Makarios congratulatory letters from the president and prime minister of Israel, with content similar to that in their telegrams of 15 August 1960. Finally, on 17 August 1960, the Israeli Foreign Minister would ask the government of Cyprus via telegram or letter, to recognize Zeev Levin as Israel's ambassador to Cyprus.

Upon his return to Nicosia, Levin found himself facing an unexpected turn of events. He was informed by Vice President Küçük and Turkish Consul Vecdi Turel on 12 August that Makarios had asked Küçük to consent to the immediate establishment of the UAR embassy in Nicosia, and to postpone the operation of Israel's embassy for six months. Küçük followed the instructions he had received from Ankara and refused to agree, telling Makarios that the two embassies must begin operations simultaneously.

Wasting no time, Levin hastened to meet with Makarios the next morning to announce Israel's decision to immediately upgrade the consulate to an embassy,

---

[102] ISA/RG130/MFA/2290/4, Fischer to Golda Meir (282/א – 8.8.1960) Cf. Israel State Archives, Gilead (ed.), *Documents*, vol. 14, 624 no. 402.

[103] Cf. 2.4.2.

[104] ISA/RG93/MFA/1008/1, Minutes of the meeting held at Israel's Ministry of Foreign Affairs on 10.8.1960, chaired by Ministry Director General Haim Yahil. Also taking part were the deputy directors general, Gideon Rafael, Moshe Bartur and Shmuel Bentzur, the adviser on political affairs, Yohanan Meroz, and Israeli consul to Nicosia Zeev Levin.

endeavouring in this way to avert any unwanted public statement by the archbishop. Having heard everything the Israeli consul had to say, Makarios responded that he was obliged to take into account the Arabs' reaction and asked him to convey to Israel's government his plea to postpone the opening of the embassy in Nicosia for six months. After hearing Levin's arguments, Makarios seemed to back down. 'If pressed by Israel', Levin reported, 'he said he would not be able to refuse, but that he was much afraid of the Arab reaction'.[105]

Israel's fears that Makarios would ultimately succumb to pressure from the UAR were all but confirmed. Quick action was required in order to avoid any further unpleasant developments with irreversible consequences.

Seized by panic, Levin suggested that Foreign Minister Meir send two separate telegrams recognizing the Cypriot Republic – one to President Makarios and one to Vice President Küçük.[106] However, such a move was sure to further complicate the balance between Makarios and Küçük and would be a truly terrible start to Cypriot–Israeli bilateral relations, without achieving any practical or desirable outcome. Thus, the idea was promptly rejected.

With Israel fast running out of options, it was deemed essential to set yet another 'Operation Spyros Skouras' in motion.[107] On 13 August 1960, the Ambassador of Israel to Washington Avraham Harman contacted Spyros Skouras and informed him of Makarios' sudden change of heart. Harman asked Skouras to return to Cyprus immediately and to meet with Makarios in person before dawn on 16 August. However, it was impossible for Skouras to travel from New York to Nicosia on such short notice.

Nevertheless, an alternative solution was found. Skouras got in touch with his nephew, also named Spyros Skouras (son of his brother, Dimitrios Skouras), who was a businessman living in Athens. The nephew happened to be in Athens that day and immediately agreed to travel to Cyprus. On the eve of 13 August 1960, Makarios' birthday, Spyros Skouras phoned him from New York, telling him that as he could not get to the island in time for the declaration of independence, his nephew would be in Nicosia the following day to convey an important message to him.[108]

And that is exactly what happened. On 14 August 1960, the younger Spyros Skouras arrived hurriedly in Nicosia. After being briefed by Zeev Levin, Skouras met with Makarios that night, and asked him what he intended to do about establishing diplomatic relations between Cyprus and Israel, and whether anything significant had occurred to change his mind. Makarios assured him not to worry, that 'diplomatic relations between Cyprus and Israel will run smoothly'.[109]

On 16 August 1960, Levin met with Makarios, again on his own initiative, and again informed him about Israel's decision to announce the following day, along with its recognition of the Republic of Cyprus, that the Israeli consulate in Nicosia would be

---

[105] ISA/RG130/MFA/2341/2, Levin to Yahil (249/13.8.1960). Cf. Israel State Archives, Gilead (ed.), *Documents*, vol. 14, 641 no. 414.
[106] ISA/RG130/MFA/2341/2, Levin to Yahil (249/13.8.1960).
[107] Cf. 6.1.3 on the first 'Operation Spyros Skouras'.
[108] ISA/RG93/MFA/1008/1, Yahil to Levin (661/103.1קפר – 14.8.1960).
[109] Ibid., Levin to Yahil (250/103.1קפר – 15.8.1960).

upgraded to an embassy. Makarios' response was positive – and terse.[110] Immediately following the meeting, Levin contacted Fazıl Küçük, who put his mind at ease and assured him that the risk of another about-face in Makarios' stance had been decisively avoided.[111]

Thus, on 16 August 1960, President Makarios sent a telegram to his Israeli counterpart, Yitzhak Ben-Zvi, announcing the declaration of independence of the Republic of Cyprus. The same telegram was sent to all heads of the United Nations member states.[112] On the same day, Israeli Foreign Minister Golda Meir sent a congratulatory telegram to Makarios, announcing that Israel recognized the Republic of Cyprus, and proposing to establish an Israeli embassy in Nicosia.[113] The same day, Meir also sent an official letter to her Cypriot counterpart, Spyros Kyprianou, notifying him that Zeev Levin, up until then Israeli Consul, would be assuming ambassadorial duties and asking the Cypriot government to grant its *agrément*.[114]

---

[110] Ibid.
[111] Ibid.
[112] ISA/RG130/MFA/3344/58, The telegram of 16.8.1960 from President Makarios to Israel's President Itzhak Ben-Zvi:

> Nicosia, 16 August 1960
> His Excellency the President of the State of Israel
> Jerusalem Israel
>
> Have honour inform your Excellency that Independence Republic of Cyprus was proclaimed today 0001 hours.
> Formal celebrations will take place at later date.
>
> Archbishop Makarios
> President of the Republic of Cyprus.

> Cf. Israel State Archives, Gilead (ed.), *Documents*, vol. 14, 654 no. 423.

[113] ISA/RG130/MFA/3344/58, The telegram from Golda Meir to President Makarios (16.8.1960):

> Jerusalem, 16 August 1960
> His Beatitude Archbishop Makarios,
> President of the Republic of Cyprus
>
> In acknowledging your telegram of today notifying the President of Israel of the proclamation of the Republic of Cyprus I have the honour to inform Your Beatitude that my Government has decided to recognise the Republic of Cyprus.
> The people of Israel rejoice at the achievement of independence by the people of Cyprus and they look forward to close and friendly relations with the Republic of Cyprus.
> In consequence, the Government of Israel views with favour the establishment of diplomatic missions and proposes, therefore to establish its Embassy in the Republic of Cyprus.
> I have furthermore the pleasure to convey to Your Beatitude the felicitations of the President and the people of Israel and to offer their sincere wishes for the well-being of the Republic of Cyprus and for the prosperity of its people.
>
> Golda Meir
> Minister of Foreign Affairs.

> Cf. Israel State Archives, Gilead (ed.), Documents, vol. 14, 654–5 no. 424.

[114] ISA/RG130/MFA/3345/7, The telegram from Golda Meir to her Cypriot counterpart, Spyros Kyprianou (16.8.1960):

> Jerusalem, 16 August 1960
> Monsieur le Ministre,
>
> I have the honour to inform Your Excellency of the intention of the Government of Israel to appoint Mr Zeev Levin as its Ambassador Extraordinary and Plenipotentiary to the Republic of Cyprus.

The next day, 17 August 1960, Makarios approved in writing the posting of Levin to Cyprus and the same day the Cypriot Ministry of Foreign Affairs granted an *agrément* to Levin's appointment as Israeli ambassador to the Republic of Cyprus.[115] Subsequently, Zeev Levin wired the Israeli Ministry of Foreign Affairs his request to immediately send his credentials, so that he would be able to submit them to President Makarios in the following days.[116] And so, in this eventful manner, the Independent Republic of Cyprus and the State of Israel established diplomatic relations, and the Israeli consulate in Nicosia became an embassy.

On 18 August 1960, President Yitzhak Ben-Zvi sent President Makarios a congratulatory telegram.[117] Zeev Levin personally delivered a letter of gratitude to Turkish Cypriot Vice President Fazıl Küçük on behalf of Foreign Minister Golda

I have the honour, on the instructions of the Government of Israel, to request the *Agrément* of the Government of the Republic of Cyprus to the appointment of Mr Levin.
I avail myself of this opportunity to express to Your Excellency the assurance of my highest consideration.

Golda Meir
Minister of Foreign Affairs.

Cf. Israel State Archives, Gilead (ed.), Documents, vol. 14, 655 no. 425].
[115] ISA/RG93/MFA/1008/1, The *Agrément* from the Cypriot Ministry of Foreign Affairs to Israel's Ministry of Foreign Affairs (17.8.1960):

Ministry of Foreign Affairs
Nicosia, Cyprus

The Ministry of Foreign Affairs of the Republic of Cyprus presents its compliments to the Ministry for Foreign Affairs of Israel and with reference to the latter's letter dated August 16, 1960 has the honour to bring to its knowledge that His Beatitude the President of the Republic has graciously given His consent to the nomination of Mr Zev Levin as Ambassador Extraordinary and Plenipotentiary of the State of Israel to the Republic of Cyprus.
This Ministry avails itself of the opportunity to renew to the Ministry of Foreign Affairs of Israel the assurance of its highest consideration.
Nicosia, 17, August 1960

[116] ISA/RG93/MFA/1008/1, Levin to Golda Meir, Yahil and Nall (251/103.1קפר – 17.8.1960).
[117] ISA/RG93/MFA/1008/1, The telegram from President of Israel Yitzhak Ben-Zvi to President of the Republic of Cyprus, Archbishop Makarios (18.8.1960):

My great and good friend,

Holding in esteem the relations of friendship and mutual understanding existing between the Republic of Cyprus and the State of Israel and being desirous to strengthen and develop these friendly relations, I, in accordance with the Powers vested in me by Law, have decided to appoint Mr Zeev Levin to reside near Your Beatitude as Ambassador Extraordinary and Plenipotentiary. The character and abilities of Mr Levin lead me to believe that he will fulfil the mission with which he is charged in such a manner as to merit Your Beatitude's trust and approbation and prove himself worthy of the confidence I place in him.
I therefore request Your Beatitude to receive our Ambassador favourably and to give credence to all that he shall have the honour to communicate to Your Beatitude and to the Government of Cyprus on the part of the Government of Israel.
   May I express to Your Beatitude my sentiments of high esteem and send You my best wishes for your well-being and well-being and prosperity of Your Country.

Meir.[118] At Levin's suggestion,[119] the Israeli ambassador to Washington, Avraham Harman, personally thanked the Greek American millionaire Spyros Skouras for his important contribution.

6.2 Arab actions against the establishment of diplomatic relations between the Republic of Cyprus and Israel

As already described in detail, throughout the Transitional Period – from February 1959 to the declaration of independence of the Cyprus on 16 August 1960 – the Israeli government repeatedly attempted to verify that the Greek Cypriot side and Makarios personally would not raise objections, reservations or obstacles to the establishment of diplomatic relations between the Republic of Cyprus and Israel.[120] Despite the reassurances that they received from Turkey, Greece, Great Britain, the US, the Turkish Cypriot vice president and Archbishop Makarios himself, the Israelis were not complacent. In the period between December 1959 and February 1960 (due to the imminent declaration of independence on 19 February 1960), and during the July–August 1960 period, senior officials of the Israeli Ministry of Foreign Affairs repeatedly met with their counterparts in Turkey, Greece, Great Britain and the US, to confirm everything that had already been seemingly confirmed.[121] Israel's insistence cannot be completely understood without examining the corresponding Arab moves which aimed at breaking off contacts between Cyprus and Israel and preventing the establishment of normal and full diplomatic relations between these two countries.

The only Arab countries in a position to exercise considerable influence over Cyprus' foreign policy at that time were the United Arab Republic and Lebanon. Throughout the 1950s, the UAR had supported Archbishop Makarios both politically

---

[118] ISA/RG93/MFA/1008/1, The telegram of 19.8.1960, ref. no. 253/103.1קפר, from Levin to Yahil and Nall; and ISA/RG130/MFA/3344/58, Letter of gratitude from Golda Meir to Fazıl Küçük (21.8.1960, not officially logged):

> Jerusalem, 21 August 1960
> Your Excellency,
>
> It is with a sense of profound gratification that I write to express to you once more my most cordial wishes for the prosperity of the Republic of Cyprus and for your personal well-being.
> I am convinced that the relations so happily established between our two countries will develop and widen to the benefit of both countries, thus contributing to the stability and peace of the entire area. I am aware of Your Excellency's important share in the strengthening of the bonds of friendship between Israel and the Republic of Cyprus and I should like to convey to you the appreciation of the Government and the people of Israel.
> With renewed assurance of my highest consideration and esteem,
>
> Very respectfully yours,
> Golda Meir
> Minister of Foreign Affairs

Cf. Israel State Archives, Gilead (ed.), *Documents*, vol. 14, 656 no. 426.
[119] ISA/RG93/MFA/1008/1, Levin to US Division (24.8.1960, not officially logged).
[120] Cf. 6.1.
[121] Cf. 6.1.2 and 6.1.6.

and diplomatically. Then, too, Lebanon was the only Arab country which had maintained diplomatic representation on the island, after bilateral relations between Great Britain and the UAR broke off as a result of the Suez Crisis and the closure of the Egyptian consulate in Nicosia in November 1956. Since then, Lebanon had assumed the role of informal protector and guardian of Arab interests in Cyprus. Regardless of these unique circumstances, however, both Egypt and Lebanon had long-standing ties with the Cypriot community and local enterprises despite the drastic drop in commercial transactions between Cyprus and Egypt from November 1956 onwards.

In view of Cypriot independence and the transitional period, Lebanon and the UAR maintained an active diplomatic, economic and public relations presence on the island, focusing their efforts first on increasing their influence in their new neighbour state, and second, on preventing the Republic of Cyprus from establishing diplomatic, political and economic relations with Israel. The actions of the UAR and Lebanon were coordinated at every level, their common reference point being the decisions of the Council of the Arab League. These decisions condemned all aspects of Israeli policy and instituted mechanisms as early as 1945 aimed at securing the economic and political isolation of the Jewish state. The Arab boycott provided for sanctions on third-country businesses and organizations with direct or indirect dealings with Israel. Naturally, the activity of the UAR and Lebanon throughout the transitional period in Cyprus had been a matter of grave concern for Israeli diplomacy.

6.2.1 The Arab boycott on Israel

Even before Israel's declaration of independence, as relations between Jews and Arabs in Mandate Palestine were deteriorating, the Arab League adopted drastic measures to counteract the danger of a consolidated Zionist presence in the region. Initially, these measures focused on economics and commerce. The Council of the Arab League took steps to ban the movement of products and services from the Yishuv (the Jewish population in Palestine), and through Decision No. 16/2.12.1945, to boycott all '"Zionist" products and goods', effectively prohibiting their distribution through Arab markets as of 1 January 1946.[122] Pursuant to the Council's Decision No. 70/12.6.1946, every member state of the Arab League was to set up a 'Local Boycott Office' through which to coordinate activities with corresponding offices in other Arab countries under the supervision of the Central Boycott Commission based in Cairo. The same decision banned the export of raw materials to the 'Zionist entity in Palestine' by establishing special product labels used for customs clearance and banning all exchanges with banks, commercial companies, transport companies, insurance companies, suppliers and others linked to or controlled by 'Zionist capital'.[123]

After the founding of Israel in May 1948, the Arab League added new measures. Thus, during the 1950s, the Arab boycott became a significant means of exerting political and diplomatic pressure, with multiple impacts on the newly established

---

[122] Muhammad Khalil, *The Arab States and the Arab League: A Documentary Record* (Beirut: Khayats, 1962), vol. 2, 161 no. 75.
[123] Ibid., 162 no. 78.

Jewish state. They not only prohibited the movement of goods and services between Israel and Arab markets, but imposed penalties on third-country businesses for dealing in any way with public or private Israeli entities. Third-country cargo ships that docked in Israel were banned from all Arab ports. All foreign companies engaged in direct or indirect transactions with Israel were entered on a 'Blacklist' with adverse effects to their international activities. According to Decision No. 300/8.4.1950, for example, Arab states were obliged to suspend all dealings with shipping lines that carried goods to and from Israel or Jewish passengers bound for Israel and settlement there.[124] Decision No. 1075/15.10.1955 held that local Arab embassies were responsible for controlling exports to Arab markets and preventing the infiltration of Israeli products with false certificates of origin.[125] Finally, in order to enforce these decisions more effectively, a 'Central Boycott Office' was set up in Damascus to coordinate the boycott and to draft periodic reports to the General Secretariat of the League of Arab States.[126]

6.2.1.1 The political aspect of the Arab boycott and Cyprus

During British colonial rule, the Cypriot economy, which was mostly controlled by the Greek Cypriot community, had strong commercial ties with the neighbouring Arab markets. According to data collected by the Israeli Foreign Ministry, between 1950 and 1955, 15 per cent of the exportable agricultural products from Cyprus were intended for Arab countries.[127] During the 1953–6 period, Egypt absorbed 75 per cent of Cypriot exports, while from 1956 to 1958, Lebanon – the only Arab country to have maintained a diplomatic representation on the island – exported goods to Cyprus, followed by Jordan, Libya and Sudan, and to a far lesser extent to Syria and Iraq.[128] When diplomatic relations between Egypt and Great Britain were suspended in November 1956 due to the Suez Crisis, Cypriot exports to Egypt were reduced by nearly 80 per cent.[129] Between 1955 and 1959, the Cypriot economy suffered a continual recession, not just because of the turbulence on the island, but because the Egyptian market had essentially closed.

In 1958, the Cypriot trade ratio to the Arab world was estimated at 1:7.[130] At the same time, Israel's Ministry of Commerce data showed an even less favourable trade balance for Cyprus, with a ratio of 1:11.[131] From the early 1950s until just before Cypriot independence, the Israeli market had demonstrated an unwillingness to absorb more products from the island.

---

[124] Ibid., 166 no. 84.

[125] Ibid., 175 no. 101.

[126] Martin A. Weiss, *Arab League Boycott of Israel* (Washington, DC: Congressional Research Service, 2013), 5.3.2013.

[127] ISA/RG93/MFA/1008/1, Nachum Eshkol, second secretary, Israeli consulate in Nicosia, to Economic Affairs Division (636/103.1קפר – 26.4.1960).

[128] ISA/RG93/MFA/2156/7, Leshem to British Commonwealth Division (192/162/59-18.2.1959), Table comparing Cypriot exports to Arab countries and Israel in the period 1953–8.

[129] Ibid.

[130] Ibid.

[131] ISA/RG93/MFA/1428/2, Yaakov Hecht, *Ha-Mivne ha-Kalkali shel Kafrisin* [*The Economic Structure of Cyprus*] (Jerusalem: Hebrew University of Jerusalem, 1960), 15. According to data of the Israeli Ministry of Commerce, in 1958, Cypriot exports to Israel amounted to £55,931 (pounds sterling), while the respective Israeli exports to Cyprus totalled £506,370 (pounds sterling).

As a result, with the approach of Cypriot independence, Greek Cypriot businessmen pinned their hopes on the Egyptian and Lebanese markets. But although the UAR and Lebanon who wished to implement the decisions of the Arab League pressed Cypriot entrepreneurs to suspend all contact with Israel, the Cypriot market could not afford to ignore either the flow of tourists or the large volume of imports from Israel.

During the Transitional Period, pressure from the Arab world on Cypriot political leadership was both economic and political. The UAR and Lebanon appeared eager to develop close economic ties with the new republic but expected Cyprus to impose the Arab boycott on Israel – an action that was certain to shape its foreign policy in a decisive way. Cairo thought the time had come for Nicosia to give something in return for the political and diplomatic support it had received from Nasser because of his personal friendship with Archbishop Makarios and the positive image the UAR enjoyed at all levels of Greek Cypriot public opinion. On the other hand, if the newly established and economically weak Republic of Cyprus dismissed Arab demands, it would likely weaken Nasser's regional influence as well as the effectiveness of the Arab boycott on Israel. Likewise, since the harbours and airports of Cyprus were just a 'stone's throw' away from Israeli shores this would eventually render the Arab boycott a 'dead letter'. Lebanon as well as Nasser's Egypt, Israel's most formidable opponent in the region, wished to prevent such an eventuality at all costs.

6.2.2 Relations between the UAR and Cyprus during the Transitional Period in Israeli diplomatic reports

In September 1959, the Arab League advised all member states to recognize the Republic of Cyprus immediately after its declaration of independence, establish full diplomatic relations with it, support its candidacy for full membership in the United Nations; and conclude economic cooperation agreements with it in order to prevent any Israeli political or financial activity on the island.[132] In the run-up to the initial date of the Cypriot declaration of independence (19 February 1960), the General Secretariat of the Arab League in Cairo made the above recommendation binding on all Arab governments.[133]

The decision issued by the General Secretariat of the Arab League in January 1960 was not merely symbolic. At the end of that month, US Ambassador to Nicosia Taylor Belcher informed his Israeli counterpart, Zeev Levin, that the US Embassy in Cairo had been informed by reliable sources that all member countries of the Arab League were about to recognize the Republic of Cyprus. The first Arab country to open an Embassy in Nicosia would be the UAR and Egypt's top priority was the enhancement of ties with Cyprus through the economically powerful Greek Cypriot community in Alexandria.[134] The information provided by Belcher was also verified by Israeli sources.[135] The Greek Cypriot community of Alexandria issued a request for a Cypriot

---

[132] Yitzhak Oron (ed.), *Asia: Middle East Record 1960* (Jerusalem, Tel Aviv and London: Israel Oriental Society, Reuven Shiloah Research Center and Weidenfeld & Nicolson, 1962), vol. 1, 181.
[133] Ibid.
[134] ISA/RG93/MFA/1007/3, Levin to British Commonwealth Division (101/110.1קפ – 20.1.1960).
[135] Ibid., Sufott to Levin (60/110.1קפפ – 21.1.1960).

consulate to be established in their city so as to alleviate the workload of the future Cypriot embassy in Cyprus.[136]

Because the declaration of independence initially scheduled for February 19, 1960 was postponed,[137] the Egyptian consulate in Nicosia did not open on 1 February 1960, as had been reported in the Cairo newspapers a month earlier.[138] Nevertheless even before, during the summer of 1959, Egyptian diplomacy, had begun to set its own terms and prepare its official representation in Cyprus. Specifically, in his interview on 30 June 1959 with *Al-Ahram* newspaper, Nasser defined the ideological framework for bilateral relations between the UAR and the future Republic of Cyprus and highlighted the anti-colonialist stance he had maintained throughout the 1950s towards the Cyprus question. To this, he contrasted Israel's alliances with the colonial powers of the West and its consequent 1959 UN vote against recognizing independence for Algeria and Cameroon as 'a recent example of the Jewish state's pro-colonial attitude'[139] in order to show that anti-colonial Egypt, and by extension, the Arab world, and not Israel, were the true supporters of the Cypriots in the region.

Naturally, the Israelis did not expect words of praise from the Egyptian president. However, they were concerned that the Cypriot political leadership appeared not to disagree with the views Nasser expressed in the interview. At least, that is how Makarios' statements, published in the *Washington Star* on 5 July 1960 were interpreted. As he explained it, he would need the consent of the Arab countries and primarily the Nasserist UAR, to establish diplomatic relations with Israel. These statements resulted in a flurry of activity at the Israeli Ministry of Foreign Affairs, as they were seen to coincide with Nasser's views published in *Al-Ahram*.[140]

The way in which Nasserist Egypt perceived its bilateral relations with the Republic of Cyprus had become clear during the official Cypriot representation's stay in Cairo to celebrate the eighth anniversary of Nasser's triumphant military coup. That delegation had included only Greek Cypriot ministers of the Transitional government.[141]

In a relevant report, Israeli Consul Zeev Levin includes the impressions of Deputy Minister of Agriculture Andreas Azinas, who had participated in the delegation along with fellow ministers Paschalis Paschalides, Antonis Georgiades and Nikos Kranidiotis.[142] During their stay in Cairo, the Greek Cypriot ministers met with UAR

[136] ISA/RG93/MFA/1431/23, *Fileleftheros*, 'The Cypriots from Alexandria are asking for a Cypriot Consulate in their city', 28.1.1960.
[137] Cf. 6.1.2 on Israel's diplomatic actions in view of the declaration of independence of Cyprus on 19.2.1960.
[138] ISA/RG130/MFA/3570/12, Research Division (1407/א – 15.11.1959), Publication in the Egyptian newspaper *Al-Ahram* (7.11.1959), according to which the UAR intended to open a consulate in Cyprus on 1 February 1960.
[139] ISA/RG93/MFA/2156/7, Sufott to Levin (1263/28.7.1959). The document sent by the Press Office of the Israeli Ministry of Foreign Affairs to the Asia-Africa Division which included an excerpt of Nasser's interview in *Al-Ahram* on 30.6.1959 is attached.
[140] Cf. 5.2.1.4.
[141] Cf. 5.2.2, Fazıl Küçük turned down Makarios' suggestion to have the Turkish Cypriot community represented on the delegation travelling to Cairo in July 1959.
[142] ISA/RG93/MFA/263/7, Levin to British Commonwealth Division, notification to the Middle East Division and Research Division (801/59-30.7.1959, confidential report).

Minister of Foreign Affairs, Mahmood Fawzi, on 24 July 1959. Fawzi seemed particularly annoyed by the contacts between Cypriot and Israeli officials, and also by the commitments that the Cypriot leadership had made to the West after the signing of the London–Zurich Agreements. He criticized the Cypriot leadership, first for agreeing to the retention of the British military bases on the island, and second for not obstructing Israel's economic presence, though it was known that Israel sought to apply the same persuasive economic and political practices it was implementing in Ghana and Burma at the time.[143] The Egyptian foreign minister told the Greek Cypriot ministers in no uncertain terms that such actions or omissions ran against the spirit and letter of the Arab League's decisions on the economic and diplomatic boycott of Israel. Moreover, he reminded them that before the Suez Crisis, Egypt had continued to buy overpriced Cypriot products and to sell Egyptian products to Cyprus at lower than market prices. At the same time, the trade balance between Cyprus and Israel throughout the 1950s had never benefited Cypriot producers.

When Mahmood Fawzi called the Greek Cypriots on the carpet and told them to choose 'whose friendship they respected more', the Cypriot reply was interesting. As confided to Israeli Consul Zeev Levin by Charles Foley, a reporter with the English-language daily *Times of Cyprus* who had accompanied the Cypriot representation to Cairo,[144] Minister of Commerce and Industry Paschalis Paschalides had told Fawzi that Cyprus' aim was to maintain its independence 'even if this meant conceding on the issue of the bases'. In fact, he noted, the Greek Cypriots had also offered their good services to Egypt in the recent past, reminding Fawzi that during the Suez Crisis in November 1956, EOKA had intensified its armed action against the British on the island. In this way, the British were forced to respond to the distraction in Cyprus, allowing the Egyptian Army to achieve important victories on the battlefield.[145] Paschalides also assured Fawzi that Cyprus wished to be included in the Afro-Asian Bloc and it therefore went without saying that it wanted to maintain close ties with the UAR. Nevertheless, he said in defence of contacts with Israel that Cyprus wished to maintain friendly relations with all neighbouring countries.

The Egyptian foreign minister's straightforward expression of concerns to the Greek Cypriot ministers revealed yet another important factor. The UAR's support of Archbishop Makarios throughout the 1950s and Nassar's positive attitude toward the island allowed Egypt to interact comfortably with all political currents in the Greek Cypriot community.[146] Thus, although the Egyptian government welcomed the ministers of Makarios' Transitional government to Cairo in July 1959, nothing had prevented the – obviously pro-Nasser – leadership of the Greek Cypriot community in Egypt from inviting Georgios Grivas[147] a month earlier, despite notable tensions

---

[143] Cf. 5.2 and 6.1.5, on Israel's penetration into Ghana and Burma in the areas of economy and organizing local armed forces.

[144] ISA/RG93/MFA/263/7, Levin to British Commonwealth Division, copies to the Middle East Division and Research Division (801/59-30.7.1959, confidential report). Levin had been impressed by what Paschalis Paschalides had to say.

[145] Cf. Sakkas, *Kypriako kai o Aravikos Kosmos*, 62–3.

[146] Cf. 5.2.1.4.

[147] ISA/RG130/MFA/3570/12, Research Division 1170/λ – 15.6.1959). *Al-Ahram*, 6.6.1959.

between the latter and the archbishop.[148] Meanwhile, the friendship between Nasser and Makarios himself did not stop Mahmood Fawzi from chastising the ministers of Makarios' Transitional government for not having suspended contact with Israel. The left-wing Cypriot newspapers took every opportunity to praise Nasser's regime and its good relations with Makarios, regardless of the fact that the archbishop had avoided including a leftist minister in the Transitional government.[149] On the other hand, Israel had not managed to develop a reliable channel of communication with Makarios. Israel had already ascertained that it could not work with the anti-Makarios Right led by Themistoklis Dervis[150] yet it had not cultivated substantive relations with the Greek Cypriot Left,[151] nor did it seek to foster relations with communist AKEL.[152] Owing to all these factors, Israel had no choice but to trust in the Turkish Cypriot leadership of Cyprus which made clear from the outset that it did not share the Greek Cypriots' pro-Nasserist leanings.[153]

The signing of the tripartite Greece–Turkey–Cyprus defence agreement on 28 October 1959 prompted the displeasure of the UAR, which saw the NATO military presence in the Eastern Mediterranean increase.[154] Although such a development might have provoked a crisis in UAR–Cypriot relations, nothing of the kind occurred. Egypt denounced the machinations of the West in seeking to establish a military presence on the island but carefully avoided any criticism of Makarios. Similarly, the Greek Cypriot newspapers, regardless of their political affiliations, appeared sympathetic to Egyptian concerns. A typical example was the commentary on the tripartite defence agreement in the pro-Makarios Cypriot daily *Ethnos*, in its 1 November 1959 edition:[155]

> The Arabs, who are our candid friends and our fervent supporters in the UN in our claim for self-determination, are rightly annoyed due to the military cooperation agreement between Cyprus, Greece and Turkey, which was signed in Athens four days ago. And the radio station in Cairo quite rightly posed the question: What are the objectives of this alliance?

Thus, not only were relations between the UAR and Cyprus unaffected by this development, but in January 1960, Egypt advanced the decision of the Arab League, encouraging the member states to provide political and diplomatic support for independent Cyprus with a view to enhancing the Arab presence on the island and

[148] Cf. 5.2.1.4, on Makarios' statements in the US newspaper *Washington Star* and journalist Marie Grebenc about Grivas' role in Cypriot political life.
[149] Cf. 6.1.2, Açıkalın's assessment of relations between the UAR and the Greek Cypriot opposition.
[150] Cf. 5.2.1.2.
[151] ISA/RG93/MFA/2156/7, Minutes from the meeting held on 2.7.1959 at the Israeli Ministry of Foreign Affairs. Highlights by Zeev Levin regarding the absence of substantive contact between Israel and the communist faction in Cyprus. Cf. 5.2.1.3 and 6.1.1.
[152] Cf. 5.2.1.3.
[153] Cf. Nikos Stelgias, *O Thanatos tou Anepithymitou Vrefous* [*The Death of the Unwanted Infant*], (Athens: Papazisis, 2015), 104, and cf. 5.2.2.
[154] Cf. 6.1.1.
[155] ISA/RG93/MFA/263/7, *Ethnos*, 1.11.1959.

preventing Israeli infiltration.[156] During the same period, in anticipation of the declaration of Cypriot independence, claims in the Greek Cypriot press that Lebanon, Iraq, Jordan and Libya were all preparing to open embassies in Nicosia, at Nasser's prompting, grew more frequent.[157]

Another aspect of bilateral relations between Cyprus and the UAR during the Transitional Period was the presence of Cypriot representatives at conferences of Afro-Asian countries where Nasser exerted significant influence. On the initiative of Andreas Araouzos, Makarios' close associate who represented the Egyptian airline company *Misr* in Cyprus, the Cyprus Federation of Commerce and Industry decided to send its General Secretary, Costas Montis to the second Afro-Asian Economic Conference in Cairo in April 1960.[158] That month, Makarios assigned the general secretary of the Cyprus Workers Confederation (SEK), Michalakis Pissas, to represent Cyprus at the second Conference of the Afro-Asian People's Solidarity Organization (AAPSO), held in Conakry, Guinea, where the UAR also enjoyed a leadership role.[159]

Israeli diplomacy kept a close eye on the eager participation of the Greek Cypriots in Afro-Asian conferences, particularly as these conferences always adopted resolutions condemning Israel.[160] Both the US and Turkish consuls in Nicosia, along with Stephen Hastings, a senior member of the British secret services posted in Cyprus at the time, attempted unsuccessfully to convince Makarios not to associate himself diplomatically with the anti-West positions of the Afro-Asian countries.[161] The Israelis expressed deep concerns to Turkey, Britain and the US about the nature of the foreign policy independent Cyprus intended to adopt. On the other hand, it was true that the Afro-Asian conferences were also attended by countries which did not belong to the Eastern Bloc, countries which had recognized Israel and whose relations with the Jewish state were not influenced by the pro-Arab resolutions adopted at each conference. More specifically, the preparatory committee charged with organizing the Afro-Asian Economic Conference of 1959 which took place in Cairo, included Japan, India, Ethiopia and Ghana – all countries friendly towards Israel.[162] Similarly, the conference in Conakry was attended by Turkey, Ghana, Ethiopia, Ivory Coast, Japan, Sierra Leone and Iran, all of which had recognized Israel.[163] The Israelis tried to put their minds at ease with the thought that the ties between Archbishop Makarios and the Afro-Asian People's Solidarity Organization were not new, but dated back to the Bandung

[156] Oron (ed.), *Middle East Record*, 181.
[157] ISA/RG93/MFA/1007/6, Reports in Greek Cypriot newspapers, January 1960.
[158] ISA/RG93/MFA/1008/4, Levin to British Commonwealth Division (26.2.1960).
[159] Ibid., Levin to British Commonwealth Division (621/103.1קפר – 22.4.1960).
[160] Ibid., Research Division to Levin (955/2-27.3.1960).
[161] Ibid., Levin to British Commonwealth Division (419/110.10קפר – 10.3.1960), Levin's contacts with Belcher, Türel and Hastings, who told him of their efforts to convince Makarios not to send a representation to the Afro-Asian Economic Conference to be held in Cairo in April 1960.
[162] Ibid., Research Division (500/ס – 21.12.1959), On the Afro-Asian Economic Conference in Cairo (30.4.1960–3.5.1960). Also taking part in the preparatory committee that met in Damascus (14–19.12.1959) were countries not friendly to Israel: the People's Republic of China, Indonesia, Iraq, Libya, Sudan and the UAR.
[163] ISA/RG93/MFA/1008/5, Research Division (534/ס – 11.5.1960), Extensive report on the proceedings of the 2nd Conference of the Afro-Asian People's Solidarity Organisation [AAPSO] in Conakry, Guinea (11–15.4.1960).

conference of 1955.[164] On the other hand, the fact that Cyprus was known as being pro-Arab and pro-Asian at an international level boosted the appeal of Nasser's Egypt – a fact which indirectly yet clearly harmed Israel on a diplomatic level.

When it was announced in January 1960 that the initial date for declaring Cypriot independence (19 February 1960) was to be postponed and while negotiations about the expanse and legal status of British bases on the island had stalled, the UAR seized the opportunity to level harsh criticism at the terms of the London–Zurich Agreements regarding the retention of the British military presence in Cyprus.[165] Egypt's anti-colonialist arguments were shared by all the Greek Cypriot newspapers, which even called on Makarios to seek guarantees from the British that their bases would not target the territorial integrity of the UAR. During the period that negotiations were at a standstill, public figures in the Greek Cypriot community who were not usually critics of Israel also began to express pro-Arab views. A typical example of such views was an open letter by SEK General Secretary Michalakis Pissas, published in the Cypriot press, stating that:

> The Cypriot people will not allow the military bases to pose a threat to the safety of the Arab people or serve as a springboard for a new adventure in Suez [...]. We know that the British do not wish to have close friendly relations with the Arabs. It suffices that we once again restate our friendship and gratitude to the Arab people for its sincere support of the Cypriot struggle.[166]

Similarly, the AKEL's daily *Haravgi* applauded Egypt's criticism of the unresolved issue of the British bases, while Nasser himself highlighted his good relations with political figures from the Left and publicly congratulated the mayor of Famagusta, Andreas Pouyuros, on his missive to the United Nations in favour of the decolonization of the Arab countries triggered by developments in Algeria – an issue spearheading the UAR's anti-West policy.[167] All this took place in a very volatile and polarized climate, as disagreements between the British and Makarios implied the London–Zurich Agreements might not be implemented.[168]

An anti-West (and thus pro-Nasser) climate also began to develop amongst Cypriot trade unions. During the last three months of 1959, the idea of establishing a joint body linking the trade unions of Yugoslavia, Greece, Cyprus and the Arab states of North Africa and the Eastern Mediterranean had come to the forefront once again. The first steps in this endeavour were taken by Fotis Makris, general secretary of the General Confederation of Greek Workers (GSEE), who had met with his counterparts from

---

[164] Cf. 1.1.3, 3.3.1 and 3.3.2.2.
[165] ISA/RG93/MFA/1008/4, *Haravgi*, 'On the issue of the military bases: President Nasser did address a message to Archbishop Makarios. The Arab people are concerned about the land that will be conceded in Cyprus for the British military bases', 7.4.1960.
[166] ISA/RG93/MFA/1008/4, *Eleftheria, Ethnos* and *Fileleftheros*, 20.4.1960. Also: Michalakis Pissas, 'The Arabs and Cyprus', *Fileleftheros*, 28.4.1960, and Levin to British Commonwealth Division (621/22.4.1960). Text of Michalakis Pissas' speech at the Conakry Conference, 13.4.1960.
[167] ISA/RG130/MFA/3570/12, *Times of Cyprus*, 'Nasser writes to Mayor', 11.11.1959.
[168] Cf. 6.1.4, Period of stagnation in negotiations (February–July 1960).

Yugoslavia, Turkey, Bulgaria, Romania and the UAR.[169] On the Cypriot side, Michalakis Pissas of SEK was pursuing similar contacts with trade unions in Syria.[170] In May 1960, Makris and Pissas travelled to Cairo, and according to Israel's diplomatic reports, the plans seemed to be taking shape.[171]

As previously noted, Israel's consul to Nicosia, Zeev Levin, a long-standing member of Israel's workers federation, the Histadrut, was particularly aware of the issues. In 1958, he had been quite active in Greece and Cyprus as an ICFTU representative, and had made a number of gains in Israel's image.[172] Disturbed by the new initiatives, Levin predicted that the planned regional trade union organization in the works would be controlled politically by the UAR, Yugoslavia and pro-Arab Greece. In January 1960, he contacted ICFTU headquarters in Brussels for the purpose of neutralizing the actions of Makris and Pissas. Instead, he proposed the establishment of a regional trade union organization under the auspices of ICFTU which would be based in Cyprus and include members of Israel's Histadrut, along with labour unions from Cyprus, Turkey, and the European countries of the Mediterranean – possibly including Greece.[173]

Based on Israeli assessments of the situation, the ongoing deadlock in negotiations over the size and legal status of the British bases, together with the delay in financial assistance from Britain to Cyprus, was of some benefit to the UAR which was systematically hastening the process of turning the island into an Arab satellite. In the unlikely event that the London–Zurich Agreements were not implemented and Makarios decided to adopt a purely pro-Nasserist line, the safeguard of the Turkish Cypriot veto would be a non-starter. The military coup in Turkey and the determination of the Gürsel regime to exercise behind-the-scenes pressure to conclude negotiations in Cyprus and pave the way for independence essentially 'saved' not just the London–Zurich Agreements, but also Israeli aspirations.[174]

A few days after the change of regime in Turkey, the Greek government invited Nasser for an official visit to Athens on 7 June 1960. Needless to say, the Greek Cypriot newspapers covered the event extensively and stressed the friendly ties between Greece, Cyprus and Egypt. According to a report by the Athens correspondent for the Cypriot daily *Fileleftheros*, Nasser had warned Karamanlis that the development of friendly relations with Israel would jeopardize Cyprus' relations with the UAR,[175] while the

---

[169] ISA/RG93/MFA/1432/5, Israel's embassy in Brussels to West Europe Division, with copy to Levin (109/4.1.1960), and the English-language bulletin *Weekly Athens Newsletter* (119/5.12.1959), published by the Hellenews-Hellenic News Centre and distributed to all diplomatic missions in Belgium.

[170] ISA/RG130/MFA/3570/12, Levin to British Commonwealth Division (1092/59-17.9.1959).

[171] ISA/RG93/MFA/1008/4, Levin to British Commonwealth Division (791/110.10קפ – 25.5.1960).

[172] Cf. 3.6.1.1.1 and 4.3.1 On Levin's activity as special ICFTU envoy to Greece and Cyprus.

[173] ISA/RG93/MFA/1432/5, Correspondence between Levin, the central administration of ICFTU, Israel's Federation of Workers *Histadrut*, the competent departments of the Ministry of Foreign Affairs and the various local diplomatic missions, during the period 4.1.1960–28.12.1960. Israel's actions aimed to neutralize the efforts being made by the UAR, in collaboration with left-wing trade unions, to hold a meeting in Rome in February 1961 that would lead to the establishment of a joint trade union body for workers in the Eastern Mediterranean, with an anti-Israeli political focus.

[174] Cf. 6.1.4, On Israel's views of the impact of the Gürsel coup on progress of negotiations in Cyprus.

[175] ISA/RG93/MFA/1008/4, *Fileleftheros*, 'During his talks with the Greek government, UAR President Nasser brought up the issue of the British bases in Cyprus – He also broached the issue of Cyprus-Israel relations', 9.6.1960.

overall impression given by Cypriot newspapers was that relations between Greece and the UAR were better than ever.

Nevertheless, Greek Consul to Nicosia Georgios Christopoulos pointed out an important point to his Israeli counterpart: the Cypriot reports focused on Nasser's statements in Athens, but not on the views of the Greek government.[176] One exception was the report by Evripidis Ioannou, for the newspaper *Alithia*, which described precisely the points of disagreement between Athens and Cairo. In its 13 June 1960 edition, *Alithia* published the following:

> It was established that Nasser and the Greek government share exactly the same views as regards dealing with the current situation in the Eastern Mediterranean, and both recognise the important role which the Republic of Cyprus could play as a pillar of stability and peace in this sensitive region, in defending the free world. [...] Regarding the foreign policy of both countries [Greece and the UAR] vis-à-vis the East and West coalition, it was found that there was agreement only in supporting the countries of the UN Charter on freedom, self-determination and independence of the peoples. This means that each country has remained committed to its points of focus abroad, Greece within the framework of its obligations to its allies, and the United Arab Republic within the camp of neutralist countries, far from any political and military coalitions and totally free to exercise its foreign policy.[177]

According to Christopoulos, 'the Greek government was facing several difficulties with Makarios' other than the issue of British bases and the manner in which Makarios had negotiated with the British. Zeev Levin became even more concerned when Christopoulos told him that 'it will be very hard for anyone to change Makarios' mind, if he has indeed settled on a specific line regarding his foreign policy'.[178]

In order to fully clarify the positions of Makarios as well as Greece, a few days after Nasser's departure from Athens, Maurice Fischer, assistant director general at Israel's Ministry of Foreign Affairs, arrived in Athens. Evangelos Averoff told Fischer that Greek–Israeli relations suffer from 'a chronic disease' which should not be transmitted to relations between Cyprus and Israel. The Israelis interpreted this statement to mean that Greece would urge Makarios to maintain 'equal friendship with everyone'.[179] Despite the newspaper reports, the Israeli Ministry of Foreign Affairs concluded that Athens had made no promises to Nasser during his visit to Greece – or vice versa – about how Cypriot–Israeli relations might unfold.[180] Nevertheless, it appeared certain that with the approaching date of the Cypriot declaration of independence, 16 August

---

[176] ISA/RG93/MFA/1008/4, Levin to British Commonwealth Division (882/110.10קפר – 15.6.1960), Levin's conversation with Christopoulos.

[177] Evripidis Ioannou, 'The United Arab Republic anxious for full independence in Cyprus – Conclusions from talks between President Nasser and the Greek government', *Alithia*, 13.6.1960.

[178] ISA/RG93/MFA/1008/4, Levin to British Commonwealth Division (882/110.10קפר – 15.6.1960), Levin's conversation with Christopoulos.

[179] Ibid. (635/110.10קפר – 18.7.1960). Cf. ISA/RG130/MFA/2293/8, Fischer to Yahil (394/ב – 18.7.1960), and Israel State Archives, Gilead (ed.), *Documents*, vol. 14, 640 no. 412. Cf. 6.1.6.

[180] ISA/RG93/MFA/1008/4, Levin to Yahil (935/110.10קפר – 27.6.1960).

1960, the UAR would increase pressure on Makarios to suspend all contact with the Israelis.

Israel's assessments were confirmed. On 9 June 1960, while Nasser was in Athens, Burhan Dajani, the president of the Arab Chambers of Commerce, Industry and Agriculture, who was of Palestinian origin, and Malek Shahab, adviser to the Chamber of Commerce in Beirut, arrived in Nicosia.[181] After a week of meetings with entrepreneurs and officials, they held a press conference that had quite an impact. After outlining the opportunities opening up for the Cypriot economy in the extensive Arab market, they also noted that all Cypriot companies or individual entrepreneurs who continued to have dealings with Israel or falsified the certificates of origin of Israeli products and diverted them to Arab countries would be put on the 'Black List' and suffer the consequences, and that if Cyprus wished to attract Arab tourists, it would have to first stop the flow of tourists from Israel.[182]

The statements issued by Burhan Dajani and Malek Shahab provoked a strong reaction from Israeli Consul Zeev Levin, who accused them of trying to 'disrupt the smooth commercial life of Cyprus through words of hate'.[183] The Turkish Cypriot newspaper *Bozkurt* responded similarly with comments which were reprinted by Greek Cypriot newspapers. The threat of being blacklisted had terrified many entrepreneurs, a fact widely cited in the local press.[184]

Aside from those severe warnings directed at the island's business community, the Egyptian side sought to establish official mechanisms that would monitor compliance with the Arab embargo on Israel. Moreover, Israel's consulate had been informed that within the framework of the meetings of the second Afro-Asian Economic Conference which took place in Cairo from late April to early May 1960, high-ranking officials from the Egyptian Ministry of Commerce explored the possibility of establishing a permanent Arab boycott office in Nicosia to verify on the spot whether or not Cypriot businesses were adhering to the boycott.[185] Such a step would potentially cause great difficulties for local business owners who maintained trade relations with Israel. At the receiving end of these unofficial exploratory talks was the general secretary of the Federation of Trade and Industry of Cyprus, Costas Montis, who represented Cyprus at the conference. The Israeli consulate knew that Montis was in favour of developing stronger economic ties between Cyprus and the Arab world. His stance was not politically nuanced but based exclusively on the economic conditions of the times and the fact that the Arabic market was much larger than Israel's.[186] Nonetheless, when

[181] ISA/RG93/MFA/1007/11, Transcripts of recorded statements made by Burhan Dajani and Malek Shahab at the press conference they gave in Nicosia on 12.6.1960 (document not officially logged).
[182] ISA/RG93/MFA/1007/6, Levin to Political-Financial Planning Division (884/110.12קפר – 15.6.1960). *Fileleftheros, Ethnos, Ethniki, Haravgi* and *Eleftheria*, 15.6.1960.
[183] Ibid.
[184] ISA/RG130/MFA/8317/7, *Times of Cyprus*, 'Arab Challenge to Cyprus – Visiting trade chief says "be careful, or we won't like it" – "We'll blacklist if you touch Israel" warning', 11.6.1960.
[185] ISA/RG93/MFA/1007/11, Eshkol to Political-Financial Planning Division (780/553.1קפר – 25.5.1960), Eshkol did not name his sources in his report. Cf. *Fileleftheros*, 'The United Arab Republic sends trade delegation to Cyprus – The Archbishop's message to the Afro-Asian Conference was enthusiastically received – The actions of the Cypriot delegation at the conference', 10.5.1960.
[186] ISA/RG93/MFA/1007/11, Eshkol to Economic Affairs Division (1446/553.1 – 24.10.1960), and Research Division to Israel's Embassy in Nicosia (965/ערב – 2.12.1960).

Egyptian officials explained their thinking to him, he tried to discourage them, in an apparent effort to protect his compatriot entrepreneurs who happened to have commercial ties with Israel. According to information collected by Israel's consulate in Nicosia, Montis cleverly countered the Egyptian proposal with the specious argument that the establishment of an Arab boycott office in Cyprus to monitor the embargo against Israel would run contrary to Makarios' commitment to follow a policy of neutrality on the Arab–Israeli dispute. According to Montis, there would be negative reactions not only from the Israelis but also from the Turkish Cypriots, who were friendly to Israel. The most important counterargument, however, was based on the belief that Greek Cypriot entrepreneurs would also react, whether they supported Makarios or not. This would damage the positive image of the UAR and Nasser in Cyprus and would have a negative long-term impact on economic dealings with the Arab world.[187]

When Costas Montis returned from Cairo, the adviser on Economic Affairs to the Israeli consulate, Nachum Eshkol, asked to meet with him and ask him directly whether the Egyptians were in fact planning to set up such a control mechanism on the island. Perhaps because Montis did not want to become further involved, he refuted the information. Nevertheless, Eshkol, believing that the sources who had informed him were more reliable, was not convinced by what Montis had to say and in his report stated with certainty that the UAR was planning to open a 'Boycott Compliance Office' in Cyprus.[188] Despite everything, the supposed undertaking never materialized.

Until then, offices monitoring compliance with the boycott on Israel operated in all member states of the Arab League, supported by their local embassies and consuls around the world. The fact that Egypt was planning to establish similar mechanisms in a non-Arab country shows the extent to which the UAR wished to control independent Cyprus' international trade, and, ultimately, to shape its foreign policy against Israel.

The arrival in Cyprus of the adviser to the UAR embassy in Athens, Salahaddin Al-Sahrawi, in late July of 1960 – two weeks prior to the declaration of Cypriot independence – was viewed by the Israelis as an attempt by the Nasser regime to assuage the fears of Greek Cypriot entrepreneurs. In an interview in *Fileleftheros* published on 10 August 1960, Al-Sahrawi made no reference to relations between Cyprus and Israel. He focused on the hopeful prospects opening up for Cyprus and the UAR in the area of trade, with reference to the impending provision of logistic assistance and the arrival of Arab tourists on the island. He did not neglect to mention the British bases, which threatened the national sovereignty and security of the UAR, pointing out that his country trusted the people of the island never to 'allow Cyprus to become a springboard for aggressive action against the Arabs'.[189]

Al-Sahrawi's statements were well received by the Greek Cypriot press but not by the Turkish Cypriot *Bozkurt* which spoke of 'Egyptian fellahs with expansionist views'

[187] Ibid., Eshkol to Political-Financial Planning Division (780/553.1קפר – 25.5.1960).
[188] Ibid.
[189] ISA/RG93/MFA/1008/4, *Fileleftheros*, 'Salah Al-Din Al-Sahrawi speaks to "Fileleftheros" on relations between Cyprus and the UAR – They will cover all activities and all sectors – "Ready to also provide technical assistance if asked". Cyprus in a position to develop its tourism', 10.8.1960.

whom Cyprus would nevertheless 'manage to deter, with assistance from Greece, Turkey and the British bases'.[190] It would seem that *Bozkurt* accurately represented the anti-Arab sentiments of the Turkish Cypriot leadership. Indicatively, the formal meeting between Al-Sahrawi and Fazıl Küçük lasted 'barely five minutes' as noted with satisfaction by the Israeli consul in his report.[191]

When the day for declaring independence drew near, and on the face of it, relations between Makarios and Nasser continued to be excellent, something seemed to have changed. Contrary to what had taken place in 1959, at the ninth anniversary celebration of the Nasserist military coup on 23 July 1960, the UAR decided not to invite the ministers of the Makarios Transitional government this time. Invited to Cairo in their stead was Nikos Sampson, a member of EOKA and a Grivas follower, who was given a medal 'in recognition of his services during the Anglo-French attack on Suez in 1956'.[192]

This tactic was not resorted to out of the blue. As Zeev Levin had been informed by the US consul to Nicosia, Taylor Belcher, on 22 July 1960 – the eve of the UAR national holiday – Nasser warned Makarios that relations between Cyprus and the UAR would be suspended if Cyprus established any form or level of diplomatic relations with Israel.[193] For his part, Makarios sent a congratulatory telegram to Nasser on the national holiday while all Greek Cypriot newspapers dedicated full-page features describing the celebrations taking place in Cairo – including the bestowal of the medal on Samson.

On 2 August 1960, and after a delay of ten days, Nasser sent a telegram of thanks to Nicosia. However, the contents were addressed primarily to the Greek Cypriot residents of the island, and only then to the leadership of the country about to become independent:

> I was deeply touched by Your congratulatory message and Your noble sentiments on the occasion of our celebrations. I thank You warmly and take this opportunity to stress that the people of the UAR have warm and heartfelt feelings for the People of Cyprus and share their joy in view of the acquisition of their own independence. We admire the heroic struggle of the Cypriots and hope that, under Your leadership, they will gain the position they deserve without delay. I have the pleasure of addressing to You my most sincere wishes for personal health and happiness and wish for the People of Cyprus the realisation of their expectations of grandeur and glory.[194]

[190] ISA/RG93/MFA/1008/4, Levin to Middle East Division (1187/110.10קפר – 15.8.1960). Cf. *Times of Cyprus*, 'Arab envoy hits back at report', 11.8.1960.
[191] ISA/RG93/MFA/1008/4, Levin to British Commonwealth Division(1099/110.10קפר – 25.7.1960), and Levin to Middle East Division (1187/110.10קפר – 15.8.1960).
[192] ISA/RG93/MFA/1008/4, *Fos*, 'Great honour bestowed on a Cypriot fighter by President Nasser – Mr Nikos Sampson officially invited to the 9th anniversary of Egypt's independence in recognition of his services during the period of the Anglo-French attack against Suez', 20.7.1960.
[193] ISA/RG93/MFA/1008/4, Levin to Yahil and British Commonwealth, Middle East, Western Europe, US divisions (143/144-24.7.1960).
[194] ISA/RG93/MFA/1008/4, *Fileleftheros* and *Eleftheria*, 'Nasser's heartfelt message to the people of Cyprus', 3.8.1960. *Ethnos*, 'Nasser to the Ethnarch', 3.8.1960.

On the eve of the declaration of Cypriot independence, the UAR could not have harboured any illusions. The Republic of Cyprus would establish diplomatic relations with Israel, as there was no way to avoid doing so. The initiative of recognizing the newly established Cypriot state came from the Israeli side, but Israel's ten-year diplomatic presence on the island was in any case one of several pro-West legacies of British sovereignty. Egypt's persistent efforts to terminate any contact between Israel and Cyprus proved ineffective, particularly since the Turkish Cypriot vice president had the constitutional right to exercise a veto against any attempt by Makarios to give in to Nasser's demands.

Makarios was well aware of how important the UAR was – and would continue to be – for his homeland. Yet at the same time he knew that if the new state were to become a satellite of the Arab world, it would draw Cyprus into the endless Ara–Israeli dispute, with unpredictable future consequences. After all, the constitutional rights instituted in favour of the Turkish Cypriot vice president provided Makarios with a valid alibi – if not an ostensible one, which institutionally at least, 'required' the Republic of Cyprus to maintain 'an equal friendship with all peoples in the region', regardless of the personal intentions of its Greek Cypriot president. This would explain what proved to be the completely sincere assurances Spyros Kyprianou offered Zeev Levin: that the UAR would not impose sanctions on Cyprus if the latter established diplomatic relations with Israel as well. Kyprianou had cited the words of UAR Foreign Minister Mahmood Fawzi.[195] Thus, since Egyptian diplomacy was fully aware of the real situation, it is logical to assume that the same was true for the president of the UAR, Gamal Abdel Nasser.[196]

Nevertheless, the Israeli Ministry of Foreign Affairs reports under review do not reveal the reasons that led Makarios to decide on 12 August 1960, that the UAR embassy in Cyprus should first become operational and only then, after a six-month delay, would the Israeli embassy in Nicosia be opened. Küçük's persistent refusal to agree to the solution Makarios had proposed to the 'Israeli problem' and the resourceful intervention on Israel's behalf by the Greek American Spyros Skouras shed light on one side of a series of behind-the-scenes diplomatic manoeuvres, just a few days before the Cypriot Republic was due to declare its independence, 16 August 1960.[197] The archival sources of the Egyptian and Cypriot foreign ministries from that time would surely have much to add.

6.2.3 Lebanon's policy in Cyprus during the Transitional Period, in Israeli diplomatic reports

As a result of the outbreak of the Suez Crisis in October 1956, diplomatic relations between Britain and Egypt were suspended, and Egypt's Consulate in Nicosia was

---

[195] Cf. 6.1.5.
[196] ISA/RG93/MFA/1007/15, Levin to Nall, 799/103.2קפר – 27.5.1960). During his meeting with Zeev Levin, Spyros Kyprianou cited a conversation he had had with UAR Foreign Minister Mahmood Fawzi. Cf. 6.1.6.
[197] Cf. 6.1.6.

closed. In consequence, the Greek consulate in Nicosia administered the bureaucratic matters of Egyptian citizens which were later handled by the United Arab Republic, established through the union of Egypt and Syria on 1 February 1958. After Egypt, Lebanon was the second Arab country with official diplomatic representation in Cyprus. When the Egyptian consulate closed, the Lebanese consulate assumed the role of guardian of Arab interests on the neighbouring island.

When Israel's consulate was opened in Nicosia[198] on 28 August 1950, the Consul of Lebanon did not maintain any contact, official or social, with his Israeli counterpart. Following the signing of the London–Zurich Agreements and during the Transitional Period, the Lebanese consulate, in coordination with the UAR and the Arab League, moved systematically to avert the formation of bilateral diplomatic relations between Cyprus and Israel, to reduce Israel's economic presence on the island and to improve the Arab position locally at a political, economic and public relations level.

From February 1959 to August 1960, the actions of the Lebanese consulate in Nicosia focused on two key issues: improving the political role of the Cypriot Maronites, who had strong historical, cultural and religious ties with the Maronites of Lebanon – and implementing the decisions of the Arab League which had instituted the economic boycott on Israel.

6.2.3.1 Lebanon and the Cypriot Maronites

6.2.3.1.1 Lebanon's interest in the status of Maronites in the Cypriot political system

The settlement of the Cypriot dispute achieved in Zurich and London in 1959 formalized the political coexistence of the two major ethnic communities on the island: The Greek Cypriots and the Turkish Cypriots. The principle of bicommunalism serves as the fundamental basis for the provisions of the Cypriot Constitution which establish the competences of the Greek Cypriot President and the Turkish Cypriot vice president, the composition of the House of the Representatives, the Ministerial Council, the judicial system, public services, local administrative authorities and so on. Greek and Turkish were recognized as the official languages of the Republic of Cyprus,[199] and it was stipulated that two Communal Chambers would be established, one Greek and one Turkish, charged with preserving the cultural identity of each community

---

[198] Cf. 2.3.
[199] According to the Cyprus Act enacted by the British Parliament of 27.7.1960 (*Part II – Appendix E: Statement of Her Majesty's Government Concerning the Rights of Smaller Religious Groups in Cyprus*), all minority rights that were already protected in the constitution and the law during the British rule would continue to be protected in the Republic of Cyprus. The British colonial law was laid down in the letter and spirit of the pre-existing Ottoman edict *Hatt-ı Hümmayun* of 18.2.1856. Cf. Cypriot Constitution/1960, Article 110, para. 3, Cypriot Constitution/1960, Article 111, Kriton Tornarites, *To Politeiakon Dikaion tis Kypriakis Dimokratias* [*The Constitutional Law of the Cypriot Republic*] (Nicosia: Kentron Epistimonikon Erevnon, 1982), 18; and Alexandros-Michael Chatzilyras, *I Kypriaki Dimokratia kai oi Thriskeftikes Omades* [*The Cypriot Republic and the Religious Groups*] (Nicosia, 2012), 40 and 86–8.

separately, (the curriculum for both Greek and Turkish schools, cultural and athletic associations for both communities and so forth).[200]

However, in addition to the Greek and Turkish Cypriots living in Cyprus in 1960, there were other population groups with a discrete identity. The London–Zurich Agreements had not stipulated an institutional framework that would govern these groups after the declaration of independence.

According to the census carried out in 1960 by the British, the people living on the island were as follows: 3,608 Armenians, the majority of whom were Orthodox Christians belonging to the Armenian Apostolic Church and the rest, Catholics and Evangelicals;[201] 2,752 Maronite Catholics;[202] and 4,505 Roman Catholics mostly from European countries (France, Italy, Austria, Britain, the Dalmatian coast and Malta). British colonial law stipulated the status of these ethno-religious groups according to the letter and spirit of the Ottoman edict *Hatt-ı Hümmayun,* ratified by the Sublime Porte on 18 February 1856 immediately after the end of the Crimean War. Therefore, during the long period of British colonial rule on the island, discrete freedoms were recognized for the Armenians, Maronites and Latins of Cyprus as well as the administrative independence of their ecclesiastical bodies. However, this did not mean that there had been no cases of discrimination from time to time against one or the other population group at a local or pan-Cyprian level when local authorities had their own political interests to serve.[203] The mixed committee charged with preparing the final text of the Cypriot Constitution was called upon to decide what the status of certain discrete groups would be in the new Cypriot polity.

During the Transitional Period (February 1959–August 1960), the only third country to express a special interest in this particular issue was Lebanon. The Beirut government focused its attention on the political status of the Cypriot Maronites, a community with historical ties to the politically and financially strong Maronite community of Lebanon.[204] Lebanon's interest in the Maronites of Cyprus was based on the following key factors:

Under the first Lebanese Constitution of 1926 and up to the present time, ethnic origin is the primary criterion for determining the composition of state institutions, proportional parliamentary representation and staffing of the public sector. The Cypriot bicommunal system instituted by the London–Zurich Agreements was completely understandable to Lebanon, as it bore significant similarities to its own constitutional model. The Lebanese, and particularly the Lebanese Maronites, considered it a given that the Cypriot followers of the same religious dogma were entitled to have an independent role in their country's political system.

The US invasion of Lebanon in July 1958[205] occurred following an appeal by the country's pro-West Maronite President, Camille Chamoun. The ethnic conflict in Lebanon between the pro-West Christians and the pro-Nasser Muslims had worsened

[200] Tornarites, *Politeiakon Dikaion,* 19–20.
[201] Chatzilyras, *Thriskeftikes Omades,* 45.
[202] Ibid., 59.
[203] Ibid., 71.
[204] Ibid., 55–67.
[205] Cf. 3.6.4.

dangerously. The departure of American forces and the national unity government formed under the moderate Sunni leader Rashid Karami failed to dampen political passions. Despite the difficulties he faced, Karami had managed to keep his country away from major involvements, maintaining a fine balance both at home and at a regional level. Thus Lebanon, through subtle diplomatic manoeuvring, ultimately evaded becoming overly identified with the UAR's anti-West rhetoric, while also avoiding the hard-core pro-West Baghdad Pact. This did not mean that the risk of yet another civil war had been eliminated. When the London–Zurich Agreements were signed, the Beirut government needed an important pretext to unite divided public opinion in the country. In an attempt to foster a sense of national unity, Beirut and the Lebanese media pointed to the necessity for safeguarding the constitutional rights of Maronites living in Cyprus. As a result, the Cypriot Maronites were perceived as an ethnic minority that also warranted the protection of Lebanon – their own mother country.

Lebanon's ambition to improve the political role of Maronites in neighbouring Cyprus was in line with the Arab League's intention to strengthen Cypriot ties with the Arab world and to halt Israel's political and economic penetration of the island. Lebanon found an important supporter in Nasser due to his influence on the Greek Cypriot community and Archbishop Makarios in particular.

Finally, of critical importance were the strong ties between the Cypriot Maronites and the Maronite Church of Lebanon. The decision by the Ottomans in 1673 to move the seat of the Maronite Archbishopric of Cyprus to Lebanon proved fateful. Since that time, and over the next three centuries, their distinctive religious identity was shaped by the neighbouring Arab country. The Maronite Archbishop of Cyprus was represented on the island by the vicar general (the protopriest of the village of Kormakitis at any given time), but the most critical decisions that determined Maronite interests on the island were made in Lebanon, and the Maronite Church of Lebanon in particular.[206] The Maronite Church of Lebanon had always greatly influenced the Cypriot Maronites through education and the preservation of religious customs. At the same time, Cypriot Maronites were outward-looking and very active in trade and the public life of their island, eventually becoming an integral part of the multicultural Cypriot reality. Once the Lebanese state was created, the Maronite Church there acquired strong political influence, cultivating relations of interdependence with the higher echelons of government.

Since it first opened (in late August 1950) and until the beginning of the Transitional Period, the Israeli Consulate in Nicosia had not paid any attention to the political role of the local Maronite element and had not developed contacts with any of its members. Israel's contact with the powerful community of Maronites in Lebanon was equally non-existent. It was only fifteen years later, in 1975, when the Lebanese Civil War broke out that an alliance was formed between the Maronites of Lebanon and the State of

---

[206] Ibid., 63. The seat of the Maronite Archbishopric of Cyprus returned to Cyprus in 1988 which has been based in Nicosia since that time.

Israel.[207] If that rapprochement had taken place during the period 1958–60, it is possible the Israelis would have looked more kindly on the enhancement of a political role for the Maronites of Cyprus.

During the Transitional Period, the Israelis carefully monitored Lebanon's attempts to improve the Maronites' position in the Cypriot political system. Noting the sudden activity of the Lebanese Consulate, Israel could see that Beirut, with Cairo's help, wanted to highlight the Lebanese origins of the island's Maronites in order to secure a permanent pro-Arab element that could influence local decision-making centres. If such a role were enshrined politically and institutionally, Maronite influence would be able to serve as an additional obstacle to the establishment of normal diplomatic relations between the Republic of Cyprus and Israel. Moreover, the Israelis believed the local Maronite community, having secured the support of Lebanon, or even Nasser would be able to act as a permanent pro-Arab lever to put pressure on the local political leadership of both Greek and Turkish Cypriots.

Being aware of these facts, the Israeli Ministry of Foreign Affairs adopted a 'wait-and-see' approach, closely monitoring the impact Lebanon's diplomatic activity would have at a local level, as well as on Athens and Ankara. At the same time, it tried to reach the mixed committee, which had not yet completed its work on the Cypriot Constitution – but without success.

At this point, it is worth noting that Lebanon did not express the same interest in the political role of the Armenians of Cyprus, even though the Armenian community in Lebanon also played a significant role in that country's political system. The meagre information included in related reports from the Israeli Consulate in Nicosia indicates that Lebanese diplomacy had tried to rally the Armenians of Cyprus in its favour. Those who belonged to the leftist *Tashang* political faction seemed to respond positively. Such was not the case, however, with Armenians who were more prosperous and more sympathetic to the Right-liberal *Ramgavar* faction. According to the only report filed by Israeli Consul Zeev Levin on this particular issue,[208] his Lebanese counterpart, Michel Farah, had threatened to revoke the Lebanese citizenship of certain Armenian businessmen who were permanent residents of Cyprus and had relatives and considerable wealth in Lebanon because they had business transactions with Israel.[209] Michel Farah's threats at that time seriously upset the Lebanese consulate's relations

---

[207] Around the late 1950s, Israel slowly began to cultivate behind-the-scenes contacts with non-Arab and/or non-Muslim minorities living in the Arab countries of the Middle East and North Africa. In the 1960s, those contacts were developed further as part of the so-called 'Periphery Doctrine', meaning Israel's overall effort to develop strategic cooperation with the governments of non-Arab countries in the greater region (e.g. Iran, Ethiopia), in order to diplomatically and militarily hold off hostile Arab countries. As part of this effort, Israel developed unofficial alliances with the Druze in Syria, the Kurds in Iraq, the Christians in South Sudan and isolated Berber tribes in Algeria. When the Lebanese Civil War broke out in 1975, the Maronites of Lebanon requested Israeli military assistance, which was given to them up to 1982. Cf. Yosef Olmert, *Miutim ba-Mizrakh ha-Tikhon* [*Minorities in the Middle East*] (Tel Aviv: Misrad ha-Bitakhon, 1986), 83–95, on the historical background of the Maronites' place in the Lebanese political system. Alper, *Medina Bodeda*, 72–81, on the non-Muslim/non-Arabic minorities in the Levant as a means of exercising regional policy by Israel in the 1950s and 1960s.

[208] ISA/RG93/MFA/1431/19, Levin to the West Europe Division (19.1.1961, not officially logged).

[209] Oron (ed.), *Middle East Record*, 181; and report in the Lebanese *Akhbar al-Usbu'*, 8.7.1960.

with a significant number of local Armenian businessmen in Cyprus.[210] In addition, they rekindled pre-existing political passions and personal rivalries between the right-wing *Ramgavar* and the leftist *Tashang* within the Armenian community of the island which expressed a more pronounced pro-Nasserist leaning, as Zeev Levin implies in his report.[211] In commenting on the stance of the right-wing *Ramgavar*, Levin counted this group among elements that supported the Cypriot–Israeli rapprochement, the establishment of bilateral diplomatic relations and the need for the Cypriot Republic to keep a safe distance from the Arab world. The result of all these variables – including the rather ill-fated actions of Consul Michel Farah – was Lebanon's failure to rally the Armenians of Cyprus to its side, even though they were greater in number and also wealthier than the Maronites of the island.

6.2.3.1.2 Maronite parliamentary representation in Cyprus as a Lebanese priority

A few weeks after the mixed committee commenced its work on the final text of the Cypriot Constitution, Maronite Archbishop Elie Farah made an official eight-day visit to Cyprus, the first such visit after the signing of the London–Zurich Agreements.[212] On 17 May 1959, he officiated at the Divine Liturgy of the Cathedral of Saint George in the Maronite village of Kormakitis, with Archbishop Makarios and the consul of Lebanon in Nicosia, Michel Farah, attending. At the end of the mass, the Maronite Archbishop made a reference to the excellent relations between the Maronites and Greek Cypriots, stressing that: 'We unite with the Greek community, to whose glorious fight for liberation we contributed as best as we could, we now stand with you, ready to help with all our forces to establish our Republic.'[213] Makarios, in his reply, thanked the Cypriot Maronites 'for their contribution to the fight for liberation of the Cypriot people' and assured them that the Maronites would have equal rights with the other citizens of the Republic of Cyprus.[214]

In anticipation of welcoming the Maronite Archbishop, Kormakitis had been decorated with the flags of Greece, Great Britain, the Vatican and Lebanon.[215] That semiological decoration with flags and the content of the speeches of Farah and Makarios about the contribution of the Maronites in EOKA's struggle against the British attracted the interest of Israeli diplomacy, which only then began to follow this new dimension of the Lebanese presence on the island with interest – but also with

[210] Cf. 6.2.3.2, the case of Cypriot impresario, Enger Krikor Mandossian, of Armenian descent.
[211] ISA/RG93/MFA/1431/19, Levin to the West Europe Division (19.1.1961, not officially logged). Report for 1960: 'we took advantage of the polarisation between "Tashang", which enjoys the Lebanese support, and the anti-Lebanese "Ramgavar", to intensify our activities against Lebanon'.
[212] *Fileleftheros*, 'The Maronite community enthusiastically welcomed Archbishop Farah yesterday – The Maronite Archeparch praised the Ethnarch Makarios and Dr Küçük – He proposed harmonious co-existence', 13.5.1959. *Haravgi*, 'The Maronite Archeparch arrived yesterday in Cyprus', 13.5.1959. *Eleftheria*, 'The Maronite Archeparch arrived yesterday in Cyprus – He wished progress and prosperity for the Republic of Cyprus', 13.5.1959.
[213] *Ethnos*, 'The Maronites standing by the Ethnarch – The visit on the day before yesterday in Kormakitis', 19.5.195.
[214] Ibid.
[215] ISA/RG93/MFA/2156/7, Leshem to British Commonwealth and Middle East divisions (102/495/59-18.5.1959). Cf. *Neoi Kairoi*, 'The Archbishop and the Governor visited Kormakitis yesterday', 18.5.1959.

surprise. That celebratory mass in Kormakitis was the first opportunity for the Israeli Ministry of Foreign Affairs Research Division to begin systematically monitoring reports in the Lebanese press related to the Maronites in Cyprus. Certain pointed comments published in Greek Cypriot newspapers, which were less than complimentary about the Maronite stance during British rule also made quite an impression. In particular, they described Maronite relations with the colonialist regime as inordinately smooth. Indicative of this was a humorous column in *Fileleftheros* under the pseudonymous byline '*Djiypriotis*' ('Cypriot') explaining why the anonymous author, a Greek Cypriot, did not attend the Divine Mass held in honour of the Maronite Archbishop, and insinuating the 'Anglophile' stance of the local Maronite element.[216] The caustic comments of *Djiypriotis* apparently correlated with the attitudes of some Greek Cypriots at the time. Also of interest was an excerpt from a speech by a British MP who, in addressing the House of Representatives in March 1960, argued in favour of supporting the Cypriot Maronites (economically or politically) after the declaration of Cypriot independence, saying that 'the Maronite Community had shown constant loyalty, especially during the last few years'.[217]

Following Maronite Archbishop Elie Farah's visit to Cyprus in May 1959, and over the next four months, the issue of the Maronites' political role in the developing political system of independent Cyprus came under discussion more and more frequently in Lebanon. According to Lebanese newspaper articles, the topic had been raised by a member of the Beirut government directly with the ministers of the Cypriot Transitional government, Tassos Papadopoulos, Paschalis Paschalides, Glafcos Clerides and Fazıl Plümer, as well as with the head of the Greek delegation on the mixed constitutional committee, Themistoklis Tsatsos, when they arrived in Lebanon in mid-August 1959[218] at the government's invitation to attend the arts festival in the city of Baalbek.[219] Tassos Papadopoulos made repeated visits to Lebanon in September 1959, after which the Lebanese press announced that by the middle of the month, Lebanese officials would visit Cyprus to 'continue talks' without any official announcement of the issues to be discussed.[220]

According to a confidential report by Israeli consul, Zeev Levin, the frequent contacts between Cypriot and Lebanese officials focused on the issue of parliamentary representation for Cypriot Maronites.[221] The confidential information collected by the Israelis was soon confirmed: In early September 1959, three days before Tassos Papadopoulos' departure for Beirut, Consul Michel Farah arrived in the Lebanese capital for consultation on this very topic.

[216] *Fileleftheros*, column, 'Kypriaka imeronychtia' ['Cypriot days and nights'], 20.5.1959.
[217] *Cyprus Mail*, 'Financial aid for Maronites', 11.3.1960.
[218] ISA/RG130/MFA/3570/12, Levin to the British Commonwealth Division, copies to the Middle East Division and Research Division (951/59-27.8.1959 confidential report). Cf. *L'Orient*, 25.8.1959.
[219] Cf. 6.2.3.2, on the invitation from the Lebanese government to the Cypriot ministers and Themistoklis Tsatsos to attend the cultural festival of Baalbek (20.8.1959–24.8.1959).
[220] ISA/RG130/MFA/3570/12, Research Division (1257/ג – 11.9.1959). Cf. *Al-Hayat*, 9.9.1959.
[221] ISA/RG130/MFA/3570/12, Levin to British Commonwealth, Middle East, West Europe divisions (1050/59-10.9.1959, confidential report).

On 3 September 1959, the Beirut newspapers openly broached the subject of the 'Lebanese minority in Cyprus', the protection of which was directly linked for the first time with the need to prevent Israeli encroachment on the island.[222] There was no longer any room for doubt that Lebanon attached a national identity to the Maronite religious community in Cyprus, aspiring to include it in the general framework of the Arab–Israeli diplomatic tug of war so critically important at the time for the Cypriot political leadership and Archbishop Makarios personally. The Greek Cypriots would have to deal with one more issue of separate communal representation with constitutional implications, while the Turkish Cypriots were concerned that with the emergence of a 'third community' in Cyprus, they might lose some of the privileges they had secured with the London–Zurich Agreements. These concerns may have been the true reason behind the refusal of Rauf Denktaş, Nihat Erim and Suat Bilge – all members of the mixed constitutional committee – to attend the Baalbek festival in August 1959.[223] Apparently, they had declined the invitation in order to avoid any attempt by the Lebanese government to extract a commitment or at least a statement regarding the parliamentary representation of the Maronites – an issue that was increasingly on the Lebanese agenda.

As the Israelis followed Lebanon's movements, mainly through reports in the Lebanese newspapers, they realized that Beirut was taking a belated interest in the Cypriot Maronites. Their assessment was that Lebanon had decided to follow the example of other countries in the region which in order to intervene in the internal affairs of their neighbours, elevated distinct ethnic or religious groups to national minorities in need of protection. Iran followed a similar tactic with the Shia Muslims of Iraq, Syria with the Arab inhabitants of the Turkish Hatay Province (Alexandretta) and Turkey with the Turkomans of Syria and Iraq. On the other hand, it was impressive that a small, multi-ethnic and divided country like Lebanon dared to imitate the policies followed by far stronger countries, as it sought to acquire a role in the Cypriot political landscape. The Israelis believed that the Beirut government would not have dared to harbour such ambitions without first securing the support of a truly powerful country. Their suspicions centred on Nasser's Egypt, the only Arab country in the region that was also seeking to establish a presence on the neighbouring island at a political and economic level.

The Israeli Ministry of Foreign Affairs knew that if it expressed its opinion on Lebanon's pursuits publicly, it would be handing the Arab-friendly voices in Cyprus a chance to accuse Israel of interfering in their internal affairs. Besides, the matter of the Cypriot Maronites' constitutional position was indeed an internal matter for the Republic of Cyprus, and on the face of it, did not directly impact bilateral Cypriot–Israeli relations. On the other hand, it was clear to the Israelis that Lebanon's real interest – and consequently that of the UAR – was not the defence per se of the minority rights of the Cypriot Maronites. According to Israel's line of thinking, Beirut and Cairo aimed at

---

[222] ISA/RG130/MFA/3570/12, Research Division (1272/ג – 20.9.1959). Cf. *Al-Sahafa*, 'The Consul of Lebanon in Cyprus about Zionist activity on the island', 3.9.1959.

[223] Cf. 6.2.3.2, on the refusal of Rauf Denktaş, Nihat Erim and Suat Bilge to go to Lebanon in August 1959.

making the independent Republic of Cyprus a satellite country, and thus give its foreign policy a distinctively anti-Israeli character.[224] A 'pro-Arab' Maronite community with a strong political presence in Cyprus would certainly help achieve such an objective.

On 22 September 1959, Lebanese Ambassador Fouad Ammoun visited Cyprus for seven days as an envoy of the Beirut government. Although the precise reason for his visit was not announced, Cypriot newspapers reported his meetings on the island would focus mainly on the constitutional status of the Maronite community,[225] something which was confirmed by the Research Division of the Israeli Ministry of Foreign Affairs.[226] Although in response to questions from Cypriot reporters, Ammoun refuted any connection between his visit to the island with this particular issue, he also added cryptically that he had come to Cyprus merely as 'a simple messenger of the President of Lebanon', and that 'the Maronites are Cypriot citizens of the Republic of Cyprus and constitute part of the Cypriot people'.[227]

According to off-the-record information gathered by the Israelis, leading members of the local Maronite community laid out the following demands to the Lebanese envoy:

> To have the 'Maronite Community' constitutionally recognized as a distinct community – exactly as the Turkish Cypriots had been – differentiated from other Christian inhabitants of the island, Armenians and European Roman Catholics ('*Latins*').
> To constitutionally establish the proportional representation of Maronites in the Cypriot government, as provided for the Turkish Cypriots.
> To set up separate Maronite schools staffed by Lebanese teachers to teach the Arabic language.
> To appoint a permanent representative of the Cypriot Maronites in Lebanon who would be in close contact with the Beirut government.
> To determine a distinct proportion of Maronite participation in Cypriot public administration.[228]

Upon hearing these demands, Fuad Ammoun allegedly kept his distance. Without rejecting them outright, he promised to convey them to the Lebanese government so it could make decisions. At the same time, though, Ammoun assured the Maronites that one way or another the Cypriot political leadership planned to appoint instructors of Arabic – not only from Lebanon but from other Arab countries – to teach in Cypriot

---

[224] ISA/RG130/MFA/3570/12, Avraham Cohen, first assistant, Middle East Division, to Levin (14עמ׳.מ- – 23.9.1959).

[225] *Ethnos*, 'The Ambassador from Lebanon arrived yesterday in Cyprus', 23.9.1959.

[226] ISA/RG130/MFA/3570/12, Research Division to Levin (94-2576/27.10.1959).

[227] *Fileleftheros*, 'Lebanon will be amongst the first countries to recognize the Republic of Cyprus – Dr Ammoun conveyed the warm greetings of President Chehab to the Archbishop and Dr Küçük – Statement of Lebanon's special envoy', 24.9.1959. *Haravgi*, 'Mr Ammoun wishes the development of relations between Cyprus and Lebanon', 24.9.1959. *Ethnos*, 'Relations between Cyprus and Lebanon will be enhanced', 24.9.1959.

[228] ISA/RG130/MFA/3570/12, Research Division to Levin (94-2576/27.10.1959).

secondary schools, in view of the imminent expansion of economic relations between the Republic of Cyprus and the sizeable Arab market.[229]

As Israeli Consul Zeev Levin wrote in a confidential report, the Lebanese special envoy did not manage to extract a specific commitment from Makarios as to the exact way the Maronites would be represented (in the House of Representatives or the Communal Chambers and the number of Members of Parliament or representatives they would have) and by what process (election or appointment).[230] Levin also confirmed that the issue of teaching Arabic in Cypriot secondary schools had indeed been raised in the mixed constitutional committee. Although no specific decision had been reached by October 1959, the matter was to be reviewed in March 1960. However, in the event that it was approved, Arabic would not be taught at all Cypriot schools but only those with Maronite students.[231]

During the same period, Israel's interest had turned to the difference of opinion between the Maronites and the Latins. According to another confidential report by Levin, the Latins submitted a proposal to Maronite Archbishop Elie Farah, whereby all Roman Catholics on the island would have one common representative in the Cypriot Parliament. Farah refused their proposal, countering that 'the Maronites do not define themselves only as a religious community but also as an ethnic-Lebanese community' and that 'their Lebanese ethnic origin is the criterion that distinguishes the Maronites from the rest of the island's Roman Catholics'. However, relations between Latins and Maronites were further exacerbated by their split over which of the two communities would exercise more influence at the Terra Santa Catholic School in Nicosia.

These were the developments that ultimately led the Latins to take a separate position. Under these circumstances, they asked President Makarios to be recognized as a distinct religious community, to have their rights in the Terra Santa School legally established and to be considered members of the Greek Cypriot community with regard to the electoral process. The requests of the Latins were immediately accepted both by Makarios and the mixed constitutional committee – with the consent of the Turkish Cypriots and the representatives of Turkey.[232] However, the issue of the parliamentary representation of the Maronites was still unresolved.

Following this development, pressure exerted by the Lebanese Consul on Makarios intensified in November 1959, while the latter continued to hold his cards close to the vest.[233] According to a relevant report from Levin, a significant member of the Maronite community named Joseph Yamakis appeared to be strongly critical of Makarios' approach and threatened that unless Makarios committed to a distinct Maronite representation in the House of Representatives and the Communal Chamber – though without

---

[229] Ibid.

[230] ISA/RG130/MFA/3570/12, Levin to British Commonwealth, Middle East, West Europe divisions (1465/59-19.10.1959, confidential report).

[231] Ibid., Levin to the Middle East Division (1257/59-26.10.1959, confidential report).

[232] Ibid., Levin to British Commonwealth, Middle East, West Europe divisions (1465/59-19.10.1959, confidential report).

[233] Ibid., Levin to British Commonwealth, Middle East divisions (1341/59-5.11.1959).

clarifying which of the two – the entire community would abstain from all future elections.[234]

December 1959 was marked by a climate of underlying tension, until Makarios expressed his opinions at a meeting on 9 January 1960 with Lebanese Consul Michel Farah and Vicar General Ioannis Foradaris, in the presence of the head of the Greek delegation to the mixed constitutional committee, Themistoklis Tsatsos, and delegation member Konstantinos Hoidas. Makarios proposed that the Maronites be represented with one seat in the Communal Chamber, exactly as the Armenians were. The Maronite side counter-proposed one seat in the House of Representatives and another in the Communal Chamber.[235]

That meeting did not result in a mutually acceptable solution. Ten days later, the Maronite Archbishop Elie Farah, stated in the Lebanese press that during his visit to Cyprus in May 1959, he had discussed with Makarios, Küçük and Sir Hugh Foot the issue of the future constitutional status of the Maronite community in the independent Cypriot Republic. Farah stated that all three had committed to constitutionally ensuring Maronite representation by one or two seats in both the House of Representatives and the Communal Chambers, without specifying whether he was referring to the Greek Communal Chamber, the Turkish one, or both.[236]

In early March 1960, Zeev Levin was informed by a source allegedly close to the Maronite community that on the initiative of Nasser's Egypt, the Lebanese government had approved 10,000 Lebanese pounds to fund the instruction of the Arabic language in Cyprus.[237] This alleged intervention by the UAR, which may have contributed to the specific funding, confirmed Israel's speculation[238] that in reality, Lebanese protection of the Cypriot Maronites was one of various efforts by Nasser to turn the Cypriot Republic into an Arab satellite. According to Levin's source, the teaching of Arabic was initially to be assigned to local Maronite priests but in due course, Lebanese teachers would be sent to the island. It is worth noting, however, that on the eve of Cypriot independence, the mother tongue of the Cypriot Maronites was not Arabic. The residents of Kormakitis, the largest Maronite village on the island, spoke a distinct dialect with significant Arabic influences, whilst at the Maronite villages of Asomatos, Karpasia and Agia Marina, spoke the Greek Cypriot idiom.[239]

[234] Ibid., Levin to British Commonwealth, Middle East, West Europe divisions (1465/59-19.10.1959, confidential report).
[235] ISA/RG93/MFA/1431/25, *Haravgi, Ethnos* and *Ethniki*, 10.1.1960.
[236] ISA/RG93/MFA/1432/8, Department of Research (1507/ג – 22.1.1960), Lebanese *Al-Hayat*, 'Demand for constitutional rights for the Maronites in Cyprus', 17.1.1960. Cf. *Eleftheria*, 'Departing for Lebanon', 15.8.1959, and *Ethnos*, '27-member Cypriot delegations returned yesterday from Lebanon', 25.8.1959.
[237] ISA/RG93/MFA/1007/5, Levin to British Commonwealth Division (356/101.11רפק – 2.3.1960).
[238] ISA/RG130/MFA/3570/12, Cohen to Levin (14-פכ.מ – 23.9.1959).
[239] Decades later, in 1993, UNESCO named this Arabic-derived dialect spoken in Kormakitis as Cypriot Maronite Arabic (KMA), classifying it that same year as an endangered language. In 2004, the Council of Europe, following an on-site survey, included KMA (also known as *Sanna* – author's note: 'our language') in the category of regional-minority languages. In 2007, Maltese linguist Alexander Borg proposed the written form of KMA using Latin letters, enhanced with phonetic symbols similar to those used to accurately pronounce the Maltese language (also a Semitic and Arabic-

In London that month, following an initiative by members of the coalition government, the issues of parliamentary representation for the Maronites in Cyprus, and whether Britain would grant the request for a one-time payment of £80,000 (pounds sterling) in aid, was discussed in the House of Commons. After agreeing that relations between the Maronites and the British authorities in the recent past had been excellent, and that the older Radcliffe Plan provided for their representation with one seat in the House of Representatives, British Colonial Secretary Iain Macleod determined that the top priority going forward was to safeguard the Maronites' constitutional rights within the new Cypriot political system. Macleod was against the idea of providing the Maronites with financial assistance, 'as something like that could lead to further complications at an intercommunal level'.[240]

While the issue of Maronite representation continued to hold the interest of the Cypriot and Lebanese press, information began to leak regarding the Turkish Cypriots' view of developments and their strong reservations about the number of Maronite and Armenian parliamentary representatives and how they would be chosen.[241] Later, the Greek Cypriot press reported that the Greek Cypriots and the British agreed either to increase the number of Greek Cypriot seats in the House of Representatives from 35 to 37 or the joint concession of two seats – one by the Greek Cypriots and one by Turkish Cypriots – so that the Maronites and the Armenians would be represented by one member each.[242] Responding indirectly to such scenarios, the Turkish Cypriot newspaper *Bozkurt* made it clear from the start that the Turkish Cypriots would not agree to any change in the 35:15 ratio in the Cypriot Parliament, adding that, 'If the Armenians and the Maronites must be represented in the House of Representatives and the machinery of Government according to a specific ratio, this must be examined separately'.[243]

The Turkish Cypriots did not want to redefine the controversial issue of institutional community representation, perhaps because it might bring to light additional disagreements that were liable to compromise their position. Without discounting the possibility that the Greek Cypriots were also reluctant to enter additional negotiations, the sense derived from Greek Cypriot reports was that it was mainly the Turkish

related language). In 2008, the Republic of Cyprus recognized KMA as a minority language in Cyprus, based on the European Charter of Regional or Minority Languages of the Council of Europe. Cf. Chatzilyras, *Thriskeftikes Omades*, 62; and Alexander Borg, *Cypriot Arabic: A Historical and Comparative Investigation into the Phonology and Morphology of the Arabic Vernacular Spoken by the Maronites of Kormakitis Village in the Kerynia District of North-Western Cyprus* (Stuttgart: Komissionsverlag Steiner Wiesbaden, 1985). Cf. Brian Bielenberg and Costas Constandinou (eds), *The Sanna Project – Empowerment through Language Revival: Current Efforts and Recommendations for Cypriot Maronite Arabic* (Oslo: International Peace Research Institute, 2010); and Costas Constandinou, 'Why does the government refuse to protect Cypriot Maronite Arabic?', *Cyprus Mail*, 3.2.2008.

240 ISA/RG93/MFA/1007/14, *Fileleftheros*, 'The rights of the Maronites', 11.3.1960. *Cyprus Mail*, 'Financial aid for Maronites', 11.3.1960.
241 ISA/RG93/MFA/1007/14, *Eleftheria*, 'Representation of the Maronites in Ankara', 15.3.1960.
242 ISA/RG93/MFA/1007/14, *Eleftheria*, 'Turkish reservations about the Armenian and Maronite representation', 16.3.1960.
243 ISA/RG93/MFA/1007/14, *Fileleftheros*, 16.3.1960. Reprinted excerpts of the main article in the Turkish Cypriot newspaper *Bozkurt*.

Cypriots who were averse to Maronites in the House of Representatives. Although this conclusion was not entirely accurate, in comparison to the Greek Cypriots (who publicly maintained a more moderate stance), the Turkish Cypriots were quite vocal in numerous newspaper articles about their strong reservations while enjoying the ongoing support of Ankara.

In order to overcome Turkish Cypriot objections, Lebanese President Fuad Chehab sent former Lebanese ambassador to Turkey, Sheikh Khalil Takiedinne, to Ankara in mid-March 1960,[244] where he was soon joined by Lebanon's Consul to Nicosia, Michel Farah.[245] Their talks with the Turkish Minister of Foreign Affairs, Fatin Zorlu, and President Celâl Bayar did not bear fruit, and notwithstanding Takiedinne's optimistic statements to the press,[246] the Lebanese newspaper *Al-Hayat* began to prepare public opinion by predicting that no positive outcome was visible on the horizon.[247] Turkey continued to procrastinate in an effort to show the Lebanese envoy, that Ankara would not accept any change to the allocation of seats in the Cypriot Parliament.[248] The bicommunal Cypriot arrangement was already complicated enough and there was no room for a third, additional community.

The Turkish position on the representation of the Maronites in Cyprus played a pivotal role, as outlined in a confidential report by Israel's chargé d'affaires to Ankara, Moshe Alon, drafted right after the failure of the initial mediatory attempts by Takiedinne and Farah. According to that report, Turkish diplomat Hakki Aldin, who had formerly served in Beirut and was aware of the political balance in Lebanon, believed that Ankara, while seeming to understand the demands of the Maronites and Lebanese motives would never under any circumstances agree for a third community to sit in the House of Representatives. Nevertheless, Turkey was reluctant to discourage the special envoy sent by the president of Lebanon, first, so as not to disrupt Turkey's relations with pro-West Lebanon and second, so as not to force Beirut to seek Egyptian assistance and align itself with Nasser's regional ambitions. A characteristic example of Turkey's intentions was the fact that its administration did not reject the Lebanese envoy's proposal to revisit Ankara on 4 April 1960, because it wished to create the impression that there was still a chance of settling matters with Beirut. However, both Ankara and Athens knew perfectly well that the work of the mixed constitutional

---

[244] *Ethnos*, 'Representative of Lebanon in Turkey to discuss the Maronites of Cyprus', 13.3.1960. *Fileleftheros*, 'Sheikh of Lebanon travels to Ankara – Will discuss matters concerning the Maronites of Cyprus – Conveys message by Chehab', 13.3.1960.

[245] ISA/RG93/MFA/1007/14, *Fileleftheros*, 'The Consul to Cyprus departs for Ankara', 15.3.1960. Cf. *Haravgi*, 'The Consul General of Lebanon goes to Ankara – Will hold talks on the Maronites of Cyprus', 16.3.1960.

[246] ISA/RG93/MFA/1007/14, *Ethnos*, 'Talks in Ankara on the Maronites of Cyprus – The Lebanese envoy Mr Takiedinne expresses his satisfaction', 20.3.1960.

[247] ISA/RG93/MFA/1007/14, Research Division (1610/ג – 23.3.1960), Lebanese *Al-Hayat*, 'Turkey opposed to Maronites' representation in the House of Representatives', 20.3.1960.

[248] *Ethnos*, 'Talks in Ankara on the Maronites of Cyprus – The Lebanese envoy Mr Takiedinne expresses his satisfaction', 20.3.1960. *Fileleftheros*, 'The President of Lebanon sends message to Bayar on the rights of the Maronites in Cyprus', 20.3.1960. *Fileleftheros*, 'The rights of the Maronites in Cyprus', 23.3.1960. *Haravgi*, 'Yet unknown when talks will resume', 23.3.1960. Cf. ISA/RG93/MFA/1007/14, *Ethnos*, 'The Lebanese envoy to re-visit Ankara on the rights of the Maronites in Cyprus', 23.3.1960.

committee was essentially done, and a mere 48 hours later, on 6 April, the mixed committee approved the final text of the Constitution of Cyprus.[249]

Essentially, according to Aldin, the burden of rejecting Lebanon's proposals was taken on by Ankara rather than Athens, since the latter wished at all costs to avoid disrupting its relations with the Arab world. He also claimed that Greece and Turkey had already agreed not to allow any other community groups in the House of Representatives, and not to agree to any change in the 35:15 ratio of parliamentary seats.[250] At the same time, the Research Division of Israel's Ministry of Foreign Affairs confirmed that the Turkish government intended to propose formalizing the right of both Maronites and Armenians to choose through which of the two Communal Chambers[251] they would be represented.[252] It was this proposal that ultimately prevailed.[253]

In light of the above, Lebanon's efforts to provide for a distinct Maronite parliamentary presence were doomed to fail. Nevertheless, the final draft of the Cypriot Constitution introduced the concept of 'Religious Group', defined as:

> a group of persons ordinarily resident in Cyprus, professing the same religion and either belonging to the same rite or being subject to the same jurisdiction thereof, the number of whom, on the date of the coming into operation of this Constitution, exceeds one thousand out of which at least five hundred become on such date citizens of the Republic.[254]

According to the Cyprus Act, passed by the British Parliament on 29 July 1960, the constitutionally recognized religious groups of Cyprus were three: Armenians, Maronites and Latins.[255] All Cypriot nationals who belonged to these three religious groups, based on Article 3 of the Law on Religious Groups and Citizens (Method of Option) of 1960, were called upon to select by secret vote a representative of their religious group and to which of the two Communal Chambers (Greek or Turkish) their elected representatives would belong.[256] Indeed, a secret vote took place on 13

---

[249] Cf. 6.1.4.

[250] ISA/RG93/MFA/1007/14, Alon to Middle East Division (113.12/22.3.1960, strictly confidential telegram).

[251] The provisions of Articles 86–108 of the Cypriot Constitution of 1960 detail the competences and function of the Greek and Turkish Communal Chambers. In brief, their competences focus on handling all religious, cultural and educational issues, as well as the operation and supervision of charitable, cultural and athletic associations of a communal nature, the composition of courts entrusted with personal status decisions, etc.

[252] ISA/RG93/MFA/1007/14, Avraham Kidron, director of Research Division, to Levin (965/20-24.3.1960).

[253] ISA/RG93/MFA/1007/14, *Ethnos*, 'The Turks now accept the representation of minorities in the Communal Parliament', 29.3.1960. In the Cypriot journalistic parlance of that period, the 'Communal Chamber' was often referred to as the 'Communal Parliament'.

[254] Constitution of the Republic of Cyprus, 1960, Article 2 (3).

[255] Cyprus Act, 29.7.1960 (Part II – Appendix E: Statement concerning the Rights of Smaller Religious Groups in Cyprus). Cf. Achilles Emilianides, 'Legal Opinion on the Legal Personality of the Karpasha Church Committee of the Maronite Church of Cyprus', *Epitheorisi Kypriakou ke Evropaikou Dhikeou* [*Cyprus and European Law Review*], 11, *EKEΔ* 6 (2010): 164–9.

[256] Cypriot Law No. 7/1960, *Nomos peri Thriskeftikon Omadon kai Politon (Tropos Epilogis)* [*Law on Religious Groups and Citizens (Method of Option)*] was published in Appendix A of the *Official Gazette of the Republic of Cyprus* (No. 16/10.11.1960).

November 1960, and all three religious groups in Cyprus elected their representatives and all three decided to be represented in the Greek and not the Turkish Communal Chamber.[257]

Israel's interest was not limited to the way in which the negotiations were conducted, and the solution finally given to the question of Maronite representation in Cyprus; it was mainly focused on the extent to which Lebanon and the UAR were in a position to impose their own terms – as insignificant as they may have been – on the Cypriot political system. As Fazıl Küçük was alleged to have said to Zeev Levin, 'not even Makarios would want a proliferation of communities in the House of Representatives'.[258] Küçük had correctly surmised that Makarios, either through his enigmatic behaviour vis-à-vis the Lebanese and Maronite demands, or by speciously highlighting Turkish Cypriot objections to them, had ultimately led the Turkish Cypriot community and Turkey itself to become the main bulwark against any further Arab involvement in the intercommunal status quo that was then taking shape.[259]

The conclusions Israel drew from the way in which the matter of the Maronites' institutional representation was settled were optimistic. Both Makarios and Küçük, each in his own way, had finally rebuffed the efforts of both Lebanon and the UAR to infiltrate the mechanisms shaping Cyprus' system of government. By acting independently, Makarios and Küçük had maintained the intercommunal balance, as defined by the London–Zurich Agreements. Although it might easily be assumed that Makarios and Küçük had arranged this in advance, there was nothing in Israel's diplomatic reports from that period to indicate that this was so.

Meanwhile, Athens adopted a stance similar to that of Makarios, essentially letting Ankara set limits to Arab invasiveness. This served Israel's purposes as well, as it was not obliged to take steps to contain Arab efforts regarding the Maronite issue which would in any case have had little chance of succeeding. Although Israel's diplomats had realized early on that defending the minority rights of the Maronites was a pretext for establishing a permanent Arab presence in the Cypriot state system, they chose not to express any official position so as not to be accused of meddling in an issue that was clearly an internal one for Cyprus.

The Lebanese pursuit in the matter of Cypriot Maronites was assessed by the Israelis as an 'Arab failure'. The mild containment Makarios demonstrated vis-à-vis Lebanon's aims (and by extension, the aims of the UAR) was a pleasant surprise for the Israelis.

---

[257] According to the official announcement by the Public Information Office of the Republic of Cyprus on the results of the secret ballot conducted on 13.11.1960, 1,077 Armenians, 1,046 Maronites and 322 Latins chose to be represented by the Greek Communal Chamber, as opposed to 5 Armenians and 1 Latin who chose the Turkish Communal Chamber. Nevertheless, the actual rate of abstention remains unknown, though it appears it was particularly high amongst the Latin religious group. The census conducted that year recorded 3,628 Armenians, 2,752 Maronites and 4,505 Latins living in Cyprus (cf. 6.2.3.1.1). The census data do not provide a precise number of Armenians, Maronites or Latins who had acquired Cypriot nationality and had a right to vote on 13.11.1960.

[258] ISA/RG93/MFA/1007/14, Levin to Middle East Division (521/113/12קפר – 29.3.1960).

[259] Cf. 6.1.2, Views of Mehmet Cevat Açıkalın, Turkish ambassador to Rome, to his Israeli counterpart Eliahu Sasson on the need for Makarios to get support from anti-Nasserist regional factions (ISA/RG130/MFA/3736/3, Eliahu Sasson to Fischer – 51/מפר – 25.12.1959).

Makarios' position was seen as a positive indicator of the subsequent course of bilateral relations between Cyprus and Israel, only four months prior to the declaration of Cypriot independence. Nonetheless, their assessment proved overly optimistic.

In view of the first elections of 31 July 1960 – the first to elect the members of the House of Representatives – and given that, on the one hand, the anti-Makarios right-wing 'Democratic Union' party would not be in the running, while on the other hand a majority voting system would apply, it was clear in advance that all 35 candidates of Makarios' 'Patriotikon Metopon' ('Patriotic Front') party (which included 5 candidates nominated by AKEL), would take all 35 Greek Cypriot seats. Since mid-July, it had been rumoured that the ticket would also include a representative of the Maronites.[260] This information was not officially confirmed.

According to a relevant report by Zeev Levin,[261] on 20 July 1960, just two days prior to the official announcement of the election ballot line-ups, Makarios caught everyone off guard by suddenly replacing a candidate from his list for the Nicosia constituency with the Maronite economist Joseph Yamakis, who had criticized Makarios strongly in the recent past about his handling of the state representation of his community.[262] According to the information gathered by Levin, when Makarios' associates asked him why he had made this sudden move, he answered that 'he had promised the Lebanese'. This laconic answer, as Levin observed, put an end to any further questions, reactions or doubts.[263] Makarios had the first and final word on everything.

Indeed, when Cypriot newspapers published the official announcement of the party tickets on 24 July 1960, Joseph Yamakis was included in the Patriotikon Metopon line-up for the constituency of Nicosia.[264] During the election campaign, news reports described Yamakis as 'a "Patriotikon Metopon" candidate representing the Maronite community in the in Nicosia province'.[265] This was the wrong phrasing since the Constitution of Cyprus recognized a 'Maronite Religious Group', not a 'Maronite Community'. There was no provision for any community in the House of Representatives, other than the Greek and Turkish Cypriot communities. Therefore, the seats of the House of Representatives had to be filled by candidates from the constitutionally

[260] *Fileleftheros*, 'Talks continue regarding the Patriotic Front candidates – The Provincial Committees prepare a list for the Central Committee – 318 election centres all over Cyprus', 15.7.1960.
[261] ISA/RG93/MFA/1007/14, Levin to British Commonwealth Division (1095/113.1קפר -25.7.1960).
[262] ISA/RG130/MFA/3570/12, Levin to British Commonwealth, Middle East, West Europe divisions (1465/59-19.10.1959, confidential report).
[263] ISA/RG93/MFA/1007/14, Levin to British Commonwealth Division (1095/113.1קפר – 25.7.1960).
[264] *Fileleftheros*, 'The Elections Law (House of Representatives and Communal Chambers), 1959', 24.7.1960.
[265] *Fileleftheros*, pre-election entry of candidates' photographs, 22.7.1960. *Eleftheria*, '45 candidacies were submitted yesterday for the 35 Greek seats in the Central Parliament – No elections to be held in Paphos since the candidacies do not exceed the number of seats – Independent candidates submitted in Nicosia, 1 in Famagusta, 2 in Limassol, 2 in Larnaca and 2 in Kyrenia – The Turkish candidates', 22.7.1960. *Ethnos*, 'Landslide victory of the Patriotic Front expected in tomorrow's parliamentary elections', 30.7.1960. *Fileleftheros*, 'Election campaign ends with rallies for the Patriotic Front – The people will come to vote with indescribable enthusiasm – How the elections will run tomorrow', 30.7.1960. *Alithia*, 'Parliamentary elections held yesterday all over the island with exceptional order and peace – Very low voter turnout noted in the towns and rural areas – The election results in the various constituencies', 1.8.1960.

recognized communities, Greek and Turkish – and not from the three constitutionally recognized religious groups in Cyprus. The Israelis interpreted Yamakis' inclusion on the Patriotikon Metopon ticket and the 'inaccurate wording' in the press as Makarios' roundabout way of satisfying the Beirut government.

As expected, Yamakis was elected to Parliament, which meant that the Cypriot Maronites were represented 'twice', both in the House of Representatives, and in the Greek Communal Chamber, by the elected representative of their constitutionally established Religious Group, Ioannis Mavridis.[266]

Yamakis' election was particularly gratifying to the Lebanese press which presented the news as a national victory. In fact, two days before the elections, the Beirut paper *Al-Hayat* reported in its 29 July 1960 edition that:

> Thanks to the talks between the Ministry of Foreign Affairs and the government of Cyprus, a solution was found to the problem of the Maronites in Cyprus being represented in the Cypriot Parliament. It was announced that Archbishop Makarios has agreed to include a candidate from the Maronite community in the Greek party ticket in the next elections for the House of Representatives. The candidate is Joseph Yamakis. Furthermore, it has been decided that another Maronite candidate will be included in the Communal Chambers.[267]

This peculiar 'double' parliamentary representation of the Maronites led the Israelis to conclude once again that Makarios wished to avoid displeasing the regional Arab governments.[268] Given that there were only six weeks between the parliamentary elections of 31 July 1960 and the official declaration of Cyprus' independence, this particular move by Makarios only increased Israel's concerns about 'unpleasant' last-minute surprises, stemming from the archbishop's political omnipotence, regardless of what the relevant constitutional provisions did or did not dictate. In light of the above, Israel's apprehension focused on the credibility of Makarios' oft repeated assurances that he intended to establish normal diplomatic relations with Israel – while Arab diplomatic pressure was expected to increase in the period leading up to the official declaration of the independence of the Republic of Cyprus on 16 August 1960.[269]

6.2.3.2 Lebanon, the Arab boycott and Cypriot–Israeli relations

A few weeks after Makarios' return to Cyprus in April 1959, the Israeli Consulate in Nicosia, in collaboration with Israel's Tourism Organisation and the national air carrier El-Al, invited Greek and Turkish Cypriot tour operators and journalists to visit Israel. The reaction of Lebanese Consul Michel Farah was immediate.[270] He called the Greek

---

[266] It is noted that the Armenian religious group, although larger than the Maronite group, did not enjoy similar privileges and was represented exactly as stipulated by the Constitution, meaning by its elected representative in the Greek Communal Chamber.
[267] ISA/RG93/MFA/1007/14, Research Division (2038/ג – 2.8.1960), Lebanese *Al-Hayat*, 'The Maronites' representation in the legislative bodies of Cyprus', 29.7.1960.
[268] ISA/RG93/MFA/1007/14, Levin to British Commonwealth Division (1095/113.1קפר – 25.7.1960).
[269] Cf. 6.1.6.
[270] Cf. 6.1.

Cypriot travel agents who had been invited and warned them that if they visited Israel, their companies would immediately be placed on the 'Blacklist' of the boycott declared by the Arab League,[271] and all transactions between them and Lebanon or other Arab countries would be terminated. As a result, the main travel agencies on the island, namely Amathus Navigation Co. Ltd., Hull Blyth & Co., A.L. Mantovani & Sons Ltd. and Thornton & Pengelley, which were affiliates of Air Liban, Middle East Airlines, MisrAir (United Arab Airlines) and Air Jordan, respectively, did not send representatives to Israel. Only two small Turkish Cypriot travel agencies accepted Israel's invitation.[272]

This development was widely publicized by the press in Cyprus,[273] and troubled Israel greatly. It was a definite indication of how much influence the Lebanese Consulate exerted over the island's entrepreneurial activity. At the same time, it highlighted the inability of the Greek Cypriot Minister of Commerce and Industry, Paschalis Paschalides,[274] and the British Secretary for Economic Affairs, David A. Percival, to prevent similar occurrences in future.[275] In fact, when Percival asked the Lebanese consul to explain his intervention, Michel Farah countered with the claim that it was the Greek Cypriot travel agents who had contacted him to inquire whether there would be consequences if they were to accept Israel's invitation. Farah added that owing to his official capacity, he was obligated to inform them about the decisions of the Arab League and Lebanon regarding the sanctions they had imposed on entrepreneurs from third countries who violated the Arab boycott of Israel.[276]

At the same time, the Lebanese press began to comment on the risks involved in Israel's activities in Cyprus. *Al-Hayat* warned strongly and repeatedly about Israel's intentions to create a stable market for its products in Cyprus, to install special technical advisers there and to ensure the supply of cheap raw materials, similar to its solid presence in the developing countries of Asia and Africa. With regard to Cyprus in particular, the newspaper noted the island's ports which could be used as major transit points for Israeli imports and exports, or even as ideal sites for the falsification of certificates of origin for Israeli products in order to distribute them to Arab markets.[277] Such concerns were not unreasonable. It was true that the nearby Cypriot ports and airports, and Israel's increasing exports to the island were factors that could render the Arab boycott on Israel virtually ineffective.

A few weeks after Israel issued its invitation to the Cypriot tour operators, Lebanon countered with an invitation of its own. On 20 August 1959, a 27-member delegation from Cyprus left to attend the four-day art festival in Baalbek as official guests of the Lebanese government. The delegation included four ministers of the Transitional

[271] ISA/RG130/MFA/3570/12, Leshem to British Commonwealth Division with copy to the Middle East and Economic Affairs divisions, the Israeli Tourism Organisation and the national airline El-Al (41א/315/59-5.4.1959). Cf. 6.2.1.

[272] ISA/RG130/MFA/2570/12, Leshem to British Commonwealth Division (41א/328/59-8.4.1959).

[273] *Times of Cyprus*, 'That Israel trip "ban" could hit Cyprus tourist plans', 10.4.1959; and *Times of Cyprus*, 'Travel row: Israel protest', 15.4.1959.

[274] ISA/RG93/MFA/2156/7, Leshem to British Commonwealth Division (102/352/59-14.4.1959).

[275] Ibid., Leshem to British Commonwealth Division, with copy to the Middle East and Economic Affairs Divisions (102/333/59-10.4.1959).

[276] Ibid., Leshem to British Commonwealth Division (102/465/59-11.5.1959).

[277] ISA/RG130/MFA/3570/12, Research Division (1116/א-13.4.1959), Lebanese daily *Al-Hayat*, 8.4.1959.

government: Paschalis Paschalides, Tassos Papadopoulos, Andreas Azinas and Fazıl Plümer. They were joined by Themistoklis Tsatsos, the head of the Greek delegation which had participated in the mixed constitutional committee, by Dr Konstantinos Spyridakis, President of the Greek Education Council which had undertaken the planning of the educational system in the Greek Cypriot community during the Transitional Period, and numerous other Greek Cypriot entrepreneurs.[278]

Nevertheless, before the Cypriot delegation travelled to Lebanon, there had been some behind-the-scenes diplomatic activity about which the Turkish Cypriot side hastened to inform Israeli Consul Zeev Levin in detail. The Lebanese Consulate had initially invited fifty Greek Cypriot officials to Baalbek, as opposed to only six Turkish Cypriot officials. This was taken as an insult by the Turkish side. Consequently, Rauf Denktaş and Turks Nihat Erim and Suat Bilge refused to accept the Lebanese invitation, citing prior commitments as members of the mixed constitutional committee.[279] The unpleasant atmosphere that ensued between Lebanon's consulate and the Turkish Cypriots once again confirmed Israel's conviction that the Turkish Cypriots would not hesitate to publicly express their dissatisfaction, any time the possibility of rapprochement between Cyprus and the Arab countries arose.[280]

In Lebanon, the guests from Cyprus were received with honour and met with the country's president, Fuad Chehab, and Prime Minister Rashid Karami. Nevertheless, certain similarities were noted between this visit and the earlier visit by the Cypriot delegation to Cairo in July of 1959 for the eighth anniversary of Nasser's military coup.[281] According to Israeli diplomatic reports citing an unnamed 'reliable source from Cyprus', the Speaker of the Lebanese Parliament, Sabri Hamadeh, essentially reiterated the warnings of UAR Minister of Foreign Affairs Mahmood Fawzi,[282] and called upon Cyprus to decide whether it wished to maintain trade relations with Israel or with the Arab countries. Cypriot minister of commerce and industry, Paschalis Paschalides, took the initiative to respond, as he had in Egypt the previous year.[283] In fact, he added that Cyprus was not yet in a position to determine the focus of its foreign policy, as it was still in a Transitional Period, and that 'in any event, the soledeterminant of the Cypriot Republic's actions would always be what is best for Cyprus'.[284]

Meanwhile, throughout the first six months of 1960, the consulates of Israel and Lebanon in Nicosia engaged in a fierce public relations competition, endeavouring to impress Greek Cypriot public opinion any way possible. Thus, in January, a few days after Israel's Symphony Orchestra performance in Cyprus,[285] the Lebanese Consulate invited 54 political and business figures from both communities to spend the last weekend of that month at the recently opened Beirut casino – all expenses paid. In fact,

[278] Ibid., Levin to British Commonwealth, Middle East and Research Divisions (102/1012/59-4.9.1959).
[279] Ibid.
[280] Ibid., Levin to British Commonwealth, Middle East Divisions (102/912/59-20.8.1959).
[281] Cf. 6.2.2.
[282] Ibid.
[283] Ibid.
[284] ISA/RG130/MFA/3570/12, Levin to British Commonwealth and Middle East and Research Divisions (951/59-20.9.1959, confidential report).
[285] ISA/RG93/MFA/1431/19, Levin to West Europe Division (19.1.1961, not marked as official entry).

a rumour circulated through newspaper gossip columns that the list of esteemed guests would include Aristotle Onassis – a fact which was never verified.[286]

The peculiar rivalry between Israel and Lebanon unfolding in Cyprus during the summer of 1960 caught the attention of the foreign press. On 10 June 1960, the London *Daily Telegraph*, in a lengthy and scathing report, revealed the true reason behind the cancellation of a scheduled appearance by the Stuttgart Symphony Orchestra. The scandal involved a Cypriot impresario of Armenian origin, Enger Krikor Mandossian,[287] who in January of the same year was to arrange for the Israel Philharmonic Orchestra to perform at the Pallas Theatre in Nicosia.[288] At that time, relations between Lebanese Consul, Michel Farah, and the Armenian community in Cyprus were strained.[289] That aside, Farah allegedly warned the German symphony orchestra that if it chose to collaborate with that particular impresario in Cyprus, it would never appear in Lebanon again. Thus, the famed German orchestra cancelled its appearance in Cyprus.[290]

The performance of a dance group from Tel Aviv[291] was immediately followed by an announcement from the Lebanese consulate that a 100-member traditional dance troupe would appear in Nicosia on the day of the declaration of Cyprus' independence,[292]

---

[286] ISA/RG93/MFA/1007/5, Levin to British Commonwealth Division (102/110.11קפר – 20.1.1960), and press release from the consulate of Lebanon in Nicosia (no. 6/ 16.1.1960). *Times of Cyprus*, 'They're off to the Casino', 17.1.1960.

[287] Enger Krikkor Mandossian was born in Jerusalem on 1.10.1923. In the late 1950s, he settled in Cyprus where he acted as empresario for cultural events. He was an active member of the local Armenian community and a member of the liberal Armenian movement, Ramgavar (ADLP). At the end of the 1960s, he settled permanently in Vancouver, Canada, where the Armenian community numbered a mere 100. He was active in community institutions and an initiator of the building plan for an Armenian church in Vancouver, dedicated to Saint Vartan. He established a local branch of the Ramgavar movement and served as its chairman for a number of years and was likewise a founder of Vancouver's Tekeyian Armenian Cultural Center. While living in Cyprus and Canada over the years, he maintained a close relationship with the president of Cyprus, Makarios. He died in Vancouver on 11.7.2014. *The Armenian Mirror – Spectator*, 'Obituary – Krikkor Mandossian', vol. 85, no. 18, issue 4361, 11.11.2014, 7. Details of his political activity in Cyprus are available on the Armenian Community Website, www.hayem.org (accessed 6 October 2022).

[288] ISA/RG93/MFA/1007/11, Levin to Political-Financial Planning Division (96/553.1קפר – 21.6.1960). *Fileleftheros*, 'Yesterday's concert by Israel's Philharmonic', 21.1.1960. The Israel Philharmonic Orchestra performed in Cyprus for the first time on the evening of 20.1.1960 at the Pallas Theatre in Nicosia. After the concert, Israel's consulate general held a reception at the Ledra Palace Hotel, which was attended, inter alia, by the ministers of the Transitional government, Tassos Papadopoulos, Paschalis Paschalides and Andreas Azinas, Consul General of Greece Georgios Christopoulos and the president of the Hellenic Educational Council, Dr Konstantinos Spyridakis.

[289] Cf. 6.2.3.1.1.

[290] Oron (ed.), *Middle East Record*, 181.

[291] *Fileleftheros*, 'Yesterday's performance by the folk dancers from Hapoel-Israel', 12.5.1960. *Haravgi*, 'An artistic extravaganza – The folk-dance group "Hapoel"', 13.5.1960. *Ethnos*, 'The Hapoel dance group in Limassol', 15.5.1960. *Haravgi*, 'Limassol warmly welcomes Israel's folk-dance group – Reception and artistic events in the Public Gardens following two successful performances by the group – Addresses by Messrs. Partassides and Levin', 15.5.1960. The consulate general of Israel in Cyprus arranged for two performances of Israel's folk-dance group, Hapoel, in Nicosia (Pallas Theatre, 11.5.1960) and Limassol (Rialto Cinema, 14.5.1960). In Limassol, the Hapoel group was joined by the traditional dance group of the AKEL youth organization, EDON Agias Fylas.

[292] ISA/RG93/MFA/1007/5, Research Division (1094/110.1קפר – 25.7.1960) *Fileleftheros*, 'The famous Lebanese folk-dance group "Al-Anouar" in Cyprus', 22.7.1960. *Haravgi*, 'On the occasion of the visit by "Alanouar" group from Lebanon – Cyprus to establish its own folk-dance group to perform abroad – How the Lebanese set up their famous 120-member dance group – A matter of national pride to perform their national dances – What we should do – A representative meeting to be called to discuss the matter', 4.8.1960.

as a 'celebratory gift from Lebanon'. As August 16, 1960 approached, Israeli and Lebanese sports and cultural associations also visited the island's major cities in quick succession.

6.3 The impact of diplomatic relations between Cyprus and Israel on the Arab world, Greece and Turkey

On 17 August 1960, President Makarios recognized Zeev Levin as Israeli ambassador to Nicosia, and thus the two countries established diplomatic relations.[293] This fact did not go unnoticed in the Arab world[294] though at first it showed restraint. On 19 August the Arab League press officer merely expressed surprise at the news, did not confirm it and said that, if verified, it would be a topic of discussion during the forthcoming meeting of the foreign ministers of the Arab League member states, to be held in Beirut on 22 August 1960.[295]

The reactions of the Arab press varied in the days that followed. The Egyptian press kept silent about it until 19 August. The Cairo *Al-Hayat* referred on 20 August to the 'big surprise experienced by the UAR'.[296] The Lebanese newspapers were more outspoken. *Al-Hayat* of Beirut commented on the astonishment expressed by the Arabs about this adverse development, wondering 'what exactly the topics of concern had been during the Arab meetings about Cyprus after the signing of the London–Zurich Agreements if not Israel's pervasive presence on the island'. A short article on 20 August accused Makarios of hypocrisy, concluding that by accepting the Israeli Ambassador in Nicosia, he had essentially clarified 'his real stance on the Arab-Israeli conflict'.[297] *Al-Anwar*, on the other hand, justified Makarios' decision, placing full blame on Turkish Cypriot Vice President Fazıl Küçük.[298]

The reaction of the Jordanian press was interesting. *Falastin* wrote self-deprecatingly that 'the Jews are faster at acquiring friends', and urged all Arab League countries to take a common stand with regard to the current development.[299] It likewise cautioned that that a termination of relations with Cyprus might result in 'losing a friend and in a missed opportunity for Cyprus to restore relations with us Arabs'. At the same time, the newspaper speculated that 'because Cyprus had always been a centre of espionage and contraband, an Arab diplomatic presence on the island was essential to monitor Israeli activity there'.[300] A self-critical attitude was also evident in a question *Al-Difaa*

---

[293] Cf. 6.1.6.

[294] *Fileleftheros*, 'The appointment of the Ambassador of Israel in Cyprus causes surprise and disappointment in Cairo – This topic shall be discussed next Monday in Beirut by the Council of the Ministers of Foreign Affairs of the Arab countries', 20.8.1960.

[295] ISA/RG93/MFA/1008/2, Research Division to Middle East Department of the Mossad and to the Embassy of Israel in Nicosia (2086/ג – 22.8.1960). Overview of Egyptian, Lebanese and Jordanian reports on the establishment of diplomatic relations between Cyprus and Israel.

[296] Ibid. Lebanese *Al-Hayat*, 19.8.1960.

[297] Ibid. Lebanese *Al-Hayat*, 20.8.1960.

[298] Ibid. *Al-Anwar*, 21.8.1960.

[299] Ibid. *Falastin*, 21.8.1960.

[300] Ibid. *Falastin*, 20.8.1960.

raised: 'As the Arabs did not impose any sanctions on France about the Algeria issue, what right do they have to demand that non-Arab countries impose sanctions on Israel?'[301]

Finally, *Al-Manar* noted that 'the Arabs have lost their momentum in Cyprus. But now, they must work hard to become active there, otherwise, if they depart from the island, they will only make Israel the happier.'[302]

The first reactions from the Cypriot side came from the community of 15,000 Greek Cypriots living in Egypt. The Greek Cypriot associations in Cairo and Alexandria sent strongly worded telegrams to Makarios, warning him that establishing diplomatic relations with Israel would place the Greek Cypriots of Egypt in the UAR in jeopardy.[303] The fate of the Greek Cypriots in Egypt was the main topic of concern in all Cypriot newspapers immediately after the establishment of diplomatic relations with Israel became known. The anti-Makarios *Ethniki* newspaper, whose major shareholder was Themistocles Dervis, wrote characteristically that Makarios, 'by establishing diplomatic relations with Israel, sold out 17,000 ethnic Greek Cypriots in Egypt'. The pro-Makarios *Ethnos*, which criticized Israel for its decision to recognize the Cypriot Republic, was interesting. It called on the Israeli government, first, to 'consider the impact their action would have on Cypriots abroad', and second, 'not to exert pressure to have its embassy opened in Nicosia'.[304] Meanwhile, the Turkish Cypriot paper *Halkın Sesi*, whose editor in chief was Fazıl Küçük, posited the argument that Cyprus, precisely because of its Turkish Cypriot community which shared the same religion as the Arabs, 'should seek close relations with the Arab countries while also maintaining close relations with Israel, from which it has a lot to learn'.[305] *Bozkurt* expressed a like sentiment, namely that 'it would not be proper to ignore the friendship of 60 million Arabs versus 2 million Israelis', but that, 'nevertheless, from a moral point of view, the question is: why should Cyprus turn away from Israel under Arab pressure?'[306]

Similar arguments were expressed over the days that followed by other pro-Makarios Greek Cypriot newspapers, but only after Zeev Levin had hastened to meet their chief editors in person. In fact, Levin made sure to personally meet with Dervis, who explained that what had been published in *Ethniki* about 'Makarios selling out the Cypriots living abroad'[307] was not a dart aimed at the establishment of diplomatic relations with Israel per se, but at Makarios' policies in general. In his report to the Israeli Ministry of Foreign Affairs, Levin wrote that at the meeting with Dervis, he had extracted a promise that *Ethniki* would not touch on that specific issue again in future. Dervis kept his promise.[308]

---

[301] Ibid. *Al-Difaa*, 21.8.1960.

[302] Ibid. *Al-Manar*, 21.8.1960.

[303] *Fileleftheros*, 'The 15,000 Cypriots of Egypt are very much upset by the appointment of the Ambassador of Israel in Cyprus – They sent a telegram to the Archbishop stating the imminent dangers because of the Israeli actions', 21.8.1960. *Haravgi*, 'The Cypriot Brotherhood of Alexandria opposes the appointment of the Israeli Ambassador', 21.8.1960.

[304] ISA/RG93/MFA/1008/1, Levin to Yahil (1246/103.1קפר – 31.8.1960), Review of the Greek Cypriot press on the reaction of the Greek Cypriot community in Egypt.

[305] *Eleftheria*, 'Halkın Sesi about the relations of Cyprus with Israel and the Arab countries', 2.9.1960.

[306] *Ethnos*, 'The Turkish newspapers on the issue', 24.8.1960.

[307] ISA/RG93/MFA/1008/1, Levin to Yahil (1279/102.1קפר – 7.9.1960), Review of articles printed in *Halkın Sesi, Fos, Ethniki* and the Athenian *Kathimerini*.

[308] Cf. 5.2.1.2 Themistoklis Dervis' visit to Israel in June 1959.

A sensation was caused by an interview with Makarios in the Egyptian newspaper *Al-Gumhuriya*, published on 25 August 1960, which was reprinted the very next day in the Cypriot *Eleftheria*. In response to a question posed by an Egyptian reporter as to whether the Israeli embassy would open in Nicosia, Makarios avoided answering directly. *Eleftheria* reprinted this excerpt from the archbishop's interview with the Egyptian newspaper:

> Al-Gumhuriya's correspondent in Nicosia, Mr Farah Gubran, writes: In the interview with me on the topic of relations with Israel, President Makarios said that the Arabs should know that he is not completely free to decide on his own about the relations between Cyprus and Israel, as the Turkish Vice-President, Dr Küçük, also has his own opinions. I knew, writes the correspondent, that Dr Küçük was instructed by the Turkish Government to support the establishment of relations with Israel and apply the same policy Turkey has towards Israel.[309]

As the Israeli diplomatic mission in Ankara learned from the Turkish Ministry of Foreign Affairs,[310] Makarios' statements caused resentment not just on the part of the Turkish government, but mainly on that of Fazıl Küçük who accused Makarios of using 'hypocritical words to justify himself to the Arabs by placing all the blame on the Turkish Cypriots'. Küçük likened such tactics to the way Makarios had handled the parliamentary representation of the Maronites.[311] But apart from that, the Turkish vice president had his own serious personal reasons to worry: His elder brother, Ahmet Küçük, who had been working in Egypt for many years, lived permanently in Alexandria and had acquired considerable wealth.[312]

As Zeev Levin noted in a related report, Makarios appeared very ill at ease when asked to speak before Greek Cypriot journalists and take a specific position on the issue of diplomatic relations with Israel. Specifically, at a press conference he held in Nicosia on 24 August 1960, he was quoted as saying:

> The Arabs have known for months now about my intention of establishing normal diplomatic relations with Israel and their surprise, therefore, is unjustified. Cyprus shall stay out of the Arab–Israeli conflict, and the Arab countries, if they so wish, can open six embassies in Cyprus. That does not mean they will prevent the opening of the Israeli embassy. I hope that the Arab countries will not take measures against Cyprus, but my decision on this is clear.

---

[309] *Eleftheria*, 'Arab newspapers react against Makarios' policy towards Israel', 26.8.1960.
[310] ISA/RG93/MFA/1008/1, Eytan Ronn, first secretary of the Diplomatic Mission of Israel in Ankara, to Fischer and the Middle East and Consular Affairs divisions (331/א – 31.8.1960). Ronn was informed about the impact of Makarios' statements in Turkey and the reactions of Fazıl Küçük by Haluk Bayülken, a member of the Turkish Foreign Ministry's Middle East Division Office for Cypriot Affairs.
[311] Cf. 6.2.3.1.2, On the position of Makarios towards Lebanon on the issue of parliamentary representation of the Maronites.
[312] ISA/RG93/MFA/1008/1, Eytan Ronn, first secretary of the Israeli diplomatic mission in Ankara, to Fischer and the Middle East and Consular Affairs divisions (331/א – 31.8.1960).

However, as Levin writes in his report, immediately after these statements, Makarios asked the journalists present not to publish them – and they obeyed.[313]

A few days before the foreign ministers of the Arab League member states convened in Beirut on 22 August 1960, Israeli Prime Minister David Ben-Gurion assured the English-language Athenian *Daily Post* that the Arab threats against Cyprus were made solely for domestic consumption. 'If Cyprus says "we are independent, do not get involved", said Ben-Gurion, 'then they [the Arabs] will finally understand. They are not so foolish as not to establish diplomatic relations with Cyprus'.[314] Israeli Foreign Minister Golda Meir expressed the same views in an interview with the Athenian paper *Ethnos*, which was reprinted a few days later in Cyprus by a pro-Makarios Cypriot newspaper of the same name.[315] Nevertheless, neither Ben-Gurion's statements nor Meir's appeased the Greek and Turkish Cypriot ministers, or for that matter, the Cypriot organizations in Egypt, which quickly sent a delegation to Nicosia to speak to Makarios about the community's fears of a possible retaliation by Nasser.[316]

The anxiety felt by the Greek Cypriots, both within and outside of Cyprus, was not without substance, judging by the local front-page news during the second half of August 1960. Not a newspaper on the island failed to warn of serious diplomatic complications for the newly established Cypriot state in the event that Makarios refrained from re-evaluating his policy towards Israel.[317] Meanwhile, the Israelis observed that with growing frequency the Arab news reports created the impression that 'although Israel had recognised Cyprus, Cyprus had not yet recognised Israel'. In reality, though, this was not the case, given that only a pre-existing state can recognize a newly established one – not the reverse.[318]

---

[313] ISA/RG93/MFA/1008/1, Levin to Yahil (1246/103.1קפר – 31.8.1960).

[314] Statements by Ben-Gurion to the English-language Greek newspaper *Daily Post* were reprinted in Cyprus by the pro-Makarios press: *Kypros*, 'Statements of Ben-Gurion about the relations between Cyprus and Israel and the Arab countries', 22.8.1960. *Ethnos*, 'Ben-Gurion does not believe the threats of the Arab countries about not establishing diplomatic relations with Cyprus. He believes that the relations between Israel and the Arab people shall improve', 22.8.1960.

[315] *Ethnos*, 'Statements by Foreign Minister Meir on Cypriot–Israeli relations – I see no reason not to have close relations', 25.8.1960. Reprint of Golda Meir's interview in the Athenian newspaper *Ethnos*.

[316] *Fileleftheros*, 'Delegation of the Greek Cypriots of Egypt comes to Cyprus – for talks with the President – the concerns of the Cypriot Community about the relations of Cyprus with the UAR', 13.9.1960.

[317] Indicatively: *Ethnos*, 'The Republic of Cyprus is in a difficult position due to the Arab–Israeli competition – The Arabs threaten not to enter into diplomatic relations with Cyprus, if an Ambassador of Israel is appointed on our island', 20.8.1960. *Fileleftheros*, 'The Arabs see dangers for the Republic of Cyprus because of Israel – The views of the Egyptian newspaper "Journal d' Egypt" expressed in an open letter to His Beatitude Archbishop Makarios', 26.8.1960. *Ethnos*, 'The Arabs invited Makarios again to reconsider his stance about Israel – Egyptian journalist launches indirect threats for the Greeks of Cyprus', 26.8.1960. *Eleftheria*, 'Warning of the Arab League to Cyprus', 28.8.1960. *Ethnos*, 'The Ministers of Foreign Affairs of the Arab League countries delved into the relations between the Arabs and Cyprus – Warning to Cyprus about the Zionist objectives – The support of Arabs to the fight of the Cypriot people', 28.8.1960. *Kypros*, 'The Arabs shall present a demarche to Nicosia, Athens and Ankara about the relations between Cyprus and Israel – A relevant resolution was unilaterally approved by the Council of the Ministers of Foreign Affairs of the Arab countries', 29.8.1960. *Neoi Kairoi*, 'The Arab countries warn Cyprus about the establishment of diplomatic relations with Israel', 29.8.1960.

[318] ISA/RG93/MFA/1008/1, Levin to Yahil and British Commonwealth Division (266/103.1קפר – 8.9.1960).

As the days passed, however, instead of anticipated Arab reprisals, both the Arab League and the UAR, along with Lebanon, Iraq, Sudan and other Arab countries limited themselves to announcing their regrets over the diplomatic relations between Israel and the Republic of Cyprus, without further comment. Gradually, the disquieting Cypriot news diminished and the verbal Arab threats against Cyprus lessened, too.

The first clear sign that relations between Cyprus and the Arab countries would not be affected came on 6 September 1960. The official Egyptian Middle East News Agency (MENA) announced that Mustafa Lutfi would be appointed UAR ambassador to Nicosia the following month; the news was quickly disseminated by Cypriot state radio,[319] and the next day by all the local newspapers.[320] The same news was also published by the Lebanese *Al-Hayat*, which added that 'Cyprus has not recognised Israel yet' and that 'representatives of Lebanon and Egypt are continuing to make contacts in Athens and Ankara wishing to deter such an eventuality'.[321]

A fortnight of complete news silence followed until 21 September 1960 when the arrival of the first delegation of Egyptian entrepreneurs in Cyprus was announced. The head of the delegation was a senior official of the UAR Ministry of Finance which aimed at exploring the possibilities of forging business relations with the Republic of Cyprus.[322] The visit of the first official delegation of technocrats from the UAR was sealed with the signature of the Memorandum of Cooperation between Cyprus and the UAR in the area of trade on 29 September 1960.[323]

While all indications were that the tension between the newly established Republic of Cyprus and the Arab countries had been overcome, there was still one formal issue pending in the relations between Cyprus and Israel. A month had passed since the declaration of independence, but President Makarios had not yet set the date for the credentials ceremony of the Israeli ambassador. By contrast, all of other ambassadors placed in Nicosia had already presented their credentials a few days after 16 August 1960, and although no Cypriot official said as much, the Israelis had the impression that this delay was clearly linked to the successive postponements of the arrival of UAR Ambassador Mustafa Lutfi. Zeev Levin, along with senior officials at the Israeli Ministry of Foreign Affairs, grew concerned about the quality the Cypriots seemed to want to assign to their relations with Israel. On the other hand, the Israeli consulate had already been upgraded to an embassy and the appointment of Zeev Levin to Nicosia had been ratified on 17 August 1960.[324] The fact that the Cypriot side wanted to delay the credentials ceremony for Levin as long as possible, though a mere formality in order to avoid caustic remarks in the Arab press, raised the Israeli ambassador's suspicions

[319] Ibid.

[320] Indicatively: *Fileleftheros*, 'Participant of the Egyptian Revolution was appointed Ambassador of the UAR in Cyprus – Mr Mustafa Lutfi assumes his diplomatic duties next month', 7.9.1960.

[321] ISA/RG93/MFA/1008/1, Research Division to Levin (1866/8.9.1960).

[322] *Ethnos*, 'Commercial delegation of UAR to Cyprus', 21.9.1960. *Fileleftheros*, 'Towards forging economic relations of the UAR with Cyprus – The appointment of the Ambassador of the UAR shall be announced soon', 22.9.1960.

[323] Indicatively: *Fileleftheros*, 'A memorandum was signed yesterday by Cyprus and the UAR for the development of the commercial relations – the Arab Economic Delegation left yesterday', 30.9.1960.

[324] See 6.1.6.

because time was passing and diplomatic protocol had not yet been implemented for his own country.

The newly established Republic of Cyprus was forced to engage in highly nuanced diplomatic moves which had been determined by general developments in the Middle East only a few weeks prior to 16 August 1960. To better understand the circumstances of the time – which Nicosia could neither predict nor influence – the following must be briefly noted.

Around mid-July 1960, the Shah of Iran Mohammad Reza Pahlavi, was asked by journalists whether his country would establish full diplomatic relations with Israel and he answered, 'Iran has long recognised Israel.'[325] The underlying meaning of the Shah's statement was that Iran would not proceed with de jure recognition of the Jewish state, as it had already recognized it de facto a decade earlier, in 1950, under the Mosaddegh government.[326] Nasserist Egypt, however, chose to take advantage of the Iranian monarch's statement and protested – a decade after the fact – against the existence of Iranian–Israeli diplomatic contacts, about something which was already widely known. The UAR's Foreign Ministry portrayed the Shah's words as 'an admission of guilt'. This quickly led to an unprecedented diplomatic crisis between the UAR and Iran, resulting in the recall of the Egyptian ambassador from Teheran, and the departure of his Iranian counterpart from Cairo on 31 July 1960.[327] In this abrupt manner, diplomatic relations between Egypt and Iran were suspended for the next decade. It was never made clear that the true reason the Nasser regime pushed its relations with Iran to the limit was to stop Iran's pervasiveness in the Gulf countries.[328]

The unexpectedly tense diplomatic rift between the UAR and Iran occurred only two weeks before 16 August 1960, the day Cypriot independence would be declared. Undoubtedly, Nasser wanted to establish full diplomatic relations with Cyprus right away. However, it was very difficult for him to justify to the Arab world and to the public opinion of his country that he would have to be lenient with President Makarios. This, given that the latter had already established de jure diplomatic relations with Israel, and the Israeli consulate had been upgraded to an embassy, despite the severity shown two weeks earlier towards the Shah and Iran – a much more powerful country than Cyprus which after all, had never recognized Israel de jure.

Essentially, Egyptian diplomacy had backed itself into a corner. It was trying to find the appropriate time and way to establish full diplomatic relations with the newly established Republic of Cyprus. But it had to wait until the effects of the diplomatic crisis it had caused with Iran settled down. It appears that those were the concerns that were the topic of extensive discussions in New York between Zenon Rossides, Cypriot ambassador to Washington and the head of the permanent delegation to the United Nations, and Nasser himself, in October 1960. According to the Greek secret service,

[325] Trita Parsi, *Treacherous Alliance: The Secret Dealings of Israel, Iran and the United States* (New Haven, CT, and London: Yale University Press, 2007), 27.
[326] Barouch Gilead, 'Yakhasey Israel-Iran (1949–1979): Diplomatia be-Makhteret' ['Israeli-Iranian Relations (1949–1979): Underground Diplomacy'], in *Misrad ha-Khutz*, ed. Yeger, Govrin and Oded, 251–4; and Alper, *Medina Bodeda*, 37–52.
[327] Cf. *Neoi Kairoi*, 'After the suspension of Iranian-Egyptian relations', 1.8.1960.
[328] Parsi, *Treacherous Alliance*, 28.

the procedure to establish diplomatic relations between Cyprus and the UAR was hammered out at that very meeting. The Greek Central Intelligence Service (KYP) informed the Greek Ministry of Foreign Affairs and Prime Minister Konstantinos Karamanlis on 21 October 1960 that Nasser and Rossides 'had settled the pending issues' between Cyprus and the UAR, 'primarily the thorny issue of the exchange of diplomatic envoys'. KYP added that in fact 'the first Ambassador of the UAR, Brigadier General Mustafa Lutfi, a fellow student and associate of Nasser's who was providing him with confidential information, is already expected in Nicosia'.[329] Nevertheless, Lutfi only arrived in the Cypriot capital several months later.

Once Cyprus and Israel had established diplomatic relations, Athens had to maintain its delicate balance in relation to the Arab world and Israel. Concerns about the future of the Greek community in Egypt were deep and justified. Foreign Minister Evangelos Averoff, in welcoming to Athens the newly appointed Israeli chargé d'affaires, Shmuel Kapel in early September 1960, tried to persuade him that Greece was obliged to practice restraint under the circumstances. He also told Kapel that he had personally advised Makarios that if he intended to establish diplomatic relations with Israel 'it would be preferable to do so now rather than later'.[330] Averoff essentially reaffirmed the opinion he had expressed in July 1960 to Maurice Fischer, assistant secretary general of the Israeli Ministry of Foreign Affairs, that with regard to Cypriot–Israeli diplomatic relations, 'it would be preferable to deal with a wave of wrath from the Arabs once and for all, than a chronic disease later on'.[331] There is no doubt that the 'disappointment' Athens expressed publicly to Makarios regarding the establishment of diplomatic relations with Israel a few days after the meeting between Averoff and Kapel was nothing more than a smokescreen intended to avoid stirring up the Arab countries and preventing reprisals from Nasser against the Greek community in Egypt.[332]

In contrast to Greece, Turkey's position vis-à-vis the Arab world was perfectly clear. The secretary general of the Turkish Ministry of Foreign Affairs, Zeki Kuneralp, informed Moshe Alon, the Israeli chargé d'affaires that on 12 September 1960, the ambassadors of all the Arab countries posted to Ankara had visited Minister of Foreign Affairs Selim Sarper.[333] Their common request was for Turkey to pressure Fazıl Küçük to withdraw his consent to the issuance of Makarios' *agrément* accepting the appointment of an Israeli ambassador to Nicosia.

---

[329] Manos Iliadis, *To Aporrito Imerologio tis KYP gia tin Kypro* [*The Classified KYP Record on Cyprus*] (Athens: I. Sideris, 2007), 319–20. Greek Central Intelligence Service (KYP) to Greek Ministry of Foreign Affairs, copy to Prime Minister Konstantinos Karamanlis (Memo on Cyprus Region, 21.10.1960).

[330] ISA/RG93/MFA/1008/1, Research Division to Levin (603/103.1קפר – 4.9.1960). An excerpt from the report by the newly appointed Israeli diplomatic envoy to Athens, Shmuel Kapel, to the West Europe Division, Cf. 6.1.6.

[331] ISA/RG93/MFA/1008/4, British Commonwealth Division to Levin (635/18.7.1960) Content of Fischer-Averoff meeting in Athens. Cf. 6.1.6; ISA/RG130/MFA/2293/8, Fischer to Yahil (394/ג – 18.7.1960); and Israel State Archives, Gilead (ed.), *Documents*, vol. 14, 640 no. 412.

[332] ISA/RG130/MFA/2341/2, Levin to the British Commonwealth Division (265/7.9.1960). The director general of the Cypriot Ministry of Foreign Affairs informed Levin that the Greek government was said to have expressed its disappointment about the establishment of diplomatic relations between Cyprus and Israel. Cf. Israel State Archives, Gilead (ed.), *Documents*, vol. 14, 644 no. 416.

[333] ISA/RG130/MFA/2290/5, Alon to Yahil (383/אי –15.9.1960).

Having already successfully handled the issue of parliamentary representation of the Cypriot Maronites,[334] Turkey was experienced in setting limits to Arab pursuits. Indirectly albeit clearly, Selim Sarper ruled out the possibility of taking the initiative in this direction. In fact, he reached the point of saying that 'the Arab countries have rather overestimated the influence Turkey can exercise, not only over decisions made by Fazıl Küçük, but over the Turkish citizens of the island in general'. The Turkish foreign minister justified the Cypriot Republic's decision to accept the appointment of the Israeli ambassador to Nicosia and explained to the Arab ambassadors that:

> because of the special regime in Cyprus and the problems related to it, the Cypriot government does not wish to get involved in the Arab-Israeli conflict and, as it seems, it chose to establish diplomatic relations with Israel as well. That does not mean, however, that the Cypriot Republic does not wish to develop good diplomatic relations with the Arab countries. Quite the opposite.[335]

Again and again, from September 1960, and over the next four months, Israeli Ambassador Zeev Levin asked President Makarios, Turkish Vice President Küçük and Foreign Minister Spyros Kyprianou when exactly he would be able to formally present his credentials. In contrast to the vague responses he received from Kyprianou and Makarios, Fazıl Küçük never missed an opportunity to offer a detailed account of his efforts to speed up the process in order to show the Israelis that the only reliable partners on the island were the Turkish Cypriots and nobody else.

The unusual delay was due to intensive behind-the-scenes talks between Nicosia, Cairo and Beirut which ultimately resulted in a solution: the UAR ambassador would be the first to present his credentials to President Makarios, after which his Israeli counterpart would do likewise. Thus, after a series of postponements, Mustafa Lutfi arrived in Nicosia in January of 1961, and on the 14 of that month he presented his credentials to President Makarios.[336] Then, six days later, at the Presidential Palace in Nicosia, Israeli Ambassador Zeev Levin presented his credentials to President Makarios in the presence of Vice President Küçük, Deputy Minister Apostolos Kontos, Deputy Minister Cemal Müftüzade, Minister of Foreign Affairs Spyros Kyprianou and the Director General of the Ministry of Foreign Affairs Costas Ashiotis.

As Zeev Levin described the day in his report:

> The presidential car, with a small Israeli flag waving, accompanied by four motorcycles, arrived at the agreed time to take us to the Presidential Palace. I was accompanied by the Director-General of the Cypriot Ministry of Foreign Affairs. At the entrance, we were met by an honour guard of the Cypriot Police. The Police Band played only the Israeli national anthem – as there is no Cypriot national anthem yet.

---

[334] Cf. 6.2.3.1.2, contacts between Turkey and Lebanon on the issue of the Maronites' role in the Cypriot political system (March–April 1960).

[335] ISA/RG130/MFA/2290/5, Alon to Yahil (383/א – 15.9.1960).

[336] ISA/RG93/MFA/1008/1, Levin to Yahil (31/103.1קרפ – 19.1.1961).

Standing in the Presidential Palace hall were Makarios, Dr Küçük, the Minister of Foreign Affairs, the Director-General of the Ministry of Foreign Affairs and the deputy ministers of the President and Vice President.

When I presented my credentials, I expressed the hope of close bilateral relations and Makarios answered extensively. After a few minutes, the ceremony was over. It was a formal affair but also pleasant and very friendly.

The Cypriot press covered the credentials ceremony extensively.

Cyprus radio reported it in all news bulletins of the day, emphasising my statements and Makarios' answer.

And that is how this affair ended.[337]

[337] ISA/RG130/MFA/3345/7, Levin to West Europe Division (87/103.1-26.1.1961). Cf. Barouch Gilead, 'Ha-Maarakha al Yitzug Israel be-Kafrisin' ['The Campaign for Israel's Representation in Cyprus'], in *Misrad ha'Khutz*, ed. Yeger, Govrin and Oded, 374–6, and articles published in the newspapers *Ethniki, Machi, Haravgi* and *Fileleftheros*, 21.1.1961.

Overview of Israel's Foreign Policy towards Cyprus, 1946–60

7.1 Western guarantees for Israel's security and the background to regional collaboration between Turkey and Israel during the 1950s

In early 1949, the Armistice Agreements between Israel, Egypt, Lebanon, Syria and Jordan sealed the outcome of the First Arab–Israeli War, or as it is known in Israeli historiography, the War of Independence. The de facto land borders of the newly established Jewish state and its diplomatic recognition by the two superpowers, the United States and USSR, created a new status quo in the Middle East and the Eastern Mediterranean. Israel was called upon to decide its position toward the international community, that is, whether to align itself with the East, the West or the so-called Third World which was gradually ridding itself of colonial rule. The answer to this question was not self-evident. The focus of Israel's foreign policy was a particularly controversial issue amongst the various ideological trends in the collective arms of the governing Centre-Left party, Mapai, under the leadership of David Ben-Gurion.

The USSR and the People's Republics of Eastern Europe provided military, economic and diplomatic support in the early months of the young state which found itself at war on the very day after the declaration of its independence. The Jewish armed struggle against the British in Palestine had been viewed by Moscow as a fight against the Western colonialist presence in the Middle East. At the same time, various trends of the Zionist movement in Palestine, dominated by the kibbutz farming communities, had a clear socialist focus, on an ideological as well as a purely practical level. Notwithstanding the various diplomatic congruencies noted between Israel and the Soviet Union during the 1948 War, it soon became apparent that Israel was not inclined to join the so-called 'Eastern Bloc'. Moscow was unwilling to support Israel demographically by allowing its Jewish citizens to emigrate or to provide weapons to Israel's armed forces. With nothing more to expect from the USSR, the Ben-Gurion government openly expressed its decision to adopt the political models of Western Europe. The first multi-party parliamentary elections on 25 January 1949 showed clearly that Israel was not about to come under the Soviet sphere of influence.

On the other hand, Israel's initially restrained ideological distancing from the Eastern Bloc countries did not signify its immediate and complete integration in the post-Second World War 'Western World'. Memories of the armed struggle against the British in Palestine were still fresh. London's coldness on a bilateral and international level with regard to Israel's interests did not go unnoticed by the country's decision-makers nor by its public opinion. Nevertheless, Ben-Gurion did not hide the fact that allying with the United States was the only viable option for the newly established vulnerable Jewish state's foreign policy. The powerful Jewish element in the US was in a position to effectively influence decisions taken at the White House. Ben-Gurion's visit there in late April of 1949, a year after Israel declared independence and only three months after the signing of the 1949 Armistice Agreements with the neighbouring Arab states, proved decisive. The Israeli Prime Minister's arguments did not fall on deaf ears in Washington. However, in order to further its position, Israel had first to smooth relations with the British government and prove that it was indeed able to function as the most reliable Western ally in the Middle East, which was a very important and unstable region.

In the early 1950s, the only other important non-Arab country in the region that sought the trust of the West was Turkey. The Korean War had provided both Turkey and Israel an opportunity to prove their intention of joining the post-war 'West' in practical terms by strengthening the Western Bloc as much as possible. Turkey sent combat ground forces to Korea, and Israel filled significant shortages in medical units behind the front lines. The goals Israel shared with Turkey contributed to a further strengthening of ties. Moreover, Israel hoped Turkey's geographical position and military power would offer protection in a potential conflict with the Arabs while Turkey hoped a regional alliance with Israel would leverage the strong Jewish lobby in the US to support its own interests. However, such a regional accord would be short-lived if London continued its cold-shoulder policy. Post-war Britain still controlled key positions in the Middle East and the Eastern Mediterranean, one of which was Cyprus – an island only a few nautical miles off the Mediterranean coast of Israel and Turkey.

Although post-war Britain was clearly weakened, it had no intention of renouncing its privileges in the Middle East. Given the close relations between London and Ankara, a regional rapprochement between Turkey and Israel was encouraged by the Foreign Office. Despite its mortifying withdrawal from Palestine, Britain still sought reliable allies in the region, knowing full well that the pro-West Arab regimes were threatened by internal political instability and that their communities appeared susceptible to Soviet influence and Arab nationalism, as expressed then by Gamal Abdel Nasser. It was within this carefully balanced framework that relations between Israel and Britain were restored, affording Israel its only access to the West, the ports and airports of Cyprus whose territorial integrity was still extremely precarious.

Throughout the 1950s, two factors above all others guaranteed Israel's security: the British military and political presence in Cyprus, and the multi-level regional collaboration between Israel, Turkey and Britain. As such, a potential British withdrawal from Cyprus would leave Israel even more exposed, in the event that neighbouring Arab countries, led by Nasser's Egypt, decided to launch a coordinated military attack.

7.2 Israel's stance on the Cyprus issue up to 1957

Enosis, the movement for the unification of Cyprus with Greece and the demand of Greek Cypriots to have done with British colonialism brought the Israeli government up against some crucial moral dilemmas. There were clear historical parallels: The 'Enosis Plebiscite' of January 1950 was held only 18 months after Britain's hasty withdrawal from Palestine and Israel's subsequent declaration of independence. Ending British rule had been a goal shared by the Greeks in Cyprus and the Jews in Palestine. Still vivid in Israel were memories of the support shown by the Greek Cypriots to the Jewish Holocaust survivors detained in the British camps of Karaolos, Dhekelia and Xylotymbou between 1946 and 1949.

Consequently, when the results of the Enosis Plebiscite of 1950 were announced and the Ben-Gurion government was called upon to determine its position, it had to consider both the deeply rooted anti-British sentiments of the Israeli people and the unsentimental rationale of maintaining regional alliances. In order to restore good relations with London, Israel had to solidify its position vis-à-vis the West, gain favour with the United States and achieve a geopolitical alliance with powerful, pro-West Turkey. The continued presence of British military forces in Cyprus served as a guarantee for Israel's extremely vulnerable territorial integrity whereas Enosis, given Greece's pro-Arab foreign policy, would in all likelihood bring about the exclusion of Israel from the ports and airports of Cyprus. Greece had voted against the Partition Plan of 1947, which involved the establishment of a Jewish state in Palestine; it maintained a consistently pro-Arab stance at international fora and was one of few countries in Western Europe which had not recognized Israel on a diplomatic level. As a result, it was logical for Israel to conclude that in the event of an Arab attack, their territorial integrity would be better safeguarded by a Cyprus under British rule than a Cyprus belonging to pro-Arab Greece.

Based on these considerations, the Israeli government was unwilling to support Enosis. On the other hand, it did not wish to rule out the possibility of improving relations with the Greek regional element, particularly at a time when the Israeli public was well aware of the plebiscite results and the local media spoke favourably of the Greek Cypriot demand for Enosis. Illustrative of this dilemma were some very carefully worded statements issued by Israel to calls for political support from Makarios II, as well as from Kleopas, locum tenens of the archbishopric throne and Bishop of Paphos, and from the newly elected Archbishop Makarios III addressed to Prime Minister Ben-Gurion and Minister of Foreign Affairs Moshe Sharett. While Israel showed sympathy for the Greek Cypriot demand to overthrow colonial rule, it recommended a political solution that would allow the population to participate in a system of self-governance, thereby indirectly, albeit clearly, advocating the preservation of British rule on the neighbouring island.

Between 1950 and 1954, while the Greek governments were concerned about how to enact Enosis without disturbing relations with London and Ankara, Britain clarified that it was unwilling to withdraw from Cyprus. The British position was a relief to Israel, which was broadening its presence on the island meanwhile. It had established its own consulate in Nicosia on 28 August 1950, and Israeli companies were undertaking the construction of military-related public works. Moreover, Cyprus was now the last transit station for many Jews prior to permanent settlement in Israel, and the Cypriot market was proving particularly profitable for Israeli exports.

Israel was called upon to voice its views on the Cyprus issue for the first time in 1954 when the Greek government put Cyprus's right to self-determination before the 9th Session of the UN General Assembly. At the time, Israel was unwilling to take a clear stand on this, first, because London was not prepared to leave the island soon. Moreover, the continuing cold shoulder from Athens engendered no feelings of obligation on Israel's part. On the other hand, adopting an openly negative position with regard to Cyprus' right to self-determination would make the possibility of improving Greek–Israeli relations even more remote.

Regardless of the above assessments, Israel's Permanent Representation to the UN believed that the Greek claim was basically a pretext. Its real objective, Israel suspected, was to annex Cyprus, not just to defend the islanders' rights. Furthermore, a group of Israeli diplomats argued that Israel had to support Turkey, with which it maintained excellent relations at the time. The view that finally prevailed was that, in view of Britain's discomfort at having to explain why it was holding on to one of its few remaining colonies, this might be the right time to request London's further facilitation of Cyprus' ports and airports in exchange for Israel's positive vote at the General Assembly. Thus, the Israeli side decided to stand in favour of entering the Greek claim on the General Assembly agenda for December 1954, allowing the Cyprus question to be debated for the first time before the UN, which would be the right moment to ask Britain for concessions.

Israel did indeed vote in favour of including the Greek claim on the agenda before the 9th Session of the General Assembly, surprising Alexis Kyrou, director general of the Greek Ministry of Foreign Affairs, and encouraging Archbishop Makarios who hastened to write a note of thanks to the Israeli government in an effort to gauge whether Greece could expect a positive vote from Israel before the Plenary. Israel did not encourage any further courtesies from the Greek Cypriots nor was it shocked by the understandably cold response from Athens which had turned its attention to garnering votes from the Arab, Latin American and Eastern European countries. In the end, Britain did not ask for Israel's support in view of the December vote on the Cyprus issue, depriving it of the opportunity to ask for something in exchange. Turkey adopted the same tactics, relying on the belief that in any case, Ben-Gurion's government would not wish to upset the British. As a result of all this, Israel chose to abstain, thus avoiding a clear-cut stand on the Cyprus problem which was the focus of the UN meetings and at the centre of highly charged confrontations.

By 1955, Israel had fewer dilemmas regarding the Cyprus issue. It had been troubled by Turkey's improved relations with the Arab world, particularly after the signing of the military cooperation agreement signed between Ankara and Baghdad. Although Israel's initial concerns had lessened considerably when Britain acceded to the Baghdad Pact, its suspicions about Turkey had not. Turkey's participation in the clearly pro-Arab Bandung Conference of Afro-Asian Countries and the pro-Arab statements made by senior officials in Turkey helped fuel Israel's suspicions. Moreover, Turkish President

Celâl Bayar's statement implying that his country's army would support Jordan in the event of Israeli aggression likewise created a stir. As a result, Israel decided not to support Turkey's positions when it became known that Greece would again put forward the Cyprus issue at the upcoming 10th Session of the UN General Assembly. Israel had no particular reason to support Greece's positions either. Besides, Athens seemed uninterested in securing Israel's support – particularly as the Arab and Latin American countries reassured it of their positive intentions. Furthermore, EOKA's struggle had already begun, which meant that the Greek demand at the UN would take on strongly anti-colonialist overtones. By that time, Israel and Britain had fully restored bilateral relations.

In view of the inclusion of the Greek claim regarding the Cyprus question on the agenda of the 10th Session of the UN General Assembly, Israel had two options: Either to abstain or to support Britain. However, if it chose to support the British positions, which essentially served Turkey's interests, Israel would be giving Ankara the impression that it was not bothered by its rather late interest in the Arab world. The Israelis may well have been placated by the fact that the Baghdad Pact would serve the interests of the West in the Middle East. But this did not mean that Israel should applaud Turkey's pro-Arab orientation. With these thoughts in mind, Israel chose to abstain from the vote on including the Greek claim on the agenda of the 10th Session of the UN General Assembly. Ultimately, this claim was rejected by the US and the other countries of the West. At the same time, however, no one – including Israel of course – could overlook the unwavering support the Greek claim had garnered amongst the Arab and Latin American countries.

Turkey's deepening ties with pro-West Arab regimes in the region had sparked Israeli suspicions. On the other hand, Israel could not ignore the British guarantees of its territorial integrity, which to a large extent were linked to smooth relations between London and Ankara. Thus, Israeli diplomatic views of developments on the Cyprus front, particularly of the outbreak of EOKA's armed struggle, were greatly influenced by British assessments. Indicative of this was Israeli Prime Minister and Minister of Foreign Affairs Moshe Sharett's comparison of the situation for the Turkish Cypriot minority vis-à-vis the Greek Cypriot majority with the aggression inflicted on Jews by the Arab majority during the 1920s and 1930s when Palestine was under the British Mandate. Such comparisons were unflattering both with respect to the EOKA struggle and to Greek positions on the Cyprus issue. Sharett's explicitly anti-Greek view of events as they unfolded in Cyprus during the second half of 1955 stemmed, firstly, from the significance for Israel of its regional collaboration with Turkey, and secondly, from the fact that Greece, in its desire to gather as many Arab votes as possible at the UN and to protect the Greek diaspora in Egypt, consistently assumed an anti-Israeli stance in its foreign policy. But Israel's Ministry of Foreign Affairs never actually voiced Sharett's views on the Cyprus issue, although they were revealed internally to the Israeli diplomatic service. And it is impossible to assess whether these views would ever have been publicly expressed since Sharett withdrew from active politics in June 1956, following intense intra-party disputes.

When Sharett left the government, the pro-Turkish views on the Cyprus question seemed to become more moderate. Developments in Cyprus also contributed to this, with suppressive British measures becoming harsher by the day. Makarios' exile and the hanging of Karaolis and Dimitriou drew the sympathy of Israelis to the anti-colonialist struggle of the Greek Cypriots. Meanwhile, Turkey continued to strengthen its ties with the Arab countries, raising apprehensions in Israel. When Golda Meir succeeded Sharett as foreign minister in June 1956, a new era dawned in Israel's foreign policy, with a number of fresh prospects. From that year onwards, Israel shifted its attention to former colonies in Africa and Asia which had recently gained independence and began to provide them with significant logistic support and technical advisers. In this way, Israel endeavoured to secure diplomatic solidarity at international fora. Given the context, it was natural during that period for Israel's foreign policy to become more sensitive to demands for decolonization.

In 1956, on the eve of the 11th Session of the UN General Assembly, and under its new leadership, Israeli diplomacy had decided to support Greece's position on the Cyprus issue. The exile of Makarios and the severely suppressive measures enacted in Cyprus had drawn a range of criticism against Britain's policies, both in Israel and around the world. The Israelis began to realize there was no reason to oppose the wishes of the Cypriot population for self-determination. They also realized that even if they supported Turkish positions on the Cyprus question, Ankara would continue its affiliation with the numerous Arab votes at the UN for precisely the same cause. The new leadership in Israeli diplomacy calculated that by supporting anti-colonialist Greek positions for Cyprus, Israel would strengthen its ties with the vocal anti-colonialist governments in Asia, Africa and Latin America. Finally, Israel believed that an unexpected positive vote would be a pleasant surprise for Athens and go a long way to thawing icy Greek–Israeli diplomatic relations. Besides, the Israelis' first impressions of the newly appointed Greek Minister of Foreign Affairs Evangelos Averoff were encouraging.

But a few weeks before the vote at the UN, Meir's decision to maintain a pro-Greek stance on the Cyprus issue changed radically. The reason for this was the international outcry raised by the Suez Crisis in October 1956, and pressure from the US for the withdrawal of the Israeli, British and French troops from the Egyptian territory they had occupied. Israel's Permanent Representation to the UN could not ignore the Foreign Office's demand to support British positions on the Cyprus question. It was self-evident that it would be inconsistent and damaging for Israel to side diplomatically with the critics of British policy in the region, particularly under these circumstances.

At the same time, Israel's abandonment of its pro-Greek line on Cyprus was essentially to Turkey's advantage; the latter had recalled its ambassador from Tel Aviv during the Suez Crisis as a way of expressing solidarity with the Arab World. Nevertheless, in the days before the vote to include the Greek claim on the General Assembly agenda, it became apparent that the Israeli–Turkish rift would not last for long. The head of Turkey's permanent representation to the UN, Selim Sarper, admitted, though a little belatedly, that recalling the Turkish ambassador from Tel Aviv had been 'a mistake that would soon be remedied'. Thus, at the 11th Session of the UN General Assembly, Israel again chose to abstain from the vote on the Cyprus issue. It is worth noting that the review of the archival material does not indicate whether Athens was ever informed about the original intentions of Israel's Ministry of Foreign Affairs, under its new leadership, to support the Greek positions. If Israel had expressed the decision it had adopted through its vote, or at least had it been more open about its intentions with Athens, the course of Greek–Israeli relations over the next few years, particularly during the critical year of 1958, may have been different, and more beneficial to Greek pursuits.

Having monitored developments in Cyprus throughout 1957, Israel came to the conclusion that despite Britain's intense clashes with EOKA, to a large extent, it was still in a position to determine developments on the island. On the one hand, the British clearly wished to disentangle themselves in a dignified way from the impasse that had been created. On the other, the Israeli Ministry of Foreign Affairs believed that, regardless of what form the future political situation would take, Britain would maintain a military presence on the island. In view of the anticipated status quo which had not yet been specified, Israel's consulate in Nicosia began for the first time to map out the political trends surfacing in Greek and Turkish Cypriot societies.

The 12th Session of the UN General Assembly was fast approaching. Ankara and Athens were striving to secure the Arab votes. Israel had no particular reason to support either of the two mother countries, since its relations with both were shaky. Meanwhile, the appointment of the more moderate Sir Hugh Foot as Governor of Cyprus signalled Britain's desire to extract itself from the diplomatic quagmire, albeit maintaining its military presence – a fact that set Israel's mind at ease. Yet given the above, and since the situation was still volatile, Israel was once again reluctant to take a specific stand on the Cyprus issue, and once again, abstained.

Israel's Ministry of Foreign Affairs explained the decision in an internal document, claiming that, as regards a resolution of the Cyprus question in general, the most appropriate approach would be for the parties concerned to negotiate directly. Such reasoning was completely in line with Israel's standing position: to seek direct peace talks with the Arabs without terms and conditions. This position was based on the argument that vital issues, such as territorial integrity, should not be decided by incidental majorities formed in UN bodies. With this reasoning, the Israelis determined that the future status of Cyprus should not be put to a vote at the UN but should rather be a subject for discussion between the countries with a vested interest in the problem, Britain, Greece and Turkey.

7.3 Israel's reasons for supporting Turkey's positions on the Cyprus issue at the 13th Session of the UN General Assembly, 1958

The year 1958 proved fateful for the Middle East, for Turkish–Israeli relations and of course for the Cyprus issue. Of catalytic importance was the decision made by Egypt and Syria in February of that year to join forces and form the United Arab Republic (UAR). The UAR aspired to become the precursor of a united pan-Arab state, which would include all Arab countries, under the leadership of Egyptian President Gamal Abdel Nasser.

Nasser's plan for regional expansion was clearly revealed in the summer of 1958, when the pro-West regimes of Jordan and Lebanon were threatened by subversive political forces incited by Cairo. The West immediately discerned Nasserism as a precursor to Soviet predominance in the Middle East. Britain accepted Jordan's request for military reinforcements to quell the insurgents who were trying to overturn the Hashemite monarchy. Similarly, the US sent military forces to Lebanon, following an appeal by the Beirut government. The result was that the UAR's attempts to bring the two countries into its sphere of influence were blocked. But such was not case in Iraq, where the pro-West Hashemite monarchy did not succeed in maintaining control and was overthrown by a pro-Soviet military coup in July of 1958. This was the beginning of the end for the Turco-Iraqi regional entente upon which Turkey's entire network of relations with the Arab world had hinged at the time.

When Syria fell under the sway of Egypt, Israel was forced to address the threat of Nasserism not only at its southern and western borders, but in the north as well. If the pro-West regimes of Jordan and Lebanon had been overthrown by the Nasserists, Israel would have found itself essentially surrounded by the UAR and UAR satellite states. Britain's military intervention in Jordan and that of the US in Lebanon brought to light again the inextricable link between Israel's regional security and the interests of the West. Turkey arrived at the very same conclusion when Iraq's pro-West monarchy was overturned.

Following these dramatic developments in the summer of 1958, it was only to be expected that Turkey and Israel would want to put an end to the diplomatic stand-off which had been in effect since November 1956. The cooling of relations had ostensibly been perpetuated by Ankara in an effort to ensure the long-term prosperity of pro-West Arab regimes. But in reality, behind-the-scenes contact between Turkey and Israel had never ceased. After the formation of the UAR and the collapse of the Iraqi monarchy, communication between Turkish and Israeli senior diplomats intensified and led to the conclusion of a peripheral pact, signed in Ankara in utter secrecy by prime ministers Ben-Gurion and Menderes in August 1958. Most of the contents of that agreement have remained secret to this day.

At this crucial turning point, according to declassified documents from the Israeli Ministry of Foreign Affairs, Ankara added the Cyprus question to the bundle of items in the agreement, and for the first time, asked directly for Israel's diplomatic support at the upcoming 13th Session of the UN, where the Cyprus issue was to be discussed. The traditionally anti-colonialist Latin American Bloc consistently supported the Greek positions on Cyprus not only because of the influential Greek diaspora there but owing to the popularity Makarios had acquired when the British exiled him to the Seychelles. At this time, Turkish diplomacy had zero presence in Central and South America, and it sought to take advantage of the powerful ties Israel had been cultivating there since its early years of independence.

Israel agreed to Turkey's request for the following reasons.

First of all, neither Britain nor Greece nor any other country had asked Israel to assume an important role when the Cyprus issue came before the UN. Britain had its own, more effective ways of securing votes in its favour, and did not need Israel's vote in order to achieve its goals. Greece had voted against the Partition Plan in 1947, and was one of the Western countries which had not yet recognized Israel de jure though it had recognized it de facto in 1952 under pressure from the US. Throughout the 1950s,

Greece had made clear that it did not wish to further improve bilateral relations with the Jewish state, and maintained an explicitly pro-Arab position at international fora and at the UN. Consequently, every year from 1954 onward, Athens leveraged these factors to garner as many Arab votes as possible in support of its positions on the Cyprus issue.

As for Turkey, after recalling its ambassador from Tel Aviv in November 1956 in a show of solidarity with the Arab world, it turned its efforts to strengthening the Baghdad Pact in order to curb the pro-Soviet Nasserist influence in the Middle East. In this way, while boosting the pro-Arab profile of its foreign policy, in reality it served the regional interests of Britain, and maintained an ostensibly cold stance towards Israel in order to mislead the Arabs. Where the Cyprus issue was concerned, Ankara believed that keeping Israel at arm's length would persuade pro-Arab countries not to vote in favour of the Greek positions.

Thus, following its secret rapprochement with Turkey in August 1958, Israel agreed to the request for support and speculated that this would establish a basis for a fresh start in Turco-Israeli relations, with the ultimate goal of gradually distancing Turkey from the Arab world. Furthermore, the Israelis knew that, by supporting Turkey on the Cyprus issue, they were essentially serving US plans for the region in the sense that Washington did not want three NATO members, Britain, Turkey and Greece, to waste time on a public squabble that would allow the Soviet Union and its satellites to insinuate their way into an issue that could easily be resolved within the 'NATO family of nations', through direct negotiations and away from the public eye.

Israel had now been asked to prove its credibility and pervasiveness on the diplomatic chess board. Memories of the general outcry at international fora following the Suez Crisis were still raw. So was Foreign Minister Golda Meir's realization that Israel was essentially a country without stable diplomatic alliances, 'without a family', as she concluded, and Turkey's call for help was an opportunity to create a 'family' on a solid geopolitical footing.

Israel might have dropped the Cyprus matter from its complicated network of relations with Turkey and opt once again for the safe and familiar route of abstaining and holding its cards close to the vest. Such a decision would surely not have impinged on Turkish pursuits, since Ankara was in a position to secure the mediation both of Britain and the US, two countries that were far more important than Israel and could easily and effectively break through the Latin American Bloc.

Nevertheless, as Israel took stock of changing circumstances during the summer of 1958, it believed it had an additional reason not to support Greece's interests in the Cyprus issue. On the eve of the official announcement of the Macmillan Plan, Archbishop Makarios expressed his doubts that Greece was in a position to put up a strong enough resistance against the British, and therefore decided that diplomatic support from the UAR would provide him with the scope to negotiate. Consequently, over the objections of the Greek government, he paid an official visit to Cairo in early June 1958. He countered the urging of Greece to refrain from such a move by asking what alternative its 'natural' Western partners proposed for defending Greek Cypriot claims. To this question Athens had no persuasive answer. Meanwhile, Gamal Abdel Nasser's United Arab Republic grasped the opportunity to convince Makarios that, with Cairo's assured support, the Greek Cypriots had nothing and no one to fear.

Makarios was one of the first foreign leaders to arrive in Egypt after the establishment of the UAR. Beyond the symbolic aspect of his visit to the Egyptian capital, it coincided with Nasser's ever-increasing influence over Jordan and Lebanon – which a few weeks later mobilized the British and American military machine to contain Nasser's plans for regional expansion. With his triumphant presence in Cairo in June 1958, Makarios created – perhaps unintentionally – a negative impression on the Israelis, who saw their land borders gradually surrounded by Nasserist expansionism. The Israeli Ministry of Foreign Affairs had been aware of the strong ties the UAR was fostering with the Greek Cypriots, regardless of political ideologies. However, Israeli concerns grew stronger when Nasser and Sadat linked the security of the UAR to the island's freedom from the British military presence there, and the possibility of providing Cyprus with every sort of assistance to achieve 'full independence'.

The heartfelt solidarity expressed in Cairo by Makarios, Nasser and Sadat in June of that year, was perceived by Israel as yet another indication of the UAR's expansionist programme, which aimed at compromising Israel's national sovereignty. If Nasser's regime were in a position to control not only Israel's land borders but its maritime boundaries as well, and the UAR and its affiliates saw fit, the Jewish state might become a tiny dispensable enclave. Hence, notwithstanding the secret pact entered into by Menderes and Ben-Gurion in August of 1958, another reason for Israel's consent to Ankara's request for diplomatic support at the UN on the Cyprus issue was its fear of the potential 'Nasserization' of the neighbouring island which was of paramount importance for Israel.

In light of the above, it is easy to understand the events that followed. In December 1958, on the eve of the vote on the Cyprus issue, Israel's Permanent Representation to the UN offered to assist Turkish diplomacy any way it could. The Israelis mobilized their contacts, and the Turkish Minister of Foreign Affairs Fatin Zorlu travelled to New York to meet in person with the Latin American diplomats posted at the UN. Concurrently, Israel's missions in the various Latin American capitals tried to sway government ministries and the media in Turkey's favour. The Israelis' main argument was that the interests of the West in the Eastern Mediterranean would be more effectively safeguarded by Turkey, which was the only country capable of halting Nasser's pro-Soviet expansionism. In contrast, Greece was portrayed as a country which had failed to prove its reliability to the West.

The behind-the-scenes activities of the Israeli diplomats advocating for Turkey's positions seem to have contributed to the breakup of the Latin American Bloc, which had previously been pro-Greek. This meant that Greece lost several favourable votes it had been counting on. Nevertheless, it would be an exaggeration to say that the Greek diplomatic failure at the 13th Session of the UN General Assembly was due exclusively to clandestine Turco-Israeli collaboration. According to Israeli diplomatic reports, Evangelos Averoff's so-called 'new views' on the 'conditional independence of Cyprus' and 'a *sine die* presence of the military forces of Britain or other NATO member-states' raised concerns amongst the Latin Americans. Regardless of this, both Britain and the US had engaged in behind-the-scenes lobbying, so that Greece was unable to secure the majority of the Arab votes it needed. It was indicative that of all the Arab League member states, only the UAR and pro-Nasser Yemen remained loyal to their commitments to the Greek government.

7.4. Israeli foreign policy and Cyprus in the Transitional Period

The results of the 1958 vote on the Cyprus issue at the UN opened the way for direct negotiations between Great Britain, Turkey and Greece, with the latter in a diplomatically weakened position. In February 1959, the London–Zurich Agreements were signed, giving Cyprus its independence. Israeli regional policy was now required to adapt to the new state of things.

First, Israel very quickly ascertained that Turkey was not inclined to restore bilateral diplomatic relations as promised, despite Israel's assistance before the UN vote on Cyprus. The Ministry of Foreign Affairs realized, albeit belatedly, that Turkey was going to perpetuate its chilly diplomatic relations with Israel, not out of concern that the Arab countries would support Greece on the Cyprus issue, but for fear of upsetting good relations with the pro-West Arab regimes of the region.

The stance taken by Athens came as no surprise. The Greeks had made clear that a de jure recognition of Israel would be addressed in future, and that what had impeded the normalizing of relations with Israel was their need to secure Arab votes on the Cyprus issue. The Greeks, as Israel realized once again, were caught up in the uncertainty of Nasser's intentions vis-à-vis the Greek diaspora in Egypt.

Still, there was one very positive and important outcome of Israel's pursuits. Both Athens and Ankara confirmed that they would not discourage the newly established independent Cypriot state from entering into full diplomatic relations with Israel. Turkey's position was self-evident, in the aftermath of the secret rapprochement of August 1958, but Israel was pleasantly surprised by the stance taken by Greek Foreign Minister Evangelos Averoff, who advocated establishing diplomatic relations between the Republic of Cyprus and Israel, because 'it would be preferable to deal with a one-time wave of wrath from the Arabs, rather than a chronic disease later on'. Averoff likewise assured the Israelis that he had advised Makarios not to postpone the establishment of full diplomatic relations with Israel so that the Republic of Cyprus would not be faced with the same difficulties as Greece in terms of maintaining an even-handed policy vis-à-vis the Arab–Israeli conflict.

Despite behind-the-scenes reassurances from Greece and Turkey, the Israelis took nothing for granted. While Fazıl Küçük and Rauf Denktaş were clearly in favour of establishing diplomatic relations with Israel, Archbishop Makarios told the *Washington Star* in July of 1959 that Cyprus would establish diplomatic relations with Israel only with the consent of the UAR and the Arab world. Naturally, this was quite disturbing to Israel. At about the same time, the Israelis realized they could not rely on any substantive help from either London or Washington. Britain was focused on the terms of its military presence on the island, and the United States wanted to retain all the practical advantages it had under British rule.

In attempting a preliminary reading of the new Cypriot political reality, Israel realized that the only players it could rely on without reservation were the Turkish

Cypriots. For the Israelis, the Turkish Cypriot vice president's veto power was the strongest guarantee that Makarios would not succumb to Arab pressure and that Israel would maintain its diplomatic presence of ten years which had begun with the opening of its consulate in Nicosia on 28 August 1950.

Israel's top priority was to prevent Cyprus from becoming a satellite of Nasserist Egypt, particularly as Cyprus was the only non-Arab state in the region with a non-Moslem majority with which Israel had a common maritime boundary. If such a prospect could not be avoided, then the hitherto 'open' Cypriot ports and airports would close to Israel and 'Nasserized' Cyprus would be independent in name only. The first indications were worrisome. Makarios forbade all Greek Cypriot members of the bicommunal Transitional government to visit Israel, while official Cypriot delegations comprising both Greek and Turkish Cypriot ministers met with senior officials in Lebanon and Egypt. Concerns grew as the Israelis wondered how far the Greek Cypriots or Makarios himself might go in their resentment of Israel's pro-Turkish manoeuvres at the UN prior to the vote on the Cyprus issue. Everything that had taken place at the time cast a shadow over relations between the Greek Cypriots and Israel. This particular topic was never raised, either during the Transitional Period or later. The fact was, however, that the Turkish–Israeli entente occurred in December of 1958 in the back stages of the 13th Session of the UN General Assembly would never be forgotten by Greece and Makarios himself.

It took a while for the Israeli side to realize that during the long and difficult Transitional Period – from the signing the London–Zurich Agreements in February 1959 to the declaration of independence of the Republic of Cyprus on 16 August 1960 – Makarios had painstakingly walked a tightrope in the Arab–Israeli conflict, and made sincere efforts to stay clear of their chronic discord. But the Israelis gradually realized that they would have to adapt to Makarios' centralized decision-making process, seeing that he had sole control of political developments on the island. Besides, it was becoming increasingly clear that the Israeli assessment of reality had little in common either with the anti-Makarios right-wing opposition led by the Mayor of Nicosia, Themistocles Dervis, or with the leftist AKEL. Thus, Israel's Ministry of Foreign Affairs reluctantly accepted the situation when Makarios forbade his ministers to visit Israel during the Transitional Period. Meanwhile, Israeli officials were developing significant contacts with their Greek Cypriot counterparts without any restrictions and with Makarios' knowledge. The aim of these contacts was to prepare the soon-to-be-established Cypriot public service for the adoption of useful practices, similar to those operative in Israel. Furthermore, the Israelis were pleasantly surprised to see Greek Cypriot officials who were part of Makarios' inner circle setting appropriate limits to Arab claims in order to prevent Cyprus from being completely dependent on the Arab world at an economic, political and diplomatic level.

It was not easy for Makarios or for his inexperienced associates to maintain the right balance between Israel, the UAR and Lebanon. The undertaking was made even more difficult because the representatives of the Turkish Cypriot community, in cooperation with Ankara, were plainly pro-Israel in their stance. At the same time, the Israeli side was required to dampen the eagerness of the Turkish Cypriots to strengthen ties with Israel. A conscious decision had been made to keep up appearances in the sense that Cyprus should not be given the impression that Israel was supporting the Turkish Cypriot minority over the Greek Cypriot majority, since the latter would ultimately shape the new state and assume complete control over the economy and trade. It was a well-kept secret that Israel had first penetrated the Cypriot economy under British rule when the British authorities were expanding their military infrastructure. The slightest public relations faux pas during the Transitional Period might have evoked unpleasant historical memories – resulting in Israel's exclusion from the loop once and for all.

Another question that clearly concerned Israelis and Arabs was how the independent Cypriot Republic would position itself vis-à-vis the ongoing Arab–Israel conflict. Throughout the Transitional Period, the UAR and Lebanon had taken every opportunity to impress on Makarios and every other Greek Cypriot official or entrepreneur that independent Cyprus would have to decide 'whose friendship it respected more'. Cairo and Beirut demanded that Cypriot–Israeli contact should cease at every level. In contrast, the tactic used by Israeli diplomats was to avoid calling on Cypriot leaders to choose between the regional camps, most likely because they speculated that Greek Cypriots had more reasons to choose Nasserist Egypt, not only for sentimental and financial reasons but for the sake of the Greek Cypriot community there. On the other hand, the Israelis insisted that their diplomatic representation in Cyprus should be equal to that of the Arab countries – and this point was non-negotiable.

In order to confirm the verbal commitments made by Makarios, Athens, London, Washington and Ankara (the latter in fact reiterated that Turkish Vice President Fazıl Küçük would veto any decision by Makarios to give in to the demands of the UAR and Lebanon), Israel did not hesitate to stray from prescribed diplomatic methods. Specifically, the Israeli Embassy in Washington contacted Greek American multimillionaire Spyros Skouras and asked him to go meet his friend Makarios in Nicosia. On the eve of 19 February 1960, the date on which Cypriot independence was supposed to be declared, Skouras met with Makarios with the aim of informing the Israelis of the archbishop's true intentions. Makarios offered assurances that no obstacles would be raised to the establishment of full diplomatic relations between the Republic of Cyprus and Israel. 'Operation Spyros Skouras', as Israeli classified diplomatic documents referred to the undertaking, was repeated a few days before 16 August 1960 – the date on which the independence of the Republic of Cyprus was actually declared – as soon as it appeared that Makarios had again begun to waver. This time, for purely practical reasons, Spyros Skouras' entrepreneur nephew of the same name who lived in Athens went off to Nicosia and met with Makarios, who confirmed yet again that there would be no hindrance to establishing diplomatic relations with Israel.

A secondary but extremely interesting aspect of the delicate balance between Israel and the Arab world in Cyprus during the Transitional Period was the handling of Lebanon's demand for recognition of the Maronite religious group as a distinct national 'Lebanese-Arabic' community in Cyprus, with its own representation both in the House of Representatives and in one of the two Communal Chambers. While the mixed committee charged with finalizing the articles of the Cypriot Constitution was still deliberating, Lebanon asked for special regulations to be included for the Maronites, similar to those that defined the status of the Greek and Turkish Cypriot communities.

The Beirut government went to great lengths to establish Lebanon as a third 'mother country' of the citizens of the Cypriot Republic, working in cooperation with Nasser's Egypt to have Arabic taught in Cypriot schools. The persistent actions of the Lebanese Consul in Nicosia and the Maronite Archbishop, whose seat was in Lebanon, were a source of concern for President Makarios and Vice President Küçük, as well as for Ankara and Athens. The Israelis watched the Lebanese efforts with bated breath, fearing that a permanent anti-Israeli, Arab factor might become constitutionally enshrined in the Cypriot political system. In fact, the Israelis believed – and not without reason – that Lebanon's delayed interest in the Cypriot Maronites was part of the UAR's scheme to put the Cypriot Republic under Nasser's influence.

While Israeli diplomacy kept a vigilant eye on the progress of the Lebanese efforts, it was surprised to see that both Makarios and Küçük, each for his own reasons, refuted every attempt to change the bicommunal political status quo, which had been created with a great deal of hard work and arduous negotiations. The seemingly contradictory – but fully harmonized – actions of Makarios and Küçük were bolstered by both the specious objections of Ankara and the purposeful silence of Athens.

Thus, after some delay, Lebanon's failure to intrude institutionally on the Cypriot political system led Israel to this conclusion: Aside from the Turkish Cypriots and Turkey, which had maintained a clear anti-Arab stance throughout the Transitional Period, neither Athens nor President Makarios really wanted Cyprus to fall under Arab influence, whether it came from the pro-Soviet, Nasserist UAR or pro-West Lebanon.

7.5 Conclusions

Israel's foreign policy regarding the Cyprus issue can be separated into four time periods.

7.5.1 1946–1949

The initial experience of the Zionist leadership with Cyprus spanned three years, 1946 when Jewish Holocaust survivors illegally tried to enter Palestine under the British Mandate, up to 1949, when the survivors wished to join Israel's newly established regular army while they were detained in camps set up by the British authorities around Famagusta, Karaolos, Dhekelia and Xylotymbou. Israel's diplomatic confrontation with Britain over the liberation of the Jewish detainees in Cyprus influenced of Israeli public opinion regarding the Greek Cypriot quest for Enosis. While the Arab–Israeli War of 1948 was underway, the Greek Cypriots of Famagusta had provided significant support to members of Israel's armed forces who illegally landed on the island to train the Jewish detainees – eligible men and women – so they would be ready to join the ranks of Israel's army as soon as they escaped from the camps to the shores of northern Israel. In the minds of both the Jewish detainees in Cyprus and the Israeli public following events on the island with great interest, Cyprus was inextricably linked to Hellenism. Judging from Israeli press reports of that period, the Greek Cypriot demand to have done with British domination and unite with Greece seemed perfectly valid to the Israeli public.

7.5.2 1950–1957

During the seven-year period between 1950 and 1957, Israeli diplomacy viewed Cyprus in the context of its participation in a regional cooperation with Britain and Turkey. Despite the obvious historical association of the anti-colonialist struggle in Cyprus and that of the Jews against Britain in Palestine, Israel's political leadership knew full well how serious the impact on Israeli security would be if the British ultimately withdrew from the neighbouring island.

The cold relations between Israel and Greece and the Greek pro-Arab stance at international fora left no room for doubt. While Israeli Minister of Foreign Affairs Moshe Sharett objected to Enosis, Golda Meir, who succeeded him in June 1956, seriously considered supporting Greece's position at the UN, in the belief that it would improve Israel's image in the Third World – with numerous benefits to be reaped. However, the diplomatic isolation which followed the Suez Crisis left Israel no margin whatsoever to displease Britain. Meanwhile, in the period 1955–7, Turkey, in full coordination with Britain, was used as a rallying point for the pro-West Arab regimes, leading to the cooling of Turco-Israeli relations. As such, Israel maintained a position of positive neutrality vis-à-vis Britain on the UN votes about the Cyprus issue from 1954 to 1957. Israel wished to avoid upsetting the Turkish side but not to dismiss the possibility of improving relations with Greece at some future point – although this seemed unlikely at the time.

7.5.3 1958

The year 1958 was one of catalytic activity with regard to Israel's position on the Cyprus issue. The potential expansion of Nasser's influence to neighbouring Arab countries and the dissolution of the Turco-Iraqi agreement led Israeli diplomats to seek a rapprochement with Turkey. As a result, Ben-Gurion travelled to Ankara in August 1958 under absolute secrecy in order to sign a clandestine cooperation agreement with his Turkish counterpart, Adnan Menderes. Most of the content of that pact remains confidential to this day.

Israeli diplomatic reports show that this was the first time the Cyprus issue was at the epicentre of Turco-Israeli relations. More specifically, Turkey asked Israel to exert pressure on the countries of Latin America so that they might support Turkey's positions on Cyprus at the impending 13th Session of the UN General Assembly, rather than those of Greece – which they had supported in previous years. In exchange, Turkey promised Israel that their bilateral relations would be normalized and that the Turkish ambassador, who had been recalled from Tel Aviv in November 1956, would resume his post.

Israel responded to Turkey's claim with particular care. Behind-the-scenes manoeuvring by Israel's Permanent Representation to the UN successfully augmented and coordinated contacts in London and Washington, as a result of which the overwhelming majority of Latin American countries did not support the Greek draft resolution or the draft resolution put forward by India approved by Greece but rather took a firm stand in favour of Turkey's positions on Cyprus. In this way, Israeli diplomacy had hoped to achieve full normalization of Turco-Israeli relations.

The events of the 13th Session of the UN General Assembly proved decisive for the outcome of the Cyprus issue. They paved the way for negotiations between Britain, Turkey and Greece, and led to the signing of the London–Zurich Agreements in February 1959. Israel's decision to support Turkey behind the scenes at that important point in time, though never openly discussed, cast a shadow over Israel's relations with Greece and the Greek Cypriots for decades.

7.5.4 1959–1960

The signing of the London–Zurich Agreements satisfied the Israelis for a variety of reasons: The settlement ensured that British troops would remain in the Eastern Mediterranean. In addition, the political solution in Cyprus was the result of direct negotiations – a fact which reinforced the standard Israeli argument at the time that the Arab–Israeli conflict could only be resolved through direct talks with the Arab countries, rather than through the UN majority system. For the first time, Israel would border on a non-Arab country with which there was potential for developing good relations. The Turkish Cypriot vice president had the right to veto any issue impacting the Republic of Cyprus' international relations, which set Israel's mind at ease given that the Turkish Cypriot community would faithfully adhere to instructions from Israel-friendly Turkey. The excessive powers granted to the Turkish Cypriot vice president would keep in check any Greek and Greek Cypriot pro-Arab tendencies. Thus, the risk of the neighbouring island becoming an Arab satellite would be significantly downscaled, and Cypriot ports and airports would continue to serve Israeli economic interests in the Eastern Mediterranean. With the London–Zurich Agreements, yet another non-Arab state with a Western European constitutional and economic structure that was fully compatible with Israel's political and cultural model, was established in the region. Nevertheless, the establishment of full and normal diplomatic relations between Israel and the newly formed independent state of Cyprus was a prerequisite for the above to work. This critical detail was not self-evident.

During the Transitional Period of February 1959–August 1960, Israel had to ensure the continuation of its diplomatic presence in Cyprus, uninterrupted since the operation of the consulate in Nicosia on 28 August 1950. All directly involved countries, Britain, Turkey and Greece and the US reassured the Israelis that they would support the establishment of normal diplomatic relations between Cyprus and Israel. Makarios remained equivocal, however, and the Israelis realized that, from a practical standpoint, only the Turkish Cypriot vice president and the powers granted him by the Cypriot Constitution would be able to prevent Makarios from succumbing to anti-Israel Arab pressure. Israel feared that the strong ties between the Greek Cypriots and Egypt on a political and economic level, and the personal friendship between Archbishop Makarios and President Nasser might turn independent Cyprus into a satellite of the Nasserist UAR.

During the Transitional Period, both the UAR and Lebanon increased their presence on the island and Greek Cypriot entrepreneurs and ministers of the Transitional government frequently met with their Egyptian and Lebanese counterparts who demanded that future Independent Cypriot should sever all ties with the State of Israel. Repeated Arab warnings seriously worried the Greek Cypriot officials and President Makarios. Meanwhile, Israel endeavoured to ensure its continuing diplomatic representation on the island. Obviously the UAR and Lebanon could not prevent Israel from recognizing the Republic of Cyprus, but if Makarios did not agree to upgrade Israel's consulate to an embassy, Israel would perceive such a step as hostile – something both Makarios and Israel hoped to avoid.

Observing the reluctance of the British and Americans to prevail on Makarios to resist regional Arab pressure, the Israelis realized that they could not rely on vague foreign assurances. Thus, Israel entered an intense communications contest with the UAR and Lebanon to highlight the benefits the Republic of Cyprus would reap by strengthening its ties with Israel.

The key difference between the Israeli and Arab approach was this: Israel did not ask Cyprus to make an immediate decision about the regional camp it would support, but it did ask permission to maintain a diplomatic presence in Nicosia equal to that of the Arab countries. This, while the UAR, Lebanon and the Arab League were threatening to impose diplomatic and economic sanctions if Cyprus failed to sever all contact with the Israelis.

As Makarios struggled to find a balance, Fazıl Küçük took a clear stance in favour of establishing full and normal diplomatic relations with Israel and, encouraged by Ankara, took advantage of every opportunity to put forward his objections to any effort to strengthen Cyprus' relations with the Arab world.

After numerous meetings, Israel's Ministry of Foreign Affairs decided to present Makarios with a *fait accompli*. Israel would recognize the Republic of Cyprus on the day of the declaration of its independence, but asked Makarios to upgrade Israel's consulate in Nicosia to an embassy and recognize the promotion of Zeev Levin from consul to ambassador. The formal presentation of Levin's credentials to President Makarios would then be scheduled as soon as possible, and thus, on August 16, 1960, Israel recognized the Cypriot Republic.

The next day, after several changes of heart, Makarios finally ordered Foreign Minister Spyros Kyprianou to send the *agrément*, to Israel's Ministry of Foreign Affairs, accepting Israel's recognition and the posting (essentially, the promotion) of Levin as Israel's ambassador to Nicosia. And so, on 17 August 1960, Cyprus and Israel established diplomatic relations.

It seems Makarios decided to follow the purported advice of Greek Foreign Minister Evangelos Averoff that 'it would be preferable to deal with a wave of wrath from the Arabs once and for all, than a chronic disease later'. Arab wrath, as noted *ex-post*, was limited to a host of articles published in the Cairo and Beirut newspapers which appeared with decreasing frequency as the end of August approached. By early September 1960, it looked as if the UAR would likewise establish diplomatic relations with the Republic of Cyprus. The Arab world did not blame Makarios, since he had no room to manoeuvre.

A full five-month period followed, during which the inexperienced Cypriot administration had to deal with the rules of diplomatic protocol. Israel's Ambassador was expecting to present his credentials to President Makarios any day, while the UAR, citing various pretexts, postponed the arrival of its ambassador to Nicosia, Mustafa Lutfi. At the same time, unconfirmed information was leaked to the press, according to which the UAR was allegedly trying to convince Makarios to revoke the *agrément* with Israel. But their demand was unrealistic. The UAR delay in posting its ambassador was in fact an attempt to avoid conceding a diplomatic defeat to Israel which had just established diplomatic relations with Cyprus.

In the end, the solution was provided by the Cypriot Ministry of Foreign Affairs: In order to bring an end to the months-long delay in UAR Ambassador Mustafa Lutfi's arrival in Nicosia and the presentation of his Israeli counterpart's credentials, Cyprus suggested that Lutfi submit his credentials on 14 January 1961, and that his Israeli counterpart, Zeev Levin, should do likewise a week later, on 20 January. Cairo agreed to Cyprus' proposal and Israel consented.

Nicosia's breakthrough solution demonstrated the new republic's desire to safeguard the political prestige of Gamal Abdel Nasser and the traditionally friendly UAR, while providing an excellent indication of the newly established Cypriot diplomatic service which had been called upon to handle as effectively as possible one of many Middle Eastern aspects of the Cyprus issue.

And this was only the beginning.

Archival Sources and Bibliography

Primary sources

Unpublished

IDFA – Israel Defense Forces Archive
    IDFA-481   Operations Directorate
    IDFA-922   Operations Directorate
    IDFA-1003   Human Resources Department
    IDFA-1042   Human Resources Department
ISA – Israel State Archives, Jerusalem
    ISA/RG43/G   Interministerial Correspondence
    ISA/RG59/GL   Interministerial Correspondence
    ISA/RG93/MFA   Ministry of Foreign Affairs
    ISA/RG105/PRES   Office of the President of the State of Israel
    ISA/RG130/MFA   Ministry of Foreign Affairs

Archives of the Greek Orthodox Patriarchate of Jerusalem
    Greek Orthodox Patriarchate of Jerusalem Monastery, List of Monks [*monachologion*]
Archives of the Holy Archbishopric of Cyprus, Nicosia
Archives of the Municipality of Rhodes
    Archive of minutes from the Municipality of Rhodes council meetings
Author's family archives
Historical Archives of the Pancyprian Federation of Labour (PEO), Nicosia
    International Relations sub-section / File: Israel, 1946–1962
MAA – Milli Arşiv ve Araştırma Dairesi / National Archives and Research Department, Kyrenia

    MAA-GZ Newspaper archives
Public Information Office (PIO), Ministry of Interior, Republic of Cyprus, Nicosia
    Cypriot Press Archives

Published

Archbishop Makarios III Foundation, Ourania Kokkinou, ed. *Apanta Archiepiskopou Kyprou Makariou III* [*The Collected Works of Archbishop Makarios III of Cyprus*]. Vol. 1. Nicosia: Archbishop Makarios III Foundation, 1992.
Archbishop Makarios III Foundation, Ourania Kokkinou, ed. *Apanta Archiepiskopou Kyprou Makariou III* [*The Collected Works of Archbishop Makarios III of Cyprus*]. Vol. 2. Nicosia: Archbishop Makarios III Foundation, 1992.

Archbishop Makarios III Foundation, Ourania Kokkinou, ed. *Apanta Archiepiskopou Kyprou Makariou III* [*The Collected Works of Archbishop Makarios III of Cyprus*]. Vol. 3. Nicosia: Archbishop Makarios III Foundation, 1992.

Archbishop Makarios III Foundation, Ourania Kokkinou, ed. *Apanta Archiepiskopou Kyprou Makariou III* [*The Collected Works of Archbishop Makarios III of Cyprus*]. Vol. 4. Nicosia: Archbishop Makarios III Foundation, 1992.

Bernadotte, Folke. *To Jerusalem*. London: Hodder and Stoughton, 1951.

Colony of Cyprus. *The Cyprus Gazette (Extraordinary)*. Nicosia: Government Printer, 1960.

Colony of Cyprus. *Legislation of the Year 1959*. Vol. 2: *Subsidiary Legislation*. Nicosia: Government Printer, 1960.

Cyprus Department of Public Relations. *Lord Radcliffe's Terms of Reference: Cyprus Embargoed*. No. 5. 14.9.1956. Pamphlet. Nicosia: [Government of Cyprus].

Galambos, Louis, and Daun Van Ee, eds. *The Papers of Dwight David Eisenhower: The Presidency: Keeping the Peace*. Vol. 18. Baltimore, MD, and London: Johns Hopkins University Press, 2001.

Ha-Lishka ha-Leumit li-Statistika [Central Bureau of Statistics]. *Shishim Shana bi-R'ey ha-Statistika* [*Sixty Years from a Statistical Perspective*]. Jerusalem: Central Bureau of Statistics, 2008.

Hakki, Murat Metin, ed. *The Cyprus Issue: A Documentary History, 1878–2007*. London and New York: I.B. Tauris, 2007.

Hellenic Parliament. *Gazette of Parliamentary Debates: 3rd Term, Session C*. Vol. A. Athens: Printed 1955.

Her Majesty's Stationary Office (HMSO). *Constitutional Proposals for Cyprus. A report Submitted to the Secretary of State for the Colonies by the Rt Hon. Lord Radcliffe, G.B.E.* London: HMSO, 1956.

Israel State Archives (ISA), Naomi Barzilai, ed. *Documents on the Foreign Policy of Israel*. Vol. 9. Jerusalem: Government Printer, 2004.

ISA, Barouch Gilead, ed. *Documents on the Foreign Policy of Israel*. Vol. 11. Jerusalem: Government Printer, 2008.

ISA, Barouch Gilead, ed. *Documents on the Foreign Policy of Israel*. Vol. 13. Jerusalem: Israel State Archives, Government Printer, 2001.

ISA, Barouch Gilead, ed. *Documents on the Foreign Policy of Israel*. Vol. 14. Jerusalem: Israel State Archives, Government Printer, 1997.

Khalil, Muhammad. *The Arab States and the Arab League: A Documentary Record*. Vol. 2. Beirut: Khayats, 1962.

State of Israel. *Government Year-Book 5714 (1953–54)*. Jerusalem: Government Printer, 1953.

State of Israel. *Government Year-Book 5715 (1954)*. Jerusalem: Government Printer, 1954.

State of Israel. *Government Year-Book 5717 (1956)*. Jerusalem Government Printer, 1956.

State of Israel. *Government Year-Book 5718 (1957)*. Jerusalem: Government Printer, 1957.

State of Israel. *Government Year-Book 5719 (1958)*. Jerusalem: Government Printer, 1958.

State of Israel. *Government Year-Book 5720 (1959/60)*. Jerusalem: Government Printer, 1960.

State of Israel. *Government Year-Book 5721 (1960/61)*. Jerusalem: Government Printer, 1961.

United Nations (UN). *Yearbook of the United Nations, 1957*. Part 1, chapter 6, 76. New York: UN, Department of Public Information, 1957.

UN. *Yearbook of the United Nations, 1958*. Part 1, chapter 6, 76. New York: UN, Department of Public Information, 1958.

United States Department of State, John P. Glennon, ed. *Foreign Relations of the United States, 1955–1957: Soviet Union, Eastern Mediterranean*. Vol. 24. Washington, DC: United States Government Printing Office, 1989.

United States Department of State, Glenn W. LaFantasie, ed. *Foreign Relations of the United States, 1958–1960: Eastern Europe Region, Soviet Union, Cyprus*. Vol. 10, part 1. Washington, DC: United States Government Printing Office, 1993.

United States Department of State, Glenn W. LaFantasie, ed. *Foreign Relations of the United States, 1958–1960: Eastern Europe, Finland, Greece, Turkey*. Vol. 10, part 2. Washington, DC: United States Government Printing Office, 1993.

Secondary sources

Monographs

Alastos, Doros. *Cyprus in History*. London: Zeno Booksellers and Publishers, 1976.

Alper, Yossi. *Medina Bodeda [A Country Alone]*. Tel Aviv: Matar, 2015.

Alteras, Isaac. *Eisenhower and Israel: US-Israeli Relations, 1953–1960*. Gainesville, FL. University Press of Florida, 1993.

Aridan, Natan. *Britain, Israel and Anglo-Jewry, 1949–1957*. New York: Routledge, 2004.

Ben-Gurion, David. *Beayot ha-Medina: Mediniut Khutz shel Israel [Problems of the State: Israel's Foreign Policy]*. Jerusalem: Intelligence Services, 1951.

Bengio, Ofra. *The Turkish–Israeli Relationship: Changing Ties of Middle Eastern Outsiders*. London: Palgrave Macmillan, 2004.

Bialer, Uri. *Our Place in the World: Mapai and Israel's Foreign Policy Orientation, 1947–1952*. Jerusalem: Magnes Press and Hebrew University of Jerusalem, 1981.

Bielenberg, Brian, and Costas Constandinou, eds. *The Sanna Project – Empowerment through Language Revival: Current Efforts and Recommendations for Cypriot Maronite Arabic*. Oslo: International Peace Research Institute, 2010.

Bitsios, Dimitri S. *Cyprus: The Vulnerable Republic*. Thesssaloniki: Institute for Balkan Studies, 1975.

Borġ, Alexander. *Cypriot Arabic: A Historical and Comparative Investigation into the Phonology and Morphology of the Arabic Vernacular Spoken by the Maronites of Kormakitis Village in the Kerynia District of North-Western Cyprus*. Stuttgart: Komissionsverlag Steiner Wiesbaden, 1985.

Bozdağlıoğlu, Yücel. *Turkish Foreign Policy and Turkish Identity: A Constructivist Approach*. New York and London: Routledge, 2003.

Caroz, Yaacov. *Ha-Ish Baal Shnei ha-Kovaim [The Man with Two Hats]*. Tel Aviv: Misrad ha-Bitakhon [Israeli Ministry of Defense], 2002.

Chrissochoidis, Ilias, ed. *Spyros P. Skouras, Memoirs (1893–1953)*. Stanford, CA: Brave World, 2013.

Cohen-Hattab, Kobi. *La-Tur et Irushalayim: Ha-Tayarut be-Eretz Israel bi-Tkufat ha-Mandat ha-Briti, 1917–1948 [Touring in Jerusalem: Tourism in Eretz-Yisrael during the British Mandate, 1917–1948]*. Jerusalem: Yad Yitzhak Ben Zvi Institute, 2006.

Crouzet, François. *Le Conflit de Chypre 1946–1959 [The Cyprus Conflict, 1946–1959]*. Vol. 2. Brussels: Émile Bruylant, 1973.

Eytan, Walter. *Bein Israel la-Amim [Between Israel and the Nations]*. Tel Aviv: Masada, 1958.

Eytan, Walter. The First Ten Years: A Diplomatic History of Israel. London: Weidenfeld and Nicolson, 1958.

Finkelshtein, A. *Shurot ha-Meginim be-Makhanot Kafrisin* [*The Defenders' Line at the Cypriot Detention Camps*]. Tel Aviv: Tzva ha-Haganah le-Israel/ Agaf Mivtzayim /Agaf Mateh [Israeli Army / Operations Branch / General Staff Branch], 1954.

French, David. *Fighting EOKA: The British Counter-Insurgency Campaign on Cyprus, 1955–1959*. Oxford: Oxford University Press, 2015.

Galambos, Louis, and Daun Van Ee, eds. *The Papers of Dwight David Eisenhower – The Presidency: Keeping the Peace*. Vol. 18. Baltimore, MD, and London: Johns Hopkins University Press, 2001.

Galnoor, Yitzhak, and Diana Blander. *Ha-Maarekhet ha-Politit be-Israel* [*The Political System in Israel*]. Tel Aviv and Jerusalem: Am Oved and Israel Democracy Institute, 2013.

Hatzivassiliou, Evanthis. Britain and the International Status of Cyprus, 1955–59. Minneapolis, MN: University of Minnesota, 1997.

Herzog, Chaim. *The Arab–Israeli Wars: War and Peace in the Middle East from the War of Independence through Lebanon*. New York: Vintage Books, 1984.

Holland, Robert. *Britain and the Revolt in Cyprus, 1954–1959*. Oxford: Clarendon Press, 1998.

Ioannides, Christos P. *In Turkey's Image: The Transformation of Occupied Cyprus into a Turkish Province*. New Rochelle, NY: Caratzas, 1991.

Jessup, John. *An Encyclopaedic Dictionary of Conflict Resolution, 1945–1996*. Westport, CT: Greenwood Press, 1998.

Karsh, Efraim. 'Israel'. In *The Cold War and the Middle East*, ed. Yezid Sayigh and Avi Shlaim, 156–87. Oxford: Clarendon Press, 1997.

Kimmerling, Baruch, and Yoel Migdal. *Falastinim: Am be-Hivatsruto* [*Palestinians: A People on the Making*]. Jerusalem: Keter, 1999.

Kochavi, Arieh. *Post-Holocaust Politics: Britain, the United States & the Jewish Refugees, 1945–1948*. Chapel Hill, NC: University of North Carolina, 2001.

Kyle, Keith. *Suez: Britain's End of Empire in the Middle East*. London and New York: I.B. Tauris, 2003.

Laub, Morris. *Last Barrier to Freedom: Internment of Jewish Holocaust Survivors on Cyprus, 1946–1949*. Berkeley, CA: Judah L. Magnes Museum, 1985.

Levinshtein, P. *More-Derekh ba-Khok ha-Eretz Israeli* [*Digest of Palestinian Law under the British Mandate*]. Jerusalem: Rubin Mass, 1947.

Manus, William. *This Way to Paradise*. Athens: Lycabettus Press, 1998.

Meir, Golda. *My Life*. New York: G. P. Putnam's Sons, 1975.

Miller, John Donald Bruce. *The Politics of the Third World*. London: Oxford University Press, 1967.

Morris, Benny. *Medina Akhat, Shtei Medinot: Yisrael-Falastin* [*One State, Two States: Israel-Palestine*]. Tel Aviv: Am Oved, 2012.

Nachmani, Amikam. *Israel, Turkey and Greece: Uneasy Relations in the East Mediterranean*. London: Frank Cass, 1987.

Namir, Mordechay. *Shlikhut be-Moskva* [*Mission to Moscow*]. Tel Aviv: Am Oved, 1971.

Nicolet, Claude. *United States Policy towards Cyprus, 1954–1974: Removing the Greek-Turkish Bone of Contention*. Mannheim and Mohnesee: Bibliopolis, 2001.

Ofir, Adi, ed. *Khamishim le-Arbaim u-Shmone: Momentim Bikortiim be-Toldot Medinat Israel* [*Fifty Years since Forty-Eight: Critical Moments in the History of the State of Israel*], Jerusalem: and Tel Aviv: Van Leer Institute and Ha-Kibbutz ha-Meukhad, 1999.

Olmert, Yosef. *Miutim ba-Mizrakh ha-Tikhon* [*Minorities in the Middle East*]. Tel Aviv: Misrad ha-Bitakhon [Israeli Ministry of Defense], 1986.

Olmert, Yosef. *Suria ha-Modernit* [*Modern-Day Syria*]. Tel Aviv: Misrad ha-Bitakhon [Israeli Ministry of Defense], 1997.

Parsi, Trita. *Treacherous Alliance: The Secret Dealings of Israel, Iran and the United States*. New Haven, CT, and London: Yale University Press, 2007.

Rappas, Alexis. *Cyprus in the 1930s: British Colonial Rule and the Roots of the Cyprus Conflict*. London and New York: I.B. Tauris, 2014.

Republic of Turkey. *Turkey and Cyprus: A Survey of the Cyprus Question with Official Statements of the Turkish Viewpoint*. London: Press Attaché's Office, Turkish Embassy, 1956.

Reuveni, Yaakov. *Mimshal ha-Mandat be-Eretz Israel: Nituakh Histori-Medini* [*Administration of the British Mandate in Palestine: A Historical-Political Analysis*]. Ramat Gan: Bar-Ilan University, 1993.

Rosenne, Shabtai. *Basic Elements of Israel's Foreign Policy*. New Delhi: Indian Council of World Affairs, 1962.

Sachar, Howard. *A History of Israel: From the Rise of Zionism to Our Time*. 3rd edn. New York: Knopf, 2007.

Sayıl, Altay. *Dr. Fazıl Küçük'ün Anıları ve Siyasal Örgüt Çalışmaları* [*The Memoirs and Political Formations of Dr Fazıl Küçük*]. Lefkoşa, 2010.

Sharett, Moshe. *Yoman Ishi 1955* [*Personal Diary 1955*]. Tel Aviv: Sifriat Maariv, 1955.

Shay, Aharon. *Sin ve-Israel* [*China and Israel*]. Tel Aviv: Yedioth Akharonot & Chemed, 2016.

Uzer, Umut. *Identity and Turkish Foreign Policy: The Kemalist Influence in Cyprus and the Caucasus*. London and New York: I.B. Tauris, 2011.

Weinstein, Menachem. *Tzionut Datit be-Shulei Eretz-Israel: Tnuat Tora va-Avoda be-Makhanot ha-Maatsar be-Kafrisin* [*Religious Zionism in the Periphery of Eretz Yisrael: The Tora and Labour Movement in the detention camps of Cyprus Camps*]. Beit ha-Edot le-Moreshet ha-Tzionut ha-Datit ve-ha-Shoa. Nir Galim: Jewish Centre for the Cultural Heritage of Religious Zionism and the Holocaust, 2001.

Weiss, Martin A. *Arab League Boycott of Israel*. Washington, DC: Congressional Research Service, 2013.

Xydis, Stephen G. *Cyprus: Conflict and Conciliation, 1954–1958*. Columbus, OH: Ohio State University Press, Columbus, 1967.

Xydis, Stephen G. *Cyprus: Reluctant Republic*. The Hague and Paris: Mouton, 1973.

Yeger, Moshe, Yosef Govrin and Arieh Oded, eds. *Misrad ha-Khutz: 50 ha-Shanim ha-Rishonot* [*Ministry of Foreign Affairs: The First 50 Years*]. Jerusalem: Keter, 2002.

Greek and Greek Cypriot bibliography

Alexandrakis, Menelaos, Vyron Theodoropoulos and Efstathios Lagakos. *To Kypriako 1950–1974: Mia endoskopisi* [*The Cyprus Question: An Introspection*]. Athens: Elliniki Evroekdotiki, 1987.

Argyriou, Sofia. *To Ethniko Kinima ton Ellinokyprion* [*The National Movement of the Greek Cypriots*]. Athens: Asini, 2017.

Averoff, Evangelos. *Istoria Hamenon Efkairion (Kypriako 195–1963)* [*A Story of Missed Opportunities (Cyprus Question 1950–1963)*]). Vol. 1, 2nd edn. Athens: Estia, 1982.

Averoff, Evangelos. *Istoria Hamenon Efkairion (Kypriako 1950–1963)* [*A Story of Missed Opportunities (Cyprus Issue 1950–1963)*]. Vol. 2, 2nd edn. Athens: Estia, 1982.

Chatzilyras, Alexandros-Michael. *I Kypriaki Dimokratia kai oi Thriskeftikes Omades* [*The Cypriot Republic and the Religious Groups*]. Nicosia, 2012.

Chorafas, Vangelis, and Lefteris Rizas, eds. *Kypros. Geopolitikes exelixeis ston 21o aiona* [*Cyprus: Geopolitical Developments in the 21st Century*]. Athens: Monthly Review Imprint, 2009.

Christodoulides, Nikos. *Ta Schedia Lysis tou Kypriakou (1948–1978)* [*Plans for Solution of the Cyprus Problem*]. Athens: Kastaniotis, 2009.

Christopoulos, Georgios, and Ioannis Bastias, eds. *Istoria tou Ellinikou Ethnous* [*History of the Greek Nation*]. Vol. 15. Athens: Ekdotiki Athinon, 1978.

Christopoulos, Georgios, and Ioannis Bastias, eds. *Istoria tou Ellinikou Ethnous* [*History of the Greek Nation*]. Vol. 16. Athens: Ekdotiki Athinon, 2000.

Frezis, Raphael. *I Israilitiki Koinotita Volou* [*The Israelite Community of Volos*]. 2nd edn. Volos: Epikoinonia, 2002.

Hatzivassiliou, Evanthis. *To Kypriako Zitima, 1878–1960: I Syntagmatiki Ptychi* [*The Cyprus Question, 1878–1960: The Constitutional Aspect*]. Athens: Ellinika Grammata, 1998.

Iliadis, Manos. *To Aporrito Imerologio tis KYP gia tin Kypro* [*The Classified KYP Record on Cyprus*]. Athens: Sideris, 2007.

Katsonis, Konstantinos. *I Kypros stous Dromous tis Istorias* [*Cyprus on the Roads of History*]. Larnaca, 2002.

Kızılyürek, Niyazi. *Kemalismos* [*Kemalism*]. Athens: Mesogeios, 2006.

Kızılyürek, Niyazi. *Oi Tourkokyprioi, i Tourkia kai to Kypriako* [*The Turkish Cypriots, Turkey and the Cyprus Question*]. Athens: Papazisis, 2009.

Koudounaris, Aristeidis, ed. *Vivliografikon Lexikon Kyprion 1800–1920* [*Cypriot Bibliographic Dictionary 1800–1920*]. Nicosia, 2010.

Koutsis, Alexandros. *Mesi Anatoli: Diethneis Scheseis kai Politiki Anaptyxi* [*Middle East: International Relationships and Political Development*]. Vol. 1. Athens: Papazisis, 1992.

Kranidiotis, Nikos. *Oi Diapragmatefseis Makariou-Harding, 1955–1956* [*Negotiations between Makarios and Harding, 1955–1956*]. Athens: Olkos, 1987.

Kyrou, Alexis. *Elliniki Exoteriki Politiki* [*Greek Foreign Policy*]. Athens, 1955.

Makridimitris, Antonis. *Oi Ypourgoi ton Eksoterikon tis Elladas 1829–2000* [*Foreign Ministers of Greece 1829–2000*]. Athens: Kastaniotis, 2000.

Moudouros, Nikos, and Michalis Michail, eds. *I Nea Tourkiki Igemonia* [*The New Turkish Hegemony*]. Athens: Papazisis, 2014.

Pikros, Yiannis P. *O Venizelos kai to Kypriako.* [*Venizelos and the Cyprus Question*]. Athens: Filippotis, 1980.

Sakkas, Giannis. *I Ellada, to Kypriako kai o Aravikos Kosmos 1947–1974* [*Greece, the Cyprus Question and the Arab World*]. Athens: Patakis, 2012.

Stelgias, Nikos. *O Thanatos tou Anepithymitou Vrefous.* [*The Death of the Unwanted Infant*]. Athens: Papazisis, 2015.

Tornarites, Kriton. *To Politeiakon Dikaion tis Kypriakis Dimokratias* [*Constitutional Law of the Cypriot Republic*], Kentron Epistimonikon Erevnon, Nicosia, 1982.

Varnava, Pantelis. *Koinoi Ergatiki Agones Ellinokyprion kai Tourkokyprion: Gegonota mesa apo tin Istoria* [*Common Labour Struggles of Greek Cypriots and Turkish Cypriots – Events in History*]. Nicosia, 1997.

Veremis, Thanos, and Odysseas Dimitrakopoulos, eds. *Meletimata gyro apo ton Venizelo and tin Epohi tou* [*Studies on Venizelos and His Era*]. Athens: Filippotis, 1980.

Vlachos, Angelos. *Mia fora ki enan kairo enas diplomatis* [*Once Upon a Time a diplomat*]. Vol. 4. Athens: Estia, 1999.

Vlachos, Angelos. *Deka Chronia Kypriako* [*Ten Years of the Cyprus Question*]. Athens: Estia, 2003.

Doctoral dissertations and university research

Hecht, Yaakov. 'Ha-Mivne ha-Kalkali shel Kafrisin' ['Structure of the Cypriot Economy']. MA diss., Hebrew University of Jerusalem, Jerusalem, 1960.

Kazamias, Giorgos, and Giorgos Antoniou, eds. 'Historical Perspectives on Cypriot-Jewish Relations', Conference on the Historical Perspectives on Cypriot–Jewish Relations, Department of History and Archaeology, University of Cyprus, Nicosia, 30 October 2015.

Levey, Zach. 'Israel's Foreign Policy Orientation, 1952–1959'. PhD diss., Hebrew University of Jerusalem, Jerusalem, 1993.

Limor, Yehiel, and Rafi Mann. *Itonaut Isuf Meida, Ktiva va-Arikha' ha-Universita ha-Ptukha* [*Journalism: Information Gathering, Writing and Editing*]. Tel Aviv: Open University of Israel, 1997.

McHenry, James Allen Jr., 'The Uneasy Partnership on Cyprus, 1919–1939: The Political and Diplomatic Interaction between Great Britain, Turkey and the Turkish Cypriot Community'. PhD diss., University of Kansas, Lawrence, KS, 1981.

Articles and periodicals

Atun, Ata. 'Initiative to Colonize Cyprus with Jews in the 20th Century', *International Journal of Academic Research*, 3, no. 3 (2011): 790–4.

Emilianides, Achilles. 'Legal Opinion on the Legal Personality of the Karpasha Church Committee of the Maronite Church of Cyprus', *Epitheorisi Kypriakou ke Evropaikou Dhikeou* [*Cypriot and European Law Review*], 11, *EKEΔ* 6 (2010): 164–9.

Gordon, Joseph. 'Soviet Union', *American Jewish Year Book, 1950*. Vol. 51, 336–40. (New York: American Jewish Committee, 1950).

Haritos, Gabriel. 'The Jewish Community in a Multicultural Turkey', ELIAMEP *Middle East Mediterranean*, 3, no. 2 (May–August 2013): 17–20.

Haritos, Gabriel. 'I Araviki Psifos for Israil: Apo ta "Kommata-Doryforous" tis Dekaetias tou '50 ston Eniaio Araviko Syndyasmo tou 2015' ['The Arab Vote in Israel: From the "Satellite Parties" of the 1950s to the Joint Arab List of 2015'], Policy Paper 5/2015. Cyprus Centre for European and International Affairs, University of Nicosia, April 2015.

Kabha, Mustafa. 'Khavrei ha-Kneset shel Reshimot ha-Lavian ha-Araviot bi-Tkufat ha-Mimshal ha-Tzvai, 1948–1966' ['Knesset Members of Arab Satellite Parties and Their Activity during the Era of the Military Administration, 1948–1966']. In *Etgarim Bitkhoniim u-Mediniim be-Mivkhan ha-Metsiut: Yisrael bein ha-Olam ha-Aravi ve-ha-Zira ha-Benleumit* [*Security and Policy Challenges in Practice: Israel between the Arab World and Global Reality*], ed. Michael Laskier and Ronen Yitzhak, 203–18. Ramat Gan: Bar-Ilan University, 2012.

Kimmerling, Baruch. 'Al-Naqba'. In *Khamishim le-Arbaim u-Shmone– Momentim Bikortiim be-Toldot Medinat Israel* ['Nakba'. In *The Fifty Years since Forty-Eight: Critical Moments in the History of the State of Israel*], ed. Adi Ofir, 33–8. Jerusalem and Tel Aviv: Van Leer Institute and Ha-Kibbutz ha-Meukhad, 1999.

Laskier, Michael, and Ronen Yitzhak, eds. *Etgarim Bitkhoniim u-Medinim be-Mivkhan ha-Metsiut: Israel bein ha-Olam ha-Aravi ve-ha-Zira ha-Benleumit* [*Security and Policy*

Challenges in Practice: Israel between the Arab World and Global Reality]. Ramat Gan: Bar-Ilan University, 2012.

Levy, Zach. 'Israel's Entry into Cyprus, 1959–1963: Diplomacy and Strategy in the Eastern Mediterranean', *Middle East Review of International Affairs*, 7, 3 (2003): 73–87.

Lowenberg, Helmuth. 'Israel', *American Jewish Year Book, 1950*. Vol. 51, 394–5. New York: American Jewish Committee, 1950.

Markides, Diana. 'I Metavatiki Periodos, Fevrouarios 1959 – Avgoustos 1960' ['The Transitional Period February 1959 – August 1960']. In *Istoria tis Kypriakis Dimokratias* [*History of the Republic of Cyprus*], ed. Petros Papapolyviou, vol. 1, 21–31. Nicosia: Fileleftheros Publishing, 2010.

Ofir, Adi. 'Sh'at ha'Efes'. In *Khamishim le-Arbaim u-Shmone:- Momentim Bikortiim be-Toldon Medinat Israel* ['Zero Hour', in *Fifty Years since Forty-Eight: Critical Moments in the History of the State of Israel*], ed. Adi Ofir, 15–32. Jerusalem and Tel Aviv: Van Leer Institute and Ha-Kibbutz ha-Meukhad, 1999.

Oron, Yitzhak, ed. *Asia: Middle East Record 1960*. Vol. 1, 181. Jerusalem, Tel Aviv and London: Israel Oriental Society, Reuven Shiloakh Research Center and Weidenfeld & Nicolson, 1962.

Örs, Yaman. 'Certain Basic Misconceptions in the Field of History: Ancient Greeks, the West and the Modern World'. *The Turkish Yearbook of International Relations*, University of Ankara, Faculty of Political Science, 14 (1974): 93–117.

Persson, Sunne. 'Folke Bernadotte and the White Buses'. *Journal of Holocaust Education*, 9, no. 2 (2000): 237–68.

Rodan, Yadin. 'The Forgotten Jews of Cyprus', *Eretz Magazine* (July–August 2001): 26–36.

Sam Ma, Young. 'Israel's Role in the UN during the Korean War'. *Israel Journal of Foreign Affairs*, 4, no. 3 (2010): 81–9.

Seltenreich, Yair, and Yossi Katz. 'Between the Galilee and Its Neighbouring Isle: Jules Rosenheck and JCA Settlements in Cyprus, 1897–1928'. *Middle Eastern Studies*, 45, 1 (2009): 87–109.

Shapiro, Leon. 'World Jewish Population'. *American Jewish Year Book, 1951*. Vol. 52, 194–200. New York: American Jewish Committee, 1951.

Shub, Louis, 'Israel and the United Nations'. *American Jewish Year Book, 1950*. Vol. 51, 385–6. New York: American Jewish Committee, 1950.

Srebrnik, Henry. 'Birobidzhan: A Remnant of History – The Jewish Autonomous Region in the Russian Far East'. *Jewish Currents* (July–August, 2009): 16–18.

Xydis, Stephen G. 'The UN General Assembly as an Instrument of Greek Policy: Cyprus, 1954–1958'. *Journal of Conflict Resolution*, 12, no. 2 (1968): 141–58.

Newspaper and periodical articles

Cypriot Press Archive registered

Public Information Office, Republic of Cyprus

Alithia	1959
Cyprus Mail	1954, 1959
Eleftheria	1958, 1959
Ethnos	1958, 1959
Fileleftheros	1958, 1959, 1960
Haravgi	1958, 1959

Kypros	1958
Neoi Kairoi	1959, 1960
Times of Cyprus	1958, 1959

Israel State Archives listed

Cyprus

Alithia	1960
Ethniki	1960, 1961
Ethnos	1956, 1959, 1960
Eleftheria	1957, 1960
Kypros	1960
Machi	1961
Fileleftheros	1960, 196
Foni tis PEO	1958
Haravgi	1959, 1960, 1961
Bozkurt	1960
Halkın Sesi	1958, 1960
Cyprus Mail	1959, 2008
Cyprus Pictorial	September 1959
Times of Cyprus	1958, 1960

Egypt

Al-Ahram	1954, 1959
Al-Hayat	1960
Al-Qahira	1954
Egyptian Gazette	1954
Fos	1960

Great Britain

The Times	1951, 1956

Greece

Athens News	1958
Estia	1956
Kathimerini	1956, 1960, 2014, 2015
Vima	1959
Weekly Athens Newsletter	1959

Israel

Al ha-Mishmar	1948, 1949, 1950, 1951, 1958, 1959
Davar	1948, 1949, 1950, 1953, 1955, 1958, 1959, 1960
Ha-Aretz	1959, 2007
Ha-Boker	1956, 1959

Ha-Tzofeh	1949
Heruth	1948, 1949, 1950
Jerusalem Post	1959
La-Merkhav	1958
Maariv	1950, 1959, 1960

Jordan

Al-Difaa	1960
Al-Manar	1960
Akhbar Al-Usbu'	1960
Falastin	1954, 1960

Lebanon

Al-Anwar	1960
Al-Hayat	1959, 1960
Al-Sahafa	1959
Daily Star	1954
L'Orient	1959

Turkey

Cumhuriyet	1957
Hakimiyet	1957
Ulus	1957

USA

| Washington Star | 1959 |

Milli Arşiv National Archives, Kyrenia, registered

| Halkın Sesi | 1958 |

Newspaper Archives, Central Public Library of Rhodes registered

| Proodos Dodekanisou | 1954 |

Internet

Digital databases

Armenian Community of Cyprus (Cyprus Armenians-Gibrahayer). Available online: www.hayem.org (accessed 6 October 2022).

Centre Virtuel de la Connaissance sur l'Europe (CVCE). Available online: http://www.ena.lu (accessed 6 October 2022).

Church of Cyprus. Available online: http://churchofcyprus.org.cy (accessed 6 October 2022).

Cyprus Bar Association. Available online: http://www.cylaw.org (accessed 6 October 2022).

Fazıl Küçük Müzesi. Available online: http://www.fazilkucuk.com (accessed 6 October 2022).

Hellenic Republic, Ministry of Foreign Affairs. Available online: http://www.mfa.gr (accessed 6 October 2022).

Internet Movie Database. Available online: http://www.imdb.com (accessed 6 October 2022).

Israel National Library, Tel Aviv University, Historical Jewish Press. Available online: http://web.nli.org.il/sites/JPress/Hebrew/Pages/default.aspx (accessed 6 October 2022).

Jewish Community of Rhodes. Available online: http://www.jewishrhodes.org (accessed 6 October 2022).

Milli Arşiv ve Araştırma Dairesi. Available online: http://www.arsiv.gov.ct.tr (accessed 6 October 2022).

Moshe Sharett Heritage Society – Ha'Amuta le-Moreshet Moshe Sharett. Available online: http://www.sharett.org.il/cgi-webaxy/item?index (accessed 6 October 2022).

Navy, Army & Airforce Institute – NAAFI. Available online: http://www.naafi.co.uk (accessed 6 October 2022).

Republic of Cyprus, Ministry of Foreign Affairs. Available online: http://www.mfa.gov.cy (accessed 6 October 2022).

Republic of Cyprus, Municipality of Famagusta. Available online: http://www.famagusta.org.cy (accessed 6 October 2022).

Republic of Cyprus, Press and Information Office. Available online: http://www.pio.gov.cy (accessed 6 October 2022).

Republic of Lebanon, Presidency. Available online: http://www.presidency.gov.lb (accessed 6 October 2022).

Republic of Turkey, Ministry of Foreign Affairs. Available online: http://www.mfa.gov.tr (accessed 6 October 2022).

Society for Preservation of Israel Heritage Sites, Atlit Detention Camp, 'Bintivey ha-Apala' – Clandestine Jewish Immigration Information and Research Center. Available online: http://maapilim.org.il (accessed 6 October 2022).

State of Israel, Israel State Archives. Available online: http://www.archives.gov.il/ArchiveGov (accessed 6 October 2022).

State of Israel, Ministry of Foreign Affairs. Available online: http://mfa.gov.il/memorial/Pages/Home.aspx (accessed 6 October 2022).

State of Israel, The Knesset. Available online: http://main.knesset.gov.il/Pages/default.aspx (accessed 6 October 2022).

Syrian Social Nationalist Party. Available online: http://www.ssnp.net (accessed 6 October 2022).

Tidhar, David, ed. 'Entsiklopedia le-Khalutzey ha-Yeshuv u-Vonav', Tel Aviv, 1952. Available online: http://www.tidhar.tourolib.org/tidhar/view/5/2288 (accessed 6 October 2022).

US Department of State, Office of the Historian. https://history.state.gov (accessed 6 October 2022).

Yad VaShem, Shoah Resource Center. Available online: http://www.yadvashem.org (accessed 6 October 2022).

News websites

Karyos, Andreas. 'Cyprus' Black October', 1 March 2015. Available online: http://www.kathimerini.gr/805532/article/epikairothta/kosmos/o-mayros-oktwvrhs-ths-kyproy (accessed 6 October 2022).

Kathimerini, newspaper, Athens. Available online: www.kathimerini.gr (accessed 6 October 2022).

Papapolyviou, Petros. 'Makarios' Exile to the Seychelles', 1 June 2014. Available online: http://www.kathimerini.gr/771762/article/epikairothta/ ellada/o-ektopismos-toy-makarioy-stis-seuxelles (accessed 6 October 2022).

The Armenian Mirror – Spectator. Available online: www.mirrorspectator.com (accessed 6 October 2022).

Email

Wirthlin, Benedikt, Swiss Embassy. 'Swiss Ambassador – February–March, 1959', attached with email to Gabriel Haritos, 2015.

Index of Names